Increasingly, political scientists are describing their e........ ....
soning behind their choices in empirical research using the terms "experiment"
or "experimental." One of the primary reasons for doing so is the advantage of
experiments in establishing causal inferences. In this book, Rebecca B. Morton and
Kenneth C. Williams discuss in detail how experiments and experimental reasoning with observational data can help researchers determine causality. They explore
how control and random assignment mechanisms work, examining both the Rubin
Causal Model and the Formal Theory Approach to causality. They also cover general
topics in experimentation such as the history of experimentation in political science;
internal and external validity of experimental research; types of experiments – field,
laboratory, virtual, and survey – and how to choose, recruit, and motivate subjects
in experiments. They investigate ethical issues in experimentation, the process of
securing approval from institutional review boards for human subject research, and
the use of deception in experimentation.

Rebecca B. Morton is a Professor in the Wilf Family Department of Politics at
New York University. She received her Ph.D. from Tulane University and has held
academic positions at Tulane, Texas A&M University, the University of Iowa, the
University of California in San Diego, and the University of Houston. She was a
Visiting Scholar at the Center for the Study of Democratic Politics at the Woodrow
Wilson School at Princeton University, the Russell Sage Foundation, and the
Hanse-Wissenschaftkolleg in Delmenhorst, Germany. Her book *Learning by Voting:
Sequential Choices in Presidential Primaries and Other Elections* (with Kenneth
C. Williams, 2001) addresses the effects of voting sequentially, as in presidential
primaries in the United States. Her more recent book, *Analyzing Elections* (2006), is
a comprehensive study of the American electoral process. Morton also considered
the complexity of empirical evaluation of formal models in her book *Methods
and Models: A Guide to the Empirical Analysis of Formal Models in Political Science*
(Cambridge University Press, 1999). Her research has appeared in the *American
Economic Review*, the *American Journal of Political Science*, the *American Political
Science Review*, the *Journal of Law and Economics*, the *Review of Economics and
Statistics*, and the *Review of Economic Studies*.

Kenneth C. Williams is currently a Professor of Political Science at Michigan State
University. He received his Ph.D. from the University of Texas at Austin and did a
postdoctoral fellowship at Massachusetts Institute of Technology. He was a visiting
professor at the University of California at Santa Barbara and also taught several
summer courses at Birkbeck, University of London. He has published articles in
the *American Political Science Review*, the *American Journal of Political Science*,
Experimental Economics, *Economics and Politics*, the *Journal of Theoretical Politics*,
and *Public Choice*. He is also co-author of *Learning by Voting: Sequential Choices in
Presidential Primaries and Other Elections* (with Rebecca B. Morton, 2001).

Experimental Political Science and the Study of Causality

From Nature to the Lab

REBECCA B. MORTON

New York University

KENNETH C. WILLIAMS

Michigan State University

CAMBRIDGE UNIVERSITY PRESS
Cambridge, New York, Melbourne, Madrid, Cape Town,
Singapore, São Paulo, Delhi, Mexico City

Cambridge University Press
32 Avenue of the Americas, New York, NY 10013-2473, USA

www.cambridge.org
Information on this title: www.cambridge.org/9780521136488

First published 2010
Reprinted 2012

A catalog record for this publication is available from the British Library.

Library of Congress Cataloging in Publication Data

Morton, Rebecca B., 1954–
Experimental political science and the study of causality : from
nature to the lab / Rebecca B. Morton, Kenneth C.Williams.
   p. cm.
Includes bibliographical references and index.
ISBN 978-0-521-19966-7 – ISBN 978-0-521-13648-8 (pbk.)
1. Political science – Methodology. 2. Political science – Research.
3. Thought experiments. I. Williams, Kenneth C. II. Title.
JA71.M675   2010
320.01–dc22   2010019826

ISBN 978-0-521-19966-7 Hardback
ISBN 978-0-521-13648-8 Paperback

Contents

IV ETHICS

Acknowledgments

We began work on this book more than 10 years ago and many have helped us in that process along the way. We especially have benefited from the valuable comments of several anonymous reviewers, James Druckman, Guillaume Fréchette, Jorge Gallego, Macartan Humphries, Gary King, Kathleen McGraw, Elinor Ostrom, Ingo Rohling, and Dustin Tingley. We also thank participants at the NYU Politics Department In-House Seminars and in graduate and undergraduate classes on the subject at the Michigan State University, New York University, the University of Essex, and the University of Ljubljana.

PART I

INTRODUCTION

The Advent of Experimental Political Science

1.1 The Increase in Experimentation in Political Science

In some sense every empirical researcher is reporting the results of an experiment. Every researcher who behaves as if an exogenous variable varies independently of an error term effectively views their data as coming from an experiment. In some cases this belief is a matter of *a priori* judgement; in some cases it is based on auxiliary evidence and inference; and in some cases it is built into the design of the data collection process.

(Harrison and List, 2004, p. 1009)

Increasingly, political scientists are thinking about their empirical research as in the quotation from Harrison and List, using the terms experiment or experimental to describe their approach or the reasoning behind their choices. In the coming chapters we explore in depth what researchers often mean when they use these terms (which varies depending on the researcher's perspective) and our own definitions of these terms.[1] But before undertaking that task, which is more complicated than some readers might expect, it is noteworthy that the increasing use of these terms to describe a study, although somewhat ambiguous in meaning, suggests that a significant change in perspective in the discipline of political science is occurring. Until the past decade, experimentation seemed to have a low standing within the discipline. For example, McDermott (2002) surveyed a set of political science, psychology, and economics journals and found only 105 experimental articles by political scientists she labels as "established" from 1926 to 2000, with only 57 of these in political science journals.[2]

---

[1] We formally define experiments in Section 2.4.2 and discuss some of the controversies over defining experimentation in that section as well.

[2] McDermott's restriction by unexplained characteristics of the author results in serious undercounting of experimental research, which we discuss in the next section. For example,

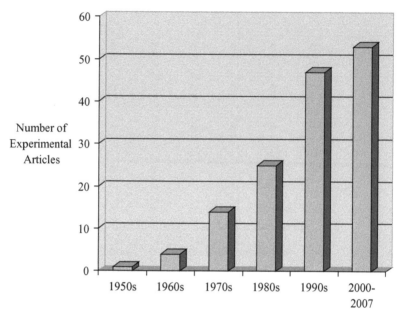

Figure 1.1 Experimental Articles in the American Political Science Review, American Journal of Political Science, and the Journal of Politics.

Yet many see evidence of the increase in the ranking of experimentation within the discipline. For example, Druckman et al. (2006) document the increase of experimental research papers in the discipline's arguably premier journal, the *American Political Science Review* (APSR). They found that more than half of the experimental articles that they classify as a "conventional experiment" appeared in the APSR after 1992. The APSR is not the only premier journal in political science where experimentation appears to have increased. According to McGraw and Hoekstra (1994), from 1950 to 1992, 58 journal articles with experiments appeared in the three major mainstream journals – APSR, the *American Journal of Political Science* (AJPS), and the *Journal of Politics* (JOP). In the next five years (1993–1997), 28 such articles were published (approximately 33% of the total from 1950 to 1997).

Figure 1.1 shows the number of experimental articles published by decade in these three journals through 2007 and that number has increased at an

she reports that in the 1990s only five experimental papers were published in the APSR. According to our count, excluding survey experiments, there were thirteen experimental papers published in the APSR during this period, with at least one in every year with the exception of 1996, although a survey experiment was published in that year.

astonishing rate.[3] These figures do not include the use of so-called survey experiments, as in 14 additional articles published from 2000 to 2005 in the APSR, AJPS, and JOP, making the total of experimental publications in the first five years of the twenty-first century equal to 47, which equals the entirety published in the 1990s. The evidence suggests, as Druckman et al. (2006) have argued, that experimentation is receiving new prominence within the discipline of political science. They conclude from their study that "[e]xperiments in political science have progressed from a method used in the occasional anomalous study to a generally accepted and influential approach" (p. 634). Recognition of the status of experimentation in political science is exemplified in the pride that many political scientists have taken in the awarding of the 2009 Nobel Prize in Economics to an experimental political scientist, Elinor Ostrom.

1.2 Is the Increase in Experimentation Real?

1.2.1 How "New" Is Experimental Political Science?

Is the increase in experimentation in political science real or is it just becoming more acceptable to do experiments within the mainstream of the discipline? The increase in prominence of experimentation is evidenced by the increase in visibility in the major journals, as supported by Druckman et al., Hoekstra and McGraw, and our own analysis. But such studies, by focusing on major journals, tend to understate the long history of experimental work in political science. Moreover, a closer look at experimental work in political science shows that the literature is not nearly as small nor is it as occasional in previous years as these studies would suggest. Experimentation in political science has been large enough to generate several articles on the method and reviews of the literature such as Brody and Brownstein's (1975) chapter in the *Handbook of Political Science*, Miller's (1981) chapter in the *Handbook of Political Communication*, and Bositis and Steinel's (1987) review article in *Political Behavior*. In 1991, Thomas Palfrey edited the volume *Laboratory Research in Political Economy*, highlighting experimental work evaluating formal models in political science, and in 1993a Donald Kinder and Palfrey edited a volume on experimental political science, *Experimental Foundations of Political Science*, which contained 20 experimental studies in political science and encompassed experimental work by both political economists

---

[3] McGraw and Hoekstra limit their search to experiments they classify as randomized. As noted earlier, in the coming chapters we discuss these classifications.

and political psychologists. All of these appeared more than 15 years ago, clearly before the perceived recent increase in experimental political science.

Bositis and Steinel's (1987) extensive review of the experimental literature in political science provides strong evidence for the longevity and size of experimentation. They analyzed 217 political science–related experiments that had been published from 1924 to 1985 (but note that these are just a subset of more than 300 such experiments that they found, as discussed later). Of these, they identified nine published experiments in political science prior to 1950, which most date as the beginning of the behavioral revolution in political science. Most political scientists are aware of Harold Gosnell's 1920s field experiment on the effect of information and encouragement on voter turnout in Chicago – the first known experiment in political science.[4] But less well known are the early experiments conducted by Lund (1925), Rice (1929), Hartmann (1936), and Hovland et al. (1949), which Bositis and Steinel also classified as political science–related. This is probably because these experiments appeared not in political science journals, but in social psychology or sociology journals, or, in the case of Hovland, in a monograph on communication.

These experiments are noteworthy not only because they appeared early, but also because some illustrate types of experiments that are not that different from the types of experiments observed in political science today. For example, Lund manipulated arguments in a political debate to see if the order in which they were presented affected political attitudes, and Hartmann compared the effects of emotional and factual leaflets on voting behavior and electoral outcomes in the 1936 state and local elections in Allentown, Pennsylvania. Lund's work is a clear forerunner of the many priming and framing experiments that have been conducted in political science in the past and present. Similarly, Hartmann's work, like that of Gosnell, is an early example of conducting a field experiment in the context of a naturally occurring election, something that is now quite popular in twenty-first-century political science.

1.2.2 Political Science Experiments in the 1950s and 1960s

Bositis and Steinel contended that the 1950s' behavioral revolution was "a watershed period in the development of political science experiments."

---

[4] Some do not classify Gosnell's study as a "real" experiment because it did not use random assignment. We discuss the issue of defining what is a "real" experiment and the importance of random assignment in the coming chapters.

They focus on 26 published political science experiments during the 1950s and 34 in the 1960s, although as noted earlier, most were published in social psychology, sociology, or communication journals and monographs. One noteworthy exception was the first experimental paper to appear in the APSR, Eldersveld's (1956) study of the use of propaganda and voting in field experiments conducted during elections in Ann Arbor, Michigan. Bositis and Steinel found that experimentalists examined questions of group conformity, opinion formation, and jury behavior in these two decades.

Most striking during the 1950s and 1960s was the beginning of a sizable experimental literature evaluating game-theoretic work, particularly in international relations. The *Journal of Conflict Resolution* was founded in 1957 with a strong interest in publishing both game-theoretic work and work using experiments to test the predictions of such games, publishing the first experimental paper in 1959. For more on the large experimental literature produced in the 1950s and 1960s studying game-theoretic models of international relations, see Mahoney and Druckman (1975), Guetzkow and Jensen (1966), and Guetzkow and Valadez (1981). Coupled with the focus on international relations, more generally political scientists began during this period to conduct experiments on game-theoretic models with other applications. For instance, in the 1960s, William Riker conducted experimental studies of three-player bargaining games using both male undergraduates and graduate evening business students at the University of Rochester (see Riker [1967]).

The literature on game-theoretic experiments by 1985 was substantial enough that Bositis and Steinel decided to limit the number of studies they included in their analysis of experimental political science and these are not included in their counts. They remark:

A large number of experiments of interest to political scientists appear in the voluminous literature on gaming. For example, the *Journal of Conflict Resolution* alone has published over 100 such experiments. In view of our intention to provide a broad perspective of political science experiments, we have included only a sample of the gaming experiments in our corpus of experiments, since their great number would overwhelm and distort the distribution of experiments over time. (p. 280, note 4)

1.2.3 The Rise in Experimentation in the 1970s and 1980s

A Journal and a Notable Field Experiment

Thus, during the 1950s and 1960s, experiments were conducted that examined a wide variety of political science questions. Bositis and Steinel reported a tripling of non-game-theoretic experimental research in the 1970s, with a count of 96 publications and another 52 publications from 1980 to 1985. In the 1970s, experimental research in political science even had its own journal, *The Experimental Study of Politics*, which was out of existence by 1981.[5] Bositis and Steinel contended that the passing of the journal was actually a positive sign of the acceptance of experimental work in mainstream research since they found that the number of experimental publications continued to increase despite its demise and they argued that a specialized journal suggested that experiments were not a conventional method. However, the demise of the journal does illustrate a lack of interest at the time among political scientists in the methodology of experiments.

One notable field experiment published at this time in the *Midwest Journal of Political Science* (the forerunner of the AJPS) is Blydenburgh's (1971) study of campaign techniques in a naturally occurring legislative election in Monroe County, New York. Blydenburgh was able to secure the cooperation of both candidates to manipulate their methods of contacting voters between in-person meetings and telephone calls according to the experimental design. He found something that has been the focus of recent experimental work on turnout in political science – that personal contacts did affect voter preferences, but that telephone solicitation had no effect.

The Increase in Laboratory Work

The 1970s also saw sizable growth in laboratory experimental work with a considerable spread of such work to a number of political science departments. Political psychology began to emerge as a separate field, with researchers receiving training in psychological experimental methods.[6] During the 1970s, an experimental laboratory focused on political psychology experiments was set up by Joseph Tanenhaus and Milton Lodge at the State University of New York (SUNY) at Stony Brook, where experimental research continues to be a strong interest.[7] In the late 1970s, Donald Kinder and Shanto Iyengar collaborated on experiments on the effects of the news media on public opinion at Yale University. Kinder went on to develop

---

[5] Iyengar (forthcoming) reports that the journal was founded by James Dyson and Frank Scioli and that other noted political scientists involved in the enterprise were Marilyn Dantico, Richard Brody, Gerald Wright, Heinz Eulau, James Stimson, Steven Brown, and Norman Luttbeg.

[6] Iyengar (forthcoming) cites the Psychology and Politics Program at Yale University, founded by Robert Lane, as an "important impetus" for political psychology.

[7] Iyengar (forthcoming) reports that when SUNY Stony Brook was founded in the early 1960s, "the political science department was given a mandate to specialize in behavioral research *and* experimental methods" and that in 1978 "the department moved into a new building with state-of-the-art experimental facilities."

a strong program in experimental political psychology at University of Michigan and Iyengar joined David Sears at the University of California, Los Angeles (UCLA), to promote experimental political psychology. A large number of political science experimentalists received their training at Stony Brook, Michigan, and UCLA.

Related to the experimental literature on games in international relations that began in the 1950s and 1960s is the continued growth of experimental research by political economists in the 1970s and 1980s. At this time, Charles Plott established an experimental laboratory for political science and economics at the California Institute of Technology.[8] Numerous political scientists have been trained in experimental political economy at Caltech. In the 1980s, future Nobel Prize winner Elinor Ostrom at Indiana University began collaborating with experimental economists to study common pool resource and public goods problems. In the late 1980s, her student Rick Wilson at Rice University began to build a program in experimental political science and collaborate with experimentalists in sociology and economics. And at Michigan State University one of us (Williams) began to build an experimental political science agenda. In 1991, Thomas Palfrey, also at Caltech, produced his edited volume on laboratory experimental political economy.

1.2.4 Not New Research, But New in Prominence

In summary, experimental work in political science has a long history and has been more substantial than most recognize. Many who focus on the recent increase in experimental research in major political science journals implicitly understate and minimize the large quantity of experimental work of all types conducted in the latter half of the twentieth century. Yet, there is no question that, even as much experimental work was being produced within the discipline, prominent political scientists questioned its value and it was not considered a mainstream approach into the late 1990s. Much experimental work seems to have been ignored. As evidence of this view, Druckman et al. quote Lijphart's (1971, p. 684) remark that experiments "can only rarely be used in political science because of practical and ethical impediments," and point out that one principal methods text from 1994, King et al. (1994, p. 125), claimed that experiments were useful primarily in understanding nonexperimental design.

---

[8] We focus on the growth of experimental laboratories especially designed for political science research. The pathbreaking work of Vernon Smith in economics and Daniel Kahneman in psychology led them to jointly receive the Nobel Prize in Economics in 2002. For a history of experimental economics, see Guala (2005) and Roth (1993, 1995). For a history of experimental social psychology, see Rodriguez and Levine (1999).

A sign of the increasing interest in experiments occurred in 1996–1997, when Elinor Ostrom served as president of the American Political Science Association. However, she found when she addressed most of the regional association meetings, as is the norm, that many reacted negatively to her emphasis on the value added from experiments (Ostrom, 2007). So the question is, why the recent change in the perceived value of experiments in political science? Why are the mainstream journals and prominent political scientists more friendly to experiments now?

1.2.5 Is It the Artificiality?

A discipline becomes experimental when the variables of theoretical interest are susceptible to experimental control and manipulation.[9] For example, as Friedman and Sunder note: "Experimentation in physics became routine only after Newton and others created theoretical concepts (such as force, mass, etc.) suitable for controlled manipulation" (1994, p. 122). Similarly, psychology became an experimental science when psychologists switched from an emphasis on studying "consciousness," using introspection, to studying behavior, using experiments. Psychology became an experimental science in the latter half of the nineteenth century. The advent of statistical measures to facilitate experimentation led to experimental work in social psychology in the 1930s and 1940s through the influence of Kurt Levin and others. Political science also seemed ripe for an increase in the prominence of experimental work.

Yet, the hypotheses of concern to political scientists during much of the 1950s, 1960s, and 1970s (and that continue to be most important for many political scientists) generally are viewed as especially inappropriate for experiments because experiments would be too divorced from the naturally occurring political environment. Political science, as opposed to psychology, is organized around the study of a specific "real-world" behavioral domain. For this reason, political scientists have traditionally and reasonably worried about artificiality of any sort. Experimentation, by introducing artificiality, seemed hardly useful as a method.

The unwillingness to strip to an artificial world cannot be a complete explanation for why experimental political science did not become prominent earlier. For example, during the same period when political science mainstream researchers avoided experiments, microeconomic theory was similarly nonexperimental despite the fact that the discipline was built

---

[9] We discuss the role of control and manipulation in experimentation in Section 2.4.2.

on formal assumptions of a stylized artificial world. Because economists, like political scientists, were primarily interested in empirical research that could answer their hypotheses about the real-world domain that they cared about, they were uninterested in experimental research even though they were comfortable with theoretical models that were highly artificial.

Yet, although the resistance to experimental economics was strong for many years, experimental economics became prominent in the mid-1990s when a *Handbook of Experimental Economics* was published, along with several textbooks, and the journal *Experimental Economics* started publication in the late 1990s and appears in little danger of demise. Seven years before the Nobel Prize committee honored Elinor Ostrom, Vernon Smith received a Nobel Prize for his experimental research; Reinhard Selten, who is a prominent experimental economist, also has received the Prize (1994). Of particular note is the fact that experiments conducted by Roger Myerson (a 2007 Nobel Prize winner) were political economic experiments on voting. Thus, while prominent economists and political scientists may have been equally unfriendly to experiments until the twenty-first century, experimental economics has arguably advanced significantly. In so doing, experimental economics has had a strong influence on experimental political science, as we explore in this book.

1.3 Why Experiments Have Received More Interest

1.3.1 Is It Technology?

Despite these preferences for survey, archival, and other observational data, political scientists are turning to experiments as a mainstream approach. One seemingly obvious explanation is the technological advances that have made it easier to conduct some experiments, lessening the practical impediments mentioned by Lijphart. For computer-assisted (CATI) survey experiments (discussed in Section 8.2.1), technology no doubt is one of the driving factors behind their increased use, as remarked by Sniderman and Grob (1996). They note that, prior to the invention of CATI, surveys had to be printed and distributed in advance and were very difficult to use as an experimental instrument. In the nine years since their review of survey experiments, technology has made them even more useful as a technique because researchers can now use web-based instruments via private entities such as Knowledge Networks and Harris Interactive.[10]

---

[10] See, for example, Clinton and Lapinski (2004) in Example 2.3.

Technology has also allowed for greater variety in laboratory experiments. For example, Lau and Redlawsk (2006) use a unique computer software environment for their experiments on how voters process campaign information, which we discuss in Example 4.2. Charles Holt at the University of Virginia has created a web-based platform for researchers to use for many standard political science experimental questions with very little effort in programming.[11] More complex software programs have been created that can be easily used to create unique experimental designs, such as the Zurich Toolbox for Ready Economic Experiments, or z-Tree developed by Urs Fischbacher. Creators like Fischbacher have been willing to share the programs widely at low to zero cost to the user.[12] Thus, it is now cheaper and easier to program complex games, create virtual laboratories for such experiments, and administer previously impossible survey experiments.

But technology cannot be the primary answer for why experiments have increased in standing. Other research has become easier as well through technology, although technological advances may have reduced the relative cost of experimental research. But one of the more recent trends in experimental political science is the use of technologically unsophisticated field experiments, as in Gerber and Green's work on field experiments on voter mobilization, going back to the old methods used by Gosnell, Eldersveld, and Blydenburgh, and an increased interest in so-called natural experiments, research that could have been conducted in the 1980s as easily as today.

There are two principal reasons beyond technological advances for the increased prominence of experiments: (1) nonexperimental methods have failed to answer some significant research questions, particularly causal ones, and (2) there are now new research questions of interest to political scientists which are particularly suitable for experimental study.

1.3.2 Inability of Existing Data to Answer Important Causal Questions

During the last decades of the twentieth century, some political scientists began to worry that the restrictiveness of nonexperimental data prevented researchers from asking important causal empirical questions. For example, Kinder and Palfrey (1993) illustrate the problem of determining

[11] See http://veconlab.econ.virginia.edu/admin.htm. accessed May 16, 2010.
[12] See http://www.iew.unizh.ch/ztree/index.php. accessed May 16, 2010.

the influence of television on American public opinion by using only survey data. They argue that a survey on media habits and public opinion (p. 14)

cannot establish causal relationships. Observing that television news coverage and viewers' beliefs are correlated is not the same as establishing that television coverage influences viewers' beliefs. Citizens who rely primarily on television may differ in many ways from those who obtain their information elsewhere, and it may be these differences that are responsible for generating different outlooks on national problems.

Because of the belief in the inability of survey data to answer causal questions, some researchers turned to experimental methods. Iyengar and Kinder (1987) conducted a number of experiments in which citizens viewed television newscasts that were unobtrusively altered. By randomly assigning the citizens to different treatments and controlling the content of the newscasts, the researchers were able to determine the extent that the television newscasts affected citizens' political views.

Gerber and Green (2000) make a similar justification about an inability to establish causality using observational data in their efforts to determine the causes of the decline in turnout in U.S. presidential elections in the 1960s. They note that Rosenstone and Hansen (1993) argue that a significant portion of the decline occurred because of changes in mobilization strategies of candidates and political parties but that their use of survey research does not allow for a clear test of their contentions. Gerber and Green contend that Rosenstone and Hansen's research suffers from two problems: (1) the independent variable in their analysis, whether a voter was contacted by a party or candidate, may not be a truly exogenous variable because the mobilizers may be contacting those more likely to vote and (2) the voters in the surveys may be more likely to report contact by mobilizers if they voted (are politically active) or voters may overreport voting and political contact. Gerber and Green, through using a randomized experiment, were able to control for these problems and to demonstrate support for Rosenstone and Hansen's contention about the effect of mobilization strategies on turnout.

These are just two examples of how experimental research has been used to answer causal questions where traditional methods were deemed inadequate and the establishment of causality has been used as a justification for experimental methods over research with observational data. The role of experimental political science in discovering causal relationships is central to the increased focus on experiments in the discipline, which is why we emphasize causality in the title to this volume. Furthermore, we explore in depth what it means to measure causal relations using quantitative data, both observational and experimental, and return to these issues repeatedly in subsequent chapters.

1.3.3 New Research Questions

The Underpinnings of Political Behavior
The second reason for the increasing perceived value of experimental work in political science is that new research questions have begun to receive emphasis. Two changes in research focus are particularly noteworthy causes for the turn to experimental work: (1) an increased interest in the underpinnings of political behavior and the implications for what we observe and (2) the renewed attention to the role played by institutions in understanding political behavior.

Although political science research, like psychology, has focused largely on behavior, recently there has been renewed interest in theories of the sources of observed political behavior. That is, political scientists in the past twenty years have become more concerned with underlying assumptions about the nature of political behavior and the implications these assumptions have for the choices political actors make under different circumstances. For example, Lodge et al. (1989), Lodge et al. (1995), and Lau and Redlawsk (2006) considered experimentally how voters integrate information into summary evaluations in political contexts. Similarly, a number of researchers have begun to use experiments to explore the assumptions about individual behavior underlying game-theoretic and rational choice models in an effort to better understand political choices. For instance, Dickson et al. (2008) use experiments to test whether individuals rationally interpret the use of arguments by other speakers when engaging in deliberation. Both are research questions that individual surveys or archival research are less able to answer.

Some political scientists are turning to sophisticated technologies to explore individual decision making. For example, Mutz (2007) measures the responsiveness of subjects to videotapes using skin conductance levels assessed by attaching two electrodes to the palm of each subject's nondominant hand. We present Mutz's experiments in Example 2.5. Spezio et al., discussed in Example 3.1, incorporate the use of functional magnetic resonance imaging during experiments to measure brain activity. Because political scientists have become more interested in questions such as the process by which voters use information in an election, either at the individual level or as a group, and experimentation is an advantageous method for studying these questions, it is becoming more popular.[13]

The New Institutionalism and Experiments

The preceding discussion highlights the increased stress on assumptions underlying individual behavior in political science theory. Nevertheless, this is not the only way in which research questions in the discipline have changed, leading to more experimentation. Political science research has also begun to focus more on the effects of institutions on political behavior. The "new institutionalism" contends that institutions matter and influence norms, beliefs, and actions of individuals. In some cases, experimental research is a better way to evaluate these institutional differences. As Przeworski (2004) reviews, if the endogeneity of institutions is strong, it is difficult to determine by cross-country observations whether they matter and have causal efficacy of their own, and thus cross-country comparisons of political institutions can be problematic. In contrast, experiments can provide empirical results about individual behavior where the institutional rules are exogenously determined. Fréchette et al. (2005), for example, consider how different legislative bargaining institutions affect the distribution of resources. Thus, experimental research on institutions can fundamentally address issues about the importance of institutions in affecting political behavior.

Ostrom (1998) remarked in her presidential address to the American Political Science Association in 1997 that she turned to experimental work to supplement her years of field research on collective action because of the difficulty in evaluating complex theoretical hypotheses in the field. She remarks:

As an avid field researcher of the past 35 years, I know the importance and difficulty of testing theory in field settings – particularly when variables function interactively. Large-scale field studies will continue to be an important source of empirical data, but frequently they are a very expensive and inefficient method for addressing how institutional incentives combine to affect individual behavior and outcomes. We can advance much faster and more coherently when we examine hypotheses about contested elements among diverse models or theories of a coherent framework.

---

[13] A case can be made that experimental economics became most accepted when experimentalists demonstrated through carefully constructed game-theoretic experiments some of the disconnects between human behavior and the assumptions underlying economic models.

Careful experimental research designs frequently help sort out competing hypotheses more effectively than does trying to find the precise combination of variables in the field. By adding experimental methods to the battery of field methods already used extensively, the political science of the twenty-first century will advance more rapidly in acquiring well-grounded theories of human behavior and of the effect of diverse institutional arrangements on behavior.

Furthermore, some contend that new institutional designs, which do not or rarely exist in the observational world, may have desirable properties. By using experiments, comparative institutional analysis of hypothesized institutions can be conducted (see, for example, Gerber et al.'s [1998] experiments on cumulative voting or Casella et al.'s [2008] study of storable votes)[14] where without experiments little or no data would exist.[15] This advantage of experimental analysis is also elaborated on in later chapters. In summary, as the research questions of interest to political scientists have changed, the comparative advantage of experimental research to answer some of the new questions has led to increased emphasis on experimentation in the discipline.

1.4 Is Political Science Now an Experimental Discipline?

The dramatic escalation in interest in experimental research in political science should not be overstated, however. Despite the remarkable growth in prominence, the view that Ostrom found, that experimental methods have less use in political science as compared to other sciences, is still prevalent. The modal political scientist has not conducted an experiment and experimental work is still not seen as being that relevant to some weighty political science questions of interest. For example, consider John Gerring's (2004) discussion of case study research methods in the *American Political Science Review*, "What Is a Case Study and What Is It Good For?" where he remarks that experiments are always desirable, but not often possible in political science (see p. 351). And in Rogers M. Smith's (2002) essay in *PS: Political Science and Politics*, "Should We Make Political Science More of a Science or More about Politics," he expresses a view about field experimentation: "Throughout the realms of science, this [randomized field experiments] is the methodology that has the best prospect of identifying causal relationships actually at work in the world," but nevertheless he

---

[14] We present this experiment as Example 8.6.
[15] Cumulative voting allows voters in a single election with multiple positions to cumulate more than one vote on one candidate. Storable votes are votes that can be cumulated over issues in separate elections across time.

concludes that this type of experiment can only be conducted on no "more than a small, relatively minor fraction of the political questions that most interest people" (see p. 200; we discuss field experiments as a distinct type more expansively in Section 8.2, as well as other types of experimentation).

Smith's general view about experimentation probably sums up the stance of many in the discipline about experimental political science – remaining skeptical about the value of some of experimental political science but interested in the potential and excited about the possibilities. Smith remarks:

> I do think there are important questions that we cannot hope to answer via any form of true experimentation, only "thought experiments" and other kinds of "quasi"-experimentation. But I'm not only in favor of people pursuing experimental designs to answer political questions – I'm thrilled when they find creative new ways to do so. I don't want experimentation to be the only thing that counts as part of political science, but I do want us to do more![16]

1.5 Why Study Causality?

1.5.1 What Is Experimental Reasoning?

Gerring and Smith's remarks are noteworthy not just because they present a pervasive perspective that in political science research experiments are sometimes simply not possible, but because they also imply that if experiments were possible for a wide range of political science questions, then their use would be justified, particularly to establish causal relationships. That is, experiments are seen as the best method to establish causality even if they are also seen as not that useful for some of the questions that political scientists study. Experiments are presented as an ideal method for the study of causality, but one that is sometimes not unusable.

One consequence of this assessment has been what Druckman et al. labeled a "rapid evolution of experimental reasoning"; that is, there is a growing perspective like that expressed by King, Keohane, and Verba that experimental methods can be used as a guide in nonexperimental research designs to establish causality even if the method itself is seen as unusable. Harrison and List, in the quotation at the start of this chapter, express the essence of an "experimental reasoning" approach to empirical research, whether experimental or not. Essentially, the idea is that if we cannot do experiments, then trying to transform our analysis of nonexperimental data to give us results equivalent to those we would get if we could run

---

[16] Quoted from email with the authors.

experiments is the next best choice. Druckman et al. point out that there has been "a growing interest in the statistical underpinnings of causal inference and increasing awareness that even nonexperimental research borrows its logic and assumptions from experimental analogs." This growth can be seen by examining the number of political science articles with the words "natural experiment" (which we define in Section 2.4.4, but roughly implies that nonexperimental data look like experimental data) in their title from the Social Science Citation Index. According to the Index, ten such articles have been published in political science journals for all the years indexed, seven of which were published in the twenty-first century.[17]

Even when researchers do not make the claim that their data are like experimental data, they often use a statistical method that they claim transforms the data to better meet the standards that experimental data can achieve. An example is provided in Jason Barabas' (2004) *American Political Science Review* article, "How Deliberation Affects Public Opinion." Barabas states that he uses the statistical technique of propensity score matching (which we discuss in Section 4.6.1) because some of his data do not come from an experiment and this method, he contends, corrects for the deficiency between experimental and nonexperimental data to better make causal inferences.[18]

1.5.2 Using Experiments as a Guide for Research Broadly

The increasing reference to experiments as a benchmark for nonexperimental research is not limited to research using quantitative data. Gerring and McDermott (2007) suggest that qualitative research would benefit from a reconceptualization of case study research "according to an experimental template" which they describe. They explain their goal as follows:

We wish to enlist the experimental ideal as a way of identifying the strengths and weaknesses of all research into causal analysis, with special focus on the case study

---

[17] If we expand the count to articles where the term "natural experiment" appears in the abstract or as a topic of interest, the count expands to 45 such political science publications, 34 of which were published post-1999. We also searched for political science articles with the topic "quasi-experiment." Of the eight articles found, five were published post-1999.

[18] Barabas remarks (p. 692): "Matching techniques reduce bias by adjusting estimates of the treatment effect as if the whole study were a randomized experiment." Interestingly, the data Barabas uses for his analysis are from an experiment conducted by a nonpartisan group. However, because of the mechanism by which subjects were recruited to the experiment, the possible effects of confounding variables are insufficiently controlled for according to Barabas, and thus it is necessary to use the statistical technique of matching. We discuss this experiment further in Section 2.4.2.

format. The most useful methodological question, in our opinion, is not whether a case study is experimental or nonexperimental but rather how experimental it is, and in what respects. We regard the traditional experimental model as a heuristic tool – an ideal-type – by which to understand a wide range of empirical studies. . . . In particular, we have suggested a reconceptualization of research design in terms of the extent to which projects deviate from the classic experiment.

(Gerring and McDermott, 2007, p. 698)

We maintain in this book that the principal reason for this growth in "experimental reasoning" as a basis for nonexperimental research is because of the perception that the experimental method is the best way to establish causal relationships. Are experiments the ideal method of establishing causality? Should nonexperimental work try to be like this ideal? And if so, what is meant by an ideal experiment? In this book we consider these issues because they are central questions of concern to both experimentalists and nonexperimentalists. Thus, our book is about not just experimental political science but also the study of causality using experimental reasoning, and the relationship between the two.

1.6 The Welcoming Discipline

1.6.1 Heritage Matters

Political science is a discipline that is defined by the substance of what we study, politics. Beck remarks that researchers "freely use whatever methodological solutions are available," drawing from other social sciences like economics, sociology, and psychology as well as statistics and applied mathematics to answer substantive questions. Experimental political science draws primarily from three major distinctive heritages – experimental and social psychology, experimental economics, and statistics. If we were to do a Poole and Rosenthal (1997) analysis of experimental research in the discipline similar to their study of congressional voting where they determine how much such voting can be explained by one dimension, we would likely find that most of the variation in experimental design can be explained by whether the researcher was trained as a political psychologist, a political economist, or came to experiments from a statistical background.

In political psychology experiments, researchers usually pay subjects a flat fee and the presumption is that the subjects will respond sincerely. The experiments are often conducted in a laboratory, although a significant number are embedded in surveys. Sometimes students in classes are given extra credit for participation, or they participate in experiments as part of a class exercise. Typically the experiments involve individual decision-making situations, although some political psychologists are calling for more group decision-making experiments (see Mendelberg, 2005). Often-times researchers use hypothetical situations such as fictional candidates and elections or fake newspaper articles and quotes and engage in decep-tion, telling the subjects that the materials used in the experiment are real. Rarely is the experiment tied to an explicitly stated formal mathematical model or theory, although many times the experimentalists engage in test-ing nonformal theories. Political psychologists generally tie the experiment to a specific real-world political context. It is easy for them to randomly assign subjects to different situations when they arrive for the experiment. Most subjects' choices are observed only once and the subjects participate in only one situation.

In political economic experiments, experimentalists usually pay subjects based on their choices. The experiments are frequently conducted in a laboratory, although some are conducted outside the laboratory. The pre-sumption is that payments must be salient to motivate subjects to choose as if the situation was "natural." Many political economists avoid using students in their own classes and most do not give extra credit for participa-tion in experiments. Although experiments might be conducted in classes, they are typically treated as an educational device and the data are not used for research purposes. Researchers conduct both group and individual decision-making experiments, although most of the ones in political sci-ence are group experiments. Researchers rarely use hypothetical situations or deceptive materials. Often the experimental evaluations and designs are tied to a formally derived mathematical model and used to test theories, although occasionally experimentalists engage in some fact finding, which is less connected to theory. Efforts are not generally made to make the exper-iment like a real-world political situation, although sometimes this is done. Most subjects engage in repeated activities and more than one observation is collected per subject. Sometimes subjects also participate in more than one situation.

Experiments conducted by researchers who come from a background focused on statistical methods tend to be embedded in surveys or conducted in the field, such as Gerber and Green's study of mobilization. Subjects are not paid for their participation and in many cases are unaware that they are participating in an experiment. Most of the experiments are individual decision-making experiments and are not typically tied to a formally derived model or theory. The experiments tend to be closer to what some believe is a classical experiment – one treatment versus a baseline and random assignment, since this is the ideal that statisticians tend to emphasize. These experiments are generally "searching for facts" without theory. Sometimes the goal is to actually influence government policies through experimental evidence. Considerable care is taken to use statistical methods to control for possible nonresponse or noncompliance of subjects so that the sample estimates of behavior are accurate. Subjects typically engage in only one choice, although sometimes subjects are asked to make a series of choices over time to judge the effects of nonexperimental events such as campaigns and elections on their choices in the experiment. Finally, many of the political scientists who have begun to focus on "experimental reasoning" in their research also come from a statistical tradition.

1.6.2 The Advantages of the Welcoming Nature

The welcoming nature of methodology in political science has a number of advantages that have positively influenced experimental political science. First, it is cheaper for political scientists to draw on the labor of researchers outside the discipline and as a result to use rather sophisticated methods faster than if these approaches had been internally developed, given the statistical and mathematical training of most in the discipline. Our graduate students and faculty can concentrate on building the detailed substantive knowledge that is often needed to address political science questions, particularly in comparative politics work where training in languages and institutional, historical, and cultural nuances may be required. Second, looking at an old political science research question from the perspective of a method derived to address a different question can force researchers to confront old assumptions or results from tried-and-true methods used within the discipline, possibly leading to new advances in the field. Third, dissatisfactions with methods from other disciplines can plant the seed for methodological research that is more appropriate to research questions within political science and lead to new developments in methodology more generally.

The advantages are exhibited in the way in which political scientists conduct and use experimental research. Political science has seen a rise in experimental research, and experimental reasoning influenced research even though few departments have experimentalists or, even more unusual, offer courses in experimental methods. The escalation in clout of experimental research has focused more attention within political science on the complexity of measuring causality, something that traditional political science research rarely discussed. And finally the development of computerized survey experiments and National Science Foundation–sponsored programs such as TESS (Time-sharing Experiments for the Social Sciences), by political scientists Arthur Lupia and Diana Mutz, are efforts made by political scientists to devise experimental methods that are more specific to research questions of interest to the discipline.

1.6.3 The Disadvantages of the Welcoming Nature

Unfortunately there are disadvantages to being a welcoming discipline as well. First, the reliance on methodological training in other disciplines may impede the development of such courses and training within political science when it is accepted that interested students take methods courses in other departments or faculty in political science courses use texts written for other disciplines. Since many political science students may find such courses more difficult because of their substantive focus on questions that do not interest them, fewer students will take these classes or do well in them. Second, methods designed to ask questions in other fields may make assumptions or take approaches that limit their applicability to political science questions. And because the development of a method was accomplished in a different discipline, many who use it within political science may be unfamiliar with the assumptions that underlie the approach and limit its applicability, resulting in claims made by the researchers that are unwarranted given these limitations (particularly if they have not taken the methods courses in the discipline from which the method arose).

Third, if most methods come from outside a discipline, then there can be less development of methods designed to address research questions that are particularly located within that discipline and not of much interest in other disciplines and, as a consequence, those questions can receive less attention. Fourth, methodological borrowing leads to disputes within a discipline as researchers who use methods with different heritages and underlying assumptions have difficulty working together to answer research questions. Finally, graduate student exposure to the range of methods can vary depending on the heritage of the faculty in charge of the training.

The disadvantages are exemplified in the way experimental research in political science has developed as well. Whereas most graduate-level departments offer training in advanced methods or at the minimum encourage their students to take such classes at summer programs for example, at universities in Michigan, Essex, or Ljubljana, few offer classes in experimental methods for graduate students; so students who want such training are generally forced to seek it outside the discipline. Some summer programs are beginning to offer training in experimental methods in their standard curriculum, but such courses are still relatively rare even in these venues. No texts exist on experimental methods specifically geared to political scientists and political science research questions (something this book obviously hopes to address). More problematic is the fact that a growing number of political scientists are either attempting to use experimental approaches or evaluate them with only a cursory knowledge of the underlying assumptions used in the experimental approach or how to evaluate it in comparison to other approaches to research questions. Although the development of computerized survey instruments is laudatory, most experimental research in political science adapts approaches from other fields rather than internally developing new methods, which fuels the increasing ignorance.

Finally, there are big divides within the experimental community that are in large part driven by differences between the experimental approaches used by social psychologists, economists, and statisticians, the three main sources of the experimental approach within political science. Experimentalists from the social psychology tradition and those from an economics background attend different specialized conferences and publish in different specialized journals, while those from a statistical background attend and participate in conferences on political methodology that usually have few experimental papers presented.

The research from the different heritages often takes dissimilar approaches in answering common research questions. This can be good for the body of knowledge, but so far there has been little effort to do a synthesis of what the three approaches learn as a whole because researchers from one perspective are unlikely to read, understand, or value the work from the other. More important, there are disputes as well over basic issues in the experimental method that stem from these different heritages: differences over how to motivate subjects, how to randomize treatments, how control and manipulation works, how realistic to make the environment, whether field experiments are superior to laboratory ones or vice versa, and so on. One notable effort to bring the experimental community together was the production of the 1992 volume jointly edited by Palfrey, a political economist, and Kinder, a political psychologist (Kinder and Palfrey, 1993b). Recently the different groups of experimentalists have begun to collaborate and explore commonalities.[19] However, as experimentation and experimental reasoning grow in authority, communication between the

[19] In February 2007, New York University's Center for Experimental Social Sciences began sponsorship of an annual conference on experimental political science, which included experimentalists from all three heritages, and Druckman et al. plan to produce an edited volume on experimental political science with a diverse set of authors.

different types of experimentalists has lagged as the growth of each group leads to more specialization in terms of conferences and interactions. Sometimes this means that experimentalists themselves who work from a given heritage have only cursory knowledge about the methods and techniques used in other heritages and are likely to have a bias that the other perspective is not as useful as their own. In such cases, experimentalists can unfortunately increase divisions between experimentalists through their own lack of information and biases.

1.7 Purpose of This Book

Political science experimentalists have had either training in experimental methods from other disciplines (typically social psychology, experimental economics, or statistics) or the fortune of learning from one of the few practicing political science experimentalists in the discipline. Others are self-taught. Many who use an experimental reasoning approach to political science research have never conducted an experiment and have little formal training in experimental methods.

It is our view that a guide to experimental methods and experimental reasoning in political science will help facilitate political science research by making experimental methods and experimental reasoning more widely accessible and providing us with a common language to discuss these methods. Furthermore, when a discipline becomes experimental, it faces unique situations and concerns particular to the discipline's research questions. It is important that political scientists have a common understanding of the methods to deal with these situations and concerns. Because of differences in the research interests of psychologists, economists, and statisticians, when political scientists' training is exclusively in one of these areas, experimentalists within the discipline have trouble communicating. In this book, we hope to furnish a guide that addresses both general issues in experimental methods that are relevant across disciplines and those singular to political science. In the coming chapters we discuss in detail how experiments can help researchers determine causality and how to develop an experimental design; to select, recruit, and motivate subjects; to establish control and avoid bias; and to run experiments. We also discuss how to analyze and evaluate the data generated in an experiment.

Our book also has a related purpose: to address the measurement of causality in quantitative political science research, using both experimental and observational data. As noted earlier, the increase in experimentation is coupled with an increase in focus on measuring and determining causal relationships in quantitative research in political science. Although many political scientists freely accept the advantages that experiments can provide in measuring causality, the assumptions necessary for measurement of causality under the various procedures that are used for quantitative data (both experimental and observational) are not well understood within the discipline. Thus, we also discuss experimental reasoning, how researchers working with nonexperimental data use experimental reasoning, and the limits of experimental reasoning.

Finally, we take a broad view of experimental political science, including in our review discussions of natural experiments which are not technically experiments according to our definition (see Section 2.4.2). We discuss survey experiments as well as the more traditional field and laboratory experimental approaches in our study of experimental political science (these distinctions we explore in the next chapter). We also include experiments in which nonnatural manipulation occurs but assignment is not random.[20] We do so because we see an increase in these types of experiments as part of the general trend toward a focus on the experimental approach to political science research to answer questions of causality. That is, the desire to seek out observational data that is close to an experiment or to change traditional surveys into more experimental instruments are efforts both to better measure causality and to answer new research questions concerning causality. The focus of these research approaches is experimental in the use of manipulated variables and thus part of experimental political science, as we discuss in the next chapter. Moreover, by examining experimental political science as a whole, rather than just the narrow segment of work that can be classified as a laboratory or field experiment, we can better understand how laboratory and field experiments fit into a larger research agenda, which is in our view experimental and directed toward understanding causal relationships. We see these classifications as lines in the sand, rather than inherent and uncrossable divisions.

1.8 Our Audience

Most of our book is written to be accessible to a wide audience interested in how experiments work in political science. Some of the material assumes

---

[20] Shadish, Cook, and Campbell (2002) call these quasi-experiments. In political science the term quasi-experiment is sometimes used to refer to any observational study where manipulation occurs, whether experimental or not, so we avoid the use of this term because of the confusion.

some prior exposure to probability and statistics of the level taught to masters and first-year graduate students in political science, particularly in Chapters 4, 5, and 6. We expect that readers of these chapters have some prior knowledge of multiple regression analysis. We believe that such statistical training is essential for anyone who plans to do experimental research and should be required of graduate students using this book as a text in experimental political science research. Statistical training is also a necessary requirement for researchers who intend to address issues of causality using quantitative data, either experimental or observational. Moreover, we expect that graduate students will take courses in experimental political science after completion of such material. However, these more technical sections can be skipped without loss of an understanding of the basic points we address for someone who simply wants a basic comprehension of the field or for undergraduate students who do not have the training in statistics.

1.9 Plan of This Book

Our book has five main parts. The first part contains this introductory chapter, and the conclusion to the book is presented in Part V. In Part II we explore experimental reasoning about causality in Chapters 2–6. Chapter 2 discusses types of causal relations, defines experimentation, and presents a basic model of causal relations in the context of an example of the relationship between information and voting. We note that experiments and experimental reasoning use two different methods to establish causality: control and random assignment. We present the basic problem of causal inference and the Rubin Causal Model (RCM), which is an approach used by many political scientists to understand causality, using our information and voting example in Chapter 3. In Chapter 4 we explore how control is used to establish causality in both experimental and nonexperimental data using RCM, and in Chapter 5 we consider how randomization and pseudo-randomization are used to establish causality using RCM as well. We turn to the formal theoretical approach to establishing causal relationships in Chapter 6, discussing how formal theory is used to investigate causal relationships in both experimental and observational data.

In Part III we deal with experimental design issues. We begin with Chapter 7, which presents a detailed examination of the concepts of internal and external validity of experimental research. The remaining chapters of this part of the book address particular issues in the validity of experiments: whether the experiment is conducted in the field or the lab, how artificial the experiment's environment is for subjects, whether the experiment uses a baseline for comparison, whether the subjects are students, and how the subjects are motivated in the experiment. The first three issues are addressed in Chapter 8, the fourth in Chapter 9, and the fifth in Chapter 10.

We consider the ethics of experimentation in Part IV of the book. Chapter 11 provides a history of the regulation of human-subjects experiments with a detailed presentation of the current governmental regulations governing human experimentation, Chapter 12 delineates the costs and benefits of human-subject experimentation and provides some guidance for political scientists considering experimental research, and Chapter 13 focuses on the debate over the use of deception in experimentation. Finally, Part V contains our concluding chapter, which looks to the future of experimental political science, and an appendix with "The Experimentalist's To Do List."

Throughout the book we use numerous examples. We have attempted to focus on experiments conducted fairly recently, rather than classics, because we want to acquaint readers with examples of current practices. In these cases we have tried to present a summary of these examples, although we encourage readers to seek out the original research papers or monographs for more details. To use a coherent example to compare the various approaches with experimental and nonexperimental data that have been used to study a single research question, many of our examples concern experiments that explore the effects of information, either in content or presentation, on voter choices. However, we discuss other examples from political science as well: we hope to demonstrate the wide variety of research questions that can be addressed with experiments as well as the diversity of approaches that experimentalists in political science have taken. We also present examples of experiments from other relevant disciplines such as psychology and economics when they illustrate a particular approach relevant to experimental political science.

PART II

EXPERIMENTAL REASONING
ABOUT CAUSALITY

2

Experiments and Causal Relations

2.1 Placing Experimental Research in Context

In typical discussions of estimating causality, social scientists who come from a statistics perspective often begin with a review of the experimental approach in an idealized setting that rarely exists, argue that the experimental approach as idealized is not feasible in social science, and then go on to discuss how causality is measured in observational data. For example, Winship and Morgan (1999) begin their otherwise excellent review of the literature in social science on measuring the effects of causes with the statement (p. 660), "sociologists, economists, and political scientists must rely on what is now known as observational data – data that have been generated by something other than a randomized experiment – typically surveys, censuses, or administrative records." This tendency to bracket off measuring causality in experimental social science from measuring causality in observational data presumes that experiments are "either-or propositions": a researcher can either conduct an "ideal" experiment, which we argue in this book would not be ideal for many questions in which political scientists are interested, or work with observational data.

Most of experimental social science is not the hypothesized ideal or classical experiment, usually with good reason. The bracketing off prevents a discussion of how causality is measured in experiments as they exist in social science and a realistic comparison of those methods to research with observational data. Moreover, many of the methods that are used to measure causality in observational data are also relevant for experimental work in social science, and researchers must understand the relationships between experimental design and these methods and how they interact.

As discussed in Section 1.5.1, if you ask political scientists what is the principal advantage of the experimental approach to political science, most

would answer that it can better measure causality than is possible with observational data. Yet, the relationship between the experimental approach to
establishing causality and other methodological approaches to causality
used in political science is not well understood and misunderstandings exist
between experimentalists whose approach builds on work in social psychology or statistics and those whose approach builds on work in economics
over how causality can be measured in experiments. A significant source of
this lack of a common understanding is related to the welcoming-discipline
nature of political science, as mentioned in Section 1.6.

Both the advantages and the disadvantages of being a welcoming discipline are also exhibited in the ways in which political scientists have
addressed questions of causality. Political scientists rely on approaches to
causality, which originated in statistics and biostatistics, sociology, psychology, and economics. This borrowing has benefited political scientists'
research as the discussion of particular examples in Chapter 1 demonstrates.
However, little has been written about how these approaches fit together or
make sense for political science questions in a comprehensive sense (Zeng
[2003] is exception) or how these approaches compare to the experimental
approach. In this chapter, we explore how causality is measured (or not) in
political science research and place the experimental approach within that
context.

The importance of a discussion of measuring causality in a general sense
for both experimental and observational data was highlighted by the recent
exchange between Imai (2005) and Gerber and Green (2000) in the *American Political Science Review* on how to interpret the estimated effects in field
experiments on mobilization. We thus discuss measuring causality in a general sense for a given data set, not making any assumptions about whether
the data are observational or experimental. From this general perspective
we then place the experimental approach to measuring causality – its advantages and disadvantages compared to observational data – in context.

2.2 Technical Background

The statistical and econometric literature on causality is built on existing
knowledge in probability theory, procedures such as ordinary least squares,
methods such as probit and logit, the maximum likelihood approach to data,
nonparametric estimation techniques, and graph theory. As such, some of
the material in this and following chapters necessarily refers to these techniques and for the more technical sections we assume that readers have prior
exposure to probability theory and basic multiple regression techniques and

can work with simple mathematical models.[1] It is necessary to present this technical material because of the importance of the assumptions underlying the techniques for how we interpret data on causality, even assumptions that to an outside observer would appear to be innocuous. We attempt to make the material accessible to readers who have less exposure to these techniques in our interpretations.

Two important caveats about our discussion of causality are in order. First, we only discuss quantitative approaches to causality because our emphasis is on the measurement of causal relations through the analysis of data generated by manipulations either by an experimentalist or nature acting in a similar fashion. We do not address qualitative approaches to causality used in political science. Second, we primarily focus on studies of causality using cross-sectional and panel data rather than time-series data because most empirical studies with experimental data involve the use of such data. Specifically, when we have observations over a period of time, we are interested in cases for which it is reasonable to argue that it is more likely that the number of observations per time period approaches infinity faster than the number of time periods and panel data methods are appropriate.[2]

2.3 Causes of Effects Versus Effects of Causes

2.3.1 Causes of Effects and Theoretical Models

When addressing causality we must distinguish between investigations of the causes of effects and investigations of the effects of causes. If we are asking what causes turnout, we are asking a question about the causes of effects (turnout), but if we ask if making a voter more informed increases his or her probability of voting, then we are asking more narrowly about the effects on turnout of a cause (information). Heckman (2005a) presents a view from econometrics when he argues that ultimately we are interested in the causes of effects. He remarks (p. 2): "Science is all about constructing models of the causes of effects." Heckman also (2005b) contends that

"causality" is not a central issue in fields with well formulated models where it usually emerges as an automatic by-product and not as the main feature of a scientific investigation. Moreover, intuitive notions about causality have been dropped in

---

[1] In some discussions, knowledge of logit and probit is helpful, although not required.
[2] Hence, the asymptotic properties of estimators are evaluated as the number of observations approach infinity, holding time constant. In time-series data, the opposite is the case.

pursuit of a rigorous physical theory. As I note in my essay with Abbring (2007), Richard Feynman in his work on quantum electrodynamics allowed the future to cause the past in pursuit of a scientifically rigorous model even though it violated "common sense" causal principles. The less clearly developed is a field of inquiry, the more likely is it to rely on vague notions like causality rather than explicitly formulated models.

The emphasis on models of causes of effects as the primary goal of study is no doubt the main reason why Heckman advocates what he calls the structural approach to causality, which with observational data is close to the formal theory approach and which we explore in detail in Chapter 6.

In the formal theory approach to causality, an empirical researcher works with a model of the causes of effects from previous theoretical and empirical work and then evaluates that model (predictions and assumptions) with available data, either observational or experimental. The model usually makes a number of causal predictions rather than just one, but all are logically consistent with each other and with the model's assumptions. The causality in the model is often conditional to given situations; that is, some variables may be simultaneously determined. The evaluation of the model leads to further research, both theoretical and empirical. Sometimes theoretical investigators may think like Feynman; that is, envision situations that are beyond common sense in order to explore the logical implications of the model in these nonsensical worlds. Empirical investigations, however, tend to use applied versions of the model (although experiments can allow for the researcher to move beyond the observed world in the same way theory allows, if the researcher desires). This approach is also presented in political science by Morton (1999) and Cameron and Morton (2002) and is the basis of most laboratory experiments conducted by political economists and some by political psychologists (although with nonformal rather than formal models).

The weight on modeling the causes of effects in economics explains why many experimentalists who come from an economics tradition do not appear to be terribly interested in using their experiments to study a particular single cause-and-effect relationship in isolation but instead typically study a host of predicted relationships from some existing theory, as discussed in Chapter 6. These experimentalists usually begin with a formal model of some process, derive a number of predictions from that model, and then consider whether the behavior of subjects is in line with these predictions (or not) in their experiment. To researchers who have been trained to think of experiments as single tests of isolated cause-and-effect relationships as in the so-called classical experiment, these experiments appear wrongheaded. But this failure is one of understanding, not of a method, which we hope our discussion of the formal theory approach to causality in this book will help reduce.

2.3.2 Effects of Causes and Inductive Research

However, not everyone agrees with Heckman's emphasis on theoretical models and the causes of effects. In his critique of Heckman's essay, Sobel (2005, p. 103) argues that many scientific questions are not causal, but purely descriptive. He remarks that "NASA...crashed a probe from the Deep Impact spacecraft into comet Tempel1 with the objective of learning more about the structure and composition of cometary nuclei." Sobel continues by pointing out that modeling the causes of effects is not important unless the effects of causes are sizable, noting that studying the causes of global warming is important because of the effects of global warming.

A lot of political science quantitative research – we would say the modal approach – is not so much into modeling or thinking beyond causality but instead focuses on investigating the effects of particular causes. Sometimes this activity is advocated as part of an effort to build toward a general model of the causes of effects, but usually if such a goal is in a researcher's mind, it is implicit. In experimental research, Gerber and Green (2002) advocate this approach in their call for use of field experiments to search for facts, as we discuss further later. Gerber and Green contend that experiments are a particularly useful way to discover such causal relationships, more useful than research with observational data. Experimentalists who have been largely trained from a statistical background and some political psychologists also tend to take this approach. The implicit idea is that eventually systematic reviews would address how these facts, that is, causes, fit together and help us understand the causes of effects.

Is there a "right" way to build a general model of the causes of effects? Morton (1999) maintains, as do we, that both approaches help us build general models of the causes of effects. Moreover, as Sobel holds, sometimes purely descriptive studies, which are not interested in causal questions, are useful. But it is a mistake to think that piecemeal studies of the effects of causes can be effectively accomplished without theorizing, just as it is a mistake to think that general models of the causes of effects can be built without piecemeal studies of effects of causes in the context of the models. To make this point, we explore how piecemeal studies of the effects of causes and approaches to building models of the causes of effects work in this and the following chapters.

2.3.3 An Example: Information and Voting

To illustrate how causal inference in political science research is conducted, we focus on a research area that has received significant attention, using both observational and experimental data and from researchers who use methods from a range of disciplines: What is the causal effect of information on voting behavior? What are the causes that determine how individuals vote in elections? We later elaborate on the nature of the research questions in terms of causality.

The Effects of a Cause Question

Elections often involve fairly complicated choices for voters. Even in simple two-candidate contests, voters vary in the degree over which they know the policy preferences of the candidates and how the candidates are likely to govern if elected. When elections involve more than two candidates or are referenda over specific legislation, voters' information about the consequences of their choices also varies. What is the effect of information about choices in elections on how voters choose? We know that uninformed voters are more likely to abstain; Connelly and Field (1944), in one of the first survey analyses of the determinants of turnout, found that nonvoters were two-thirds more likely to be uninformed about general political matters than those who participated. But, as Connelly and Field noted, the effect they discovered may simply reflect the fact that nonvoters are also less educated. Connelly and Field could not conclude that a lack of information caused voters to abstain. Much subsequent research has reported that this relationship is robust across election contests and years of study. Are these individuals not voting because they are less educated and, as a consequence, choosing to be uninformed because they are not voting or are they uninformed because they are less educated and, as a consequence, choosing not to vote? Or is there another factor, such as cognitive abilities or candidate strategies, that affects both whether someone is informed and whether they vote or not?

Furthermore, what is the effect of information on voting choices if voters do participate? Some uninformed individuals do vote. Do less informed voters choose differently than more informed voters who are similar in other ways, choosing different candidates as Bartels (1996) contends? Or do uninformed voters choose "as if" they are informed using simple cues like party labels or poll results, as argued by a number of scholars?[3] How much information do voters need to make "correct" decisions (decisions they would make if they were fully informed)? Can voters use simple cues

---

[3] See, for example, Berelson et al. (1954); McKelvey and Ordeshook (1985); Page and Shapiro (1992).

and cognitive heuristics as described by Kahneman et al. (1982) to make "correct" decisions? If uninformed voters would choose differently if they were fully informed, then does the distribution of information affect the ability of different voters to have their preferences affect electoral outcomes resulting in election outcomes that are biased in favor of the preferences of other, more informed voters? The answers to these questions are fundamental for understanding how electoral processes work and how elections translate voter preferences into outcomes. All of these answers hinge on how information influences voter choices, a question that turns out to be extremely difficult to determine and the subject of much continuing controversy.[4]

The Causes of an Effect: Questions and Theories of Voting

Furthermore, the relationship between information and voting is highly relevant to the task of building a general model of turnout and voting behavior in elections. Why do people vote? What determines how they vote? There are a number of competing explanations for voting behavior, most of which have specific implications for the relationship between information and voting. We explore the main ones because they are relevant for some of the examples that we use throughout this text.

The Expressive Voter. One explanation of how voters choose in elections is that voters choose whether to participate and how they vote for expressive purposes, which we label the Expressive Voter Theory.[5] Voters receive some value from participation and expressing their sincere preferences, and this induces them to do both. A version of this theory argues that one implication is that the more informed voters are, the more they are likely to participate in elections because they receive more utility from expressing preferences when they are informed about the choices.[6] Expressive voters are also predicted to make the choice that their information leads them to believe is ex ante their most preferred choice.

The Cognitive Miser. An explanation of how voters choose from political psychology is the view that voters are "limited information processors" or "cognitive misers" and make voting decisions based on heuristics and cues

---

[4] Contrast, for example, the conclusions of Bartels (1996), Lau and Redlawsk (2001), and Sekhon (2005) on whether uninformed voters vote "as if" they are informed and the literature reviewed on this subject. We address the reasons for these different conclusions subsequently.

[5] See Schuessler (2000), for example.

[6] See Matsusaka (1995).

as described earlier. These heuristics may lead to more informed choices with limited information or they may lead to systematic biases in how voters choose. As Lau and Redlawsk (2001, p. 952) remark: "Heuristics may even improve the decision-making capabilities of some voters in some situations but hinder the capabilities of others." Thus, the theory contends that how voters use these cognitive heuristics and whether they can lead to biased outcomes influences how information affects voters' choices. We label this the Cognitive Miser Theory.

The Primed, Framed, or Persuaded Voter. An extension of the Cognitive Miser Theory is the view that in politics, because voters are cognitive misers they can be easily influenced by information sources such as campaign advertising and the news media. That is, as Krosnick and Kinder argue, one heuristic that voters might use "is to rely upon information that is most *accessible* in memory, information that comes to mind spontaneously and effortlessly when a judgement must be made" (1990, p. 499, emphasis in the original). Because information comes to voters selectively, largely through the news media or advertising, biases in this information can have an effect on voter behavior. The contention is that the news media, by choosing which stories to cover and how to present the information, can "frame" the information voters receive, "prime" them to think about particular issues, or "persuade" voters to value particular positions, such that they are inclined to support political positions and candidates.

Chong and Druckman (2007) review the literature on framing and explain the distinctions among framing, priming, and persuasion as used in the psychology and communications literatures. Loosely, framing effects work when a communication causes an individual to alter the weight he or she places on a consideration in evaluating an issue or an event (e.g., more weight on free speech instead of public safety when evaluating a hate group rally), whereas priming in the communication literature refers to altering the weight attached to an issue in evaluations of politicians (e.g., more weight on economic issues than on foreign affairs in evaluating the president). Persuasion, in contrast, means changing an actual evaluation on a given dimension (e.g., the president has good economic policies). Thus, the theory argues that biases in the content of the information presented to voters and differences in presentations of the information can bias how voters choose in elections.

Effects of Negative Information. One particular aspect of information during election campaigns has been the subject of much disagreement in the political behavior literature – the effects of negative campaign advertising. Ansolabehere and Iyengar (1997) suggest that some advertising can actually decrease participation. Specifically, they argue that negative advertising actually demobilizes voters by making them apathetic. The exposure to negative advertising, according to this theory, weakens voters' confidence in the responsiveness of electoral institutions and public officials generally. The negative advertising suggests not only that the candidate who is the subject of the negative ads is not someone to trust, but also that the political system in general is less trustworthy. Negative advertising then makes voters more negative about politics, more cynical, and less likely to participate. In contrast, others such as Lau (1982, 1985) have argued that negative advertising actually increases voter participation because the information provided can be more informative than positive advertising. The debate over the effects of negative advertising has been the subject of a large experimental literature in political science and is also a case for which a notable number of observational studies exist that use experimental reasoning. We discuss some examples from this literature.

The Pivotal Voter. An alternative theory of voting from political economics is what we label the Pivotal Voter Theory. In this model, voters' choices, whether to turn out and how to vote, are conditioned on being pivotal. That is, whether or how an individual votes does not matter unless his or her vote is pivotal. So when choosing whether and how to vote, an individual votes "as if" he or she is pivotal and does not vote at all if the expected benefits from voting (again conditioned on pivotality) are less than the cost. In a seminal set of papers, Feddersen and Pesendorfer (1996) apply the pivotal voter model to understand how information affects voters' choices. They show that the theory predicts that uninformed voters may be less likely to vote than informed voters if they believe that informed voters have similar preferences because they wish to avoid affecting the election outcome in the wrong direction. Moreover, the less informed voters may vote to offset partisan voters whose votes are independent of information levels. According to the theory, then, it is possible that less informed voters may purposely vote against their ex ante most preferred choices to offset the partisan voters. These particular predictions about how less informed voters choose has been called by Feddersen and Pesendorfer the Swing Voter's Curse.

The Voter as a Client. Electoral politics in many developing countries has been theorized by comparative politics scholars as a clientelist system. Clientelism is when the relationship between government officials and voters is characterized as between a rich patron who provides poor clients with jobs, protection, and other specific benefits in return for votes. Thus, in such systems, campaign messages are about the redistributive transfers that the elected officials plan to provide to their supporters. Voters choose candidates in elections that they believe are most likely to provide them with the most transfers. Information about what candidates will do once in office in terms of such transfers can thus affect voters' choices to the extent that they value the transfers.

Of course, because voting is a fundamental part of political behavior and has been the subject of extensive theoretical examination, other theories exist of how people vote, such as group models of voting described by Feddersen and Sandroni (2006), Morton (1987, 1991), Schram (1989), and Uhlaner (1989). We focus on the aforementioned theories because they have been addressed using experimental work that we use as examples in this chapter.[7]

The Broader Implications

Evaluating the causal effect of information on turnout and how individuals vote in the ballot booth provides evidence on whether these particular implications of the more general models of the causes of voting are supported. Such research, combined with evaluations of other implications of these theories, works to determine what causes turnout and what causes how voters choose in the ballot booth.

Furthermore, the answers to the questions of effects of a cause and the causes of an effect also affect how we answer other important policy questions about elections and campaigns. For example, how do campaign advertisements influence voters' choices (if at all)? Do ads need to be substantively informative to influence uninformed voters to choose as if they are informed or can voters use simple ads that mention things like party or other simple messages to make "correct choices?" Is it important that the media provide detailed substantive information on candidate positions? Can biased media reporting on candidate policy positions influence voters? How important are debates in which candidates discuss substantive issues in the electoral process? These policy questions depend not only on the particular causal effect of information on voting but also how we answer the questions about why voters turn out and the determinants of how they vote.

These questions are also useful for an exploration of how causality is investigated in political science using both experiments and nonexperimental

---

[7] Feddersen et al. (2009) provide an interesting experimental test of a theory of voting related to the Feddersen and Sandroni model of ethical voting.

empirical studies since many researchers have tackled them using both types of data, including even natural experiments. Thus, we can use these studies as examples in our exploration. However, it is important to recognize that the examples are not necessarily ideal cases; that is, researchers have made choices that may or may not have been optimal given the question at hand, as we note. The examples are meant as illustrations of how actual research has been conducted, not always as exemplars for future research.

2.4 Setting Up an Experiment to Test the Effects of a Cause

2.4.1 The Data We Use

The Data Generating Process
We begin our study of causality with the effects of a cause question. We use our example of information and voting as an illustration. We also show how experimental reasoning works within our example. We consider an election in which there are two or more options before voters who must choose only one. The election might be for President of Mexico, Mayor of Chicago, a member of the British Parliament, a referendum on a policy proposal, or an election created by an experimentalist in a laboratory (where what we mean by a laboratory experiment is defined more precisely later). That is, it may be the case that individuals, which we call subjects, have been brought to the laboratory and asked to choose between a set of candidates in an election set up by a researcher. The candidates could also be subjects or they might be artificial or hypothetical actors. Voters face a choice over whether to vote, and if they vote, which candidate to vote for. We think of the data generated by the election as created by a general data generating process (DGP) that provides the source for the population of data that we draw from in our research.

Definition 2.1 (Data Generating Process or DGP): *The source for the population of data that we draw from in our empirical research.*

The Target Population
The DGP is the source for lots of populations of data, not just one election. When we think of the DGP we think of data generated in all the countries of the world (and possibly outside our world). But we are typically interested in just a subset of the data that is generated. What population are we interested in? We have to choose a particular target population to study. If the election we are studying is a U.S. presidential election, then our target population includes the data generated by that election. Alternatively, if we are conducting an election in a laboratory, then the target population would

be the population of observations that are generated by such an election set up by the researcher in the laboratory. When we choose to study a particular election or set of elections, we effectively choose a target population. In our analyses, we typically use a sample of data drawn from the target population of data, which is a subset of the target population. The extent that the sample represents the target population is a question of statistical validity and is addressed in Chapter 7.

Definition 2.2 (Target Population): *The population of observations generated by the DGP that an empirical researcher is addressing in his or her analysis.*

2.4.2 What Is an Experiment?

Intervention and Manipulation in the DGP
In an experiment, the researcher intervenes in the DGP by purposely manipulating elements of the environment. A researcher engages in manipulations when he or she varies parts of the DGP so that these parts are no longer naturally occurring (i.e., they are set by the experimenter). We might imagine an experimenter manipulating two chemicals to create a new one that would not naturally occur to investigate what the new chemical might be like. In a laboratory election experiment with two candidates, a researcher might manipulate the information voters have about the candidates to determine how these factors affect their voting decisions. In both cases, instead of nature choosing these values, the experimenter chooses them. Our laboratory election is a particular type of experiment in the social sciences in which subjects are recruited to a common physical location called a laboratory and the subjects engage in behavior under a researcher's direction at that location.

Definition 2.3 (Experiment): *When a researcher intervenes in the DGP by purposely manipulating elements of the DGP.*

Definition 2.4 (Manipulation in Experiments): *When a researcher varies elements of the DGP. For a formal definition of the related concept, manipulated variable, see Definition 3.3.*

Definition 2.5 (Laboratory Experiment): *Where subjects are recruited to a common physical location called a laboratory and the subjects engage in behavior under a researcher's direction at that location.*

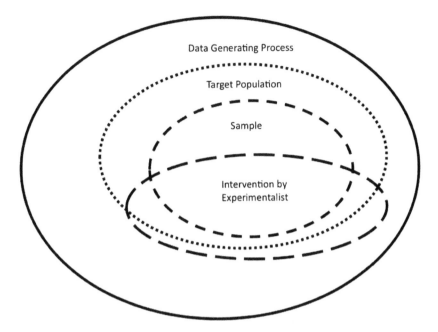

Figure 2.1 Relationships between the Data Generating Process, Target Population, Sample for Study, and Experimental Intervention.

The intervention and manipulation of the experimenter ideally principally affect the target population in the study (and the sample drawn from that population that is studied by the researcher). However, the intervention and manipulation may also affect other parts of the DGP by affecting choices of individuals outside of the target population. For example, when a researcher pays subjects for their participation in an experiment, the payments may affect the income and choices of individuals who are not part of the target population of the experiment as the subjects spend the money given to them. Figure 2.1 above illustrates the case in which the intervention affects observations outside the target population (and outside the sample drawn by the experimentalist).

Experimental Control
Confounding Factors. Experimenters worry (or should worry) about factors that might interfere with their manipulations. For example, trace amounts of other chemicals, dust, or bacteria might interfere with a chemist's experiment. That is, the chemist may plan on adding together two chemicals, but when a trace amount of a third chemical is present, his or her manipulation is not what he or she thinks it is. Similarly, if a researcher is manipulating the

information that voters have in a laboratory election, factors such as how the individual receives the information, the individual's educational level, how much prior information the individual has, the individual's cognitive abilities, the individual's interest in the information, or the individual's mood at the time he or she receives the information all may interfere with the experimenter's ability to manipulate a voter's information. The researcher intends to manipulate voter information but may or may not affect voter information as desired if these confounding factors interfere.

Definition 2.6 (Confounding Factors): *Factors that can interfere with the ability of an experimentalist to manipulate desired elements of the DGP.*

Early experimenters were aware of these possible confounding factors. As a result, they began to control possible confounding factors when they could. Formally, a researcher engages in control when he or she fixes or holds elements of the DGP constant as he or she conducts the experiment. A chemist uses control to eliminate things that might interfere with his or her manipulation of chemicals. In a laboratory election, if a researcher is manipulating the information voters have about candidates, the researcher may want to hold constant how voters receive the information and how much other information voters have so that the researcher can focus on the effects of information on how voters choose in the election.

Definition 2.7 (Control in Experiments): *When a researcher fixes or holds constant elements of the DGP to better measure the effects of manipulations of the DGP.*

Observable Versus Unobservable Confounding Factors and the Advantage of the Laboratory. The confounding factors can be of two types: observable and unobservable. Observable factors are simply things that the researcher is able to measure with only random error. For example, in a laboratory election, how the individual receives the information or the individual's educational level are things the researcher can measure arguably with only random error. In contrast, the individual's interest in the information or mood may be something that the researcher cannot observe with confidence. We would call such a factor an unobservable factor. What is observable and unobservable depends on the circumstances of the manipulation and the target population studied. That is, some potential confounding factors such as an individual's educational level may be observable in an experiment conducted with voters participating in a U.S. presidential election as well as in a laboratory election, but it might be easier to observe how much prior information voters have in a laboratory election than in an experiment that is part of a U.S. presidential election. Thus, in the first case, prior information may be observable, but in the latter case, it is unobservable.

As a consequence, to facilitate control, most early experiments in the social sciences, as in the physical sciences, were conducted in laboratories. In the laboratory, many confounding factors can be made observable and the experimentalist can then control for their possible interference. As noted in the preceding example, in a laboratory election a researcher can, by creating the election that takes place, make observable voters' prior information, allowing the researcher to better control voters' prior information, which may be unobservable outside of the laboratory.

Definition 2.8 (Observable Confounding Factors): *Confounding factors that a researcher is able to measure in the target population with only random error given the experimental manipulation.*

Definition 2.9 (Unobservable Confounding Factors): *Confounding factors that a researcher cannot measure with any confidence in the target population given the experimental manipulation.*

Baselines in Experiments. One method of controlling confounding variables is to compare experimental results to outcomes in which manipulations do not occur but all other observable conditions are identical. That is, if all the other conditions are held constant – are identical – and the only difference between the two outcomes (the outcome when the manipulation did not occur and the outcome when the manipulation did occur) is the experimental manipulation, then the researcher can argue that the effect he or she is measuring is truly causal; that is, the manipulation has caused any differences between the two outcomes. Oftentimes experimentalists call the outcome in which a manipulation did not occur the "control" and the experiment a "controlled experiment." However, because control is a more than just a comparison, but involves other ways that experimentalists attempt to control confounding variables, we label such a comparison a "baseline comparison." Also, the word control is used in observational studies in the same general sense: as a method of holding constant the effects of possible confounding variables. We discuss baselines more expansively in Section 8.3.

Definition 2.10 (Baseline): *A manipulation in an experiment designated by a researcher as being particularly relevant for comparisons. For a formal definition of the related concept, baseline treatment, see Definition 8.7.*

Random Assignment

Moving Out of the Laboratory. As Shadish et al. (2002; hereafter SCC) observe, when experimentation moved out of the laboratory and expanded to disciplines such as agriculture, public health, education, and so forth, researchers were no longer able to control adequately aspects of the DGP that might interfere with their manipulations. Researchers could not always find observations with identical observables, and they encountered more unobservable possible confounding factors. A field experiment using human subjects – the name probably comes from agricultural use – is a researcher's intervention that takes place in subjects' natural environments and the researcher has only limited control beyond the intervention conducted.

Definition 2.11 (Field Experiment): *Where a researcher's intervention takes place in subjects' natural environments and the researcher has only limited control beyond the intervention conducted. Usually the relationship between the researcher and the subject is conducted through variables outside of the researcher's control.*

In field experiments in agriculture, it was difficult to use control to account for differences in soil, farming abilities, and so on. It was not possible to find two fields with exactly the same observable conditions and unlikely that unobservable conditions were the same, and researchers expected that these factors could confound the manipulations. Thus, when comparisons were made between the baseline outcome that resulted from no manipulation and outcome that occurred as a consequence of a manipulation, the experimenter could not be sure if the difference was due to the manipulation or to the differences in the fields that he or she could not control.

In field experiments in public health and education, researchers similarly lost the ability to control for variables that could confound their manipulations. It was not possible for them to compare individuals who were exactly the same, living in exactly the same environment, eating the same food, with the same prior health conditions, psychological makeup, or cognitive abilities. Similarly, if a researcher wished to manipulate the information voters have in an election that is naturally occurring as part of the DGP, then the researcher no longer has as much control over how the voters receive information and how much other information voters have in the same way as the researcher can control the information in the laboratory. That is, suppose the information is provided through a mailing about candidate positions on issues. Some voters may not receive the mailing because of mistakes in addresses, others may not check their mail, and still others may throw the mailing away without reading it. Furthermore, some voters may already know the information. These disconnects would occur to a much smaller extent in the laboratory.

As a result of the inability to control factors outside the laboratory and the difficulty in comparing human subjects, researchers in agriculture, biomedicine, and social sciences began to develop techniques such as random assignment as substitutes. Random assignment is when the researcher uses a randomization mechanism to assign subjects to manipulations, one of which might be a baseline manipulation. In our simple example, the researcher may randomly assign some subjects to receive the information manipulation about the candidates and others to receive no information (a baseline).

Definition 2.12 (Random Assignment): *When a researcher uses a randomized mechanism to assign subjects to particular manipulations in the experiment to better measure the effects of manipulations of the DGP.*

Is Random Assignment Essential for an Experiment? As shown in Section 5.2.2, random assignment can facilitate the ability of researchers to establish causal inferences. Essentially, because the information is randomly assigned across subjects, then the factors that might interfere with the effects of the manipulation, such as whether the subjects actually received the information or already knew the information, are in expectation mitigated (the effects do not disappear, but on average are controlled assuming the randomization is effective). The importance of random assignment for experiments conducted outside of the laboratory in public health, education, and similar disciplines led some to restrict the definition of an experiment using human subjects to one in which random assignment is used. For example, SCC define an experiment explicitly as an intervention that uses random assignment, and an intervention that does not is defined as a quasi-experiment because their focus is largely on experiments conducted in these disciplines. Many political scientists have adopted the same convention. Certainly SCC are correct to say, as we explore later in this book, that when one compares two experiments conducted outside the laboratory that are exactly alike except that manipulations in one experiment are assigned randomly and in the other they are not, the one in which the manipulations are assigned randomly is likely to do better in establishing causal inferences than the other, and can certainly do no worse.

However, if we were to compare a laboratory experiment that did not use random assignment but the researcher engaged in significant control over the elements of the DGP to an experiment outside the laboratory in which little control is exercised but random assignment is used, the answer is not so clear. Any experiment with random assignment does not always make "better" causal inferences than any experiment without random assignment. Why? There are two reasons. First, control also facilitates causal inferences, as we discuss in Section 4.1.1. For example, in some laboratory experiments, researchers use what is called a within-subjects design (defined and discussed in Section 3.3.3), which can have advantages over simple random assignment in establishing causality because the same subjects experience all manipulations even if everything else about an experiment is held constant. Subjects serve as their own baselines. Random assignment implies that subjects in expectation have the same probability of experiencing a manipulation, but a within-subject design makes that probability equal to 1 for both manipulations across all subjects.

Second, operationalizing random assignment in experiments is not simple and involves a number of decisions, about what to randomize, across what groups of subjects, and so on, that can affect the value of the inferences made through random assignment. Furthermore, when researchers conduct experiments, especially when the experiments are conducted in the field, issues of response and compliance become important. Nonresponse is when a subject's choices, given manipulations, are not observable, and noncompliance occurs when a subject fails to comply with the manipulation given by the researcher. Random assignment, particularly in field experiments, is thus rarely as ideal for establishing causal inferences as the statistical theory that underlies it would suggest. Thus, both control and random assignments are methods used to deal with factors that can interfere with manipulations; neither is perfect, but both are extremely powerful.

Definition 2.13 (Nonresponse): *Nonresponse is when a subject's choices, given manipulations, are not observable.*

Definition 2.14 (Noncompliance): *Noncompliance occurs when a subject fails to comply with the manipulation given by the researcher.*

Consider some well-known deliberative polling experiments (see Fishkin, 1991, 1993 to 1997; Luskin et al. 2002). In these experiments, a random sample of subjects was recruited to participate in an event to discuss and deliberate public policy on a particular issue. The early experiments suffered from the lack of an explicit baseline sample, noncompliance when subjects who were selected to attend did not, and nonresponse when subjects who attended did not respond to surveys after the event. As a result, many have argued that these events are not experiments, labeling them quasi-experiments, as in the discussion by Karpowitz and Mendelberg (forthcoming). We agree that the methodological concerns of the critics are justified. The design of the deliberative polls makes it difficult to draw causal inferences about the effects of deliberation on public opinion. However, not all of these experiments lacked a baseline group and an attempt at random assignment. For example, Barabas (2004) reports on a deliberative poll event in which a baseline group was surveyed and random samples of subjects were recruited to both a baseline group and a group that participated in the deliberative poll. However, the random assignment was problematic because some subjects (fewer than 10%) were recruited to participate independently by interest groups, some subjects chose not to participate (noncompliance), and others did not respond when surveyed post-poll (nonresponse). Barabas labels the experiment a quasi-experiment as a consequence of these problems with the attempt at random assignment despite the efforts of the researchers to draw random samples for both the baseline and manipulated groups. Since almost all field experiments suffer from similar problems in implementing random assignment, it would seem that a strict interpretation of what is an experiment along these lines would ultimately mean that only a few real field experiments exist in political science.

Some important and useful experiments have been conducted that do not use random assignment or baselines or that fail to fully implement random assignment, yet they have added significantly to our understanding of political behavior and institutions just as many experiments in which the researcher has little control over variables not manipulated also have provided useful knowledge. The fact that a study does not include randomization or baselines or the randomization suffers from problems, in our view, does not make it less of an experiment, just as an experiment in which control is minimal is not less than an experiment. As we explain in Section 8.2.4, we think it is important not to confound definitions of experiments with normative views of desirable properties because what is desirable in an experiment depends on the research goal – what the researcher seeks to learn – as well as the opportunities before the researcher. What is ideal in an experiment also depends on where it is conducted. In field experiments, random assignment can be extremely valuable, although difficult, because control is less available; in the laboratory, the opposite relationship holds although both control and random assignment can be much easier to implement. It would be unreasonable for us to define interventions outside the laboratory, where there are disconnects between manipulations, and what happens to subjects because of a lack of control or problems with the implementation of random assignment as not really experiments, just as we think it is unreasonable to define interventions without random assignment and baselines as not really experiments. Thus, we define experiments broadly following the traditional definition: an experiment is simply an intervention by a researcher into the DGP through manipulation of elements of the DGP.[8] We further define control and random assignment with or without baselines as usual and important tools by which a researcher can more fruitfully make causal inferences based on his or her interventions. But we recognize that both control and random assignment are rarely implemented perfectly, especially when the experiment is conducted in the field, and thus defining an experiment by whether it contains either one is not useful.

2.4.3 Examples of Information and Voting Experiments

In the Appendix to this chapter contains seven examples of experiments on the relationship between information and political choices. In some cases, the subjects voted in an election conducted by the experimenters; in other cases, subjects reported on their preferences over choices that were presented to them as candidates or choices, sometimes in a hypothetical election, sometimes in an upcoming naturally occurring election in which the subjects would vote or had voted. In some cases turnout decisions, rather than choices between candidates or parties, were measured or surveyed. In all the examples, the experimenters manipulated or attempted to manipulate the information the subjects possessed about the choices before them, how the information was presented to the subjects, or both. All seven used some form of random assignment to manipulations and comparison of manipulations.

The examples, however, illustrate the wide variety of experimental approaches used in political science. Three of the example experiments were conducted during elections in the field. Example 2.1 presents an experiment by Gerber et al. (2007) in which they provided subjects with free newspaper subscriptions during a Virginia gubernatorial election; Example 2.2 concerns an experiment by Wantchekon (2003) during a presidential election in Benin in which he manipulated the campaign messages used by some of

---

[8] Our definition of an experiment is also traditional in that researchers used experimentation for many years before the advent of random assignment as a tool in establishing causal inferences in the early twentieth century. If we label interventions into the DGP as nonexperiments if they do not use random assignment, many famous and infamous research trials would be considered nonexperiments, such as Edward Jenner's research leading to the smallpox vaccine and the Tuskegee syphilis study discussed in Section 11.4.1.

the political parties; and Example 2.3 discusses an experiment by Clinton and Lapinski (2004) during the 2000 U.S. presidential election, in which Clinton and Lapinski showed subjects negative campaign advertisements. Clinton and Lapinski's experiment is an Internet survey experiment because it is embedded in a survey and conducted via the Internet. We discuss these particular types of experiments more expansively in Section 8.2.1.

The other four examples are laboratory experiments. However, they vary across important dimensions. Two were conducted by political psychologists involving hypothetical candidates (Example 2.4, experiments conducted by Kulisheck and Mondak (1996), Canache et al. (2000), and Mondak and Huckfeldt (2006), and Example 2.5, conducted by Mutz (2007)). Mondak and his coauthors varied how much information subjects had about candidate qualities, whereas Mutz varied the visual mechanism by which subjects learned about candidates. The remaining two examples were conducted by political economists in which subjects chose in a laboratory election and were given payments based on which choices won (Example 2.6, conducted by Battaglini, Morton, and Palfrey, and Example 2.7, conducted by Dasgupta and Williams [2002]). In Dasgupta and Williams's experiment, the choices before voters were called candidates, and voters were told they were voting in an election, whereas in Battaglini, Morton, and Palfrey's (2008, 2010) study, subjects were asked to guess the color of an unseen jar given information provided to them and the "winner" was the color that received the majority of guesses. Some of the experiments were conducted via computer networks. (Battaglini et al., Dasgupta and Williams, and Mondak et al. used computers in a laboratory; Clinton and Lapinski's experiment was conducted via the Internet). Mondak et al. and Mutz also used other methods to measure how subjects used or responded to information: Mondak et al. measured the time taken by subjects to respond to various questions and Mutz measured skin reactions to visual presentations of information.

We can also see tremendous variation in the control used in the experiments. In Examples 2.1, 2.3, and 2.5, Gerber et al., Clinton and Lapinski, and Mutz, respectively, designate one of the manipulations as a baseline manipulation. In other examples, although comparisons are made, the manipulation that one would call a baseline is not so obvious, as in Dasgupta and Williams's and Wantchekon's experiments. In the field experiments, the researchers generally had little control over many possible confounding variables. For instance, in Example 2.1, Gerber, Kaplan, and Bergan have little control over what is reported in the newspapers about the election, whether subjects read the newspaper articles about the election, and to some extent whether their access to the newspaper is manipulated. In contrast, in the laboratory experiments in Example 2.5, the subjects came to Mutz's laboratory and watched videos she had prepared in a controlled setting. In studies by Dasgupta and Williams and Battaglini et al., the researchers used financial incentives in an attempt to control subjects' preferences over their choices in the elections, which was not possible in the other five examples. That is, in the other five examples, the researchers must account for partisan preferences held by the subjects that may also affect their choices but cannot control them explicitly.

The seven examples also differ in the types of subjects used. The field experiments used residents in the localities where they were conducted, whereas the laboratory experiments generally used students, with the exception of Mutz's experiment which used nonstudents recruited via employment agencies or civic groups. Clinton and Lapinski used a national sample from an Internet survey organization. Some of the laboratory experiments that used students drew subjects from multiple universities: Mondak et al. used students from the United States, Mexico, and Venezuela, and Battaglini et al. used students from Princeton University and New York University. We discuss the advantages and disadvantages of different types of subjects in Chapter 9.

Finally, all seven examples reference to varying degrees one or more of the theories of voting mentioned in Section 2.3.3. Gerber et al., Mondak et al., and Mutz reference either explicitly or implicitly Cognitive Miser views of voting in which information primes, frames, or persuades voters. Clinton and Lapinski contend that their experiment provides important new evidence on negative advertisements, while Wantchekon argues that his work similarly informs our understanding of how clientelism works. Dasgupta and Williams and Battaglini et al. relate their experimental work to pivotal voter models. And both Gerber et al. and Battaglini et al. discuss expressive theories of voting. We address these and other variations in the examples (and additional examples presented later) throughout the text.

2.4.4 What Is Not an Experiment?

Qualitative Research and Traditional Surveys
Although our definition of experiments is encompassing, it excludes other research with human subjects in the social sciences such as interviews and qualitative, soak-and-poke, political science research that aims not to intervene in the DGP but to measure and observe how the DGP operates through close interaction with human subjects. Manipulations that occur in these types of research studies are not generally purposeful, but accidental. Whether, of course, it is possible to observe in close interaction without manipulating the DGP is an important issue in such research, but the overall

goal, as we understand it, is access to human subjects in the DGP as if the researcher were not there, rather than to manipulate the DGP. If qualitative researchers see themselves as intervening with the purpose of altering the DGP, we call that research an experiment. Similarly, a traditional survey is not an experiment because the goal of the researcher is to measure the opinion of the respondents, not to intervene or manipulate elements of the DGP that affect these opinions. When a researcher does purposely attempt to use a survey to manipulate elements of the DGP that theoretically affect respondents' opinions, we call this an experiment. We discuss experiments in surveys more expansively in Section 8.2.1.

Note that we recognize that the goal of many experimental manipulations is to better measure political behavior or preferences, as in many of the political psychology experiments which use implicit messages in an attempt to better measure racial prejudices (see, for example, Lodge and Taber, 2005). Yet the means of achieving the goal is through manipulation, not passive observation, which makes this research experimental rather than observational, in our view.

Natural and Policy Experiments and Downstream Benefits of Experiments

Sometimes nature acts in a way that is close to how a researcher, given the choice, would have intervened. For example, hurricane Katrina displaced thousands of New Orleans residents and changed the political makeup of the city, as well as having an impact on locations that received large numbers of refugees. Although no political scientists we know would wish such a disaster to occur in a major city, many find the idea of investigating the consequences of such a manipulation an exciting opportunity to evaluate theories of how representatives respond to changing constituencies, for example. Katrina was an act of nature that was close to what a political scientist would have liked to have done if he or she could – intervening and changing the political makeup of several large U.S. cities such as New Orleans, Houston, and Atlanta.

Natural manipulations might also occur in our information and voting example. For instance, in the case where the mailing described earlier in a naturally occurring election is provided without input by a researcher, then it is a natural manipulation. When natural manipulations occur, sometimes researchers argue that the manipulation is "as if" an experimentalist manipulated the variable. The researcher often calls the manipulation a "natural experiment," although the name is an oxymoron because by definition an experiment cannot be a situation where the DGP acts alone and thus we do not call these experiments, according to our definition. The researcher is contending that nature has two sides: the side that generates most data, and then the interventionist side that occasionally runs experiments like academics, messing up its own data generating process. Even though in this case the researcher is not doing the intervening, the approach taken with the data is as if the researcher has. When does it make sense for a researcher to make such a claim and approach his or her observational data in this fashion? The answer to this question is complicated and we address it fully in Section 5.4.3. Example 2.8 in the Appendix presents a study of a natural experiment involving the effect of information on voter turnout by Lassen (2005).

Definition 2.15 (Natural Experiment): *Nonexperimental or observational data generated by acts of nature that are close to the types of interventions or manipulations that an experimentalist would choose if he or she could.*

A special type of natural experiment occurs when government officials manipulate policies. For example, in Lassen's experiment, the natural manipulation occurred when government officials varied the ways in which public services were provided. Similarly, De La O (2008) exploits governmental policy changes in Mexico to consider how different governmental services impact voter participation. We call such a manipulation a policy experiment when it is undertaken by government officials without academic involvement.

Definition 2.16 (Policy Experiment): *A field experiment in which a government agency or other institution chooses to intervene and act "like an experimentalist."*

More recently, governments and other nonacademic institutions have formed collaborations with academic researchers to conduct experimental manipulations. An example of such a collaboration is provided in Example 12.1, where Olken (2008) collaborated with officials to manipulate the mechanisms by which villages in Indonesia made decisions about which public projects to fund. When such collaboration occurs and the researcher is directly involved in consciously choosing the design of the manipulation, the manipulation is an experiment, as we have defined. If the collaboration does not involve a researcher in the design process but simply allows a researcher the opportunity to gather data on a manipulation already planned and designed for a different purpose, the research is a natural experiment and not an experiment, as we have defined.

Occasionally researchers might use the manipulation of an experiment conducted in the past to investigate either a new hypothesis or the long-term implications of the original manipulation. Gerber and Green (2002) label such research downstream research and the results of these investigations the downstream benefits of experimentation. The use of previous experiments in this fashion certainly has advantages in the same ways that natural and policy experiments can be useful in empirical analysis. See Sondheimer (forthcoming) for a discussion of how researchers can benefit from prior manipulations.

Definition 2.17 (Downstream Benefits): *The benefits of analysis of prior experiments, either conducted by academics for research or conducted by government as a policy experiment.*

Computational Models and Simulations

Occasionally political scientists who use computational or agent-based models to numerically solve formal models of politics call the output "experiments," or others who run counterfactual analyses using parameters estimated from an empirical model call their analyses "experiments" (see, e.g., Kollman and Page, 1992). Computer simulations to solve formal models are aids in solving a model, not in "testing" the model with empirical data. These simulations are an extension of the researcher's brain. Similarly, counterfactual simulations using parameters from estimated empirical models are aids to understanding the empirical model estimated using either observational or experimental data and are an extension of the analysis of those data, not the generation of new experimental data. In experiments the subjects make "real" decisions and choices and are independent of the researcher, and new data are generated. The subjects are not simulating their behavior, but engaging in behavior. The environment created by the experimentalist is not an observational environment but it is real in the sense that real individuals are involved. Thus, simulations and experiments serve entirely distinctive purposes.[9]

Counterfactual Thought Experiments

Related to the use of computational or agent-based models to solve formal models are what have been called counterfactual thought experiments, in which nonformal theorists hypothesize the effects of situations in which

---

[9] Some experimentalists believe that this also means that it is important that the experimentalist not "hard-wire" the experiments by telling subjects how to choose or behave. However, there is no hard-and-fast rule on such suggestions, because in some cases doing so may be an important part of the experiment and is the subject of the experimental investigation.

one or more observables takes on values contrary to those observed (see, e.g., Tetlock and Belkin [1996] and Tetlock et al. [2006]). For example, what would have happened if Great Britain had confronted Hitler more before World War II? Again, these are not experiments as we have defined them because they are extensions of the researcher's brain – theoretical speculation about what would have happened historically if a variable had been manipulated.

2.4.5 Experimental Versus Observational Data

In most experimental research, the variation in the data is partly a consequence of the researcher's decisions before the data are drawn and measured. If we think of the DGP before or without intervention as nature acting alone, then the DGP after intervention is nature and the researcher interacting. We call the data generated by such intervention "experimental data." So for instance, in Clinton and Lapinski's experiment, Example 2.3, the 2000 presidential election without the experiment would be nature acting alone, but with the intervention of the researchers is nature and Clinton and Lapinski interacting. Data on the presidential election that do not involve such interaction are observational data (such as who the candidates were), but data generated through the interaction (such as how the subjects voted after having the campaign advertisements they saw manipulated by the researchers) are experimental data.

Definition 2.18 (Experimental Data): *Data generated by nature and the intervention of an experimentalist.*

Nonexperimental empirical research involves using only data drawn from the population in which all variation is a consequence of factors outside of the control of the researcher; the researcher only observes the subset of data he or she draws from the DGP but does not intervene in that process or if he or she does so, it is an accidental intervention, not purposeful. There are many observational studies of the 2000 U.S. presidential elections of this sort. This approach assumes, of course, that the researcher can and will choose to measure the data perfectly; clearly, choices made in measurement can result in a type of post-DGP intervention, but the data are still not experimental data because the data are generated without intervention.

Some distinguish between experimental and "naturally occurring" data. Others talk of the "real world" versus the experimental world. Such terms are misleading because nature is also involved in determining variation in experimental data. Even in laboratory experiments, although the experimenter may intervene in the data generating process, the subjects in the experiment who make decisions are "real" and their decisions occur "naturally," albeit influenced by the experimental environment. Since as political scientists we are interested in human behavior, we should recognize that the humans participating in an experiment are as "real" as the humans not participating in an experiment.[10] A more neutral description of research using only data where the variation is a consequence of factors outside of the control or intervention of the researcher is research that uses observational or nonexperimental data; we use that terminology.

Definition 2.19 (Nonexperimental or Observational Data): *Data generated by nature without intervention from an experimentalist.*

2.5 Chapter Summary

Fundamentally, scientific research is about building and evaluating theories about the causes of effects. Political scientists are interested in studying why and how people vote, for example. One of the ways we build toward such theories and evaluate them is to study the effects of causes. Many theories of why and how people vote make causal predictions about how information, a cause (either in content or presentation), affects voters' choices, an effect. In this chapter we have reviewed some of these theories of voting and their predictions about the relationship between information and voting as an illustration. To evaluate theoretical predictions, or sometimes just hunches, about the relationship between information and voting, many political scientists have used experiments. We have discussed examples of these in this chapter and the examples are presented more fully in the Appendix.

In this chapter we have also surveyed the features of the experimental method used by researchers to address predictions. In summary, the standard use of the experimental method in political science typically involves the following four principal features:

1. Designating a target population for the experimental study,
2. Intervention and manipulation in the DGP,

---

[10] We discuss in Chapter 7 whether the experimental environment leads subjects to make choices they would not make if the same changes in their environment would occur via nature or the DGP, rather than through experimental intervention. Even if "being in an experiment" has such an effect, this does not mean that the subjects' choices are less real or less human. It means that we must understand that sometimes the aspects of the experiment itself that cause such effects are treatments that must be considered explicitly.

3. Controlling observable confounding factors, and
4. Random assignment of subjects to manipulations to control for unobservable confounding factors and observable confounding factors that are difficult to control for otherwise.

In Chapter 9 we comprehensively investigate the choice of a target population. But we have argued that the key component of experimentation is the second feature, intervention and manipulation in the DGP. Some research with human subjects, where such intervention and manipulation is not the intended goal, we do not include as experiments. Similarly, other research activities that have the label experiment, such as natural experiments and computer simulations, we also do not include because they do not involve intervention or manipulation in the DGP by a researcher.

Furthermore, we have argued that although the second two aspects – control and random assignment – are valuable features of experimentation, experiments can vary significantly in how these two components are manifested. Sometimes control is manifested in the use of baseline manipulations and a high degree of control over the environment of the experiment; other times control is only minimally used by an experimentalist. Correspondingly, sometimes random assignment is implemented nearly perfectly, in which all subjects comply with assignments and their choices are fully observable; other times experimentalists must deal with noncompliance with manipulations and an inability to observe subjects' behavior (nonresponse).

Because these two aspects of experimentation are not binary but are closer to continuous variables, we do not define experiments by whether they have a given level of control or random assignment. Instead, we argue that the degree that control and random assignment are used depends on the goal of the experiment, something that we explore more expansively in the chapters to come, with an extensive discussion of control in Chapter 4 and random assignment in Chapter 5. Before we turn to our detailed examination of these aspects of experimentation, we present the Rubin Causal Model, which is one of the main approaches that underlies causal inference in experimental political science. We discuss the second approach to causality in experimental political science, the Formal Theory Approach, in Chapter 6.

2.6 Appendix: Examples

Example 2.1 (Newspaper Field Experiment): *Gerber et al. (2007) report on an experiment conducted during the 2005 Virginia gubernatorial* *election, designed to see if biased information sources affected voter behavior.*

Target Population and Sample: *Gerber, Kaplan, and Bergan selected a set of residents in Prince William County, Virginia, which is 25 miles from Washington, D.C. The subjects were selected about one month before the gubernatorial election in two waves from two different lists – a list of registered voters and a consumer database list. The registered voter list provided names of 54% of the first wave and 46% of the second wave; the consumer database provided the other names. Once these names were selected, the residents were surveyed in September 2005 and were asked if anyone in the household received either the* Washington Post *or the* Washington Times *newspapers. Respondents who answered "yes" or refused to answer any one of the questions in the survey were excluded from the study. The other questions were about the respondent's newspaper readership in general, the respondent's gender, whether he or she had voted in previous elections, and who she or he supported in the coming gubernatorial election.*[11] *This yielded a total of 3,347 subjects.*

Environment: *Gerber, Kaplan, and Bergan make use of the fact that Washington, D.C., has two national newspapers, the* Washington Post *and the* Washington Times; *the first is generally viewed as a liberal newspaper and the second is widely viewed as a conservative paper. Furthermore, researchers have found empirical evidence in support of the popular perceptions. Groseclose and Milyo (2005) compare the similarity of the experts used by media outlets with those cited by conservative and liberal members of Congress. From this comparison, they construct a measure of the ideological bias of newspapers. They find that the* Times *is the most conservative of the six papers they evaluate and the* Post *is much more liberal. Furthermore, the* Post *had endorsed the Democratic candidate for the Virginia gubernatorial election and the* Times *had endorsed the Republican. Thus, they have the opportunity to compare the effects of exposure on voting behavior in the Virginia gubernatorial election of two apparently very different news sources where the framing of stories, priming on issues, and persuasive efforts are arguably biased toward different candidates.*

Procedures: *The subjects were randomly assigned to one of three groups: a group that received a free one-month subscription to the* Post, *a group that received a free one-month subscription to the* Times, *and a group that received neither offer. Prior to the randomization, the sample was stratified into groups based on who they planned to vote for, whether they subscribe to another*

---

[11] Initially half of the subjects were to be asked if they would like a free one-month subscription to a national newspaper as a thank you for completing the survey. But this question was dropped early in the study.

(*non*-Post, *non*-Times) *newspaper, whether they subscribe to news magazines, and whether they were asked if they wished they read the paper more (50% of the subjects were asked this question). The stratification was designed so that Gerber, Kaplan, and Bergan had a balance on these covariates across the groups and the proportion of subjects in the groups was constant across strata. This randomization took place in two waves to maximize the time that subjects received the newspapers. We discuss such stratification techniques in Chapter 6. Households were given the option of canceling the subscriptions; approximately 6%, roughly equal between the* Post *and* Times, *canceled.*

The newspapers were unable to deliver to some of the addresses (76 of those assigned to the Times *and 1 of those assigned to the* Post). *Gerber, Kaplan, and Bergan employed a research assistant to monitor the delivery of newspapers to a random sample of households in the newspaper groups. While the* Post *had been delivered, the* Times *was not observed at all of the assigned addresses. Gerber, Kaplan, and Bergan spoke to the* Times *circulation department and called a small random sample of households assigned to receive the* Times *to verify their delivery.*

Moreover, when the lists of households to receive the newspapers were sent to the newspapers, 75 of the households assigned the Post *were reported to already subscribe to the* Post *(although it is unclear if they were subscribers only to the Sunday Edition or to the regular newspaper as well) and 5 of those assigned the* Times *were reported to already subscribe to the* Times.

After the gubernatorial election, Gerber, Kaplan, and Bergan reinterviewed 1,081 of the subjects, a response rate of approximately 32%. Gerber, Kaplan, and Bergan reported that (p. 11)

[t]*he remainder was not reached because the individual refused to participate in the follow-up survey (29.7%), the individual asked for was not available at the time of the call (10.3%), the operator reached an answering machine (9.8%), or the individual only partially completed the survey (6%). The operators were unable to reach the remainder for a number of different reasons, including reaching a busy signal, being disconnected, or getting no answer on the phone.... The follow-up survey asked questions about the 2005 Virginia Gubernatorial election (e.g. did the subject vote, which candidate was voted for or preferred), national politics (e.g. favorability ratings for Bush, the Republicans, the Democrats, support for Supreme Court nominee Samuel Alito), and knowledge of news events (e.g. does subject know number of Iraq war dead, has subject heard of I. Lewis Libby).*

Results: *Gerber, Kaplan, and Bergan found that those assigned to the* Post *group were eight percentage points more likely to vote for the Democratic candidate for governor than those not assigned a free newspaper. They also found similar evidence of differences in public opinion on specific issues and attitudes, but the evidence was weaker.*

Comments: *The results provide evidence that the biases in the news can affect voting behavior and political attitudes. The experiment is also a good illustration of randomization within strata and the measurement of causality using Intention-to-Treat, both of which we discuss in Chapter 5.*

Example 2.2 (Clientelism Field Experiment): *Wantchekon (2003) reported on a field experiment in Benin during a naturally occurring election in which candidates manipulated their campaign messages to test voter responses to messages of clientelist versus public policy messages.*

Target Population and Sample: *With the help of consultants, Wantchekon approached the leaders of four of the six political parties in Benin, which included the candidates of the two major parties. In Benin, voters are divided into eighty-four electoral districts. Wantchekon chose eight districts that are noncompetitive: four dominated by the incumbent government and four dominated by the opposition government. He also chose two competitive districts. The selection of districts was done in consultation with the campaign managers of the candidates. Within these districts, Wantchekon drew random samples for his postelection survey using standard survey sampling methods.*

Environment: *Benin is considered one of the most successful cases of democratization in Africa with a tradition of political experimentation. The election was a first-round election in which all expected a subsequent run-off election between the two major parties' candidates. Finally, candidates typically use a mixture of clientelism and public policy appeals in their election campaigns.*

Procedures: *Within each experimental district, two villages were chosen. In noncompetitive districts, one village was exposed to a clientelist platform, and the other a public policy platform. In the competitive districts, the manipulation differed; in one village one candidate espoused a clientelist platform and the other candidate a public policy platform, and in the other village the roles were reversed. The remaining villages in the selected districts were not exposed to the manipulation. The noncompetitive districts were ethnically homogenous and were less likely to be exposed to the nonexperimental manipulated campaign. The villages within each district were similar in demographic characteristics. Wantchekon took care to select villages that were physically distant from each other and separated by other villages so that, given normal communications, the manipulation was contained.*

The experimental platforms were carefully designed in collaboration with the campaign managers. The public policy message emphasized "national unity and peace, eradicating corruption, alleviating poverty, developing agriculture and industry, protecting the rights of women and children, developing rural credit, providing access to the judicial system, protecting the environment, and fostering educational reforms." The clientelism message consisted of a specific promise to the village for things like government patronage jobs or local public goods, "such as establishing a new local university or providing financial support for local fishermen or cotton producers."

After devising the platforms, ten teams of campaign workers were created and trained. Each team had two members, one a party activist and the other a nonpartisan research assistant. The team trained, monitored, and supervised campaign workers. There were also statisticians who served as consultants. Wantchekon (p. 410) describes how the messages were conveyed to voters:

> During each week for three months before the election, the campaign workers (one party activist and one social scientist) contacted voters in their assigned villages. With the help of the local party leader, they first settled in the village, contacted the local administration, religious or traditional authorities, and other local political actors. They then contacted individuals known to be influential public figures at home to present their campaign messages. They met groups of ten to fifty voters at sporting and cultural events. They also organized public meetings of fifty to one hundred people. On average, visits to household lasted half an hour and large public meetings about two hours.

In the post-election surveys, voters were asked demographic characteristics, degree of exposure of messages, and voting behavior.

Results: Wantchekon found that clientelism worked as a campaign message for all types of candidates but was particularly effective for regional and incumbent candidates. He also found that women had a stronger preference for public goods messages than men.

Comments: Wantchekon's experiment is an unusual example of a case where political candidates were willing to manipulate their messages substantially in a naturally occurring election. The experiment raises some ethical issues of the influence of experimentalists in the DGP, although most of the manipulation took place in noncompetitive districts in an election that was widely seen as not significantly consequential given the likelihood that a run-off election would be held. We return to these ethical issues in Chapters 11 and 12.

Example 2.3 (Negative Advertising Internet Survey Experiment): *Clinton and Lapinski (2004) report on an Internet survey experiment on the effects of negative advertising on voter turnout.*

Target Population and Sample: *Clinton and Lapinski used a national panel in the United States created by Knowledge Networks (KN). Information on KN can be found at http://www.knowledgenetworks.com/index3.html. Another Internet-based survey organization which has been used by political scientists is Harris Interactive (see http://www.harrisinteractive.com/). The* panelists were randomly selected using list-assisted random-digit-dialing sampling techniques on a quarterly updated sample frame from the entire U.S. telephone population that fell within the Microsoft Web TV network, which at the time of the study was 87% of the U.S. population. The acceptance rate of KN's invitation to join the panel during the time of the study averaged 56%. Clinton and Lapinski randomly selected eligible voters from the KN panel for their study.

Subject Compensation: The panelists were given an interactive television device (Microsoft Web TV) and a free Internet connection in exchange for participating in the surveys. Participants are expected to complete one survey a week to maintain the service.

Environment: Clinton and Lapinski conducted their experiment during the 2000 presidential general election campaign and they used actual advertisements aired by the two major candidates, Bush and Gore. Subjects took part in the experiment in their own homes, although the subjects had to use the Web TV device to participate in the experiment. This somewhat reduced the variance in subjects' survey experience.

Procedures: An email was sent to the Web TV account of the selected subjects, informing them that their next survey was ready to be taken. Through a hyperlink, the subjects reached the survey. The response rate was 68% and on average subjects completed the survey within 2.7 days of being sent the email. The subjects were asked a variety of questions, both political and nonpolitical, for other clients of KN, but Clinton and Lapinski's questions were always asked first. During the survey, those subjects who had been randomly chosen to see one or more political advertisements were shown a full-screen advertisement and then asked a few follow-up questions.

The subjects were approached in two waves. The two waves in the experiment tested between different manipulations. In wave I, Clinton and Lapinski investigated the effect of being shown a single or pair of advertisements on Gore on the likelihood of voting, and in wave II, Clinton and Lapinski investigated the effect of seeing a positive or negative Bush advertisement conditioned on seeing a Gore negative advertisement. In wave I, subjects were divided into four groups depending on the types of advertisements shown: manipulation A (Gore negative and positive), manipulation B (Gore positive), manipulation C (Gore negative), and a group that was not shown an advertisement. Wave I took place between October 10, 2000, and November 7, 2000, with the median respondent completing his or her survey on October 12, 2000. In wave II, subjects were divided into three groups: manipulation D (Gore negative, Bush positive), manipulation E (Gore negative, Bush negative), and a group that was not shown an advertisement. Wave II took place between October 30,

2000, and November 5, 2000, and the median respondent completed his or her survey on November 1, 2000. Overall 2,850 subjects were assigned to groups A, B, and C; 2,500 were assigned to groups D and E. In wave I, 4,614 subjects did not see an advertisement; in wave II, 1,500 did not see an advertisement.

After being shown the ad or ads in both waves, subjects were asked the likelihood that they would vote in the presidential election. The question wording was slightly different in the two waves, with five options in wave I, and ten options in wave II. Finally, after the election, subjects were surveyed again, asking whether they had voted; 71% of the subjects responded to the post-election survey request.

Results: *Clinton and Lapinski found no evidence that the negative advertisements demobilize voters either using the initial probability of voting question or the post-election self-reported turnout question. They also found, when they controlled for respondent characteristics, that there is no mobilization effect of the campaign advertisements either. They argued that their results suggest that the effects of the manipulations are dependent on voter characteristics and the issues discussed in the advertisements and not the overall tone of the ads.*

Comments: *The group that did not see an advertisement in wave I was not a random sample devised by Clinton and Lapinski, but due to a technical difficulty that was known prior to the administration of the survey. However, Clinton and Lapinski state that the group was "essentially" random and that they used demographic controls in the analysis. Clinton and Lapinski analyzed the data using both the manipulations as independent variables and other demographic variables that can matter for turnout and that varied by manipulation group. We discuss the reasoning behind these estimation strategies in Section 4.2.8.*

Example 2.4 (Candidate Quality Lab Experiment): *Kulisheck and Mondak (1996), hereafter Mondak1; Canache et al. (2000), hereafter Mondak2; and Mondak and Huckfeldt (2006), hereafter Mondak3, reported on a series of experiments investigating how voters respond to information about the quality of candidates, independent of issue positions. Mondak et al. refers to all three experiments.*

Target Population and Sample: *Mondak et al. used as subjects undergraduate students enrolled in political science classes at universities in Mexico, Venezuela, and the United States. Mondak1 used 452 students at the University of Pittsburgh; Mondak2 used 130 students at two universities in Caracas (Univeridad Católica Andrés Bello and Universidad Simón Bolívar) and 155 students at three universities in Mexico (Universidad de las Américas, Universidad Autónoma de Méjico-Xochimilco, and Centro de Investigación y Docencia Económica de Méjico); and Mondak3 used 223 students at Indiana University.*

Subject Compensation: *Mondak et al. did not report whether the subjects were compensated for their participation. Presumably, however, they were compensated by credit in the political science classes they were taking.*

Environment: *The experiments reported on in Mondak1 and Mondak2 were conducted in classrooms using pen and paper. The experiments reported on in Mondak3 were conducted using computers. In all of the experiments, the candidates that subjects were presented with were hypothetical. In Mondak1 and Mondak2, subjects were given detailed information about the hypothetical candidates and asked to read material similar to what would appear in a local newspaper in a "meet the candidates" format. In Mondak3, subjects were presented information about the candidates via computer, but the information was more limited. An important factor in the experiments was that while in the United States there is usually much discussion about personal skill and the integrity of candidates for Congress, for legislative positions in Mexico and Venezuela the electoral system in place at the time of the experiments did not encourage voter discussion of these issues and voters rarely had this sort of information about the candidates.*

MediaLab and DirectRT are computer software programs designed for psychology experiments and used by political psychologists like Mondak et al. Information on this software can be found at http://www.empirisoft.com/ medialab.aspx and http://www.empirisoft.com/DirectRT.aspx.

Procedures: *First subjects took a survey about their political attitudes and attentiveness. Then subjects were presented with the information about the hypothetical candidates, either in paper form or via computer. All of the experiments varied the content of the information presented and subjects were randomly assigned to these manipulations. In all of the experiments, the researchers focused on manipulations of evaluations of the skill and integrity of the candidates. In Mondak1, the subjects were asked to give feeling thermometer-like ratings to the two candidates in each set and to identify which one would receive their vote. In Mondak2, the subjects were only asked which candidate they would vote for. And in Mondak3, subjects were asked whether they favored or opposed each candidate on an individual basis; that is, the candidates were presented not as pairs but singly on the computer screens. Also in Mondak3 the researchers measured the response time of subjects (how long it took for a subject to express his or her choice after seeing the information about a candidate).*

Results: *Mondak1 and Mondak2 found significant evidence that the qualities of the candidates affected the subjects' choices. They found this result was robust even when controlling for the importance of political issues for subjects and the distance between subjects' views on ideology and the candidates. Mondak3 found a similar effect but also found that subjects' attitudes toward candidates' competence and integrity were highly cognitively accessible* *(as measured by the response time). But they found no evidence that candidate character serves as a default basis for evaluation when things like partisanship and ideology are unavailable.*

Comments: *In Mondak3, the researchers also reported on survey evidence that supports their conclusions.*

Example 2.5 ("In-Your-Face" Discourse Lab Experiment): *Mutz (2007) reported on laboratory experiments designed to evaluate the effects of televised political discourse on awareness of opposing perspectives and views of their legitimacy.*

Target Population and Sample: *At least 171 subjects were recruited from temporary employment agencies and community groups. Mutz did not report the community from which the subjects were drawn, although probably they were from the area around her university.[12]*

Subject Compensation: *Subjects from the temporary employment agencies received an hourly rate that depended on whether the subjects came to campus to participate in this particular experiment or a set of studies over several hours. The subjects from civic groups participated as a fund-raising activity for their organizations.*

Environment: *The experiments took place in a university facility where subjects were shown a 20-minute mock television program while sitting on a couch. The program was produced professionally with paid actors and a professional studio talkshow set was used to tape the program. The program was also professionally edited. The program was an informal political discussion between two "candidates" for an open congressional seat in a distant state, with a moderator who occasionally asked the candidates questions. Subjects were led to believe that the program and candidates were "real."*

The candidates in the video had opposing views on eight different issues. The views drew on arguments from interest groups and the issues were topical at the time of the experiment. Four versions of the video were produced; two were civil versions and two were uncivil ones. In all four the same issue positions and arguments were expressed in the same words. As Mutz relates (p. 625):

> The only departures from the script that were allowed for purposes of creating the variance in civility were nonverbal cues (such as rolling of the eyes) and phrases devoid of explicit political content (such as "You have completely missed the point here!"). The candidates in the uncivil condition also raised their voices and interrupted one another. In the civil version, the politicians spoke calmly throughout and were patient and respectful while the other person spoke.

---

[12] Mutz did not report the number of subjects who participated in experiment 3, so this sum only includes the participants in experiments 1 and 2.

Mutz did a manipulation check with pretest subjects who rated the candidates on measures of civility.

Mutz also manipulated the camera perspective. That is, in one of the civil versions and one of the uncivil versions there was an initial long camera shot that showed the set and location of the candidates and moderator, and then the subsequent shots were almost exclusively tight close-ups. In contrast, in the medium version the candidates' upper bodies were shown.

General Procedures: *After giving consent to participate, subjects were seated on the couch and given a pretest questionnaire. They were then asked to watch the video program and informed that they would be asked some questions after the program was concluded. Afterward, a paper-and-pencil questionnaire was administered. Subjects only saw four issues discussed, which varied by experimental session. In the questionnaire, Mutz asked open-ended questions designed to measure the extent that subjects recalled the arguments and the legitimacy of the arguments. Mutz also asked subjects to rate the candidates on a feeling thermometer. Using these basic procedures, Mutz conducted three different experiments.*

Experiment 1 Procedures: *In the first experiment, which used 16 subjects, the subjects saw a discussion using all four different combinations of camera perspective and civility (the issues also varied). These subjects' arousal during the video was measured using skin conductance levels by attaching two electrodes to the palm of each subject's nondominant hand. According to Mutz (p. 626), "Data collection began at the start of each presentation, with a 10-second period of baseline data recorded while the screen was blank prior to the start of each debate."*

Experiment 2 Procedures: *The second experiment used 155 subjects and the subjects saw only one of the four possible experimental manipulations. Subjects were randomly assigned to manipulations. Also included was a group of subjects who were randomly assigned to watch a nonpolitical program for the same amount of time and received the same questionnaire.*

Experiment 3 Procedures: *Mutz did not report the number of subjects used in this experiment. Experiment 3 is a partial replication of experiment 2 with one exception: in this experiment, all subjects saw the close-up versions of the videos and were randomly assigned to either civil or uncivil discourse.*

Results: *In experiment 1, Mutz found that uncivil discourse was significantly more arousing than civil discourse and that the close-up camera perspective was also significantly more arousing than the medium perspective. In experiment 2, she found that the awareness of rationales for arguments was also affected by the manipulations in the same direction, and uncivil close-up conditions led to the most recall. Furthermore, she found that the difference in thermometer ratings between the subjects' preferred and nonpreferred candidates* *was not affected by civility in the medium camera perspective. However, in the close-up camera condition, this difference was significantly greater in the uncivil condition. The effect worked in both directions; that is, in the civil close-up condition the difference in ratings fell and in the uncivil close-up condition the difference rose, in comparison to the medium camera condition. Mutz found a similar relationship in the perceived legitimacy of opposing arguments in both experiment 2 and experiment 3.*

Comments: Mutz's experiments are a good example of how control can be exercised over unobservable variables in experiment 1, which we discuss further in the next two chapters. Experiment 3 is an interesting instance of a researcher replicating a previously found result, something we discuss in Chapter 7.

Example 2.6 (Swing Voter's Curse or SVC Lab Experiment): *Battaglini et al. (2008, 2010) report on a series of experiments conducted to evaluate the predictions from the Swing Voter's Curse.*

Target Population and Sample: *Battaglini, Morton, and Palfrey recruited student volunteers at Princeton University (84 subjects) and New York University (NYU; 80 subjects) from existing subject pools which had been recruited across each campus. No subject participated in more than one session. The subject pool for the experiments had been recruited via email to sign up for experiments conducted at either the Princeton Laboratory for Experimental Social Sciences at Princeton or the Center for Experimental Social Sciences at NYU. One free online recruitment system is ORSEE (Online Recruitment System for Economic Experiments, devised by Ben Greiner at the University of New South Wales; see ttp://www.orsee.org/).*

As is typical in political economy laboratory experiments, more subjects than the required number were recruited because the experiments were designed for specific numbers of participants. Subjects were chosen to participate on a first-come/first-serve basis, and subjects who arrived after the required number of participants had been met were given the show-up fee as payment.

Subject Compensation: *Subjects were paid in cash based on their choices during the experiment as described in the procedures. Average earnings were approximately $20. In addition, subjects were also given a show-up fee of $10. Subjects were assigned experiment-specific identification (ID) numbers and payments were made to subjects by ID numbers such that records were not kept that could be used to match subject identity with payments received or choices in the experiment.*

Environment: *The experiments used a standard setup for computerized laboratory experiments by political economists. That is, the experiments were conducted in computer laboratories via computer terminals and all* communication between the experimenter and subjects was conducted via the computer interface. Each subject's computer screen was shielded from the view of other subjects in the room through privacy screens and dividers. Subjects were first presented with instructions about the experiment and then took a short quiz regarding the information in the instructions before they were allowed to continue to the experiment. Subjects were told all the parameters of the experiment as described in the procedures. The experimental parameters were chosen specifically to evaluate game-theoretic predictions and a formal model was used to derive these predictions explicitly. The software used for the experimental program was multistage, which is an open-source software program for laboratory experiments developed at the California Institute of Technology (see http://multistage.ssel.caltech.edu/). Of particular usefulness for experiments is the free software z-Tree for the Zurich Toolbox for Readymade Economic Experiments (see http://www.iew.uzh.ch/ztree/index.php), which was devloped by Urs Fischacher.

Procedures: Before the experiment began, one subject was randomly chosen to be a monitor. The monitor was paid a flat fee of $20 in addition to his or her show-up fee. Each session was divided into periods. In five of the sessions conducted at Princeton University, 14 subjects were randomly assigned to two groups of 7 voters. The group assignments were anonymous; that is, subjects did not know which of the other subjects were in their voting group. In two sessions at Princeton, only 7 subjects were in each session, so in each period the group of voters was the same. At NYU all subjects in each session were in the same group; three sessions used 21 subjects and one session used 17 subjects.

In each period and group, the monitor would throw a die to select one of two jars, red or yellow. Although subjects could see the monitor making the selection, they were not able to see the selection made. The red jar contained two red balls and six white balls, the yellow jar contained two yellow balls and six white balls. These were not physical jars, but were represented on the computer monitors. Subjects then were shown the jar with eight clear balls, that is, a jar without the colors. They then could click on one of the balls and the color of the ball selected would be revealed. If a red or yellow ball was revealed, they learned which jar had been chosen. If a white ball was revealed, they did not learn which jar had been chosen.

After choosing a ball and finding out its color, the group members simultaneously chose where to abstain, vote for red, or vote for yellow. The computer casts a set number of votes for the red jar. The jar that received the majority of the votes was declared the winner, including the computer votes (ties were broken randomly by the computer). If the jar chosen by the majority was the correct jar, all the subjects earned a payoff of 80 cents in the period, and if the *jar chosen by the majority was the incorrect jar, all the subjects earned a payoff of 5 cents in the period.*

Subjects were told the outcome of the period in their group. They were then randomly reassigned to new groups for the next period if applicable and the procedure was repeated. The colors of the balls within each jar were randomly shuffled each period so that if a subject repeatedly chose to click on the same ball, whether they were revealed a white ball was randomly determined by the percentage of white balls in the jar (i.e., the probability of observing a white ball was always 75%). A check of the data shows that the procedure worked as desired: approximately 75% of subjects saw a white ball and 25% saw either a red or yellow ball. There were a total of 30 periods in each session.

Each session was divided into three subsessions of ten periods each. In one of the subsessions, the computer had zero votes. In sessions with groups of 7 voters, in one subsession the computer had two votes and in one subsession the computer had four votes. In sessions with groups of 17 and 21 voters, in one subsession the computer had six votes and in one subsession the computer had twelve votes. The sequence of the subsessions varied by session. The following sequences were used depending on the number of voters in the groups: (0,2,4), (0,4,2), (2,4,0), (4,0,2), (4,2,0), (0,6,12), and (12,6,0).

Battaglini, Morton, and Palfrey also varied the probability by which the monitor would pick the red jar. In some sessions, the probability of a red jar being selected was equal to the probability of a yellow jar, which was equal to 1/2. This was done by having the monitor use a six-sided die; if 1, 2, or 3 were shown, the red jar was selected, and if 4, 5, or 6 were shown, the yellow jar was selected. In other sessions the probability of a red jar being selected was equal to 5/9 while the probability of a yellow jar was equal to 4/9. This was done by having the monitor use a ten-sided die; if 1, 2, 3, 4, or 5 were shown, the red jar was selected; if 6, 7, 8, or 9 were shown, the yellow jar was selected; and if 10 was shown, the die was tossed again.

Results: Battaglini, Morton, and Palfrey found that subjects who were revealed either a red or yellow ball voted for the red or yellow jar, respectively. They also found that when the number of computer votes was equal to zero, most of the subjects who were revealed a white ball abstained. As the number of computer voters increased, uninformed voters increased their probability of voting for the yellow jar. These results occurred even when the probability of the red jar was 5/9.

Comments: The results strongly support the SVC theoretical predictions. Uninformed voters are more likely to abstain than informed voters, but when there are partisans (as operationalized by the computer voters), the uninformed voters appear to vote to offset the partisans' votes, even when the probability is higher that the true jar is the red jar (the partisans' favorite). Battaglini, Morton, and Palfrey also considered some alternative theoretical models to explain some of the subjects' errors, an analysis that we explore in Chapter 6.

Example 2.7 (Polls and Information Lab Experiment): *Dasgupta and Williams (2002) reported on a laboratory experiment that investigates the hypothesis that uninformed voters can effectively use cues from public opinion polls as an information source to vote for the candidate they would choose if informed.*

Target Population and Sample: *Dasgupta and Williams recruited 119 undergraduate student volunteers at Michigan State University. The authors recruited subjects who were unaccustomed to psychological experiments and were unfamiliar with spatial voting models and formal decision theory.*

Subject Compensation: *Subjects were paid based on their choices as described in the procedures. As in many political economic experiments, the subjects' payoffs were denominated in an experimental currency that was then converted at the end of the experiment into cash. Dasgupta and Williams called this experimental currency "francs." We discuss reasons for using an experimental currency in Section 10.1.4; one reason for doing so in the Dasgupta and Williams experiment is that it allowed them to have different exchange rates for different types of subjects, as described later. The exchange rates were fixed and known by subjects. Subjects earned on average $22 for the two-and-a-half hours plus a show-up fee.*

Environment: *As in Example 2.6, the experiment was conducted via a computer network. Subjects were seated so that they were unable to see the computer monitors and choices of other subjects. The experimental parameters were chosen to fit the formal model presented by Dasgupta and Williams.*

Procedures: *Dasgupta and Williams conducted six experimental sessions with 17 subjects in each session. At the beginning of a session, two subjects were chosen to be incumbent candidates; the remaining subjects were assigned as voters. The sessions were divided into two subsessions lasting 10 periods each. The incumbent candidates were randomly assigned to separate subsessions and only participated in the experiment in the subsession to which they were assigned. At the beginning of each subsession, the incumbent candidate was assigned an issue position of either 0 or 1000, which was held fixed throughout the subsession. This issue position was publicly announced to all subjects. In each period in a subsession, the subjects were randomly divided into three equal-sized groups of 5 voters each with issue positions of 250, 500, and 750, respectively. So in each period, a subject's issue position was a new random draw. All subjects knew the distribution of issue positions of voters.*

Table 2.1. *Voters' payoffs*

Incumbent Quality	Incumbent's issue position = 0					
	Voter issue positions					
	Incumbent wins			Challenger wins		
	250	500	750	250	500	750
10	40	10	10	25	10	20
20	45	45	25	30	45	40
30	50	50	50	35	50	60

Before the subsession began, the incumbent candidate was provided with an initial endowment of 900 francs. The candidate chose an "effort" level equal to either 10 or 20. Effort levels were costly to the candidate; if he or she chose an effort of 10, the cost was 30 francs. The cost of an effort of 20 was 170 in one subsession and 90 in the other. The cost of the effort chosen by the candidate was deducted from his or her endowment. The computer program then assigned the candidate a "quality" of either 10, 20, or 30, with equal probability. Note that the incumbent candidate was not told his or her quality before choosing an effort level. The effort level and quality were combined to produce an "output." Three voters in each of the voting groups were randomly chosen to be told the output. The remaining two voters in each voting group received no information about the output and were uninformed.

Voters then participated in an election. They could either vote for the incumbent or the challenger (who was an artificial actor). If the incumbent won the election, he or she would receive 300 francs. The voters' payoffs depended on their own issue position, the issue position of the incumbent candidate, and the quality of the incumbent. Table 2.1 presents the payoffs to voters by issue position when the incumbent candidate's issue position equals 0 (the case where the incumbent candidate's issue position equals 1000).

Before the election was held, three separate opinion polls were taken. In each poll, voters were asked which of the two candidates – incumbent or challenger – he or she currently preferred. All subjects were revealed the aggregate outcomes of the polls. After the polls were completed, the election was held, which was decided by majority rule (ties were broken randomly by the computer). The incumbent candidate and the voters received their respective payoffs and a new period began with voters reassigned to new voter types.

Dasgupta and Williams also conducted an additional seventh session which was the same as the other sessions except that the candidate's issue position was held constant at 0 in both subsessions and all voters were uninformed.

Results: *Dasgupta and Williams found significant support for the theoretical argument that uninformed voters will use poll information to make more accurate voting decisions and that the electorate's behavior is consistent with complete information. Compared to the session in which no voters were informed, voters were much more likely to choose optimally. However, voters make errors when incumbent candidates choose suboptimally. Specifically, in the low-cost subsessions, according to the theory, the candidates should always choose a low level of effort and in the high-cost trials the candidates should choose a high level of effort. The majority of the time candidates chose effort levels as predicted, with errors occurring early in the subsessions. Voters' mistakes were most likely to occur when candidates did not choose effort levels as predicted.*

Comments: *The experiments are an extension of earlier experiments and theoretical work reported by McKelvey and Ordeshook (1984, 1985a,b, 1986a,b), and Collier et al. (1987) on a rational expectations model of the relationship between voting and information. Dasgupta and Williams also compared the predictions of several alternative models in which uninformed voters are uninfluenced by polls and found support for the rational expectations model.*

Example 2.8 (Decentralization Experience and Turnout Natural Experiment): *Lassen (2005) presents a study of the effects of information on voter turnout in Copenhagen. He exploits a naturally occurring situation that affected voter information in a naturally occurring referendum and studies the effect of the information on turnout in the referendum.*

Target Population and Sample: *Lassen used a telephone survey of voters in the city of Copenhagen. The voters in the city were partitioned into five strata reflecting five different areas of the city. In Denmark every citizen has an identification number. Everyone eligible to vote automatically receives a ballot card at their address in the census registry. The voter then presents the ballot card at their local polling station and if the individual votes, it is registered. The survey was commissioned by the city, so the sample was drawn from the city's list of eligible voters in the election. The response rate to the survey was 55%, resulting in a sample of 3,021 observations. Of this sample, one-third refused to answer questions about their yearly income or whether they had voted in the referendum, which left 2,026 observations. Lassen used the larger sample for some analysis as well as the smaller sample.*

Environment: *In 1996 the city of Copenhagen decided to conduct a policy experiment in decentralization of city government by having some areas of the city experience decentralized services while other areas continued to experience centralized services. The policy experiment lasted for four years and in 2000 a* *citywide consultatory referendum was held on whether the program should be extended to or abolished in the entire city.*[13]

Procedures: *The city was divided into fifteen districts (divisions which did not exist prior to the policy experiment): eleven districts where government services continued to be centrally administered and four districts where approximately 80% of government services were administered by locally elected district councils, which are labeled pilot city districts or PCDs. The designers of the policy experiment attempted to choose four districts that were representative of the city. The strata for the survey were the four PCDs and the rest of the city.*

The consultatory referendum was held on the same day as a nationwide referendum on whether Denmark should join the common European currency. It was possible for individuals to vote in only one of the referenda if they wished.

The survey asked respondents if they voted in the last municipal election, whether they voted in the nationwide referendum, whether they voted in the municipal referendum, their opinion of the decentralization experiment, their opinion of the responsiveness of municipal council members, how interested they are in political issues, and a set of demographic questions.

Results: *Lassen found that turnout was significantly higher among informed voters than in the districts where services remained centralized. The effect is robust to a number of different specifications and is strongest among those voters who had zero cost of voting; that is, those who voted in the nationwide referendum and so had paid the cost of going to the polling place.*

Comments: *Lassen dealt with a wide variety of methodological issues in identifying and estimating the causal relationship between information and voting. We discuss his study more expansively as we explore these issues. As in the other experiments we have so far discussed, in Lassen's study the manipulated variable is not the same as the treatment variable. The manipulated variable is whether the respondent lived in the district that experienced the decentralization policy experiment, whereas the treatment variable is the information level of the respondents. As a proxy for the treatment variable, Lassen uses whether a respondent reported an opinion of the decentralization experiment, classifying those with no opinions as uninformed. He cites empirical evidence that finds a strong correlation between other measures of voter information and the willingness to express an opinion. Lassen also finds, however, that this treatment variable is endogenous and affected by other observable variables from the survey. We discuss how Lassen deals with this endogeneity in identifying and estimating the causal effects of information on turnout in Chapter 5.*

---

[13] The referendum was nonbinding because the Danish constitution does not allow for binding referenda at the municipal level.

3

The Causal Inference Problem and the Rubin
Causal Model

In this book we concentrate on two prominent approaches to causality that underpin almost all of the work in political science estimating causal relationships: the Rubin Causal Model (RCM) and the Formal Theory Approach (FTA).[1] In this and the next two chapters, we focus on the RCM model. In Chapter 6 we discuss FTA. RCM is an approach that has its genesis in the statistical literature and early studies of field experiments,[2] whereas FTA comes primarily from the econometric literature and is the approach used by experimental economists in many laboratory experiments (although statisticians such as Pearl [2000] are also advocates of an approach that is similar to FTA).

We begin our presentation of RCM by defining some basic variables and terms used in the approach.

---

[1] There are other approaches to causality; see Winship and Morgan (1999) for a review of the literature and Dawid (2000) for a critique of current approaches. RCM and FTA are by far the most prevalent ones used in political science.

[2] Although RCM is named after his work, Rubin (1990) notes that the ideas behind the approach precede his work and were first applied to experimental research (see Neyman, 1923). Because of Neyman's contribution, some call the model the Neyman–Rubin Causal Model. Rubin receives due credit for providing a formal foundation for use of the approach with observational data. However, the use of counterfactuals and potential outcomes can also be found in formal models of the early econometrics literature (see Roy, 1951; Quandt, 1958, 1972; and Lewis, 1963). Heckman (2005a) reviews this literature in economics and also points to early work in mathematical pyschology on counterfactuals (Thurstone, 1930). For a review of the statistical literature, see Rubin (1990), Winship and Morgan (1999), and Wooldridge (2002, chapter 18). Sometimes the model is also called the Rubin–Holland approach in recognition of Holland's noteworthy (1986) formalization. (Holland is credited with naming the model after Rubin.)

3.1 Variables in Modeling the Effects of a Cause

3.1.1 The Treatment Variable

We are interested in the effect of information on how voters choose in the election studied or target population; that is, information is our possible causal variable. To simplify our analysis, we think of being informed as a binary variable (later we discuss analyses where this assumption is relaxed). We can think of there being two states of the world, one in which an individual i is informed about the choices before them in the election and the other in which the individual i is uninformed. In a naturally occurring election, the information the voter may or may not have may be about the policy positions of the candidates on the issues they care about or some overall quality of the candidates that matters to voters such as honesty, integrity, or the ability to manage the economy or national defense. In the referenda example, the voter may or may not have information on aspects of the proposed law. And in the laboratory election, similarly, the subject may or may not have information about the choices before him or her in the election.

In general, we can denote the two states of the world that a voter can be in as "1" or "0" where 1 refers to being informed and 0 refers to being uninformed or less informed. Let $T_i = 1$ if an individual is in state "1"; $T_i = 0$ otherwise. So in an experiment like Example 2.4, in which Mondak et al. provide subjects with information about hypothetical candidates' qualities, 1 would mean that a subject read and understood the information provided and 0 would mean otherwise.

Typically we think of T_i as the treatment variable. In political science we often refer to it as the main or principal independent variable. We are interested in the effect of the treatment variable on voting choices.

Definition 3.1 (Treatment Variable): *The principal variable that we expect to have a causal impact.*

3.1.2 Variables That Affect Treatments

Because we are interested in both experimental and observational data, it is useful to think of T_i as an endogenous variable, which is a function of a set of observable variables, Z_i; a set of unobservable variables, V_i; as well as sometimes a manipulated variable, M_i, which may be manipulated by a researcher or by nature. The manipulated variable describes whether the subject was assigned to view a campaign advertisement by the researchers. In a laboratory experiment, as in that of Dasgupta and Williams, the manipulated variable is whether subjects were told the quality of the candidates directly by the experimenter. We call this an experimental manipulation. In observational data without manipulation, T_i is only a function of Z_i and V_i; we call this a natural manipulation.

Definition 3.2 (Manipulated Variable): *A variable that has an impact on the treatment variable that can be manipulated either naturally or by an experimenter.*

Definition 3.3 (Experimental Manipulation): *When the manipulated variable is fixed through the intervention of an experimentalist.*

Definition 3.4 (Natural Manipulation): *When the manipulated variable is part of nature without intervention of an experimentalist.*

The observable variables, Z_i, are observable confounding factors as defined in Definition 2.8, and the unobservable variables, V_i, are unobservable confounding factors as defined in Definition 2.9. In the case of an experiment during an election in the field, as in Clinton and Lapinski's experiment (see Example 2.3), observable variables might be the individuals' level of education, their income, or their place of residence whereas unobservable variables might be the individuals' cognitive abilities, interest in politics, or free time.[3]

3.1.3 The Dependent Variable

We are interested in the effects of a cause and we call the dependent variable the variable that represents or measures the effects, essentially. In our running example of information and voting, the dependent variable is the voting behavior upon which we expect information to have an effect. Whether informed or not, our individuals have choices over whether to vote or abstain, and if they vote, which candidate or choice to vote for. If our target election is a U.S. presidential election with three candidates, then the voter has four choices: abstain, vote for the Republican candidate, vote for the Democratic candidate, or vote for the minor party or independent

---

[3] Of course we may attempt to measure some of these unobservables and make them observable; the point is that there are always some influences that will be unobservable.

candidate. So in standard political science terminology, our dependent variable is a random variable, Y_i, that can take on four values $\{0, 1, 2, 3\}$, where 0 denotes individual i choosing abstention, 1 denotes individual i voting for the Republican, 2 denotes individual i voting for the Democrat, and 3 denotes the individual voting for the minor party or independent candidate. Denote Y_{i1} as the voting choice of i when informed and Y_{i0} as the voting choice of i when uninformed.

Definition 3.5 (Dependent Variable): *A variable that represents the effects that we wish to explain. In the case of political behavior, the dependent variable represents the political behavior that the treatment may influence.*

Note that in some of the experiments in our examples in the appendix to the Chapter 2, the dependent variable is a survey response by subjects as to how they would choose rather than their actual choice, since observing their actual choice was not possible for the researchers.

We hypothesize that Y_{ij} is also a function of a set of observed variables, X_i, and a set of unobservable variables, U_i, as well as T_i. For example, Y_{ij} might be a function of a voter's partisan affiliation, an observable variable, and it might be a function of a voter's value for performing citizen duty, an arguably unobservable variable. Note that we assume that it is possible that Z_i and X_i overlap and could be the same and that U_i and V_i overlap and could be the same (although this raises problems with identification of causal relationships, as discussed in the following chapters).

3.1.4 Other Variables and Variable Summary

Occasionally we also discuss two other variables: W_i, the set of all observable variables, and P_i, the probability that $Y_i = 1$. We define and use W_i when the analysis makes no distinction between X and Z. In some of the examples and sometimes for ease of exposition, we focus on the case where Y_i is binary – it can be either 0 or 1. This might be the case where the dependent variable is turnout and 0 represents abstention and 1 represents voting as in the study of Lassen (2005) discussed in the next chapter. In other situations, 0 might represent voting for a Democratic candidate and 1 voting for the Republican, as in the analysis of Bartels (1996) discussed in the next chapter. When the choice is binary, the dependent variable is often assumed to be the probability that Y_i equals 1, which we designate as P_i. Denote P_{i1} as the value of P_i when i is informed and P_{i0} as the value of P_i when i is uninformed. Table 3.1 presents a summary of this notation, which is used throughout Chapters 3–5.

Table 3.1. *Variable definitions*

Variable	Definition
T_i	Treatment of unit of observation i In our example, $T_i = 0$ if an individual is uninformed, $T_i = 1$ if an individual is informed
Z_i	Observable variables that partly determine T_i
V_i	Unobservable variables that partly determine T_i
M_i	Manipulated variable that partly determines T_i This could be manipulated by an experimenter or nature
Y_i	The actual outcome or choice of the unit In our example, the vote choice of the individual
Y_{ij}	The hypothetical outcome or choice of the unit when $T_i = j$ In our example, the hypothetical vote choice of the individual when $T_i = j$ (which may not be observed)
X_i	Observable variables that partly determine Y_{ij} There may be overlap between X_i and Z_i
U_i	Unobservable variables that partly determine Y_{ij} There may be overlap between V_i and U_i
W_i	$X_i \cup Z_i$
P_i	The probability that $Y_i = 1$ when $Y_i = \{0, 1\}$
P_{ij}	The hypothetical value of P_i when $T_i = j$

3.2 Manipulations Versus Treatments

3.2.1 Why Are Manipulations Sometimes Called Treatments?

Many would argue that in the ideal experimental manipulation $M_i = T_i$, and Z_i and V_i have no effect on T_i. But this ideal experimental manipulation is impossible when we think about voter information as the treatment and, as we argue later, may not be the best option for the study under question. But even if we have this as a goal, that our manipulation variable is equivalent to our treatment variable, it is not possible when examining human behavior. The most ideal case for such a situation would be in the laboratory, but even there we find disconnects between the two. For instance, in Example 2.6, the subjects' education and income levels, cognitive abilities, interest in the laboratory election, and belief about the experimenter's truthfulness can vary and affect whether the subjects are able to comprehend the information provided to them by the experimenter. In general, for experiments in social sciences, there are usually some observable and unobservable aspects of humans that affect our ability to manipulate the treatments the subjects experience.

Often experimentalists, ourselves included, use the term treatment to refer to the manipulated variable itself or a particular experimental manipulation. For example, Gerber, Kaplan, and Bergan in Example 2.1 refer to the groups to which subjects are assigned as "treatment" groups. When an experimentalist does so, then the implicit presumption is that the manipulated variable is the treatment and that the researcher has complete control over the treatment variable. Because we know that the treatment and manipulation are two different things – that voter information is affected by observable and unobservable variables independent of the manipulation in the experiment – why would an experimentalist ignore this reality? The answer lies in random assignment of the manipulations. In Chapter 5 we explore in more detail how well random assignment works.

3.2.2 When Treatment Variables Cannot Be Manipulated

When we think of treatment variables, we also allow for those that arguably cannot be manipulated through experimentation (or can only be manipulated with great difficulty). Thus, it is possible in our model of causality for the treatment to be things like gender, race, ethnicity, and so on. This is in contrast to Holland (1986, 1988), who argues that there can be no causal effect of gender on earnings because it is not possible to assign gender to subjects. However, it is possible to assign subjects with particular genders to different work situations and measure their earnings. Consider, for example, the experiment of Michelitch (2010) in Ghana. She investigates the effects of ethnicity on bargaining behavior. Specifically, when two individuals are bargaining over a price, say a taxi ride, if they are in the same ethnic group, is the price lower? In her experiment she assigns people to bargaining situations by their ethnic type to determine the answer to her question. Although she cannot assign ethnicity to an individual, she can choose the combinations of ethnic identities of the individuals in the bargaining situations.

Heckman (2005a,b) and Heckman and Vytlacil (2007a,b) point out, and we agree, that the view that ethnicity cannot be a treatment variable conflates the difficulty in identifying causal effects with defining causal effects. It may be that identifying the causal effect of gender, race, or ethnicity on something like earnings, in political science voting, is difficult, but that does not mean it is not an interesting question that we can imagine asking.

3.2.3 When Manipulations Affect Treatments Only Indirectly

In the example experiments we have discussed so far, the manipulations all affect the treatment variable in a straightforward manner. In Example 2.6, the manipulation directly provides subjects with information about the true jar; in Example 2.1, the manipulation directly provides subjects with newspapers containing information about the election; in Example 2.3, the manipulation directly provides subjects with campaign advertisements; and in Example 2.8, the manipulation directly provides subjects with information through the experience of living with the policy experiment.

In some experiments, the researcher engages in manipulations, but the manipulations do not directly affect the treatment variable the researcher is focusing on in a straightforward way. Example 3.1 presents two studies where the researchers use an experimental laboratory to investigate voter brain responses to candidate appearances using functional magnetic resonance imaging (fMRI) equipment. The treatment variables that are under study by the researchers (candidate appearances) are not directly manipulated.

Example 3.1 (Brain and Candidate Image Lab Experiment): *Spezio et al. (2008) report on an experiment using brain imaging (fMRI) equipment to determine whether positive or negative attributions of candidate images play a primary role in how candidate appearance affects voting.*

Target Population and Sample: Spezio et al. did not report how their subjects were recruited. They used two separate samples of participants in California. In study 1 they used 24 subjects aged 18–38, seven of which were female. In study 2 they used 22 white women aged 20–35, who were all registered to vote and had voted in one or more of the following national elections: 2000, 2002, and/or 2004. In both studies the participants had no history of neurological or psychiatric illness and were not on antipsychotic medications. The participants also had no prior knowledge of any of the political candidates whose images were used and reported no recognition of the candidates.

Compensation: Spezio et al. did not report if the subjects received compensation for their participation.

Environment: The experiments were conducted at the California Institute of Technology using a Siemens 3.0-T Trio MRI scanner.

Procedures: The researchers conducted two studies. In study 1, subjects were shown "200 grayscale images of political candidates who ran in the real 2006 U.S. midterm elections for either the Senate (60 images), the House of Representatives (74 images), or Governor (66 images). The stimuli were collected from the candidates' campaign Web sites and other Internet sources. An electoral pair consisted of two images of candidates, one Republican and one Democrat, who ran against one another in the real election. Due to the racial and gender composition of the candidates, 70 of the 100 pairs were of male politicians, and 88 of 100 pairs involved two Caucasian politicians. An independent observer classified 92% of the images as 'smiling'. In 57% of the pairs, both candidates were frontal facing, in the rest at least one was facing to the side. Except for transforming color images into a gray scale, the stimuli were not modified. Images were presented using video goggles. . . .

The study was conducted in the month before the 2006 election. An effort was made to avoid pairs in which one of the candidates (e.g. Hillary Clinton) had national prominence or participated in a California election, and familiarity ratings collected from all of the participants after the scanning task verified the stimuli were unfamiliar. . . .

Participants were instructed that they would be asked to vote for real political candidates who were running against each other in the upcoming midterm election. In particular, they were asked to decide who they would be more likely to vote for given that the only information that they had about the politicians were their portraits.

Each trial consisted of three events. . . . First, a picture of one of the candidates was centrally presented for 1 s. Second, after a blank screen of length 1–10 s (uniform distribution), the picture of the other candidate in the pair was presented for 1 s. Third, after another blank screen of length 1–10 s, the pictures of both candidates were presented side by side. At this point, participants were asked to cast their vote by pressing either the left or right button. They had a maximum of 2 s to make a decision. Participants made a response within this time frame in 100% of the trials. Trials were separated by a 1–10 s blank screen. The order of presentation of the candidates as well as their position in the final screen was fully randomized between participants" (pp. 350–351).

Similarly, study 2 used "60 grayscale images of smiling political candidates who ran in real U.S. elections for the House of Representatives or Senate in either 2000, 2002 or 2004 (30 pairs of opponents)." The images were a subset of those used in a previous study of candidate images on voter choices by Todorov et al. (2005) for comparative purposes. The images were selected such that "both images in an electoral pair (i) were frontal facing, (ii) were of the same gender and ethnicity and (iii) had clear, approximately central presentation of faces that were of approximately the same size." Again the pairs matched Republicans and Democrats who had actually run against each other. "Due to the racial/ethnic and gender composition of the original image library, all stimuli were of Caucasian politicians, and 8 of the 30 pairs were of female politicians. Stimuli were preprocessed to normalize overall image intensity while maintaining good image quality, across all 60 images. All images were presented centrally, via an LCD projector and a rear-projection screen, onto a mirror attached to the MRI head coil, approximately 10 inches from a participant's eyes. . . . A pilot behavioral study confirmed that the social judgments made about our selected stimuli were representative of the entire set of face stimuli from which they were drawn....

Participants were instructed that they would be asked to make judgments about real political candidates who ran against one another in real elections. They were told that they would only be given the images of the politicians to inform their judgments. Image order was counterbalanced across participants. Participants made judgments about candidates' attractiveness (Attr), compe-tence (Comp), public deceitfulness (Dect) and personal threat (Thrt) in four separate scanning sessions" (pp. 352–353). Specifically, the participants were asked which candidate in a pair looked more physically attractive to them, more competent to hold national office, more likely to lie to voters, and more likely to act in a physically threatening manner toward them. *"Each session took approximately 9 min to complete"* (p. 353).

Spezio et al. used a protocol that had been used successfully in prior studies of fact preference. That is, *"[e]ach trial in a decision block consisted of the sequential presentation of two images in an electoral pair, image A then image B, until a participant entered a decision about the pair via a button press.... An A/B cycle on a given trial proceeded as follows: (i) central presentation of a fixation rectangle that surrounded the area in which an image was to appear; (ii) after 4–6 s, a 30 ms display of image A surrounded by the fixation box, accompanied by a small black dot in the lower left corner (indicating that this was image A); and (iii) after 3–4 s, a 30 ms display of image B surrounded by the fixation box, accompanied by a small black dot in the lower right corner (indicating that this was image B). Cycles were separated by 4–6 s and continued until a participant entered a button press or until 30 s had elapsed, whichever came first (no participant ever took the 30 s). Participants were asked to attend overtly to the space inside the rectangle in preparation for a candidate image."* The authors used eye tracking to ensure that participants were looking at the stimuli.

Results: In study 1, Spezia et al. found that images of losing candidates elicited greater brain activation than images of winning candidates, which they contend suggests that negative attributions from appearance exert greater influence on voting than do positive. In study 2, Spezia et al. found that, when negative attribution processing was enhanced under the threat judgment, images of losing candidates again elicited greater brain activity. They argue that the results show that negative attributions *"play a critical role in mediating the effects of appearance on voter decisions, an effect that may be of special importance when other information is absent."*

Comments: In study 2, the researchers had to reject the neuroimaging data from 6 participants due to excessive motion. The behavioral data of these *participants were not significantly different from the 16 used in the analysis, however.*

Is Example 3.1 an experiment? Certainly it does not fit what some would consider a classic experiment because the treatments investigated – candidate images – are not manipulated directly by the experimenters. The authors have subjects experience a large number of choices and make multiple judgments in study 2, but they do not manipulate those choices to investigate their hypotheses and instead measure the correlation between brain activity and votes and judgments made by the subjects.

Yet we consider it an experiment because the researchers intervene in the data generating process (DGP) and exert control over the choices before the subjects, as discussed in Section 2.4.2. There is no perfect or true experiment. The appropriate experimental design depends on the research question, as is the case with observational data. In fact, the variety of possible experimental designs and manipulations is in some ways greater than the range of possibilities with observational data, as we discuss. It is true, as we show in the following chapters, that when a researcher is investigating the effects of a particular cause, then having the manipulation directly affect the treatment variable (i.e., the proposed causal variable) provides advantages to the researcher in identifying that causal relationship. And it is true that Spezia et al. lost those advantages by not directly manipulating the treatment variable in this fashion.

3.3 The Rubin Causal Model

We have now defined the terms of our model of the effects of a cause. Usually the next step is to discuss how to measure the causal effect of treatments on the dependent variable (i.e., the effect of T_i on Y_i, within a given target population). But before moving on to the issues of identification and estimation, we address the theoretical foundations of studies of causality in political science – the foundations behind different identification and estimation strategies. It is important to discuss these foundations because of the underlying assumptions and the implications these assumptions have for the interpretation of estimated results.

3.3.1 Defining Causal Effects

Our first step is to formally define what we are interested in, the causal effect. In RCM, the causal effect of the treatment for each individual is defined as the difference between the individual's choices in the two states of the world:

$$\delta_i = Y_{i1} - Y_{i0}.\tag{3.1}$$

The main issue in causal inference is figuring out how to measure δ_i.

3.3.2 The Causal Inference Problem and Observational Data

In observational data, an individual can only be in one of the two states of the world at a given time; in our running example, the individual is either informed or uninformed. It is also possible that we have no observations at all for one state of the world if we are considering proposed treatments that have never been used. Thus, with observational data the observed voting choice of an individual, Y_i, at a given point in time is given by

$$Y_i = T_i Y_{i1} + (1 - T_i) Y_{i0}.\tag{3.2}$$

As a result, we cannot observe directly the causal effect of information on any given individual's voting choice because for each individual we only observe one value of Y_i. How can we deal with this problem? RCM conceptualizes the individual as having two potential choices under the different information situations and that the causal effect is the effect of the treatment on the difference between these two potential choices.[4] RCM is also called the counterfactual approach to causality because it assumes that counterfactuals are theoretically possible; that individuals have potential choices in both states of the world even though we only have factual observations on one state.[5] As Winship and Morgan (1999, p. 664) note, the value of the counterfactual approach is that we can summarize causal inference in a single question (using our notation): "Given that δ_i cannot be calculated for any individual and therefore that Y_{i1} and Y_{i0} can be observed on mutually exclusive subsets of the population, what can be inferred about the distribution of the δ_i from an analysis of Y_i and T_i?" It is at this point that RCM requires thinking theoretically or hypothetically to measure causal effects.

---

[4] Most, including Rubin, credit Neyman (1923) as the first to formalize this idea, but see also Thurstone (1930).

[5] Heckman (2005a,b) prefers the term hypothetical because the potential outcomes may not be contrary to certain facts, just hypothetical. We use both hypothetical and counterfactual to describe the potential choices.

Definition 3.6 (Rubin Causal Model or RCM): *The causal effect of the treatment for each individual is defined as the difference between the individual's potential or hypothetical choices in the two states of the world as given by Equation (3.1) and we can use observations of actual choices given treatments as given by Equation (3.2) to make inferences about the size of the causal effect of the treatment.*

3.3.3 Causal Inference Problem and Experimental Data

Within-Versus Between-Subjects Designs
What about experimental data? In many field experiments, as in the newspaper experiment of Gerber, Kaplan, and Bergan in Example 2.1, subjects are only in one state of the world during the experiment. That is, subjects either receive one of the newspapers during the campaign of the Virginia gubernatorial election or they do not. This is also true in many decision-making experiments conducted by political psychologists, as in Mutz's second and third experiments in Example 2.5 in which subjects were assigned to watch only one of the videos.

Such a design is called a "between-subjects" experimental design in which we only observe subjects in one state of the world. In such a case, the researcher faces the same causal inference problem that a researcher faces with observational data and must think counterfactually or hypothetically about what would have happened if a subject had been in a different state of the world.

Definition 3.7 (Between-Subjects Experimental Design): *Subjects in an experiment make choices in only one state of the world.*

Can we observe subjects in two states of the world simultaneously in experiments? In some experiments, subjects make choices in multiple states of the world in what is called a "within-subjects" experimental design. In Mutz's first experiment, subjects viewed all four of the videos. Both Battaglini et al. and Dasgupta and Williams use within-subjects designs in their experiments. In Battaglini et al.'s Swing Voter's Curse (SVC) lab experiment in Example 2.6, the same subjects were informed in some periods and uninformed in others, as given by the random assignment of the colors in the jars; in Dasgupta and Williams's polls and information lab experiment in Example 2.7, subjects experienced both cost treatments. So these experiments used a within-subjects design and data were gathered on subjects in multiple states of the world during the course of the experiment.

This means that many unobservable and observable characteristics that are subject specific are thus the same for observations in both states of the world.

Definition 3.8 (Within-Subjects Experimental Design): *Subjects in an experiment make choices in multiple states of the world.*

Multiple-Choice Procedures and the Strategy Method
However, in Examples 2.5, 2.6, and 2.7, the choices in the multiple states of the world are made sequentially. It is possible that learning or some other time-related variable can affect the choices of subjects in later periods so that they are not the same as they would have been in the same state of the world in earlier periods. A special type of within-subjects design is when subjects simultaneously choose in both states of the world, as used by Kagel and Levin (1993) in an economics experiment with buyers and sellers. Subjects chose both as buyers and sellers simultaneously. We call this a multiple-choice procedure.[6]

Definition 3.9 (Multiple-Choice Procedure): *Subjects in a within-subjects experimental design make choices in multiple states of the world simultaneously.*

An example of a multiple-choice procedure is when subjects are asked to give strategies that are then implemented by the experimenter in a game-theoretic or decision-theoretic experiment, which is called the strategy method and was pioneered by Selten (1967). The strategy method can be useful for providing information on what subjects would have chosen in situations that do not occur when choices are sequential.

Definition 3.10 (Strategy Method): *A version of the multiple-choice procedure in which subjects choose a strategy to be implemented in an experiment that tests a game-theoretic situation. The strategy is a set of choices conditional on hypothetical information or previous choices that subjects may face when the choice situation occurs in the experiment.*

In contrast, game-theoretic experiments in which subjects choose only when the decision situation occurs in the experiment, given the information

---

[6] They call this a "dual markets" design because subjects make choices as buyers and sellers simultaneously.

and previous choices made by other subjects, as done in the SVC experiment in Example 2.6, the subjects' choices are made using the decision method.

Definition 3.11 (Decision Method): *When subjects in an experiment evaluating a game-theoretic model make choices when the decision situation for the choice occurs in the experiment given knowledge of the information available at that time and actual previous choices made by other subjects.*

How does the strategy method work? Consider a simple bargaining game, called the ultimatum game. In the ultimatum game a proposer is told to make a proposal on how to divide a fixed sum of money, say $10, between him- or herself and a second player, called the responder. The responder can either accept or reject the proposal. If the responder rejects the proposal, the responder and the proposer get a reversion amount of money that is typically much smaller than half of the total sum to be divided, say $1.

The subgame perfect equilibrium of this game is that the responder will accept any sum offered to him or her by the proposer greater than $1 and the proposer will offer the responder just as little as possible.[7] However, in ultimatum games, responders often reject proposals that are small but exceed the reversion amount, "leaving money on the table," and proposers typically offer responders more than the minimum amount given by game theory (see Oosterbeek et al. 2004).[8] Responders are generally thought to reject proposals because of concerns about fairness, whereas proposers are generally believed to be concerned about both the possibility of rejection of an unfair proposal and a preference for fairness. Again, evidence suggests that the behavior in this game can be quite sensitive to differences in experimental protocols, which we return to in later chapters.

The ultimatum game has particular relevance to political science. The experimental results demonstrate that the equilibrium concept of subgame perfection may not be a good predictor of human behavior in certain bargaining or trust situations. This particular equilibrium concept has been used in a number of formal theoretical models in political science. In fact, the situation faced by subjects in the ultimatum game is closely related to the Baron–Ferejohn legislative bargaining game and other similar models of bargaining used in political science. Experimental results

---

[7] As noted by Binmore (2005), any proposal made by the proposer is a Nash equilibrium to this game.

[8] For early experiments on the ultimatum game see Güth et al. (1982); Kahneman et al. (1986); Ochs and Roth (1989); Binmore et al. (1991); Forsythe et al. (1991), and Hoffman et al. (1994).

have demonstrated similar disconnects between predicted behavior in the Baron–Ferejohn game and subjects' choices (see, e.g., Diermeier and Morton, 2005), where subjects displayed a similar tendency toward "fairer" divisions within coalitions than theoretically predicted.

An experiment that uses the decision method would only have observations on responders' choices given the proposals actually made in the experiment. Thus, using the decision method, the experimenter gains limited information on how responders would have reacted in some of the possible theoretical situations that may occur. Moreover, the experimenter cannot compare how one subject might have behaved under different situations and thus consider the effects of differences in proposal offers on responder behavior.

An experimenter can use the strategy method for recording the responders' possible choices for many proposals at once. That is, instead of simply telling the responder the proposal made, the experimenter asks the responder to indicate whether she or he would reject a set of possible proposals that could be offered. The understanding is that, once the proposal is made, the responder's previously given schedule will be implemented. As noted earlier, besides appearing to deal with the aforementioned causal inference problem by having subjects be in multiple states of the world simultaneously, the strategy method allows for a researcher to gather more data on rare cases. For this reason, many experimenters find the strategy method a useful approach. In Example 8.5, Bahry and Wilson (2006) use the strategy method, as we discuss later.

An interesting example in which the strategy method was used in combination with the decision method is Example 3.2. In this experiment, Stanca (2009) compared choices of subjects in a gift exchange situation in which subjects were either first or second movers.[9] Subjects who were first movers had a choice of whether to give second movers a gift from an endowment they were given. Their gift was then tripled by the experimenter. Subjects who were second movers then chose how much of their endowment to give to first movers, also tripled by the experimenter. Stanca manipulated whether second movers gave their gift to the first mover who had given to them or to a different first mover and whether they had information about the gift they had received or instead the gift another second mover had received when they made their decision. Second movers made their gift choices first using the strategy method for the possible gifts that the

---

[9] The gift exchange game is a variant of the trust game, which is discussed in Section 8.2.2, and in Example 8.2.

first mover they would observe could give; then they were told the information about the actual first mover's choice and made a choice using the decision method. The experimenter then tossed a fair coin to determine which method, strategy or decision, would be used to determine the payoffs in the experiment. Subjects played the game only once. Stanca found that the choices subjects made in the two methods, strategy and decision, were highly correlated and that there were no significant differences across manipulations in the relationship between choices in the two methods.

Example 3.2 (Gift Exchange Lab Experiment): *Stanca (2009) conducted an experiment in which he used the strategy method to gain observations on the extent that individuals are willing to engage in indirect reciprocity.*

Target Population and Sample: Stanca used undergraduate students of economics at the University of Milan Biocca. The students were recruited by email from a list of volunteers. Stanca ran six sessions with a different set of 24 subjects each, for a total of 144 subjects.

Subject Compensation: Subjects were paid based on their choices as described in the procedures that follow. As in Dasgupta and Williams (see Example 2.7), Stanca used experimental tokens that were converted to euros for an exchange rate of 2 tokens per euro. Subjects were not given a show-up fee. Subjects' payments ranged from 0 to 40 euros, with an average of approximately 14 euros.

Environment: As in Example 2.6, the experiment was conducted via a computer network. Subjects were seated so that they were unable to see the computer monitors and choices of other subjects.

Procedures: Upon arrival, subjects were randomly assigned to a computer terminal and assigned a role as an A or B player. The subjects were matched into groups of four with two A players, labeled A1 and A2, and two B players, labeled B1 and B2. All subjects were given an endowment of 20 tokens. The players participated in a two-stage game called a gift exchange based on the work of Fehr et al. (1993) and Gachter and Falk (2002).

First Stage: Players A1 (A2) were told to choose an amount a_1 (a_2), an integer between 0 and 20, that would be sent to player B1 (B2). The amount sent is subtracted from the payoff of A1 (A2), multiplied by 3 by the experimenter, and added to the payoff of B1 (B2).

Stanca conducted three different versions of the second stage.

Direct Reciprocity Second Stage: Bi must choose an amount b_i to send to Ai. The amount sent is subtracted from the payoff of Bi, multiplied by 3 by the experimenter, and added to the payoff of Ai. Bi makes this decision in two ways. First, Bi is given a table with all the possible amounts (0 to 20) *that Ai might have chosen to give to Bi and to indicate the amount Bi would give to Ai in response to each amount. Thus, Stanca uses the strategy method to elicit Bi's responses to each of Ai's possible offers. Then Bi is informed of the actual amount Ai has given to Bi and asked to respond using the decision method. Before B players choose, all B players are informed that their payoffs would be determined on the basis of one of the two methods which is randomly selected by publicly tossing a coin. A players, although they knew that B players would have a choice of sending money in the second phase, did not know that B players' choices were based on a random draw between the strategy method and the decision method.*

Indirect Generalized Reciprocity Second Stage: This stage is exactly the same as the direct reciprocity second stage except that Bi chooses how much money to send to Aj based on how much money Ai has sent her.

Indirect Social Reciprocity Second Stage: This stage is exactly the same as the generalized reciprocity second stage except that Bi chooses how much money to send to Aj based on how much money Aj has sent to Bj.

Results: Stanca found that, in all three manipulations, reciprocity was evident. Furthermore, he found that B subjects sent significantly greater amounts in the generalized reciprocity manipulation than in either the direct reciprocity manipulation or the social reciprocity manipulation and that reciprocity was significantly stronger in the generalized reciprocity manipulation than in the other two using data both from choices made in the strategy method and the decision method.

Comments: Of significance for our discussion of the strategy method, Stanca found that there were no significant differences across manipulations in the relationship between strategies and actual decisions.

In a within-subjects design with the multiple-choice procedure we might reasonably argue to have a good measure of δ_i, assuming that nothing else about the experimental design makes the choices different than they would have been if made in isolation. However, even in that case there is evidence that subjects do not make the same choices in multiple-choice procedures as they do in single-choice procedures. Although Stanca found a significant positive relationship between choices in the strategy and decision methods, the choices were not always identical. Furthermore, in an analysis of many ultimatum game experiments, Oosterbeek et al. (2004) found that proposers offer significantly more to responders when the strategy method is used than when responders only respond to the actual offer made by the proposer. In Stanca's procedure, first movers were unaware when they chose their gifts that second movers' choices would be with some probability determined by the strategy method. His instructions used deception in that they implied that second movers' choices would be made only through the decision method. Doing so allowed Stanca to avoid the problem found by Oosterbeek et al. but may have created future problems with subjects not believing experimenters, as we discuss in Chapters 8 and 10.

Crossover Procedures and the Importance of Sequence

It is sometimes the case that the best a researcher can do is to conduct a within-subjects design where subjects choose in multiple states of the world sequentially, as in Examples 2.5, 2.6, and 2.7. This is called a "crossover" procedure. In the crossover procedure, we can use our data to provide an estimate of δ_i as well, although besides the learning that can occur during the experiment mentioned earlier, the fact that subjects have experienced a previous state of the world might affect their choices in a subsequent stage as they learn about the choice process. Typically to try to estimate the effects of sequence in experiencing states of the world, experimenters conduct experiments with variations in the sequential order to control for these possible effects. But then the researcher is using a between-subjects design to estimate the effect of sequence because subjects can only experience one sequence of states of the world.

Definition 3.12 (Crossover Procedure): *Subjects make choices in states of the world sequentially.*

In Example 2.6, Battaglini, Morton, and Palfrey varied the number of computer voters over time within sessions with the same subjects, but varied the sequence of these manipulations. In their analysis of the results, they used between-subjects comparisons to see if sequence matters and found that the qualitative results are robust to variation in the sequence of manipulations, but that the quantitative results are affected.

In another example, Holt and Laury (2002) conducted experiments in which they presented subjects with different risky situations and varied the situations over time. They used a within-subjects design where subjects were asked to choose over a succession of lotteries in which the payoffs were varied. They then estimated the effects of increasing payoffs on risk preferences. The subjects always began the treatment with low payoffs. Harrison et al. (2005b) pointed out that the use of the same ordering for all subjects led to an overestimation of the effects of varying payoffs and that to control for this possibility, different orderings of treatments should also

Figure 3.1. Stages in Experimental Research.

be considered. Holt and Laury (2005) and Harrison et al. (2005b) presented results that control for the ordering effects. In the new experiments, the qualitative results of the first study are supported, but the effects of increasing payoffs on risk preferences is less than previously estimated. Thus, there is evidence that sequence can matter.

In conclusion, even when working with experimental data, a researcher has to think theoretically about the causal inference problem; the researcher has to imagine or theorize about the situations that he or she cannot observe when subjects cannot make choices in multiple states of the world simultaneously. Even if subjects can make choices in multiple states of the world simultaneously as in the strategy method, a researcher needs to consider whether the fact that the subjects can do so makes their choices different from those that would be observed if the subjects could not. Experimental data cannot speak for themselves; the researcher must theorize about counterfactual choices to interpret the data.

3.4 Design Versus Analysis

Thus, to make causal inferences, both in experimental and in nonexperimental research, researchers take leaps of faith and make assumptions about the choices they do not observe and how they relate to those choices they do observe. Given these assumptions, both use knowledge from statistics to establish their results. In what way then can experiments be advantageous? A key difference between experimental and nonexperimental research is when statistical tools are used to understand the data. In experiments we can think of research taking place in three stages, as illustrated in Figure 3.1. In the first stage of an experiment, a researcher creates the design of the intervention; in the second stage, the intervention occurs and the data are generated; and in the third stage, the researcher analyzes the data. In the analysis stage, researchers typically use statistical tools, often making unverified assumptions about the data to rely on these tools.[10] In nonexperimental research, the data are generated without researcher intervention, so the only relevant stage in which the researcher can use statistical tools is in this last stage.

---

[10] All assumptions are either unverified or false. If an assumption is known to be true, then it would be a fact, not an assumption.

The tools that are primarily used involve statistical methods that attempt to control for confounding observable and unobservable variables (Chapter 4) or to sidestep them using methods that attempt to simulate random assignment (Chapter 5). But in experiments a researcher can also use statistical tools in the design stage. A researcher can use experimental control and random assignment (also explored in Chapters 4 and 5), such that the researcher does not need to rely as much on unverified assumptions about the data in conducting post-experiment analysis in interpreting the data. As a result, when we discuss how researchers establish causal inferences in experiments, we focus considerable attention on the design stage and the decisions that experimentalists make in that stage.

Definition 3.13 (Design Stage): *The period before an experimenter intervenes in the DGP in which he or she makes decisions about the design of the experiment such as the extent to use experimental control and/or random assignment.*

Definition 3.14 (Analysis Stage): *The period after data have been generated, either by an experiment or without experimental intervention, in which a researcher uses statistical tools to analyze the data such as statistical control and statistical methods that attempt to simulate random assignment.*

3.5 Measures of Causality

3.5.1 Average Unconditional Treatment Effects

The causal inference problem as defined by RCM is that δ_i is a random variable that we cannot measure directly in observational or in a lot of experimental data. In experiments and nonexperimental research we can try to measure features of its distribution. But what features? A number of researchers have proposed features to estimate. The most commonly estimated feature is the average treatment effect (ATE), which is defined as follows:

$$\text{ATE} = E\left(\delta_i\right). \tag{3.3}$$

Another commonly estimated feature is the average treatment effect on the treated (ATT), which is defined as follows:

$$\text{ATT} = E\left(\delta_i | T_i = 1\right). \tag{3.4}$$

Thus, ATE estimates the causal effect of treatment on a randomly drawn individual in the population whereas ATT estimates the causal effect of treatment on a randomly drawn untreated individual.

3.5.2 Average Conditional Treatment Effects

Sometimes researchers are interested in conditional measures of causality. Recall that W_i is a set of observable variables that the researcher believes affects potential choices Y_{ij}. Then we can define conditional treatment effects as functions of W:

$$\text{ATE}\,(W) = E\,(\delta_i | W_i) \tag{3.5}$$

$$\text{ATT}\,(W) = E\,(\delta_i | W_i, T_i = 1), \tag{3.6}$$

where ATE(W) is the average effect of information given W_i and ATT(W) is the average impact of information on those who actually are informed given W_i.

3.5.3 Other Treatment Effects

A number of other measures of causality are utilized in the literature. Researchers may hypothesize that the causal effect of the treatment on outcomes is accomplished via what is called a mediating variable (see Definition 4.6) and wish to estimate the direct causal effect of the mediating variable or the effect of treatment on outcomes through the mediating variable. We discuss estimates of these types of treatment effects in Section 4.7.

Imbens and Angrist (1994) define a treatment effect, called the local average treatment effect (LATE), that is relevant to instrumental variable estimation, and Heckman and Vytlacil (2001, 2007a,b) define a treatment effect called the marginal treatment effect (MTE). Heckman and Vytlacil (2001, 2007a,b) discuss the relationship between LATE and MTE. We discuss LATE in Section 5.4.3. Recall that when researchers conduct experiments in the field, they sometimes have to deal with noncompliance and nonresponse (discussed in Section 2.4.2). Sometimes researchers are interested in the effect of the assignment of treatment independent of such realities or the intention-to-treat (ITT) effect.

When researchers try to measure the actual effect of treatment in the face of nonresponse (missing data) and noncompliance, they try to measure what has been defined as the complier average causal effect (CACE). Abstracting from differences in assumptions underlying how these effects are measured, LATE and CACE are actually equivalent concepts, which relates to the fundamental relationship between instrumental variable estimation and experimental work, as we discuss in Section 5.4.3. We discuss both ITT and CACE and how they are measured in the context of instrumental variable analysis and experiments in Section 5.4.3.

3.6 The Stable Unit Treatment Value Assumption

3.6.1 What Does It Mean for δ_i to Represent the Causal Effect?

The conclusion that δ_i represents the causal effect of information on voter choices is generally called the stable unit treatment value assumption (SUTVA). SUTVA is actually a collection of implied assumptions about the effect of treatments on individuals. As Rosenbaum (1987, p. 313) summarizes: "This assumption concerns the notation that expresses treatment effects as comparisons of two potential responses of each subject; it says that this notation is adequate for the problem at hand. One might say it is the assumption, or perhaps the indefinite collection of assumptions, implicit in the notation."[11]

What assumptions are implicit in assuming that δ_i represents the causal effect of information on voter choices? Rubin (1980) highlights two implicit assumptions in particular: (1) that treatment of unit i only affects the outcome of unit i (thus, it does not matter how many others have been treated or not treated) and (2) that, for ATE and ATT, the treatment is homogeneous across voters. Sekhon (2005) points out that the first of these is unlikely to be satisfied in observational data on voters in our example because individuals may be influenced by the treatment effect on family members or friends. Sekhon argues then that what is measured by estimates of Equation (3.1) is a "local" effect of information on voting and we cannot use it to aggregate the effect of increasing levels of voter information in the population and

---

[11] Rosenbaum goes on to discuss the difficulty of defining SUTVA in a general sense and the problems that can result when researchers fail to understand what SUTVA might imply for their particular application using an interesting analogy that is worth repeating: "I do not love SUTVA as a generic label for all of these, for it seems to bear a distinct resemblance to an attic trunk; what does not fit is neatly folded and packed away. The more capacious the trunk, the more likely we are to have difficulty remembering precisely what is packed away. Periodically, we might open the lid and scan the top layer to illustrate what the trunk contains, but because it is so large, we are not inclined to take everything out, to sort the contents into piles: useful in season, useful if altered to fit, damaged beyond repair; still less are we inclined to begin the alterations, for the repair of each garment entails considerable effort."

to answer questions as to what happens if the entire electorate is informed or uninformed, because of the cross-effects or interference of the treatment of one individual upon another's choice. Obviously this significantly limits what we can conclude from the RCM approach to estimating causal effects of information on voting and answering many of the questions we posed earlier.

Heckman (2005a,b) points out four additional implicit assumptions in RCM that are worth noting. First, Equation (3.1) implies that treatment of unit i is invariant with respect to the mechanism by which the treatment is provided. That is, suppose that we are counting a voter as informed if he or she were told specific information about a candidate. If the information is told verbally it may have a different effect than if an individual is given the information to read, which depends on the cognitive abilities of the voter. If we define treatment as the general provision of information, then this assumption may not be reasonable. Second, there is the presumption that all the possible states of the world are observed – there exist both informed and uninformed units. This is not possible if we wish to investigate the effect of a change in information that affects all potential voters.

Third, Equation (3.1) assumes that the only causality question of interest is a historical one: the evaluation of treatments that exist in reality on the population receiving the treatment, either observational or experimental. Equation (3.1) alone says nothing about the treatment effect on other populations of interest or of other possible interventions that have not been historically experienced, either in an undisturbed DGP or a DGP manipulated by a researcher. Thus, the equation in itself does not ensure external validity or robustness of the results, which we discuss more fully in Section 7.3.2. Fourth, Equation (3.1) assumes a recursive model of causality. It cannot measure the causal effects of outcomes that occur simultaneously. For example, if the choices an individual plans to make if informed are a function of the amount of information a voter has, Equation (3.1) cannot estimate the effect of information on voting choices when these choices are made simultaneously.

Definition 3.15 (Stable Unit Treatment Value Assumption or SUTVA):
Assumptions implicit in the assertion that δ_i represents the causal effect of a treatment. These assumptions typically involve the following:

1. *Treatment of unit i only affects the outcome of unit i.*
2. *In estimating ATE or ATT, the treatment is homogeneous across individuals.*

3. *Treatment of unit i is invariant with respect to the mechanism by which the treatment is provided.*
4. *All possible states of the world are observed.*
5. *The only causality question of interest is a historical one for the data set analyzed.*
6. *The only causality question of interest is one in which treatment is received before a choice is made; there are no simultaneous relations between treatment and choice.*

3.6.2 Implications of SUTVA for Inductive Experimental Work

Gerber and Green remark (2002, p. 820): "The beauty of experimentation is that one need not possess a complete theoretical model of the phenomenon under study. By assigning . . . at random, one guarantees that the only factors that could give to a correlation . . . occur by chance alone." Although they go on to recognize the value of having theoretical underpinnings to research in general as a guide, they clearly see this as simply being more efficient, not as a necessary component for experimental searching for facts (p. 821):

Granted, the design and interpretation of experiments benefits enormously from sound theoretical knowledge. To the extent that we begin the process with intuitions . . . we may design experiments to isolate high-effect and low-effect circumstances. . . . Theoretical reflection on the conditions under which a treatment is likely to be effective may prevent us from drawing inferences that do not generalize to other situations. The point remains, however, that the experimental method could discover these nuances merely by trial and error, as researchers make sense of why a sequence of experiments produces different results. By clarifying both what experimental results mean and what kinds of experiments are likely to yield the most fruitful parameter estimates, good theories provide a more efficient path to knowledge about the underlying causal process.

As we see in Section 5.2.2, Gerber and Green are of course correct about the value of random assignment, when it is successful, in identifying and estimating causal relationships using an RCM approach. But how necessary is a well-articulated theory for learning from experiments? Is it possible to discover knowledge without theory? Is theorizing merely an aid to experimental political science, but not a requirement? The argument that searching for facts is possible in an atheoretical setting is based on the presumption that causality can be determined without theory; the claim is that, by trial and error of manipulating various causes and determining their effects using experiments, facts and nuances can be accumulated, eventually leading to greater knowledge with or without theory. However, as we have shown, measuring causality requires that a researcher think hypothetically or theoretically both about counterfactual events that do not occur and to assume SUTVA. Searching for facts, even in experiments, requires that a researcher theorize; it is not possible to search for facts and through trial and error discover nuances of the DGP without theorizing about that process even when using experiments.

3.7 Advantages of RCM

RCM has advantages. It allows researchers to narrow the focus of causality to a single cause-and-effect relationship and it provides researchers with a definition of causal effects and quantities such as ATE and ATT that researchers can attempt to identify and estimate. It does not require that a researcher present a fully developed formal model of hypothesized causal relationships before empirical study, and it allows for nonparametric estimation of the causal effects. However, RCM requires that a researcher first theorize that potential outcomes exist and that they are all observed in actuality in the population, although not in the same unit of observation. That is, RCM requires that a researcher take a theoretical leap. The researcher hypothesizes that missing data (potential outcomes) exist, and the researcher hypothesizes how those missing data are related to the data he or she can measure. Without the theoretical leap, the researcher is unable to measure causality. Data do not speak for themselves under RCM, but rather through the unverified assumptions use of RCM requires a researcher to make. To the extent that those assumptions are incorrect, the inferences are questionable.

In summary, RCM assumes that the causal effect that a researcher is interested in is a narrow one, limited to the population experiencing a known cause that is recursive and not simultaneous; that the cause is uniformly administered to the units potentially affected; that other possible administrations of the cause do not matter to how the units respond; and that there are no cross-effects between units. RCM is purely a model of the effects of causes. It does not have anything to say about how we move from a set of effects of causes to a model of the causes of effects.

3.8 Chapter Summary

In this chapter we have presented the RCM approach to causality, defining the terms in that method. We have described the different measures of causality used in RCM. We have also discussed SUTVA, the implied assumptions a researcher makes when using RCM. The implied assumptions narrow significantly what we learn about the effects of a cause under RCM.

Moreover, RCM requires that researchers think theoretically; the method does not allow the data to speak for themselves. Only in the rare cases of within-subjects experiments using multiple-choice procedures can one observe subjects making choices close to simultaneously in multiple states of the world. Otherwise, one must theorize that counterfactual events occur and that comparisons of individuals' choices can be used to estimate the effects of a cause on the unobservable difference between what we observe and what would have happened otherwise.

In the next chapter we discuss the methods that researchers use that attempt to identify and control for confounding variables. As noted earlier, these methods are both statistical and experimental, with experimental methods primarily used in the design stage and standard statistical methods used in the post-data-generation analysis stage. We assume with a few noted exceptions that the researcher is taking an RCM-based approach. In Chapter 5 we bring in methods in which researchers attempt to avoid or sidestep confounding variables while usually also controlling for others, such as instrumental variables and random assignment in experiments. And in Chapter 6 we discuss the use of formal theory to estimate causal relationships.

4

Controlling Observables and Unobservables

4.1 Control in Experiments

4.1.1 Controlling Observables in Experiments

We begin our analysis of the Rubin Causal Model (RCM)-based approaches to estimating the effects of a cause with a review of those that work through the control of observable variables that can make it difficult to estimate causal effects. Specifically, using the notation of the previous chapter, there are two types of observable variables that can cause problems for the estimation of the effects of a cause, Z_i and X_i. Recall that Y_i is a function of X_i and T_i is a function of Z_i. That is, X_i represents the other observable variables that affect our dependent variable besides the treatment variable and Z_i represents the set of observable variables that affect the treatment variable. Moreover, these variables may overlap and we define $W_i = Z_i \cup X_i$.

In experiments researchers deal with these observable variables in two ways – through random assignment and through the ability to manipulate these variables as they do with treatment variables. In the next chapter we show how such random assignment sidesteps both observable and unobservable variables that can interfere with measuring the causal effect of the treatment.

But experimenters also can manipulate some of the observable variables that might have an effect on treatments or directly on voting behavior and thereby reduce their effects. For instance, one observable variable that might affect the treatment variable is the mechanism by which a voter learns the information. We can imagine that if the information is told to subjects verbally, the effect might be different than if the subjects read the information or if it is shown to them visually. In a naturally occurring election without experimental manipulation or in a field experiment in which the researcher cannot control the mechanism of manipulation, this information may reach voters in a variety of ways, affecting the treatment. In a laboratory experiment, and to some extent in a field experiment, a researcher can control the mechanism so that it does not vary across subjects. Or, if the researcher is interested in the effects of different mechanisms as well as information itself, the researcher can randomly assign different mechanisms to the subjects.

An observable variable that might affect subjects' voting behavior independent of treatment could be the language used to describe the candidates in the election and the other aspects of the election environment. In a naturally occurring election, different voters may be exposed to different descriptions of the candidates and other aspects of the environment that affect their voting behavior. In a laboratory, and to some extent in a field experiment, a researcher can control this language and the other aspects of the election environment that have these effects so that they do not vary across subjects. We call the information provided to subjects during an experiment the script. Or a researcher might randomize the language to reduce possible effects as with the mechanism of providing information. In this way experimentalists can control for W_i. Guala (2005, p. 238) remarks: "[T]he experimental method works by eliminating possible sources of error or, in other words, by controlling systematically the background factors that may induce us to draw a mistaken inference from the evidence to the main hypothesis under test. A good design is one that effectively controls for (many) possible sources of error."

Definition 4.1 (Controlling Observables in Experimentation): *When an experimentalist holds observable variables constant or randomly assigns them to evaluate the effect of one or more treatments on subjects' choices.*

Definition 4.2 (Script): *The context of the instructions and information given to subjects in an experiment.*

4.1.2 Controlling Unobservables in Laboratory Experiments

Control can also mitigate problems from subject-specific unobservable variables when a laboratory researcher uses a within-subjects design as discussed in Section 3.3.3. That is, by using a within-subjects design a researcher can hold constant things about the subject that are unobservable such as interest in the experiment, overall mood, and cognitive ability.

Sometimes laboratory experiments can make some variables observable that are typically unobservable without experimental manipulation and, thus, enable a researcher to control these typically unobservable variables, as discussed in Chapter 2. For example, in political economy laboratory experiments, as we saw in the Battaglini, Morton, and Palfrey experiment (Example 2.6), the researchers use financial incentives to motivate subjects to take their choices in the experiment seriously, to make the choices salient to the subjects. Holding these financial incentives constant, Battaglini, Morton, and Palfrey then manipulated other aspects of the experimental environment. Thus, Battaglini, Morton, and Palfrey control subjects' motivations to some extent.

Why might financial incentives help control unobservables? Suppose that we suspect that voters who have more intense preferences for candidates are more likely to be informed and more likely to vote, but there is no way to accurately measure variation in voter preference intensity in observational data. Without being able to control for intensity, it is possible that this unobservable is confounding the observed relationship between information and voting. In a laboratory or web-based election, voters can be paid based on the outcome of the election, and the size of the payoff can be set to control for intensity effects. (That is, the researcher can hold voter payoffs according to preference orderings equal across voters such that each voter receives the same payoff if her first preference wins, and so forth.) In this fashion, voter intensity can be held constant across voters. Of course, this raises other issues about the comparability of such experiments to voter intensities in observational data. Nevertheless, many of the measures used in laboratory and virtual laboratory experiments on the web are used to control both observable variables and, in particular, unobservable variables outside the laboratory. Through control, then, the researcher can more safely calculate treatment effects than with observational data.

Definition 4.3 (Controlling Unobservables in Experimentation): *When an experimentalist attempts to control typical unobservables through within-subjects designs, by manipulation, or by observation to evaluate the effect of one or more treatments on subjects' choices.*

Another example of control over a normally unobservable variable is how much time and effort individuals spend on a task. In a laboratory experiment, researchers can manage how subjects spend their time on various tasks and actually measure how much time subjects spend on one task instead of another, whereas outside of the laboratory, researchers cannot typically observe how subjects or individuals in general allocate their time to various tasks. We discuss Example 4.2 later in this chapter, in which researchers both control and monitor the time that subjects spend on various pieces of information during a laboratory election campaign.

Finally, we present an especially interesting method that political psychologists have used to measure racial attitudes through the use of subliminal primes (words displayed to subjects that are viewed unconsciously) coupled with implicit measures of responses in Example 4.1. In a set of experiments, Taber (2009) evaluates the theory that racism and prejudice are no longer significant reasons why individuals object to policies such as affirmative action and that instead conservative principles such as individualism and opposition to big government explain such objections. However, measuring racial prejudice is extremely difficult observationally or in simple surveys given the stigma attached to such preferences. In one of the experiments he conducts, Taber exposes subjects to the subliminal prime of affirmative action and then measures the time it takes for them to identify words related to racial stereotypes, conservative principles, and a baseline manipulation of unrelated words. The subjects are told that their job is to identify words versus nonwords, and they are exposed to nonwords as well.

Example 4.1 (Subliminal Priming Lab Experiment): *Taber (2009) conducted a series of experiments in which he measured the effects of subliminal primes of the words affirmative action and welfare on implicit responses to racial and gender stereotypes and conservative individualist principles.*

Target Population and Sample: *Taber used 1,082 voting-age adults from five U.S. cities (Portland, Oegon: 90; Johnson City, Tennessee: 372; Nashville, Tennessee: 132; Peoria, Illinois: 138; and Chicago, Illinois: 350). The subjects were recruited by print and Internet advertisements in the summer of 2007. "The sample included: 590 men, 492 women; 604 whites, 364 blacks, 104 other; 220 self-reported conservatives, 488 liberals, 332 moderates; 468 with household income below \$15,000, 260 with income \$15,000–30,000, 354 with income greater than \$30,000; 806 with less than a college diploma. The mean age was 40 years with a range of 18 to 85 years."*

Subject Compensation: *Subjects were paid \$20 for participating.*

Environment: *"Participants came to an experimental location at an appointed time in groups of no more than eight. Laptop computers were set up in hotel or public library conference rooms in a configuration designed to minimize distractions. The . . . experiments were programmed in the MediaLab and DirectRT software environment and run on identical Dell laptop computers,* proceeded in fixed order, with the pace controlled by the participant. All instructions appeared onscreen. Participants were consented before the session, debriefed and paid $20 after." We discuss the benefits of debriefing in Sections 12.1.2 and 13.6.3.

Procedures: *The subjects participated in six consecutive experiments in a single, one-hour session. Subjects were also given a survey of political attitudes, demographics, and so on. We describe each experiment in the order in which it was conducted.*

Study 1: *Subjects were first given a subliminal prime of the phrase "affirmative action" and then a target word or nonword, which the subject was asked to identify as either a word or nonword. The target words came from six sets of words with an equal number of nonword foils. The nonwords were pronounceable anagrams. The six sets were (p. 10) "Black stereotype targets (rhythm, hip-hop, basketball, hostile, gang, nigger); White stereotype targets (educated, hopeful, ambitious, weak, greedy, uptight); female stereotype targets (caring, nurturing, sociable, gossipy, jealous, fickle); individualism targets (earn, work-ethic, merit, unfair, undeserved, hand-outs); egalitarianism targets (equality, opportunity, help, need, oppression, disadvantage); big government targets (government, public, Washington, bureaucracy, debt, mandate); and pure affect targets (gift, laughter, rainbow, death, demon, rabies). . . . In addition to these affirmative action trials, there were also interspersed an approximately equal number of trials involving the prime 'immigration' and a different set of targets" which Taber (2009) does not discuss. "In total, there were 72 affirmative action/real target trials, 72 baseline/real target trials, and 144 non-word tries, not including the immigration trails. On average study 1 took approximately ten minutes to complete."*

Note that the target words were of three types: stereotype targets, principle targets, or baseline targets.

The prime and target were presented (pp. 7–8) "*in the following way . . . : a forward mask of jumbled letters flashed center screen (e.g., KQHYTPDQF-PBYL) for 13 ms, followed by a prime (e.g. affirmative action) for 39 ms, a backward mask (e.g. DQFPBYLKQHYTP) for 13 ms, and then a target (e.g., merit or retim, rhythm or myhrth), which remained on screen until the subject pressed a green (Yes, a word) or red (No, not a word) button. Trials were separated by a one second interval. Where precise timing is critical, masks are necessary to standardize (i.e., overwrite) the contents of visual memory and to ensure that the effective presentation of the prime is actually just 39 ms. Conscious expectancies require around 300 ms to develop.*"

Taber measured the response times on word trials, discarding the nonword trials.

Study 2: Subjects "were asked to think about affirmative action and told that they might be asked to discuss this issue with another participant after the study. One third were told that this discussion partner would be a conservative opponent of affirmative action, one third were told to expect a liberal supporter of affirmative action, and for one third the discussion partner was left unspecified." Then subjects completed the same task of identifying words and nonwords as in study 1 without the subliminal primes.

Study 3: In this study Taber used the race stereotype words as primes for the principle targets and vice versa, mixed in with a larger set of trials designed to test unreported hypotheses. He used the same procedure in the subliminal primes as in study 1.

Study 4: This study used black and white stereotype words as primes for pure affect target words using an equal number of positive and negative examples.

Study 5: Taber conducted a replication of a famous experiment conducted by Sniderman and Carmines (1997). "Participants... read a realistic one-page description of a fictional school funding proposal that sought to provide $30 to $60 million per year to disadvantaged school districts in the participant's home state. The proposal was broken into an initial summary, which manipulated whether the program would be publicly or privately funded, and a brief case study of a particular school that would receive funding through the proposed program, which manipulated race of recipients in three conditions...: the school was described as predominantly white, black, or racially mixed.... After reading the summary and case study, participants were asked a single question...: Do you support of [sic] oppose this proposed policy? Responses were collected on a 7 pt. Likert-type scale" (p. 21).

Study 6: This study replicated study 5 "with a simpler affirmative action program using different manipulations." Taber manipulates "need versus merit, and target race, but this time the brief proposal mentions a particular disadvantaged child as a target recipient. The race of the child is subtly manipulated by using stereotypical white, black and racially-ambiguous names (Brandon, Jamar, and James, respectively). The child is described either as struggling academically with a need for special tutoring he cannot afford or as a high achieving student who would be targeted by the program because of exceptional ability and effort" (p. 23). Subjects were asked again whether they support or oppose the proposed program on a seven-point scale.

Results: In study 1, Taber found evidence that both conservative opponents of affirmative action and liberal supporters of affirmative action had shorter response times to black stereotype targets as compared to other targets. In study 2, he found that explicitly thinking about affirmative action in the absence of an expectation about the discussion partner led to shorter response times to *principle and race stereotype targets. When conservative opponents expect to talk to a like-minded partner, only response times for black stereotype targets are shorter; when they expect to talk to a liberal supporter, black stereotype target response times are shorter than the baseline but also are principle target response times. Liberal supporters' response times are shorter for black and principle targets regardless of whom they expect as a discussion partner. In study 3, Taber found that race primes reduced reaction times on principle targets, particularly for conservatives.*

Taber used the data from study 4 plus survey data on the subjects to devise a measure of implicit affect toward African Americans. He found that white respondents had more negative implicit attitudes toward African Americans than black respondents and that conservative opponents of affirmative action were significantly more negative toward blacks than white supporters. Taber's analysis of the data from studies 5 and 6 supports previous results found by Sniderman and Carmines and Feldman and Huddy (2005) that conservatives prefer private to public funding, white liberals prefer public funding, and neither group has a significant preference for racial targets. However, he finds that conservatives who are politically sophisticated strongly oppose spending public funds when it targets black schools (students) but not when white or mixed race schools (students) are targeted.

Comments: *Taber's studies are a good example of building on previous research in psychology on the subliminal prime effects on response times. By using the primes and measuring response times to particular types of words that have known connotations, he was able to make observable how subjects respond to these words. In studies 1–4 he made use of a within-subjects design, whereas in studies 5 and 6 he used a between-subjects design (see Section 3.3.3).*

Taber found that response times for words related to racial stereotypes are affected by the subliminal primes for conservative opponents of affirmative action as compared to other words, which he argues suggests that racial prejudice is a factor in explaining conservative opposition to the policy. Observing such response times to subliminal primes would be difficult to accomplish outside of a laboratory environment. That said, Taber took the lab to his subjects to some extent, recruiting the subjects to temporary laboratories set up in local library or hotel conference rooms in five U.S. cities. Such an experiment is what is often called a "lab in the field" experiment, which we investigate more fully in Section 8.2.3 and define in Definition 8.5.

Taber's experiment is also a good example of how a researcher working with naturally occurring words and situations may need to conduct a manipulation check to be sure that the manipulation he or she is conducting captures the manipulation he or she wishes to conduct. He used as his primes words that had been shown in previous psychological studies to fit the categories of interest. He also checked that the names he assigned to the child in study 6 implied a particular race for the child; he found that 73% of the participants in the Brandon Smith condition perceived him as white, 88% perceived Jamar Smith as black, and 64% were uncertain about James Smith.

Definition 4.4 (Manipulation Check): *A survey or other method used to check whether the manipulation conducted in an experiment is perceived by the subjects as the experimenter wishes it to be perceived.*

The same degree of control is not generally possible when conducting field experiments. First, it is not generally possible to gather repeated observations on the same subject and control for unobservables in this fashion when an experiment is conducted in the field, although it may be possible via the Internet. While in the laboratory or via the web, a researcher can induce preference orderings over candidates; in field experiments, researchers investigating the effect of information on voting must work within the context of a given election that he or she cannot control or of a set of elections and the unobservable aspects of voter preferences in those elections. Hence, researchers using field experiments focus more on how random assignment can help determine causality rather than the combination of control and random assignment, whereas researchers using laboratory experiments (both physical and virtual) use both control and random assignment in designing experiments. Unfortunately, random assignment is harder to implement in the field as well because experimenters confront problems of nonresponse and noncompliance, so in many cases field experimentalists must often also rely on the statistical methods discussed earlier to deal with these problems, and these statistical methods require making untestable assumptions, as we show below.

4.2 Control Functions in Regressions

4.2.1 When an Observable Variable Cannot Be Controlled or Manipulated

What happens when a researcher is investigating the effects of information on voting behavior in observational data or in some cases experimental data gathered through a field experiment in which the researcher did not have the ability to control observable variables or to randomly assign them? For example, a researcher might survey subjects as to their level of political sophistication or partisan identification and the researcher believes that these subject-specific observables might confound the relationship between the causal effect of information on voting.

The modal method for exploring hypothesized causal relations in political science in such a situation is the use of control functions in regressions. That is, the modal method in political science is to estimate an ordinary least squares (OLS) multiple-regression equation of the dependent variable on the treatment variable plus a function of observable variables (the control function). So the researcher would estimate a regression with voting choice as a dependent variable and information as an independent variable with the other observable variables also as independent variables. Researchers then interpret the coefficient on the treatment variable as measuring the causal effect of the treatment on the dependent variable, controlling for the possible confounding observable variables. Most who use this approach in political science are working within an RCM basis either implicitly or explicitly.

Definition 4.5 (Control Function Approach in Regressions): *When a researcher includes in a regression a function of observable variables in an attempt to better measure the causal effect of the treatment variable, which is used as an independent variable, on the dependent variable in the regression.*

Is it accurate to interpret the coefficient on the treatment variable as the causal effect of the treatment on the dependent variable? Under some restrictive assumptions, the answer is yes, which we explore in this section. Before doing so, however, we need to digress and discuss the difficulties of working with dependent variables that are discrete using standard empirical techniques. Because much of political science empirical research, both observational and experimental, is about voting and other discrete choices, such a digression is useful as well.

4.2.2 A Digression on Dealing with Voting as a Dependent Variable

Most political scientists use OLS regression to estimate causal effects based usually only implicitly on RCM. One problem with our analysis so far is that the dependent variable, voter choices, is an unordered multinomial response and thus OLS is an inappropriate estimation procedure. The standard line of attack is to concentrate on the probability of each voter choice, or what is typically called the response probabilities. The response probabilities are then assumed to be a function of explanatory variables, which sum to 1. The response probabilities are typically estimated using maximum likelihood procedures such as multinomial logit, conditional logit, or multinomial probit.[1]

Another solution is to focus more narrowly on the effect of information on a binary choice, within our general choice context. For example, Bartels (1996) examines the effect of information on voters' choices in American Nation Election Study (ANES) surveys between major party candidates in presidential elections from 1972 to 1992, excluding voters who report no preference or a preference for minor party or independent candidates.[2] Alternatively, we could restrict our analysis to the effect of information on the decision to turn out alone, also a binary choice, as in Example 2.8 and Larcinese (2007). A significant body of empirical research focuses on participation decisions.

For expositional purposes, we restrict our examination to the effect of information on turnout. We assume then that our dependent variable, Y_i, can only take two values, 0 or 1, and we are interested in the probability of voting. One simple approach to estimating this probability is the linear probability model (LPM), for which we assume that the response probabilities are a linear function of explanatory variables, which can be estimated using OLS. For example, this is the approach used to estimate causal effects of media exposure on voting in Example 2.1. For now, we use this approach because of its expositional clarity, although it has known limitations.[3] We are interested in the causal effect of information on the probability that a voter chooses to turn out in an election assuming that LPM accurately measures this probability.

4.2.3 The Switching Regression Model

Following the LPM, we assume that the probability of voting is a linear function of observables and unobservables. As we noted in Chapter 2, we define that probability as P_i, and P_{ij} is the probability of voting for

---

[1] See Wooldridge (2002, chapter 15) for a discussion of the assumptions needed for these procedures.

[2] In footnote 14, Bartels reports results from a multinomial specification for 1992 that includes Perot supporters.

[3] Many researchers now typically use probit or logit estimation techniques to estimate probability models. We discuss such models subsequently. See Wooldridge (2002, chapter 15) for a discussion.

individual i in information state j. The causal effect we are interested in when we use P as our dependent variable is defined as $\delta = (P_{i1} - P_{i0})$. Also, to make our exposition simpler, we drop the i's from our notation and refer to P_0 as the probability of voting when an individual is uninformed and P_1 as the probability of voting when an individual is informed.

Can we just add in our treatment variable – information – as one of these observable variables and use the effect of information on P_i as measured in a linear regression as our measure of the causal effect, assuming that the LPM is an accurate assumption about how the probability of voting is determined? The answer is yes, under certain additional assumptions. What are those assumptions?

First, it is useful to decompose the two probabilities, P_0 and P_1, into their means and a stochastic part with a zero mean:

$$P_0 = \mu_0 + u_0, \tag{4.1}$$

$$P_1 = \mu_1 + u_1, \tag{4.2}$$

where μ_j is the mean value of P in state j, u_j is the stochastic term in state j, and $E(u_j) = 0$.

Furthermore, we assume that the probability of voting that we observe, P, depends on the state of the world for a voter as in Equation (3.2) in Chapter 3:

$$P = TP_1 + (1 - T)P_0. \tag{4.3}$$

We can then plug in Equations (4.1) and (4.2) into Equation (4.3), yielding

$$P = \mu_0 + (\mu_1 - \mu_0)T + u_0 + (u_1 - u_0)T. \tag{4.4}$$

In econometrics, Equation (4.4) is called Quandt's switching regression model (see Quandt, 1958, 1972) and the coefficient on T is thus the causal effect of information on the probability of turnout.

4.2.4 Selection on the Observables or Ignorability of Treatment

However, most political scientists would assume, unlike the assumption underlying Equation (4.4), that the stochastic nature of the probabilities of voting in the two states, u_j, would depend on X, our set of observable exogenous variables that also affect the decision to turn out, and Z and M, our sets of observable and manipulated exogenous variables that affect the decision to be informed when this decision is endogenous, such that the means of the stochastic terms are not zero. Because the focus in this chapter is on control of observables, for ease of exposition we drop M from our analysis for the rest of this chapter. However, inclusion of M is straightforward whenever Z is included or discussed.

If a political scientist thinks that these variables are related, can he or she simply estimate an OLS regression with T as an exogenous variable, using the coefficient on T as an estimate of the causal effect as in Equation (4.4)? The answer is no. The main problem is that now the potential choices, P_j, may be correlated with the treatment variable, making it difficult to determine treatment effects. Thus, we may not be able to estimate causal relationships. How can we deal with the problem? The principal assumption necessary is called ignorability of treatment by statisticians Rosenbaum and Rubin (1983) and selection on the observables by econometricians Heckman and Robb (1985) and Moffitt (1996). There are two forms of this assumption, which are given in the following axioms.

Axiom 4.1 (Ignorability of Treatment or Selection on the Observables): *Conditional on W, T and (P_0, P_1) are independent.*

Axiom 4.2 (Mean Ignorability of Treatment or Mean Selection on the Observables): $E(P_0|W, T) = E(P_0|W)$ *and* $E(P_1|W, T) = E(P_1|W)$.

Mean ignorability of treatment is sufficient for the estimation of a regression function with T and W as independent variables (recall that $W = X \cup Z$). We also need a second assumption, that $(u_1 - u_0)$ has a zero mean conditional on W, although we relax this assumption in what follows. Therefore, given mean ignorability of treatment and the assumption that $E(u_1|W) = E(u_0|W)$, then ATE = ATT and

$$E(P|T, W) = \mu_0 + \alpha T + h_0(W)\beta_0, \tag{4.5}$$

where $\alpha = $ ATE and $h_0(W) = E(u_0|W)$.[4]

What does this mean? It means that if the predicted individual specific effect of information given W is zero, the coefficient on the treatment variable in a regression can be used to estimate ATE.

Equations like Equation (4.5) are estimated frequently in political science. The function $h_0(W)$ is generally called a control function, as in Definition 4.5. If mean ignorability of treatment and $E(u_1|W) = E(u_0|W)$ are both true, then when the control function is added to the regression of P on

---

[4] See Wooldridge (2002, propositon 18.1).

1 and T, biases are controlled, allowing for α to serve as a consistent estimator of ATE and ATE(W).

4.2.5 How Reasonable Is the Ignorability of Treatment Assumption?

One of the things that the strict version of ignorability of treatment implies is that the conditional treatment effects are equal; that is, ATT(W) = ATE(W). As Heckman (2005a) points out, this means that the conditional marginal treatment effect (MTE) also equals the conditional average treatment, ATE(W), which is arguably an unattractive assumption because it implies that the average individual is indifferent between being treated or not – in our analysis, being informed or not. For example, it means that the effect of information on the person who is just indifferent between voting and not voting is the same as the effect of information on a person who is a priori inclined to vote.

When is ignorability of treatment likely not to hold? If we believe that whether an individual is informed or not (treatment choice) is related through unobservables to her potential choices if informed or not (whether she would vote), then ignorability of treatment does not hold. Suppose that Louise and Sam are identical on observable variables such as gender (we assume both are female in this example), race and ethnicity, income, home ownership, and partisan identification. What is unobservable is the value they place on being a "good citizen" by voting and by being informed about political matters. Louise values being a good citizen but Sam places no value on it. For Louise, the value of being a good citizen by voting outweighs the cost of voting, so whether she is informed or not, she will vote. Also assume that she receives more utility from casting an informed vote than an uninformed vote (the value she places on being a citizen is higher). So she will choose to be informed. Her decision to be informed is a function of the choices she would make if informed or uninformed and the value she places on citizen duty.

In contrast, Sam places zero value on being a good citizen by voting or by being informed. For Sam, the cost of voting outweighs the benefit from voting, whether she is informed or not. So whether she is informed or not, she will not vote. However, we assume that if she is informed and does not vote, she will experience some regret from not participating, so she receives greater utility from being an uninformed nonvoter than being an informed nonvoter. So, given that she will not vote regardless of whether she is informed, and that she receives higher utility from being an uninformed nonvoter than from being an informed nonvoter, she will choose to be uninformed. On measurable variables, Louise and Sam are identical except one is informed and the other is not and the one who is informed votes and the other does not. Because being informed (treated) is a function of Louise and Sam's potential or counterfactual choices even when controlling for all observable variables, ignorability of treatment does not hold. The control function approach to establish the causal effect of information on voting, which assumes that Louise's behavior is the counterfactual of Sam's behavior if informed and Sam's behavior is the counterfactual of Louise's behavior if uninformed, would be an overstatement of the effect of information on voting.[5]

Citizen duty is just one hypothesized example of an unobservable variable that can lead to problems with the control approach to establishing causality. Earlier we noted that unmeasurable differences in cognitive abilities may also affect both whether an individual is informed and how he or she votes. Lassen (2005) suggests that simple measurement error in evaluating voter information can lead to violations of mean ignorability of treatment and cause attenuation biases in estimating causal effects. That is, the researcher does not actually observe the decision to be informed but usually measures whether individuals appear informed in response to survey questions. Thus, measurement error of the decision to be informed can lead to correlation between U and V. As Sekhon (2005, p. 6) remarks, "there is little agreement in the literature . . . on the best way to measure levels of political information." Such disagreement is evidenced in the variety of measures of voter information used in the studies cited in this chapter. The assumption of ignorability in studies that use such measures is unlikely to be satisfied simply because estimating individuals' true informational choices often involves misclassifications by researchers.

If strict ignorability of treatment is unlikely to hold, what about mean ignorability of treatment? Mean ignorability of treatment implies that the expected voting choices of voters with observables like Louise and Sam if informed and the expected choices if uninformed are independent of whether they are informed and that the distribution of effects on potential voting choices of the unobservables is such that they are random. This assumption is, in our opinion, a strong one that is unlikely to hold for many situations in political science. In voting, if we think that factors like the value individuals place on citizen duty or cognitive limitations have effects

---

[5] Information or treatment can affect the utility Louise and Sam receive from voting or not voting that can have a causal effect in this example and have a causal effect on the probability of turnout. The point is that confounding by unobservable variables can bias our estimate of the causal effect of information, in this case overstating that effect.

on both information levels and potential voting choices in the aggregate, then mean ignorability of treatment does not hold.

Although ignorability is not directly testable, there are sensitivity tests to determine if ignorability holds (see Rosenbaum, 2002). The Rivers and Vuong procedure discussed in the next section is an illustration of how one might test for exogeneity of treatment given a set of controls in a regression model. Heckman (2005a) argues that these sensitivity tests are variants of control functions that resemble a structural approach (discussed in Chapter 6) and certainly the Rivers and Vuong test does have that resemblance.

4.2.6 When Ignorability of Treatment Holds but Observables Affect Potential Choices

However, it might be the case that $E(u_1|W) \neq E(u_0|W)$. For example, we can imagine that the probability of voting is affected by an observable when informed in a different way than when uninformed. Consider the case in which an observable variable is gender and that women are more likely to vote than men, but only when they are also informed. In that case, the expected value of the stochastic part of the probability of voting when informed is greater than the expected value of the stochastic part of the probability of voting when uninformed for women. We assume though that, conditioned on gender, we have mean ignorability of treatment. That is, we assume that factors like citizen duty and cognitive ability wash out.

A recent trend in political science empirical research is to use multiple interaction terms as an effort to loosen some of the restrictiveness of the assumption $E(u_1|W) = E(u_0|W)$ described earlier, particularly if we think that the effect of the causal variable, the treatment, is mitigated or part of some general imprecise process including some other observable variables. This is the approach followed by Basinger and Lavine (2005) in their study of political alienation, knowledge, and campaigns on voting behavior. Can we use interaction terms and relax some of the preceding assumptions? Using interaction terms does allow us to relax the assumption that $E(u_1|W) = E(u_0|W)$. If we do so, we lose the equality between ATE and ATT but we can devise a regression equation that estimates these values. That is, if $E(u_1|W) \neq E(u_0|W)$, then[6]

$$E(P|T, W) = \mu_0 + \alpha T + h_0(W)\beta_0 + T[h_1(W) - h_0(W)], \quad (4.6)$$

where $\alpha = \text{ATE}$, $h_0(W) = E(u_0|W)$, and $h_1(W) = E(u_1|W)$.

---

[6] See Wooldridge (2002, proposition 18.2).

We can estimate the treatment effect if we include in our standard regression analysis interaction terms between the control function and the treatment variable. Wooldridge (2002, p. 613) points out that if linearity is assumed so that the coefficient on T measures ATE, the researcher should demean the values of W. (He discusses procedures that can be used to do so and adjustments to standard errors that might be necessary.) Assuming that these adjustments are appropriately made, then we can estimate ATE(W) for given ranges of independent variables by combining both the coefficient on T and the coefficients on the interaction terms times the different values of the independent variables that interest us.[7] For more information on how to use and interpret interaction terms in political science, see Brambor et al. (2006). Druckman and Kam (forthcoming) discuss how interaction terms can be useful in estimating the effects of uncontrolled observables in experiments that can allow for better comparisons of subject pools.

In summary, if mean ignorability of treatment is true, then the standard political science approach of estimating causal effects through including control variables and interaction terms can provide estimates of ATE and ATE(W, M). The assumption of mean ignorability of treatment is important for making these statements. If this assumption does not hold, and as we see later there are good reasons for thinking that it does not, then the estimating equations, even including interaction effects, cannot give us accurate estimates of causal effects.

4.2.7 Political Science Examples

Bartels' Study of Information and Voting
Do Uninformed Voters Vote as if They Are Informed? An innovative example of the type of control function estimation in political science is found in Bartels (1996), where he evaluates the effect of information on major party voting choices in presidential elections using the ANES survey data. He restricts his analysis to respondents who gave a choice of a major party candidate (thus excluding nonvoters and those who voted for minor party candidates). He uses a probit equation instead of LPM. As his information variable he uses the interviewer ratings of subject information. Interviewers rate subjects' information levels from "very high" to "very low." He assigns voters cardinal information scores to represent each of the five levels

---

[7] This is often not done in political science applications, however. Instead, political scientists usually evaluate effects with the independent variables at their means to show the same relationships.

possible: 0.05, 0.2, 0.5, 0.8, or 0.95. To keep within the notation used in this chapter, we label this variable T. However, these numbers are best viewed as approximate assignments in an unspecified interval of information ranges around them because within these categories respondents vary in information level. So, for example, some of those classified as very high information and assigned $T = 0.95$ may have information levels above 0.95 and some may have information levels below 0.95. Bartels assumes that the variable T is bounded between 0 and 1; when $T = 1$, a voter is fully informed, and when $T = 0$, a voter is fully uninformed.[8]

As control variables in the probit equations, Bartels includes demographic variables that measure the following characteristics: age (which is entered nonlinearly), education, income, race, gender, marital status, homeownership, occupational status, region and urban, and religion. In the probit, he interacts these independent variables with both T and $(1 - T)$ so assigned. This is a generalization of the switching regression model in Equation (4.4). Bartels argues then that the coefficients on the independent variables when interacted with T are the effects of these variables on voting behavior when a voter is fully informed and that the coefficients on the independent variables when interacted with $(1 - T)$ are the effects of these variables on voting behavior when a voter is completely uninformed. He then compares the goodness of fit of the model with the information variable as interacted with the goodness of fit of a probit estimation of voting choice as a function of the independent variables without the information variables; he finds that in every presidential election year from 1972 to 1992 the estimation including information effects improves the fit and that in 1972, 1984, and 1992 the improvement is large enough to reject the hypothesis of no information effects.

Using simulations and the clever way that he has coded and interacted the information variable, Bartels then makes a number of comparisons of how different types of voters, according to demographic characteristics, would or would not change their vote choices if they moved from completely uninformed to fully informed and how electoral outcomes may actually have been different if the electorate had been fully informed. He finds that there are large differences in how his simulated fully informed and fully uninformed women, Protestants, and Catholics vote but that the effects of education, income, and race on voting behavior are similar for the simulated fully informed and fully uninformed voters. He argues that his results show

---

[8] In private communication with the authors, Bartels reports that alternative assignments of the values do not change the results significantly as long as the order is maintained.

that incumbent presidents received about 5% more support and Democratic candidates almost 2% more support than they would have if voters had been fully informed.

The Problem of Generalizing from Individual Results.   Although the implications from the analysis about the effect of having a fully informed electorate are interesting, they hinge crucially on belief in the stable unit treatment value assumption (SUTVA), as Sekhon (2005) notes. It is extremely doubtful that we can assume that the treatment effects are fixed as we vary the number of informed voters in the population and, thus, it is highly speculative to argue what would occur in the two worlds. How then can we estimate the effect of large, aggregate changes in information on voting behavior? To aggregate up from individual-level data, we need to assume SUTVA, which is highly suspect. Thus, the answer must be to use data at an aggregate level. If the unit of the analysis is at the aggregate level, then the measured effect will be at the aggregate and take into account possible equilibrium and cross-effects from changing aggregate information levels.

Even though political scientists have devoted considerable attention to the problems of ecological regression – how do we infer individual behavior from aggregate analysis – little attention has been paid to the problem of moving from the individual to the aggregate. Because of excessive worry about the problem of ecological regression, the assumptions necessary for generalization are often ignored. Furthermore, by focusing excessively on the individual-level effect, the fact that the effect measured depends crucially on the current distribution of variables across the population implies that even the individual effect is highly conditional on that distribution. An individual-level model that ignores equilibrium and cross-effects across individuals yields results about causal effects only at the individual level given the current information level that exists in the population analyzed. It is not clear, if the population information level changed, that even the individual-level effect would be the same, much less clear what the aggregate effect of the change would imply. These lead to problems of external validity or robustness of the results, which we discuss in Chapter 7.

What can be done? Certainly it is easy to measure aggregate voting behavior, but then the problem is measuring aggregate levels of voter information and, even more difficult, having significant enough variation in voter information to discern treatment effects, as well as having a large enough data set to be able to show results that are statistically significant.

Mediating Variables in Control Functions.   Sekhon (2005) also asserts that, because Bartels' estimation does not include known variables that can affect

Figure 4.1. Control and Endogenous Variables.

voter choices such as partisan identification, the results overstate the effect of information on voting behavior. The reasons for excluding these variables are not in contention; that is, the values of these variables are likely to be affected by voter information and thus mask the effect of information on voting behavior in the survey data. Partisan identification is a mediating variable, a variable which is a function of treatment that affects potential outcomes as well. This issue is an important one in choosing control variables in analysis of causal effects that is often ignored in political science research.

Definition 4.6 (Mediating Variable): *A variable through which treatment variables can affect potential outcomes. Mediating variables are functions of treatment variables and potential outcomes are functions of mediating variables.*

We use a simple graph to illustrate why Bartels omits the mediating variable partisan identification. In Figure 4.1 we are interested in the causal effect of T, say information, on Y, say voting behavior, which is represented by the arrow that goes from T to Y. Variable Y is also a function of an observable variable, X, say partisan identification, and unobservable variables, U, which we assume do affect X but not T. Thus, U is not a confounder of the relationship between T and Y. But if we control for X, partisan identification, in estimating the effect of information on voting behavior, then because X is a descendant or a function of both U and T, and U and T are independent, then U and T are associated through Y. Controlling for X makes U a confounder of the relationship between T and Y. Intuitively, when measuring the effect of T on Y and including X as a control variable, we remove part of the effect of information on voting behavior that is mediated through partisan identification because of the confounding. Greenland and Brumback (2002) note a similar problem when researchers analyze the effects of weight on health and the researcher adjusts for serum lipids and blood pressure.

However, leaving out these variables does result in models of voting behavior that do not fit well and there can be numerous missclassification errors, which bothers Sekhon. This is probably why many political scientists tend to include variables that arguably create such confounding. Bartels' work is exceptional in this respect. Yet, can the poor fit be a problem in itself? Sekhon argues that the estimated effects Bartels finds may be inaccurate if the consequences of the misclassifications are not considered. Sekhon reestimates the model with a matching procedure designed to determine treatment effects that are robust to these errors (which we explore in Section 4.6.3) and finds that the information effects are not significant.

Sometimes researchers may be interested in identifying the effect of the mediating variable on outcomes or measuring the effects of treatment as transmitted through the mediating variable (as independent of the direct effects of treatment). We discuss how researchers attempt to estimate these particular causal effects in Section 4.7.

Reduced-Form Equations and Implicit Models. Bartels contends that the estimating equation he uses can be thought of as a reduced-form version of a more elaborate model, as we discuss in Chapter 6, but that is unspecified. His argument is that by including only as control variables "essentially fixed" demographic and social characteristics and using a flexible estimation procedure, and multiple experimentation with alternative specifications which yield similar results, he can accurately detect the effect of information on voting behavior in the reduced-form estimation. Many political scientists estimate equations similar to Equation (4.6), with multiple interaction effects, as implicit reduced-form representations of unstated more elaborate models. However, because the reduced-form equation estimated is not actually solved for from a fully specified more elaborate model, but just hypothesized to be the solution to one, the researcher is still using an RCM approach to the problem. He or she is implicitly assuming SUTVA as well as some version of ignorability of treatment, which may be untrue and, thus, the estimates may be inconsistent.

How might ignorability of treatment be false and the results not be consistent in equations that are reduced-form versions of unstated models? To see how estimating treatment effects using reduced-form equations that are not explicitly derived from a formal model might lead to inconsistent estimates of effects, we construct a simple example with a binary treatment variable that can take on either 0 or 1. In our simple model, we allow for the treatment variable to be endogenously determined and a function of the same demographics that affect voting behavior as well as other factors, which is a reasonable assumption. Suppose the underlying model is given by the following equations (using notation from Chapter 3):

$$Y_j^* = X\beta_{Yj} + u_j, \tag{4.7a}$$

$$T^* = X\beta_T + Z\theta + v, \tag{4.7b}$$

$$Y_j = 1 \quad \text{if} \quad Y_j^* > 0, \ 0 \text{ otherwise}, \tag{4.7c}$$

$$T = 1 \quad \text{if} \quad T^* > 0, 0 \text{ otherwise}, \tag{4.7d}$$

$$Y = TY_1 + (1 - T)Y_0, \tag{4.7e}$$

where Y_j^* is the latent utility that a voter receives from voting for the Republican candidate over the Democratic opponent under treatment j and Y_j is a binary variable that represents whether an individual votes Republican or Democrat under treatment j. Define $u = Tu_1 + (1 - T)u_0$. We assume that (u, v) is independent of X and Z and distributed as bivariate normal with mean zero and that each has a unit variance. Because there is no manipulation by an experimenter or nature, we do not include M as an exogenous variable in Equation (4.7b); however, if there was manipulation, then M would be included there. In our formulation, the equivalent equation to what Bartels estimates is the following probit model:

$$\Pr(Y = 1) = \Phi((1 - T)X\beta_{Y0} + TX\beta_{Y1}), \tag{4.8}$$

where Φ is the cumulative normal function.

Because T is an endogenous variable in the underlying model, can the estimation of Equation (4.8) yield consistent estimates of the effect of information on voting behavior? Define $\rho = \text{Corr}(u, v)$. If $\rho \neq 0$, then u and v are correlated, and probit estimation of Equation (4.8) is inconsistent for β_{Yj}. Why might this occur? If we think that there are unobservable variables that affect both whether a voter is informed and how he or she votes, then these errors may be correlated. For example, one such variable is cognitive abilities. We might expect cognitive abilities would affect both how informed a voter is and how he or she votes in an election. (Voters who have low cognitive abilities may have difficulty processing information they receive and making calculations about how best to vote in an election given their information levels.) Another unobserved variable that might lead to problems is the value that individuals place on citizen duty. We might expect that individuals who value citizen duty are more likely both to vote according to their preferences and to be informed about politics.

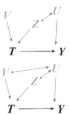

Figure 4.2. Ignorability of Treatment.

Thus, unobserved variables like cognitive abilities and the value that voters place on citizen duty might lead to a correlation between the error terms and inconsistent estimations of the effect of information on voting.[9]

Again the problem can be illustrated using a simple graph. In Figure 4.2 we are interested in the effect of T on Y, where T is a function of observables, Z, and unobservables, V, and Y is a function of T and U, which contains both observables and unobservables. Note that we allow for Z to be related to U and even overlap with some of the observables; U and T are correlated through the observables. When we use control functions, we are controlling for these effects. The assumption of ignorability of treatment is that this is the only avenue through which U and T are correlated. If U and V are correlated, then selection on unobservables is occurring and there are common omitted variables in the estimation of the treatment effect. In the top graph of Figure 4.2, ignorability of treatment holds – there is no arrow connecting U and V – but in the bottom graph of Figure 4.2, ignorability of treatment fails – there is an arrow connecting U and V.

How can a researcher find out if $\rho \neq 0$? Rivers and Vuong (1988) propose a test of exogeneity that can be applied to our problem. To do so, a researcher first estimates a probit of T on X and Z and saves the residuals. The researcher then estimates Equation (4.8), including the residuals as an additional independent variable. If the coefficient on the residuals is significantly different from zero, then the researcher has an endogeneity problem. Evidence suggests that, in studies of the effect of information on voting behavior, endogeneity can be a problem. For example, Lassen (2005), in Example 2.8, conducts such a test in his work on the effect of information on voting behavior and finds evidence that supports endogeneity of voter information. As Wooldridge (2002, chapter 15) discusses, consistent estimates

---

[9] Lassen (2005), Example 2.8, suggests that systematic measurement error in calculating voter information is another unobservable that may cause estimation of Equation (4.8) to be inconsistent. We return to this point when we discuss his empirical estimation more fully.

of the causal effect of information in the underlying model can be obtained through maximum likelihood methods that explicitly incorporate and estimate ρ.

Laboratory Experiment on How Voters Use Heuristics in Making Voting Choices
Bartels (1996), by investigating whether uninformed voters choose as if they are informed, evaluates an implication of the hypothesis that uninformed voters use heuristics and information shortcuts to vote correctly; recall the theories of voting discussed in Section 2.3.3. In Example 4.2, Lau and Redlawsk (1997, 2001, 2006), tackle how voters use heuristics from a different perspective. They point out that research from political psychology suggests a number of heuristics, which uninformed voters might use in making voting choices such as party, ideology, endorsements, polls, and candidate appearance. Furthermore, this research indicates that sometimes voters use these heuristics incorrectly. To evaluate how voters use heuristics, they create a computer-generated hypothetical campaign where voters are exposed to these heuristics and have opportunities to acquire more substantive information. In the laboratory, they exposed subjects to this campaign and were able to monitor electronically which heuristics subjects use and how often. The subjects then voted in a hypothetical election. They constructed measures of whether subjects voted correctly in two ways – a subjective measure by revealing complete information to voters about the candidates and asking them if they voted correctly given the complete information, and a normative measure in which they used information from a pretreatment survey of political attitudes and preferences.

Example 4.2 (Cognitive Miser Experiment): *Lau and Redlawsk (1997, 2001, 2006), hereafter LR, reported on a series of laboratory experiments conducted at Rutgers University, evaluating the extent that voters use cognitive heuristics to vote correctly in a mock presidential election.*

Target Population and Sample: LR recruited individuals from the central New Jersey area who were American citizens, at least 18 years old, and not currently going to college. The recruiting was conducted via ads in local newspapers and through churches, parent teacher associations, and the American Legion. LR (1997) reported on the results from 293 subjects and later (2001) they reported on the results from 657 subjects, which includes the first 293 subjects. In LR (2006) the authors report on the results from 664 subjects which includes subjects recruited by students in research methods classes taught at Rutgers University. Subjects were paid $20 for participating, which some donated to *the charitable organization through which they were recruited. Some subjects were unpaid volunteers, although this was a small percentage of the sample. The experiment did not attempt to recruit a random sample but did gather demographic information on the subjects that suggested a diverse population.*

Environment: *The candidates in the election were hypothetical, but given characteristics to make them realistic. The experiment used a technique to measure the effects of voter information on voter choices developed by LR, called a dynamic processing tracing methodology, which is a variant of the "information board" used by behavioral decision theorists for studying decision making.[10] LR (2001, pp. 955–956) described the technology as follows:*

"The standard information board presents decision makers with an m by n matrix, with [sic] the columns of the matrix are headed by the different alternatives (e.g. candidates) and the rows of the matrix are labeled with different attributes (e.g. issue stands, past experience, and so forth). None of the specific information is actually visible, however, and decision makers must actively choose what information they want to learn by clicking on a box on a computer screen. The researcher can record and analyze what information was accessed, the order in which it was accessed, how long it was studied, and so on.... Our dynamic process-tracing methodology retains the most essential features of the standard information board while making it a better analog of an actual political campaign. Our guiding principle was to devise a technique that would mimic crucial aspects of an actual election campaign while still providing a detailed record of the search process employed by voters.... We accomplished ... [this] by designing a radically revised information board in which the information about the candidates scrolls down a computer screen rather than being in a fixed location. There are only a limited number of attribute labels (six) visible on the computer screen – and thus available for access – at any given time.... The rate of scrolling is such that most people can read approximately two labels before the positions change. Subjects can 'access' (i.e., read) the information behind the label by clicking a mouse.... The scrolling continues while subjects process the detailed information they have accessed, so that typically there is a completely new screen when subjects return to scrolling – thus mimicking the dynamic, ongoing nature to the political campaign.... [A]t periodic intervals the computer screen is taken over by a twenty-second political advertisement for one of the candidates in the campaign. Voters can carefully watch these commercials or avert their eyes while they are on the screen, but they cannot gather any other information relevant to the campaign while the commercial is on."

---

[10] See Caroll and Johnson (1990) for more details.

Procedures: The experiment proceeded as follows. First, subjects completed a questionnaire about both their political attitudes and media usage. Then subjects participated in a practice session in which they accessed information using the technology about the 1988 presidential election. Next, subjects were randomly assigned to different experimental conditions, although these assignments were unknown to subjects. Subjects then registered for either the Democratic or Republican party. In the primary elections there were two candidates in one party's primary and four in the other (randomly determined). After 22 minutes of experiencing the primary election campaign through the dynamic process-tracing procedure, the subjects voted in the primary election and evaluated all six of the candidates. Then subjects participated in a general election campaign involving two of the candidates (selected by the experimenters) for 12 minutes. At the conclusion of the general election campaign, subjects voted in the general election and evaluated all six candidates. After voting, subjects were asked to remember as much as they could about the two general election candidates. Next, subjects were presented with complete information about two candidates from the primary (the one they voted for and the one in the same party who was closest to the subject on the issues) and asked to decide who they would have voted for if they had full information. Finally, the subjects were debriefed and asked what their general impressions were about the experiment and if they had any questions about the experiment. Debriefing is discussed more extensively in Section 13.6.3.

Results: LR compared the voting behavior of the subjects in the mock elections to two measures of full information voting – the self-reported full information voting behavior at the end of the experiment and a theoretically predicted full information voting choice based on their answers to the questionnaire at the beginning of the experiment. They found that the majority of subjects voted "correctly" using these two measures. LR also considered several additional hypotheses about the use of heuristics as well as the effects of primaries with more candidates on the ability of voters to choose "correctly."

Comments: Because they did not manipulate heuristic use but instead manipulated other dimensions of the election (number of candidates, for example), to evaluate the effect of heuristic use on whether a subject voted correctly they estimated a logit regression with voting correctly as a dependent variable and heuristic use as an independent variable. They also interacted heuristic use with a measure of subject political sophistication.

Although we consider Lau and Redlawsk's hypothetical election an experiment, the researchers did not manipulate heuristic exposure, allowing subjects to choose which heuristics to use; thus their choices on information were endogenous. That said, through controlling the information subjects had about the election beyond the heuristics and the cost to the subjects of using heuristics, they attempted to control for confounding that may have occurred because of the endogeneity. Lau and Redlawsk estimated a version of Equation (4.5), implicitly assuming mean ignorability of treatment and SUTVA. They found that heuristic use does increase the probability of voting correctly if voters are more politically sophisticated, suggesting that unsophisticated voters are less able to use heuristics.

4.2.8 Using Regression Control Methods with Experimental Data

Although LR's experiment is a particular example of a case in which treatment is endogenous, in many cases researchers using experiments estimate regression equations with control functions to deal with observable variables that they think might be confounders. For example, Gerber, Karlan, and Bergan, in Example 2.1, use the control function approach when they estimate the effects of their manipulation of newspaper subscriptions on voter behavior in Northern Virginia. They report that they included as control variables gender, reported age, indicators for whether a voter turned out in previous years, and many other indicators and survey responses. Clinton and Lapinski, in their Internet survey experiment on negative campaign advertising (see Example 2.3), also use a control function regression without interaction terms to deal with possible confounding of observable variables. As in Gerber, Karlan, and Bergan, they implicitly assume both mean ignorability of treatment plus $E(u_1|W) = E(u_0|W)$. The latter assumption may not hold, of course, as we observed earlier. Humphreys (2009) presents a number of examples in which $E(u_1|W) = E(u_0|W)$ does not hold, although mean ignorability holds because manipulations are randomly assigned. He derives a monotonicity condition and shows that when the condition holds, the estimated treatment effects are guaranteed to lie between estimates of ATT and the average treatment effects for nontreated subjects.

Hence, if a researcher feels confident that $E(u_1|W) = E(u_0|W)$ is true, including control variables as independent variables and estimating Equation (4.5) results in an estimate of ATE. If $E(u_1|W) \neq E(u_0|W)$, then a researcher should consider adding in interaction terms (see Section 4.2.6) or using nonparametric methods such as matching (discussed in Section 4.6) for estimating treatment effects if he or she is worried about possible confounding uncontrolled observables. Alternatively, the researcher might randomize within strata of observable variables that he or she believes ex ante are likely to be confounders. Gerber, Karlan, and Bergan randomized within some of the observable variables in their sample from the initial survey – a subject's intention to vote, whether a subject receives a paper (non-*Post*/non-*Times*), mentioned ever reading a paper, received a magazine, or were asked whether they wish they read newspapers more. Gerber, Karlan, and Bergan also include strata indicators as control variables in the regression (we discuss design methods of dealing with the problem in Section 5.3.2).

Random assignment of manipulations when implemented ideally, as discussed in the next chapter (see Section 5.2.2), allows one to compute ATE as the simple average of choices of subjects given their assignments. In this case we can estimate the simple bivariate regression equation, Equation (4.4), and with an estimate of ATE. We may have a host of covariates on our subjects and we may think that estimating Equation (4.5) will increase the precision of our estimates, as advocated by Maxwell and Delaney (2004) and others. However, in finite samples, as Freedman (2008a,b) shows, including the controls results in biased OLS estimates even when manipulations are randomly assigned, although it does yield consistent estimates under the aforementioned assumptions. Freedman argues that the bias can be substantial for sample sizes of less than 500, which is relevant for experimentalists who sometimes do not have such large sample sizes. Yet, the worry about small sample sizes is not as problematic as Freedman suggests. Green (2009) shows that in simulated and in actual examples the biases tend to be negligible for sample sizes greater than 20. He further notes that cases where biases might occur in larger experiments are cases with extreme outliers that he suggests would be readily detected through visual inspection.

4.3 Using Time to Control for Confounding Unobservables

4.3.1 Time and Data Structures

In the preceding examination of regression procedures, we assumed that the researcher was using a single cross-sectional random sample similar to that used by Bartels. But often researchers have data over time and can exploit the time dimension to determine causal effects. At one extreme, when a researcher has time-series data, where the number of cases is small relative to the time periods examined, the researcher can turn to time-series methods of establishing causality. Although there are a host of issues to consider when using time series to establish causal relationships, these issues are not particularly relevant to experimental political science where researchers normally have a much larger set of cases relative to the time periods examined. We thus concentrate on those situations and, as a consequence, we do not need to worry about unit root processes. For more detail on such processes and the methodological issues involved, see Hamilton (1994) and Enders (2003).

There are two types of data sets that are relevant – pooled cross-sectional data and panel data. Pooled cross-sectional data are obtained when we have a new random sample from the relevant population for each time period. The observations are thought of as independent but not identically distributed. In contrast, panel data are obtained when we have observations on the same group of individuals, geographical locations, and so forth, over time. One of the ways that researchers evaluate the effects of manipulations by nature, or natural experiments, is through the use of pooled cross-sectional data. We discuss these methods in the next chapter when we review procedures used to estimate causality by sidestepping confounding variables. In this chapter we explore panel data methods that primarily are used to aid in the control of confounding variables and to better determine causal effects by controlling for unobservables. Panel data methods are also useful for analyzing experimental data generated through repeated choices of the same subjects.

4.3.2 Panel Data and Control of Unobservables

As we have discussed, one problem with trying to determine the effect of information on voters' choices is that some unobserved variable might affect both how informed voters are and the choices they would make given their informational choices. This individual-specific variable could be cognitive ability or the value the individual places on citizen duty or some other unobservable characteristic. If we have repeated observations on individuals for whom we can observe differences in voter information over time and we assume that the individual-specific variable is constant, then having a panel data set can perhaps allow us to control for the observable variable. Experimental data generated in crossover designs with multiple periods discussed in the previous chapter also can be analyzed in this fashion.

To see how this works, assume that we expect that our dependent variable, P, according to the LPM, is given by the following simple model:

$$P_t = \alpha + \beta T_t + I + U_t, \tag{4.9}$$

where t denotes the time period of the observation, T_t represents the information state of an individual at time t, I is the unknown characteristic that is individual-specific and constant across t, and U_t is the time and individual-specific unobservable error. So that our analysis is clear, we are assuming that the only thing that affects voters' choices is their information and their individual characteristics. The problem is that if I is correlated with T_t, then if we just have I in the error term we cannot consistently estimate the effect of information on voting behavior. If we just have a single cross section, then our estimate of the effect of information on voting behavior is problematic unless we come up with a good proxy for I or take an instrumental variable approach (discussed in the next chapter).

Can we estimate Equation (4.9) if we have panel data, using repeated observations for the same individuals as a way to control for I? A number of relatively common estimation procedures are used by political scientists to control for I such as random-effects estimators, fixed-effects estimators, dummy variables, and first differencing methods.[11] All of these methods assume at the minimum strict exogeneity; that is, once T_t and I are controlled for, T_s has no partial effect on P_t for $s \neq t$.

Formally, in OLS, researchers assume the following:

$$E(P_t | T_1, T_2, \ldots, T_s, I) = E(P_t | T_t, I) = \alpha + \beta T_t + I. \quad (4.10)$$

The second equality is an assumption of linearity. When Equation (4.10) holds, we say that T_t is strictly exogenous conditional on the unobserved effect.

Definition 4.7 (Strict Exogeneity): *Once T_t and I are controlled for, T_s has no partial effect on P_t for $s \neq t$.*

How reasonable is strict exogeneity? The assumption implies that the explanatory variable or variables in each time period – in this case, a single one, information – is uncorrelated with the idiosyncratic error in each time period. It is relatively simple to show that if we include a lagged dependent variable, then the error terms will necessarily be correlated with future explanatory variables and strict exogeneity does not hold. So strict exogeneity rules out a type of feedback from current values of the dependent variable to future values of the explanatory variable, a feedback from current voting

---

[11] Wooldridge (2002, chapter 10) provides a review and discussion of these methods and their underlying assumptions.

choices to future information levels. We can imagine that such feedback does occur. For example, if individuals who have voted in the past are more likely to be informed about future choices as may occur if individuals who vote are more informed than nonvoters, then such feedback occurs.

It is possible to estimate the partial effect of an explanatory variable relaxing strict exogeneity, and Wooldridge (2002, chapter 11) reviews the various assumptions involved; usually these methods involve adding in instruments or making specific assumptions about the relationship between the observable explanatory variables and the unobservable variable. The upshot is that panel data can allow a researcher to control for these individual unobservables, but a researcher must be extremely careful to understand the assumptions behind the estimation procedure and the reasonableness of these assumptions for the particular data set and research question. When these assumptions do not hold or are unlikely to hold, then the conclusions of the analysis are suspect.

Finally, when these methods are used with panel data to control for unit-specific unobservables, it makes it impossible for a researcher to determine the effect of observable variables that do not vary over time by unit. Thus, panel data can be used to control for unobservables if the treatment variable – the independent variable of interest – varies over time by unit. For example, if a researcher wished to use panel data to control for unobservable individual-specific effects in studying the effect of information on voting, the panel data approach would only work if the information levels of the voters varied over the time period in the panel.

4.3.3 Political Science Example: A Panel Study of Turnout

The analysis of Holbrook and McClurg (2005) is an example of the use of panel data in a regression to estimate the causal effects of presidential campaign activities on voter turnout across states. Their panel consists of the 50 states for the presidential elections in 1992, 1996, and 2000. They assume (p. 702) "that the link between campaign activity and the mobilization of core voters is based on the information transmitted by campaigns." However, the causal effect they investigate is not of information-level variations across states but of campaign activity across states. They use a modification of a first differencing method to attempt to control for unobservable state variables. That is, in the differencing method, a researcher drops the first period of observations and then uses as dependent and independent variables the change from period to period in place of the original dependent and independent variables. In this way, effects are controlled that are unit specific – in this case states – and that could confound the causal effect as discussed earlier.

Holbrook and McClurg use as a dependent variable the first difference in turnout, but they do not difference their independent variables. They do include lagged turnout as an independent variable, which, because it is a function of the other independent variables in the previous period, is an indirect method of first differencing. Because lagged turnout is also a function of the state-specific unobservable variable, including lagged turnout also includes that variable in the estimation and there is the possibility of correlation across years in the error terms because of its inclusion.[12]

A potential problem with Holbrook and McClurg's analysis is the endogeneity of campaign activities, which are probably functions of the expected turnout effects, even when differenced. That is, campaign activities are clearly choices that candidates make to maximize their probability of winning. Work by Stromberg (2008) demonstrates that campaign visits and advertisement choices closely match those predicted by a game-theoretic model in which candidates make these choices strategically in reaction to both anticipated effects on voter choices in a state and the activities of their competitors. Thus, an estimate of the causal effect of campaign activities should take this endogeneity into account, which is not possible in a single-equation regression. We deal with models of causality that allow for such endogeneity in Chapter 6.

4.4 Propensity Scores in Regressions

An alternative to the standard control function approach discussed earlier is to use propensity scores as control functions in the regression equations. What are propensity scores? Propensity scores are estimates of the probability of receiving treatment as a function of W, which we define as $\pi(W)$. Rosenbaum and Rubin (1983) suggest that they be estimated using a flexible logit model, where W and various functions of W are included. Others have estimated them using nonparametric methods (see Powell, 1994; Heckman et al., 1997). Wooldridge (1999) shows that if we assume (1) mean ignorability of treatment, (2) that $E(P_1 - P_0 | W)$ is uncorrelated with $\text{Var}(T | W, P)$, and (3) that the parametric estimator of the propensity score is consistent, then the OLS coefficient on T is also a consistent estimator of ATE.

---

[12] By not first differencing all of the variables, they are able to have 150 observations instead of 100 because they do not have measures of the campaign activities prior to 1992, so true first differencing would reduce their observations by one-third.

Definition 4.8 (Propensity Scores): *Propensity scores are estimates of the probability of receiving treatment as a function of W, which we define as $\pi(W)$.*

Ho et al. (forthcoming) point out that the last assumption, that the parametric estimator of the propensity score is consistent, is something that is untestable. As they demonstrate, if the parametric estimation of the propensity score is inaccurate, then the causal effects estimated are inconsistent. They advocate that researchers make use of what they call the "propensity score tautology"; that is, they note that (p. 219)

The estimated propensity score is a balancing score when we have a consistent estimate of the true propensity score. We know we have a consistent estimate of the propensity score when matching on the propensity score balances the raw covariates. Of course, once we have balance on the covariates, we are done and do not need to look back. That is, it works when it works, and when it does not work, it does not work (and when it does not work, keep working at it).

Ho et al. suggest that researchers first begin with a simple estimation of the propensity score using a logistic regression of T on W. To check for balance, the researcher matches each treated unit to the control unit with the most similar value of the estimated propensity score (nearest-neighbor matching on the propensity score).[13] If the matching shows that W is balanced (Ho et al. discuss how to check for balance), then the researcher should use the propensity scores. If not, the researcher respecifies the estimation by adding in interaction terms, squared terms, or both and checks balance again. If this fails, the researcher turns to more elaborate specifications.

Which is better in regressions estimating treatment effects – standard control functions or propensity scores as control functions? Sekhon (2005) contends that an advantage of propensity scores is that they are estimated independently of outcome or choice data whereas control functions in regressions are not. This approach allows for the application of a standard for determining the optimal model that balances the covariates, independently of the outcome data. Propensity scores also appear parsimonious as compared to the kitchen sink–like regression with control functions.

The appearance of parsimony is deceiving because the propensity scores themselves are estimated in a similar fashion. If the propensity score is estimated in linear regressions without interaction effects as in Equation (4.6), the estimations are identical. Moreover, the standard errors in the

---

[13] We discuss matching more extensively later. Ho et al. provide free software for such matching and in the documentation to the software discuss different techniques in matching.

kitchen sink regression have known reliability, and adjustments for problems can be made as is standard in regression analysis. However, in regressions with propensity scores, the first-stage estimation is sometimes ignored in computing the standard error and the proper adjustments are not made. Researchers who use propensity scores need to be careful in the construction of the standard error and in making these adjustments. Furthermore, the two techniques rely on different assumptions and arguably the ones underlying propensity scores are more restrictive and less likely to be satisfied. Finally, the use of propensity scores depends on the assumption that the parametric model used is consistent.

4.5 Use of Controls and Propensity Scores Without Regression

The preceding control function analysis focuses on regression approaches to estimating causal effects. There are also nonregression methods, which are attractive because they do not require that assumptions be made about linearity as in most regression analysis used in political science. Nonparametric approaches are particularly useful for discrete dependent variables such as voting behavior. That is, recall that we needed to restrict our attention to a binary dependent variable and then assume that the probability of turnout was given by LPM, even though we knew that this placed unrealistic assumptions about that probability. If we use as our estimating equation a more realistic probit, logit, or multinomial variant, then the linearity assumptions break down and estimating ATE is more complicated.

We can avoid this problem by noting that if we assume mean ignorability of treatment, then it can be shown that the conditional treatment effects, ATT(W) and ATE(W), are equal, although the unconditional ones are not necessarily equal. Specifically, ATE $= E[\text{ATE}(W)]$ and ATT $= E[\text{ATE}(W)|T = 1]$. If ATE(W) can be estimated, then the average treatment effects can be estimated. It turns out that, if we have a random sample, then $E[\text{ATE}(W)|T = j]$ are nonparametically identified and from them the average treatment effects can be estimated as well.[14] However, obtaining the asymptotically valid standard errors using this approach can be very difficult, making nonparametric estimation less desirable than the standard regression approach.

Alternatively, rather than including the propensity score in a regression, propensity scores can be used directly to estimate causal effects nonparametrically if we assume ignorability of treatment in its stricter version, that

---

[14] See Härdle and Linton (1994).

propensity scores are bounded between 0 and 1 (that is, every observation has a positive probability of being in either state of the world), and that the parametric estimation of the propensity score is correct such that the propensity scores are consistent. Then[15]

$$\text{ATE} = E\left(\frac{[T - \pi(W)]P}{\pi(W)[1 - \pi(W)]}\right) \tag{4.11}$$

and

$$\text{ATT} = \frac{E\left(\dfrac{[T - \pi(W)]P}{\pi(W)[1 - \pi(W)]}\right)}{\Pr(T = 1)}. \tag{4.12}$$

These can then be estimated after estimating the propensity scores, both nonparametically and using flexible parametric approaches. Again, note that both of these approaches assume ignorability of treatment, with the propensity score approach making the more restrictive assumption and that the propensity score estimates are consistent.

4.6 Control by Matching

4.6.1 Propensity Scores and Matching

An alternative use of propensity scores in estimating the effects of a cause is through the process of matching on propensity scores, as we discussed earlier. Again, this can be useful if the dependent variable is, as in our case, discrete. The idea behind matching is simple: suppose that we randomly draw a propensity score from the population and then match two voting choices from the population, where one individual is informed and the other individual is uninformed. If we assume ignorability of treatment in the stricter form as earlier, that the propensity scores are bounded between 0 and 1, and that the propensity score estimates are consistent, then we know that

$$E[P|T = 1, \quad \pi(W)] - E[P|T = 0, \quad \pi(W)] = E[P_1 - P_0|\pi(W)]. \tag{4.13}$$

By doing this iteratively and averaging across the distribution of propensity scores, a researcher can compute ATE. Matching implicitly assumes that, conditioned on W, some unspecified random process assigns individuals to be either informed or uninformed. Because the process of assignment is

---

[15] See Ho et al. (forthcoming) and Rosenbaum and Rubin (1983).

random, the possible effects of unobservables on voting choices wash out, allowing for accurate estimates of the causal effect of information on voting. If we assume just mean ignorability of treatment, then we can estimate ATT (see Heckman et al., 1997; Ho et al., (forthcoming)).

The process is actually more complicated because it is difficult to get exact matches for propensity scores, which of course must be estimated as discussed earlier. Thus, most researchers who use matching procedures also use some grouping or local averaging to determine similarities in terms of propensity between treated and nontreated observations as well as exact matching on certain selected variables. The methods employed are discussed by Heckman et al. (1997); Angrist (1998); Dehejia and Wahba (1999); and Ho et al. (forthcoming). Ho et al. provide free software for matching and in the documentation explain these procedures in detail.

4.6.2 Nonparametric Preprocessing and Matching

Ho et al. (forthcoming) also propose that researchers use matching as a nonparametric preprocessing approach to deal with all data before estimating causal effects regardless of the parametric analysis the researcher plans to undertake. The idea of preprocessing (as they note on p. 211, using our notation) is

to adjust the data prior to the parametric analysis so that (1) the relationship between T and W is eliminated or reduced and (2) little bias and inefficiency is induced. . . . An assumption of ignorability is still necessary, but we would no longer need to model the full parametric relationship between the dependent variable and the multidimensional W. This also eliminates an important source of model dependence in the resulting parametric analysis stemming from the functional form specification and the curse of dimensionality. For data sets where preprocessing reduces the extent of the relationship between T and W but is unable to make them completely unrelated, model dependence is not eliminated but will normally be greatly reduced. If nonparametric preprocessing results in no reduction in model dependence, then it is likely that the data have little information to support causal inferences by any method, which of course would also be useful information.

How is the preprocessing accomplished? Assuming ignorability, a researcher can select, duplicate, or drop observations from the sample based on T and W without bias. The goal would be to use matching to make these choices so that the following relationship holds:

$$\tilde{p}(W|T=1) = \tilde{p}(W|T=0),$$

where $\bar{p}$ refers to the observed empirical density of the data. Again, Ho et al. provided advice and software for accomplishing such preprocessing through matching http://gking.harvard.edu/matchit/.

4.6.3 Political Science Example

Matching and the Effect of Information on Voting
Sekhon (2005) addresses the question of how information affects voter decisions in survey data using a matching procedure he developed for the statistical software program R. The procedure produces standard errors that take into account ties and sampling controls with replacement when finding matches. Sekhon matches the observations using a combination of variables and propensity scores that are estimated using principal components of the baseline variables. He uses a general procedure to estimate the principal components, including first-order interactions and nonlinear specifications of continuous variables. As Sekhon points out, one of the unique advantages of the matching procedure is that there is no need to discard observations with missing data; they can be matched on and included in the analysis. Thus, matching allows for a wider use of data from surveys, something particularly attractive to political scientists.

Sekhon tests his use of the matching procedures for balance. He first uses a number of nonparametric tests: (1) the Wilcoxon rank sum test for univariate balance, (2) the McNemar test of marginal homogeneity on paired binary data, and (3) the Kolmogorov–Smirnov test for equality. He also estimates a logistic model in which the dependent variable is treatment assignment and the baseline variables are explanatory. Unlike the control function approach in regressions, the tests of balance are conducted independently of the examination of the relationship between information and voting. Sekhon assumes mean ignorability and thus reports only ATT(W) rather than ATE(W).

Panel Data Redux
As noted earlier, Bartels (1996) restricted the independent variables he used to those that could be considered exogenous and not influenced by voter information levels, which led to a high number of missclassification errors and poor general goodness of fit compared to other models of voting behavior. Sekhon avoids this problem by using panel survey data and matching on the baseline survey or "pretreatment" survey. Using panel surveys from three ANES data sets – 1980, 1972–1974–1976, and 1992–1994–1996 – Sekhon finds that there are not significant differences between the choices of

informed and uninformed voters in U.S. elections at the time of the election (he finds effects at earlier points in the election campaign). In contrast, he finds that a similar analysis of Mexican voters in 2000 at the time of the election shows significant differences. Sekhon conjectures that in more advanced democracies it is easier for voters to vote as if they were informed, even if they are not, due to communications that occur during election campaigns in advanced democracies. Sekhon uses panel data as a way to control for observables, not unobservables. He explicitly assumes, as in other matching procedures, mean ignorability of treatment.

4.7 Causal Effects Through Mediating Variables

Earlier, in Section 4.2.7, we noted that sometimes researchers believe that there exists a mediating variable through which treatments affect outcomes. We gave as an example partisan identification and noted that Bartels did not include partisan identification in his control function approach to estimate the causal effect of information on voting because of the endogenous nature of this mediating variable.

However, suppose a researcher is particularly interested in identifying the causal effect of information on voting through partisan identification or the causal effect of partisan identification on voting. More generally, we may be interested in what are called causal mediation effects. Assume that X is a mediating variable. Since X is now a function of T, then we can think of two potential values for X: X_0 when $T = 0$, and X_1 when $T = 1$. As with Y, we only observe one value of X for each individual, which is given by[16]

$$X = TX_1 + (1 - T)X_0. \tag{4.14}$$

We can also think of potential outcomes as functions of the values of both the mediating variable and treatment, such that Y_{jX_j} is the potential value of Y given that $T = j$. We define the observed outcome as

$$Y = TY_{1X_1} + (1 - T)Y_{0X_0}. \tag{4.15}$$

The causal mediation effect (CME) is the effect on the outcome of changing the mediator value as affected by the treatment without actually changing the treatment value. That is, CME is given by

$$\text{CME}(T) = Y_{TX_1} - Y_{TX_0}. \tag{4.16}$$

---

[16] We draw from Imai et al. (2009) discussion of mediators in a counterfactual framework.

Of course, because we cannot observe counterfactual situations, we cannot observe CME(T). Instead, we might attempt to estimate the average causal mediation effect, or ACME(T), which is given by

$$\text{ACME}(T) = E(\text{CME}(T)).$$

Imai et al. (2008) and Imai et al. (2008) considered what assumptions are necessary to estimate ACME(T). They pointed out that random assignment of values of the mediator value holding T constant or randomizing T cannot measure ACME(T) because the point is to measure the effects of the changes in the mediator value as a consequence of changes in T. Thus, to estimate ACME(T), a researcher must adopt a control approach. Imai et al. (2008) showed that if the following axiom of sequential ignorability holds, then ACME(T) can be easily estimated (where W does not include X).

Axiom 4.3 (Sequential Ignorability): *Conditional on W, $\{Y_{T'X}, X_T\}$ are independent of T and $Y_{T'X}$ is independent of X.*

Imai et al. (2008) call this "sequential ignorability" because it comprises two ignorability assumptions that are made sequentially. The first assumption is that treatment assignment is ignorable with respect to both potential outcomes and potential mediators, and the second assumption is that the mediator values are also ignorable with respect to potential outcomes. As Imai et al. observed, these are strong and untestable assumptions which are not likely to hold even if random assignment of treatment is conducted perfectly. Furthermore, they point out that a linear regression procedure commonly used in causal mediation analysis from Baron and Kenny (1986), linear structural equation modeling (or LISREL for Linear Structural Relations) requires additional assumptions of linearity and non-interaction effects to interpret coefficient estimates as ACME. Imai et al. advocate using sensitivity analysis and provide computer software that allows for the computation of ACME without making the additional linearity and noninteraction effect assumptions.

4.8 Chapter Summary

In this chapter we have discussed how control is used in both experimental and observational data to establish causal relationships using the RCM approach. Table 4.1 summarizes these methods of control and their assumptions. In experiments, researchers can control explicitly many observable

Table 4.1. *Summary of control methods*

Method	Assumptions	Helps control
Approaches with Experimental Data Only (Design Solutions)		
Manipulation of observables in lab	Can manipulate relevant variable	Observables
Cross-over within-subjects design	No effects from sequence variation	Both
Multiple-choice within-subjects design	No effects from choice elicitation method	Both
Financial incentives based on choices	Can overcome unwanted confounders	Both
Approaches with Both Experimental and Observational Data (Analysis Solutions)		
Control functions in regressions without interactions	Mean ignorability $E(u_1\|W) = E(u_0\|W)$	Observables
Control Functions in Regressions with Interactions	Mean ignorability	Observables
Panel data methods	Strict exogeneity	Both
Regression with proximity scores	Mean ignorability Proximity scores consistently estimated	Observables
Nonparametric matching methods	Matches accurate and consistent Strict ignorability for ATE Mean ignorability for ATT	Observables
Causal mediation analysis	Sequential ignorability for ACME	Observables
Both = Unobservables and Observables		

variables, they can make some variables that are normally unobservable observable, and they can use within-subjects designs and financial incentives to control for other unobservables. In observational data, researchers use statistical methods to attempt to control for observable variables. These measures typically make strong assumptions about unobservable variables and how observable variables affect treatments and potential choices. Regression methods rely on the assumption of mean ignorability of treatment and in most cases the assumption that the expected effects of observable variables on potential choices are equivalent. Most of the control and matching methods based on RCM also rely on the assumptions of ignorability of treatment or mean ignorability of treatment. Regressions with panel data typically assume strict exogeneity. Propensity score and matching methods that estimate ATE rely on the stricter version combined with the assumption that all observations have some positive probability of existing in either state of the world (being either informed or uninformed). Some assume only mean ignorability, as in Sekhon (2005), and report ATT(W) rather than ATE(W).

Ignorability of treatment, mean ignorability of treatment, and strict exogeneity are all assumptions that are essentially untestable, although researchers can explore through sensitivity analysis whether they are likely to hold. We have discussed some examples of how these assumptions are unlikely to hold for the relationship between information and voting behavior.

In this chapter we have explored how researchers use control either with observational or experimental data to estimate causal relationships using an RCM approach. In the next chapter we turn to the use of randomization and pseudo-randomization techniques under RCM.

5

Randomization and Pseudo-Randomization

5.1 RCM-Based Methods and Avoiding Confounding

In the previous chapter we reviewed the methods used to estimate the effects of causes using control either through untested statistical assumptions about the relationships between observable and unobservable confounding variables, principally ignorability of treatment, or through the use of laboratory experimental designs that allow a researcher to set values of unobservables and observables directly or to control for them through repeated observations of subjects. We have also examined a number of studies using observational and experimental data, which have used control as a method of trying to discern the effect of changing voter information on voter behavior.

Suppose that, instead of trying to measure all the possible covariates that might confound the effect of information on voting decisions and then just assuming that the unobservables do not confound the effect or running an experiment in the laboratory where we are able to both control for observable and unobservable variables that affect the relationship between information and voting, we could find a variable that was related to the information levels of voters but independent of the choices voters make that depend on the information as well as the unobservables. That is, suppose we could find a variable or set of variables that are ignorable in the determination of P_j but have a consequential effect on T. Another way to think of the variable or set of variables in relationship to P_j is that they are redundant in the determination of the potential choices given information levels. If we could find such a variable, then maybe we could use it as a substitute for information and avoid or sidestep the problem of confounding that occurs when we use information.

The goal of sidestepping confounding by finding such a variable is the basis for two principal methods used to establish causality: (1) random assignment to manipulations in experiments and (2) statistical analysis incorporating instrumental variables (IVs) in observational data. Although in political science these two methods are often considered separately, the theoretical basis underlying the two approaches when based on a Rubin Causal Model (RCM) of causality is identical, as a growing body of literature in statistics and econometrics has established.[1] In the literature on measuring causality through experiments, the assignment to manipulations is used in the same way as an instrumental variable is used in observational data without experimental manipulation. Moreover, we believe, as argued by Angrist et al. (1996), hereafter AIR, that examination of IV approaches from the perspective of experiments and the requirements for establishing causality in that context can help a researcher better understand when IV methods are appropriate in a given observational data set and when they are not.[2] Thus, we discuss these two methods in a general formulation rather than separately and illustrate how random assignment is a special type of IV. We begin with a characterization of an ideal IV and then consider how IV estimation can work when circumstances are less than ideal.

5.2 The Ideal Instrumental Variable

5.2.1 Definition of an Ideal IV

In our notation, the candidate IV is designated as M. It is useful to be clear about the definition of an ideal IV because then we can consider how relaxing that definition affects the ability of a researcher to estimate causal effects. So that we can take a general approach that incorporates both experimental research and statistical analysis of observational data, we define an ideal IV independent of estimation procedures. That is, explanations of IV approaches usually begin with particular models of the data generating process and the assumptions about functional forms and correlations between variables that allow for IV estimation given those models. Instead

---

[1] The seminal works combining the two approaches in an RCM context are that of Imbens and Angrist (1994) and Angrist et al. (1996).

[2] AIR (1996, pp. 444–445) summarize this view: "Standard IV procedures rely on judgments regarding the correlation between functional-form-specific disturbances and instruments. In contrast, our approach [incorporating RCM and an experimental framework] forces the researcher to consider the effect of exposing units to specific treatments. If it is not possible (or not plausible) to envision the alternative treatments underlying these assumptions, the use of these techniques may well be inappropriate."

we begin abstractly, independent of a particular functional form of the data generating process or estimation procedure, and focus on the properties of an ideal IV. We classify M as an ideal IV if the following three conditions are satisfied.

Condition 1 (Independence): *M is statistically independent of the potential choices; that is, in the situation where the potential choices are designated as P_j, we assume $M \perp (P_0, P_1)$ where $\perp$ denotes statistical independence.*

Condition 2 (Perfect Substitute): *M is a perfect determinant of who receives treatment, that is, T.*

Condition 3 (No Missing Data): *We can perfectly observe the choices made by those affected by M. That is, define P^{OBS} as the choices observed by the researcher and P^{ACT} as the actual choices made by the units of study. When there are no missing data, then $P^{OBS} = P^{ACT}$ for all units.*

The first condition is obvious because the point of seeking out an IV is to avoid the problem of confounding by other variables (particularly unobservables) that can occur between the independent variable of interest, T, and the potential choices of interest, in our analysis either Y_j or P_j. Ideally, we would like an instrument that suffers from zero confounding. The second condition, that M is a perfect substitute for T, is straightforward because unless M is a determinant of T, we cannot use M to estimate the effects of T on P. The ideal substitute is a perfect substitute. The third condition simply requires that we can measure the treatment effect with accuracy and there are no missing data in that measurement.

If these three conditions hold, then it is straightforward to show that the average treatment effect (ATE):

$$\text{ATE} = E(P|M=1) - E(P|M=0). \tag{5.1}$$

Definition 5.1 (Ideal Instrumental Variable): *We classify M as an ideal IV if the following three conditions are satisfied.*

Independence: M is statistically independent of the potential choices; that is, in the situation where the potential choices are designated as P_j, we assume $M \perp (P_0, P_1)$, where $\perp$ denotes statistical independence.

Perfect Substitute: M is a perfect determinant of who receives treatment, that is, T.

No Missing Data: We can perfectly observe the choices made by those affected by M. That is, define P^{OBS} as the choices observed by the researcher and P^{ACT}

Figure 5.1. The Ideal Instrumental Variable.

as the actual choices made by the units of study. When there are no missing data, then $P^{OBS} = P^{ACT}$ for all units.

A graph helps illustrate how an ideal IV can work. In Figure 5.1, M is the potential instrument and is assumed independent of U; M only affects Y through T, the treatment whose effect we wish to measure. But since V and U are correlated, we cannot use control functions since ignorability of treatment does not hold (see the discussion in Chapter 4). Contrast Figure 5.1 with Figure 4.2, where Z is strongly correlated with U, and U and V are uncorrelated. IVs and control functions serve opposite purposes, both with the same aim.

5.2.2 Is Random Assignment of Manipulations in Experiments an Ideal IV?

Is there an M that could possibly satisfy the three conditions for an ideal IV discussed in the previous section? Random assignment of manipulations in an experiment satisfies the three conditions (is an ideal IV) when (1) subjects are assigned simultaneously, (2) the manipulation assignments are independent of random assignments of manipulations of other treatment variables, (3) we can enforce perfect compliance with manipulations, and (4) we can observe all the choices of the subjects. Simultaneous random assignment of manipulation and independence between manipulations of various other treatment variables ensures independence between treatment and potential outcomes, satisfying the first condition for an ideal IV. Enforcing perfect compliance ensures perfect substitutability, satisfying the second condition for an ideal IV. Finally, observing all choices ensures no data are missing, satisfying the third condition for an ideal IV.

When are these four aspects of random assignment most likely to exist? When subjects are recruited at the same time for all possible manipulations, the subjects are randomly assigned to manipulations simultaneously and independently of assignments to other manipulations of other treatment variables, when there are no cross-effects between subjects, and when all subjects comply as instructed (none exit the experiment before it has ended and all follow directions during the experiment), random assignment comes as close as possible to an ideal IV. Unfortunately, only a subset of usually simple laboratory experiments are likely to be conducted in this fashion. A number of laboratory experiments and almost all field experiments are not ideal IVs because they violate one or more of these conditions.

Furthermore, if a researcher is working with observational data in which treatment is not randomly assigned by the researcher, violations of these conditions are likely as well. Later we discuss how such violations occur in random assignment and in natural manipulations that researchers use as IVs. We explore the various methods, either in the design of random assignment or after the experiment in statistical analysis, that researchers can use to deal with these problems.

5.3 When Assignment of Treatment Is Not Independent of Potential Choices

5.3.1 Potential Violations of Independence in Random Assignment

We begin our discussion of how experimentalists can deal with the cases when random assignment is not an ideal IV or how researchers using observational data can deal with instrumental variables that are not ideal, with a discussion of violations of condition 1 in section 5.2.1, independence. We first explore the possible situations in which independence may be violated and then discuss how these situations can be handled.

Timing Issues and How Random Assignment Is Operationalized in the Laboratory
The first step for researchers who conduct laboratory experiments is to recruit a subject pool. Since agreeing to be in the pool of subjects is voluntary, it is never possible or conceivable to think of such experiments as random draws from the population at large. However, this is not a violation of random assignment although it may mean that the pool of subjects is not representative of some desirable target population. What is required by independence in random assignment is that, of those subjects who participate in the experiment, the manipulations are randomly assigned so that the observable and unobservable factors within that set of subjects do not confound the measurement of the effect of the manipulation.

Within the subject pool, a subset can be randomly drawn to be contacted for a given experiment, but the willingness to participate in a given experiment on a given day will vary. If the experiment is simple and the researcher is running only a few manipulations, then it is possible for the researcher to randomly assign subjects to manipulations at the same time, mitigating the nonrandomness in the sample that shows up on a given day. Simple decision-theoretic experiments clearly have an edge in this regard.

However, sometimes researchers conducting even these simple experiments do not have large enough laboratories or enough research assistance to run multiple manipulations. Consider, for example, Mutz's experiment on the effects of video presentations on voters' preferences (Example 2.5). In her second experiment, she used 155 subjects, who were randomly assigned to view the five video manipulations she had prepared. Although she does not report the timing of the manipulations, it is likely that the subjects were not assigned simultaneously because it is unlikely that she had the ability to simultaneously randomly assign 155 subjects to videos and for the subjects to watch the videos simultaneously in the comfortable living room setting she had devised. Thus, even in decision-theoretic political psychology experiments, most researchers conduct the experiment over time, with subjects' time in the experiment partly determined by their own choice and schedule.

Similarly, in many game-theoretic experiments, manipulations must necessarily be conducted at separate times simply because of physical constraints. This is true for the Swing Voter's Curse experiments of Battaglini, Morton, and Palfrey (Example 2.6) in which the experimenters ran separate sequential sessions of 7 to 22 subjects each. Furthermore, the researcher may wish to expose the same subjects to different manipulations (a within-subjects treatment design, which we discussed in Section 3.3.3) and, thus, may need to run a subsequent experiment that reverses the order of manipulations. This was the case for Battaglini, Morton, and Palfrey. Finally, a researcher may not anticipate fully the range of manipulations required by the experiment and may need to run additional manipulations after learning the results from one experiment. Again, for Battaglini, Morton, and Palfrey, this was also true. In response to reviewer comments on a working paper version of the first set of experiments, Battaglini, Morton, and Palfrey ran additional sessions of new manipulation configurations.

Hence, in most laboratory experiments, subjects are randomly assigned to manipulations not simultaneously but over time and their assignments can then depend on variables related to the timing of their participation choice. Subjects who participate on Monday morning might be differently affected by manipulations than those who participate on Thursday evening. Subjects who participate in the summer one year might also be differently affected than those who participate several years later in the winter.

Timing in the Field

Timing issues in manipulations in the field can also mean that random assignment does not ensure the independence of manipulation and potential outcomes; that is, field experiments are often conducted in waves, over a period of time, as well. In the experiment in which Gerber, Kaplan, and Bergan manipulated subjects' subscriptions to newspapers in Example 2.1, the authors contacted subjects in two waves a week apart due to capacity constraints at the newspapers in starting the subscriptions. If the experimenters also varied the manipulation assignments across waves, which does not appear to have been the case, or if the subjects contacted successfully in one week were arguably different than in the subsequent week (for example, if the first week had been before schools had begun their new year and many families were on summer vacation), then conducting the experiment in two waves may have meant a violation of independence. Similarly, Clinton and Lapinski, in their Internet experiment on negative campaign advertising, used two separate waves of subjects (see Example 2.3). The two waves involved separate manipulations rather than one common manipulation over time, as in Gerber, Kaplan, and Bergan's study. To the extent that Clinton and Lapinski treated each wave as a separate experiment, then the separation into two time periods is unlikely to cause a problem with independence. Thus, if a field experiment is conducted over a period of time, it is important that the manipulations be randomized within given time periods. Nevertheless, within a given time period some subjects may be manipulated on a Monday morning whereas others may be manipulated on a Thursday afternoon.

Assignment of Other Manipulated Variables

Even if the set of subjects who experience manipulations is arguably randomly assigned such that unobserved and observed variables are controlled, independence may be violated through poor experimental design of how other manipulated variables are set; that is, the experimentalist could vary another controlled variable such that it is correlated with both the potential choices and the manipulation assignment. Consider the experiment conducted by Dasgupta and Williams, presented in Example 2.7. In that experiment, subjects were randomly assigned to be either informed or uninformed about the choices made by an incumbent candidate that affect their payoffs. Then, given their information levels, they voted on whether to reelect the incumbent candidate and, depending on the voting outcomes, they were then paid. The researchers are interested in determining the causal effect of information on how the subjects voted. If the individual payoffs from the individual voting choices had been affected by the random assignment mechanism that determined which voters were informed or not, then the treatment assignment mechanism affects their potential choices and the first condition for an ideal IV is violated.

In some laboratory experiments, of course, payoffs are manipulated as subjects may be randomly assigned to particular roles and the role would imply a different payoff matrix (Dasgupta and Williams randomly assign roles as well). In Dasgupta and Williams's study, however, these two random assignments were independent, which is required if the causal effect of information in this case is to be accurately measured. If the experiment does not maintain that independence in the two random assignment mechanisms (i.e., is poorly designed), then assignment to treatment is correlated with potential outcomes and is no longer an ideal IV. Obviously, maintaining independence of manipulations is also important in field experiments that evaluate more than one treatment effect or a complexity of treatment effects. If the assignments are correlated, then independence of the manipulations can be violated.

When Random Assignment Probabilities Vary

In some cases random assignment probabilities are a function of an observable variable. If that variable also affects potential outcomes, then we may have a violation of independence. Humphreys (2009) reviewed a number of examples of such cases in experiments. One example he provided is an experiment in which the manipulation is a technology that is distributed randomly to children but the experimenter is interested in the effects of the manipulation on the children's parents. In this case, parents with more children are more likely to be exposed to the technology. If having more children is related to the potential outcomes that are of interest, then we have a violation of independence.

Can the problem occur in our information and voting example? Consider the situation in which an experimenter has two data sources for an experiment – one data source comes from a consumer list provided by a marketing agency and the other from a voter registration list as in Gerber, Kaplan, and Bergan's experiment (Example 2.1). Suppose that the list provided by the marketing agency is primarily dominated by voters who have completed college, whereas the registration list is balanced among voters who have not completed high school; voters who have completed high school, but not college; and voters who have completed college. The experimenter randomizes such that half of the subjects come from each list. Suppose further that information only affects voters who have completed college. Because the researcher has not randomized within these educational categories, randomization is more likely to select college-educated voters and, as a result, we no longer have independence between the manipulation and potential outcomes. We have independence within, but not across, educational categories.

When Random Assignments Are Made at Aggregate Levels
If the assignment of manipulation is made at a group level rather than an individual level and the choice is not fully randomized, a researcher may have problems with independence when attempting to make causal inferences at the individual level. For example, in the policy experiment that Lassen studied (Example 2.8), the manipulation was necessarily at the city district level although Lassen studied the effect of the manipulation at the individual level. If there is a relationship between living in a particular city district and the potential outcomes studied, then there is a violation of independence. Michelson and Nickerson (forthcoming) point out that in some mobilization experiments, randomization is done at the precinct level or some other aggregate level to avoid other problems in implementing the randomization such as mobilizers contacting subjects who were designated not to be contacted (see, e.g., Arceneaux, 2005; Imai et al., 2009; King et al., 2007). Green and Vavreck (2008) and Panagopoulos and Green (2008) conducted experiments on campaign advertising in which the randomization occurs at the level of the media market. If residence in these aggregate groups is related to potential outcomes, then independence is violated.

Mechanisms and Manipulations
It may be possible to contend that there is an independence between M and P_0 but not between M and P_1. The previous example of sampling variation within educational categories is such a case because M has a differential effect only on P_1. Another example can occur when those who do not receive the treatment are unaffected by the manipulation but those who receive the treatment may make different choices than they would if they had received the treatment but not through the manipulation. For example, suppose that the manipulation provides a group of potential voters with campaign material, where some voters receive the material and others do not. The material provides the voters with factual information about the candidates. The voters who do not receive the information do not know that the manipulation is being carried out, and their choices are unaffected. But the voters who receive the information are told that the campaign

material is being mailed by a particular nonprofit, nonpartisan group. Just that knowledge may affect their willingness to vote or how they cast their vote. It may, for example, reinforce a view that voting is a norm that they should engage in. If they had become informed via a different mechanism, then their voting choices may be differently affected. Thus, their potential choices are affected by M. (We assume in this example that the information is not available to the subjects independent of the mailing, so this is the only way they can become informed of this piece of information.)

Effects from Knowledge of Manipulations

However, if random assignment takes place publicly and subjects know that others are affected, the random assignment can affect the behavior of both those treated and those not treated differently than if the treatment had occurred without the random assignment, which may violate the independence between M and both P_0 and P_1. For example, AIR and Heckman (1997) discuss problems with using draft lottery numbers as an instrumental variable for enlisting in the military. Men with low lottery numbers, who expect to be drafted, may get more education as a way of avoiding service through deferment, and men with high numbers may have received more on-the-job training by employers who were more confident that they would not be leaving their jobs.

In most web and field experiments, it is probably unlikely that assignment to a manipulation affects the behavior of outsiders toward a subject in the case where the subjects are individual voters as is typically conducted. Field experiments involving candidate or party behavior in elections may be more problematic. For example, in Example 2.2, candidates were experimentally induced to vary their messages to voters across election districts. Because the variation could be observed by other candidates and parties as well as other elites involved in the election process, their behavior with respect to the voters may have been affected. It turned out that this did in fact happen in some of the districts where some candidates used experimental strategies and others did not and, thus, Wantchekon excluded those observations from his analysis of the results.

5.3.2 Using Experimental Design to Solve Independence Problems

In the previous section we noted the many ways that independence problems may occur. How can researchers deal with these problems? As we noted in Section 3.4, experimentalists have two stages in which they can deal with problems in establishing causal inference: the pre-experiment design stage

(Definition 3.13) and the post-experiment analysis stage (Definition 3.14). We address ways in which researchers deal with independence problems first in the design stage and second in the analysis stage.

Solving Problems in Timing Through Design

How can laboratory experimentalists deal with timing differences across manipulations? First, if the experimenter believes that the subjects' types are affected by the day and time of the experiment, the researcher should try to run manipulations on the same day or at the same approximate time. Second, it is advantageous for researchers to have a subject pool from which to draw from that is likely homogeneous in possibly confounding unobservables and observables over time. This is the principal methodological advantage of using undergraduate students as subjects in experiments; it increases our ability to compare the effects of different manipulations carried out over time. We also note this advantage when we explore the use of undergraduate students as subjects in Section 9.1. Because Battaglini, Morton, and Palfrey had conducted the initial sessions at Princeton University using a subject pool drawn from those students, in conducting the additional manipulations suggested by the reviewer, Battaglini, Morton, and Palfrey returned to the same laboratory and subject pool so that the results would likely be comparable and the benefits of random assignment would be maximized. Although student subject pools can be significantly advantageous in this regard, it is also possible to build a nonstudent subject pool, as did Mutz, that is arguably homogenous on observables over time.

What can be done if randomization within time periods is not possible in the field? In this case, the researcher needs to attempt to draw samples of subjects across time periods that are likely to be homogenous on observables and unobservables, as is done in laboratory experiments that use a standard homogenous subject pool. This can be more difficult in the field than in the laboratory, when a designated common subject pool may not be the basis for the experiment. Although it may be possible for the researcher to control for variations in observables over time, if there is sufficient variation within each time period (see Section 4.2.8), confounding unobservables that vary over time can be controlled for ex post in this fashion.

Solving Other Problems Through Design

As noted earlier, it is important that a researcher maintain independence between random manipulations; otherwise the experimentalist has violated the first condition of an ideal IV. Other problems with violations of independence can also be dealt with through better experimental design. For example, if a researcher expects that randomization will vary within observable variables that also affect potential outcomes, and the researcher is interested in the aggregate effect across observable variables, then the researcher can condition his or her randomization within these observable variables. In our example in which randomization probability varied within educational categories, the researcher might condition his or her randomization within educational category by the distribution of such categories within the target population of the experiment. In this way, the randomization should be independent of potential outcomes for the target population (assuming the sample of subjects is randomly drawn from the target population). In the newspaper experiment, Gerber, Kaplan, and Bergan randomized within some of the observable variables in their sample from the initial survey – a subject's intention to vote, or whether a subject receives a paper (non-*Post*/non-*Times*), mentioned ever reading a paper, received a magazine, or was asked whether they wish they read newspapers more. Correspondingly, if a researcher thinks that randomization at the group level is likely to cause a problem with independence in measuring the causal effect at an individual level that is of interest, the researcher should attempt to avoid randomizing at the group level if possible.

Furthermore, in our other previous example of the mailing that both provided information to randomly selected voters but also may have affected the potential choices of those manipulated by the appearance of being sent by a nonprofit group, one way to solve the problem through design is to vary the mechanisms by which the manipulation occurs. That is, a researcher could send mailings from an anonymous source or a source that is ambiguous. Or the researcher could send mailings that are reported to come from a partisan source (although there may be difficulties in the ethics of doing so because of potential harms to the political parties, as considered in Section 12.1.3). In this fashion the experimentalist can use design to determine whether the source of the mailing interferes with the independence of the random assignment of information on potential choices.

Finally, experimentalists should be aware of the potential problems with independence when their random assignments of experimental manipulations are public information. In many field experiments, subjects often have no idea they are participating in an experiment (although in some cases the point of the experiment is to evaluate how subjects' knowledge of being in an experiment affects their behavior, as in Gerber et al). Minimizing the knowledge of random assignments of course can lead to ethical concerns, however, as noted in Section 12.2.2.

5.3.3 Solving Independence Problems After an Experiment or with Observational Data

Sometimes independence violations cannot be solved through pre-experiment design, either by choice because of the research question studied or ethical concerns or because of an inability to control the relevant factors that would prevent violations. We also may be using data from a previous experiment or natural experiment and we suspect there is an independence violation. Can we deal with the independence problem in our analysis of the data we have?

When Only P_0 is Statistically Independent
If only P_0 is independent of M, we can still consistently estimate ATE on the treated (ATT) from the difference in sample means. That is, the difference in sample means can be expanded as follows:

$$E(P|M=1) - E(P|M=0)$$
$$= E(P_0|M=1) - E(P_0|M=0) + E(P_1 - P_0|M=1). \qquad (5.2)$$

If $E(P_0|M) = E(P_0)$, then

$$E(P|M=1) - E(P|M=0) = \text{ATT}. \qquad (5.3)$$

Although ATT can be estimated in this fashion, estimating ATE can be problematic, even if a researcher uses a control function approach (but without interaction terms) as noted by Humphreys (2009). To see why this is true, we revisit the previous example with randomization probabilities varying within educational categories. Suppose that we have a total of 12 observations that are a random sample from our target population distributed as in Table 5.1.[3]

In this simplistic example $W = 0$ represents an individual without a high school degree, $W = 1$ represents an individual with a high school degree only, and $W = 2$ represents an individual who is college educated. P equals 0 if an individual does not turnout, $= 1$ if an individual votes. $\text{Pr}(T = 1)$ is the probability of receiving the manipulation. We assume that the manipulation is a perfect substitute for treatment. We also assume that within each educational category we have zero variance in the potential voting choices, so it does not matter which of the individuals within each educational category is selected by the randomization procedure.

---

[3] We thank Macartan Humphreys for the example.

Table 5.1. *Hypothetical sample*

P_0	P_1	W	$\Pr(T=1)$	T	P	$P_1 - P_0$	$(P_1 - P_0)\,|\,T=1$
0	0	0	0.25	1	0	0	0
0	0	0	0.25	0	0	0	
0	0	0	0.25	0	0	0	
0	0	0	0.25	0	0	0	
0	0	1	0.25	1	0	0	0
0	0	1	0.25	0	0	0	
0	0	1	0.25	0	0	0	
0	0	1	0.25	0	0	0	
0	1	2	0.5	1	1	1	1
0	1	2	0.5	1	1	1	1
0	1	2	0.5	0	0	1	
0	1	2	0.5	0	0	1	

From this example it is straightforward to observe that if we knew P_0 and P_1 we should estimate a value of ATE (assuming that the distribution of individuals by educational categories is equivalent in the sample to the distribution in the target population) of $\frac{4}{12} = \frac{1}{3}$. However, if we just summed the means using the P's we observe without recognizing the differences in randomization across educational categories or estimated a simple ordinary least squares (OLS) equation with T as our independent variable [Equation (4.4)], we would estimate ATE as 0.5, which is the value of ATT (which we can estimate accurately from the P's we observe) but not ATE.

What happens if we use the control function approach without interactions and estimate Equation (4.5)? Unfortunately, such a regression would yield a coefficient on T that is again biased; our estimated value of ATE would be 0.43.

The problem is that, because of the way the randomization has occurred, $E(u_1|W) \neq E(u_0|W)$, the equality of which is a necessary condition for the control function regression without interaction terms to yield an estimate of ATE. Why is this so? It is because information has a different effect on college-educated voters than on non-college-educated ones. If information did not have this differential effect, the control function regression would estimate ATE accurately. What can be done? Researchers can estimate a control function with interaction terms such as Equation (4.6), although they must be careful about the standard errors as explained. Nonparametric matching procedures are also an option; however, these only yield ATT when assuming mean ignorability of treatment, which is no better than estimating the bivariate equation, Equation (4.4). (For matching to yield an estimate of ATE one needs to assume strict ignorability of treatment, as discussed in Section 4.6.)

Minimal Conditions on the Relationship Between M and Potential Choices

Is it still possible to estimate ATE(W) when there is some violation of independence? In the preceding example, our sample means within educational categories give us accurate estimates of ATE(W) because we assume no variation within each educational category. Even if variation occurs, it may be possible to estimate ATE(W) if independence is maintained within values of W. However, if the variable that is causing the dependence between M and potential choices is unobservable, then we could have a problem, even with ATE(W). It is useful to again express the observed data on the choice to vote, P, as in a linear probability model (LPM) and in terms of means, variances, and treatment as in Equation (4.4):

$$P = \mu_0 + (\mu_1 - \mu_0)T + u_0 + (u_1 - u_0)T. \tag{5.4}$$

Instrumental variable approaches can generally estimate causal effects using an IV approach (which we discuss more expansively in the next section) if a researcher assumes, at the minimum, conditional mean redundancy.

Axiom 5.1 (Conditional Mean Redundancy): $E(u_0|W, M) = E(u_0|W)$ *and* $E(u_1|W, M) = E(u_1|W)$

In some cases it may be possible to estimate causal relationships with only the first part of (Axiom 5.1) assumed (see Wooldridge, 2002, pp. 632–633).

In summary, we can allow for some effects of M on potential choices through observables if we condition on these observables in the estimation. However, we must maintain the untested assumption that there are no unobservable effects that can confound the redundancy of M to use an IV approach to estimating causality with M.

5.4 When an IV or Assignment Is Not a Perfect Substitute for Treatment

5.4.1 Potential Problems of Substitutability in Random Assignment

What Is Noncompliance?

Substitutability might be violated if subjects do not comply with their assignments. We remarked that noncompliance can be a problem in field experiments and defined the concept in Definition 2.14. Noncompliance can occur in the following four ways: pretreatment of subjects, subjects who always take assignments, subjects who never take assignments, and subjects who choose the opposite of their assignments.

Definition 5.2 (Pretreated Subject): *Subject who has experienced the desired manipulation prior to his or her random assignment.*

Definition 5.3 (Always-Taker): *Subject who chooses an assigned manipulation independent of his or her random assignment.*

Definition 5.4 (Never-Taker): *Subject who chooses against an assigned manipulation independent of his or her random assignment.*

Definition 5.5 (Defier): *Subject who chooses the opposite of the manipulation assigned to him or her.*

Noncompliance in the Laboratory

When might noncompliance occur? Consider first laboratory experiments. Some laboratory experiments use naturally occurring candidates as Spezio et al., in Example 3.1. In this experiment, the researchers used images of candidates in actual 2006 U.S. elections as their manipulations to determine how simple differences in images can affect subjects' evaluations of the candidates. If subjects had already been exposed to these candidates, then they would be pretreated. As for the problems of always taking, never taking, or defying, these may occur in the laboratory if subjects fail to pay attention during instructions in the sense that they fail to read something they are told to read, or fail to listen when told to listen.

In some game-theoretic experiments in the laboratory, a form of non-compliance may occur when subjects interact repeatedly and subjects can make inferences based on previous behavior, which can influence their behavior in later periods. For example, suppose that subjects are playing a game in which they are choosing whether to cooperate. The experimenter has manipulated the information subjects have about the benefits from cooperation, so that some subjects know the benefits, but others do not. If the subjects play the game repeatedly, however, subjects who are not told the benefits from cooperation could possibly infer those benefits from observing the behavior of informed subjects in earlier periods. Of course, the point of the experiment may be to study the effects of repetition in such a situation and whether such inferences occur and affect behavior in later periods.

But if that is not the purpose of the experiment, then these inferences mean that the data gathered from the later periods may be suspect and not useful.

A similar problem can occur when researchers wish to investigate communication during an experiment. For example, suppose that researchers are interested in how communication might affect the likelihood that subjects are willing to cooperate in the aforementioned game. But the uninformed subjects might learn more from the communication – learning about the information other subjects have about the benefits of cooperation – which could interfere with the design of the experiment to manipulate which subjects are informed. Again, this may be the purpose of the experiment (to measure how information is transferred through communication), but if it is not, then the researcher needs to be concerned about the possible effects of the communication on information levels.

In other laboratory experiments, noncompliance can also occur when subjects are asked to return for a subsequent session. In such a situation, a subject is participating in a sequential experiment. Consider Example 5.1. In the experiments discussed, Druckman and Nelson (2003) contacted subjects in a survey 10 days after an experiment to determine whether framing effects observed in the original experiment diminish over time, and Chong and Druckman (2009) had subjects participate in two sequential sessions three weeks apart. In both cases some subjects failed to comply in the second round.

Definition 5.6 (Sequential Experiment): *Experiment in which subjects participate in manipulations conducted either over time or at separate time intervals.*

Example 5.1 (Dynamic Public Opinion Laboratory Experiment):
Druckman and Nelson (2003) and Chong and Druckman (2007, 2009), hereafter Druckman et al., reported on a set of experiments on framing in which subjects were either contacted after the experiment to participate in an additional manipulation or surveyed to determine the extent that the effects of the original experiment survived over time.

*   **Target Population and Sample:** *Experiment 1 [first reported by Druckman and Nelson, also analyzed in Chong and Druckman (2009)] was conducted at a large Midwestern university and used 261 student and nonstudent subjects in the area. They reported that most of the subjects were students and that (footnote 9) "the participants' demographics reveal a heterogeneous and fairly representative group that compares favorably with the 2000 National*

Election Study sample." In the follow-up second stage of the experiment, only 70 subjects participated.

Experiment 2 [first reported by Chong and Druckman (2007) and also analyzed in Chong and Druckman (2009)] recruited a combination of 869 students at a large public university and nonstudents in the area. They do not report the exact numbers of each type of subject, but report the following about the subjects (footnote 7): "Overall, aside from the disproportionate number of students, the samples were fairly diverse, with liberals, whites, and politically knowledgeable individuals being slightly over-represented (relative to the area's population). We checked and confirmed that adults and nonadults did not significantly differ from one another in terms of the experimental causal dynamics presented later." The follow-up experiment involved 749 of the original participants.

Subject Compensation: *Subjects were paid an unspecified amount in cash for their participation. In experiment 1, subjects who responded to the post-experiment survey were entered in a lottery for an unspecified payment. In experiment 2, subjects were paid an extra $5 for taking part in the second round and participants, if they responded, were entered in a lottery where they could win an additional $100.*

Environment: *The experiments took place at university political psychology laboratories. Experiment 1 took place during the period in which the U.S. Senate was considering new legislation on campaign finance reform, the McCain–Feingold bill, with sessions beginning about a week after the Senate introduced the bill and ending before the Senate debate began. The experimenters used articles on the McCain–Feingold bill that were made to resemble as closely as possible articles from the New York Times' Web site. The researchers drew from recent similar reports, copied an actual article from the site, and then replaced the original text with their text. Finally, the experimenters reported that there was "a flurry of media coverage" that preceded the experiment and did not begin again until the experiment was over. Experiment 2 used fake editorials about a hypothetical urban growth management proposal for the city in which the experiment took place and subjects were told that the editorials were from a major local newspaper.*

Procedures: *We report on the two experiments highlighted by Chong and Druckman (2009) in which subjects were called back for a post-election survey or second experiment. Chong and Druckman reported on a third experiment, which we do not discuss.*

Experiment 1: *Subjects were randomly assigned to one of seven manipulations. In six of the manipulations, subjects received an article to read about the McCain–Feingold bill. The articles were either framed to emphasize the "free-speech" arguments against campaign finance reform or to emphasize the "special-interest" arguments in favor of campaign finance reform. "Specifically,* the free-speech article uses a title that emphasizes free-speech considerations and includes a quote from a Harvard law professor who argues for the precedence of free-speech considerations (citing the Supreme Court's Buckley v Valeo opinion)" (Druckman and Nelson, 2003, p. 733). The special-interests article has an analogous title and quote but instead of free speech, it focuses on limiting special interests (citing Supreme Court Justice White's opinion). The subjects were "also assigned to one of three conversational conditions – a 'no discussion' group, an 'unmixed' discussion group, or a 'mixed' discussion group. The no-discussion group participants read the articles and did not engage in discussion, while the unmixed and mixed discussion participants took part in small group discussions after reading an article. . . . In the unmixed frame discussion groups, all participants had read the same article – either the free-speech or special-interests article" (Druckman and Nelson, 203, pp. 733–734). The mixed frame discussions included two participants who had read the free-speech article and two participants who had read the special-interests article.

After completing the experiment, subjects received a questionnaire that asked demographic variables as well as political knowledge and had items designed to measure whether framing effects occurred. The discussion group manipulations were crossed with the article framing manipulations to yield six manipulations. In the seventh manipulation, subjects only received the questionnaire.

Ten days after the initial experiment, they conducted a follow-up survey to see if framing effects had persisted, during which time the major local newspapers made no mention of campaign finance reform.

Experiment 2: Based on survey of the literature and pretests on the issue of urban growth, the authors selected four frames for use in the experiment. "One 'Pro' proposal frame was the 'open space' frame, which emphasized that development was rapidly consuming open space and wilderness, and that it was necessary to conserve the natural landscape that remained. A second Pro frame emphasized building 'stronger communities' by concentrating development in more compact neighborhoods that foster social interaction and active community participation." The authors note that the pretest showed that the two frames did not significantly differ in their direction of support but that the open-space frame was viewed as a stronger argument.

The authors also used two Con frames: "'an economic costs' frame that used the law of supply and demand and economic studies to argue that growth boundaries would inflate the cost of housing and place first homes beyond the reach of young families; and a 'voter competence' frame that criticized the policy on the grounds that it required participation of citizens in arcane issues of regulation beyond their interest and competence" (Druckman and Chang, 2009, p. 17). The pretest showed no significant difference in the perceived direction of the two Con frames but that the economic costs frame was viewed as a significantly stronger argument. Some subjects were assigned the baseline condition and were simply given a neutral description of the issue. The experimenters varied the combined number of frames exposed to (0, 1, 2, or 3 frames), strength (weak or strong), and direction (pro or con) of the frames received for 17 distinct manipulations.

Before being given the assigned readings, participants completed a short background questionnaire and, after reading the editorials, a second questionnaire. "The first questionnaire included standard demographic questions and a battery of factual political knowledge items. The questionnaire also included a value question that measured the priority each participant assigned to competing values on the issue under consideration. In the urban growth experiment, respondents were asked: 'In general, what do you think is more important: protecting the environment, even at the risk of curbing economic growth, or maintaining a prosperous economy, even if the environment suffers to some extent?' Respondents rated themselves on a 7-point scale, with higher scores indicating an orientation toward maintaining a prosperous economy.... The second questionnaire contained various items, including our key dependent variables measuring overall opinions on the issues. We asked participants in the urban growth experiment to indicate their answers to the question 'Do you oppose or support the overall proposal to manage urban growth in the city?' on a 7-point scale, with higher scores indicating increased support." The authors also included measures of the perceived importance of various beliefs.

The researchers contacted the subjects again three weeks later. Participants had initially consented to participate in both sessions but were not given the details about the second session in advance. Participants in the baseline group were resurveyed without any additional manipulation. Participants in the 16 other manipulations read an additional article on the urban growth issue that drew on one of the original four frames. In some cases the new editorial repeated a frame that had been received earlier and in other cases the frame had not previously been encountered. Subjects were asked to complete a brief second-round questionnaire that included the same policy question about the proposal and some factual questions about the second-round article to evaluate the extent to which participants read and comprehended the article. The subjects were also asked whether they had encountered or sought out more information about the issue in the interim between the two sessions.

Results: In experiment 1, Druckman and Nelson found elite framing effects when subjects engaged in conversations with individuals with common frames, but the effects were eliminated by conversations with individuals with mixed frames. They found in the post-experiment follow-up that the elite framing effects in the first case diminished to statistical insignificance. Chong and

Druckman (2009), in a reanalysis of the data, found that the effects depended on the type of information processing used by the subjects; that is, subjects who used a more memory-based method of processing new information were less affected by the frames, but the effect that did occur persisted longer. In experiment 2 for the first session, Chong and Druckman (2007, 2009) found that framing effects depend more heavily on the strengths of the frames than on their frequency of dissemination and that competition alters but does not eliminate the influence of framing. In evaluating the two sessions together, they find again that strong frames play a larger role in affecting opinions and that subjects who used a more memory-based method of processing new information responded more strongly to recent frames.

Comments: Chong and Druckman (2007, 2009) presented a nonformal theory of how framing works over time and derived a number of hypotheses that form the basis of the experimental tests. To increase compliance of subjects to show up for the second treatment in experiment 2, Chong and Druckman sent reminders every three days, with up to a total of three reminders (if necessary).

Noncompliance in the Field

Pretreatment, always-taking, never-taking, and defying are more likely to be manifested in field experiments. How can noncompliance occur? For example, consider the newspaper experiment of Gerber, Kaplan, and Bergan (Example 2.1). A subject is not complying with the manipulation if he or she already subscribes to the newspaper. In this case the subject has been pretreated. A subject who chose to start his or her own subscription to the newspaper during the experiment or purchased the newspaper daily at a newsstand regardless of his or her assignment would be a noncomplier of the second type, and a subject who refused to accept the newspaper when offered (either by not bringing it in the home or by throwing it away once it arrived) and never purchased the newspaper when not offered would be a noncomplier of the third type. A subject who only chose to subscribe to the newspaper or purchase it daily when it was not assigned to him or her but chose to refuse to accept the newspaper when assigned to him or her would be a noncomplier of the fourth type.

However, sometimes noncompliance occurs in field experiments not because of subjects willfully choosing contrary to their assigned manipulations, but because of a researcher's inability to control the randomization process or because of social and other relationships between subjects assigned to different manipulations. Many of the recent voter mobilization field experiments that have been conducted in the United States have involved researchers working with nonacademic groups interested in evaluating different mobilization strategies. However, it can be difficult to convey to the nonacademics the value of following a strict randomization strategy, which can lead to instances of noncompliance. Michelson and Nickerson (2009) highlighted a number of the situations that can occur, such as mobilizers enthusiastically contacting voters who were designated not to be contacted because of their desire to increase voter participation, having difficulty identifying subjects by names from lists, and failing to locate subjects' addresses.

Similarly, subjects in field experiments may be "treated" when someone who is in a close relationship with them either personally or professionally is treated. Providing information to one subject who is friends or colleagues with another subject who is not provided information as a baseline may result in the baseline subject similarly learning the information. In the newspaper experiment, if subjects shared their newspapers with neighbors, friends, or colleagues, and these individuals were in the sample as baseline subjects, then noncompliance could occur. In mobilization experiments such cross-effects are well documented. For instance, Nickerson (2008) found higher levels of turnout in two-person households when one member was contacted. Specifically, he argues that 60% of the propensity to vote can be passed on to the other member of the household. Green et al. (2003) estimated an increase of 5.7 percentage points for noncontacted household members among households of younger voters.

5.4.2 Using Experimental Design to Solve Substitutability Problems

Dealing with Pretreated Subjects
How can experimentalists deal with problems of noncompliance? Consider first subjects who have been pretreated. This problem is usually avoided in laboratory experiments that use nonnaturally occurring choices, as in the laboratory experiments like Mutz (Example 2.5) or Battaglini, Morton, and Palfrey (Example 2.6). But in other cases a researcher may worry that using nonnaturally occurring choices introduces some measure of artificiality into the experiment, which we discuss in Section 8.4. In Example 5.1, Druckman and Nelson went to great lengths to use as their manipulation a naturally occurring issue before voters, campaign finance reform. Druckman and Nelson argued that doing so motivates subjects to make decisions in the same way that they would outside the laboratory. Sometimes researchers wish to use naturally occurring candidates to compare with observational

data using the same candidates. Spezio et al., by using naturally occurring candidates, compared the choices of the subjects between candidates with who actually won election. Spezia et al. avoided candidates who had national prominence or had participated in a California election (the experiment was conducted in California). The researchers also collected familiarity ratings from all of the participants in an attempt to verify that none of the subjects had been pretreated.

In the field, avoiding pretreatment of subjects can be more difficult. Gerber, Kaplan, and Bergan attempted to deal with pre-treatment by excluding subjects that already subscribed to the newspapers and they also attempted to control for subjects' existing knowledge from other news sources by measuring and randomly assigning subjects within strata by their use of sources. Gaines and Kuklinski (2008) suggest that researchers deal with pretreatment by explicitly considering the effects of treatment as the effect of an additional treatment given prior to treatment. In either case, the recommendation is for researchers to attempt to measure when subjects have been pretreated in conducting the experiment and to consider the data from these subjects separately from those who have not been pretreated.

Dealing with Other Types of Noncompliance
In the Laboratory
Using Randomization with Repetition. To reduce cross-effects in game-theoretic experiments in which subjects play the same game repeatedly, researchers who are interested in studying one-shot game behavior often randomly assign subjects to roles in each period and take pains to make the periods equivalent to a one-shot game. In some of the sessions in Example 2.6, 14 subjects participated, and in each period they were randomly rematched in two groups of 7 subjects with new randomly assigned roles so that each group was probabilistically distinctive. In experiments with smaller groups, such as subjects playing two-person games, an experimenter can ensure that subjects in a session in which one-shot games are repeated never play each other twice and that the order of matching of subjects is such that when subject n meets a new subject, say m, m has not previously played the game with a subject who has previously played with n. This is a procedure used by Dal Bo in Example 6.1 to reduce possible cross-effects in studying the effects of manipulations on the extent of cooperation in prisoner's dilemma games. When such procedures are used, it is important that subjects fully understand how randomization occurs so that the cross-effects are indeed minimized. One solution is to only conduct one-shot games; however, there may be good reasons to allow subjects to

play the games more than once to facilitate possible learning, as explained in Chapter 6.

Randomization has its limits in reducing such cross-effects that can limit the ability of experimentalists to manipulate subjects independently. For instance, suppose that two subjects are playing the ultimatum game repeatedly (see Section 3.3.3), but each period they are randomizing between being the proposer and the responder. The experimenter wants to manipulate the size of the amount of money the proposer is dividing and in some periods the proposer has a larger pie to divide. Even if the experiment is set up so that subjects always play a new subject with no possibility of contamination from previous play as in Dal Bo's experiment, it may be the case that subjects perceive the game as a larger supergame and choose to always divide the pie in half regardless of the size of the pie or who is the proposer. Thus, if the game is to be repeated, the experimenter may want to not randomize the roles and to always have the same subjects serve as proposer and the same ones as receiver, and assign pairings as in Dal Bo's experiment (always ensuring new matches with no cross-effects). Of course, in this case, subjects assigned to be proposers will likely earn more than those assigned to be receivers (based on previous experiments), which can lead to some inequities in how much subjects earn during an experiment. As a result, an experimenter may have to pay more on average to all subjects as a consequence so that subjects still earn enough to be motivated to participate in the experiment even when their earnings are low relative to other subjects.

Controlling Communication Between Subjects. To prevent possible cross-effects that occur with communication, experimenters can use their ability to control that communication by setting what can be communicated, how, and when in the design of the experiment. In almost all game-theoretic laboratory experiments, communication between subjects is not allowed except under particular controlled circumstances. Of course, if the goal of the experiment is to evaluate communication without such control, then experimenters can loosen these controls. The important issue for the design of the experiment is to carefully consider how allowing less controlled communication may interfere with other manipulations that the experimenter is investigating.

Using Financial Incentives and Other Motivation Techniques. One of the benefits of financial incentives and other motivational techniques in laboratory experiments is that these can motivate subjects to pay attention by reading or listening when told to do so. Many laboratory experimentalists usually give subjects a short quiz after going over the instructions and set up the quiz so that subjects are not allowed to participate until they have answered all questions correctly, as a method to reduce noncompliance of this sort. We discuss methods of motivating subjects in laboratory experiments further in Chapter 10.

In terms of sequential experiments in the laboratory as in Example 5.1, researchers can use various motivational techniques and financial incentives to minimize drop-off. In Druckman and Nelson's study, the drop-off is more than half but in Chong and Druckman's study, nearly 85% complied. Chong and Druckman had informed subjects at the beginning of the experiment that there would be a second session three weeks later and they sent reminders to subjects every three days, up to a total of three reminders.

In an innovative experiment, presented in Example 5.2, Casari et al. (2007) report on a sequential experiment in which they evaluated the effects of different incentive mechanisms on possible selection bias and compared the design method to traditional post-experimental statistical analysis to control for selection bias. In the experiment, subjects participated in a series of auctions in which subjects bid on the value of unknown objects. Before each auction, each subject received a private signal about the value of the object. If a subject made the highest bid, he or she was forced to pay for the object. Earlier experimental research had demonstrated that subjects often overbid such that the winner ends up paying more for the object than it is worth in terms of payoffs. Why? Most theorize that subjects overbid because they fail to account for the implications of making a winning bid. That is, suppose as a subject you receive a signal that the object has a high value. If you just bid your signal, and everyone else does, in the event that you win the auction, you are likely to have received a signal that is inaccurate – an extreme one, much higher than the average signal and higher than the other subjects' signals. It is likely that the object is worth less than your signal in this case. Ignoring these implications and overbidding by bidding one's signal has been labeled the "winner's curse" result.

Example 5.2 (Selection Bias in Auction Laboratory Experiment): *Casari et al. (2007), hereafter Casari et al., report on an experiment in which they use design of incentives to measure selection effects during a sequential experiment in which subjects exit due to bankruptcies and may not choose to participate in the second stage.*

Target Population and Sample: *A total of 502 subjects were recruited from The Ohio State University student population with nearly 93% undergraduates, the remainder either graduate students or of unknown status. Casari et al. collected demographic and ability data on the subjects. They compared the sample on these values with the target population. They report that "[m]en comprise 59.7 percent of the sample, with the breakdown by major being 30.2 percent economics/business majors, 23.4 percent engineering and science majors, and 46.4 percent all other majors. There are more men in the sample than in the university population, as well as a much larger percentage of economics and business majors than the university population (30.2 percent versus 12.3 percent). . . . Some 20.2 percent of the sample are in the top 5 percent (of the national average) with respect to composite SAT/ACT scores (versus 4.9 percent for the university), with less than 8.9 percent scoring below the median (versus 20.9 for the university), and 13.3 percent not having any SAT/ACT scores (versus 21.1 percent for the university). The last group are primarily transfers from regional campuses, as these students are not required to take these tests when transferring to the main campus. If their SAT/ACT scores were available, they are likely to be lower, because a number of these regional campus transfers were ineligible to enter the main campus when they originally applied to college. Thus, our sample includes students with significantly higher ability than the university population as measured by the percentage of students scoring in the top 5 percent on composite SAT/ACT scores and below median SAT/ACT scores."*

Subject Compensation: *Subjects received cash payments based on their choices as described in the procedures that follow. Subjects also received cash show-up fees, which varied according to manipulation as described later.*

Environment: *The experiment was conducted in a computer laboratory in an environment similar to that discussed in Example 2.6.*

Procedures: *In each experimental session, subjects were given a starting capital balance which varied as described later. In each period, two auctions were conducted simultaneously with six bidders each. Assignments to each market varied randomly between periods. The subjects submitted simultaneous bids for the item and if they won the auction paid their bid and received the item. The value of the item, x_0, in terms of payoffs was the same for all bidders but unknown to them. The value was chosen randomly from a uniform distribution with support [\$50, \$950]. Each subject was told prior to bidding a signal that was drawn independently for each subject from a uniform distribution with support $[x_0 - \$15, x_0 + \$15]$. All this information was conveyed to subjects in the instructions. At the end of each auction, all bids were posted from highest to lowest, along with the corresponding signal values (bidder identification numbers were suppressed) and the value of x_0. Profits (or losses) were calculated for the high bidder and reported to all bidders.*

Subjects participated in two sessions, week 1 and week 2. In the week 1 sessions, subjects first participated in two practice auctions, which were followed by 30 auctions played for cash. "Earnings from the auctions, and lottery earnings, were added to starting cash balances. Once a bidder's cash balance was nonpositive, bidders were declared bankrupt and no longer permitted to bid." Week 2 sessions "employed an abbreviated set of instructions, a single dry run, and 35 auctions for cash."

Because of the potential bankruptcies, Casari et al. recruited extra bidders, so that bidders randomly rotated in and out of the active bidding by period.

Subjects also gave their consent for the researchers to collect demographic data on gender, SAT and ACT scores, major, and class standing (freshman, sophomore, etc.) from the University Enrollment Office.

Control Manipulation: "[A]ll subjects were given a starting capital balance of $10 and a flat show-up fee of $5. All subjects participating in week 1 were invited back for week 2, when all subjects were again given starting capital balances of $10 and a flat show-up fee of $5."

Bonus Manipulation: "Starting cash balances were either $10 or $15, with half the subjects randomly assigned to each cash balance level. Further, following each auction, active bidders were automatically enrolled in a lottery with a 50 percent chance of earning $0 or $0.50 in order to provide additional exogenous variation in cash balances. In addition, a show-up fee of $20 was paid only after completing week 2's session, with 50 percent of week 1 earnings held in escrow as well."

Random Manipulation: "This was the same as the bonus [manipulation] with the exception that (a) bidders were given a $5 show-up fee in week 1 along with all of week 1's earnings; and (b) when inviting bidders back for week 2, half the subjects (determined randomly) were assigned a show-up fee of $5, with the other half assigned a show-up fee of $15."

Results: Casari et al. found evidence that economics and business majors, subjects with lower SAT/ACT scores, and inexperienced women tended to overbid and make more losses. They also found that there were strong selection effects for estimating the bid functions of inexperienced and experienced subjects due to bankruptcies and bidders who have lower earnings returning less often than experienced subjects.

Comments: Casari et al. showed that their experimental design allowed them to estimate the selection effects, but the standard statistical techniques used on observational data did not identify the selection effects. They note that estimates of learning during the experiment with the standard statistical techniques were misleading as a result.

Auction experiments are particularly interesting cases in which noncompliance may be a problem for establishing results in a laboratory experiment (see Kagel and Levin [2009] for a review of the literature). First, some auction experiments have been sequential experiments in order to evaluate whether experience in previous auctions leads to less overbidding in a subsequent experiment. Researchers have found that indeed experienced subjects, when they return for a second auction experiment, are less susceptible to the winner's curse. But it could be that the subjects that show up for the second experiment are simply the ones that did well in the first experiment, and the ones who did not do well chose not to show up.

Second, subjects during an auction experiment can go bankrupt and exit the experiment before it is finished. In a typical auction experiment, subjects are first given a cash balance and then participate in a series of auctions. However, because of the overbidding, some subjects go bankrupt during the experiment. Once bankrupt, subjects are unlikely to believe that experimenters will demand money from them at the end of the experiment and subjects may change their risk behavior (see Chapter 9 for more discussion of risk preferences and experimental choices), so typically these subjects are no longer permitted to participate in the experiment. Previous researchers were interested in whether learning occurred during an auction experiment: are subjects less susceptible to the winner's curse in later round than in earlier rounds? In general, there is evidence that subjects overbid less in later rounds; however, this may be simply a selection effect because it may be that the only subjects who stayed to the later rounds (did not go bankrupt) were subjects who were less likely to make mistakes and no learning occurs.

Casari et al. (2007) varied both the starting balance that subjects had in the experiments and the incentives to show up for the second session. When subjects had a greater incentive to show up for the second session, they found that subjects who made poorer choices in the first session were more likely to show up, demonstrating that selection effects do occur in sequential auction experiments and that estimates of the effect of experience were previously overstated. Furthermore, when subjects had higher initial balances and were less likely to go bankrupt during a session, subjects at the end of a session made poorer choices than when bankruptcy was more likely, demonstrating that selection effects also occur within an auction experiment and that estimates of learning during a session were previously overstated as well. Finally, Casari et al. found that standard econometric estimators designed to identify selection effects did not find these effects in their data from the experiment. They argue that the sample sizes in experiments such as theirs, although relatively large compared to many other laboratory experiments, are not large enough for these econometric techniques. Their results suggest that if a researcher is worried about noncompliance in a laboratory experiment, design solutions such as theirs are much more likely to yield useful answers than econometric or statistical techniques after the experiment.

In the Field. In the field, researchers can try to avoid problems of noncompliance that occur when collaborating with nonacademics through education, extensive training, and close monitoring. When researchers are aware of potential cross-effects within social or professional groups, researchers can attempt to choose subjects who are unlikely to have interactions with each other or use a multilayered randomization strategy as advocated by Sinclair (2009). To see how this works, consider an example in which there are just two levels at which individuals interact and cross-effects might occur: household and neighborhood. Assume that the researcher is conducting one manipulation and choosing other subjects to serve as a baseline (not manipulated). First, the researcher randomly assigns neighborhoods to be either manipulated or serve as baselines, then the researcher repeats the random assignment by household within the nonbaseline or manipulated neighborhoods, and finally randomizes again by individual within the nonbaseline or manipulated households. Only the subjects who were chosen for manipulation in the final randomization are actually manipulated, but in this fashion the researcher has created baselines at each level where these individuals interact.

Sinclair contends that doing so allows for the identification of both the spillover effects and the true treatment effect while removing the potential bias associated with the spillover. To use the procedure, a researcher must assume that there exists a level at which no subjects interact, that each lower-level group is a subset of a next higher-level group (that the groups are nested), and that there is no intersection between groups at the same level of hierarchy. Sinclair discusses some strategies for conducting such a randomization. For example, she points out that a researcher can avoid the household-level randomization issue by selecting only one subject per household, thereby reducing some of the complications of the design.

Definition 5.7 (Multilevel Experiment): *An experiment in which subjects are randomly assigned to manipulations using a layered approach in which subjects are viewed as interacting in definable separate groups in a hierarchy of* *groups such that lower-level groups are nested. Randomization occurs within groups by layer.*

Designing an Experiment with Noncompliance

Gaines and Kuklinski (2008) argue that instead of considering noncompliance as a problem in measuring the causal effect of a treatment, in many cases the relevant question is the effect of treatment on those who choose to comply – those who self-select to receive treatment. For instance, suppose that we are interested in the effects of negative campaign advertising on voter turnout, as examined by Clinton and Lapinski in the experiment in Example 2.3. Gaines and Kuklinski provide an example of how self-selection may affect how we interpret the results from an experiment (p. 16):

Suppose... that some unobserved factor strongly affects whether or not people see negative ads in the real world. For example, some people conceivably strive to avoid being exposed to any behavior or rhetoric that smacks of conflict or incivility. To be concrete and realistic, yet simple, suppose that conflict-avoiders, in the event that they are actually subjected to negative advertising, react strongly; their probability of voting falls by 10 percentage points. Negative ads slightly demobilize conflict-neutral types; when they see any negative advertisements, their intention to vote falls by 5 points. Conflict lovers, by contrast, are mobilized, and become slightly more likely to vote (their probability of voting rises by 5 points).

Gaines and Kuklinski point out that, in a world in which conflict-averse people do not choose to see ads (select out of receiving treatment) and all conflict-lovers and half the conflict-neutral people choose to see the ads (select in to receive treatment), the effect of negative advertising is to mobilize voters in the aggregate. They argue that an experiment in which all people, regardless of their conflict preferences, are forced to view the ads could suggest that negative advertisements have the opposite effect (demobilize voters) and thus the results from the experiment would give misleading results as to the effects of campaign advertising in the aggregate observationally. They contend that allowing subjects to "noncomply" or self-select into treatment gives a better measure of the causal effects of treatment as applied to many political science research questions. They suggest that researchers conduct experiments in which subjects are both forced (to the extent possible) to comply and ones in which subjects can choose whether or not to comply to treatment as a way of measuring the effects of treatments in situations where self-selection is prevalent in the observational world.

However, Gaines and Kuklinski note that, in many cases in which subjects are not revealed the true treatment, allowing for self-selection may change the nature of the experiment and be difficult to operationalize. Consider, for example, a laboratory experiment in which subjects are randomly assigned to watch campaign ads, some of which are negative. To give subjects a choice whether to watch a negative ad before the ads are shown would make subjects more aware than is typically the case that the negative nature of the ad is the experimental treatment. If subjects are not told in advance, technically subjects are always able to cease their participation in an experiment at any time. Yet, because subjects have already agreed to participate and are physically at the laboratory, they may be less likely to choose not to watch ads than they would be outside the laboratory.

Noncompliance in some field experiments may be similar to noncompliance in an observational study given that subjects have greater opportunities to select out of treatments. To some extent, as we discuss in Section 5.4.3, experimentalists already measure the effect of assignment to treatment, which measures the causal effect allowing for some endogenous selection to treatment as an arguably better measure of the causal effect of interest to the researcher.

We agree that Gaines and Kuklinski have a useful point that in some cases we are interested in the causal effect of treatment only on those who would self-select into treatment if no intervention by an experimentalist had occurred. That said, we believe that to understand why it is that someone may choose not to select the treatment observationally it is useful to understand more fully the effect of treatment if they were forced to receive treatment. Such information can help us to understand why they may choose not to select treatment and to better evaluate the effects of treatment on those who do select treatment. If we restrict our experiments to only those situations that would occur without intervention, then we limit our ability to think abstractly about the possibilities that can occur in counterfactual situations. For instance, if we discover that voters who are conflict-averse are demobilized by negative campaign advertising but that voters who are conflict-loving are mobilized, by studying the effects of campaign advertising on both types of voters we better understand how campaign advertising works to mobilize those voters who select to watch the ads – the conflict-loving voters. In the absence of an experiment that considers the effects of negative ads on conflict-averse voters, we do not have good evidence about the relationship between conflict preferences, mobilization, and negative campaign ads. Thus, although we agree with Gaines and Kuklinski that in some cases the relevant question is the effect of treatment on those who would select to be treated observationally, we believe that understanding the effect of treatment on those who would not select to be treated observationally is as useful in building a general understanding of the causal effects of treatments.

5.4.3 Solving Substitutability Problems After the Experiment

Weak Instruments

How badly are our causal inferences if M is only weakly related to T – not a very good substitute? Bound et al. (1995) show that when an IV is only weakly correlated with the treatment variable, then the causal estimates have large inconsistencies. Furthermore, in finite samples, the causal estimates using an IV in a two-stage regression process are biased in the same direction as OLS estimates that use treatment as an explanatory variable. They find that the magnitude of the bias approaches the OLS estimates' bias as the R^2 between the instruments and the treatment variable approaches zero.[4] What can be done then?

When the decision to receive treatment is endogenous, then we can no longer use manipulation assignment, M, as a perfect substitute for treatment itself, and a researcher must deal with the confounding or endogeneity of T. In the experimental literature the obstacle is labeled noncompliance, as we have discussed earlier. In the IV literature it is called a selection bias problem. The difficulty is the same.

Researchers have managed this problem in three ways. Some focus on what is called the intention-to-treat or the causal effect of M on the dependent variables. Others make assumptions about the data generating process and then use IV estimation techniques that control for compliance or selection bias and estimate ATE. Still others focus more narrowly on the causal effect of treatment on a subpopulation of those for whom treatment has an effect. We discuss each of these tactics in this chapter.

The Causal Effect of M

Intention-to-Treat Measures. To avoid the problem of noncompliance or selection bias, some researchers estimate the causal effect of intention to treat, the causal effect of M, rather than the causal effect of treatment, T. This is a particularly attractive measure when researchers are confident that M is independent of potential choices, as in an experiment with random

---

[4] Angrist and Kreuger (2001) point out that the bias in the IV case with observational data is related to the difference between the number of instruments and endogenous variables. If the number of instruments is equal to the number of endogenous variables, the bias is zero. They discuss the use of a number of approaches to control for the bias when this is not the case.

assignment of treatment. Assume that $M = 1$ if a subject is assigned the treatment; $M = 0$ otherwise. Define P^k as the value of P when $M = k$. So P^k is a potential value of P for each value of M in the same way that P_j is a potential value of P for each value of T. We can define $\delta^M = (P^1 - P^0)$. The intention-to-treat causal effect is simply the ATE for M. We can also have versions of intention to treat that are equivalent to ATT for M. Formally, the effect of intention to treat is defined as ITT and ITT(W) as follows:

$$\text{ITT} = E(\delta^M), \tag{5.5}$$

$$\text{ITT}(W) = E(\delta^M | W). \tag{5.6}$$

In some political science empirical studies, it could be argued that treatment assignment better captures the causal effect of interest. To some extent, treatment assignment may also get at the causal effect that concerns Gaines and Kuklinski (2008), discussed in Section 5.4.2. That is, if the research question is if providing voters with campaign material increases their probability of voting, then the causal effect of interest is ITT or ITT(W) and random assignment of intention to treat can be sufficient to estimate that effect. We are not interested in the effect with compliance as an endogenous variable.

Note that, as with δ, we cannot measure δ^M for any single individual because individuals cannot be in both assignment states simultaneously. Thus, assuming that ITT measures the causal effect of the assignment, it also means that we make the stable unit treatment value assumption (SUTVA), as discussed in Section 3.6. The presumption is that there are no cross- or equilibrium effects from the assignment, that the assignment is homogeneously administered across individuals, and that the host of other usually unstated implications of SUTVA apply when a researcher uses ITT to measure the causal effect of treatment assignment.

If treatment assignment is considered independent of the potential voting choices, then it appears that we can straightforwardly estimate these causal effects. However, if some of the data on the units' choices are missing, and there is a relationship between the potential choices and whether data are missing, then the measurement of ITT and ITT(W) must be adjusted for the missing data. We discuss how this is done when we discuss dealing with missing data more fully in a later section.

Political Science Example: Field Experiment on the Effect of the Media on Voting. In the newspaper experiment in Example 2.1, Gerber, Karlan, and Bergan focused on ITT as their measure of causality of the effects of media coverage on voting. They measured ITT and ITT(*W*) using OLS and a control function, as explained in Section 4.2. Thus, they included those in the group who canceled the subscription or perhaps did not receive the paper regularly through delivery problems as "manipulated" subjects and could rely on the random assignment of intention to treat to justify their assumption of ignorability of treatment assignment in their case. Furthermore, they estimated that 8% of the subjects who were given free subscriptions already subscribed to one of the newspapers (more often the *Post*), either weekly or the Sunday edition only. Finally, 55.8% of the individuals in the sample did not answer the post-election survey and thus they had a high nonresponse rate, which can be a problem in measuring ITT and ITT(*W*) as we observed earlier. We discuss the implications of nonresponse for measuring treatment effects and Gerber, Karlan, and Bergan's efforts to control for problems nonresponse causes more fully later.

Gerber, Karlan, and Bergan found that the manipulation did not have a significant effect on turnout but they did find that the manipulation appeared to increase the probability that subjects favored Democrats even for those assigned to the *Washington Times*. However, they speculate that the reason was that even though the *Times* may have presented a conservative biased version of reality, the period of the study (October 2005) was a particularly bad month for President Bush, in which his overall approval rating fell approximately 4 percentage points nationwide. Thus, they contend that exposure to the news media increased voters' awareness of the problems that Bush faced and increased their probability of favoring Democrats even when the media source was arguably biased in favor of Bush.

Using IV Estimation Procedures to Measure Average Treatment Effect

Required Assumptions. Although calculating ITT is one solution to the problem of noncompliance or selection bias, other researchers are more interested in the effect of actual treatment rather than just the intention to treat. They may wish to evaluate a theory about the effect of actually increasing voter information or to discover facts that can help develop new theories about the relationship between information and voter choices. If a researcher is using a manipulation by nature, she may see the effect of the manipulation itself as less interesting than the treatment effect, in contrast to the aforementioned examples. Furthermore, if we know more accurately how M translates to T, then we can compare various alternative M's or, even more useful, the characteristics of M to determine which characteristics of a manipulation most affect voter information as well as the direct effect of information on voter behavior. Hence, it is extremely useful to carefully study all three aspects of the causal relationship when we have an independent variable – in our example, the overall effect of M on voting behavior, the specific effect of M on T, and the effect of T on voter behavior controlling for M.

What assumptions do we need to make about M to use it as an instrumental variable that allows us to establish causality when we have to worry about compliance or selection bias? A myriad of different assumption configurations have been examined that allow for the estimation of ATE using an RCM approach and instrumental variables. As remarked earlier, these assumption configurations generally involve requirements about functional form and relationships between variables. Next we present a common approach using a first-stage nonlinear estimation to highlight the overall features of IVs to establish causal effects.[5]

Again, we express the observed data on the choice to vote, P, as in an LPM and in terms of means, variances, and treatment as in Equation (5.4) and make the following five assumptions.

Axiom 5.2 $u_1 = u_0$.

Axiom 5.3 (Redundancy or Exclusionary): $E(u_0 | W, M) = L(u_0 | 1, W)$.

Axiom 5.4 (Substitutability): $\Pr(T = 1 | W, M) \neq \Pr(T = 1 | W)$.

Axiom 5.5 $\Pr(T = 1 | W, M) = G(W, M; \gamma)$ *is a known parametric form such as probit or logit.*

Axiom 5.6 $\mathrm{Var}(u_0 | W, M) = \sigma_0^2$.

$L(u_0 | 1, W)$ is the linear projection of u_0 on 1 and W in which the disturbance term has a zero mean and is uncorrelated with W.

The second assumption is a redundancy assumption: M is redundant in the estimation of voting choices, given T and W. It is also sometimes called an exclusionary assumption. It is the version of the statistical independence assumption of the ideal IV in this particular application and similar to the conditional mean redundancy assumption discussed earlier. This version

---

[5] Wooldridge (2002, pp. 621–636) presents an excellent review of this literature and the different estimation approaches that have been developed.

of the exclusionary assumption, because it also imposes linearity, does not hold for a discrete choice model as in the case where the dependent variable is voting behavior unless we assume an LPM. More general formulations can be found in Wooldridge (2002).

The third assumption is a looser version of the substitutability assumption; that is, M has predictive power in determining T. From Axioms 5.2, 5.3, 5.4, and 5.6, we can write

$$P = \theta_0 + \alpha T + W\beta_0 + e_0, \tag{5.7}$$

where $\alpha = \text{ATE}$, $e_0 \equiv u_0 - L(u_0|W, M)$, $E(e_0|W, M) = 0$, and $\text{Var}(e_0|W, M)$ is constant. Furthermore, given Axiom 5.5, it can be shown (see Wooldridge, 2002) that the optimal IV for T is $\Pr(T = 1|W, M) = G(W, M; \gamma)$.

Thus, we can estimate the binary response model for $E(T|W, M) = G(W, M; \gamma)$ by maximum likelihood, obtaining the fitted probabilities. Then we can estimate Equation (5.7) by IV using instruments 1, the fitted probabilities, and W. The preceding assumptions are fairly restrictive. Wooldridge (2002) discusses more general assumptions that allow for IV estimation of ATE with interaction effects and so forth, but the general procedure is along the lines just discussed.

Is First-Stage Probit or Logit Always Preferred over Two-Stage Least Squares? It is important to note that a researcher should not just plug the fitted values from the nonlinear estimation directly into the second step of the two-stage procedure. If the researcher does so, and the nonlinear model is not exactly right, the researcher risks specification error and the causal effect is not accurately estimated. The researcher should use the fitted values from the nonlinear model as an instrument for the endogenous dummy variable, provided that a linear model (per our earlier assumption) is used to generate the first-stage predictions of the endogenous dummy variable from these nonlinear fitted values and all other exogenous covariates in the second-stage equation. Because of these concerns, some researchers prefer to use two-stage least squares instead of the aforementioned nonlinear procedure. From Kelejian (1971) we know that the two-stage least-squares consistency of the second-stage estimates does not depend on getting the first-stage functional form right. Therefore, a linear regression in the first stage generates consistent second-stage causal inferences even with a dummy endogenous variable. As Wooldridge (2002) discusses, the aforementioned approach may give more efficient results, but not necessarily more consistent ones.

Political Science Example

Nature Manipulates Voter Information. Lassen (2005) performed an interesting study of the effects of information on turnout in the city of Copenhagen that is an especially exemplary application of the method discussed earlier (see Example 2.8). Recall that Lassen had observational data from a telephone survey of Copenhagen voters carried out after the election commissioned by the four pilot city districts (PCDs). To measure whether a voter was informed or not, Lassen used a question that asked their opinion on the decentralization experiment. If they answered with a particular opinion (either the experiment went well, medium well, or bad), they were coded as informed, and if they responded that they did not have an opinion, they were coded as uninformed. Lassen then posits that voters' net benefit from voting is given by a latent variable, which in our notation is Y^* and is a function of how informed the voter is and X as follows:

$$Y^* = \beta_Y X + \alpha T + u \tag{5.8}$$

The decision to vote, turnout, in our notation is represented by Y, which equals 1 if Y^* is greater than or equal to zero and 0 otherwise.

Lassen expects that the decision to be informed may be endogenous and a function of whether a voter lived in a PCD. As with turnout, he posits that voters' net benefit from being informed is also given by a latent variable, which in our notation is T^* as follows:

$$T^* = \beta_T Z + \theta M + v, \tag{5.9}$$

where T equals 1 if T^* is greater than or equal to zero and 0 otherwise. In his study, M equals 1 if the voter lives in a PCD and 0 otherwise. Note that Z and X may overlap as in the previous discussion.

As in the Swing Voter's Curse lab experiment in Example 2.6, Lassen is interested in evaluating the theoretical arguments made by Feddersen and Pesendorfer (1996), Ghirardato and Katz (2002), and Matsusaka (1995) that uninformed voters are less likely to vote (see also the pivotal voter theory discussed in Section 2.3.3). Thus, he is not interested in ITT as are Gerber, Kaplan, and Bergan, because the theory is about the effect of being informed, not the effect of providing voters with information, and the potential endogeneity of being informed could be a problem if he simply estimated the probability of turnout as a function of voter information level as measured in the survey. As noted earlier, Lassen conducted a Rivers–Vuong test and found evidence of endogeneity. He thus used an IV-probit estimation strategy to determine the effect of information on turnout decisions.

Are the Assumptions Satisfied? To use PCD residence as an IV, Lassen
needs to make four assumptions: (1) that SUTVA holds; (2) that PCD has
an effect on voter information, that is, $\Pr(T = 1 | W, M) \neq \Pr(T = 1 | W)$;
(3) that M is redundant on potential voting choices [Equation (22)]; and
(4) that monotonicity holds, that is, informed voters who reside in a non-
PCD would also be informed if they resided in a PCD. We discuss the
monotonicity assumption in more detail in the next section. Lassen does
not attempt to prove that SUTVA holds. It is likely that SUTVA is violated
in this analysis as in most observational studies of the effect of information
on voting, because the informational effect on voters of living in a PCD
probably influenced the voting behavior of non-PCD residents through
polls and other preference reports. Hence, the informational effect on an
individual voter using PCD as an instrument is conditioned on the overall
information level in the population at that point in time, and we should be
careful not to generalize to situations where the information distributions
across the population are significantly different. Lassen claims in a footnote
that the externalities mean that the estimate can be seen as a lower bound
of the effect of information, but this assumes that increasing information
beyond the distribution at the time of the study would have no additional
external effect, which is unlikely.

Evaluating the second assumption is more straightforward; Lassen estimates a probit regression with whether a voter is informed as the dependent
variable and PCD residence as an independent variable among other explanations. He finds that, after controlling for other independent variables,
PCD residence does have a significant positive effect on whether a voter is
informed. Similarly, he notes that the fourth assumption seems intuitively
reasonable and we agree.

In contrast, evaluating the third assumption is the more difficult issue
in IV estimations like Lassen's because it involves proving a negative or
nonexistence of a relationship. Lassen considers three ways in which redundancy might be violated: (1) there may be unobserved differences in political interest or activism that resulted in districts being classified as PCDs,
(2) the assignment of the PCD may have been nonrandom for other reasons, and (3) the policy experiment may have caused voters in the PCDs
to be more interested in local politics or may have affected other variables that affected interest in politics. Since the districts did not exist as
entities prior to the policy experiment, the first possible violation is not
relevant. As for the second and third violations, Lassen finds no substantial differences between PCD and non-PCD respondents on a variety of
measures of political attitudes and interest. Lassen also uses an indirect

test for redundancy suggested by Evans and Schwab (1995) – testing for overidentification in the linear two-stage OLS model. To do so he creates multiple instruments by using each PCD as an instrument as well as whether a PCD resident was a user of services that were particularly decentralized (child and elderly care, elementary schools). He finds significant evidence of overidentification.

Particularly noteworthy is the care Lassen takes to consider alternative estimating strategies, which he compares with his IV-probit estimation. As noted earlier, there are concerns about variations in efficiency and consistency in these procedures, and in some cases two-stage OLS may be more appropriate even with an endogenous dummy variable. He estimates (1) a single-equation probit of the effect of information on voter choices assuming that information choices are exogenous, (2) a two-stage linear regression equation, (3) a full bivariate probit which assumes that the error terms are jointly normal, (4) inclusion of the alternative instruments described earlier, and (5) nearest-neighbor propensity score matching on a larger sample that includes respondents who refused to answer questions about their income. Too often researchers focus on only one estimation strategy to establish causality. Given the conditional nature of causal estimates and the implicit and untested assumptions that most of these procedures make, use of a variety of procedures can help mitigate concerns about the robustness of the analysis.

Lassen finds that the differences in specification do not alter the conclusions; that is, he finds that the effect of being informed significantly increases the probability of voting by around 20 percentage points, although this effect is smaller in the estimation that includes respondents who refused to state their income, which is likely a consequence of the fact that these are respondents who are also less likely to vote.

Estimating the Effect of Treatment on the Subpopulation of Compliers

Definition of LATE. The two methods described earlier measure overall population effects of treatment, either ITT or ATE. Imbens and Angrist (1994) and AIR introduce the concept of the local average treatment effect (LATE), which they and others also sometimes call the complier average causal effect (CACE). The term LATE is usually used when a researcher is taking an IV approach to estimating causality using observational data, whereas the term CACE is usually used when a researcher is using random assignment as an implicit IV in estimating causality using experimental data. We use the term LATE, because it is a more general sounding description, it is used in the larger observational data literature, and the measure applies to both observational and experimental studies. In the next subsection we discuss the assumptions necessary for estimating LATE. For now, we focus on defining the effects independent of the estimation issues.[6]

Imbens and Angrist and AIR advocate LATE as a useful measure of causal effects when there is noncompliance or selection bias. Moreover, they suggest that measurement of LATE forces a researcher to think more clearly about the assumptions she is making about the relationship between M and T, whereas the assumptions discussed earlier about functional form and correlations in measuring ATE are less clear in their implications about individual behavior and theoretical presumptions.

What is LATE? Recall that when we discussed ATE and ATT we noted that to think about causal effects we have to think about the counterfactuals – hypotheticals, the values of P_j, where j denotes the treatment received. We also had to think about counterfactuals when defining ITT. To formally think about the disconnect between the instrumental variable, M, and T, we need to introduce more complex hypothetical or potential choices. Denote T_M as the counterfactual treatment variable for a given M. So $T_0 = 0$ if $M = 0$ and $T = 0$, and $T_0 = 1$ if $M = 0$ and $T = 1$. Similarly, $T_1 = 0$ if $M = 1$ and $T = 0$, and $T_1 = 1$ if $M = 1$ and $T = 1$. That is, suppose an individual is not manipulated; that is, $M = 0$. Then T_0 is his actual choice of whether to receive treatment given that he is not manipulated and T_1 is his hypothetical choice of whether to receive treatment if he had been manipulated. Similarly, suppose an individual is manipulated; that is, $M = 1$. Then T_0 is his hypothetical choice of whether to receive treatment if he had not been manipulated, and T_1 is his actual choice of whether to receive treatment given that he was manipulated.

Individuals for whom $T_0 = 0$ and $T_1 = 1$ are compliers; they always comply with treatment assignments. In terms of a natural experiment, we would say that changing M always changes T for these individuals. While compliers are alike, noncompliers can vary. For example, noncompliers might be always-takers, such that $T_0 = 1$ and $T_1 = 1$; never-takers, such that $T_0 = 0$ and $T_1 = 0$; or defiers, such that $T_0 = 1$ and $T_1 = 0$. LATE is the causal effect of treatment on compliers only. Formally, LATE is defined as

$$\text{LATE} = E(\delta \mid T_1 = 1, T_0 = 0). \qquad (5.10)$$

---

[6] As we have done previously, it is useful to define the causal effects first and then discuss the assumptions underlying estimating causal effects. See, for example, the presentation of ATE, ATT, and MTE in Chapter 3. This separates the questions of defining causal measures from estimation issues.

Recall that δ is the difference in potential choices as treatment changes. In terms of P, $\delta = P_1 - P_0$, which is the difference in voting choice between whether a voter is informed (treated) and whether a voter is uninformed (untreated).[7] So LATE is the difference in potential choices for the set of individuals who would comply with treatment. LATE is the difference in potential choices for those individuals who, if they were manipulated, would choose to be treated and, if they were not manipulated, would choose not to be treated. Note that in most cases no individual is both manipulated and not manipulated; so this difference for any single individual cannot be measured, just as discussed in Chapter 2. Furthermore, as AIR observe, the subpopulation for which LATE is defined is not generally an identifiable population because we can never know whether an individual is a member of this subpopulation. This limits the generalizability of LATE significantly as compared to concepts such as ATE, which are defined for all units in the population studied.

The assumption that LATE tells us the causal effect of treatment for that unidentifiable subpopulation, as with ATE in Chapter 2, is a SUTVA-type assumption about the causal effect of T conditional on $T_1 = 1$ and $T_0 = 0$. As we remarked in Chapter 3, SUTVA is a host of unspecified, implicit assumptions such that δ measures the causal effect of treatment. With respect to ATE, we listed a number of implications of SUTVA. Some of these also apply to LATE: (1) treatment of unit i only affects the outcome of unit i (thus, it does not matter how many others have been treated or not treated) and equilibrium and cross-effects are assumed to not exist; (2) there exist both units who are manipulated and informed and units who are not manipulated and uninformed; (3) the only causality question of interest is a historical one, that is, the evaluation of treatments that exist in reality on the population receiving the treatment, either observational or experimental; and (4) causality is recursive; treatment choices are not simultaneously chosen with outcome choices.

Estimation of LATE. Imbens and Angrist (1994) and AIR present general assumptions that allow for the estimation of LATE.

Axiom 5.7 (Independence): *M is statistically independent of the potential choices of both P_j and T_j.*

Axiom 5.8 (Monotonicity): $T_1 \geq T_0$.

---

[7] Notice that since we condition on T_1 and T_0, and Z are explanatory factors determining T, we do not condition on Z explicitly, although there is an implicit assumption.

The independence assumption implies that expectations involving functions of P_j and T_j conditional on M do not depend on M. The monotonicity assumption rules out defiers. Given these two assumptions, a consistent estimator of LATE is given by LATE*:

$$\text{LATE}^* = \frac{(\overline{P}_1 - \overline{P}_0)}{(\overline{T}_1 - \overline{T}_0)}, \tag{5.11}$$

where $\overline{P}_j$ is the sample average of P_j when $M = j$ and $\overline{T}_j$ is the sample average of T_j when $M = j$. LATE* is also identical to the IV estimator of α in the simple equation $P = \theta_0 + \alpha T + \text{error}$, where M is the IV for T. Thus, LATE* can be estimated rather simply by only assuming independence and monotonicity.

5.5 Missing Data

5.5.1 When Might Data Be Missing?

In all the foregoing estimating procedures, we assumed that the researcher could accurately measure treatment effects; there were no missing data for the choices made. Missing data is rarely a problem in laboratory experiments unless there is a serious computer failure or a researcher loses data – events that are uncommon. In field experiments, however, it may not be possible to observe all of the choices made by the units of observation in the population of interest. For example, some subjects given treatment may fail to respond to post-treatment surveys or other measurement instruments as Gerber, Karlan, and Bergan discovered when only 55.8% of their subjects participated in the post-treatment survey. But it is also a problem with nonexperimental data, where nature is conducting the manipulation. For example, in Lassen's study only 55% of those surveyed responded and a simple examination of the information contained in the responses with respect to turnout in elections as compared with census data in Copenhagen suggested that responders were not representative of the population that had been subject to the manipulation.

Are Missing Data a Problem?
In a seminal paper, Frangakis and Rubin (1999), hereafter FR, show that under some general assumptions missing data can be a problem for estimating causal effects when there is also a compliance or selection bias in

the data. In field experiments, where noncompliance is likely to occur, then missing data can be a problem as well.

5.5.2 Using Experimental Design to Reduce Missing Data

As with noncompliance, incentives provided to subjects in the design of the experiment can help reduce the problem of missing data. In particular, evidence on increasing survey responses can be helpful in reducing missing data in field experiments. The evidence suggests that prepaid monetary incentives tend to have positive effects on survey responses – increasing the response rates for face-to-face interviews, mail, and telephone surveys (see Church, 1993; Fox et al., 1988; James, 1997; Kulka, 1992; Singer et al., 1999; Warriner et al., 1996; Yammarino et al., 1991). There is also evidence that these prepaid incentives increase the quality of the data generated from the surveys (see Davern et al., 2003; Shaw et al., 2001; Shettle and Mooney, 1999; Singer et al., 2000).

5.5.3 Dealing with Missing Data After an Experiment

Dropping Missing Observations and the Missing Completely at Random Assumption
FR discuss how to estimate the causal effects of treatment when data are missing. To explain their results, we need to define what we mean by response. Define R as an individual's post-treatment response. If $R = 0$, we say that data on the individual's voting choices are missing, and if $R = 1$, we say that we have data on the individual's voting choices. So if $R = 1$, then $P^{OBS} = P^{ACT}$ and if $R = 0$, then $P^{OBS} = \emptyset$.

Suppose we just drop the observations where $R = 0$ and compute the causal effects as if these observations did not exist? If we do so, then we are implicitly assuming that the observations are *missing completely at random*, which means that the probability of nonresponse is the same for all units of observation. Formally, this assumption is the following.

Axiom 5.9 (Missing Completely at Random): $R \perp M, W, T,$ *where* $\perp$ *denotes statistical independence.*

However, we know that participation in surveys and other such measurement instruments is not the same across individuals. It is well known that deletion of observations without recognizing these differences can lead to biased estimates of causality (see Rubin, 1976; Little and Rubin, 1987; Schafer, 1997).

Using Covariates and the Missing at Random Assumption

An alternative to the assumption that observations are missing completely at random is the *missing at random* (MAR) assumption (see Rubin, 1976). Assume we have some data on all subjects, all R_j. For example, Gerber, Karlan, and Bergan had demographic data from the pretreatment survey. Similarly, Lassen had basic census data on the residents of the districts of Copenhagen. A common practice when response data are missing is to condition on those covariates that are known to be important, conducting separate analyses by covariate and then weighting by the proportions in the pretreatment covariates. Doing so assumes that the probability of observing outcomes is the same for all subjects with the same value of the observed covariates, treatment assigned and treatment received. Formally, the assumption can be stated as follows.

Axiom 5.10 (Missing at Random): $P \perp R | M, W, T$.

In this fashion the response is assumed ignorable or independent of the outcome after the conditioning.

The Missing Covariate: Noncompliance

Latent Ignorability. It would seem then that missing data are not a problem if we have the important covariates from the pretreatment survey or if we can be sure that our measurement of responses is random from the population measured when the manipulation is by nature. Thus, at first glance MAR seems a reasonable assumption. But such a conclusion is premature because there is one covariate that the researcher cannot determine from pretreatment information – specifically, whether a unit complied or selected into treatment as assigned. Lassen's study measures the information of those who respond and can determine whether they complied with the treatment (that is, if the individuals in the PCDs were informed and the individuals in the non-PCDs were uninformed) but cannot measure the compliance rate of those who did not respond. Thus, missing data coupled with noncompliance can be a potential problem in estimating causal effects.

When is this likely to be a problem? Define S as a binary variable that measures whether an individual is a complier or not; $S = 0$ if an individual does not comply and $S = 1$ if an individual does comply. FR show that under quite reasonable assumptions, missing data coupled with noncompliance can be a problem in estimating causal relationships. We present a stochastic version of the FR model that is given by Mealli et al. (2004). In this representation, the FR model makes the following assumptions:[8]

Axiom 5.11 (Latent Ignorability): $P \perp R | M, W, S.$

Axiom 5.12 (Exclusion Restriction for Never-Takers): $P^k \perp M | W, S = 0.$

Axiom 5.13 (Response Exclusion Restriction for Never-Takers): $R(M) \perp M | W, S = 0.$

Recall that P^k is the value of P when $M = k$. The first assumption means that the potential outcomes and potential nonresponse indicators are independent within subpopulations of the same compliance covariate and pretreatment or assignment levels. The second assumption means that, for the subpopulations of never-takers with the same covariate values, the distributions of the two potential outcomes for each value of treatment assignment are the same. The third assumption implies that never-takers have the same response behavior irrespective of their treatment assignment. FR show that when these three assumptions hold, then the treatment effects calculated earlier, assuming only MAR, are biased. The intuition behind this result is that because we cannot observe the compliance choices of those who are not assigned treatment – that is, $M = 0$ – then we do not know how that is affecting our measures of potential choices in this case and thus we cannot ignore the missing data. This means that if compliance or selection choice is related to whether an individual responds to post-treatment measurement instruments, then causal effects that do not recognize this relationship are inaccurately measured. This is true even in the estimation of ITT.

Estimating Causal Relationships with Latent Ignorability. Estimating the causal relationships if we assume latent ignorability instead of MAR or missing completely at random is more complicated. FR present a method of moments estimation technique under the preceding three assumptions.

---

[8] FR's presentation differs in that they make an assumption called compound exclusion restriction for never-takers which is the equivalent of Axioms 5.12 and 5.13 combined.

Mealli et al. (2004) suggested that the response exclusion restriction for never-takers (Axiom 5.13) of FR is unreasonable because never-takers who are assigned to a treatment may alter their response probability. That is, their refusal to follow through with treatment may increase their unwillingness to respond to a post-treatment survey or instrument measuring outcomes because they must admit basically that they did not comply. This could be the case in a political science field experiment where subjects provided with information about an election who did not read or use the information may be less willing to answer questions about the election afterward than they would be if they had not been forced to make the choice to ignore the information. Mealli et al. propose the following substitute.

Axiom 5.14 (Response Exclusion Restriction for Compliers): $R(M) \perp M \mid W, S = 1$.

This axiom assumes that compliers' response behavior is independent of their treatment assignments. It seems more plausible because they are more willing to go through with treatment and therefore one would expect their response behavior to also be unrelated to whether they are given a particular treatment. Mealli et al. label this model the modified FR model or MFR.

Mealli et al. note that method of moments estimations such as those presented by FR are difficult to implement and present Bayesian likelihood-based estimators instead, following results of Imbens and Rubin (1997a,b) and Hirano et al. (2000). Specifically, they model the following, assuming that the variables' distributions have a logistic regression form:

$$\Pr(S = 1 \mid W, \alpha) = \pi^s = \frac{\exp(\alpha_0 + \alpha_1' W)}{1 + \exp(\alpha_0 + \alpha_1' W)}, \qquad (5.12a)$$

$$\Pr(R = 1 \mid W, M, S; \beta) = \pi_{M,S}^R = \frac{\exp(\beta_{MS0} + \beta_{MS1}' W)}{1 + \exp(\beta_{MS0} + \beta_{MS1}' W)}, \qquad (5.12b)$$

$$\Pr(P = 1 \mid W, M, S; \gamma) = f_{M,S}(1) = \frac{\exp(\gamma_{MS0} + \gamma_{MS1}' W)}{1 + \exp(\gamma_{MS0} + \gamma_{MS1}' W)}. \qquad (5.12c)$$

Note that they assume that the slope coefficients in the outcome distribution for compliers are equal: $\gamma_{011}' = \gamma_{111}'$. Given the assumptions of latent ignorability and exclusion restriction for never-takers, the likelihood function is

$$L(\theta \mid M, W, T, R, P)$$

$$= \prod_{M=1, T=1, R=1} \pi^S \pi_{11}^R f_{11}(P) \prod_{M=1, T=1, R=0} \pi^S \left(1 - \pi_{11}^R\right)$$

$$\times \prod_{M=1, T=0, R=1} (1 - \pi^S)\pi_{10}^R f_{10}(P) \prod_{M=1, T=0, R=0} (1 - \pi^S)\left(1 - \pi_{10}^R\right)$$

$$\times \prod_{M=0, T=0, R=1} \left(\pi^S \pi_{01}^R f_{01}(P) + (1 - \pi^S)\pi_{00}^R f_{10}(P)\right)$$

$$\times \prod_{M=0, T=0, R=0} \left(\pi^S \left(1 - \pi_{01}^R\right) + (1 - \pi^S)\left(1 - \pi_{00}^R\right)\right). \qquad (5.12d)$$

Paraphrasing Mealli et al. (p. 216), the first two factors in the likelihood represent the contribution of the compliers assigned to treatment, including both respondents and nonrespondents. The second two factors represent the contribution for never-takers assigned to the treatment, including respondents and nonrespondents. The last two factors represent the contribution to the likelihood function for those assigned to no treatment. This includes both compliers and never-takers, and the likelihood contributions therefore consist of averages over the distribution of compliance types. MAR is the assumption $\pi_{00}^R = \pi_{01}^R$ in estimating this equation. FR assumes $\pi_{00}^R = \pi_{10}^R$ and MFR assumes $\pi_{01}^R = \pi_{11}^R$.

Because observations are missing and we must necessarily exclude those outcomes, then Equation (5.12d) simplifies to

$$L(\theta \mid M, W, T, R, P) = \prod_{M=1, T=1, R=1} \pi^S f_{11}(P) \qquad (5.12e)$$

$$\times \prod_{M=1, T=0, R=1} (1 - \pi^S) f_{10}(P)$$

$$\times \prod_{M=0, T=0, R=1} (\pi^S f_{01}(P) + (1 - \pi^S) f_{10}(P)).$$

Incorporating the missing data structure from earlier, Mealli et al. were able to obtain maximum likelihood estimates; that is, the complete data structure in Equation (5.12d) allows them to estimate the missing values. In this section we have examined noncompliance and nonresponse as binary cases, but it is possible to estimate causal effects for when these variables are not binary as well as the treatment itself. For an example of estimation of causal effects in a more complex situation, see Barnard et al. (2002).

Political Science Example: Web Experiment on the Effect of Voter Information

Randomization Issues. In Example 5.3, Horiuchi et al. (2007) conduct an Internet survey experiment using individuals who had registered through a Japanese Internet survey company, Nikkei Research, as a subject pool. Similar to laboratory experiments, this is a volunteer subject pool and thus not representative of the Japanese population. In particular, the subject pool is more educated and has higher income levels. Similarly, Gerber, Karlan, and Bergan also use a subject pool that is not necessarily representative of the population since they chose only those subjects who did not already have subscriptions to either newspaper.

Example 5.3 (Party Platform Internet Survey Experiment): *Horiuchi et al. (2007) reported on a survey experiment conducted via the Internet in Japan, designed to test whether voters are influenced by information provided by political parties via their Web sites during Japan's 2004 Upper House election.*

Target Population and Sample: Horiuchi, Imai, and Taniguchi drew subjects from the roughly 40,000 Internet users throughout Japan who have agreed to receive occasional electronic mail asking them to participate in online surveys from a Japanese Internet survey firm, Nikkei Research. Respondents who filled out a survey questionnaire had a chance to win a gift certificate of approximately five to ten dollars. Horiuchi, Imai, and Taniguchi asked the firm to randomly select 6,000 of these subjects (equal numbers of men and women) to receive an email asking them to answer a survey about themselves and the election. The email was sent out approximately two weeks before the election. Of those asked, 2,748 completed the survey. Horiuchi, Imai, and Taniguchi randomly selected 2,000 eligible voters from this number as subjects in the experiment.

Environment: Horiuchi, Imai, and Taniguchi contend that Japanese voters make up an especially good subject pool for the experiment because a large number of voters are independents and survey evidence suggests they are uncertain how to vote (rather than either always voting for the same party or always abstaining). Thus, Horiuchi, Imai, and Taniguchi argue that these voters are likely to be influenced by the information that they would read.

Furthermore, pension reform (the issue voters received information about) was a major issue during the election and the political parties had extensive information on their Web sites about the issue and their positions.

Procedures: *The 2,000 selected subjects were randomly assigned to three groups. Two of the groups received an email invitation to participate in both a pre-election and post-election survey and the third group received an email invitation to participate only in a post-election survey. Embedded in the pre-election survey were links to the Web pages of one or both of the two major political parties in Japanese elections, the Liberal Democratic Party (LDP) and the Democratic Party of Japan (DPJ). Of two groups who were assigned to the pre-election survey, in one group there was a link to only one party Web page and in the other group there were links to both parties' Web pages.*

Similar to Gerber, Karlan, and Bergan's study, to assign subjects to the groups, Horiuchi, Imai, and Taniguchi first divided subjects by gender and whether or not the subject planned to vote in the election, which formed six blocks of subjects (there were three possible answers to the vote intention question – planning to vote, not planning to vote, and undecided). They then conducted a complete randomization within each of the six blocks such that the total numbers of subjects were 1,000 in the one-party group, 600 in the two-party group, and 400 in the group with no pre-election survey. In the one-party group, half the subjects were randomly assigned to read material on the Web page of the LDP party and the other half to read material on the Web page of the DPJ party. Within the two-party group, they also randomized which party's Web page the respondent was asked to visit first.

The pre-election survey proceeded as follows. First, subjects were given some warm-up questions on prison reform. Then they were instructed to click on a link to the assigned party Web site and were told that they would be asked their opinion about the Web site when they returned from the party's Web site. After returning from the Web site, respondents were asked additional questions about the Web site. For those assigned to both parties, the respondents received the same set of questions after they visited each site. At the end of the survey, subjects had an optional open-ended question about their opinions of the Web site(s).

The post-election survey, which all groups participated in, took place in the four days after the election. The survey was short, focusing on whether the subjects voted in the election, and the response rate was greater than 80%.

Results: *Horiuchi, Imai, and Taniguchi found evidence that information increases the turnout of voters who were exposed to both parties' Web sites. Although they found a positive relationship between turnout and visiting one party's Web site, the effect was not statistically significant.*

Comments: Horiuchi, Imai, and Taniguchi were able to measure whether and how long subjects opened the assigned Web site in their browser and when subjects chose to stop taking the survey. Sixty-three subjects in the one-party group did not visit the designated Web site, 52 in the two-party group did not visit either Web site, and 18 in the two-party group only visited one party's Web site. Horiuchi et al. also provided extensive methodological details on the methods they used to identify and estimate the causal effects given that some subjects did not complete the survey or respond to the survey request. We return to these details as we explore the difficulties in identify and estimating causal effects and refer to their study in the following chapters.

Is the fact that the subjects studied by Gerber, Karlan, and Bergan and Horiuchi, Imai, and Taniguchi are not representative a problem with their randomization procedures? Most political scientists would say yes and stop there. However, such a summary confuses the purpose of randomization in typical surveys with the purpose of randomization in experiments. That is, in traditional surveys the purpose is to measure public opinion, and simple randomization across the population is well known to be the best way to construct such measures. The spectacular failures of pollsters to predict the 1948 presidential election using designs that were not simple randomizations led researchers who work in public opinion to prize surveys based on how closely they matched fully randomized designs.[9] However, in experiments like those of Horiuchi et al. and Gerber et al., whether the subject pool is a random draw of a different population matters in drawing inferences about the application of the results beyond the subject pool, not about the robustness of the causal inferences drawn as applied to the subject pool or target population (see Definition 2.2).

For drawing causal inferences within the population subject to the experiment, different standards of randomization are important. As Horiuchi et al. noted, many researchers implicitly assume that simple randomization of treatment is the best procedure to use within the experiment, much as it is in measuring public opinion in surveys. Yet such a conclusion, as Horiuchi et al. argued, would be incorrect. Horiuchi et al. know from previous research that particular variables such as an individual's gender and vote intention are strong predictors of whether they vote in Japanese elections. Horiuchi et al. first surveyed voters about these basic variables and grouped

---

[9] The history of randomization in public opinion research is reviewed by Morton (2006, chapter 10).

them into strata. They then randomized treatments within the blocks using a complete randomization procedure (that is, they randomized treatments across all subjects at once rather than assigning them subject-by-subject). By doing so, the resulting estimates of causal effects are more efficient than those if subjects were assigned treatments individually.[10] Their use of control, mixed with random assignment, also shows how these two aspects of experimental procedure work together and the importance of control in experimental design. Again, their use of control is not the standard narrow view of most political scientists, where control is simply a comparison of different treatments or a treatment and a baseline, but a broader perspective where control of observables allows for more efficient estimation of causal effects.

Dealing with Noncompliance and Nonresponse. In Horiuchi et al.'s study, subjects were assigned to three different treatments: (1) visit a Web site containing the party manifesto of one party, (2) visit the Web sites containing the party manifestos of two parties, or (3) no assignment to visit a Web site. As in most such experiments, the subjects did not always comply with their treatments. Horiuchi et al. assumed there were no defiers and no always-takers. They based this assumption on empirical evidence that extremely few Japanese voters were aware of the Web sites and the information contained on them about the party platforms. Such an assumption would certainly not be realistic in Gerber et al.'s study, for example, because subjects may choose to begin a newspaper subscription independent of whether they were given a free subscription. Lassen similarly cannot rule out non-PCD voters gaining information. Hence, Horiuchi et al. have a particularly useful manipulation where noncompliers can only be of one type – never-takers.

One aspect of Horiuchi et al.'s experiment is that, because of the control they have via the Internet, they can actually measure whether a subject complies or not rather than estimate compliance with treatment as in Lassen's study. But they did not have control over whether subjects responded and had the same missing data problem that Gerber et al. and Lassen experienced. Horiuchi et al.'s analysis is particularly noteworthy because they follow FR and take into account the impact of both noncompliance and nonresponse when they estimate the causal effects of their treatments.

Horiuchi et al.'s study is also significant because they were able to measure the amount of time subjects spent visiting the Web sites and thus could measure heterogeneity in what subjects experienced. Next we discuss the

---

[10] See Cox and Reid (2000).

issues involved in measuring causality with such heterogeneity and how Horiuchi et al. incorporated these issues in their estimation.

Dealing with Heterogeneity in Treatment Experiences. One of the criticisms that we have noted often is that the causal effects estimated in the various procedures reviewed in this chapter and the preceding chapter assume that the experience of a particular treatment is homogeneous across subjects. But heterogeneity in manipulation experiences is obvious. For example, some subjects in Gerber et al.'s study may have read every article with political information in the newspaper whereas other subjects may have read only one or two. In one sense this is a type of noncompliance, or a generalization of noncompliance. Alternatively, we could think of the treatment as a discrete or continuous variable while the assignment to treatment is binary. It is possible to extend the methods discussed in both this chapter and the previous one to allow for such heterogeneity. Wooldridge (1999) discusses how these generalizations can be accomplished and the assumptions underlying them.

In field experiments, Mealli et al. discussed how quality of manipulation may be incorporated into their estimation of treatment effects discussed earlier. Horiuchi et al. presented two models that incorporate causal heterogeneity – one in which the treatment effect is heterogeneous and related to their pretreatment characteristics and one in which the subjects choose different levels of treatment and the heterogeneity is related to the treatment itself. They also incorporated manipulation heterogeneity in their estimation procedure and were able to use their measures of the time the subjects spent visiting the Web sites in estimating the causal effects of the treatments.

5.6 Manipulation and Time

Sekhon's use of panel data, explored in Chapter 4, draws attention to the ability of researchers to use sequential choices as a measure of causality. We also discussed how panel data allow for researchers to control for unit-specific unobservables via first differencing and fixed and random effects estimators. In this chapter we consider the fact that time can provide a researcher with a way of sidestepping confounding when we can argue that the treatment is the result of some exogenous manipulation by either nature or an experimentalist. There are two obvious advantages to exploiting sequence with manipulation: (1) we can observe the same units in both treated and untreated states (as in the between-subjects design used in within-subjects designs and discussed earlier) and (2) we can compare treated units with untreated ones, which formerly were both untreated. In this fashion a researcher exploits both manipulation to avoid confounding and panel data for control of observables that are suspected or known to confound.

The advantages of using time coupled with manipulation to establish causal effects are well known. Heckman and Robb (1985, 1986) present an excellent review of this literature and the approaches involved with observational data. A recent example of using manipulation and time is the study of the effect of the introduction of television on voter turnout by Gentzkow (2006). He exploited some exogenous factors (World War II and a technical issue in designating spectrums) that interrupted the introduction of television in the United States. This allowed him to compare counties with television to those without. He found evidence that the introduction of television reduced voters' information about politics and caused a reduction in turnout. He also reviewed the methods and assumptions necessary for establishing causality in such situations. The method Gentzkow uses is called a difference-in-differences approach.

Because our focus is more explicitly on experiments and less on the estimation of causal effects over long periods of time, we do not review the literature on these methods in its entirety here. Furthermore, many of the issues involved are similar to those discussed previously, where observations may be separated by time if we assume that the asymptotic properties of cross-sectional methods are applicable (that is, the number of observations per period is much larger than the number of periods).

5.7 Chapter Summary

We began this chapter with the definition of an ideal IV and showed that, when accomplished perfectly, random assignment to treatment can be such an ideal IV. An ideal IV allows a researcher to measure effects of treatments simply and straightforwardly. However, as we noted, random assignment is unlikely to satisfy the three conditions for an ideal IV – independence, substitutability, and no missing data – in some laboratory experiments and almost all Internet and field experiments. Researchers can deal with violations of these conditions in the design of their experiment and in the post-experiment analysis of the data. However, post-experiment analyses require that researchers make additional assumptions about the data. Table 5.2 summarizes the various approaches a researcher can use and the assumptions implied under each approach.

Table 5.2. *Solutions to deal with less than ideal IVs or random assignment problems*

Method	Assumptions	Helps*
Approaches with Experimental Data Only (Design Solutions)		
Running experiments same time and day	Other timing effects irrelevant	I
Using a subject pool homogenous over time	Subject pool relevant for research question	I
Conditioning randomization on observables	Unobservables not confounding	I
Randomizing at level of analysis	Possible to implement	I
Minimizing subject knowledge of experiment	Possible to implement and no ethical problems	I
Using non-naturally occurring choices	Relevant for research question	S
Using unfamiliar naturally occurring choices	Relevant for research question and unfamiliar	S
Excluding subjects known to be pretreated	Possible to implement	S
Using financial incentives and quizzes in lab	Effective to induce compliance	S
Measuring compliance by varying incentives	Effective to induce compliance	S
Extensive training and monitoring of collaborators in field	Effective to induce compliance	S
Conducting a multilevel experiment in field	Groups in levels are nested, superlevel exists	S
Providing incentives to subjects to respond to surveys	Effective to induce response	D
Approaches with Both Experimental and Observational Data (Analysis Solutions)		
Estimating sample means for ATT	P_0 is independent of M	I
Conditioning estimates on observables	Axiom 5.1	I
Using intention-to-treat measures	Relevant for research question	S
Using IV estimation procedures	Axioms 5.2–5.6	S
Estimating effect on compilers only	Axioms 5.7 and 5.8	S
Dropping missing observations	Axiom 5.9	D
Conditioning on covariates	Axiom 5.10	D
FR approach	Axioms 5.11–5.13	D
Mealli et al.'s approach	Axiom 5.11, 5.12, 5.14	D

* I = independence condition, S = perfect substitute condition, and D = no missing data condition.

5.8 Adding in Formal Theory

In this chapter and the previous one, we examined the identification and estimation of causal relationships using an RCM-based approach. In the RCM approach, the focus is on the effects of a single cause – a treatment. We have seen that two methods are used to deal with potential problems caused by unobservables – control and randomization. The perspective is that, through systematic explorations of different effects of cause relationships, eventually researchers can work to understand the causes of effects in a general way. This approach makes sense when the researcher is specifically interested in a particular cause. However, our analysis in these chapters has shown that using an RCM-based approach requires that the researcher typically make specific assumptions about the relationships between those things observed and those things unobserved. The researcher is required to theorize that these possible confounding variables are not a problem for the studied relationship.

In the next chapter, we discuss an alternative perspective to establishing causal results that, instead of relying on implicit unspecified assumptions about observables and unobservables as in SUTVA, uses theoretical structures to make assumptions explicit. We call this the formal theory approach to causality (as previously noted).

6

Formal Theory and Causality

6.1 What Is a Formal Model?

We turn in this chapter to the Formal Theory Approach (FTA) to causality. The key difference between FTA and the Rubin Causal Model (RCM) is that a formal model serves as the basis for the causal relationships studied. To understand what we mean by FTA, it is useful to define what we mean by a formal model. We define a formal model as a set of precise abstract assumptions or axioms about the data generating process (DGP) presented in symbolic terms that are *solved* to derive predictions about that process.[1] These predictions are of two types: point predictions and relationship predictions. Point predictions are precise predictions about the values of the variables in the model when the model is in equilibrium, whereas relationship predictions are predictions about how we may expect two variables in the model to be related. Defining what is meant by whether the model is in equilibrium can vary with the model as well; different formal models rely on different equilibrium concepts, which is something that we investigate later in Section 6.5.4. Some of these relationship predictions may be predicted to be "causal" in that changes in one variable "cause" changes in the other variable.

Definition 6.1 (Formal Model): *A set of precise abstract assumptions or axioms about the DGP presented in symbolic terms that are solved to derive predictions about the DGP.*

Definition 6.2 (Point Prediction of a Formal Model): *A precise prediction from a formal model about the values of the variables in the model when the model is in equilibrium.*

---

[1] For a definition of DGP see Definition 2.1. Our definitions of formal and nonformal models follow Morton (1999) with some minor changes.

Definition 6.3 (Relationship Predictions of a Formal Model): *Predictions from a formal model about how two variables in the model will be related.*

Definition 6.4 (Causal Relationship Predictions of a Formal Model): *Relationship predictions in which the changes in one variable are argued to "cause" the changes in the other variable.*

In contrast, a nonformal model is a set of verbal statements or predictions about the DGP which might involve idealization, identification, and approximation but is given in terms of real observables or unobservables rather than symbols or abstracts. The predictions may be presented in a diagram or graph or they may be presented as equations with variables representing the real observables and unobservables. The key difference is that in a nonformal model, these predictions, even when presented in equation form, are not directly derived from explicit assumptions or axioms about the DGP. The researcher may have in mind some ideas or conjectures about the implicit assumptions underlying the predictions, but the researcher has not proved that the predictions directly follow from those ideas or conjectures by stating the assumptions explicitly and solving for the predictions directly from those explicit assumptions. A nonformal model may be mathematical in presentation, but that does not make it a formal model if the assumptions behind the predictions made are not stated unambiguously and the predictions directly derived from those assumptions.

Definition 6.5 (Nonformal Model): *A set of verbal statements or predictions about the DGP that involve idealization, identification, and approximation but are given in terms of real observables or unobservables rather than symbols or abstracts. The predictions may be presented in a diagram or graph or they may be presented even as mathematical equations with variables representing the real observables and unobservables. Although the researcher may have in mind some implicit assumptions underlying the predictions, the researcher has not proved that the predictions directly follow from those assumptions by stating them explicitly and solving for the predictions.*

6.2 Using an RCM Approach with Predictions from Nonformal Models

6.2.1 The Theoretical Consistency Assumption

We have already presented some experiments that investigate predictions derived from formal models in Examples 2.6, 2.7, 3.2, and 5.2. Most of the other examples that we have explored so far investigate predictions that are from nonformal models. The experiment of Clinton and Lapinski in Example 2.3, studying the effects of negative campaign advertisements, is a typical such instance. In their experiment, the causal hypotheses or predictions are stated rather than derived from explicit assumptions, although they present verbal justifications for the predictions. Similarly, Mutz in Example 2.5 evaluates predictions that are not explicitly derived from formally stated assumptions. She does provide verbal explanations from nonformal theories, suggesting that the predictions follow from these theories.

In evaluating the causal predictions made by nonformal theory, researchers like Clinton and Lapinski and Mutz necessarily take an RCM approach, which we have discussed in Chapters 3–5. As we have seen, taking an RCM approach is not without assumptions about the DGP. The assumptions a researcher makes depend on the particular methods used by the researcher in attempting to identify the causal relationship that has been predicted. For instance, as we have seen, if a researcher uses a matching procedure under RCM to estimate average treatment effect (ATE), the researcher assumes ignorability of treatment and the stable unit treatment value assumption. Whether these assumptions are consistent with the implicit underlying assumptions from which the prediction arises is not addressed by the researcher in his or her analysis because these underlying assumptions are not stated explicitly. The researcher takes for granted that the assumptions implied by the use of the particular RCM method are not inconsistent with the implicit underlying assumptions of the causal prediction. We call this assumption the theoretical consistency assumption.

Axiom 6.1 (Theoretical Consistency Assumption): *Assumption made by researchers working with an RCM approach to causality that the assumptions underlying the causal predictions evaluated are consistent with the assumptions that underlie the methods used by the researcher to infer causal relationships.*

We have already provided an illustration of a case in which implicit assumptions underlying causal predictions may not be consistent with the assumptions underlying a method in our exploration of Bartels' study of the effects of information on voting in Section 4.2.7. In Bartels' analysis, he works directly with a causal prediction that he estimates. He suggests that the prediction be thought of as a reduced-form equation from a more general formal model. We explored what that more general model might look like and pointed out that one of the assumptions of the empirical analysis, ignorability of treatment, is likely not to be consistent with the assumptions of that model. Of course, one argument might be that our proposed general model is not the one that underlies Bartels' prediction. The point is that, unless the assumptions that underlie a prediction are stated explicitly and the prediction is shown to derive from these assumptions, there is no way for a researcher to be sure that the theoretical consistency assumption is satisfied.

6.2.2 Addressing the Theoretical Consistency Assumption

Minimizing Assumptions in Empirics
Usually researchers working with nonformal models choose to try to make as few assumptions as possible in their empirical approaches because they have no way of knowing if those assumptions are consistent or not with whatever underlies their theoretical predictions. However, as we have seen in Chapters 3 through 5, data do not speak for themselves, and all empirical methods used to estimate causal predictions make some assumptions, which may or may not be consistent with the implicit assumptions underlying the predictions a researcher is evaluating. Nevertheless, attempting to minimize assumptions in empirics is the primary way researchers in political science address possible violations of the theory consistency assumption.

Nonformal Structural Modeling
Occasionally researchers take an alternative solution; instead of trying to estimate the reduced-form version of the prediction with as few empirical assumptions as possible, they empirically estimate what we label nonformal structural models. A nonformal structural model is an empirical model created by a researcher that captures the structure he or she believes underlies the predictions he or she is evaluating. The model, however, is not solved explicitly for predictions as a formal model. We have already considered one type of nonformal structural model, an empirical model of a causal relationship with a mediating variable or variables in Section 4.7. The researchers posit that the mediating variable or variables matter under the assumptions given by the estimating procedure. They do not set up the model as a theoretical model and solve it for predictions, but they make assumptions directly in the empirical estimation, using an RCM approach.

Definition 6.6 (Nonformal Structural Model): *An empirical model created by a researcher that captures the structure he or she believes might underlie the predictions he or she is evaluating. The model is not solved explicitly for predictions as a formal model.*

Another example of a nonformal structure model is an empirical model used to estimate latent variables. A latent measurement model has a set of unobserved variables that are called "latent" variables and a set of observed variables. The latent variables are the theoretical variables that the researcher is interested in and the observed variables are assumed to be imperfect indicators of these underlying latent variables. For example, we may think of an individual voter as having some latent policy preferences in broad issue areas that we cannot observe, although we can observe his or her choices in surveys with particular questions and voting actions. These choices and actions can be considered imperfect indications of the underlying unobserved preferences. A latent measurement model is a model that attempts to use the observables to measure the unobservable latent variables. Factor analysis is an example of a latent measurement model in which all the latent and observable variables are treated as continuous, interval-level measurements that have linear relationships with each other.

Latent measurement models can be extremely useful for political scientists, particularly in analyzing survey data. In a recent important paper, Ansolabehere et al. (2008) demonstrated that much of the perceived instability of voter preferences in the United States can be explained as measurement error from the typical approach of focusing on single survey questions to measure preferences. By combining multiple measures, they are able to suggest that voters instead have stable latent preferences over broad issue areas. However, as Bolck et al. (2004) noted, measurement is not an end in itself. Usually a researcher has as a goal the estimation of some causal relationship between the latent variable and an observable variable using, say, an RCM-based approach. For example, Ansolabehere et al. (2008) use the estimated preferences on broad issue areas using factor analysis in a secondary regression explaining voters' choices in an RCM-based model. They showed that indeed voters' choices are significantly influenced by the estimated preferences on broad issues from the latent measurement model. Bolck et al. labeled the approach used by Ansolabehere et al. as a three-step approach. As they note (p. 4, emphasis in the original):

In the *three-step approach*, a stand-alone measurement model is first defined (or several measurement models, one for each latent variable) and its parameters are estimated. Next, on the basis of these parameters are estimates and the observed individual scoring patterns on the indicators, individual latent scores are computed or predicted. Finally, these predicted latent scores are treated as if they were ordinary observed scores in a causal model without latent variables and are used to get estimates for the parameters in the structural part of the model.

There are potential problems with this approach, however. As Bolck et al. explain, the use of the estimated latent variables can lead to distortions in the estimated causal relationships. They suggest a procedure that can guarantee consistent estimation of the causal relationships in a three-step approach.

In contrast, sometimes the measurement model is incorporated directly into a causal model. Bolck et al. call this the one-step approach. In this method, the researcher estimates one model, and latent variables and parameters are estimated simultaneously. These models are generally considered structural models because the researcher relies heavily on theoretical assumptions about the hypothesized structure of the relationships of the variables. However, they may or may not be mathematically derived from formal theoretical models, so they may or may not be theoretically derived structural models. The LISREL model (see in Section 4.7) is an example of this approach, where the variables are continuous. As Bolck et al. remark, "The one-step approach provides optimal asymptotically unbiased, efficient, or consistent estimates of the nature and the strength of the relationships among all variables, given that the complete measurement and structural models are valid in the population and the pertinent statistical assumptions, such as multinomial or normal sampling distributions, have been met." Skrondal and Rabe-Hesketh (2007) surveyed the various types of models that address latent variables.

The term structural model is also sometimes used to describe empirical models that are multilevel or have fixed or random effects. Again, unless the model has been first set up as a theoretical model and the predictions have been derived from that model, the researchers are still only assuming theoretical consistency; they have not proved that theoretical consistency holds. Researchers are using an RCM-based approach to evaluate the predictions, albeit augmented with additional assumptions about the structure through which the predictions arise.

6.3 Using an RCM Approach with Predictions from Formal Models

Sometimes a researcher evaluating a causal prediction from a formal model takes an RCM approach and also makes the theory consistency assumption. A case in point is Example 2.8, where Lassen investigates the effect of information about Copenhagen's policy experiment on voter turnout. Lassen notes that the prediction he is evaluating – that information increases turnout – is derived from a formal model of voting, the Swing Voter's Curse theory of Feddersen and Pesendorfer which we mentioned in Section 2.3.3

and explore more fully in Section 6.5.1. Yet, his empirical approach is what we call "inspired by" the formal model, using an RCM-based approach to investigate the causal prediction of the model. In fact, many researchers in political science who evaluate the predictions of formal models, particularly with observational data, take this approach. We too have done so in our own observational data work. In inspired-by empirical evaluations researchers, like those working with nonformal theories, make the theoretical consistency assumption but do not explicitly study whether it holds as part of the empirical evaluation.

Definition 6.7 (Inspired-By Evaluations of Formal Theory Predictions): *When a researcher evaluates a formal theory prediction using an RCM-based approach and assumes theoretical consistency but does not explicitly investigate whether it holds or not.*

Alternatively, sometimes researchers, working with formal models as a basis, conduct experiments that are what Davis and Holt (1993) call "stress tests." A stress test is distinctive from an inspired-by evaluation because in a stress test the researcher focuses on a particular aspect or aspects of where the theoretical consistency assumption might be violated to determine if the violation is important. We discuss stress tests and define them formally in Section 6.4.2.

6.4 The FTA Process

6.4.1 Essence of FTA

What makes FTA different? The crucial departure from RCM-based analysis of predictions from either nonformal or formal models is that in FTA a researcher attempts for the empirical study to be governed or directly derived from the assumptions of the formal model that he or she wishes to evaluate and to carefully select when and how these assumptions may not hold in the empirical analysis. The researcher does not make the theoretical consistency assumption but instead carefully investigates whether each assumption of the theoretical model holds for the empirical analysis and how these assumptions matter in that analysis. The researcher conducts analysis of the causal predictions of the model with this knowledge of the consistency between the empirical analysis and the formal model. Consistency is not just assumed, as in RCM or inspired-by studies, but is controlled and manipulated.

Definition 6.8 (**Formal Theory Approach to Causality**): *When a researcher evaluates causal predictions that are derived explicitly from the solution of a formal model by conducting an empirical study where either assumptions underlying the empirics are as equivalent as possible to those of the formal model underlying the predictions or the researcher has explicitly chosen which assumptions to relax. Instead of making the theoretical consistency assumption, the researcher controls the extent that the assumptions hold or do not hold so that the relationship between the empirical analysis and the formal model is explicit.*

What does it mean to make the assumptions equivalent or to allow one or more to be violated? The first step for a researcher is to identify all of the underlying assumptions of the model. Formal models should have the following five components.[2]

1. The political environment:
   (a) The institutions
   (b) The political actors
   (c) The information available to each actor
2. A list of primitives, including
   (a) Preferences of the actors
   (b) The institutional characteristics
3. Variables exogenous to actors and the political environment studied:
   (a) Constraints on actors' behaviors that are outside the environment
   (b) Other variables outside the environment that alter the behavior of the actors
4. The decision variables, time horizons, and objective functions of the actors:
   (a) What do actors choose?
   (b) How are actors choosing?
5. An equilibrium solution concept, such as[3]
   (a) Nash equilibrium or subgame perfection in games of complete information
   (b) Bayesian–Nash equilibrium in simultaneous games of incomplete information
   (c) Perfect Bayesian–Nash equilibrium in sequential games of incomplete information

---

[2] Our presentation here draws on Reiss and Wolak (2007, p. 4304) for economic models.
[3] For explanations of these equilibrium concepts, see any game theory text, such as McCarty and Meirowitz (2006).

6.4.2 Theory and Stress Tests

Once a researcher has identified all of these components, the researcher's goal is to make the assumptions underlying the empirical study as close as possible to these five components of the model or to carefully choose when and how these assumptions are violated in the empirical analysis. When a researcher attempts to make all the empirical assumptions as close as possible to the theoretical ones, we call the analysis a theory test. When the researcher chooses to allow for one or more of the theoretical assumptions to be violated or purposefully investigates situations in which the researcher is uncertain as to whether the theoretical assumptions hold, the researcher is conducting a stress test of the theory (see Davis and Holt [1993] for a similar distinction). In the examples that follow we show how theory and stress tests work.

Definition 6.9 (Theory Tests): *When a researcher investigates the predictions of a formal model while attempting to make all the assumptions underlying the empirical study as close as possible to the theoretical assumptions.*

Definition 6.10 (Stress Tests): *When a researcher investigates the predictions of a formal model while explicitly allowing for one or more assumptions underlying the empirical study to be at variance with the theoretical assumptions.*

Researchers conducting experiments to evaluate a formal model's causal predictions have two stages at which they can make the assumptions underlying the empirical evaluation equivalent to those underlying the formal model: the design stage of the experiment before manipulations occur and the analysis stage where the researcher confronts the data after the experiment has occurred (see Section 3.4). Researchers working with observational data to evaluate a formal model's causal predictions have only the analysis stage available. We begin with how researchers using FTA use the design stage and then we turn to how researchers use the analysis stage.

6.5 FTA and the Design Stage of Experimental Research

6.5.1 The Formal Model: An Example

To illustrate how an experimenter takes a formal model and creates an experimental design using FTA for a theory test, we use as an example the Swing Voter's Curse model of Feddersen and Pesendorfer (1996), mentioned in Section 2.3.3. We begin with a presentation of the model as it appears in its full-blown theoretical glory so that we can explain how an experimenter moves from a more complicated model to a version of the model that is implementable in an experiment but maintains those features of interest to the experimenter.

The model is presented by the authors as follows (pp. 411–414):

There are two states, state 0 and state 1, where $Z = \{0, 1\}$ denotes the set of states. There are two candidates, candidate 0 and candidate 1. The set of candidates is $X = \{0, 1\}$. There are three types of agents, where $T = \{0, 1, i]$ is the set of types. Type-0 and type-1 agents are partisans: irrespective of the state type-0 agents strictly prefer candidate 0 and type-1 agents strictly prefer candidate 1. Type i-agents are independents: given a pair $(x, z,)$, $x \in X$ and $z \in Z$, the utility of a type i agent is

$$U(x, z) = \begin{cases} -1 & \text{if } x \neq z \\ 0 & \text{if } x = z \end{cases}$$

Independent agents prefer candidate 0 in state 0 and candidate 1 in state 1.

At the beginning of the game nature chooses a state $z \in Z$. State 0 is chosen with probability α and state 1 is chosen with probability $1 - \alpha$. Without loss of generality we assume that $\alpha \leq \frac{1}{2}$. The parameter α is common knowledge and hence all agents believe that state 1 is at least as likely as state 0. Nature also chooses a set of agents by taking $N + 1$ independent draws. We assume that there is uncertainty both about the total number of agents and the number of agents of each type. In each draw, nature selects an agent with probability $(1 - p_\phi)$. If an agent is selected, then with probability $p_i/(1 - p_\phi)$ she is of type i, with probability $p_0/(1 - p_\phi)$ she is type 0, and with probability $p_i/(1 - p_\phi)$ she is type 1. The probabilities $p = (p_i, p_0, p_1, p_\phi)$ are common knowledge.

After the state and the set of agents have been chosen, every agent learns her type and receives a message $m \in M$, where $M = \{0, \alpha, 1\}$. Both her type and the message are private information. If an agent receives message m then the agent knows that the state is 0 with probability m. All agents who receive a message $m \in \{0, 1\}$ are informed, that is, they know the state with probability 1. Note that all informed agents receive the same message. The probability that an agent is informed is q. Agents who receive the message α learn nothing about the state beyond the common knowledge prior. We refer to these agents as uninformed.

. . .

Every agent chooses an action $s \in \{\phi, 0, 1\}$ where ϕ indicates abstention and 0 or 1 indicates her vote for candidate 0 or 1, respectively. The candidate that receives a majority of the votes cast will be elected. Whenever there is a tie, we assume that each candidate is chosen with equal probability.

A pure strategy for an agent is a map $s : T \times M \rightarrow \{\phi, 0, 1\}$. A mixed strategy is denoted by $\tau : T \times M \rightarrow [0, 1]^3$, where τ_s is the probability of taking action s.

. . .

We define a sequence of games with $N + 1$ potential voters indexed by N a sequence of strategy profiles for each game as $\{\tau^N\}_{N=0}^\infty$.

After setting up the model, the authors solve the model for the symmetric Bayesian–Nash equilibria of the game for predictions. A symmetric equilibrium requires that they assume that agents who are of the same type and receive the same message choose the same strategy. Note that voting is costless in the model. They see their model as applying to a situation where a voter is already in the voting booth or has otherwise paid the costs of voting. Certainly this and other assumptions of the model may be criticized by some researchers as unrealistic or inappropriate for the situation addressed by the model. Others may find the assumptions reasonable and useful. Our purpose here is not to defend the model but to use it as an illustration for how an experimenter moves from a formal model to a specific experimental design.

6.5.2 Summary of the Features of the Model

The formal model of politics of Feddersen and Pesendorfer has the five parts mentioned earlier: (1) a description of a political environment, (2) a list of primitives, (3) a set of exogenous variables, (4) a set of decision variables, and (5) an equilibrium solution concept.

The political environment of the model has three components: institutions, actors, and information. In the environment described by Feddersen and Pesendorfer, there is a single institution – an election. There is a set of political actors, voters (partisans and independents), two candidates, and nature. Candidates have fixed policy positions. Nature chooses the true state of the world and the numbers of voters using fixed probabilities. The voters know the candidates' positions but the voters have varying degrees of information about nature's choices. All voters know their own type but they only know the probabilities of the numbers of voters of various types, not the actual draws of nature. Some voters have full information as to the true state of the world, while others only know the ex ante probability.

The model also provides a list of primitives. The list of primitives describes two things: the actors' preferences and the institutional characteristics. The model describes the voters' preferences – partisans most want their preferred choice to win independent of the state of the world and independents would like the choice decided by majority rule to match the state of the world. Nature and candidates do not make choices and thus do not have preferences. The model assumes that the election is decided by majority rule, that the candidate with the most votes wins, and that ties are broken randomly.

In the model there are a number of exogenous variables: the candidates' choices, the ex ante probability of the state of the world, the probabilities of the numbers of each type of voter, the probability of being informed, and the cost of voting. The decision variables in the model are the vote choices of the four types of voters: type 0, type 1, informed independents, and uninformed independents. And finally the equilibrium solution concept used by the researchers is a Bayesian–Nash symmetric equilibrium.

6.5.3 Predictions of the Model

Point Predictions
Feddersen and Pesendorfer make a number of point predictions, which they derived from solving the model as follows:

1. Type 1 (type 0) agents always vote for candidate 1 (candidate 0) and all informed independent agents vote according to the signal they receive. So if an informed independent agent receives $m = 1$ ($m = 0$), she votes for candidate 0 (candidate 1).
2. (Proposition 2) Suppose $q > 0$, $p_i(1 - q) < |p_0 - p_1|$, and $p_\phi > 0$.
   (a) If $p_i(1 - q) < p_0 - p_1$ then $\lim_{N \to \infty} \tau_1^N = 1$; that is, all uninformed independent agents vote for candidate 1.
   (b) If $p_i(1 - q) > p_0 - p_1$ then $\lim_{N \to \infty} \tau_0^N = 1$; that is, all uninformed independent agents vote for candidate 0.
3. (Proposition 3) Suppose $q > 0$, $p_i(1 - q) \geq |p_0 - p_1|$, and $p_\phi > 0$.
   (a) If $p_i(1 - q) \geq p_0 - p_1$ then uninformed independent agents mix between voting for candidate 1 and abstaining; $\lim_{N \to \infty} \tau_1^N = (p_0 - p_1)/p_i(1 - q)$ and $\lim_{N \to \infty} \tau_\phi^N = 1 - [(p_0 - p_1)/p_i(1 - q)]$.
   (b) If $p_i(1 - q) \geq p_1 - p_0$ then uninformed independent agents mix between voting for candidate 0 and abstaining; $\lim_{N \to \infty} \tau_0^N = (p_1 - p_0)/p_i(1 - q)$ and $\lim_{N \to \infty} \tau_\phi^N = 1 - [(p_1 - p_0)/p_i(1 - q)]$.
   (c) If $p_0 - p_1 = 0$ then uninformed independent agents abstain; $\lim_{N \to \infty} \tau_\phi^N = 1$.
4. (Proposition 4) As the size of the electorate approaches infinity, the probability that the election fully aggregates information (i.e., that the outcome of the election is the right choice from the point of view of the independents) goes to 1.

The first point prediction follows because doing otherwise would be a strictly dominated strategy for these voters. Partisans clearly gain the highest expected utility from voting their partisan preferences and fully informed independents similarly gain the highest expected utility from voting according to their signals.

The second and third point predictions concern what uninformed independents choose to do. In equilibrium, uninformed independents condition their vote on being pivotal – they vote as if their vote can change the outcome of the election. A voter can change the outcome if in the absence of her vote the election is expected to be a tie or one vote short of a tie. Why condition one's vote on these events that might seem very unlikely? In the event that an uninformed voter is not pivotal, it does not matter how she votes; but in the event that she is pivotal, then her vote completely determines her final utility. Thus, even if the probability of being pivotal is extremely small, an uninformed voter has the highest expected utility by voting as if she is pivotal.

The fact that uninformed independents rationally condition their vote choices on being pivotal leads to what Feddersen and Pesendorfer label the Swing Voter's Curse – that uninformed voters, when indifferent, prefer to abstain. To see how this works, suppose that uninformed independents have no idea which way informed independents are voting and there are no partisan voters. If an uninformed voter chooses to vote for candidate 0 (candidate 1), and she is pivotal, she might be canceling out the vote of an informed independent for candidate 1 (candidate 0). Therefore, the uninformed independent voters, when indifferent, prefer to abstain and never adopt an equilibrium strategy of mixing between voting for candidate 1 and 0.

In equilibrium, uninformed voters' choices also depend on whether one of the candidates has an expected partisan advantage and the relative size of that advantage. Candidate 0 (candidate 1) has an expected partisan advantage when there is expected to be more type 0 voters than type 1 voters. When one of the candidates has a partisan advantage, say candidate 0, an uninformed independent has an incentive to vote to offset that advantage, voting for that candidate's opponent, candidate 1, so that the decision will be made by the informed independents. In this case, the uninformed independent is not indifferent in the case of being pivotal. To see how this is true, imagine the situation in which there is a tie election and only one uninformed independent and the number of informed independents is exactly equal to candidate 0's partisan advantage over candidate 1. For the election to be a tie, then, informed independents must be voting for candidate 1. Thus, the uninformed independent should also vote for candidate 1, breaking the tie in favor of candidate 1 in the event she is pivotal.

The second point prediction applies when the expected percentage of voters who will be uninformed is less than the expected partisan advantage for one of the candidates. In this case, Feddersen and Pesendorfer show that, as the size of the electorate approaches infinity, the optimal strategy for uninformed independents approaches the strategy of voting for the candidate who does not have the expected partisan advantage. The third point prediction concerns the case when the expected percentage of voters who will be uninformed is greater than or equal to the expected partisan advantage for one of the candidates. Feddersen and Pesendorfer show that in this situation, as the size of the electorate approaches infinity, in the limit the uninformed independent will use a mixed strategy. That is, they will vote for the candidate with the partisan disadvantage with just enough probability to offset the disadvantage and abstain with one minus that probability, so that the informed independents' votes can decide the outcome.

Feddersen and Pesendorfer's fourth point prediction follows from the strategies adopted by the uninformed independent voters. By offsetting the partisan voters, and facilitating the decisiveness of the votes of the informed independents, when the electorate is large the probability that the outcome is as independents most prefer is as high as possible.

Relationship Predictions

Feddersen and Pesendorfer also make a number of relationship predictions (holding other things constant):

1. Abstention is increasing with
    (a) increases in the percentage of independents,
    (b) decreases in the probability of being informed, and
    (c) decreases in the partisan advantage of the advantaged candidate.
2. Margin of victory is increasing with
    (a) increases in the percentage of independents and
    (b) increases in the probability of being informed.
3. From relationship predictions 1(b) and 2(b), when the percentage of independents is held constant, there is a negative relationship between the margin of victory and abstention. That is, higher margins of victory are correlated with lower levels of abstention.
4. From relationship predictions 1(a) and 2(a), when the probability of being informed is held constant, there is a positive relationship between the margin of victory and abstention. That is, higher margins of victory are correlated with higher levels of abstention.
5. When the size of the electorate is large, then small changes in the ex ante probability that state 0 is the true state, α, have no effect on voting strategies or other equilibrium predictions. When the size of the electorate is small, and α is close to zero, then a small change in α can have significant effects on voting behavior.

Relationship predictions 1 and 2 are predicted causal relations. For instance, the model predicts that when the percentage of independents increases, it will cause abstention to increase and the margin of victory to increase. In contrast, relationship predictions 3 and 4 are not causal relations, but correlations between abstention and margin of victory that may occur in response to changes in the causal variables in relationship predictions 1 and 2. The formal model allows us to distinguish between predicted relationships that are causal and those that are simply predicted correlations as a consequence of other causal relationships.

Of particular interest is relationship prediction 3, which predicts that when the percentage of independents is held constant, higher margins of victory will be associated with lower levels of abstention. This prediction is contrary to a relationship prediction that is found in some alternative formal models of elections and abstention. Take, for example, a simple model of the rational calculus of voting in which individuals vote only if the expected utility from voting is greater than the costs of voting. In such a simple model, the expected utility of voting depends on the probability of a vote being pivotal. The lower the probability of being pivotal, the higher the expected margin of victory in the election and the more likely the individual is to vote. So the simple model predicts that margin of victory and abstention are positively related in contrast to relationship prediction 3. However, relationship prediction 4 fits with the simple model's prediction.

Finally, relationship prediction 5 is a predicted nonrelationship. Perhaps somewhat surprisingly, Feddersen and Pesendorfer found that differences in ex ante probabilities have no expected effect on voting behavior in large electorates. Again, sometimes what we find in a formal model is that two variables are predicted not to have a relationship. What is important about this particular prediction is that it means that, even when state of the world 1 is ex ante expected to be more likely (i.e., $\alpha < 0.5$), if candidate 1 has a partisan advantage, for α not too small and a large enough electorate, uninformed voters should vote for candidate 0, contrary to their own limited information about the ex ante probability. Naive uninformed voters may be expected to vote their ex ante probability, voting for candidate 1, since the size of α suggests that state 1 is more likely, but Feddersen and Pesendorfer show that a rational voter would choose instead to balance out the partisan advantage of candidate 1 so that informed voters, when voting for candidate 0, are able to make a difference.

The relationship predictions that Feddersen and Pesendorfer make are called comparative static predictions. That is, time is not involved in these predictions – they are comparisons of how one variable takes a different value given changes in another variable, but they are comparisons of equilibrium predictions holding time constant, as if one could take a point in time and simultaneously observe these variables in different states. This should sound familiar. A comparative static relationship is defined as the comparison of two potential outcomes much as in defining causal effects (see Section 3.3.1). Comparative static predictions are then formal theory's equivalent to RCM's hypothesizing that two potential outcomes can be compared for the same time period even if only one can normally be observed at one point in time.

Definition 6.11 (Comparative Static Predictions in a Formal Model):
Causal relationship predictions from a formal model in which researchers compare how one variable takes a different value given changes in another variable, holding time constant.

6.5.4 Designing a Theory Test

The Feddersen and Pesendorfer model then provides a clear prediction about the relationship between information and voting behavior. In particular, the model predicts that, as the probability of an independent being informed increases, abstention should decline. The model also makes precise predictions about how different types of votes will choose and the effects of other variables on voting behavior. Some of these predictions are not obvious; for example, the prediction that uninformed voters have an incentive to vote for the candidate with a partisan disadvantage even when her prior is that the candidate with the partisan advantage is best and the prediction that under some situations margin of victory and abstention may be negatively related are predictions that have not previously been made in theoretical work on elections before. How can we use FTA in an experiment to evaluate these predictions of the model, particularly the nonobvious ones?

In this section we discuss the choices that an experimenter makes when using FTA in designing an experiment. The Feddersen and Pesendorfer model is the basis of the experiments by Battaglini, Morton, and Palfrey described in Example 2.6. As we discuss the choices to be made, we refer as well to those choices made by Battaglini, Morton, and Palfrey.

Recreating the Political Environment
Human Subjects for All Roles or Artificial Actors for Some? First, we begin with the political environment of the theory. Ideally, the researcher designs an

experiment that creates the same environment. Recall that the environment has one political institution, an election, and a number of different types of actors: candidates, nature, and four types of voters. Consider first the actors. What we are interested in is studying how humans would behave as actors within the political environment and assumptions of the model. So the actors are the roles to which our human subjects will be assigned.

But should we assign subjects to all the roles? Obviously we want to assign human subjects as uninformed independent voters because it is their choices that are the focus of the predictions we wish to investigate. However, it is less clear that we want to assign human subjects to the other roles as actors. For instance, nature is clearly not a human role but represents exogenous factors outside the model that determine which candidate is optimal for independent voters. Thus, we would not think of the choices of nature as something to study, but as part of the design of the experiment. In some cases the experimenter will make the choices of nature (by tossing a coin or a die) or have these choices computerized. In many cases, experimenters have one of the subjects serve as a "monitor" who then makes the choices of nature (by tossing a coin or a die) without discretion. Having one of the subjects make nature's choices may increase the credibility of the randomness of the choices of nature to the other subjects. Battaglini et al. use both approaches – some of nature's choices are made by the computer and others are made by a subject serving as a monitor. The monitor is then typically paid a flat fee for his or her participation, roughly equivalent to the average payment made to the other subjects.

What about candidates and partisans? Because candidates do not make decisions in the model, and their behavior is not part of the predictions of the model, the experimenter may choose to make their choices exogenous by using artificial actors to represent their choices, simply telling the subjects who are voters that they are choosing between two candidates. Similarly, although partisans do make choices in the model (choosing how to vote), the assumptions of the model are such that they should trivially always vote their partisan preferences and hence an experimenter may also want to have artificial actors as representing their choices, simply telling the subjects that (if the experiment is conducted via a computer network) the computer has a set of votes that the computer will always cast for candidate 0 or candidate 1 or both in a particular distribution. Also, the choices made by informed independents are as well boring. After all, they are given information on the true state of the world through their signals and thus have only a trivial voting choice. Clearly, one could argue that a human subject assigned the role as a partisan or as an informed independent may find the situation boring if the theoretical predictions hold and she has an obvious voting choice.

However, by filling these roles with artificial actors, the experimenter may find that the subjects who are partisans or uninformed independent voters may choose differently than they would if these roles were filled with other human subjects. Subjects may have feelings of altruism or other motivations that affect their choices when interacting with other humans, which is not the case when interacting with artificial actors. McCabe et al. (2001) studied brain activation of 12 subjects who played games with both a computer and with another subject. Based on choices of the subjects, 5 of the 12 subjects were labeled cooperators while 5 were labeled noncooperators. They found that the prefrontal regions of the brains of cooperators were more active when they were playing a human than when they were playing a computer following a fixed (and known) probabilistic strategy. However, they found that, of the five noncooperators, there were no significant differences in prefrontal activity in the two situations. Hence, it is not obvious whether using artificial actors for candidates and partisans is ideal. Moreover, if we are interested in the comparison of how voter behavior changes when a voter is informed versus uninformed, then if we did not assign subjects to the roles of informed independents we would not be comparing human behavior when uninformed with human behavior when informed in the experiment.

How did Battaglini, Morton, and Palfrey handle this question? They made the candidates and partisans artificial actors. But subjects played the roles of informed independent voters so that Battaglini et al. could compare the behavior of the subjects, both informed and uninformed.

Which Human Subjects to Use? Coupled with the question about which roles should be assigned to human subjects, an experimenter also faces a decision of which human subjects to recruit; that is, from which target population should the subjects for the experiment be drawn? Because this is a fundamental question for a lot of experimental research, we address it extensively on its own in Chapter 9. Here we focus on the answer to this question for the Feddersen and Pesendorfer theory. There are two potential answers. First, from one perspective the theory is one of how individuals vote in an election. Thus, the population that is the subject of the theory includes essentially all citizens with the right to vote in an election. This suggests that drawing subjects from any target population of eligible voters in an election, maybe not even in the same election, would be a sample of subjects addressed by the theory. Second, as noted later, the mathematical constructs of the theory are quite general and could be applied to other collective choice situations that are similar in which any human might conceivably participate. Thus, from this viewpoint, the theory applies to any target population from which the researcher wishes to draw subjects.

Battaglini, Morton, and Palfrey drew subjects from the undergraduate student populations at Princeton University and New York University. This target population fits either perspective about the application of the theory because the students are of eligible voting age. We discuss the advantages and disadvantages of using students for experiments in Chapter 9. We also discuss game-theoretic models in which one may argue that the theoretical target population should be nonstudents and what we can learn from such experiments when conducted with students.

Numbers of Subjects. Other choices in re-creating the political environment can also involve difficulties for an experimenter. Feddersen and Pesendorfer assume that the number of voters is a random draw and then the number of partisans and independents are randomly drawn as well. How can an experimenter reproduce this assumption in the laboratory? The experimenter would need to bring in $N + 1$ subjects but then for each make an independent draw whether the subject would participate in the experiment or not, presumably sending home subjects not chosen to participate. But the experimenter would have to keep secret the number of subjects drawn from the subjects who are chosen because the theory assumes that the voters do not know the total number of voters. If the experiment is conducted over computer terminals in a laboratory, it is hard to imagine how the experimenter might maintain such secrecy or be able to be prepared to have the correctly sized laboratory for the experiment. Following the theoretical assumptions about the environment to the letter would be difficult, but probably not impossible, for the experimenter.

Furthermore, many of the theoretical results concern the behavior of voters as the number of potential voters approaches infinity. But obviously in the laboratory the number of potential voters must necessarily be finite. How did Battaglini, Morton, and Palfrey deal with this problem? They used a finite number of independent voters – 7 in some sessions, 17 and 21 in others – but randomly chose which of the independents would be informed. However, because Feddersen and Pesendorfer's theory had been solved for the case where the number of voters was randomly drawn and the predictions were for limit cases as the number of potential voters approached infinity, Battaglini et al.'s experimental design with seven voters required them to prove that the same predictions held for the finite case in which the total number of voters is fixed. Battaglini et al. demonstrated that the predictions did indeed hold for the finite case examined in the experiments.

Of course, Feddersen and Pesendorfer's theory is presented as an applied theory of large elections. Certainly it is difficult to argue that elections even with 21 voters are large in a comparative sense to naturally occurring elections. Why conduct small-sized experiments of such a theory? The simple reason is cost; managing a laboratory experiment with a large number of subjects is difficult and if we move outside the laboratory the researcher loses substantial control over the manipulations administered to subjects. Furthermore, small-scale election experiments have a value in themselves. As noted earlier, the theory is a general theory of how individuals behave in a given collective choice situation that applies to both small and large electorates (as reformulated by Battaglini et al.). The experiments with small-sized electorates provide us with a test of the general theory and its predictions that are valuable. One may argue that the experiments are a strong test of the theory – that a failure of the theory's predictions in such a context would mean more than a failure of the theory in a large-sized electorate.

Dealing with the Primitives of the Model

Motivating Subjects: Should Subjects Be Told What to Choose? As noted earlier, the primitives of the model are the assumptions about the preferences of the voters and the characteristics of the institutions in the environment. The characteristics of the institution in the model are simple to operationalize in the experiment because the researcher simply conducts an election in which the voters can choose to vote for candidate 1, candidate 0, or abstain. The winner is the candidate receiving the majority of votes and ties are broken randomly.

Preference assumptions, however, are more complicated to operationalize. The model assumes that independent voters prefer to select candidate 0 in state of the world 0 and candidate 1 in state of the world 1 and that partisans always prefer their copartisan candidates. In most cases, the experimenter would like to induce subjects to have the same preferences over outcomes as assumed in the theory but at the same time not hardwire the subjects into making predicted choices to meet these goals because it is the subjects' behavior that the experimenter wants to study. The experimenter wants to motivate the subjects, if assigned as independents, to prefer to have elected candidates who match the state of the world and, if assigned as partisans, to prefer to have elected candidates who have the same partisan identities, but at the same time not tell the subjects what choices to make in the experiment.

However, in some cases subjects may be given detailed advice on what choices may work for them, depending on the question of interest to the researcher. If the researcher is focusing on the choices of some subjects given the behavior of others, they may add the extra motivation of advice to make sure that the other subjects behave as predicted. So, for example, the researcher may want to use human subjects as partisans in the experiment on Feddersen and Pesendorfer's model so that other subjects view these individuals as humans but want to be sure that as partisans they vote as predicted and thus may advise them on how to vote. Sometimes response to advice is what the researcher is interested in studying. The researcher may be interested in whether subjects pay attention to the advice or whether the advice is a motivating factor in itself. Experiments by Andrew Schotter and colleagues (Chaudhuri et al., 2009; Iyengar and Schotter, 2008; Nyarko et al., 2006; Schotter and Sopher, 2003, 2006, 2007) have focused on how subjects use advice in various economics situations.

Another reason why an experimenter may give subjects advice or tell them how to choose is to evaluate the extent that subjects understand the situation in the experiment. In Example 6.2, Chou et al. (2009) investigate how hints affect the choices of subjects as a way of evaluating whether subjects understand the experiment fully. They also manipulated aspects of the framing, which we turn to later in this chapter.

Usually experimenters working with formal models use financial incentives to motivate subjects. That is, they pay the subjects based on the outcomes so that the payoffs have the same ordering as the preferences assumed in the theory. Battaglini, Morton, and Palfrey paid independent voters $0.80 if the majority voted for candidate 0 in state 0 and candidate 1 in state 1 in a period and $0.05 if not. The presumption is that the subjects would be motivated by the financial incentives and they would be induced to have the same preferences as assumed by the theory. Is this presumption accurate? Are financial incentives a good way to motivate subjects? In Chapter 10 we explore expansively the advantages and disadvantages of using financial incentives to motivate subjects.

Dealing with Infinitely Repeated Games. The Swing Voter's Curse is a model of a one-shot game – a game played for one period only. However, many situations in politics (including elections) are situations in which people are placed repeatedly. If the game is repeated and has a known end, then it is relatively easy to design an experiment that captures this feature of the game. But in many cases repeated interactions may not have a known end. In game theory, such games are called infinitely repeated games. The name is a bit of a misnomer, because the games are unlikely to be infinitely repeated, but at each period subjects do not know exactly how long the game will continue. These situations abound in politics; for instance, we may think of party competition as such a game with an indefinite end.

How can such games be operationalized in the laboratory? One solution is to simply not tell subjects when the game will end. However, as Roth and Murnighan (1978) point out, it is apparent to subjects that the game must eventually terminate and that subjects must form their own probabilities about whether a given period is to be the last. These subjective probabilities can significantly affect the nature of the equilibrium outcome in many games. For example, subjects may be more likely to cooperate in a game that they expect with high probability to continue. A better solution is for the experimenter to randomly determine whether the game ends after completing each round using a probability that is known to the subjects. Dal Bó, in Example 6.1, uses such a procedure, in which one subject who is randomly chosen to be the monitor tosses a fair die to determine whether the game ends after each round. In this fashion, an experimenter can induce common subjective probabilities about whether the game will continue and control and manipulate that probability as Dal Bo does in his experiment.

Example 6.1 (Lab Experiment on Infinitely Repeated Prisoner's Dilemma Games): *Dal Bo (2005) reports on a laboratory experiment that compares levels of cooperation in infinitely repeated and finitely repeated prisoner's dilemma (PD) games.*

Target Population and Sample: Dal Bo recruited 398 UCLA undergraduates through advertisements on university Web pages and signs posted on campus. Dal Bo reports that 22.31% of the subjects indicated that they were majoring in economics.

Subject Compensation: During the experiment, subjects earned points that were converted into dollars at the exchange rate of 200 points to $1 and the subjects were paid privately at the end of the experiment in cash. Subjects earned an average of $18.94 with a maximum of $25.85 and a minimum of $12. Subjects also received a $5 show-up fee.

Environment: As in Example 2.6, the experiment was conducted via a computer network.

Procedures: The experiment was conducted in eight separate sessions with an average of 48.75 subjects per session with a maximum of 60 and a minimum of 30. Dal Bo reported the times and dates of the sessions, which were held in the afternoons and were in November, February, and April. Each session lasted approximately an hour including the time for instructions. In each session of the experiment, subjects were divided into two groups: red and blue. Subjects then played a game in a series of matches. In each match, every red subject was paired with a blue subject. They then played either PD Game 1 or PD Game 2 for a number of rounds (explained below) as given by the following payoff matrices:

PD Game 1				PD Game 2			
		Blue Player				Blue Player	
		L	R			L	R
Red	U	65, 65	10, 100	Red	U	75, 75	10, 100
Player	D	100, 10	35, 35	Player	D	100, 10	45, 45

The subjects assigned as red players chose either U or D and the subjects assigned as blue players chose either L or R, simultaneously. The first number in each cell is the payoff for the red player, and the second number is the payoff for the blue player. The PD game used was the same in a session, that is, in comparing PD games, Dal Bo used a between-subjects design (see Section 3.3.3).

Dice Sessions: Dal Bo also varied whether the game was played for a finite number of rounds within a match or if the number of rounds within a match could go on indefinitely. Half of the sessions used the indefinite end to the rounds. To allow for the games to possibly go on indefinitely, Dal Bo used a random continuation rule in half of the sessions, which he called the Dice sessions. Dal Bo had one of the subjects randomly selected as a monitor who publicly rolled a four-sided die after each round. He used two different probabilities of continuing the game, one in which the probability was 1/2 and the other in which the probability was 3/4. He also had the same subjects play a one-shot version of the game (i.e., with a probability of continuance of 0). In one session the sequence of the manipulations in the probability of continuance was 0, 1/2, and 3/4 and in the other session the order was reversed. Thus, he used a within-subjects design to compare the manipulations of the continuance and a between-subjects design to compare the effects of sequencing (see Section 3.3.3).

Finite Round Sessions: In the other half of the sessions, Dal Bo had subjects in each match always play a fixed number of rounds: one manipulation with just one round (a one-shot version of the game), a second manipulation with two rounds, and a third manipulation with four rounds. The number of rounds for these manipulations corresponds to the expected number of rounds in the random continuation treatment. As in the dice sessions, in one session the sequence of the manipulations in the number of rounds was 0, 2, and 4, and in the other session the order was reversed.

Matchings: Subjects were not paired with each other in more than one match and the pairings were set up so that the decisions one subject made in one match could not affect the decision of subjects he or she would meet in the future. This was explained to subjects. Given the matching procedures, the total number of matches in a session was N/2, where N was the number of subjects in a session. There were then N/6 rounds per manipulation within a session (either of the probability of continuance in the dice sessions or the number of rounds in the finite round sessions).

Public Randomization Device: "Every ten seconds a random number between 1 and 1,000 was displayed on a screen at the front of the room. Subjects were told that they could use this number to select one of the actions if they wanted." Dal Bo used this device because it is typically assumed in the theory of such games that subjects may use such devices to coordinate actions and rotate through different outcomes.

Results: Dal Bo found strong evidence that the higher the probability of continuation, the higher the levels of cooperation. Furthermore, he found that the level of cooperation in the final round of the finitely repeated games was similar to the level of cooperation in the one-shot games, and that these levels were lower than those observed in the dice games. In the first round of the games, there were greater levels of cooperation in the dice games than in the first round of the finitely repeated games of the same expected length. Dal Bo found greater evidence of cooperative behavior in PD Game 2 and that, although economics majors tended to cooperate less in one-shot and finitely repeated games, their behavior was not significantly different from that of other students in the dice games. Finally, Dal Bo found no evidence that subjects paid attention to the public randomization device.

Comments: Dal Bo's careful procedures in matching the subjects prevent supergame effects that may interfere with the effects of the manipulations. His comparison of behavior in the dice games with behavior in finite games of the same expected length is also innovative and provides important new information on the effects of indefinite endings to exchange with known finite endings to exchange on cooperative behavior.

Of course, as Dal Bo remarks (footnote 15, p. 1596): "It could be argued that the subjects understand that the experiment cannot go on forever and will end at some point. Therefore the subjects' belief in the possibility of future interactions may depend not only on the roll of the die." How useful then are these representations of infinitely repeated games in the laboratory and how much control does the experimenter have over subjects' beliefs about the likelihood that the game will end? We find Dal Bo's justification in the footnote persuasive:

> The subjects' real discount factor may have two components: one component determined by the roll of the die, and another subjective component which incorporates subjects' belief regarding the experimenter ending the experiment. (Given that subjects were paid at the end of the experiment and that there is a very short span of time between rounds, I disregard the temporal preference component of the discount factor.) It is important to note that if the subjective component is not very sensitive to changes in the random continuation rule, increases in the probability of continuation must result in increases in subjects' expectation of future interaction. Thus, by changing [the continuation rate], I affect the subjects' belief on the possibility of future interactions. In their experiments, Murnighan and Roth (1983) elicited their subjects' beliefs about continuation probabilities. They found that subjects' estimates that there would be at least two more rounds increased strongly with the probability of continuation.

Choosing and Manipulating the Exogenous Variables

Random-Assignment, and Within- and Between-Subjects Comparisons. The primary exogenous variables in the Swing Voter's Curse model are the numbers of partisans, the probability of being informed, and the ex ante probability that the true state is state 0 (i.e., α). The theory predicts that, as the probability of being informed increases, abstention should decline and the margin of victory should increase. The theory also predicts that when one of the candidates has a partisan advantage, the uninformed voters should be more likely to vote for the candidate with the partisan disadvantage. And finally the theory predicts that uninformed voters should vote to offset the partisan advantage even when it means voting contrary to their ex ante priors as to which would be the best candidate. Therefore, ideally the experimenter wishes to manipulate these exogenous variables to test these predictions: manipulating the probability of being informed, manipulating the partisan advantages of candidates, and manipulating the ex ante priors of uninformed voters. Ideally, the researcher also would like to create an experimental design in which these manipulations allow for within-subjects comparisons or between-subjects coupled with random assignment to manipulations.

What did Battaglini, Morton, and Palfrey do? They did not manipulate the probability of being informed but used a fixed probability of being informed (25%) for all sessions. Battaglini et al. did manipulate the partisan advantage, using partisan advantages of 0, 2, and 4 in the 7-voter experiments and 0,

6, and 12 in the 17- and 21-voter experiments. They also manipulated the ex ante prior, setting $\alpha = 1/2$ in some sessions and 4/9 in others. Note that because Battaglini et al. used a modified version of the Feddersen and Pesendorfer model, they first proved that, using these parameters, the predictions of Feddersen and Pesendorfer held with a finite number of voters.

Battaglini, Morton, and Palfrey also used random assignment and both within- and between-subjects comparisons of the effects of their manipulations. That is, using the 25% probability of being informed, each period subjects were randomly assigned as informed and uninformed. Because the same subjects made choices under both situations, Battaglini et al. could make use of within-subjects comparisons of the effects of information on voting choices using their crossover design. Similarly, all subjects in a session experienced all the manipulations of the number of partisans, allowing for within-subjects comparisons of these effects using a crossover design, although comparing different sequences of these manipulations required using a between-subjects design (see Section 3.3.3). The values of the ex ante prior were the same in a session, but subjects for both types of sessions were drawn from the same subject pool. See Section 5.3.1 for a discussion of the issues involved in such procedures.

Why did Battaglini, Morton, and Palfrey choose to use a within-subjects design to compare the effect of changing partisans but not for comparing the change in the ex ante prior? Certainly an alternative design could have been conducted the opposite way, keeping the number of partisans fixed in a session and varying the ex ante prior or perhaps varying both within a session. Varying both in a session may make the session too long and perhaps too complicated for subjects. Thus, it may be easier to conduct the experiment with only one of these varied as Battaglini, Morton, and Palfrey did. Arguably, the theory suggests that the ex ante prior should have little effect on behavior and thus it is unlikely that we would observe differences in behavior for different priors so one may think that it is better to vary partisan numbers within a session, which are predicted to have an effect if one must make a choice. That said, sometimes when a change in a manipulated variable occurs in the course of an experiment – when the experimenter announces as Battaglini, Morton, and Palfrey did that now there are four partisans and before there were zero – subjects may change behavior because they sense they are expected to and change more than they would if they had made choices with the new value of the variable without previous experience with an old value of the variable. Battaglini et al.'s comparison of different sequences of manipulations helps to control for these possible effects. These effects are sometimes called experimental effects and are discussed more expansively in Section 8.4.1.

Choosing the Parameters of the Experiment. As we have noted, Battaglini, Morton, and Palfrey chose not only what parameters to manipulate but also the values of the parameters. Why, for example, did they choose to use $\alpha = 1/2$ and 4/9 instead of some other possibilities? When $\alpha = 1/2$, then uninformed voters believe that each state of the world is equally likely and thus, when there are no partisans, abstaining makes sense for voters who do not take into account the probability of being pivotal and the implications of that probability. But if α is not equal to 1/2, then uninformed voters believe that one of the states of the world is more likely than the other, they have some prior information, and if they do not take into account the probability of being pivotal, they may vote that information. Thus, it is valuable to compare these probabilities. Moreover, when the number of partisans increases, for some values of α less than 1/2, but not all, uninformed voters should vote with some probability to counter the votes of the partisans, which is the counterintuitive result of the Swing Voter's Curse model. Hence, Battaglini, Morton, and Palfrey chose a value of α that was less than 1/2, but not too small so that they could evaluate this particular prediction of the swing voter's curse model. To choose the parameters, they needed to first compute the equilibrium predictions for the values of possible parameters and to be sure that the parameters that they chose evaluated adequately the theoretical predictions.

Dal Bo, in Example 6.1, chose parameters of the PD games to test the sensitivity of behavior to small payoff differences that result in large differences in theoretical predictions. That is, the equilibrium where each player cooperates (red chooses U and blue chooses L) is an equilibrium in PD Game 2 but not in PD Game 1 when the continuation probability is 0.5. Similarly, UR and LD are equilibria in PD Game 1 but not in PD Game 2 when the continuation probability is 0.5. Thus, Dal Bo could investigate the sensitivity of cooperative behavior to payoff differences, finding that indeed subjects were more cooperative in PD Game 2.

The Decision Variables and Framing the Experiment

Neutral or Political Context? The ultimate goal of the experiment on the Swing Voter's Curse is to study how the subjects choose in the election. The subjects' choices are whether to vote for candidate 0, vote for candidate 1, or abstain. But how should this choice be presented to subjects? In laboratory experiments subjects are typically given instructions that describe the choices that they will make in the experiment. Sometimes these instructions can be quite detailed when subjects participate in a game-theoretic experiment. Experimenters have a choice on how to frame the instructions: whether to frame them in terms of the political context, calling the choices before the voters candidates and the voting an election, or whether to frame the instructions in nonpolitical terms. Although the theory is explicitly about elections, the mathematical constructs of the theory are general and apply to any situation in which individuals are making collective choices by majority rule under similar circumstances, as we have already pointed out. Sometimes an experimenter may choose a neutral frame in an effort to appeal to the generality of the theory. Alternatively, others may use a political frame because they believe doing so increases the ecological validity or mundane realism of the results, concepts we discuss in Section 7.3.1.

Battaglini, Morton, and Palfrey used a nonpolitical frame for their experiments. In the experiments, subjects guess the color of balls in jars and are rewarded if the majority of the guesses are correct. Other experimenters using FTA have used a political context as in Example 2.7. Both Levine and Palfrey (2005) and Aragones and Palfrey (2004) conducted experiments evaluating two models of electoral processes; Levine and Palfrey study turnout and Aragones and Palfrey study a candidate location game, with both nonpolitical and political context frames. They found that the frame differences did not affect the subjects' choices in these experiments.

Presentations and Recognizing the Game Form. Nevertheless, in other types of experiments, frames can matter to motivate subjects to have the same preferences as those assumed in the theory. For example, Stahl and Haruvy (2008) reported on experiments on the ultimatum game (see Section 3.3.3) in which the game is presented as an abstract game tree instead of the simple verbal description that is typically used. They found in this case that the majority of behavior is consistent with individualistic preferences and subgame perfection in contrast to what is observed when the experiments are conducted using the verbal explanation. They argue that the verbal description suggests to subjects that they are in a social situation, whereas the game-tree representation reduces the tendency of subjects to see the game in a social context. They remark: "If one is asking how well game theory predicts the behavior in the abstract ultimatum game, then it is vital that the experimenter induce the payoff structure of that game. Our results show that the game-tree representation significantly reduces the unintended social context." Hence, they contend that a theory test of the ultimatum game is best conducted using the game-tree presentation.[4]

A similar example of how the presentation of instructions can matter in theory tests is found in Example 6.2. As noted earlier, Chou et al. (2009) investigate how hints and framing of the experiment affect the choices of subjects in a two-person "guessing game" that has been commonly called the beauty contest game. The game is similar to newspaper beauty contests that were conducted in Keynes's time and remarked by him as being similar to professional investment activity (see Keynes, 1936, p. 156). In the newspaper contests, readers were asked to choose the six prettiest faces from among 100 photographs, with the winner being the person whose preferences were closest to the average preferences. Nagel (1995) studied a multiperson version of the game in which subjects were told to choose a number between 0 and 100 inclusive, where the number closest to p times the mean of the responses would win a fixed prize with ties divided equally among the winners and losers receiving 0. If $0 \leq p < 1$, then there exists only one Nash equilibrium: all players announce zero. Following Costa-Gomes and Crawford (2006), we label p as the target and 0 and 100 as the lower and upper limits in the game. Grosskopf and Nagel (2008) conducted an experiment on a two-person version of the game and found significant evidence that subjects failed to choose even close to the Nash equilibrium prediction.

Example 6.2 (Guessing Game Lab Experiment): *Chou et al. (2009), hereafter Chou et al., reported on an experiment involving the effects of framing on choices in a two-person guessing game or beauty contest game.*

Target Population and Sample: Chou et al. recruited 49 subjects from the subject pool at Caltech and 179 students from a nearby community college. The subjects from the community college were recruited from economics classes with a brief introduction of the experimenters by the instructor and had no prior exposure to game theory.

---

[4] Another interesting comparison of the presentation of games to subjects is provided by Cooper and Van Huyck (2003), where they compared subjects' choices in eight two-player games when the games were presented in normal form versus extensive form (with varying information on previous subjects' choices). The games were solvable via subgame perfection and such that a choice by the first subject could end the game without a move by the second subject. They found significant differences in the choices of subjects that can be explained by the differences in presentation. They argued that the differences arise because subjects in the extensive form appear to allow the other player to make a meaningful choice.

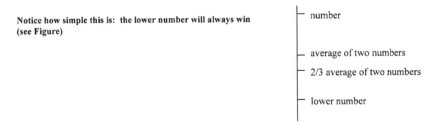

Notice how simple this is: the lower number will always win (see Figure)

- number
- average of two numbers
- 2/3 average of two numbers
- lower number

Figure 6.1. Hint Shown to Subjects in the Chou et al. Experiment.

Subject Compensation: *Subjects were paid based on their choices in the game as described in the procedures. Whether subjects received a show-up fee was not reported by the researchers.*

Environment: *The community college experiments were conducted during class time and apparently in the class rooms. Since the Caltech experiments used the standard Caltech subject pool, presumably these experiments were conducted in a laboratory. The experiments were not computerized. The experiments were conducted in November and January at Caltech and in February, March, and April at the community college.*

Procedures: *Subjects were recruited to play in a one-shot two-person guessing game. Each subject was told to guess a number between 0 and 100, inclusive. The two numbers were averaged together and the person whose number was closest to p times the average would receive $8. In the case of a tie, each would receive $4; the loser would receive $0. Chou et al. used two values of p, 2/3 and 3/4. They also varied whether subjects were given a "hint" on how to play the game. In the hint, subjects were notified in bold font "Notice how simple this is: the lower number will always win." In some of the sessions with the hint, subjects were also shown a simple figure to help them to calculate, as shown in Figure 6.1.*

The researchers varied the style of the instructions – comparing simpler instructions presented as bullet points rather than as a paragraph, whether the instructions had official Caltech letterhead, and whether they showed subjects the cash they would earn after the experiment. The experimenters also surveyed subjects at the community college who completed the standard version of the game.

Finally, the experimenters also gave some subjects a version of the game called Battle before giving them the standard game (either immediately before or a few weeks before). The instructions for Battle are shown in Figure 6.2.

Results: *Chou et al. found that the hint significantly increased the probability that subjects from Caltech chose as predicted by game theory but had no*

CALIFORNIA   INSTITUTE   OF   TECHNOLOGY

You have been chosen to play a simple strategic game. This
game is a small part of a larger project, so your performance will
not be scrutinized or manipulated. Please think strategically
about the scenario below.

C A L T E C H

Setting of the Game:

- Imagine yourself at war facing an opponent in a battle on a hill

- Both you are your opponent (a random person from this room) must locate yourselves
  on the hill

- The hill is 100 feet high

Instruction to the Game:

- Your job is to choose how high to locate your troop on the hill, from 0 feet high to 100
  feet high (both heights included).

- You win the battle if your chosen location is higher than your opponent's.

Winning Rule:

- If your location is higher than your opponent's, you will win $8 cash at the end of class
  today. If you choose the same location as your opponent, you will receive $4.

  You have five minutes to think about your answer. Write your location in the space
  below.

  LOCATION CHOSEN _____(please enter one number here)
  Group ID _____
  My Name & ID Number_____

  Please write down your motives for choosing your number on the back of the
  instructions.

Figure 6.2. Battle Version of the Guessing Game.

*effect on the choices of subjects from the community college. Simplifying the
game with bullet points and having subjects participate in the Battle version
significantly increased the probability that the community college subjects chose
as game theory predicts. Providing these subjects with hints in addition to the
simplified version after the Battle game also had a significant effect.*

Comments: *The experimenters contend that their results suggest that the
subjects did not "recognize" the game form in the standard presentation of the
guessing game and that the earlier experimental results overstate the inability
of game theory to explain behavior.*

Chou et al. compared how subjects drawn from Caltech and a local community college chose when they were provided the "hint" than when they did not. They found that the hint significantly increased the probability that subjects from Caltech chose as predicted by game theory, but it had no effect on the choices of subjects from the community college. However, other changes in the presentation and framing of the game, in response to results from a post-experiment survey, increased the probability that subjects from the community college chose the game-theoretic prediction. The found that a simplified presentation of the game using bullet points and bold coupled with the hint significantly increased the likelihood that subjects at the community college chose the game-theoretic prediction. They further discovered that when the game was presented as a battle in which the winner was the subject who picked the number closest to 100, the community college students chose as game theory predicted significantly more. Finally, they found that when subjects from the community college first played the Battle game and then the simplified version of the beauty contest game, the subjects were significantly more likely to choose according to the game-theoretic predictions in the beauty contest game.

However, questionnaire responses after the Battle game suggested that the presentation of the game in that form introduced new problems with experimental control. For instance, three subjects said they chose 50 in the battle game because it increased mobility or it was high enough to win the battle but the troop would not get tired on the way to the top, another subject chose 99 because if he or she won the battle, he or she would need to have 1 foot to put his or her flag, and a fifth chose 0 because there is no oxygen at the peak of the hill.

Chou et al. argue that the evidence from the impact of the hint on Caltech students and the framing changes on the community college students suggests that the rejection of game theory reported by previous theory testing guessing game experiments resulted from a loss of experimental control. They contend that (p. 175)

[i]f the purpose of the experiment is to test predictions of game theory, then the initial abstract instructions contain a "bug." Participants do not understand the game form and therefore a crucial assumption for solution concepts is violated. Recognition of the game form is a necessary condition for the testing of game theory. If subjects do not understand the game form, then it is unclear what behavior game theory predicts. From the point of view of game theory, one does not know what experiment is conducted. Since game form recognition is a necessary condition for the theory, its absence in an experiment reflects a lack of experimental control.

What can we conclude from the experiments of Stahl and Haruvy and Chou et al. on the effects of presentation of an experiment? Chou et al. suggested that subjects use a "recognition heuristic," following Goldstein and Gigerenzer (2002). They assert that "[s]ubjects formulate their understanding of an environment through recognition of similarities between environments. Thus, when the game is presented in the context of a battle, subjects immediately recognize the elements of the game form due to the prominence of those elements in games (sports, contests, competitions, etc.) with which they have had either experience or some sort of education (books, advisors, etc.)." The job then of a researcher in conducting an experiment where the purpose is to evaluate game theory in a theory test is to present the experiment in such a way to increase the probability that the subjects recognize the game form. Chou et al. drew the following conclusions for experimenters in designing instructions (p. 177):

(i) Post experiment questionnaires can be useful tools in helping the experimenter understand the subjects' problems. (ii) Clearly written, short instructions help but there is no guarantee that it is enough to facilitate the recognition of the game form. (iii) Subjects' ability to recognize the game form can differ from subject pool to subject pool.... This means that each subject pool might require slightly different instructions or procedures. (iv) Making the game less abstract helps with game form recognition, but it may introduce other sources of loss of control. When contextually rich instructions are used, it might be important to inform the subject that the less abstract features are included to help with the understanding and should not be taken literally.

Presentations, Stress Tests, and Political Versus Nonpolitical Frames. Of course, the goal of the experiment might be, as in the case of the work of Stahl and Haruvy and Chou et al., to investigate how much subjects "recognize" a game and the effects of different presentations of the game form. In that case, the researcher is conducting a stress test of the theory. Both Stahl and Haruvy and Chou et al. point out that their conclusions about the importance of presentation in the ultimatum and guessing games, respectively, apply only when the purpose of the experiment is to engage in a theory test. Stahl and Haruvy state (pp. 293–294):

Our results do not imply that the game-tree presentation is the only proper experimental design for the ultimatum game.... [I]f one is asking how people behave in a socially rich context of dividing a pie that activates social norms and social judgments, then obviously a context-sparse game-tree presentation would be inappropriate.

And Chou et al. remark (pp. 175–176):

[I]f the purpose of the experiment is something other than a test of game theory then the lack of recognition could be a desirable "feature." The "empirical approach" or "data first" approach in which the experimenter creates phenomena and examines a "contest" between models to determine which is more accurate (and why) has been one of the most powerful tools available for use in experimental economics since its beginning. Frequently, models work where they have no "right" to work. The models work when many of the assumptions of the theory are not satisfied, e.g. the competitive model works in the double auction with disequilibrium trades and with small numbers of agents operating under imperfect information.

We can think of the experiments of Aragones and Palfrey and Levine and Palfrey, in which the researchers compared the behavior of subjects under the neutral or objective presentation of the game with the behavior of subjects using a political context as stress tests if we think that game form recognition is affected by presentation of the game to the subjects. The fact that they found that the context does not significantly affect behavior demonstrates that game form recognition for their subjects is not affected by the presentation. We believe that more such stress tests, comparing different types of presentations, would be valuable in political science, and we turn to these again in Chapter 7 when we discuss establishing the validity of experimental results.

The Equilibrium Concept and the Experimental Design
Repetition of One-Shot Games with Randomization
How Repetition with Randomization Works. The predictions of Feddersen and Pesendorfer come from solving the game for the symmetric Bayesian–Nash equilibrium. The game is a one-shot game; that is, the actors make choices in a single election and then the game is over. This is also true for the predictions that arise from the modified version of the game that Battaglini, Morton, and Palfrey constructed and used in their experiments. Yet, in conducting their experiment, Battaglini et al. had the subjects play the game repeatedly, randomizing the role assignments (informed and uninformed) each period. In each subsession with a given ex ante probability and number of partisans, subjects participated in 10 repetitions of the one-shot game. In five of the sessions with only 7 voters, 14 subjects participated and in each period they were randomly assigned into two groups of 7 so that from period to period the subjects were in different groups in expectation. Dal Bo in Example 6.1 also had subjects engage in the finitely repeated and infinitely repeated prisoner's dilemma games repeatedly, but matched with different partners. Dasgupta and Williams similarly used repetition in Example 2.7.

Many political scientists who conduct experiments evaluating a particular one-shot game-theoretic model under a given treatment construct their experiments so that subjects play the one-shot game repeatedly in randomly reassigned groups and roles as in Battaglini et al.'s study. The groups and roles are randomly reconfigured each period to avoid possible repeated game effects; that is, if the game is repeated with players in the same roles and same groups, then there is the possibility that subjects are participating in a larger supergame and the equilibrium predictions of the supergame may be different from those of the one-shot game that the researcher is attempting to evaluate.[5] Dal Bo, as we have seen, went to great lengths to reduce the repeated game effects by having subjects always matched with new players in such a fashion that contamination, even through other players, could not occur.

Following Andreoni (1988), it is common to call matching with new randomly assigned players a "strangers matching" procedure and one in which a subject always plays a game with the same players a "partners matching" procedure. Following convention we call the procedure used by Dal Bo a "perfect strangers matching" procedure. Battaglini, Morton, and Palfrey used strangers matching in five sessions, but they used partners matching in the other sessions because of limitations on the numbers of computers and subjects. However, because each period the subjects were randomly assigned new roles (either informed or uninformed), even though the groups stayed the same, repeated game effects were unlikely and not observed by Battaglini et al.

Definition 6.12 (Strangers Matching): *Game-theoretic experiments in which subjects play a one-shot game with repetition but the other players in the game in each period are new random draws from a larger set of subjects in the experiment.*

Definition 6.13 (Perfect Strangers Matching): *Strangers matching in which researchers make sure that subjects always face a new set of other players and that contamination from previous play is not possible.*

Definition 6.14 (Partners Matching): *Game-theoretic experiments in which subjects play a one-shot game repeatedly with the same players. Subjects may be randomly re-assigned roles each period, however.*

---

[5] Here we do not mean sequential within-subjects experimental designs where subjects make choices in different treatments in sequential periods of an experiment, which we discuss in Section 3.3.3. We describe repetition in which the treatments experienced by the subjects remain constant as the groups and roles are randomized.

Using Repetition with Randomization. But why use repetition at all? Is the attempt merely to gain more observations from the subjects about their behavior given the treatment? Although gaining more observations per subject may be useful in some cases from a statistical standpoint and can help identify particular subject-specific unobservable variables (although there are problems in that the observations may not be independent; see Section 6.5.4), one reason for repetition with randomization between periods is to increase the theoretical relevance of the experiment. Almost all empirical work, both experimental and nonexperimental, that seeks to evaluate game-theoretic predictions compares observed behavior with the predictions as in Battaglini, Morton, and Palfrey's study. Yet, as Fudenberg (2006, p. 700) remarks: "Game theorists have long understood that equilibrium analysis is unlikely to be a good predictor of the outcome the first time people play an unfamiliar game." Many game theorists think of equilibrium choices as the norms of play that have developed as an outcome of repetition with randomization, learning from similar games, information gained from social learning, and other sources.[6] These game theorists think of how people play the model as distinct from how they solve the model. That is, individuals playing a game are assumed not to solve the complex optimization problems that the game theorist solves to derive his or her predictions about their behavior, but to make the equilibrium choices based on the norms of behavior that have evolved through repetition and social learning.

When subjects participate in a game-theoretic experiment that is unlikely to draw on their past experience of similar games or any social or other learning they have prior to the experiment, then if the subjects only play the game for one period and the point is to compare the predictions to equilibrium predictions, the experiment may not be theoretically relevant – an unbiased evaluation of the theory. For this reason, many experimentalists have subjects engage in repetition with randomization so that they can gain the experience that the game-theoretic equilibrium predictions assume the subjects have without the possibility of supergame effects. The experimentalists then often present results from these experiments by period or period groupings to determine if the experience has an effect on subject behavior, leading them to more or less equilibrium-predicted choices.

Do repetition and experience matter? Do subjects who have become experienced through repetition of a particular game make choices that are closer to those predicted by game theorists? The answer is yes: repetition does often lead to choices that are closer to the game-theoretic equilibrium

---

[6] See, for example, the discussion and references in Fudenberg (2006).

predictions in many types of complex game-theoretic situations. Battaglini, Morton, and Palfrey found this was indeed the case in their experiments. Even in some simple games, repetition can increase the likelihood of choosing the game-theoretic equilibrium. For instance, Grooskopf and Nagel (2008) found that subjects learn to play the equilibrium strategies in the two-person guessing game of Example 6.2 in approximately 10 periods if they are told their payoff and the opponent's options after each play. When informed only about their own payoff, convergence still occurs but at a much slower rate.

The Problem of Independence of Observations with Repetition. One criticism of repetition coupled with randomization between all subjects in a session is that the experimentalist is reducing the number of independent observations. For example, suppose a researcher wishes to investigate how 18 subjects choose in a three-player voting game under sequential voting. The researcher wishes to provide the subjects with experience through repetition but plans on randomizing each period so that there are no repeated game effects. If the researcher randomizes between all 18 subjects, then some may argue that the researcher has one observation at the session level. But if the researcher divides the subject pool into two groups of nine subjects each and then randomizes only within each group, then some may argue that the researcher has two observations at the session level. The view is that, even though randomization is used to reduce repeated game effects, repetition with randomization within a session may lead to some session-level effects that should be controlled. Furthermore, dividing the subjects into random subgroups creates an extra level of anonymity between the subjects in the experiment (assuming the experimenter does not reveal to the subjects which subjects are in which subgroup). Of course, another solution is to conduct multiple sessions with smaller numbers of subjects, but this may be more time consuming for the experimentalist and then raises issues of comparability across sessions in terms of the subjects recruited, which we addressed earlier in Section 5.3.1.

When Is Repetition Not Desirable? Is repetition always recommended for game-theoretic experiments? Most experiments using the ultimatum game, for instance see Section 3.3.3, are conducted without repetition to determine how subjects approach such a situation without prior experience or learning. The idea is to acquire a measure of altruism or fairness independent of learning to study other-regarding preferences in such a one-shot situation.

Sometimes the goal of the researcher is to explicitly study a theory of nonequilibrium choices. Chapters 12 and 13 of Camerer, Loewenstein, and Rabin's (2004)*Advances in Behavioral Economics* illustrate studies of behavior in one-shot games without repetition which consider theoretical models of nonequilibrium play. In such a case, then, repetition with randomization is not desirable. Alternatively, sometimes a researcher intends to evaluate the extent to which subjects "solve" games and make choices as if they were game theorists or use some alternative nonrational choice mental process in an experiment. In this case the experimentalist may also choose not to allow for repetition or, in some cases, may have subjects play a game repeatedly or play more than one game in the experiment, but simply not give subjects feedback during the experiment – only after all games have been completed.

In Example 6.2 (Chou et al.), most of the sessions involved non repeated versions of the guessing game so that they could focus on the effects of instructions and presentation of the game on subjects' choices independent of learning effects. Costa-Gomes and Crawford (2006) provide a good example of how to conduct an experiment with multiple observations per subject in a common game but also suppressing learning that can occur with repetition. They conducted an experiment on 16 one-shot guessing games in which they varied the targets and upper and lower limits across the games, the games were presented to the subjects in a random order, the subjects were matching using strangers matching, and, importantly, subjects were not given any feedback between games. Costa-Gomes and Crawford justify their design as follows (pp. 1741–1742):

> To test theories of strategic behavior, an experimental design must identify clearly the games to which subjects are responding. This is usually done by having a "large" subject population repeatedly play a given stage game, with new partners each period to suppress repeated-game effects, viewing the results as responses to the stage game. Such designs allow subjects to learn the structure from experience, which reduces noise; but they make it difficult to disentangle learning from cognition, because even unsophisticated learning may converge to equilibrium in the stage game. Our design, by contrast, seeks to study cognition in its purest form by eliciting subjects' initial responses to 16 different games, with new partners each period and no feedback to suppress repeated-game effects, experience-based learning, and experimentation.

Depending on the theory evaluated, then, sometimes observing how subjects choose in games without repetition is desirable.

Symmetric Equilibrium Predictions. As in many game-theoretic models, Feddersen and Pesendorfer solved for the symmetric equilibrium in the game in which subjects of the same type and the same information use the same strategies. The reason they do this is because in such games there are often many asymmetric equilibria in which subjects of the same type and information use different strategies. Solving for asymmetric equilibria in large voting games is a nearly impossible task, even using modern-day computing technology. Is it reasonable to use symmetric equilibrium predictions as a basis for comparison and as the focus of an experiment?

As of this writing, we know of no work that has investigated the reasonableness of using symmetric equilibrium predictions in either experimental or nonexperimental research (where such predictions are also often the basis for analysis). Certainly evidence suggests that there is a lot of diversity in subject behavior even when subjects are assigned the same manipulations. Battaglini, Morton, and Palfrey found evidence of such diversity. For example, some of the subjects in their experiments always abstained when uninformed and there is a partisan advantage, whereas others always voted for the candidate with the partisan disadvantage, and others use other strategy combinations, sometimes even voting for the candidate with the partisan advantage. The symmetric equilibrium prediction is that uninformed voters will use a mixed strategy in this case, mixing between voting for the candidate with the partisan disadvantage and abstaining. One perspective is that the subjects are not "really" identical in type or information; that is, even subjects who have experienced the same manipulation may be distinctive and, thus, even in a symmetric equilibrium be expected to choose differently. Using this reasoning, the true symmetric equilibrium is an extension of the one used as a theoretical basis. A researcher may solve a version of the model that includes a subject-specific parameter that may be a measure of, say, cognitive ability that means that subjects, as they vary in this parameter, vary in information and then solve for equilibrium predictions that are specific to that parameter's effect on information. In this way a researcher can evaluate whether the apparent asymmetric behavior of the subjects in the experiment can be explained by cognitive ability or some other theoretically driven factor.

Mixed Versus Pure Strategies. Some of Feddersen and Pesendorfer's predictions are that uninformed voters will use mixed strategies. In the Battaglini, Morton, and Palfrey reformulation, it is also true that, when a candidate has a partisan advantage, uninformed voters are expected to use mixed strategies. That is, the uninformed voters are theoretically predicted to place a positive probability on voting for the candidate who has a partisan disadvantage and abstaining. To evaluate these predictions, Battaglini et al.

compared the mean choices of uninformed voters with the mixed-strategy prediction. Yet, as noted earlier, many subjects chose to either always vote or always abstain, not demonstrating any mixing. How should we interpret mixed-strategy predictions in experiments?

What does it mean for an individual to choose a mixed strategy? Theoretically, when an individual chooses a mixed strategy, she is mixing between pure strategies such that the other players in the game are indifferent over their own strategies and vice versa. Actors do not mix necessarily because it is their best response; they mix because they are indifferent and mixing makes other actors indifferent as well. As such some game theorists are uncomfortable with mixed strategies and many find it desirable to find pure-strategy predictions which rely more firmly in a sense on the notion of best response. Yet, in many game-theoretic situations, equilibria only exist in mixed strategies. Moreover, there is some evidence that examination of behavior over a lengthy time period in games (more than 100 repetitions) with only mixed-strategy equilibria, individuals' choices are reconcilable with mixed-strategy predictions as Palacios-Huerta and Volij (2008) argue.[7]

It is our opinion that, in many laboratory experiments, sufficient repetition of a one-shot game is unlikely to be observed to rule out whether subjects are using mixed strategies. Each subsession conducted by Battaglini, Morton, and Palfrey lasted only 10 periods. Given that, for some of the time, subjects are learning the game, then we believe it is not reasonable to conclude that if the repetition had lasted longer, evidence of mixing would or would not have occurred based on the observations of the subjects in a subsession. We think it is reasonable to compare the mean behavior of the subjects to the mixed-strategy predictions. However, we also believe that, when working with a mixed-strategy prediction and the game is simple enough, there is merit in having subjects participate in lengthy repetition of the game to evaluate whether subjects are indeed choosing the predicted mixed strategy.

Multiple Equilibria. Feddersen and Pesendorfer are able to solve for predictions for a unique symmetric Bayesian–Nash equilibrium and Battaglini, Morton, and Palfrey also are able to solve in the reformulated model for unique symmetric equilibrium predictions. But in many cases, researchers work with models in which there are multiple equilibrium predictions, even

---

[7] We discuss their findings further in Example 9.2. Wooders (2008) has challenged their results. Contending that the soccer players' strategies did not fit the mixed-strategy equilibrium predictions.

when researchers have narrowed their analysis to symmetric equilibria. In many voting games there are multiple equilibria in the symmetric case. Voters are assigned to be one of two identities – either orange or green in Bassi, Morton, and William's study (2010, Example 6.3). In this voting game, both types of voters prefer their favored candidate to win; orange voters prefer orange to win and green voters prefer green to win, but their payoffs also depend on how they vote. If orange voters think that green is going to win, they would prefer to vote for green as well, because their payoff would be higher than if they voted for orange. Thus, the voting game has two equilibria in pure symmetric strategies, one in which all voters vote for orange, regardless of type, and the other in which all voters vote for green, regardless of type. Another example of multiple equilibria in voting games occurs in games with abstention and costly voting, but the costs of voting are fixed. Schram and Sonnemans (1996a,b) examine such a voting situation.

Example 6.3 (Lab Experiment on Identities and Incentives in Voting):
Bassi, Morton, and Williams report on a laboratory experiment on the effects of identities and incentives in voting.

Target Population and Sample: Bassi et al. used 60 students recruited from an undergraduate subject pool at Michigan State University.

Subject Compensation: Subjects were paid based on their choices as explained in the following procedures. Subjects earned on average $22.

Environment: The experiment was conducted via computers in an environment similar to that described in Example 2.6.

Procedures: Subjects were divided into groups of five voters. They chose whether to vote for one of two options, labeled green or orange (abstention was not allowed). In each period, subjects were assigned an identity: green or orange. However, draws were not purely random because the computer program's draws were designed to ensure that in each period at least one subject was of each type (that is, the possible combinations were either 4 green and 1 orange, 3 green and 2 orange, 2 green and 3 orange, or 1 green and 4 orange).

Subjects were presented with a payoff matrix of the following form:

	Winning Candidate	
Payoffs to Orange Voters	*Orange*	*Green*
If Vote for Orange	x	$x - y$
If Vote for Green	0	y
Payoffs to Green Voters	*Orange*	*Green*
If Vote for Orange	y	0
If Vote for Green	$x - y$	x

Bassi et al. used three versions of the payoffs:

1. *No-payment manipulation, where $x = y = 0$;*
2. *Low-payment manipulation, where $x = \$1.5$ and $y = \$1$; and*
3. *High-payment manipulation, where $x = \$3$ and $y = \$2$.*

Furthermore, in the no-payment manipulation, subjects were shown the low-payment manipulation payoff matrix and told that they should choose as if they were maximizing those payoffs.

Finally, Bassi et al. also manipulated how much information voters had about the types of other voters. In the complete information manipulation, subjects knew the numbers of voters of each type, and in the incomplete information manipulation, each subject knew his or her own type and the types of two other randomly selected voters.

Bassi et al. used both a within- and between-subjects design in that subjects participated in multiple manipulations, varying the sequence. Each manipulation was repeated for 8 periods with random reassignments of types each period.

Results: Bassi et al. found that subjects were influenced by their assigned identities to vote sincerely for the candidate associated with their identity and that the effect is stronger when voters have less information. Moreover, they found that financial incentives significantly reduced the influence of identity and that higher incentives reduced the effects of identity in the incomplete information manipulation.

Comments: In this voting game, there are multiple equilibria in pure strategies, one in which all voters vote for orange and another in which all voters vote for green. In both equilibria some voters will vote strategically for their second choice. Bassi et al. argue that voters are more likely to coordinate on the equilibrium in which the winner is expected first preference of the majority of voters, which they found supported.

How should an experimenter deal with multiple equilibrium predictions in designing his or her experiment? In some cases, the purpose of the experiment is to study factors that may lead subjects to choose one equilibrium rather than another. For example, Bassi, Morton, and Williams focused on the impact of being in the majority. They posited that subjects will choose to coordinate on the voting equilibrium in which all vote for the candidate who has the majority of supporters. They found that indeed subjects tend to coordinate on this particular equilibrium. When the research question is to find out what factors may cause individuals to coordinate on one type of behavior rather than another, working with an experimental design in which there are multiple equilibria may be desirable.

However, if the research question concerns predictions of behavior that occur in only one equilibrium out of multiple predicted, the experimenters may want to consider mechanisms or aspects of the design that can reduce or simplify the equilibrium predictions. For instance, if the cost of voting is a random variable and voters only know their own cost of voting but not the costs of other voters, it is possible to narrow the equilibrium predictions significantly. Levine and Palfrey (2005) conducted an experiment using random costs of voting and were better able to consider the theory's predictions versus the behavior of the subjects than if the costs of voting had been fixed.

Do FTA Theory Testing Experiments Hardwire Results?

In FTA theory-testing experiments researchers often attempt to build an experimental design as close as possible to the assumptions of the theory. As we have argued, the researcher does so to ensure that the assumptions underlying the empirical analysis are equivalent to those underlying the theoretical predictions. Otherwise, the researcher is not sure that he or she is evaluating the theory because these assumptions could quite possibly be inconsistent with each other. In doing so, is the researcher actually hardwiring the results – ensuring that the results from the experiment will validate the theory to such an extent that the empirical evaluation is meaningless? That is, what do we learn from such experiments?

It is important to remember that in such experiments the subjects are not puppets but real human beings who make real choices. The experimenter attempts to give subjects the same preferences as in the theory and to have subjects choose within the same environment as the theory. But the subjects' choices are their own. Consider, for instance, Example 6.4. Dickson, Hafer, and Landa (2008) conducted an experiment evaluating a game-theoretic model of deliberation in which individuals have incomplete information about their preferences over the choices before them and can engage in communication prior to voting over the choices. According to the rational-choice game-theoretic model, individuals can make inferences based on the information that they hear and information that they do not hear and should choose not to speak in situations where the information provided can send negative signals. However, Dickson et al. found that significant numbers of subjects spoke when it was not rational to do so, engaging in "overspeaking." Even though they had designed the experiment to closely represent the theory as much as possible, a large number of subjects' choices were at variance with the theoretical predictions, providing interesting evidence on the applicability of the theory to understanding deliberation and validating Dickson et al.'s supposition that subjects were less likely to be introspective than standard game theory assumes.

Example 6.4 (Laboratory Experiment on Deliberation): *Dickson, Hafer, and Landa (2008) report on a laboratory experiment evaluating the predictions of a game-theoretic model of deliberation.*

Target Population and Sample: Dickson et al. used 36 subjects drawn from the New York University subject pool for the Center for Experimental Social Sciences (CESS).

Subject Compensation: Subjects were paid based on their choices as described in the procedures. Sessions lasted approximately 90 minutes and on average subjects earned $26.56, including a show-up fee of $7.

Environment: The experiments were conducted at the CESS laboratory using procedures similar to those in Example 2.6.

Procedures: The experiment was conducted in two sessions with 18 subjects in each session. The subjects participated in a deliberation game that was repeated for 30 periods. At the beginning of each period, subjects were randomly matched into groups of three members. In the game, subjects were told that each member of their group was assigned a two-digit "true number." The subjects were told the distribution of possible true numbers and the probabilities of each true number. They were also told one fragment of their true number (either the first or second digit) as well as one fragment of each of the other group members' true numbers (all group members were told the same fragments). Finally they were told that they would soon vote between two of the numbers from the distribution.

Before the voting, each group member chooses whether to "speak" or "listen." If a group member has chosen to speak, then all the group members who have chosen to listen receive the following messages: they receive the fragment of the speaker if the fragment is the same as one the digits of the listener's true number, otherwise they receive the message "foreign fragment" from the speaker. Only group members who have chosen to listen receive these messages and only group members who have chosen to speak can send messages.

After the message stage, then all subjects voted for one of the two numbers (abstention was not allowed). Subjects were paid based on how close the winning number was to their true number. Specifically, they received 80 cents if the winning number was their true number. If the winning number was not their true number, they received 80 cents less 1 cent for each unit of distance between the winning number and their true number.

Dickson et al. identified four possible situations that a subject might face as given by the game-theoretic model they evaluated. The situations vary in whether game theory predicts the subject will speak or listen. In periods 1–12, subjects were assigned to fragment types and distributions such that each subject was exposed three times to each of the four situations to give subjects diverse experience with the entire range of possibilities early in the experiment. In the remaining periods, subjects were exposed to these situations as well, such that all subjects experienced each situation either 7 or 8 times in total.

Results: *Dickson et al. found that subjects were responsive to the strategic incentives of the game, but significant numbers deviated from the Bayesian predictions by "overspeaking" when speech is likelier to alienate than persuade.*

Comments: *Dickson et al. analyzed the data by subject and classified subjects according to a cognitive hierarchy in terms of their ability to make Bayesian inferences.*

Many other examples abound in which researchers have found that subjects choose at variance with the predictions of the formal theories evaluated in theory testing experiments and we do not have the space to provide all of the illustrations of these cases. The recent volume by Camerer (2003) – *Behavioral Game Theory* – and the edited volume – *Advances in Behavioral Game Theory* – provide numerous such examples.

Of course, much debate still exists over the robustness of these results and the value of the alternative theories that have developed which attempt to explain why subjects choose contrary to the predictions. Would learning through repetition, clearer presentations or presentations in different contexts, or stronger incentives result in subjects' choices closer to the predictions of the original formal theories? Which alternative theory is best? These are questions that researchers continue to consider in experiments. We have already explored how some researchers have suggested that failures of theory tests in the ultimatum game and the guessing game are due to presentation and recognition problems that can be corrected with stronger experimental control in this section. If theory tests simply hardwired their results, this extensive and growing literature would not exist.

Control, Random Assignment, and FTA

As we have reviewed the FTA process for theory tests, necessarily we have emphasized the importance of experimental control. Experimental control is the principal method by which the researcher attempts to make the empirical world and assumptions equivalent to the theoretical assumptions. We have discussed how researchers attempt to control the environment, subjects preferences, subjects understanding of the experimental situation, and so on. In many cases we have observed how experimenters also use within-subjects designs, as in Battaglini, Morton, and Palfrey's study, so that they can actually measure how the same subjects choose in different situations, gaining observations that are as close to observing counterfactuals as possible.

But in these experiments researchers also use random assignment in numerous ways to deal with those factors that they cannot control directly, primarily unobservable subject-specific factors. In all of the formal theory experiments we have discussed, subjects are randomly assigned to different manipulations. For example, in Battaglini, Morton, and Palfrey's study, whether a subject is informed or not is randomly determined each period and, under certain assumptions about commonality of the subject pool (see Section 5.3.1), we can think of the different manipulations by session as randomly assigned. Similarly, in Example 6.2, Chou et al. randomly assigned to subjects whether they received the hints in the instructions; in Example 6.3, subjects are randomly assigned identities, information, and whether they are in the majority or minority in a voting group; in Example 6.4, subjects are randomly assigned to different deliberation situations; and in Example 5.2, subjects are randomly assigned to various payoff incentives used by the authors to measure selection effects. Oddly, many assume that random assignment is only a characteristic of field experiments. But as we noted in Section 5.3.1, random assignment is often most easily implemented in the laboratory and almost all experiments from an FTA perspective use random assignment in some fashion to control for unobservable confounding variables.

6.5.5 Designing a Stress Test

Through the example of the Feddersen and Pesendorfer Swing Voter's Curse model and Battaglini, Morton, and Palfrey's experiments we have explored many of the issues a researcher faces in using FTA to estimating causal relationships in a theory test. Battaglini et al. did indeed find that the theoretical relationship predictions of Feddersen and Pesendorfer were supported in their laboratory experiments. In particular, they found that uninformed voters were more likely to abstain than informed voters; as the partisan advantage of one candidate increased, these voters were more likely to vote for the candidate with the partisan disadvantage. Importantly, they found, as predicted, that voters voted for the candidate with the partisan disadvantage even when their ex ante prior information suggested that the candidate with the partisan advantage was the better candidate. Furthermore, they compared the results to several alternative theoretical models as well.

As noted, when Battaglini, Morton, and Palfrey found that the laboratory limited their ability to devise an experiment with a randomly determined set of voters as in the theory, they reformulated the theory and solved for predictions with a finite fixed number of voters. But sometimes a researcher takes a theory and changes some aspect of the theory in the experimental design that is either not expected to change the theoretical predictions or has an unknown effect on the outcomes. Such an experiment is a stress test of the theory. For example, in the Battaglini, Morton, and Palfrey experiment, the subjects were not allowed to communicate with each other prior to voting. Such communication is not allowed in the theoretical setup. Would voters choose differently if they could communicate prior to voting? An experiment that allowed such communication would be a stress test of the theory.[8] Stress tests like these can guide us to build better theories or open up areas that have yet to be explored.

As our quote from Chou et al. noted earlier, many experiments in experimental economics have considered situations in which assumptions are violated to determine if the predictions from the formal theories still hold. One classic FTA experiment in political science by McKelvey and Ordeshook (1984) conducted such a stress test of the theory. In this experiment, the authors evaluated a two-candidate spatial voting game in which candidates knew nothing about the distribution of voter preferences in order to determine if, through learning, the candidates' choices would be drawn to the median voter position. At the time, theories of candidate choices in such a situation were relatively unexplored. Thus, their experiments provided new information about the robustness of the existing theory built on complete information to a situation of incomplete information.

Stress tests can also involve cases in which a researcher varies something that is not supposed to matter but is interested in whether it does or not. We discussed a number of examples of these types of stress tests involving variations in presentations of experiments to subjects earlier such as Aragones and Palfrey's and Palfrey and Levine's comparison of political and nonpolitical frames, Stahl and Haruvy's comparison of game-tree and verbal presentations of the ultimatum game, and Chou et al.'s comparison of various presentations of the two-person guessing game. Bassi et al.'s

---

[8] There are a few theoretical treatments of communication in similar types of voting games, although to our knowledge communication in the Feddersen and Pesendorfer Swing Voter's Curse game has not been explored theoretically.

experiment in Example 6.3 is a stress test on the effects of incentives on how subjects choose.

The beauty of stress tests is that they allow a researcher to carefully manipulate assumptions of a formal theory or aspects of a theory-testing experiment to better understand what assumptions are important in a formal theory or what aspects of an experimental design are significant in determining whether theoretical predictions are supported. By directly confronting how each assumption of the theory relates to the experimental design, the researcher can isolate the effects of particular assumptions of the theory as well as the effects of details of the design on the empirical evaluations. Such a careful understanding of theoretical assumptions is not possible in RCM-based experiments.

6.6 FTA and the Analysis Stage

6.6.1 The Growing Importance of the Analysis Stage

As we have seen, in FTA the design stage is where a lot of the action is involved in carefully considering the relationship between each theoretical assumption and the empirical evaluation in the experiment. In many FTA experiments (and almost all early ones), the analysis stage is simple – a researcher compares mean observations for different manipulations to provide estimates of ATE and sometimes ATE(W), with the strong use of control and random assignment to manipulations allowing such comparisons.

However, increasingly researchers working from FTA are turning to more sophisticated post-experimental statistical analysis. The reasons for this development are twofold. First, there is a growing interest in aspects of the behavior of subjects that are sometimes less easily controlled through experimental design, even in the laboratory. Researchers are exploring, for example, the relationship between subjects' cognitive behavioral differences, the influence of altruism or views of fairness or reciprocity, and how subjects learn and manipulations. Although clever designs can be used to distinguish and identify the effects of manipulations on subject-specific variables (in the deliberation experiment in Example 6.4, Dickson et al. use simple techniques to classify subjects according to different types by examining their choices across manipulations), sometimes more elaborate statistical approaches are needed when distinguishing between various behaviors is not so clear cut. Second, a larger number of FTA experiments are being conducted in the field (principally by economists) where control is less easily maintained and random assignment can be problematic, as we have previously discussed in Chapters 4 and 5, respectively.

Moreover, in FTA on nonexperimental data, the analysis stage is the only stage in which a researcher can attempt to consider explicitly the consistency between the theoretical assumptions and the empirical analysis. Although there are some similarities in the FTA methods used on both experimental and nonexperimental data in the analysis stage, it is useful to first discuss the methods used on experimental data in the analysis stage and then turn to those used on nonexperimental data.

6.6.2 The Analysis Stage and FTA Experiments

Analysis in FTA Versus Analysis in RCM
How is the analysis stage of FTA experiments distinctive from that of RCM-based experiments? The vital difference, again, is how FTA deals with the issue of theoretical consistency. Just as in the design stage, ideally in FTA researchers approach the empirical analysis of the data post-experiment, not just assuming theoretical consistency between the statistical equations estimated but confronting the degree to which the theoretical assumptions are consistent with the statistical analysis. If researchers fail to do this, then they are simply taking an RCM-based approach to the post-experimental analysis and that analysis is assuming theoretical consistency rather than explicitly exploring whether such consistency holds.

Given that in FTA post-experimental analysis the relationship between the theoretical and statistical assumptions are paramount, and that such theoretical assumptions vary depending on the theory evaluated, the statistical approach chosen by researchers in post-experimental analysis often varies with the theory and there is no set formula to follow. That said, as an example of how such post-experimental analysis has been manifested, it is useful to explore how researchers in FTA have dealt statistically in the post-analysis stage with one particularly vexing issue – how to measure when subjects make "mistakes."

Optimization Errors in Experiments
Game-theoretic models generally assume that subjects' choices are without error. That is, subjects are able to, without mistakes, translate their preferences into choices. Yet, from the first FTA experiments, researchers discovered that although in a number of experiments the overall predictions of the theory may be supported by the average behavior of subjects, clearly some subjects chose at variance with the predictions. Could these

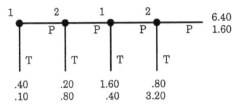

Figure 6.3. The Centipede Game from McKelvey and Palfrey (1992).

variations in subjects' choices be a consequence of errors that subjects make in translating their preferences into choices?

The Centipede Game and Strategic Errors. If subjects are making errors, then the strategic nature of the interaction between individuals as assumed in the model may differ. For example, consider the centipede game illustrated in Figure 6.3 from McKelvey and Palfrey (1992). In the centipede game, players make choices sequentially to stop the game or continue the game. If the first player chooses to stop (move T for "take" in the figure), the two players receive payoffs. The top number is the payoff received by player 1 and the bottom number is the payoff received by player 2. If the first player chooses to continue (move P for "pass" in the figure) and the second player chooses to stop, the second player receives a higher payoff but the payoff to the first player declines. However, if the second player chooses to continue, the first player will get a choice again, and if the first player chooses to take at this second option, he or she receives more than he or she would have received by taking on the first move; but the payment declines for the second player. This process continues until the end of the game, so that by the end of the game the two players' payoffs are both much higher than at the start of the game.

We can solve this game for the subgame perfect Nash equilibrium by working backward through the game. That is, we begin with player 2's last move. If player 2 chooses to pass, he or she receives $1.60. But if player 2 chooses to take, he or she receives $3.20. Therefore, player 2 should choose to take on the last move. Now, we move to player 1's choice. If player 1 chooses to pass, then player 2 will choose to take and player 1 will receive $0.80. But if player 1 chooses to take, player 1 receives $1.60. So player 1 should choose to take. Now we move to player 2's first choice. Player 2 knows that if he or she chooses to pass, player 1 will choose to take, and thus player 2 will receive $0.40. But if player 2 chooses to take instead, he or she will receive $0.80. So player 2 will choose to take. Now consider player 1's first move. If player 1 chooses to pass, player 2 will take, and player 1 will receive \$0.20. But if player 1 chooses to take, he or she will receive \$0.40. Therefore, player 1 will choose to take on the first move of the game and the game should end on the first move.

But this prediction depends crucially on the assumption that the players are fully strategic and do not make errors in their choices. What would happen if player 1 thought that player 2 might make a mistake and by accident choose to pass on player 2's moves? Depending on the size of the probabilities of mistakes, we can imagine that player 1 may actually pass on the first move in order to take advantage of player 2's errors and achieve some of the higher payoffs at later moves in the game. The implication is that if we add in some stochastic decision making by the players of the game, then the equilibrium predictions may change. While this is a stylized example, the implication holds for more complex models in political science. That is, if a researcher believes that the stochastic aspect in an empirical model has an effect on an actor's choices in the model, then if the model considers a strategic situation, that stochastic element may also affect the choices of other actors in the model as well and the equilibrium predictions of the model.

Quantal Response Equilibrium. McKelvey and Palfrey (1995, 1998) introduced the concept of quantal response equilibrium (QRE) as a game-theoretic equilibrium concept that allows for actors to make choices with errors, which they apply to data from laboratory experiments on the centipede game. QRE is a generalization of probabilistic choice models such as logit and probit to game-theoretic situations. The approach developed by McKelvey and Palfrey has also been used on nonexperimental data; see in particular the work of Signorino (1999), who develops a theoretically derived structural model applied to understanding international conflict processes. The key assumption in QRE is that actors' deviations from optimal decisions are negatively correlated with the associated costs and that, in equilibrium, players' beliefs about these deviations match the equilibrium choice probabilities. Goeree et al. (2005) provide an axiomatic definition of what they label *regular* QRE and they demonstrate that given these axioms, regular QRE exists in normal-form games.

In the logit equilibrium of QRE, for any two strategies, the stochastic choice function is given by the following logit function with the free parameter λ, which indexes the responsiveness of choices to payoffs or the slope of the logit curve:

$$\sigma_{ij} = \frac{e^{\lambda U_{ij}(\sigma)}}{\sum_{k \in S_i} e^{\lambda U_{ik}(\sigma)}} \quad \text{for all } i, j \in S_i, \tag{6.1}$$

where σ_{ij} is the probability i chooses strategy j, $U_{ij}(\sigma)$ is the equilibrium expected payoff to i if i chooses decision j, and the players in the game have a strategy profile of σ. A higher λ reflects a less noisy response to the payoffs. In the extreme, when $\lambda = 0$, subjects are choosing purely randomly and when $\lambda = +\infty$ subjects are choosing according to the Nash equilibrium.

Recently Haile et al. (2008) have criticized the original formulation of QRE by McKelvey and Palfrey (1995). In the original formulation it is possible that QRE can explain any data when the disturbances in the model are unrestricted by assumptions as in regular QRE. Thus, a QRE model with disturbances unrestricted may be unfalsifiable. However, as Goeree et al. (2005) point out, the problem with the original formulation of QRE can be easily avoided if the disturbances are assumed to be independently and identically distributed or by making a weaker assumption about disturbances called interchangeability. Alternatively, a researcher can constrain the model to hold across data sets or work directly from the axioms of regular QRE, which does impose empirical restrictions on the data. However, the criticism of Haile et al. exemplifies the importance of the assumptions made about stochastic processes when creating a theoretically derived structural model for empirical evaluation.

Using QRE in Post-Experimental Analysis. Battaglini, Morton, and Palfrey consider whether QRE can explain the variation in choices of subjects in their Swing Voter's Curse experiments. Using maximum likelihood, they estimate a single value of λ for the pooled data set of all observations of uninformed voter decisions in the seven-player voting groups. By constraining λ across manipulations and using the logit approach, which assumes that disturbances are independent and interchangeable, they avoid the criticism of Haile et al. They found that the constrained QRE-predicted choices are closer to those observed than the Bayesian–Nash predictions and other alternative theories of bounded rationality. In particular, QRE can explain the tendency for subjects to make more errors when the ex ante probability that the state of the world is the red jar is not equal to 1/2, but 5/9. In this case, although subjects' responses did follow the comparative static predictions of the theory (as the number of partisans increased, uninformed voters were more likely to vote for the yellow jar), more subjects make the "error" of voting for the red jar than in the case in which the ex ante probability equals 1/2. QRE predicts that such errors are more likely when the probability is 5/9 because the naïve strategy of voting with one's prior is less costly when the probability is 5/9, since by doing so one will vote correctly more often than not.

Bassi et al., in Example 6.3, also use QRE to understand better how subjects respond to incentives and identities in voting. They turn to QRE to distinguish between the effects of incentives and complexity on choices and the effects of identity. That is, suppose subjects receive some intrinsic utility from voting sincerely. Bassi et al. wished to discover the effects of financial incentives and incomplete information on voters' intrinsic motivations. However, if increasing financial incentives (as the authors do) or making the game more complex (as the authors do) increases the probability that subjects make errors, this can confound their ability to estimate the effects of these factors on the intrinsic utility from voting sincerely. By using a version of QRE which incorporates a parameter k that represents the additional utility a voter receives from voting sincerely, Bassi et al. were able to distinguish between sincere voting driven by errors and strategic responses to errors and sincere voting due to intrinsic utility from voting sincerely. They found that indeed the intrinsic utility from voting sincerely is affected by financial incentives and information such that this utility is reduced and when subjects have higher incentives and complete information.

To calculate the effects of increasing payoffs, Bassi et al. needed to relax one assumption in standard logit QRE: the "translation invariance" assumption. This assumption requires that adding a constant to all payoffs does not change the choice probabilities. But this is not a plausible assumption when we expect the magnitudes of perception errors to depend on the magnitudes of expected payoffs. That is, in a two-person bargaining game we might expect subjects to be highly unlikely to make a $1 error when the sum to be divided equals $1, but more likely when the sum to be divided equals $100. Bassi et al. used the regular QRE refinement discussed earlier and rescaled the payoffs such that the errors in the different games always have mean 1. Thus, the errors are linearly scale-dependent, but the choice probabilities are invariant.

6.6.3 FTA, Field Experiments, and Observational Data

To our knowledge no researcher has used FTA to examine causal relationships in a classical field experiment in political science. In Chapter 8 we present an example of a survey experiment (Example 8.1), in which Tomz and Van Houweling (2008) used FTA. In this example, they compared the predictions of several alternative formal models. The models are decision-theoretic and thus amenable to a survey experiment that is an individual decision-making experiment, as discussed further in Chapter 8. Obviously, in a field experiment a researcher has much less control in the design phase and most of the emphasis is on the analysis stage. Field experiments using FTA are more similar to when a researcher uses FTA to study causal relationships in nonexperimental data. In both cases, a researcher must be extremely careful in examining the consistency between the theoretical and empirical assumptions. A few examples exist in the political science literature where researchers have taken an FTA approach with nonexperimental data. An example is found in the work of Coate and Conlin (2004), who estimate an FTA model of voter turnout. The model of voting that they used assumes that individuals in a group adopt a rule or norm of voting that maximizes the group's aggregate utility. They assumed a game-theoretic model in which the two groups are supporters or opposers of a particular policy change. They solved the model and derived comparative static predictions about the relationships between the costs and benefits of the policy change as well as the costs of voting. They then used the theoretical model's predictions as the basis for an empirical study of voter turnout in Texas liquor referenda. They derived a maximum likelihood function from the model that they estimated with the data.

Although substantive questions in political science are of course different, many of the formal models that have been empirically evaluated in the industrial organization literature are closely related to the formal models used in political science. For example, one area that has received extensive study using theoretically driven structural models is the study of auctions. Auctions have an interesting parallel in elections. For example, a particular type of auction is called an "all-pay" auction, where everyone pays the winning bid at the end. It can be shown that theoretically an all-pay auction is equivalent to an election because in an election, everyone receives the same outcome. Furthermore, much of the theoretical work on information aggregation in elections, as in the study by Feddersen and Pesendorfer (1996), has been influenced by theoretical work on information aggregation in auctions. Political scientists have the potential of using the methods that econometricians have developed to study auctions more widely in studying elections. Economists who have worked with theoretically derived structural models of auctions include Paarsch (1992), Laffont and Vuong (1995), Guerre et al. (2000), and Athey and Haile (2002).[9]

Perhaps more obviously, theoretically derived structural models that have addressed principal agent problems in economics as in Wolak (1994) can

---

[9] Bajari and Hortacsu (2005) provide an interesting behavioral identification evaluation of methods used on auction models with experimental data. We address behavioral identification in Section 8.6.

possibly help political scientists interested in similar problems as some of the work on firm competition may be useful in constructing theoretically derived structural models of political competition as in the work of Berry et al. (1995).

6.7 Chapter Summary

In this chapter we explored how FTA works to make causal inferences. In FTA a researcher directly confronts the theoretical assumptions of a formal model which has been solved for causal and other predictions. In the empirical evaluation of these predictions, the researcher carefully considers how each aspect of the empirics satisfies these theoretical assumptions. In a theory test the researcher attempts to make the assumptions underlying the empirics as close as possible to the theoretical ones. The researcher relies strongly on control in the design of the experiment to do so but also uses random assignment to deal with unobservable variables that can confound the causal inferences the researcher wishes to investigate. Sometimes the researcher needs to re-solve the theory for the situation examined – for example, if the theory assumes an infinite number of actors, the theory will need to be re-solved to fit the finite case and the researcher will need to check to be sure the predictions of the theory still hold. The researcher also uses post-experimental analysis to sometimes distinguish relationships that are not possible to determine through the use of experimental design.

Such tests are strong tests for theories in that, if the results are contrary to those predicted, then the theory is strongly suspect. However, equally important are stress tests. In a stress test the researcher either relaxes one or more of the theoretical assumptions in the empirical analysis or changes some aspect of the design that is not predicted to have an effect theoretically but the researcher suspects might matter. Stress tests allow a researcher to meticulously investigate which aspects of the theory or the design affect individual behavior in the situation studied. Working from FTA, theory and stress tests together lead to a better understanding of the sources of the causal inferences observed and help researchers work toward the eventual building of a model of the causes of effects through the combination of theory and empirics.

PART III

WHAT MAKES A GOOD EXPERIMENT?

7

Validity and Experimental Manipulations

In the previous chapters we have examined both experimental and non-experimental research, taking a largely common perspective. Although we have mentioned some of the differences between experimental work and nonexperimental analysis and some of the different types of experimental research, we have generally focused on commonalities rather than distinctions. Yet, the differences in approaches can be important and many are controversial. In this part of the book we turn to these differences. Usually the controversies have to do with arguments about the validity, robustness, or generality of particular experimental designs. Thus, before we turn to the specific differences, we begin with a review of the concept of validity in research. Then we turn to particular and sometimes controversial issues in experimentation such as the location of an experiment (whether lab or field), the subjects recruited (whether subjects are students), and how the subjects are motivated (whether financial incentives are used).

7.1 Validity of Experimental Research

Suppose that we have conducted some empirical research with either experimental or nonexperimental data. We ideally want a research design that will provide us with *valid* results that are true for the population we are analyzing and *robust* results that *generalize* beyond our target population (see Definition 2.2).[1] So, for example, before we begin to study the effect of information on voting – the effect of changes in T_i on Y_i – we would like to come up with an experimental design that will give us results that meet these criteria.

[1] We use the term population here rather than data set because questions about how the data set relates to the population are some of the issues in establishing internal validity, which is discussed later.

Although political science has become more experimental, the most controversial questions raised about experimental research have to do with the validity, robustness, or generalizability of that research for answering substantive questions in political science. Can an experimental study of the effect of information on voting give us results that are valid and robust? We spend most of this book addressing questions of validity and robustness of all empirical research. But first we need to define these terms more precisely and deal with some of the confusions in the literature. The first such confusion is over the definitions of what we mean by validity and the types of validity. The essence of the validity of empirical research is the question: "What can we believe about what we learn from the data?" Shadish et al. (2002) or SCC (recall Section 2.4.2) use the term validity as the "approximate truth" of the inference or knowledge claim. So suppose we conduct a study, either experimental or observational, of the relationship between information and voting and we ask the validity question: What do these data tell us? This definition, however, leaves unanswered the population over which one establishes the approximate truth. We have defined the data generating process (DGP) as the source for the population from which we draw the data we use in empirical research. However, usually when we engage in empirical research we consider only a subset of the population of data generated by the DGP. For example, we may want to explain voter turnout in the United States. We probably would not be interested in the data on turnout in China in such a study.

Definition 7.1 (Validity): *The approximate truth of the inference or knowledge claim.*

When we think of validity, do we mean valid with respect to the target population of the research or is it another different population of observations? Such questions have typically been divided into two separate validity issues. This simplistic view of how to refine the concept of validity is based on the early division of Campbell (1957) and is universally used by political scientists. Specifically, political scientists generally use *internal validity* to refer to how valid results are within a target population and *external validity* to refer to how valid results are for observations not part of the target population.[2] So if our data, for example, are drawn from a U.S. election,

---

[2] Other terms have been used by researchers to capture the issues that we address about validity in this chapter. For example, Levitt and List (2007b) use *generalizability* and others use *parallelism* as in Wilde (1981) and Smith (1982).

the internal validity question would ask how valid our results are from the analysis of the data for the target population of voters in that U.S. election. The external validity question would ask how valid our results are for other populations of voters in other elections, in the United States, elsewhere in the world, or in a laboratory election.

Definition 7.2 (Internal Validity): *The approximate truth of the inference or knowledge claim within a target population studied.*

Definition 7.3 (External Validity): *The approximate truth of the inference or knowledge claim for observations beyond the target population studied.*

However, this simplistic division of validity masks the complex questions involved in establishing validity and the interconnectedness between internal and external validity. Both internal and external validity are multifaceted concepts. In this chapter we explore both types of validity.

7.2 Deconstructing Internal Validity

As SCC and McGraw and Hoekstra (1994) discuss, nearly 40 years ago Campbell abandoned the simple binary division of validity into internal and external that still dominates political science. It is ironic that political scientists typically cite him as the authority when they use the simplistic terms. Cook and Campbell (1979) extended validity into a typology of four concepts. SCC use this typology by incorporating clarifications suggested by Cronbach (1982). In this typology, validity is divided into four types: construct, causal, statistical, and external.[3] The first three of these types together are what political scientists think of as internal validity. By exploring

---

[3] Cook and Campbell (1979) called causal validity "local molar causal validity." SCC explain how the term local molar causal validity explains itself (2002, p. 54): "The word *causal* in *local molar causal validity* emphasizes that internal validity is about causal inferences, not about other types of inferences that social scientists make. The word *local* emphasizes that causal conclusions are limited to the context of the particular treatments, outcomes, times, settings, and persons studied. The word *molar* recognizes that experiments test treatments that are a complex package consisting of many components, all of which are tested as a whole within the treatment condition." SCC label local molar causal validity "internal validity" because they believe that the longer term is too unwieldy and that this is what Campbell originally viewed as internal validity. Given that many political scientists think of internal validity as whatever is left over after external validity and thus includes statistical, causal, and construct validity, we define internal validity differently from SCC. SCC also call statistical validity "statistical conclusion validity." We use the shorthand terms causal and statistical validity because they are easy to remember and capture the essence of these types of internal validity.

how each type represents a distinct question, we can better understand the different challenges involved in determining internal validity. How empirical research, either experimental or observational, establishes the validity of two of these types, causal and construct, was the focus of the previous four chapters. But before turning to these types of validity, we address statistical validity.

Definition 7.4 (Construct Validity): *Whether the inferences from the data are valid for the theory (or constructs) the researcher is evaluating in a theory testing experiment.*

Definition 7.5 (Causal Validity): *Whether the relationships the researcher finds within the target population analyzed are causal.*

Definition 7.6 (Statistical Validity): *Whether there is a statistically significant covariance between the variables the researcher is interested in and whether the relationship is sizable.*

7.2.1 Statistical Validity

Problems of Statistical Validity

Statistical validity is defined as whether there is a statistically significant covariance between the variables the researcher is interested in and whether the relationship is sizable. Suppose we find a relationship between information and voting (i.e., between T_i and Y_i) as defined in Chapter 3; statistical validity is whether the relationship is significant and sizable. Essentially this is what is often called the estimation problem of statistical analysis. Given the assumptions the researcher has made about the variables studied in the given data set, are the estimates efficient, accurate, significant, and sizable? Is the data set representative of the target population? Although these concerns seem minor compared to other matters we address later, as any empirical researcher knows, estimation is not an open-and-shut case. What does it mean when a researcher finds that the statistical relationship is just on the edge of the standard level of significance of 5%? Many now advocate an approach that focuses on reporting the actual significance level rather than just whether a result passes a threshold. Another question involved in statistical validity is whether the statistical assumptions about the distributions of the variables are supported. Are the errors estimated correctly? Is the size of the relationship consequential or not? How do we evaluate the significance of interaction terms?

Estimation issues can be important and are sometimes overlooked. As we discuss in Section 5.6, a popular method of empirical research which springs from experimental reasoning is what has been called the "difference-in-differences" approach to studying the effects of state laws or state policies. Researchers compare the difference in outcomes after and before the law or the new state policy for those affected by the law or state policy to the same difference in outcomes by those who have not been affected by the law or new state policy. The researchers often use ordinary least squares (OLS) in repeated cross sections or a panel of data on individuals before and after the passage of the law or new state policy. They then use the coefficient estimated for the dummy variable in the OLS that represents whether the law applies to the given observation as an estimate of the effects of the law or policy. However, Bertrand et al. (2004) pointed out that the OLS estimations are likely to suffer from possible severe serial correlation problems which when uncorrected lead to an underestimation of the standard error in estimating the coefficient and a tendency to reject null hypotheses that the law or policy has no effect when the null hypothesis should not be rejected.

The serial correlation occurs for three reasons: (1) the researchers tend to use fairly long time series, (2) the dependent variables are typically highly positively serially correlated, and (3) the dummy variable for the existence of the law or policy changes vary little over the time period estimated. The authors propose a solution – removing the time-series dimension by dividing the data into pre- and post-intervention periods and then adjusting the standard errors for the smaller number of observations this implies. They also point out that when the number of cases is large – for example, if all 50 states are included – then the estimation is less problematic. This is just one example of how statistical validity can matter in determining whether results are valid.

Statistical Replication
Statistical replication is a powerful method of verifying the statistical validity of a study. We follow Hunter (2001) and Hamermesh (2007) in dividing replication into two types. *Statistical replication* is when a researcher uses a different sample from the same population to evaluate the same theoretical implications as in the previous study or uses the same sample but a different statistical method evaluating the same theoretical implications (which some call verification), in both cases holding the construct validity of the analysis constant. *Scientific replication* is when a researcher uses a different sample, uses a different population to evaluate the same theoretical constructs,

or uses the same sample or a different sample from either the same or different population focusing on different theoretical implications from those constructs. We discuss scientific replication when we address external validity.

Definition 7.7 (Statistical Replication): *When a researcher uses a different sample from the same population to evaluate the same theoretical implications as in the previous study with equivalent construct validity or uses the same sample from the same population but comparing statistical techniques to evaluate the same theoretical implications as in the previous study, again with equivalent construct validity.*

It is easy to see that statistical replication is concerned with statistical validity rather than the external validity of results. In fact, researchers working with large data sets would probably be well served to engage in cross-validation, where the researcher splits the data into N mutually exclusive, randomly chosen subsets of approximately equal size and estimates the model on each possible group of $N - 1$ subsets and assesses the model's predictive accuracy based on each left out set. Although statistical replication may seem mundane, Hamermesh presents a number of interesting situations in economics where statistical replication has led to controversy.

There are examples in political science where results have been verified and called into challenge. For instance, Altman and McDonald (2003) showed that variations in how software programs make computations can, in sophisticated data analysis, lead to different empirical results in a statistical replication. In political science, statistical replication with new samples from the same target population can also lead to different results and some controversy. For example, Green et al. (1998) replicated analyses of Mac-Kuen et al. (1989, 1992) on macropartisanship using a larger data set from the same population, calling into question the original conclusions of the analysis.[4] Because of the possibility that statistical replication may lead to different results, many political science journals now require that authors make their data plus any other necessary information for replicating the analysis available to those who may be interested. There are, of course, a number of issues having to do with the confidentiality of different data sets and sources; nevertheless, the general perspective within political science is that efforts should be made to make replication of statistical analysis possible.

---

[4] See also the response by Erikson et al. (1998).

In terms of experimental work, replication can at times be a bit more complicated, unless it is the simple verification variety as in Imai's (2005) statistical replication of Gerber and Green's (2000) mobilization study.[5] Statistical replication that involves drawing a new sample from the same population requires that a new experiment be conducted using subjects from the same target population with the same experimental protocols. Oftentimes experimentalists do this as part of their research, conducting several independent sessions of an experiment using different samples of subjects from the same pool.

7.2.2 Causal Validity and the Identification Problem

Even if the results are statistically valid, if we want to be able to say something about the effects of causes, then we need for our results to have causal validity. Causal validity is the determination of whether the relationships the researcher finds within the target population analyzed are causal. Thus, suppose we find a relationship between information and voting behavior in an election, either observational or experimental. Establishing causal validity for that relationship would mean establishing that changes in one of the variables – we posit information – causes changes in the other variable – voting behavior. Formally, using the preceding notation, changes in T_i cause changes in Y_i. We have spent the previous four chapters exploring how a researcher establishes causal validity using either the Rubin Causal Model or the Formal Theory Approach (FTA).

A concept closely related to causal validity is the notion of *identification* in econometrics. As Manski (1995, 2003) explains, econometricians have found it useful to separate out the concerns of identifying relationships from the concerns in estimating relationships. Estimation problems have to do with statistical issues of whether, given the data set analyzed and the assumptions made about the relationship between the data set and the population, the parameters of interest are efficiently and consistently estimated, or statistical validity.[6] Manski remarks (2003, p. 12): "Statistical inference seeks to characterize how sampling variability affects the conclusions that can be drawn from samples of limited size."

---

[5] See also Gerber and Green's (2005) response.
[6] Consistent parameter estimates are those that, under the assumptions made about the population, converge on the true population parameters as the sample size of the data set analyzed grows without bound. Efficient estimates are loosely those that have the lowest possible variance of unbiased estimators.

In contrast, an identification problem exists when it is problematic to establish causal inferences even if the researcher has an unlimited sample from the population. Identification problems exist in many contexts. Of particular interest to political scientists is the identification problem that occurs because we cannot observe the same individual in multiple states of the world in the DGP. For example, suppose we are interested in the causal effect of education on voting. Our population is the citizens in a particular region. We cannot simultaneously observe each citizen, both educated and uneducated. Even if we have an unlimited sample from the population, we would not be able to find such observations. We can make assumptions about the probability of being educated and the reasonableness of comparing educated citizens' choices with those of uneducated citizens (and in rare cases observe them in the two states sequentially).

This type of identification problem is often labeled a selection problem because in observational analysis individuals select their education levels; they are not manipulated by the researcher. However, the problem is more fundamental than this label suggests. The difficulty arises because counterfactual observations are impossible to observe even if education could be randomly assigned to individuals – we still cannot observe the same individual both educated and uneducated. As we discussed in earlier chapters, there are experimental designs which come close to providing pseudo-counterfactual observations, and random assignment does help one "solve" the problem under particular assumptions. But even these solutions are merely close; they do not fully capture human choices in multiple states of the world simultaneously.

7.2.3 Construct Validity

Defining Construct Validity

When some political scientists think of internal validity, particularly with respect to experiments that evaluate formal models or take place in the laboratory, they are often referring to what SCC call construct validity. Construct validity has to do with how valid the inferences of the data are for the theory (or constructs) the researcher is evaluating. Essentially, establishing construct validity is an essential part of estimating causality in FTA; in FTA the goal is to investigate causal relations within a research design that has construct validity. Thus, if we think about causal validity as establishing whether changes in T_i cause changes in Y_i, construct validity takes a broader look and asks if our empirical analysis is a valid evaluation of our theory or model about why changes in T_i cause changes in Y_i.

In experimental research the question is whether the design of the experiment is such that the variables investigated are closely equivalent to the variables the theory is concerned with. Are those things that the theory holds constant held constant in the experiment? Are the choices before the subjects the same as the choices assumed in the theory? Do the subjects have the same information about each other and about the environment that the theory assumes? Are the subjects in the experiment from the same target population that the theory addresses? In other words, is there a close match between what the theory is about and what is happening in the manipulated DGP?

In observational studies, researchers who work with formal theoretical models think about the equations underlying the theory and the equations underlying the empirical analysis and their relationship. Is the estimated empirical model derived from or equivalent to the underlying theoretical model? If there are disconnects between the empirical model and the theoretical model, to what extent do these disconnects lead one to discard the results of the research as not being relevant to the theory? These are issues that we have already addressed extensively in Chapter 6.

Construct Validity and the Generalizability of Results

Although we group construct validity as part of internal validity, as do most political scientists, doing so misses an important aspect of construct validity that makes it more than just about a given experiment. Construct validity is also about generalization. The generalization is to a theoretical construct that ideally the researcher does not view as limited to the particular empirical analysis, but a more general theory. Because of this, being able to establish construct validity can actually help build answers to external validity questions about the theory and any analysis of the theory. As SCC argue (2002, p. 93):

[V]alid knowledge of constructs that are involved in a study can shed light on external validity questions, especially if a well-developed theory exists that describes how various constructs and instances are related to each other. Medicine, for example, has well-developed theories for categorizing certain therapies (say, the class of drugs we call chemotherapies for cancer) and for knowing how these therapies affect patients (how they affect blood tests and survival and what their side effects are). Consequently, when a new drug meets the criteria for being called a chemotherapy, we can predict much of its likely performance before actually testing it (e.g., we can say it is likely to cause hair loss and nausea and to increase survival in patients with low tumor burdens but not advanced cases). This knowledge makes the design of new experiments easier by narrowing the scope of pertinent patients and outcomes, and it makes extrapolations about treatment effects likely to be more accurate.

In political science this is also true when a researcher works with a well-developed theory. Results from experiments with high construct validity can help us answer more general questions than those without construct validity. For example, Wittman (1983) and Calvert (1985) demonstrate in a two-candidate model of spatial competition, if the candidates have different policy preferences independent of whether they are elected and there is uncertainty about the ideal point of the median voter in the electorate, the candidates will choose divergent policy platforms in equilibrium. However, if the candidates are certain about the location of the median voter's ideal point, then the candidates converge in equilibrium. This comparative static prediction has been supported in experiments designed to have high construct validity (see Morton, 1993).

The theoretical prediction also has implications for the relationship between factors that affect whether candidates have policy preferences (such as candidate selection mechanisms) and knowledge of voter preferences and the divergence of candidate policy positions. We can extrapolate from the theory to consider other possible relationships for future empirical investigation, such as how a change in a candidate selection mechanism that makes candidates more ideological may impact candidate policy positions. For example, we may argue that in open primaries (where all registered voters are allowed to participate in the selection of candidates) candidates are less ideological than in closed primaries (where only the voters registered in a particular party are allowed to participate in a party's primary). The theory, supported by the experimental results in one target population, would then suggest that there is more divergence between candidates in closed primaries than in open primaries. Indeed, Gerber et al. (1998) find that this new theoretical prediction is supported with data on the policy positions of congressional incumbents, a different target population. Their research shows that congressional incumbents' policy positions are closer to the estimated positions of the median voters in their districts in states with open primaries than in states with closed primaries.

Although the preceding example demonstrates how empirical research with high construct validity that supports a theory in one target population can be useful as a basis for generalizing beyond the initial empirical research to implications in other target populations, a negative result from empirical research with high construct validity can also be useful. If the empirical research shows that the theory's predictions do not hold in one target population, and the research has high construct validity, then the results from the analysis can help develop a more general and robust theory, leading again to new predictions about other populations beyond the target population in the original empirical analysis.

Construct Validity and External Validity

The previous section argues that construct validity of studies allows for generalization beyond those studies. The quote from SCC suggests that studies with construct validity can shed light on external validity questions. However, we do not believe such a conclusion should be taken too far. In our opinion, construct validity is not a substitute for external validity. To see why this is the case, consider what is implied by results from studies with construct validity. Suppose a researcher finds a situation in which the empirical research is considered to have construct validity and the theory's behavioral predictions are not supported. Does that mean that we should always change the theory once we find a single negative result? Although the empirical study may be considered to have construct validity, it is unlikely that a single negative result would be seen as decisive in determining the merits of the theory. Why? This is because all theories and models are abstractions from the DGP and, therefore, all have parts that are empirically false and can be proven empirically false when confronted with some observations of the DGP.[7] The question is not whether a theory can be proven empirically false, but when empirical inconsistencies with the theory matter enough for the theory to be modified or even discarded.

Similarly, suppose a researcher, again conducting empirical research considered to have construct validity, finds that the theory's behavioral predictions *are* supported. Does that mean that we should unconditionally accept the theory? Not necessarily. In our opinion, theory evaluation in the social sciences is a cumulative process that occurs through replication and complementary studies. However, because any theory can be disproved with enough data, the evaluation of theory is not purely an empirical question. As with Fudenberg (2006), we believe that theory should be judged on Stigler's (1965) three criteria: accuracy of predictions, generality, and tractability. In conclusion, construct validity is a property of a particular empirical study. However, negative or positive results from one such empirical study with construct validity are rarely adequate even if the results are strong and robust enough to accept or reject the theory. In our opinion, as we explain later, to establish external validity of results further empirical

---

[7] Note that a theory is always true in a theoretical sense if it is logically consistent; that is, the results or predictions follow directly from the assumptions.

study is required, both nonexperimental and experimental if possible, to fully evaluate the value of social science theories.

7.2.4 Summary of Internal Validity

When political scientists refer to internal validity, they are often referring to three distinct and important aspects of validity: statistical, causal, and construct. It is better if we think of these issues separately, because each involves a different type of answer and has a separate set of concerns. It is quite possible – in fact, highly likely given advances in estimation techniques – that an analysis satisfies statistical validity but not causal validity or construct validity, although in some cases advances in the study of identification problems (causal validity) have outpaced estimation procedures, as discussed by Athey and Haile (2002) and exemplified in the problems discussed earlier with difference-in-differences studies.

7.3 Deconstructing External Validity

7.3.1 External, Statistical, and Ecological Validity

In contrast to internal validity, external validity is a more widely understood idea among political scientists – if you asked an average political scientist the definition of external validity, he or she would probably give you something similar to what we have written earlier. But knowing a definition and applying it are not the same, and political scientists often apply the term external validity incorrectly even if they are aware of the definition. For example, sometimes when a political scientist claims that an experiment does not have external validity, he or she is making the claim that the result is not internally valid in a statistical sense – that the sample is not a random sample from the appropriate target population and thus the conclusions are not statistically valid for the appropriate target population. But random sampling from a target population does not mean that a result is externally valid. If a researcher draws a random sample from the U.S. population to evaluate a hypothesis, the results of the analysis are not necessarily externally valid to individuals in China. External validity has to do with generalizing to populations beyond the target population, so whether one has a random sample from the target population tells one nothing about the external validity for other populations for which one has not taken a random sample.

Other times political scientists confuse external validity with *ecological validity*. Ecological validity, however, is not about the validity of results from empirical research. It is about the similarity between the environment constructed in the research and a target environment. Some experimentalists call this mundane experimental realism or contextual congruence. The experimental environment is considered ecologically valid if the methods, materials, and settings of the research are similar to the target environment. Ecological validity is similar to what Harrison and List (2004) refer to as the fieldness of an experiment. For example, an experiment on voting may enhance ecological validity by being conducted in an actual polling place, using polling place equipment and registered voters.

Definition 7.8 (Ecological Validity): *Whether the methods, materials, and settings of the research are similar to a given target environment.*

However, this may or may not enhance external validity of the results because the target environment may not generalize. For example, the polling place equipment used in one jurisdiction may be different from that used in another jurisdiction. Thus, this may actually decrease the applicability of the results to different populations that use different types of equipment. Increasing ecological validity for *one* target population does not necessarily mean that the results generalize to *another* population and setting. External validity can only be established by generalizing beyond the target population and any target environment or setting. That said, increasing ecological validity and mundane realism of an experiment may help motivate subjects. We discuss this further in Chapter 10. We also return to Harrison and List's concerns about artificiality in experiments in Section 8.2.4.

7.3.2 Establishing External Validity

Suppose a researcher has been able to successfully identify and estimate a causal inference about a target population, using either experimental or nonexperimental data. Assume, for the moment, that the researcher is not engaging in theory testing and, thus, the construct validity of the initial analysis is not relevant. How can that researcher establish that the causal inference is externally valid? Or, more precisely, is it possible to establish the external validity of a causal inference that is not based on a theoretical construct without further empirical study? Without further empirical study, a researcher can only conjecture or hypothesize that his or her result has external validity based on similar studies or assumptions about the relationship between the population initially analyzed and the new population to be considered.

Is it different if the result validates a theoretical prediction and has construct validity? Although having construct validity helps us build a more general theory and provides evidence of a more general theory, we still cannot use theory to establish external validity. External validity can be conjectured or hypothesized based on similar studies or assumptions about population similarities about any study, experimental or nonexperimental, but the *proof* of external validity is always *empirical*. Debates about external validity in the absence of such empirical proof are debates about the similarity of a study to previous studies or population similarities, but there can never be a resolution through debate or discussion alone. Researchers would be better served by conducting more empirical studies than by debating external validity in the absence of such studies.

What sort of empirical analysis is involved in establishing external validity? A researcher simply replicates the empirical results on new populations or using new variations on the experiment in terms of settings, materials, and so on. With respect to establishing the external validity of results from theory evaluations, the researcher may also test new implications of the theory on the new populations as well as the old population. We discuss these processes later in this chapter.

Scientific Replication

Scientific replication is all about establishing external validity. It is when a researcher uses either a different sample or a different population to evaluate the same theoretical constructions with the same theoretical implications or uses the same or a different sample from either the same or a different population to evaluate different theoretical implications from these constructs. It is obviously less easily mandated by journals than statistical replication because it involves taking the same theoretical constructs and applying them to new populations or evaluating new theoretical implications or taking causal inferences based on fact searching and determining if they can be identified and estimated in a different data set. Often a researcher has used considerable effort to find, build, or create, as in an experiment, the data set for a study of a target population. Usually a researcher has sought all the data that he or she could find that was relevant and leaves establishing external validity through scientific replication to other researchers.

Definition 7.9 (Scientific Replication): *When a researcher uses a different sample, a different population to evaluate the same theoretical constructs with the same theoretical implications, or the same or a different sample from either the same or a different population to evaluate different theoretical implications from these constructs.*

One possible way to establish some external validity for one's own empirical results is through the use of *nonrandom holdout samples* as advocated by Keane and Wolpin (2007) and Wolpin (2007). A nonrandom holdout sample is one that differs significantly from the sample used for the estimation along a dimension over which the causal inference or theoretical prediction is expected to hold. If the empirical results from the original estimation are supported with the nonrandom holdout sample, which involves observations that are well outside the support of the original data, then the results will have more external validity along this dimension. As Keane and Wolpin remark, this procedure is often used in time-series analyses and has been used in the psychology and marketing literature. They note that such a procedure was used by McFadden (1977). McFadden estimated a random utility model of travel demand in the San Francisco Bay area before the introduction of the subway system and then compared his estimates to the actual usage after the subway was introduced. The observations after the subway was introduced composed the nonrandom holdout sample. Keane and Wolpin point out that experiments can provide an ideal opportunity for analyses with nonrandom holdout samples. One can imagine that treatments can be used as subsets of the population just as in the aforementioned cross-valuation procedure. Suppose a researcher conducts K treatments on different dimensions. Then the researcher can estimate the effects of the treatments on each of the possible groups of $K - 1$ subsets as separate target populations and then assess the predictive accuracy on the subset omitted on the dimension omitted. In this fashion, the researcher can gain some traction on the external validity of his or her results.

Definition 7.10 (Nonrandom Holdout Sample): *A nonrandom holdout sample is a sample that differs significantly from the sample used for the estimation along a dimension over which the causal inference or theoretical prediction is expected to hold.*

Although it is rare for a researcher to engage in scientific replication of his or her own research as described earlier, fortunately a lot of political science research does involve this sort of replication of the research of others. Gerber and Green's voter mobilization study was a scientific replication of the original study of Gosnell and the work of Rosenstone, as discussed previously.

Scientific replication through experimentation can occur when subjects from a different target population are used with the same experimental protocols to evaluate the same theoretical implications, or subjects from the same or different target population are used to evaluate different theoretical implications sometimes with a change in experimental protocols (maintaining the same theoretical constructs). For example, Potters and van Winden (2000) replicated an experiment they had conducted previously with undergraduate students (Potters and van Winden, 1996), using lobbyists. One advantage of laboratory experiments is that usually statistical verification with different samples from the same target population can be reasonably conducted as long as researchers make publicly available detailed experimental protocols. Such explicit publicly available protocols are also required for effective scientific replications, particularly if the experimenter seeks to replicate with a sample from a new target population using the same experimental design. It is generally the norm of experimentalists in political science to provide access to these protocols for such replication. We believe this should be required of all political science experimentalists.

Stress Tests and External Validity

Recall that in Chapter 6 we referred to a type of experiment called a stress test as part of FTA. A stress test is also a way for an experimentalist to explore issues of external validity when evaluating a formal model. For example, suppose a researcher has tested a theory of legislative bargaining in the laboratory. The model is one of complete information. However, the researcher relaxes some of the information available to the subjects to determine if the behavior of the subjects will be affected. The researcher has no theoretical prediction about what will happen. If the theory's predictions hold despite this new wrinkle, then the researcher has learned that the results of the first experiment can generalize, under some circumstances, to a less than complete information environment. The experimental results are robust to this change if the theory's predictions hold. If the theory's predictions do not hold, then the experimental results are not robust.

Another example would be to conduct the same complete-information legislative bargaining theory experiment with different subject pools by conducting what is called lab-in-the-field versions of the experiment (discussed in Section 8.2.3) to determine how robust the results are to changes in who participates in the experiment. Again, if the theory's predictions hold, we say that the results are robust to this change, and vice versa. Or the experimentalist may vary the frame of the experiment – perhaps the original experiment used a neutral frame and subjects were told they were players in a game without any political context. The experimentalist could introduce a political context to the experiment by telling the subjects they are legislators and they are bargaining for ministerial positions and see if this frame difference affects the subjects' choices.

As noted in Chapter 6, the beauty of stress tests is that the experimentalist can incorporate new features of the experimental environment on a piecemeal basis and investigate each aspect of the change in an effort to test the limits of the external robustness or validity of the results. Stress tests, then, are important tools for experimentalists to test whether their results are externally valid or robust and where in particular the robustness or validity may break down.

Analyses of Multiple Studies

Narrative and Systematic Reviews. The tendency of researchers in political science is to look for new theoretical constructs or new theoretical implications from previously evaluated constructs that then become the focus of new empirical research. Alternatively, political scientists look for new target populations to evaluate existing theoretical constructs or established causal relations. Much less often do political scientists conduct reviews of research focusing on a particular research question. Yet, such reviews can be important in establishing the external validity of empirical results. In the psychology and medical literature, these types of syntheses have become commonplace to the extent that there is now a growing literature that reports on reviews of reviews.[8] Furthermore, many of the reviews in the psychology and medical literature are quantitative in nature, using statistical methods to synthesize the results from a variety of studies, which are called meta-analysis, a term coined by Glass (1976). Researchers in the medical field also distinguish between a purely narrative review and a systematic review that includes both a narrative review and an analysis of the studies, either qualitative or quantitative. In this perspective a meta-analysis is a quantitative systematic review.

Definition 7.11 (Narrative Review): *Reviews of existing literature focusing on a particular research question.*

Definition 7.12 (Systematic Review): *A narrative review that includes either a qualitative or quantitative synthesis of the reviewed studies' results.*

Definition 7.13 (Meta-analysis): *A quantitative systematic review using statistical methods for which the researcher uses study results as the unit of observation or to construct the unit of observation.*

---

[8] For reviews of the literature on meta-analysis in other disciplines, see the special issue of the *International Journal of Epidemiology* in 2002, Bangert-Downs (1986), Delgado-Rodriguez (2006), Egger and Smith (1997), and Montori et al. (2003).

Political scientists sometimes use the term meta-analysis to refer to a literature review that is mainly narrative and qualitative. Political scientists also sometimes call a study that combines a couple of different empirical studies to address a single question, such as combining a laboratory experiment with a larger survey, a meta-analysis. Technically, neither are considered meta-analyses. In meta-analysis, usually the unit of observation is either the results of an overall study or results from distinctive parts of the study. Sometimes in meta-analysis researchers use statistical results from an overall study or distinctive parts to "approximate" data pooling (see Bangert-Downs, 1986). Other times, researchers actually pool all the data from multiple studies in cases where such data are available; such analyses are not usually considered meta-analyses but simply pooled analyses. In meta-analyses the researcher works with the reported information from the study which, of course, is secondary information, and this information serves as the basis of his or her statistical analysis. We expect that, as more political scientists begin to conduct systematic quantitative reviews as found in other disciplines, meta-analysis will have the same meaning in political science that it has in other disciplines, so we define a meta-analysis more narrowly.[9]

Definition 7.14 (Pooled Analysis): *A quantitative study that pools data from multiple studies to examine a particular research question.*

Issues in Meta-analyses. In a meta-analysis a researcher first has to decide on the criteria for including a study. Setting the criteria raises a lot of questions for the researcher. For example, suppose that the researcher is more suspect of the statistical or causal validity of some studies than others; should the researcher include all studies, but use statistics to control for these differences, or simply exclude studies with less valid results? As Bangert-Downs (1986) discussed, in psychology there has been much debate over whether low-quality studies should be included in meta-analysis – whether meta-analysis is simply "garbage in-garbage out" in such cases. Consider, for example, a meta-analysis that includes some experimental studies where

---

[9] A number of researchers have conducted systematic reviews that they call meta-analyses with case study data using case study methods. See, for example, Strandberg's (2008) study of the relationship between party Web sites and online electoral competition and Sager's (2006) study of policy coordination in European cities. Both of these studies use a method that has developed in case study research called qualitative comparative analysis (QCA). Because our focus in this book is on quantitative research taking an experimental approach, we do not include QCA approaches in our analysis.

causal validity is high with some nonexperimental studies where causal validity is not as high. Is it profitable to combine such studies for a meta-analysis? Alternatively, suppose that some of the data come from an experiment where random assignment has been utilized but another data set comes from an experiment without random assignment?

Studies also vary in the types of treatments and manipulations considered. Suppose that the treatment in a study is similar to the treatments given in other studies, but distinctive; to what extent can dissimilar studies be combined in an analysis that makes theoretical sense? One of the more seminal meta-analyses in psychology is Smith and Glass's (1977) study of the effects of psychotherapy. In this study the authors combined studies of a wide variety of psychotherapy from gestalt therapy to transactional analysis. What does such research tell us when so many different types of psychotherapy are combined? This is called the "apples-and-oranges" problem of meta-analysis. We could argue that doing so provides some overall measure of the effect of psychotherapy for policy makers who are choosing whether to support such therapies in general, but then what if one particular type of psychotherapy has been studied more often than it has actually been used, or has a bigger effect than others; does that skew the implications of the analysis?

After deciding on what types of studies to include, the researcher then faces additional statistical questions. What measures from the different studies should the research compare? Should the researcher compare significance and probabilities or sizes of effects? How does the researcher deal with publication biases? That is, suppose that studies showing no results or negative results are less likely to be published. How can the reviewer find information on such studies or, in the absence of such information, control for the possibility that they exist? Or, for example, suppose that the studies differ substantially in sample sizes, which has implications for comparisons across studies. How can a researcher control for these differences? Are there statistical techniques to estimate how robust the results of the reported studies are to unreported negative results? What happens if there is statistical dependence across different output measures?

Fortunately, the statistical methods used in meta-analysis are advanced enough in medicine and in psychology that researchers in political science who would like to conduct a meta-analysis can find a large literature on the methods that have been used to address these and many other methodological concerns. There are a number of textbooks on the subject (see, e.g., Hunter and Schmidt 1990). SCC also discussed meta-analysis at length in their Chapter 13. However, given the research interests of the other disciplines, sometimes their answers are not appropriate for political science questions because many of the questions in medicine and psychology focus on particular isolated treatment effects of manipulations on individuals, whereas much of political science research examines effects at both individual and group levels and the interactions between the two. Furthermore, in the other disciplines, especially in medicine, it is likely that there are many studies that examine a common treatment and can be easily placed on a common metric for quantitative analyses, whereas doing so in political science may be more problematic.

Meta-analyses in Political Science. It is not surprising to us that meta-analyses are still rare in political science, mainly because it is difficult to think of a research question that has been the subject of the large number of studies needed for the statistical assumptions necessary for good meta-analysis. To our knowledge, meta-analyses have appeared at this writing only three times in the top three journals in political science, once in the *American Political Science Review* (Lau et al., 1999), once in the *Journal of Politics* (Lau et al., 2007, which is a replication of Lau et al., 1999), and once in the *American Journal of Political Science* (Doucouliagos and Ulubasoglu, 2008). Examples of meta-analyses are more numerous in specialized journals on public opinion and political psychology.

The meta-analyses of Lau et al. (1999, 2007) are instructive of how such synthesizing can lead to a deeper understanding of empirical relationships and provide insight into the complex choices facing researchers in meta-analyses. In these two studies the authors consider the empirical evidence on the effects of negative campaign advertising and find little support for the common perception in journalist circles that negative campaign advertising increases the probabilities that voters will choose the candidates who choose this strategy. As discussed earlier, the first step in the research approach used by Lau et al. (2007) was to decide on the criteria with which to include a study in their analysis. They chose to include studies that examined both actual and hypothetical political settings in which candidates or parties competed for support. Thus, they excluded studies of negative advertising in nonpolitical settings or in nonelectoral settings, but included studies for which the candidates and parties were hypothetical. If a researcher had reanalyzed previous data, they used the latest such study; however, they included studies by different researchers using different methods that used the same data set. Lau et al. also required that the study contain variation in the tone of the ads or campaigns. They focused on both studies that examined voter responses to the ads as intermediate effects as well as their main interest on direct electoral effects and broader consequences on political variables such as turnout, voters' feelings of efficacy, trust, and political mood. The authors contend that these choices reflect their goal of answering the research question as to the effects of negative advertising in election campaigns. Yet, one may easily construct a meta-analysis that takes alternative focuses and uses different criteria. Ideally a researcher should consider how their criteria matter for the results provided. Lau et al. did consider the effects of using different studies from the same data set.

The second step in Lau et al.'s analysis was to do an extensive literature search to find all the relevant studies. Beyond simply surveying the literature, they contacted researchers working in the area, considered papers presented at conferences, and so on. This is a critical step in meta-analysis because it is important to avoid the "file drawer" problem of unpublished but important studies. The third step is to determine the measure for the quantitative analysis. Lau et al. focused on what is a standard technique in the psychology and medical literature, what is called Cohen's d or the *standardized mean difference statistic*, which is simply the difference in the means of the variable of interest in the treatment of interest versus the alternative treatment (or control group) divided by the pooled standard deviation of the two groups. Formally:

$$d_i = \frac{\overline{X_i^t} - \overline{X_i^c}}{s_i}, \qquad (7.1)$$

where d_i is the standardized mean difference statistic for study i, $\overline{X_i^t}$ is the mean of the treatment group in the ith study, $\overline{X_i^c}$ is the mean of the control group in the ith study, and s_i is the pooled standard deviation of the two groups.

In experiments, the d statistic is relatively easy to calculate if a researcher has knowledge of the sample sizes and the standard deviations of the two groups being compared. However, if some of the studies contain nonexperimental data and are multivariate analyses, the researcher may not be able to easily calculate these measures. Lau et al. used an approximation for d in such cases that is derived from the t statistic, suggested by Stanley and Jarrell (1989), which is called by Rosenthal and Rubin (2003) the $d_{\text{equivalent}}$. Formally:

$$d_{\text{equivalent}} = \frac{2t}{\sqrt{df}}, \qquad (7.2)$$

where t is the t statistic from the multivariate regression for the independent variable of interest and df is the degrees of freedom associated with the t

test. In their appendix, Lau et al. (1999) describe this measure in detail. This measure, of course, assumes that the independent variable associated with the t statistic is an accurate measure of the causal effect that the meta-analysis is studying. The important implicit assumptions implied by the use of this measure are explored more expansively in Chapter 5, when we discuss how causal inferences can be estimated from nonexperimental data.

After calculating the values of d, Lau et al. also had to deal with the fact that the different data sets combine different sample sizes. A number of methods exist in the literature to adjust for sample sizes (see, e.g., Hedges and Olkin, 1985). Lau et al. (1999, 2007) used a method recommended by Hunter and Schmidt (1990) to weight for sample size differences. These weights are described in the appendix to Lau et al. (1999). The authors also adjusted their measure for reliability of the variables as recommended by Hunter and Schmidt. For those outcomes for which studies report reliability, they used that measure; for studies that did not report reliability measures, they used the mean reliability for other findings within the same dependent-variable category. Finally, the authors adjusted the data for variability in the strength of the negative advertisement "treatments."

Shadish and Haddock (1994) noted that, in cases where all the studies considered use the same outcome measure, it might make sense to use the difference between raw means as the common metric. In other cases, the researcher may not be examining mean differences at all. For example, Oosterbeek et al. (2004) conducted a meta-analysis of choices of subjects in an experimental bargaining game. The analysis was a study of the determinants of the size of proposals made in the bargaining and the probability that proposals are rejected. There was no treatment or baseline in these experiments in the traditional sense because the question of interest is the extent that subjects deviate from theoretical point predictions rather than a comparative static prediction. Because the size of the bargaining pies varied as well as the relative values, Oosterbeek et al. controlled for such differences. We discuss this study more expansively in the next chapter because the study considers the effects of different subject pools in laboratory experiments.

An alternative to the d measure is the correlation coefficient as the effect size. For example, Doucouliagos and Ulubasoglu (2008) used partial correlations as their effect size measures weighted for sample size (see discussion of this measure by Ones et al. 1993; Rosenthal and Rubin, 1978). It makes sense where the studies reviewed examine the same correlational relationship among variables. Greene (2000, p. 234) provides details on how to calculate partial correlations from regression outputs of studies.

Dougcouliagos and Ulubascoglu controlled for variations across the studies they examined in the empirical analysis of the data.

The d measure assumes that the study outcome is measured continuously. If the study outcome is binary, then d can yield problematic effect size estimates (see Fleiss, 1994; Haddock et al., 1998). In this case the effect size can be measured by the odds ratio. Formally:

$$o_i = \frac{AD}{BC}, \tag{7.3}$$

where o_i is the odds ratio for study i, A is the frequency with which the treatment occurs and there is no effect on the outcome, B is the frequency with which the treatment occurs and there is an effect on the outcome, C is the frequency with which the treatment is absent and there is no effect on the outcome, and D is the frequency with which the treatment is absent and there is an effect on the outcome.

Clearly, all of the decisions that researchers like Lau et al. make in conducting a meta-analysis affect the validity of the results. SCC and Hunter and Schmidt discuss these issues in detail.

7.3.3 Is External Validity Possible Without Satisfying Internal Validity?

Many political scientists quickly concede that experimental research has high internal validity compared with research with observational data and they dismiss experimental research (especially laboratory experiments) as being low on external validity compared with research with observational data. Both opinions tend to understate and ignore the multitude of issues involved in establishing the internal validity of both observational and experimental research, which we have discussed in this chapter. In particular, in our view, external validity can only be established for results that have been demonstrated to be internally valid in the senses we have mentioned – statistical conclusion, causal validity, and, if the empirical study involves theory testing, construct validity. If a result is not statistically significant, cannot be established to be causal in the population originally investigated, or is estimated from an empirical study that has little relevance to the theory being evaluated, then how can it possibly be considered externally valid or robust as a causal relationship? It makes no sense to say that some empirical research is low on internal validity but high on external validity.

7.4 Chapter Summary

In this chapter we have reviewed the concepts of internal and external validity. Internal validity has three components – statistical, causal, and construct. In previous chapters we have considered at length the methods in which researchers use experimental and nonexperimental data to establish causal and construct validity. The main contribution of this chapter is a discussion of how a researcher establishes the external validity of his or her results. We argue that while having a high degree of construct validity facilitates our ability to generalize, the ultimate proof of external validity is always empirical. Conjectures based on whether an experiment has external validity based on the extent that the experiment has ecological validity or any of the three types of internal validity are merely conjectures that must be evaluated with data.

Many of the aspects of research that some believe add to achieving external validity (such as drawing a random sample from a target population for an experiment or designing the experimental environment to be realistic to some target environment) may increase internal validity (statistical validity in the first case, causal and construct validity by motivating subjects in the second), but they cannot tell us whether the results from the experiment are externally valid. Furthermore, it is illogical to suggest that results are externally valid if they have not been demonstrated to be internally valid.

Does it make sense for many political scientists to dismiss experiments in general or laboratory experiments in particular as not having much external validity compared to nonexperimental research? As laboratory experimentalists, obviously we disagree with such a conclusion. But because this is such a pervasive view among political scientists, we discuss some of the most important concerns political scientists have about the validity of laboratory experiments in depth in the next three chapters: Chapter 8 addresses concerns about artificiality, Chapter 9 discusses the use of undergraduates as subject pools, and Chapter 10 focuses on the motivations of subjects in laboratory experiments.

Location, Artificiality, and Related Design Issues

Experimental designs in political science vary along a number of dimensions – level of analysis, the location, whether a baseline treatment is used, how "artificial" the experimental environment appears, which subjects are recruited, how the subjects are motivated, and whether deception is used. In the next three chapters we investigate the first six of these dimensions. We discuss deception after our review of ethics in experimental research because in some cases deception is not only a design issue but also an ethical one. In this chapter we focus on the differences in levels of analysis, location in experimentation, baselines, and artificiality.

8.1 Levels of Analysis

The four lab experiments on information and voting discussed in Section 2.4.3 differ in the level of analysis. In Examples 2.4 and 2.5, the focus is on individual decision-making in how voters use information on candidate quality and react to video presentations of candidates and issues. In Examples 2.6 and 2.7, both individual and group decisions are considered because the experiments evaluate predictions from formal game-theoretic models with individual and group decisions as discussed in Chapter 6. Generally experiments on game-theoretic models use group decision-making designs, although not always. When subjects participate in a group decision-making situation, the experimenter gains data on both individual and group choices. This is an advantage in that both types of behavior can be studied and more interactive, simultaneous models of causality can be considered, as we discussed in Chapter 6.

Definition 8.1 (Individual Decision-Making Experiment): *Experiment in which the subjects' choices are not interactive and the experimenter only observes individual-level behavior.*

Definition 8.2 (Group Decision-Making Experiment): *Experiment in which the subjects' choices are interactive and the experimenter observes both individual and group choices.*

But such group experiments also have disadvantages. The experimenter gathers a smaller number of observations per subject when group decisions are compared rather than individual decisions and, thus, such designs can be more costly. The experimenter also can potentially lose some control over the manipulations for the individuals. For example, suppose that an experimenter is examining the behavior of two subjects in a sequential game. If subjects who choose first never make a particular choice or rarely do, then we are less able to gather data on how the subjects who choose second would choose if the first subject had chosen differently. This happens to some extent in Example 2.7 when candidates choose particular effort levels more often than others. It may appear that an individual decision-making experiment would be better in this case in which the second subject played against a computer or monitor. However, by moving outside the context of the interactive situation, subjects' behavior may also be affected and may be different than if the decisions had been made in the context of the interactive game. That is, in Dasgupta and Williams's study, if the subjects can anticipate candidates' effort choices, they are better able to make inferences about the candidates' qualities and may not respond in the same way to choices where the candidates are computerized or artificial as in the case where the candidates are other subjects. The decision on whether to use an individual or a group decision-making experiment thus depends on the question studied. In some cases, a researcher may find it advantageous to do both.

8.2 Location of Experiments

8.2.1 Survey Experiments

Probably the most salient dimension over which experiments differ is location. Is the experiment conducted in a laboratory where all subjects come to a common location and interact with the experimenter or does the experimenter go into the field and interact with subjects on their own turf? Is one approach better than the other? In Section 2.4.2, we defined laboratory and field experiments. We also mentioned one type of experiment that is a mixture of the two – an Internet survey experiment.

A survey experiment is a type of individual decision-making experiment in which researchers randomly assign subjects to different survey question treatments as part of a survey of public opinion. Theoretically a survey experiment could be conducted in a laboratory. However, then it is difficult to draw the distinction between a survey experiment and an individual decision-making experiment where a subject is given only a flat fee or reward for participating or is unpaid. Essentially then survey experiments are a type of individual decision-making experiment that may be conducted in the laboratory, in the field, or via the Internet. To see why this is the case, consider the experiments reported on by Mondak et al. in Example 2.4. If the same experiment had been conducted via the Internet or via survey interviews, most would call the experiment a survey experiment.

Definition 8.3 (Survey Experiment): *An individual decision-making experiment embedded in a survey.*

In a particularly significant survey experiment, Sullivan et al. (1978) compared the question format used by the American National Election Studies prior to 1964 and after. Researchers using the data had found that the two sets of surveys showed significantly different attitudes towards politics. But at the same time, the survey questions had changed. Was there really a change in attitudes or did the change in survey question format account for the results? Sullivan et al. randomly assigned respondents in a survey the two sets of questions (pre-1964 or after). The researchers found that each respondent would be asked. The researchers found that indeed the change in the format of the survey did imply that the respondents had different political attitudes and that the empirical analysis comparing the two time periods was fundamentally flawed. As noted in Chapter 1, one of the most exciting advances in survey experimental design is found in the work of Paul Sniderman with computer-assisted telephone interviewing; see Sniderman et al. (1991). Using computers, telephone interviewers can randomly assign questions to subjects, manipulating the question environment. Moreover, modern handheld computer technology also allows interviewers to engage in such random assignment in face-to-face interviews. Increasingly, survey experiments are being conducted over the Internet as in Examples 2.3 and 5.3. We turn to Internet experiments in the next section.

8.2.2 Internet Experiments

Individual Decision-Making Internet Experiments (Internet Survey Experiments)

Some of the same treatments that formerly could only be conducted in the laboratory can now be conducted via the Internet in a virtual laboratory. We define Internet experiments as experiments where the subjects' interaction with the experimenter or other subjects is largely via the Internet and the relationship between the researcher and the subject is direct, albeit through the Internet. Hence, when we discuss field or laboratory experiments in this text we mean their traditional varieties – laboratory experiments are those conducted physically in a common space and field experiments are those where the researchers' interactions with subjects and subjects' interactions take place in the context of their everyday lives but not via the Internet. For example, a field experiment would be a randomized mailing of campaign material and subsequent surveys about voter preferences, whereas an Internet experiment would be a situation in which the subjects were randomly assigned to view the campaign material on their computer and then surveyed afterward about their preferences via the computer.

Definition 8.4 (Internet Experiment): *Experiment in which the subjects' interaction with the experimenter or other subjects is largely via the Internet and the relationship between the researcher and the subject is direct, albeit through the Internet.*

We have already presented several examples of Internet experiments in Examples 2.3 and 5.3. These experiments were Internet survey experiments. Next we present a third example of an Internet survey experiment, Example 8.1. This experiment is noteworthy because the authors, Tomz and Van Houweling (2008), used the Formal Theory Approach (FTA) to establish causality, albeit in an Internet survey experiment rather than in the laboratory. They considered several non-game-theoretic models of how voters respond to information about candidate policy positions and derived from these models predictions of how individuals would choose between two candidates given their own preferences and the positions of the candidates. Using formal logic, they derived scenarios that can discriminate between the various models' predictions about how voters will choose. They devised survey questions that confront individuals with these scenarios and using their control over the scenarios coupled with random assignment they were able to draw inferences about which of the three models best fit the voters' choices. Although the control they have is less than in the FTA laboratory experiment of Battaglini, Morton, and Palfrey discussed in Chapter 6, the use of theory to derive the scenarios that subjects face follows in that tradition and they exercise control by presenting the candidates as simply A and B, without other labels, and they focus on one particular policy issue, health care. Furthermore, when they analyzed the data post-experiment, as in other work using FTA, the researchers carefully modeled how errors of subjects might affect their results and considered explicitly the relationship between the statistical model used post-experiment with the formal models evaluated.

Example 8.1 (Candidate Position Internet Survey Experiment): *Tomz and Van Houweling (2008) reported on an Internet survey experiment designed to test between several non-game-theoretic models of how voters respond to information about candidate policy positions.*

Target Population and Sample: As in Example 2.3, Tomz and Van Houweling used knowledge networks to draw a national sample of voters in the United States. The interviews took place between December 2005 and June 2006, and 3,315 subjects agreed to take a preliminary survey. Based on responses to the survey, the authors did not continue with subjects who expressed middle positions on the issue of health care (positions of 0 on a scale of −5 to 5) or the most extreme positions (positions of −5 and 5) because their positions did not allow for the evaluation of the hypotheses considered. Of those left over, 1,577 subjects were administered the experiment; 13 subjects refused to answer relevant questions and were dropped. The authors dropped an additional number of respondents who also expressed highly extreme positions on health care (positions of −4 and 4), resulting in 1,045 cases analyzed. The authors did not report demographics of the sample, but offer the information on their Web pages. In general, the sample closely mirrors the adult U.S. population on most standard demographic variables.

Subject Compensation: The authors did not report how the subjects were compensated, but presumably they were compensated in the same fashion as in Example 2.3.

Environment: Subjects completed experiments over the Internet on their personal computers.

Procedures: Subjects were asked three questions. Figure 8.1 shows an example of the first two questions asked by subjects. First, subjects were asked their position on the issue of health care policy. Conditioned on their responses, a selected group of subjects (see aforementioned target population and sample) were randomly assigned to one of three scenarios of potential locations of two

(a) Self-placement

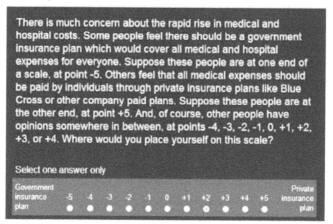

(b) Candidate choice

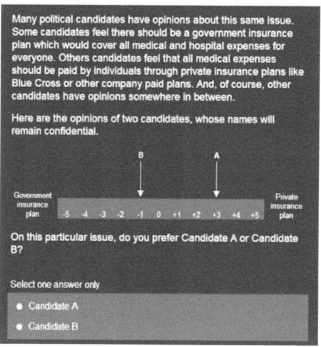

Figure 8.1. Example from Tomz and Van Houweling (2008).

candidates, A and B, on health care policy, and asked which candidate they preferred.[1] *Finally, subjects were asked their perception of the location of the status quo on health care policy.*

Results: *The authors estimated that the majority of the respondents are best viewed as preferring candidates whose policy location is closest to their ideal points, although the other models can explain nontrivial numbers of voters' preferences between the candidates. Furthermore, they found that educational attainment and degree of partisanship affected how voters chose. In particular, less educated voters and strong ideologues were less likely to vote based on proximity of candidates' positions to their ideal points.*

Comments: *Tomz and Van Houweling used FTA methods to design their Internet survey experiment evaluating non-game-theoretic models of how candidate policy positions affect voter preferences and in their post-analysis of the data.*

Obviously in Internet experiments the researcher has less control than in a physical laboratory but to some extent more control than in a traditional field experiment. We could consider Internet experiments a subset of field experiments, but Internet experiments allow for group-level experiments whereas such things are highly limited in traditional field experiments. Group-level experiments on the Internet are similar to those that take place in the laboratory because interactions of researchers and subjects take place in a common location, albeit virtually rather than physically. Traditional field experiments do not allow such a meeting of subjects and researcher. Thus, we consider Internet experiments a separate category.

Group Decision-Making Internet Experiments

Internet Experiments in Laboratories. We present three examples of game-theoretic experiments conducted via the Internet. In one case, the researchers conducted an experiment over the Internet, but subjects participated in the experiment in multiple laboratories under supervision and monitoring of the experimenters. In the second and third cases, subjects participated in the experiment outside of the laboratory. When an experiment is conducted in multiple laboratories but over the Internet between laboratories, researchers have significantly more control over subjects' choices

---

[1] Tomz and Van Houweling therefore used a between-subjects design given voters' positions on health care. They remark in footnote 8 that they used a within-subjects design. However, this is incorrect; what they meant to emphasize is that the manipulations subjects received were conditioned based on their responses, not that they observed subjects choosing given multiple manipulations.

than otherwise. However, there are still potential problems in that subjects may not believe that they are interacting with other subjects over the Internet.

The problem that subjects may not believe the experimenter that other subjects exist is confronted in Example 8.2. In this example, Eckel and Wilson (2006) conducted experiments on the trust game, which is somewhat related to the gift exchange game in Example 3.2. The trust game is a two-player game but with two sequential moves as well. In the standard trust game the first player, who is called the first mover, is given a sum of money by the researcher, again say $10, which he or she can give to a second player to invest. Whatever the first mover gives to the second player, who is called the second mover, will be increased by the experimenter, say by a multiple of 3. So if the first mover gives the second mover $5, then the second mover will receive $15. The second mover then has an option to give some of the amount he or she has received, as multiplied by the experimenter, to the first mover. The subgame perfect equilibrium predicts that the first mover will give the second mover no money because the second mover has no incentive to return any money to the first mover. Yet, first movers in trust game experiments often do give second movers money and second movers often return money to first movers (see Berg et al., 1995; Forsythe et al., 1994; Hoffman et al., 1996). The trust game is also particularly relevant to understanding delegation of authority in political systems.

Example 8.2 (Internet Trust Game Experiment): *Eckel and Wilson (2004, 2006a,b) reported on a set of trust game experiments conducted via the Internet.*

Target Population and Sample: The subjects were drawn from introductory classes in economics at Virginia Tech and dining halls at Rice University. Eckel and Wilson (2004) reported on 10 sessions using 232 subjects. These sessions ranged in numbers of subjects from 10 to 34. They reported that the subjects in these sessions were 57.3% male, 69.4% white, 9.1% African-American, 12.5% Asian-American, 5.6% Hispanic, and 3.4% foreign nationals.

Eckel and Wilson (2006a), reported on five sessions which ranged in size from 20 to 30 subjects for a total of 60 subjects. Some of these sessions appear to overlap with the sessions reported in the previous study by Eckel and Wilson (2004).

Eckel and Wilson (2006b) report on additional sessions conducted at Virginia Tech, Rice, and the University of North Carolina A&T (NCAT). The subjects from NCAT were recruited from principles of economics classes. These sessions involved 206 subjects, half from Virginia Tech, 42.2% from Rice, and 7.8% from NCAT. In these sessions the number of subjects ranged from 10 to 32. They were 55.8% male, 94% between the ages of 18 and 22, 62.6% white, 15.0% African-American, 12.6% Asian-American, 5.3% Hispanic, and 4.4% foreign nationals.

Eckel and Wilson (2006b) also recruited 296 subjects who had not participated in the aforementioned experiments who were asked to perform an evaluation task discussed in the procedures; 56.4% of the evaluators were male and these subjects were recruited over the Internet and from large classrooms at different sites.

Subject Compensation: *Subjects were paid based on their choices in experimental dollars at an exchange rate of 2 experimental dollars to 1 U.S. dollar as described in the procedures. The authors did not report whether show-up fees were given; Eckel and Wilson (2006b) reported that subjects on average earned $15.10.*

Environment: *As in Example 2.6, the experiments took place via computers in a laboratory. However, the Virginia Tech and Rice University laboratories are located off-campus and are therefore not explicitly associated with the university environment.*

Procedures: *The experiments reported all involved four basic components which were administered to subjects in the following order.*

Survey Risk Measure: *Subjects were given the Zuckerman SSS form V, which is a 40-question survey instrument designed to elicit subject preferences for seeking out novel and stimulating activities, attitudes, and values. As Eckel and Wilson (2004) report: "The survey asks subjects to choose their preferred alternative from a pair of statements about risky activities. For example, in one item the choices are (a) skiing down a high mountain slope is a good way to end up on crutches, or (b) I think I would enjoy the sensations of skiing very fast down a high mountain slope. The survey is comprised of four subfactors measuring different aspects of sensation seeking." Subjects earned 10 experimental dollars from completing the survey (the exchange rate was 2 experimental dollars per one U.S. dollar).*

Trust Game: *Subjects were randomly assigned to be either first movers or second movers in a trust game. They were paired with participants at one of the other universities. The first movers must choose whether to keep the 10 experimental dollars earned by completing the survey or to pass the money to their counterpart via the Internet. If a first mover kept the money, then that part of the experiment ended. If the first mover passed the money, the experimenter doubled the money and then the counterpart chose among nine* *different allocations of the 20 experimental dollars, ranging from sending 0 to sending 20 in increments of 2.5. The decision made by first movers was framed as a "loan."*

All subjects were then asked to predict the actions of their counterparts with first movers making the prediction after they made their decision but before finding out the second mover's decision; second movers made their prediction similarly before learning the first mover's prediction. The outcome of the game was then revealed and subjects were asked the following question: "We are very interested in what you thought about the decision problem that you just completed. In the space below please tell us what kind of situation this problem reminds you of."

Eckel and Wilson varied the information subjects had about their counterparts. Eckel and Wilson (2006a) reported on two manipulations, the first of which was a no-information manipulation in which subjects were simply told that they were participating in an experiment with subjects at another university. The subjects were not told the name of the university but simply that the other university was in Virginia or in Houston. The second manipulation was a group photo manipulation in which prior to the experiment one subject was chosen at random and asked to provide a "code word" of up to five letters. This code word was transmitted to the other site, where it was printed on a poster board and photographed with the lab and participants at the other site visible in the photograph with the faces of the persons at the other site not shown. Both photographs were uploaded to the computer server and subjects at each site then saw, on their computer screen, the photo of the other site with their own code word visible as well as the photograph of themselves holding up the other site's codeword. No other information was provided about the counterpart.

Eckel and Wilson (2004) reported on the no-information manipulation plus additional manipulations. In the information/no photo manipulation, before completing the Zuckerman scale, subjects were asked to answer eight questions with a limited number of responses. Based on these responses, subjects were told the answers to four of the questions: favorite color of their counterpart, whether their counterpart liked dogs, whether their counterpart liked movies, and their counterpart's sex. In the individual photo manipulation, subjects were photographed as part of the check-in process (the process of the photographs is described later), and observed a photograph of their counterpart just prior to making the trust decision. Eckel and Wilson (2004) did not report on the details of these manipulations and focused on the relationship between risk (as measured in the scale and in the third component of the experiments discussed later) and trust game choices in that paper.

Eckel and Wilson (2006b) reported on variations conducted on the individual photo manipulation from the previous study (Eckel and Wilson, 2004). In all the manipulations, the group photo manipulation was also used. Upon arrival at the experiment, subjects posed for four pictures – two neutral and two smiling expressions. Prior to beginning the trust game, subjects chose one of their four pictures. They were told their photograph would be seen by others during the course of the experiment. However, subjects were not told what the experiment entailed when they made their choice. Subjects were paired with up to 10 different people (the first session involved 6 trust games, the second 8, and the remainder 10), although only one of the pairings was an actual pairing and would count for payoffs (which subjects were told). The actual pairing was revealed after the trust game was over. They were asked to guess their counterpart before being informed and if they guessed correctly they would earn $1. The photos that the subjects saw who were not their partners came from the photos taken for the previous study (Eckel and Wilson, 2004). In the trust games, subjects were always either the first or second mover. In contrast to Eckel and Wilson (2004, 2006a), in the trust games first movers could send any whole experimental dollar of their survey earnings to their counterpart and the experimenter tripled the amount sent. Second movers similarly could send any amount back to the first movers. As in the preceding manipulations, subjects were asked to predict how much they would receive from their counterparts. Eckel and Wilson did not report how the choices of first movers were determined for the hypothetical pairings.

Risk Preference Measures: The subjects in all the experiments participated in two decision-making tasks. In risky decision 1, the subjects faced a set of choices between two risky lotteries for each of 10 decisions. The manipulation was a replication of a manipulation in an experiment of Holt and Laury (2002). The decision screen is shown in Figure 8.2 (we discuss these risk measures again in Chapter 10). Following Holt and Laury, subjects were told that one of the decisions would be chosen at random and then they would play the lottery they had chosen for that decision. This was implemented via choosing playing cards on the computer screen.

Before learning the outcome of the Holt and Laury procedure, subjects completed a second risky decision in which they were presented with the choice of a certain gain of 10 experimental dollars and a lottery over 0, 5, 10, 15, and 20, with the probabilities of the outcomes chosen to mimic the payoffs in the standard trust game from previous experiments. Again playing cards on the computer monitor were used to choose the outcome of the lottery if subjects chose the lottery.

Please Choose Option A or Option B for EACH Decision Below

Keep in mind that as you move down the table the chances of the higher payoff for the decision in each column increases.

	Option A	Your Choice A	Option B	Your Choice B
Decision 1	$2.00 if Card is 1 $1.60 if Card is 2-10	A: O	$3.85 if Card is 1 $0.10 if Card is 2-10	B: O
Decision 2	$2.00 if Card is 1-2 $1.60 if Card is 3-10	A: O	$3.85 if Card is 1-2 $0.10 if Card is 3-10	B: O
Decision 3	$2.00 if Card is 1-3 $1.60 if Card is 4-10	A: O	$3.85 if Card is 1-3 $0.10 if Card is 4-10	B: O
Decision 4	$2.00 if Card is 1-4 $1.60 if Card is 5-10	A: O	$3.85 if Card is 1-4 $0.10 if Card is 5-10	B: O
Decision 5	$2.00 if Card is 1-5 $1.60 if Card is 6-10	A: O	$3.85 if Card is 1-5 $0.10 if Card is 6-10	B: O
Decision 6	$2.00 if Card is 1-6 $1.60 if Card is 7-10	A: O	$3.85 if Card is 1-6 $0.10 if Card is 7-10	B: O
Decision 7	$2.00 if Card is 1-7 $1.60 if Card is 8-10	A: O	$3.85 if Card is 1-7 $0.10 if Card is 8-10	B: O
Decision 8	$2.00 if Card is 1-8 $1.60 if Card is 9-10	A: O	$3.85 if Card is 1-8 $0.10 if Card is 9-10	B: O
Decision 9	$2.00 if Card is 1-9 $1.60 if Card is 10	A: O	$3.85 if Card is 1-9 $0.10 if Card is 10	B: O
Decision 10	$2.00 if Card is 1-10	A: O	$3.85 if Card is 1-10	B: O

Thank you! You will return to this decision at the end of the session. At that time you will choose the cards that determine your earnings.

[DONE]

If you would like to review the instructions click RETURN

[RETURN]

Figure 8.2. Holt and Laury Risky Decision.

Post-Experiment Questionnaire: *"After completing all decisions, subjects were asked to complete a three part questionnaire that collected (1) demographic information, (2) answers to survey questions designed to measure trustworthiness and altruism, and (3) debriefing information."*

Photo Evaluation: *In the photo evaluations reported by Eckel and Wilson (2006b), which were conducted separately from the other experiments, each subject was asked to rate between 15 and 24 photos on a 15 word-pair items scale and was paid between $0.25 and $0.50 per photo. There were 230 photos evaluated, for a total of 5,216 evaluations. The photos and order seen were* *randomly assigned to each subject. Subjects spent an average of 80.2 seconds per photo (with a standard deviation of 64.5).*

Results: *Eckel and Wilson (2006a) found that there are significant differences between the no-information and group photo manipulations in that subjects demonstrate excessive trust in the no-information manipulation because they do not believe that another subject exists and that the experimenter is their counterpart (reported in the post-experiment survey). Eckel and Wilson (2004) found no statistical relationship between the behavioral risk measures and the decision to trust unless they add in control variables, in which case they found a weak relationship between risk measured in the survey and the decision to trust. Finally, Eckel and Wilson (2006b) found that subjects measured as attractive through the photo evaluations were viewed as more trustworthy and were trusted at higher rates and received more from first movers. However, attractiveness had a penalty in that more attractive individuals received less from second movers, holding other things constant.*

Comments: *The Eckel and Wilson experiments illustrate some of the difficulties involved in conducting experiments via the Internet. However, they also demonstrate some of the advantages – by doing so they are able to manipulate the attractiveness of subjects' counterparts in the trust games in a fashion that would not be possible if the experiment had been conducted in a single laboratory.*

Eckel and Wilson's Internet experiments have several noteworthy features. First et al. (2006a) considered the possibility that subjects may not believe that other subjects are real in an Internet game-theoretic experiment. Indeed they found evidence that supports this fact. They provided an interesting example of how one can make the subjects in an Internet game-theoretic experiment real and still maintain anonymity through the use of the group photo without faces and the codeword. Of course, given modern technologies that allow easy photo alterations, it is not clear that this method will continue to work. Their experiments demonstrate the difficulties that can be involved in Internet experiments.

Yet, their experiments also demonstrate the promise of what can be done via the Internet. That is, they are able to measure subjects' willingness to trust strangers based on physical appearance while maintaining anonymity for subjects, which for ethical reasons can be desirable in an experiment.

Internet Experiments Outside of the Laboratory. Our second example, Example 8.3, is a case of a game-theoretic experiment conducted via the Internet in which subjects did not come to a laboratory, but responded in the field.

In this experiment, Egas and Riedl (2008) investigated how punishment affects levels of cooperation in a public goods game. A public goods game is a game in which a group of people choose whether to contribute to the production of a public good. If all contribute, then everyone benefits sufficiently to offset their contribution. However, given that others are contributing, each individual has an incentive to "free ride" and not contribute. If no one is contributing, the cost of contributing exceeds the benefits that the individual would receive. The game-theoretic equilibrium prediction is for all not to contribute, or to free ride. Yet, in experiments subjects often choose to contribute in the one-shot game and at the early rounds of repeated versions of the game. Nevertheless, cooperation usually declines in such games even with subjects randomly assigned to new partners in the game. Some researchers have suggested that if punishment is allowed then cooperation may be higher in such games, which is the subject of Egas and Riedl's experiment.

Example 8.3 (Internet Public Goods Game Experiment): *Egas and Riedl (2008) reported on a public goods game experiment conducted via the Internet.*

Target Population and Sample: Subjects were recruited from the Dutch-speaking world population with Internet connections. The recruitment took place via advertisements in newspapers and on the radio in The Netherlands and the science Web site of the Dutch public broadcasting station VPRO. Egas and Riedl reported the following:

"In all recruitment announcements, we made sure that the actual content of the experiment was not revealed. The only information about the experiment given during the recruitment period was that a scientific experiment will take place with the possibility to earn money. (The title of the experiment was 'Speel je rijk', which loosely translates as 'Play to get rich'.) No further information about the content was revealed until the last experimental session was finished. Furthermore, it was announced that the experiment was going to take place from 24 to 28 May 2004, with two sessions per day (at 16.00 and 20.30): only one person is allowed to participate in one session, and that a session will take approximately 45–60 min. A person interested in participating was asked to send an e-mail and to indicate two preferred sessions (dates and times). They were then sent an acknowledgement e-mail. This e-mail contained the following information: (i) a random lottery will decide whether (s)he is chosen as an actual participant and (ii) if (s)he is chosen, this information will be transmitted shortly (usually 24 hours) before the chosen session takes place. All together more than 4000 people subscribed for the experiment. From these,

approximately 1000 were randomly selected as participants, 846 of which actually participated (not all selected people 'showed up' at the experiment)."

Egas and Riedl note that (p. 872) "[t]he average gross income of our subjects was close to the actual average gross income in The Netherlands. The average age was 35 years (range: 12–80 years), and education ranged from secondary school (3%) up to university degrees (33%). Female participants (28%) were under-represented." In the electronic supplement, the authors recounted that (p. 5) "[a] clear majority (58%) of our participants is either employed or self-employed, whereas only 29% is still in training (pupils, college and university students). The remaining subjects (13%) are either not employed, retired or are not covered by any of these categories.... The majority of participants (65%) does [sic] not have any children (likely due to the over representation of younger highly educated adults...). Nevertheless, 83% share a household with other people... and virtually everybody has at least one sibling.... Also, only 10% of the participants did not vote in the recent national elections.... The distribution of participants over the political parties shows a left-liberal bias compared to the outcome of the respective election."

Subject Compensation: Subjects were paid based on their choices as described in the procedures. The average earnings were 12.20 euros.

Environment: Subjects interacted with the experimenter and other subjects via the Internet in unknown locations. Care was undertaken so that payments were anonymous to the experimenter.

Procedures: An experimental session was conducted as follows. First all participants received an email with a password and the Web site address from where the experiment was going to start. Participants then logged into the experiment. Subjects received online instructions that explained the structure of the experiment. After having read the instructions, subjects answered a number of control questions. Only if subjects answered all questions correctly were they allowed to participate (a few subjects dropped out at this point). During the instructions and control questions, subjects could ask questions of the experimenters via a chat window built into the software.

Subjects then entered a waiting queue until a group of 18 participants was formed. Each of the 18 then played six rounds of a public good game (described next) with or without punishment, depending on the manipulation. In each session only one manipulation was implemented and manipulations were timed beforehand so that there was a balanced distribution of afternoon and evening sessions across manipulations. Subjects were unaware of other manipulations. Subjects were randomly assigned into groups of three each period to play the game, using perfect strangers matching (see Definition 6.13).

Egas and Riedl considered five manipulations – one that was a standard public goods game and four that allowed for punishment. We describe each next.

Public Goods Game: *Each subject was endowed with 20 experimental monetary units (EMUs) and could contribute between 0 and 20 of this endowment to a group project. Each EMU contributed earned 0.5 EMU for each of the three group members. After decisions were made, each group member was informed about the other group members' contributions and the resulting earnings. In the manipulation without punishment, the game ended at this point.*

Punishment Game T13: *This game was the same as the basic public goods game with the addition that after finding out the outcome of the contributions, each member had the possibility of punishing other members by assigning between 0 and 10 punishment points (PPs) to each of the two other members. Each assigned PP cost the punisher 1 EMU and reduced the payoff of the punished by 3 EMU. After the punishment stage, the game ended.*

Punishment Game T31: *This game is the same as T13 with the change that each assigned PP cost the punisher 3 EMU and reduced the payoff of the punished by 1 EMU.*

Punishment Game T11: *Same as T13 except that both costs were 1 EMU.*

Punishment Game T33: *Same as T13 except that both costs were 3 EMU.*

Results: *Only in T13 is punishment effective in that contributions increase over rounds; in all other cases, contributions decline quickly. In all manipulations, inflicted punishment strongly depends on the difference in contributions between the punisher and the punished. Actual payoffs are lowest when punishment maintains cooperation because of the payoffs destroyed through punishment. The authors examine demographic differences and find that being older and male significantly increases the amount allocated to PPs, whereas being a student significantly decreases the amount.*

Comments: *Egas and Riedl pointed out that the results from the experiment are strikingly similar to those found with students in similar games (Fehr and Gächter, 2002) reanalyzing their data.*

Like Eckel and Wilson, Egas and Riedl dealt with a number of issues in designing the experiment over the Internet. In the electronic supplement available on the Web page of the journal *Proceedings of the Royal Society*, they describe these concerns and how they used experimental control in an Internet experiment. In particular, they were concerned about the loss of control that researchers can maintain in the laboratory, which were not problems for Eckel and Wilson. As they note in the laboratory, although (p. 1) "participants know that other humans are present, . . . each participant is interacting with others through a computer interface and in a cubicle (to maintain anonymity of participants and prevent disruption of the experimental conditions by conferring, teaming up etc.). Simultaneously, the experimenter can answer questions of individual participants on the experimental procedure, and make sure that the participants stick to the rules of the experiment and do not quit before the experiment is finished."

To make the virtual laboratory similar to the environment of the laboratory, Egas and Riedl implemented the following:

- They created software that allowed a participant who accidently lost his or her connection to log in again and continue where they had left off. In the case where a participant quit during a session, the software was programmed to make the theoretically predicted decisions of no contribution and no punishment, so that the others could continue (but this never happened).
- Teaming up by participants was controlled by not revealing the content of the experiment until a session was in progress. Subjects chose two preferred sessions when they first subscribed to the experiment, but only 25% were selected to participate; thus, the probability of being in the same session as a friend was 12.5%. Subjects were told the session assignment less than 24 hours in advance. Furthermore, in each session, subjects were allocated into groups of 18 and only interacted with those in their same group.
- To reduce the possibility that subjects were participating more than once, if individuals subscribed twice under the same name but different email addresses, one of the subscriptions was dropped. Similarly, the random selection mechanism made it unlikely that an individual participated more than once. (The probability of being able to participate twice if someone signed up with two different email addresses and names was 1/16.) Ex post they found in the payment records that there were no instances of double bank accounts or double names.
- To ensure anonymity of the subjects, participants logging into the experiment were assigned an ID number for the experimental results. Participants filled in bank details at the end of the experiment and the software made a list of the bank details with the associated money to be sent without the ID numbers of subscription details attached so that experimenters were unaware of the link between a participant's decisions and his or her identity. This information was provided to participants prior to the experiment. Of course, there are limits to this

type of anonymity on the Internet as subjects necessarily need recourse if there is a problem, for example, in sending out the money.

- To allow for questions in the experiment, a chat box was built into the software such that subjects could ask questions of the experimenters during the instructions and the control questions (quiz after the instructions).

Unlike Eckel and Wilson, Egas and Riedl did not attempt to convince subjects with photos that the other participants are subjects. However, we suspect that the advertising and public notice of the experiment reduced these problems and that subjects were more likely to believe that the other subjects existed. They compared their results to previous laboratory experiments using students and found little difference, suggesting that subjects did believe that they were engaging in a game with other humans and not a computer.

One of the oldest continuing running experiments in the social sciences – the Iowa Political Stock Market, which is part of the Iowa Electronic Markets – is our last example, Example 8.4. See Berg et al. (2008) for a review of the market's history and Majumder et al. (2009) for a recent study of the dynamics of the market. In the political stock markets, subjects buy and sell contracts about an upcoming political event, usually an election. The market is nonprofit and conducted for research purposes only.[2] Note that although we consider these markets experiments, the subjects are not randomly assigned to different manipulations and there is no obvious baseline manipulation within the experiments themselves. Two baselines have been considered to evaluate the data – opinion polls and theoretical baselines. We address the use of theoretical baselines in experiments in Section 8.3.

Example 8.4 (Iowa Political Stock Market): *Forsythe et al. (1992) described the first election predictions market for research purposes at the University of Iowa which was created in 1988. The market continues in operation as part of the Iowa Electronic Markets (IEM; see http://www.biz.uiowa.edu/iem/index.cfm).*

Target Population and Sample: Originally the market was restricted to members of the University of Iowa community, but it is now open to anyone

---

[2] As described in Example 8.4, the researchers always stand ready to buy and sell a bundle or unit portfolio in the market at the aggregate liquidation price. As a result, the researchers do not earn profits and traders seeking arbitrage opportunities maintain that the prices of the contracts in the market sum to the aggregate liquidation price.

interested, worldwide. To participate, a subject opens an account and obtains and reads the Trader's Manual. The account registration form is located at http://iemweb.biz.uiowa.edu/signup/online/. There is a one-time service charge of $5 to activate an account. Subjects complete the confirmation form after registering and mail it to the IEM with a check made out to the University of Iowa with their initial investment (which can be from $5 to $500) plus the service charge. If a subject cannot send a check drawn on a U.S. bank in U.S. dollars, an electronic transfer can be arranged. After the check is received, the account is activated and the subject's IEM login and password are sent via email. In some cases, faculty have signed up classes to participate as a class exercise. To do so, a faculty member should contact the IEM office at iem@uiowa.edu. Students in classes are also required to pay the service fee. Subjects are free to close accounts and request a full or partial withdrawal of their cash balances at any time; the requests are processed twice a month.

Subject Compensation: Subjects are paid based on their choices and the outcome of the event which is the issue of the market as described in the procedures that follow. Subjects are mailed checks. Accounts that are inactive for more than six months are assessed a $5 inactivity charge.

Environment: Subjects interact using their own computers via the Internet.

Procedures: Many different prediction markets have been set up over the years. In essence, traders buy and sell contracts that are based on the outcomes of future real-world events such as elections. For example, one event might be predicting which of the two major party candidates, McCain or Obama, would receive the most votes in the 2008 presidential election as in the winner-take-all IEM market (see http://iemweb.biz.uiowa.edu/WebEx/marketinfo_english.cfm?Market_ID=149). After the outcome of the event is realized, then the market closes and subjects receive earnings based on their contract holdings (the contracts are liquidated). In our example, if a subject had a contract for Obama, after the election he or she earned $1, and if he or she had a contract for McCain, after the election he or she earned $0.

There are three ways that subjects buy and sell contracts: (1) market orders, (2) limit orders, and (3) bundle transactions. A market order is a request to buy or sell a contract at the current ask and bid prices. A limit order is a request to buy or sell an asset at a specified price for a specified period of time. A bundle (sometimes called a "unit portfolio") is a set of contracts which can be purchased from or sold to the exchange at a fixed price, which is the guaranteed aggregate liquidation value of the contracts. So in the winner-take-all 2008 presidential election market, a bundle comprised of one McCain contract and one Obama contract which was available at all times for traders to purchase *for $1. Traders were also able to sell back bundles for $1 at any point. Trading takes place 24 hours a day.*

Results: *The data from the political stock markets continue to be studied. In the first research paper on the topic, Forsythe et al. (1992) considered how well the market predicted the outcome of the 1988 presidential election as compared to opinion polls, finding that the market outperformed the polls. However, the debate on the predictive capabilities of such markets as compared to polls is continuing; see, for instance, the recent paper of Erikson and Wlezien (2008).*

Comments: *For a recent study of the dynamics of the political stock markets, see Majumder et al. (2009). Some would argue that the markets in IEM are not an experiment because there is no baseline manipulation within the experiment nor is there random assignment. That said, the baseline of opinion poll data taken during the same time period has been used as a comparison as well as theoretical baselines.*

8.2.3 Lab-in-the-Field Experiments

Another mixture of the lab and field we have explored only a little is "lab-in-the-field" experiments. We have discussed one case in which a researcher conducted a lab-in-the-field experiment, Taber (2009), presented in Example 4.1. Formerly, most game-theoretic interactive experiments took place in a laboratory at a university or a research institution. However, a growing number of researchers are taking the procedures of the laboratory into the field, using subjects from a region of particular interest. For example, Habyarimana et al. (2007) conducted a series of game-theoretic experiments in Kampala, Uganda. Whitt and Wilson (2007) conducted a set of game-theoretic experiments with Hurricane Katrina victims in Houston shelters in the period shortly after the hurricane, and Bahry and Wilson (2006) conducted game-theoretic experiments in two multiethnic republics in Russia. Usually a lab-in-the-field experiment takes place when researchers wish to conduct a traditional laboratory experiment but take advantage of a particular naturally occurring situation in the field, such as Whitt and Wilson's study of Katrina victims. In Habyarimana et al.'s case, one goal was to make sure that the subjects in the laboratory experiment were a randomized draw from a given population, which, as we noted in the previous chapter, can increase the statistical validity of the results.

Definition 8.5 (Lab-in-the-Field Experiment): *Experiment where the subjects participate in a common physical location (called the lab in the field) but the experimenter, to some degree, brings the laboratory to the subjects' natural environment more than the subjects come to the laboratory.*

Example 8.5 is a lab-in-the-field game-theoretic experiment which considers behavior in three types of simple games: dictator, ultimatum, and trust. We have already mentioned the ultimatum game in Section 3.3.3 and the trust game in Example 8.2. The dictator game is the simplest of the three and has only one move by a player. It is exactly as it sounds. A researcher gives a subject, called a proposer, a fixed amount of money, say $10, and tells the proposer that he or she can give some of that money to another subject, called a responder or receiver, and keep the rest. The responder has no choice in the game. Purely selfish behavior would result in the proposer keeping all of the money. However, as Camerer (2003, pp. 57–58) remarks, proposers often transfer money, and in some experiments more than 50% of subjects transfer money.

The interesting aspect of dictator, ultimatum, and trust games is that they are all cases in which subjects in many experiments have not chosen the subgame perfect equilibrium that is predicted by game theory; for a precise definition of subgame perfect equilibria, see McCarty and Meirowitz (2006). But in a loose sense these are equilibria in which each player is choosing the optimal strategy in all the possible subgames. Many researchers have devised models of behavior to explain the behavior in dictator games (see, e.g., Bolton and Ockenfels, 1998; Fehr and Schmidt, 1999; Andreoni and Miller, 2002; Charness and Rabin, 2002). Nevertheless, some argue that the excessive giving by proposers in the dictator game may be an artefact of the experimental design (see Bardsley, 2008), which we discuss more expansively in Chapter 10.

Example 8.5 (Trust, Ultimatum, and Dictator Games Lab-in-the-Field Experiment): *Bahry and Wilson (2004, 2006) reported on an experiment conducted in two multiethnic republics of Russia, examining trust and bargaining behavior.*

Target Population and Sample: Bahry and Wilson drew subjects from the noninstitutionalized permanent residents 18 years of age and older of two multiethnic regions of Russia, Tatarstan and Sakha-Yakutia. Both regions contain ethnic Russians – 43% in Tatarstan and 45% in Sakha-Yakutia; ethnic Tatars comprise 50% of Tatarstan's population and ethnic Yakuts comprise 40% of Sakha-Yakutia's population. A stratified random sample was drawn from this population with oversampling of the underrepresented minority in each region. The researchers first conducted a 2-hour, face-to-face survey of 2,572 people, 1,266 in Tatarstan and 1,306 in Sakha-Yakutia, with response rates of 81% and 72%, respectively. The survey "covered a number of issues ranging from work to social relations and ethnic identification to trust." Whenever possible, the interviewer was the same nationality as the subjects and conducted the interview in either Russian or the ethnic language of the subject, depending on subjects' preferences. The survey results are reported on in Bahry et al. (2005).

A subset of these subjects were invited to participate in an experiment. The subjects invited were those who lived in the capital city and another major city in each republic, some smaller towns, and some villages within a day's driving distance of the cities or towns. Villages where fewer than 20 subjects had been interviewed were excluded. At the end of the interview, the designated subjects were invited to participate in the lab-in-the-field experiments. A short time before the experiments, the subjects were contacted to set a day for them to participate.

There were 61 out-of-sample subjects, who were typically family members of friends who had come to participate in the experiment, as a substitute for the original subject or they were recruited by interviewers to ensure sufficient group size to run each session. Fifty-five of these out-of-sample subjects were contacted and interviewed with the face-to-face survey at a later date; the remaining six could not be located or refused to be interviewed. Bahry and Wilson excluded these out-of-sample subjects from their analysis.

Subject Compensation: Subjects received a 30-ruble fee when they agreed to participate and another 120-ruble show-up fee when they arrived at the experiment. Subjects were also paid their earnings from the experiment as described. The average earnings were 540 rubles in Tatarstan and 558 rubles in Sakha-Yakutia, which is between US $17.40 and $18.10. The payments were a week's wage for more than a majority of the subjects. A total of 650 subjects participated in the experiment, 254 from Tatarstan and 396 from Sakha-Yakutia.

Environment: The two regions of Russia examined were the site of ethnic revivals by the titular nationalities in the late 1980s and 1990s, so ethnicity is especially salient for the subjects. Furthermore, the region has experienced a good deal of uncertainty and growing inequality in the 10 years of Russia's market transition. The experiments were conducted mostly in schools or public libraries, which varied significantly in room size and amenities. All subjects were in the same room. The standard environment was that subjects sat at tables and had space to complete the tasks requested. Cardboard boxes were used as screens so that the subjects' decisions were confidential from other subjects. Subjects were assigned numbers as they arrived and no names were used on any of the experimental materials.

General Procedures: Bahry and Wilson conducted 42 experimental sessions (20 in Tatarstan, 22 in Sakha-Yakutia) in the summer of 2002. Each session lasted approximately 2 hours. Experimenters first ran the instructions *in Russian or the titular language and demonstrated the tasks for the subjects. The subjects played seven games in the experiment. The first five were dictator games, the sixth was a trust game, and the final one an ultimatum game. At the conclusion of the games, the subjects completed an individual decision task that measured their risk preferences (we discuss these types of measures in Chapter 10). Finally, subjects completed a one-page demographic survey. Subjects were then debriefed, thanked for their participation, and allowed to leave. Half left right away, while the other half stayed, opened their envelopes, and counted their money.*

Dictator Game Procedures: *In the first dictator game, the subjects were given eight 10-ruble notes, eight pieces of similarly sized blank paper, and two envelopes. They were asked to allocate the money and slips of paper between themselves and another subject in the same republic but not in the room. What they allocated was given to subjects in subsequent sessions in the same republic. The reason for giving the subjects pieces of paper was so that when the subjects turned in the envelopes they were given anonymity in their decisions. We discuss the importance of anonymity in these games in Chapter 10. The second dictator game was the same as the first, but the subjects were told that the other player was someone in a different region. Again, what they allocated was given to subjects in subsequent sessions in the other republic.*

The next two dictator games were the opposite; the subject received envelopes from other people with some sender characteristics on the outside of the envelope. The subjects were asked to guess how much was in the envelopes, although they were not allowed to open the envelopes until after the experiment was over. In the fifth dictator game, the subjects were given two envelopes, each with a picture of the sender on it, and were asked to choose one of the two envelopes. Again, subjects were asked to guess how much money the sender had left in the envelope chosen but were not allowed to open the envelope until after the experiment was over.

Trust Game Procedures: *In the trust game, subjects were first randomly assigned as either first or second movers by private drawing of poker chips from a hat. A blue chip meant a subject was a first mover and a white chip meant a subject was a second mover. Subjects' chips were hidden from other subjects. Subjects were told that they would be randomly and anonymously paired with partners in the same room. The anonymity was maintained by the use of secret ID numbers. After the chips were selected, subjects were given instructions about the game. Subjects were given many examples of how the experiment worked and asked questions of comprehension to be sure they understood.*

First movers were given an envelope marked "send," eight 10-ruble notes, and eight blank pieces of paper. Second movers were also given an envelope marked "send," but with the number 9999 written in the upper left-hand corner, and 16 blank slips of paper. All subjects were told to write their ID numbers in the upper right-hand corner of their send envelope and to count the number of items handed to them. Both first and second movers were asked to place eight objects, either paper or money, in the envelopes. The envelopes were then collected and given to one of the authors who was outside of the room. One of the authors recorded the information from the envelopes by ID number and tripled the amounts given by the first movers. While the information was being recorded, the subjects were given forms to fill out. First movers were asked to record how much they had put in the envelope, to triple that amount, and then predict how much they would be returned. Second movers were asked to predict how much first movers would send to them.

After the data were recorded and the money was tripled, the envelopes were shuffled and randomly distributed to second movers. At the same time, first movers received the envelopes from second movers so that player type was anonymous. In some cases there was an odd number of subjects in the room. When that was the case, the division was made such that there was one more second mover than first movers and one of the first movers' envelopes was randomly chosen and duplicated so that all second movers received an envelope. After all the envelopes were distributed, subjects were asked to write their ID numbers in the lower right-hand corner of the envelope and count the contents. First movers were asked to place eight slips of blank paper in the envelope after counting. Second movers were asked to decide how much money to return to their assigned first mover. Then the envelopes were collected and the data were recorded. The envelopes were then sealed and returned to the subjects according to the ID numbers that had been recorded.

Ultimatum Game Procedures: Subjects again drew poker chips to determine which ones would be proposers and which would be responders. Again, the assignments were kept anonymous. Forms were given to all subjects. Proposers were asked to choose one of nine possible ways to divide a sum that was approximately equivalent to a day's wage (160 rubles in Tatarstan, 240 rubles in Sakha-Yakutia) with an anonymous responder in the room. Responders were also given a list of all of the nine possible ways and asked whether they would accept or reject each one. Some responders made odd choices, such as rejecting everything but an equal split, and they were asked whether they had intended to do so and given examples of what would happen under the different scenarios. Two subjects changed their minds. The forms were taken out of the room, the subjects were randomly matched, and envelopes were delivered to the subjects based on the joint decisions made. If there was an odd number of subjects in the room, similar to the trust game, the extra player was designated a

responder. The proposer received the allocation based on one of the responders'
choices and the two responders were paid based on their decisions.

   Results: *The results from the trust games are reported by Bahry and Wilson*
(2004) and the results from the ultimatum games are reported by Bahry
and Wilson (2006). The results of the dictator games and the risk preference
information are used as measures of subject characteristics to explain behavior
in some analyses. In general, Bahry and Wilson found that the subjects in the
games are far more generous and trusting than the game-theoretic predictions
and that the behavior is similar to that found in other experimental studies
conducted at universities with student subject pools.

   Comments: *Bahry and Wilson contend that the subjects are ideal for study-*
ing variations in bargaining and trust behavior due to heterogeneity within
a population as well as such behavior in transitional societies. Particularly
interesting is that Bahry and Wilson found that there is little relationship
between survey responses on levels of trust and the behavior of the subjects,
suggesting that such survey evidence of low trust in transitional societies may
be problematic. Holm and Nystedt (2008) reported a similar finding.

8.2.4 Is Field More Than a Location?

The preceding definitions of field and laboratory experiments are what
has been the standard nomenclature among experimentalists and nonexperimentalists in the social sciences. Recently Harrison and List (2004)
challenged this perspective in experimental economics. They generalized
the concept of field experiments to encompass not only the location of the
experiment but also the nature of the subject pool, the nature of the information that subjects bring to the task, the nature of the commodity (since
they are speaking primarily to economists, most of the experiments concern
economic choices), the nature of the stakes (again, they are speaking primarily to experimentalists who use financial incentives to motivate subjects),
and finally the nature of the environment in which the subject operates
(location). They propose a taxonomy of experiments that involve these various dimensions. For example, they define a laboratory experiment as one
that uses a standard subject pool (presumably undergraduates), abstract
framing, and an imposed set of rules. They classify a laboratory experiment
which uses a "nonstandard" subject pool as an artefactual field experiment that has the other aforementioned features. They classify a laboratory
experiment which uses both a nonstandard subject pool and some other
field context (commodity, task, or information) as a framed field experiment. And finally they classify a "natural field experiment" as a framed field

experiment but one in which the subjects' choices take place outside of the laboratory in the subjects' natural environment and, importantly, where the subjects do not know they are in an experiment.

In our view, the expansion of the definition of field by Harrison and List conflates the "fieldness" of an experiment with a particular view of the determinants of the validity of an experiment's results. They state (p. 1010): "Our primary point is that dissecting the characteristics of field experiments helps define what might be better called an ideal experiment, in the sense that one is able to observe a subject in a controlled setting but where the subject does not perceive any of the controls as being unnatural and there is no deception being practiced." Harrison and List equate field with their definition of an ideal experiment. Yet, not all experiments conducted in the field meet these criteria. Sometimes field experiments use deception (in fact for subjects not to know they are in an experiment, deception is required), sometimes the control is seen as unnatural, sometimes not all subjects' choices can be observed, and sometimes the experimenter is not able to exercise the control over important variables.

Moreover, we do not agree with their definition of an ideal experiment, which suggests that this particular type of experiment, one in which subjects can be observed but do not perceive such observation, and everything about the experimental environment is "natural" is more valid than other possible experimental designs that do not meet this ideal. It is not clear that the best experiment is always one where the subject does not perceive any of the controls as being unnatural. Sometimes the best choice for a particular experimental question is to make controls extremely explicit and unnatural, as in the experiment with soccer players in Example 9.2, which we discuss in the next chapter. Recall that in Example 6.2 Chou et al. found that using the battle context for the guessing game experiment introduced new problems with experimental control such that subjects misunderstood the nature of the choice before them.

At other times the experimentalist desires to investigate a research question about a new or proposed institution that is impossible to create in the data generating processs (DGP), as in Example 8.6. In this experiment, Casella et al. (2008) investigate a voting procedure proposed by Casella (2005) called storable votes. In storable votes, individuals have a set of votes that they can cast over time on binary choices. Casella et al. showed theoretically that the ability to store votes over time can allow minority voters to express the intensity of their preferences and achieve outcomes in their favor without much loss in overall social welfare. Thus, storable votes may be a good mechanism to allow minorities influence in a fashion that treats all voters equitably. But storable votes have never been used by a political institution and it is unclear whether the theoretical predictions would hold empirically. Convincing members of a political body to adopt such a voting procedure is difficult and may be ethically problematic. Conducting an experiment designed to test the procedure has value even though there is no real-world counterpart to the voting mechanism.

Example 8.6 (Storable Votes Lab Experiment): *Casella et al. (2008) report on experiments evaluating a voting system called storable votes in which each voter has a stock of votes to spend as desired over a series of binary choices.*

Target Population and Sample: The subjects were registered students recruited through Web sites at experimental laboratories at the California Institute of Technology, UCLA, and Princeton University. Eleven sessions were conducted with 10 to 27 subjects, for a total of 167 subjects.

Subject Compensation: Subjects were paid according to their choices as outlined in the following procedures. Subjects were given a show-up payment of $10 and earned $17 on average if in the minority in the voting games and $31 on average if in the majority (see procedures). Payoffs were computed in experimental currency at an exchange rate of 100 units equals $1.

Environment: The experiment was conducted via computers in a computer laboratory using the procedures described in Example 2.6.

Procedures: Subjects participated in a series of two-stage voting games (for 15–30 rounds depending on manipulation) that proceeded as follows. First, subjects were randomly assigned as majority voters (they were told they were members of the AGAINST group) or as minority voters (they were told they were members of the FOR group). Then subjects were randomly divided into groups of 5 with 3 majority and 2 minority voters (in one session the committees were groups of 9 with 5 majority and 4 minority voters). Within each committee, subjects voted over two proposals sequentially. Subjects had one vote for each proposal plus two bonus votes that could be allocated across proposals as desired by the subject. That is, in voting over the first proposal, voters chose whether to cast 1, 2, or 3 votes. Votes were automatically cast either as for or against depending on whether they were in the minority or majority, respectively; that is, subjects only chose how many votes to cast, not how to cast them.

The payoffs for the proposals were revealed to the subjects privately before each choice and a function of the valuations which were random draws. The valuations were restricted to integer values and were drawn with equal probability from the support [−100, −1] for majority members and from [1, 100]. If a proposal passed, members of the minority received their valuation as their payoff while the majority members received 0. If a proposal did not pass, the members of the majority received the absolute value of their valuation as payoff and the members of the minority received 0. Ties were broken randomly.

After the outcome of voting over the first proposal was revealed, subjects were randomly assigned new valuations for the second proposal. All of the subjects' remaining votes were automatically cast either for or against depending on whether they were in the minority or majority, respectively. The outcome of voting over the second proposal was then revealed to subjects and they were randomly rematched into new groups of 5, and the game was repeated.

Casella et al. engaged in four manipulations. In manipulation B (for basic), each member of each group was randomly assigned a valuation drawn independently from the specified support, and in manipulation C (for correlated), all members of the same group in the same committee were assigned the same valuation and subjects were told this was the case. Manipulation C2 was exactly like manipulation C except that for each group a single voter (group representative) cast votes on behalf of all members of that group. The group representative was randomly chosen each period. Finally, manipulation CChat was also exactly like manipulation C except that before the vote on the first proposal, voters could exchange messages via computer with other members of the same group. Voters were instructed not to identify themselves, and the messages were anonymous but otherwise unconstrained. All the manipulations were conducted using a between-subjects design (see Section 3.3.3).

Results: *In the empirical analysis, Casella et al. compared both manipulations and outcomes to simple majority voting in which each voter casts only one vote sincerely. Casella et al. found that indeed storable votes helped the minority to win. Furthermore, they found that in the B, C2, and CChat manipulations there were losses in overall efficiency as compared to simple majority voting but a gain in efficiency in the C manipulation. Nevertheless, they found these losses and gains in efficiency were small in magnitude.*

Comments: *This experiment is a good example of how the experimental method can be used to investigate a proposed mechanism that has yet to be used in consequential voting situations.*

A researcher may not have a particular target field application in mind when running an experiment on a proposed institution like storable votes. For another example, a researcher may be investigating a particular political institution such as a principal agent relationship that exists between a voter and a candidate, or a legislator and a bureaucrat, or an executive and an executive agency. Which application should be given prominence to establish the "fieldness" of the experiment? Sometimes the best way to mitigate the effects of artificiality in one dimension is to increase that artificiality in another via the use of financial incentives as, for example, in voting games.

Furthermore, a number of political science experimentalists have used deception because they believed it was the ideal approach for their particular study. However, many other experimentalists, including ourselves, find deception problematic and attempt to avoid its use. Deception also creates special ethical concerns. We discuss deception more expansively in Chapter 13. Given that deception is used by some political scientists purposively and occasionally used in field experiments, it does not seem to us that the absence of deception makes an experiment more of a field experiment than its presence. Therefore, we simply define a field experiment by its location as is traditional and separately discuss issues of the validity of various experimental designs.

8.2.5 Why Laboratories?

Laboratory experiments provide a number of advantages. First and foremost, in the laboratory it is relatively easy to measure subjects' behavioral differences when manipulations are compared and subjects are randomly assigned to manipulations. In contrast, in field and Internet experiments, random assignment may not be enough for the researcher to correct for that lack of control in order to fruitfully compare manipulations. For example, suppose that a researcher is conducting a decision-making experiment that evaluates the extent that different types of campaign advertisements affect voter preferences. In the laboratory, the researcher can show the ads in a specially designed environment that can be held constant across subjects. In the field, the subjects can be shown the ads in their homes or via the Internet, but the researcher loses control over other aspects of the environment in which the ads are watched. If these environmental differences vary systematically with which ads are viewed or other factors that affect the subjects' viewing of the ads and these factors are unobservable by the researcher, then the comparison between ads can be more difficult to determine. We have already discussed these issues extensively in Chapters 4 and 5.

The advantage of control in the laboratory also extends to group experiments such as in Example 2.6. By conducting the experiment in the laboratory, the researcher is able to control the choices before voters in the election and what voters receive from the outcomes of the elections. This is control that is not generally available in the field (although it can be over the Internet) and it is highly unlikely that jurisdictions would allow for their electoral systems to be randomly manipulated by a researcher.

Second, in the laboratory (and on the Internet) the researcher has the ability to create environments that do not exist at all in observational data. For example, in the laboratory the researcher can conduct group and individual decision-making experiments on voting mechanisms, as in Example 8.6, which are used very little if at all in any country. Many have proposed that approval voting would be a better choice mechanism than plurality rule. In the laboratory a researcher can create and conduct elections using new procedures that would be difficult to convince jurisdictions of adopting on a random basis.[3]

The third advantage of laboratory (and also Internet) experiments is that the researcher can induce a wider range of variation than is possible in the field. For example, suppose a researcher theorizes that voters who choose late in sequential voting elections like presidential primaries learn about candidates' policy positions from horse race information about the outcomes of early voting and this learning affects their choices in the elections. In the field, the researcher can randomly provide horse race information to later voters during a presidential primary contest and observe via a survey how that affects their choices and information. This is similar to the experiment conducted by Tomz and Van Houweling (Example 8.1). But suppose the researcher also expects that the effect is related to the policy positions of the candidates. Like Tomz and Van Houweling he or she can randomly assign to subjects candidate policy positions to measure the effect. However, the laboratory affords the researcher the opportunity to intervene in hundreds of elections, not just a few, and expose subjects to a wide diversity of choices. Thus, the researcher in the laboratory can pick out subtle differences in predictions of theories that the researcher in the field cannot pick out because of the limitation in the number and variety of observations. In Example 2.4, Mondak et al. investigated the effects of candidate quality differences on voter choice and, in their setup of the hypothetical candidates, controlled the other aspects of the candidates that can also affect voter preferences, so that they could isolate the effects of candidate quality.

Finally, there are still some technologies and manipulations used in experiments that require subjects to go to a laboratory. Mondak and Huckfeldt (2006) were able to measure how accessible attitudes on candidate quality are by measuring the time of response in the controlled environment. In Example 4.2, Law and Redlawsk were able to measure the different heuristics

---

[3] See Brams and Fishburn (1983) and Bassi (2006).

that voters use in gathering information during a political campaign. Social scientists are beginning to use fMRI equipment and other technologies to measure brain activity as subjects make choices, as in Example 3.1, which we discuss later. In Example 2.5, Mutz uses skin conductance measuring devices to evaluate subjects' responses. Some experiments that are particularly important for political science research involve subjects in face-to-face interactions as in some free-form deliberation experiments and require that subjects be physically in the same space to test theories about the effects of such interactions. Such experiments can be difficult if not impossible to conduct outside of a laboratory.

8.2.6 Why the Field or the Internet?

Field and Internet experiments can potentially be either group or individual. Eckel and Wilson (2006a) present a nice summary of some of the advantages and disadvantages of Internet experiments for conducting experiments that evaluate game-theoretic models involving interactive behaviors. In terms of advantages they point out that Internet experiments can allow a much greater number of participants (see Plott, 2000), the comparison of subjects across countries and cultures in the same experiment, and a greater guarantee of anonymity to subjects. In terms of disadvantages, they note that in Internet experiments coordination may be difficult: subjects may be less likely to believe that promised payments are real, the identity of the subjects who are actually participating may be difficult to monitor, subjects may make decisions too quickly or be distracted, subjects may have more wariness or lack of trust toward others on the Internet, and subjects may not believe that there are other subjects involved in the experiment.

Most political science field experiments, as in the examples we have presented, are individual decision-making experiments. As discussed earlier, Harrison and List (2004) considered an ideal or natural field experiment in which subjects are unaware of the experiment and therefore unaware of the control exercised by the experimenter. In some cases this is true in the field as in Gerber and Green's (2000) voter mobilization experiment or in the study of voter reactions to campaign messages in Example 2.2. Such an experiment uses a particular type of deception. As we noted earlier, experimentation without subject consent raises particular ethical concerns, which we deal with in Chapters 11 and 12.

However, subjects in field experiments may sometimes be aware that they are participating in an experiment, particularly if the experiment is undertaken in collaboration with policy makers. This was true in the Copenhagen policy experiment in Example 2.8. Certainly in survey experiments subjects are aware they are taking part in a survey, although they are not generally told that other subjects may be receiving different questions or question orderings.

The awareness of subjects in surveys has posed a particularly difficult problem for researchers who wish to measure things such as racial prejudice when respondents may not wish to provide answers they believe will be viewed critically by the interviewer. Kuklinski et al. (1997) used a survey experiment to attempt to measure racial prejudice without requiring subjects to make prejudiced statements. In the experiment they told a subject that they were going to read to him or her a list of things that sometimes make people angry or upset and asked the subject to tell the interviewer how many of the things made the subject angry or upset, but not to identify those things. In one manipulation they gave subjects a list of three things that are unrelated explicitly to race or ethnicity and in the other manipulation, they added to the list the statement "a black family moving in next door." The researchers found that in the with the four items, southern whites demonstrated a significant probability of selecting more items compared to the manipulation with three items, suggesting that southern whites were upset or angry by the additional statement. Although subjects were aware they were participating in a survey, they were unaware that the researcher was using multiple manipulations to estimate how often the subjects were upset or angry by the additional statement and, the researchers argue, more willing to express racial prejudices.[4]

8.2.7 Which Is Better?

The popular view in political science is that field experiments have more empirical relevance or external validity (using much the same reasoning as Harrison and List) and that laboratory experiments have more coherence within their designs (because of the ability to control the environment) or internal validity. Because political science is a substantively driven field, often the perception of advantages on the empirical side trumps the perception of advantages on the control or internal side. We believe that such a view is misguided because it ignores many of the problems in establishing internal validity in the field (problems in maintaining control and conducting random assignment as discussed in Chapters 4 and 5) as well as the difficulty

---

[4] As we discussed previously, Taber uses subliminal priming to measure implicit racial prejudices in his lab-in-the-field experiment; see Example 4.1.

in establishing external validity for results that have not been demonstrated to be internally valid (a point we made in the previous chapter).

8.3 Baselines and Comparisons in Experiments

8.3.1 Making Comparisons

We have previously discussed the use of the word control to describe what we have defined as a baseline in an experiment in Section 2.4.2. In Example 2.1, Gerber, Kaplan, and Bergan used "control group" to refer to the subjects who did not receive a free newspaper. Similarly, in Example 2.2, Wantchekon labels the villages in the experimental districts that did not receive manipulated messages as control villages. Mutz in Example 2.5 refers to the group of subjects who were not exposed to any video as a control group as well. Many experimentalists use the term control to refer to a baseline treatment that allows a researcher to gather data where he or she has not intervened. In our terminology the case where $M_i = 0$ would be the baseline manipulation, and $M_i = 1$ would be the case where the subject was manipulated (received the information). Similarly, when we are investigating treatment effects and there is no manipulation or we wish to focus on the treatment comparison and not the manipulation comparison, we can think of the baseline treatment or control treatment in the same way. So the case where $T_i = 0$ would be the baseline of no treatment, and $T_i = 1$ would be the treated case.

Definition 8.6 (Baseline Manipulation): *In the case of a binary manipulation variable where 1 equals receiving the manipulation and 0 equals not receiving the manipulation, the baseline manipulation is the case where the manipulated variable equals 0.*

Definition 8.7 (Baseline Treatment): *In the case of a binary treatment variable where 1 equals receiving the treatment and 0 equals not receiving the treatment, the baseline treatment is the case where the treatment variable equals 0.*

In most of the examples on the relationship between information and voting we have presented so far, baseline manipulations are used. That is, all compare the manipulated subjects with those who are not manipulated. In Example 2.4, Mondak et al. compared subjects who receive quality information with those who do not; in Example 2.6, Battaglini, Morton, and Palfrey compared the voting behavior of subjects who revealed a white ball to those who did not; in Example 2.1, Gerber, Kaplan, and Bergan compared the voting behavior of subjects who did not receive the newspapers to those who did; in Example 2.3, Clinton and Lapinksi compared self-reported voting behavior of subjects who saw negative ads with those who did not; and in Example 2.8, Lassen compared the voting behavior of Danish citizens who lived in the districts with decentralization to those who did not. As was clear in previous chapters, such comparisons are essential for a researcher to make causal inferences.

8.3.2 Determining the "Right" Baseline

Sometimes it is not obvious what the "right" baseline or comparison should be and researchers disagree on the proper baseline. For example, Druckman (2001a, 2001b) contends that omission of baseline comparisons may lead to incorrect estimates of causal inferences in the literature on framing effects in political psychology. The issue in the framing literature is not whether a comparison was made to other experimental manipulations, but whether the proper comparison was made. That is, in most of the experiments on how elite framing affects public opinion (Tversky and Kahneman, 1981; Kinder and Sanders, 1990; Nelson and Kinder, 1996), the researchers compare alternative elite communications rather than comparing elite communication with subjects who have not received such communication. If the estimated causal relationship is the effect of elite communication framing on subjects' opinions, then arguably the proper baseline or control group is one in which subjects receive no such communication. But we believe it is important not to conflate the definition of experimentation with what is believed to be necessary to derive causal inferences. We would not define the pathbreaking work of Tversky, Kinder, Sanders, and Nelson as not qualifying as experiments simply because they may have used the wrong baseline or control in their experiment to establish a particular causal inference. We return to this argument later.

Most experiments, as in the framing experiments, involve comparisons. However, defining one of the treatments as the baseline is often not meaningful and sometimes there is no obvious baseline. Suppose a researcher is interested in evaluating how voters choose in a three-candidate election conducted by plurality rule as compared to how they would choose in an identical three-choice election conducted via approval voting. Under plurality rule, each voter has one vote that they can cast for at most one candidate, whereas under approval voting a voter can vote for as many candidates he or she wishes to vote for (essentially approves of). The researcher may conduct two laboratory elections in which subjects' payments depend on the outcome of the elections, but some subjects vote in an election with approval voting and others vote in a plurality rule election. The researcher can then compare voter behavior in the two treatments. Note that in such a case the concept of a baseline treatment is ambiguous, because the comparison is between two interventions. Because the voters' choices would necessarily need to be aggregated according to some rule, there is no comparison available that does not involve a system to aggregate voter choices.

8.3.3 Experiments with Theoretical Baselines

In Example 8.5, Bahry and Wilson engage in the manipulation of subjects – random assignment – but there is no obvious experimental baseline. There are theoretical baselines: the game-theoretic predictions for the subjects' behavior is one, and the baseline where subjects' behavior is influenced by norms that are a function of ethnicity and aspects of their social and economic environment is another. The other two example laboratory experiments by political economists, Examples 2.6 and 2.7, also compare the behavior of the subjects to theoretical baselines as well as making comparisons between manipulations. Such comparisons are evaluations of point predictions from theoretical models, which we discussed in Chapter 6.

Theoretical baselines are not exclusive to researchers who use an FTA method. For instance, in Example 4.2, Lau and Redlawsk compare their results to a theoretical baseline of correct voting using a Rubin Causal Model–based approach to causality.

8.3.4 Multiple Comparisons

When experimentalists make multiple comparisons, there is a higher probability of false significance. For example, Battaglini et al. (2007) made 15 total comparisons of subject behavior. Fortunately, methods have been developed to control for such false significance. Battaglini et al. used a nonparametric procedure described by Benjamini and Hochberg (1995). The procedure works as follows for N comparisons: Define q^* as the desired minimum false discovery rate (FDR). Rank the comparisons by their corresponding p-values (probabilities of significance), where 1 denotes the smallest and N the greatest, and denote the rank as i. Benjamini and Hochberg showed that rejection of only null hypotheses such that the p-value is less than $(i/15) q^*$ controls the FDR at q^* when the test statistics are independent. Benjamini and Hochberg (2000) further show that rejection of only null hypotheses such that the p-value is less than $(\frac{1}{15})q^*/(\Sigma_i \frac{1}{i})$ controls the FDR at q^* when the tests have dependencies.

8.4 Artificiality in Experiments

8.4.1 Experimental Effect

As political scientists we study human behavior in politics and when we intervene in the DGP there is the danger of affecting human choices in a different way than if the variables we manipulate took the same values via nature, or the DGP without the manipulation. Harrison and List (2004, footnote 6) argued that manipulation by an experimenter puts subjects on an "artificial margin" and may lead the subjects to alter behavior on unconstrained margins. Of course, this is the aim of experimental intervention – to be able to observe its effects on behavior. We fully expect that subjects will alter their behavior, so it is not obvious why this is a concern. The point Harrison and List make, though, is deeper than that. Their worry is that when intervention occurs through an experiment it may affect subjects differently than when the same changes occur via the DGP. Harrison and List contend that in an ideal experiment such intervention should appear "natural" to subjects so that their reactions are the same as those they would have taken if the same changes had occurred via the DGP.

This effect, that being in the experiment causes subjects to make choices that are different from what they would make if the manipulation occurred naturally, is sometimes called an "experimenter effect." However, usually this term is interpreted narrowly as the presence or absence of an experimenter during the experiment or the presence or absence of an experimenter's knowledge of a subjects' choices. The effect we discuss here is more general than just what is caused by the absence or the presence of an experimenter, so we call it an "experimental effect."

Definition 8.8 (Experimental Effect): *When subjects' choices in an experiment are influenced by the fact that they are participating in an experiment and are different from what they would be if the manipulations and control exercised in the experiment took place via the DGP without experimental intervention.*

The worry about experimental effects is one of the main reasons why some researchers, like Harrison and List, call for experiments to have greater ecological validity or mundane realism, as we discussed in Section 7.3.1 in the previous chapter.

8.4.2 Dealing with Experimental Effects

Attempting to make the intervention as unobtrusive and natural as possible is one possible solution to the problem that subject awareness of the experimental manipulation may affect their behavior, leading to results that would not follow if the same events occurred via the DGP. But this is not always possible to implement. Suppose a researcher is interested in studying voter choices using an untried and proposed voting mechanism like storable votes, as in Example 8.6. To our knowledge, storage votes have not been used outside of an experimental election. Should the researcher not conduct the experiment and simply wait until an observational opportunity presents itself because conducting a laboratory experiment testing the voting mechanism may have an effect different from the effect if the mechanism was implemented "naturally?"

Fortunately there are other alternatives if the goal is to reduce experimental effects on subject choices. One reason that many experimentalists use financial incentives in experiments is an effort to make the choices before the subjects salient so that they overwhelm such experimental effects. But this is just one way in which experimenters attempt to motivate subjects so that they behave "as if" the intervention were "natural" rather than experimental. We discuss the complicated topic of motivating subjects in Chapter 10. Many aspects of an experiment interact to either mitigate or increase the effect of experimental artificiality. Sometimes mitigating artificiality in one direction may lead to an increase in artificiality in another direction, as in the use of monetary incentives in a voting game.

8.4.3 Desirability of Artificiality

Sometimes artificiality in an experiment is desirable. A researcher may choose a particular "unnatural context" or desire "artificiality" in the experiment to purposely reduce the tendency of subjects to respond to the natural context which is not relevant to the purpose of the experiment. When subjects are recruited from a wide variety of experiences, avoiding a particular context that is possibly well known only to a subset of the subjects may be desirable. As we have noted, in Example 6.2 Chou et al. found that using a nonneutral context for the guessing game led subjects to make new errors that they did not make in the more neutral presentation.

Alternatively, perhaps we want to understand how an intervention in the DGP would affect individual choices with subjects knowing that such an intervention has occurred. Vernon Smith, in his Nobel Prize lecture published in the *American Economic Review* (2003, footnote 62), argues: "It is not meaningful or helpful to talk about 'experimenter effects.' There are instructional and procedural effects, including the presence or absence of an experimenter, what he/she knows or does not know . . . , and what he/she does or does not do. All of the elementary operations used to implement an experiment are treatments that may or may not have a significant effect on observed outcomes." Thus, the goal may be to see how subjects who have experience in a particular context react when that context is removed and the situation is not natural to the subjects.

For example, Palacios-Huerta and Volij (2008) reported on an experiment (which we discuss more expansively in Example 9.2 in the next chapter) for which they recruited professional soccer players to play a simple two-player game that was identical to a strategic situation the players face in soccer games. Yet the researchers presented the game to the subjects without any reference to a "soccer" context because the goal was to determine if the players' repeated experience with the strategic situation in one context influenced their choices in a different context. If they had used the context and made the experiment more like the soccer environment that subjects were familiar with, the experiment would not have addressed the research questions that interested Palacios-Huerta and Volij.

Finally, in experiments for which the manipulation is designed such that the subjects are unaware they are participating in an experiment, the experimentalist faces a number of serious ethical concerns. One of the features of an experiment that makes subjects most aware of their participation is the requirement that subjects give "informed consent" to participate in writing. When an experimentalist chooses to manipulate without the subjects' knowledge, then the experimentalist is operating without such informed consent. The experimentalist is engaging in a type of deception. It is important that such experiments be given special scrutiny. We tackle these and other ethical issues in experimentation in Chapters 11 and 12.

8.5 Experimental Cross-Effects

In Taber's experiment (Example 4.1), he conducted a series of different manipulations, each addressing a separate question. Similarly, Eckel and Wilson and Bahry and Wilson, in Examples 8.2 and 8.5, respectively, conducted several different experimental manipulations sequentially, each designed to consider a different research question (although some of the analysis compared subjects' choices across manipulations). Doing so can raise difficulties for experimentalists if the experience in a previous manipulation affects choices in a subsequent manipulation in a manner that the experimentalist does not plan or does not wish to investigate. An experimental cross-effect occurs when a subject's choices in an experiment are a function of manipulations he or she has received in previous experiments.

Definition 8.9 (Experimental Cross-Effects): *When subjects' choices in an experiment are influenced by the manipulations they have received in previous experiments.*

Taber purposefully chose the order of his manipulations with the subliminal priming and timing experiment first so that the results of this critical experiment were not confounded by the later manipulations. In the experiments by Bahry and Wilson, subjects are not told the results from any of the manipulations until the end of the experiment to reduce these cross-effects. In Example 9.3 (in the next chapter), Belot et al. also take this approach.

Ideally, a researcher should not conduct multiple unrelated manipulations if he or she thinks that such effects are possible. But sometimes an experiment is simple, not too time consuming, and the researcher believes that cross-effects are unlikely. Given that recruiting subjects and finding available space and time to conduct an experiment are sometimes difficult and costly, a researcher may be tempted to maximize what he or she can gain from the experiment. In such a case, the researcher should attempt to take procedures to minimize cross-effects if possible or consider whether the cross-effects matter in the results by comparing with another session without additional manipulations or randomizing the order of manipulations across sessions.

Cross-effects can also occur when subjects are recruited for experiments from a common subject pool containing subjects who have participated in previous experiments conducted by other researchers. The analysis of Casari et al. in Example 5.2 suggests that experience in a similar experiment can affect subjects' choices in subsequent sessions. One solution, when using students as subjects and where subjects may have such experience and the researcher prefers unexperienced subjects, is to recruit explicitly freshmen for the experiment. An advantage of student subject pools is the automatic refreshing of subjects, as we explore in the next chapter. Cross-effects can also occur in field experiments when more than one research group is studying a particular population of subjects in the field – perhaps because the subjects, like those studied by Bahry and Wilson, have had unique experiences of ethnic conflict or other experiences interesting to social scientists. As field experiments expand, such cross-effects are likely to increase and researchers working in the field need to be aware of the possible contaminations that can occur.

8.6 Experiments as a Behavioral Testbed for Methodologies

Our emphasis in this chapter and the previous ones has been on how experiments can be used to make causal inferences and work toward building theories of the causes of effects. But in the social sciences, experiments have also played an important role in the design of methodologies used on non-experimental data. In an early famous study, LaLonde (1986) demonstrated problems with using methods to deal with self-selection on observational data by estimating how well the methods work with experimental data. In Example 5.2, Casari et al. also demonstrated how some of the methods used to estimate selection bias with observational data were not able to discern selection effects in their experimental data.

One particularly noteworthy investigation of methodologies used on nonexperimental data is Fréchette et al. (2005) experiment on legislative bargaining models in Example 8.7. Fréchette et al. conducted FTA laboratory experiments evaluating two alternative models of legislative bargaining over a fixed sum, the Baron–Ferejohn model (Baron and Ferejohn, 1989) and the demand bargaining model (Morelli, 1999). The two models have distinctly different structures: in the Baron–Ferejohn model, actors make proposals about how to divide the sums that are voted over with a coalition formed when a proposal receives a majority of the votes; in the Morelli model, actors make demands and a coalition is formed when the demands have a majority of the votes and are sufficient to exhaust the sum to be divided.

Example 8.7 (Behavioral Identification Laboratory Experiment on Legislative Bargaining): *Fréchette et al. (2005) report on an experiment that compared two formal models of legislative bargaining and the ability of existing empirical methods used on observational data to test between the two models.*

Target Population and Sample: A total of 180 subjects were recruited through email solicitations and posters at the Ohio State University for sessions involving either 10 or 15 subjects.

Subject Compensation: *Subjects were paid based on their choices as described in the procedures. Subjects also received a show-up fee of $8. The sessions lasted approximately 1.5 hours.*

Environment: *The experiments were conducted in a computer laboratory using the procedures described in Example 2.6.*

Procedures: *In each session, subjects participated in a five-person legislative bargaining game for 10 periods. At the end of the session, one period was randomly selected for payment. Subjects were told they were voters and participating in a series of elections to decide how to distribute funds between themselves and the other subjects in their group. Each period, the subjects were randomly rematched into new groups of five from the either 10 or 15 subjects in the session such that their identities were anonymous. There were six versions of the bargaining game and players in a session played only one version using a between-subjects design (see Section 3.3.3). All subjects were invited back for a second session with the same manipulations received before for 15 subjects. If more than 15 subjects showed up for the second session, the subjects who were chosen to participate were randomly selected from those who showed up. Some second sessions involved only 10 subjects.*

Baron–Ferejohn Equal Weight Game: *Each subject had one vote, and a proposal had to receive at least three votes to pass. First, each subject would propose a division of $60 among the five subjects in the group. One proposal was randomly selected with all proposals equally likely to be selected. Subjects then voted whether to accept or reject the proposal. The complete voting results were posted on the subjects' screens showing the amount allocated by subject number, the number of votes the subject controlled, whether the subject voted for or against the proposal, and whether the proposal passed or not. Subjects also were able to see the results from up to three previous bargaining rounds if relevant. If the proposal was rejected, the process repeated itself. Subjects were told that the process would repeat itself until a proposal was accepted. After a proposal was accepted, then the groups were randomly redrawn and the game was repeated.*

Baron–Ferejohn Apex Game: *The game was the same as in the Baron–Ferejohn equal weight game except that four subjects had one vote, but one subject (the apex player) had three votes, for a total of seven votes. Before the games began, the apex players were chosen such that the same players were apex players throughout the session. Again, for a proposal to pass, the proposal must receive a majority (four votes). Also, the probability that a subject's proposal was selected to be voted on was proportional to the number of votes he or she controlled. After a proposal was accepted, as before, the groups were randomly* rematched with the restriction that at least one member in each group was an apex player.

Baron–Ferejohn Apex1/3 Game: *This game was the same as the Baron–Ferejohn apex game except that the apex player only received 1/3 of the money allocated to him or her in the proposal.*

Demand Bargaining Equal Weight Game: *As in the Baron–Ferejohn equal weight game, all subjects had equal votes. Otherwise, the game proceeded differently in the following steps.*

Step 1: *Each subject reported an amount of the $60 he or she requests for him- or herself. One of these requests is chosen at random and presented to the others.*

Step 2: *Again each subject reports the amount of the $60 he or she requests for him- or herself. One of the remaining voters is chosen at random and their request is presented to the others.*

Step 3: *Again each subject reports the amount of the $60 he or she requests for him- or herself. One of the remaining voters is chosen at random and their request is presented to the others. If the sum of this request and the requests in steps 1 and 2 is less than or equal to $60, the subject chosen in this step can choose to "close" the election or coalition (both words were used in the instructions).*

Step 4: *If the election is closed in step 3, and there is no money left over, the allocation is binding, and the subjects move on to a new election (randomly assigned into new groups as described earlier). If the election is closed and there is still money to be allocated, then everyone writes down a request for their share of the remaining money and each of the subjects not chosen in steps 1 and 2 will be picked in random order to get what they request until all the money has been allocated with requests that exceed the money remaining ignored.*

If the election is not closed in step 3 (either because the sum of requests 1–3 are more than $60 between them or the subject in step 3 chose not to close the election), then the request process continues. A fourth person is selected to make a request. If the sum of their requests made by any combination of subjects in steps 1–3 in conjunction with this last request is less than or equal to $60 and constitutes a majority (controls three or more votes), then the subject making the latest request can close the election. If more than one possible majority coalition exists and the decision is to close the election, then the last requester gets to decide which requests to include in their coalition. The process repeats itself until an election is closed or all five requests have been made and still no one is able to or wishes to close the election, in which case the process starts again with step 1.

Demand Bargaining Apex Game: *This game was the same as the demand bargaining equal weight game except that one of the players in each group had three votes for a total of seven votes and a majority of four votes needed for a coalition. Also, the probabilities of having one's request selected was a function of the votes a subject controlled as a percentage of the total votes controlled by subjects who had not yet had their request selected. As in the Baron–Ferejohn apex game, the apex players were chosen at the beginning of a session and stayed the same throughout the session, but each period a new random group of five subjects was drawn with at least one being an apex player.*

Demand Bargaining Apex1/3 Game: *This was the same as the demand bargaining apex game except that the apex player received only 1/3 of the money he or she requested.*

Results: *The authors found that actual bargaining behavior is not as sensitive to the different bargaining rules as the theoretical point predictions suggest, but the comparative static predictions are consistent with the theory (see Chapter 6 for a discussion of these types of predictions). Furthermore, they found that empirical approaches used on observational data cannot distinguish between the two models and that there are strong similarities between the laboratory and observational data independent of the underlying bargaining process.*

Comments: *Fréchette et al.'s paper is a good example of a behavioral identification experiment because they evaluate the methods used on observational data to identify an underlying bargaining process in a situation where, because of the control of the experiment, that process is known. The experiment also is a good illustration of how one may use laboratory experiments to compare formal models' predictions and a comparison of the laboratory data with observational data from the environment that the formal models are posited to explain.*

The Baron-Ferejohn and demand bargaining models have been proposed as explanations of the legislative bargaining process in developed countries and a number of researchers have attempted to determine which model can explain observational data about power sharing within coalition governments (Warwick and Druckman, 2001; Ansolabehere et al., 2005). Using the same data set, but different methods, Warwick and Druckman argued that the results suggest that demand bargaining explains legislative power sharing whereas Ansolabehere et al. contended that the Baron–Ferejohn model is a better fit. Fréchette et al. reran the same empirical analyses of both studies on their experimental data on each bargaining game. They found that the regressions cannot identify the DGP using the criteria commonly employed, regardless of whether the data come from the experiments using the Baron–Ferejohn setup or the demand bargaining setup.

Moreover, they showed that with simulated data, assuming that the simulated actors chose as theory would predict, the empirical methods used on observational data can distinguish between the two models. They also showed that the data from the experiments are closer to the observational data than the simulated data. They concluded that the methods used on the observational data have a behavioral identification problem with the observational data; that is, even though the methods can theoretically identify the legislative bargaining process if actors choose as theory would predict, the methods cannot identify the process given how actors actually behave within that process. Thus, Fréchette et al. not only provided experimental evidence on the predictions of the two formal models of legislative bargaining, they also provided an important evaluation of the methods used to evaluate the models on observational data. Fréchette et al.'s study is thus a behavioral evaluation of a methodology used in political science on observational data.

Definition 8.10 (Behavioral Identification Problem): *When an empirical method is unable to identify parameters of interest given how agents actually behave.*

Definition 8.11 (Behavioral Evaluation): *An evaluation of a methodology used to identify parameters from nonexperimental data with experimental data in which the parameters are already known.*

Methodologists in political science often conduct studies to determine if their methods work as predicted using data simulated for that purpose. For example, we noted in Section 4.2.8 that Green (2009) conducted such simulations to consider whether including observable variables in regressions on experimental data in which manipulations are randomly assigned is problematic. Experiments provide an additional way to evaluate methods – a way to evaluate the methods behaviorally, not simply theoretically. In some cases, as was the case in Frechette et al., methods work on simulated data but not on the behavioral data from the experiment. The behavioral data provided a stronger and more realistic test of the methods than the simulated data. The point is that experiments can have an important use in helping researchers who primarily work with nonexperimental data, independent of their ability to help establish causal inferences.

8.7 Chapter Summary

In this chapter we have explored some of the variety of experimental designs and the merits of these approaches. Experiments vary in the level of analysis, the location of the experiment, the types of baselines used, the artificiality of the environment, and the ultimate purpose of the experiment. As we have repeatedly argued, there is no ideal experiment. In some cases, the research question is best addressed using an individual decision-making experiment; in others a group decision-making experiment is required. Furthermore, there is no longer a binary distinction between field and laboratory. Increasingly, researchers are conducting experiments via the Internet or using labs in the field. The best location of a particular experiment depends on the research question asked and the degree of control desired by the experimenter.

Experiments do not always have an obvious baseline or use a theoretical baseline, depending on the research question, but such experiments are still useful, nevertheless. Artificiality in experiments can be a problem; however, the solution is not necessarily to always create experimental designs that are as close as possible to some given target environment. Reducing artificiality in one dimension may mean increasing it in another. And some experiments are by design artificial to investigate a given research question. Finally, sometimes experiments can provide important evidence on how methodologies work to identify parameters in observational data – by serving as a behavioral testbed for methodologists.

In the next chapter we turn to another dimension over which experiments vary – the subjects chosen. We deal extensively with the debate over whether experiments that use students as subjects have merit.

Choosing Subjects

Consider the perspective expressed by Brady (2000, p. 52) on the usefulness of laboratory experiments to study public opinion: "Laboratory experiments, however, produce findings of limited usefulness because the treatments are often unrealistic and sometimes mundane and the subjects tend to be samples of convenience such as the proverbial 'college sophomores.' . . . [L]aboratory experiments can seldom capture the full range of citizens' views and the variety of political stimuli found in the real world. Representative surveys are the obvious way to capture the range of citizens' perspectives." Brady's complaint that laboratory experiments are not valid can be summarized into two criticisms: Laboratory experiments rely too heavily on undergraduate students and laboratory experiments involve an artificial environment that is unrealistic and uninteresting to subjects. In the previous chapter we discussed questions of artificiality in experiments. In this chapter we explore the use of undergraduate students in laboratory experiments and in the next we address how to make experiments interesting to subjects (i.e., motivating subjects).

9.1 On the Use of Students as Subjects

9.1.1 How Often Are Students Used as Subjects?

Although some political scientists use subject pools that are drawn from a larger community surrounding their university laboratory, as in the classic work of Shanto Iyengar (1987) and the more recent study by Diana Mutz (2007), many of the subjects used in laboratory experiments are undergraduates. Kam et al. (2007) found that in the top three journals of political science, *American Political Science Review, American*

Journal of Political Science, and the *Journal of Politics,* from 1990 to 2006, approximately 25% of the articles on experimentation used student samples. However, in two more specialized journals in political psychology, *Political Behavior* and *Political Psychology,* the authors found that approximately 70% of the studies were conducted with student samples during the same time period.

Because these figures combine both laboratory and nonlaboratory experiments, such as field survey experiments which are a greater preponderance of the experimental papers in the top three journals, they understate the dominance of student subject pools in political science laboratories. Studies that have focused more exclusively on laboratory experiments show a much greater use of student subjects. For example, Danielson and Holm (2007) surveyed 60 laboratory experimental economics papers published in top experimental journals and found that only 4 did not use students as subjects. Similarly, Henry (2008a) surveyed experimental research articles on prejudice in the top-ranked empirical journals in social psychology and found that approximately 92% used student samples.

9.1.2 Why Use Students as Subjects?

The reasons for using student samples are fairly obvious – researchers are typically based at universities, students can generally easily fit a one- or two-hour-long experiment into their schedules, can be paid low wages, can be recruited in large numbers, are easy to contact for recruiting, and are often interested and excited about participating in a research endeavor. Kam et al. (2007) discuss these rationales.

However, the principal advantage of having students as a subject pool is that it increases the ability to compare experimental manipulations over time, as we discuss in Section 5.3.1. That is, it is often not possible for a researcher to anticipate the manipulations he or she would like to conduct when addressing a particular research question. Having a large subject pool that is relatively homogeneous over time increases the ability of experimentalists to think of their manipulations over time as randomly assigned. The subject pool automatically refreshes over time while maintaining the relative homogeneity, something that may not happen with a subject pool of "professional subjects" that can possibly develop with Internet experiments. Using students as a subject pool also arguably increases the comparability of experiments conducted across researchers, to the extent that undergraduate students may be similar at different institutions of higher education.

9.1.3 Worries About Students as Subjects

Using undergraduate students does make many pause, however, when considering issues of validity and robustness. For instance, McGraw and Hoekstra (1994) surveyed 18 journal editors in political science (both past and present) about reasons for rejection of experimental papers. Of the 12 that responded, 50% cited generalizability due to subject pools.

Others besides Brady have expressed these concerns about the overuse of students in laboratory experiments. Rudman (2008) remarks that concerns about the use of undergraduate subject pools have led to a devaluing of social psychology as a science.[1] In an oft-cited paper, Sears (1986) expressed a number of worries about the effects of the preponderance of use of student subjects in laboratory experiments. However, Sears's worries were speculative rather than quantifiable, as Sears (2008) later acknowledged. Henry (2008a) revisited Sears's arguments 20 years later and compared a university campus sample of subjects with a nonuniversity sample. Henry focused his analysis on social psychology research on prejudice. He provides evidence on how differences between student subjects and nonstudent subjects may bias results in several different literatures on prejudice in social psychology. Henry calls for a much greater use of nonstudents in experimental studies of prejudice.

Nevertheless, Henry (2008b) makes it clear that he does not desire that experiments with student subjects no longer be conducted. Henry states (p. 114):

> I believe it would be a mistake to stop using student samples in our research, and it is not a contradiction to my central thesis to say so. We would be fools to not take advantage of amazingly convenient, cheap, and readily available undergraduate participant pools. . . . Students are not so different from nonstudents that I would propose we should never study them. I, too, do not support the "canard" that students are, so to speak, from Mars and nonstudents are from Venus . . . and it is not my intention for a reader . . . to walk away with that message.

What does the evidence say about student and nonstudent comparisons? A growing number of studies have made such comparisons (as we review in the remainder of this chapter) and the results are mixed. In some cases students and nonstudents make significantly different choices; in other cases, there is no significant difference between their choices. When there are

---

[1] She remarks (p. 84): "The people in Washington responsible for funding decisions too often point to convenience samples as an excuse to trivialize our discipline."

significant differences between their choices, in some cases the student choices are less "rational" than the nonstudent choices; in other cases the opposite occurs. Whether students are different from nonstudents in experiments appears to depend on the types of nonstudents that students are compared with and the type of experiment conducted. We explore these answers in this chapter.

Our investigation of the impact of using students as subjects is framed by the validity questions that are relevant. Most political scientists think that concerns about undergraduate subject pools are issues of external validity or generalizability. However, often the concerns raised deal with internal validity. Specifically, using undergraduates as a subject pool typically raises concerns about construct validity and statistical validity, which are part of internal validity, as well as concerns about external validity. We deal with each in the sections that follow.[2]

9.2 Internal Validity and Subject Pools

9.2.1 Representativeness and Statistical Validity

Sampling Issues and the Target Population
As Henry (2008a, 2008b) contends, in some cases a researcher may consider the target population for their study a population larger than the undergraduate subject pool typically used by experimentalists. The researchers' goal may be to estimate the causal effect of some treatment among citizens in a particular city or region. In such an instance, of course there are sampling issues, issues of statistical validity, about the ability of the results with undergraduates to apply to the target population, because the subject pool is rarely representative. This is an internal validity concern (see Chapter 7), not an external robustness concern, because it has to do with the statistical representativeness of undergraduates to a larger, more diverse target population. The issue of representativeness of a sample to a target population can also be a possible concern when political scientists recruit subjects through newspaper advertisements, as did Iyengar (1987), or from civic groups and temporary employment agencies as Mutz has (see Example 2.5).

Some may think that calling this issue an internal validity concern is just a definitional slight of hand. Why is this not just an external validity or question about the generalizability from experiments with a target population

---

[2] There are also ethical issues in using students as subjects in experiments, which we address in Section 12.2.1.

of an undergraduate subject pool to a larger population in a region? The distinction is not merely how we think of the target population, but also how we think about the solution to the problem. If the solution is to seek out a sample that is more representative of the larger population, then clearly this larger population is the target population and we are dealing with the problem through trying to increase the statistical validity of the results. Brady, in his complaint about the representativeness of undergraduates as a subject pool in laboratory experiments, is clearly envisioning the target population as citizens and the goal of experiments to understand citizens' views. His solution is a statistical one – draw a random sample as in a standard political science survey.

Some experimentalists attempt to draw a representative sample from target populations to satisfy statistical validity, as Brady recommends. An early effort by political scientists to draw a random sample of the local population is presented in the work of Sigelman et al. (1992), who conducted their experiment in a county courthouse while prospective jurors were waiting for assignment to a jury panel. They used the reasoning that the random selection of jurors approached a random sample of the local population with driver's licenses.

Recently, Kam et al. (2007) recruited a random sample of subjects from the university staff (excluding professors, research positions, and faculty who serve as administrators) as well as a random sample from the local community surrounding the university. They then compared the subjects who responded across a number of demographic and political interest variables. They found that the university staff who volunteered for the experiment were not significantly different on these dimensions from those that volunteered from the local community except that they were younger (the local community drew also from retired persons) and more female (although this can be largely explained by a sampling disparity that oversampled women among staff compared to the local community).

Most noteworthy, they found that the response rate of university staff was higher compared to the local community, thus suggesting that recruiting among the staff may be a good option compared to student subject pools. That said, researchers should be careful not to use university employees who they interact with or for whom they have an evaluative relationship (i.e., researchers should not use employees who are staff in their own departments or institutes or otherwise find their pay or employment related to the researcher) for two reasons: (1) the employees may feel coerced into participating, an ethical issue we address further in Chapters 11 and 12, and (2) doing so may lead to experimental effects, discussed in the previous chapter.

Example 9.1 (Experiment on Subject Recruitment): *Kam et al. (2007), hereafter KWZ, reported on an experiment in recruiting subjects for a political psychology laboratory experiment.*

Target Population and Sample: KWZ drew and recruited subjects from two samples: a local residents sample and a campus employee sample. The local residents sample (N = 1,500) was drawn using a list of residents of a northern California college town and a neighboring town. The list was purchased from a reputable marketing firm and was confined to individuals with an estimated age between 24 and 80 years old. The gender of individuals on the list was identified. The campus employees sample (N = 750) was drawn using the campus directory. It omitted individuals located off-campus (e.g., the Medical Center personnel), deans (and above), professors (any rank), lecturers, and Fellows; Executive Administrative Assistants, Directors, and Associate Directors; and individuals with "Research" in their title.

Subject Compensation: Subjects were given a flat fee for participating in the main experiment ($30) and a focus group discussion ($10 and a chance to win $100).

Environment: The principal experimental manipulation reported on by KWZ is on the mechanisms by which they recruited the subjects. Therefore, the experiment took place prior to the subjects' arrival in the laboratory.

Procedures: Subjects were randomly assigned to receive three different types of recruitment letters: one that included a statement that emphasized the social utility of participating, one that included a statement that emphasized the financial incentives of participating, and one which served as a baseline manipulation that did not include either statement (although the financial incentives were mentioned).

Results: First, they found that campus employees responded significantly more to the appeals than the local residents (24.3% vs. 11.9%). They further found that the campus employees who agreed to participate were fairly similar to the local residents who also agreed to participate. KWZ compared the campus employees and local residents to the students and found that the students were younger, more nonwhite, came from families with higher incomes, and were less politically aware. The researchers found that the manipulation in the letters had no effect on recruitment of the local residents, but that for the campus employees the subjects who received the baseline letter responded most strongly to the invitation to participate; the second-highest response was to the social utility letter, and the lowest response rate was to the self-interest letter. The difference between the baseline and the self-interest responses was statistically significant, but the difference between the social utility and baseline responses were not statistically significant.

Comments: *KWZ also conducted three focus group meetings with seven, five, and four participants, respectively, with campus staff members drawn from the original campus employee sample approximately one year after the study. Included in the focus groups were individuals who had participated and not participated, and individuals who had received each of the different letter types. Each session was moderated by one of the authors. The focus groups were predominantly female. Based on the focus group responses, KWZ concluded that most of the participants were self-interested and participated for the money; the respondents preferred that the invitation letter not emphasize the monetary aspect of the study.*

Another example of experimenters using nonstandard populations is provided by Harrison et al. (2002), who use a random sample from the Danish population in an experiment to estimate discount rates for the Danish population. Similarly, Bellemare et al. (2008) used a large representative sample from the Dutch population as subjects for experiments on the ultimatum game (discussed in Section 3.3.3). They used the results to estimate inequity aversion or the desire for fairness or equity in bargains in the Dutch population. We have already discussed the Internet experiment of Egas and Riedl in Example 8.3. In political science, Habyarimana et al.'s (2007) game-theoretic experiments in Kampala, Uganda, drew from a random sample of the population in the city using methods similar to that used in survey research in that area in an effort to estimate internally valid estimates of behavior in the target population.

The growth in the ability to conduct experiments via virtual laboratories is likely to lead to more studies such as that of Egas and Riedl. Although the sample via the Internet today is far from a random sample of the population of a country, growing computer usage and the help of statistical techniques in correcting for sample biases should help us determine better in what sort of experimental tests subject pool differences matter. Of course, because virtual laboratories provide an experimentalist with less control, these disconnects may confound our ability to measure subject pool effects, as noted in the previous chapter. Ideally, researchers may conduct virtual experiments with a common pool of subjects as well to control for these differences. However, doing so may result in a subject pool primarily comprised of "professional subjects" who are less representative of the general population than desired given that automatic refreshing of the subject pool as occurs with students may not be as easy to implement.

Volunteer Subjects and Experiment Drop-off

Of particular concern for experimentalists of all types is the selection problem. That is, subjects must volunteer for laboratory experiments and in almost all field experiments can refuse the manipulation. As we discuss in Chapter 5, a selection problem can make it impossible to identify treatment effects if the determinants of participant selection are related to unobservables that interact with the treatment to affect behavior. Furthermore, in field experiments that take place over time or in virtual laboratory experiments, some subjects may choose to drop out of an experiment before the experiment is completed.

In experiments with informed consent (which may be conducted in the laboratory, via the Internet, or in a lab in the field) the selection problem is particularly obvious because subjects must volunteer. Although we know of no political science studies that have considered how participation from a voluntary subject pool may affect the results of the experiments, psychologists have investigated this issue for the subjects they use in their experiments and for different types of psychological experiments. In general, and not surprisingly, there are differences between those who participate and those who do not; the characteristics of volunteer participants can be significantly different from those who choose not to participate. Levitt and List (2007a,b) review some of this literature and conjecture that the differences may affect the interpretations of the results in the laboratory experiments in economics. However, the most recent such study cited by them was conducted in 1975, which gives one pause when extrapolating to experiments of a completely different type conducted 30 years later. Levitt and List also note two studies in economics on the effects of financial incentives on subject recruitment and subject type (see Harrison et al., 2005a; Rutstrom, 1998). We discuss financial incentives and subject motivations more expansively in the next chapter.

A few more recent studies in psychology have examined particular aspects of subject pool selection issues with mixed results. One of the difficulties in conducting these studies is gathering data on subjects who choose not to volunteer. Therefore, experimentalists investigating this question usually compare subjects who volunteer for at least part of the experiment or consider questions of balance in recruitment or timing of recruitment. Furthermore, although these studies typically demonstrate significant differences across the subject pools, they rarely consider the effects these differences may have on experimental results. The few that do, do not show a significant bias in experimental results.

For example, Pagan et al. (2006) compared peer evaluations of subjects who signed a consent form to participate in an experiment but failed to follow through with the peer evaluations of subjects who did participate in the experiment fully. They found that, according to peers, the subjects who failed to follow through were considered to be higher on narcissism or nonassertiveness. Porter and Whitcomb (2005b) compared the voluntary participation of subjects in four separate student surveys. They found that the subjects who participated most were more likely to be female and socially engaged, less likely to be on financial aid, more likely to be an investigative personality type, and less likely to be an enterprising personality type. Wang and Jentsch (1998), Zelenski et al. (2003), and Aviv et al. (2002), considered issues such as the time of day or year that subjects participate. They found that there are significant personality differences across subjects that can be explained by these variables. However, Wang and Jentsch found that these did not have a significant effect on the subjects' choices in their particular decision-making experiment. In a similar study, McCray et al. (2005) consider the possible consequences of overrepresentation of psychology majors in psychology experiments. They found that in the particular types of decision-making experiments they conducted, nonpsychology majors' choices were not significantly different.

Thus, the effects of selection bias on results in laboratory experiments in political science can at best only be conjectured because little research has been conducted on these sorts of questions with respect to political science experiments. It is an area ripe for empirical study, which we advocate.

Assuming that researchers are concerned about selection bias, can laboratory experimentalists use methods employed by field and survey experimentalists to solve selection bias problems? A large literature addresses the issues in response to surveys and how researchers can use advances in statistics to mitigate for possible selection problems (see, e.g., the work of Berinksy, 2002). These approaches are now being applied to understanding selection problems in field experiments as discussed in Chapter 5. These methods assume much larger sample sizes than are standardly available for a researcher conducting a laboratory experiment and thus may not help in solving problems of selection bias as found by Casari et al. (see Example 5.2).

9.2.2 Construct Validity

When the Target Population Is Humanity

Many research problems in political science have a specific target population. Researchers may have as a goal explaining choices of members of the European Parliament, American public opinion, or actions of terrorist cells, for example. In this case, as discussed earlier, establishing an internally valid inference for that target population suggests that one should try to achieve a representative sample of that population. But in other situations the researcher does not have a specific target population. For example, Bassi (2006) evaluates different alternative voting mechanisms such as Borda count, plurality rule, and approval voting. Her research goal is not to explain how these voting mechanisms affect behavior in a specific target population because no specific target population exists in which voters have a choice between such mechanisms. In that case, pursuing a representative sample of some broad population makes little sense. She is interested in an existence result; that is, given some sample of humans, do the theoretical predictions about these different voting mechanisms receive support? It does not matter to the research where the sample of humans comes from for such an initial study. Similarly Casella et al.'s investigation of storable votes in Example 8.6 has no specific target population.

Blanton and Jaccard (2008, p. 100) make a similar point about the reasons why social psychologists often use student subjects:

> If pressed to identify the population they are trying to target, many of the social psychologists who rely on college student samples would probably respond that they are interested in studying basic processes that are true of human beings in general. . . . [S]ocial psychologists rarely concern themselves with the task of trying to represent a known population. . . . [T]hey more typically are interested in testing the link between their findings and a broader theory than between their findings and a broader population.

For many political psychologists and political economists who use student subjects in laboratory experiments, the goal of the experiment is this sort of theory testing enterprise. However, as Blanton and Jaccard note, it would be wrong to suggest that these researchers are uninterested in broader populations or how well the results generalize. The issue for an experimentalist in this case is, once the results of an experiment are determined, how robust or general are these results? Blanton and Jaccard state this argument as follows:

> It would be wrong, however, to say that social psychologists have no interest in populations. The fact that they use inferential statistics reveals their own tacit assumption that the individuals they study are a random sample from a population. The question then becomes "Who is this population?" Stated another way, social psychologists turn the traditional approach of specifying a population and then seeking a random sample on its head. They instead start with a sample and then argue that the sample can be construed as a random sample from some population of individuals. The task then turns into one of figuring out who that population might

be. The focus is on generalizability of the results, rather than the representativeness of a sample.

Although this is a view expressed about social psychology research, it is similar to the perspective of many political scientists who conduct laboratory research with students. These researchers usually work from a carefully constructed theory that they wish to evaluate either using the Formal Theory Approach or the Rubin Causal Model method. For reasons of control and observability, they choose the laboratory as a way in which the theory can be evaluated. They seek a sample of humans for their study of the theory. They care about generalizability, not in the internal validity sense just presented, but in an external validity sense. That is, to them it does not matter from what population of humans the initial study draws its sample. We can assume that there is a population for which the sample used in the experiment is a random draw. Once the study is completed, then through scientific replication with other samples from other populations, stress tests, and meta-analyses, the external validity and generalizability of the results can be determined.

Is there a danger in this type of approach to theory evaluation? There are potential problems. It could be the case that the convenience sample of students leads to a bias in the theories that receive further investigation in either theoretical or empirical research. That is, suppose that researchers are interested in studying turnout and voting decisions in sequential versus simultaneous elections under incomplete information as in Battaglini, Morton, and Palfrey's study (2007). The question of the research is how much can voting lead to information aggregation as voters update their beliefs about unknowns through sequential voting, which is not possible under simultaneous voting. Suppose the researchers find that the subjects' choices are less "rational" than predicted and as a result the sequential voting mechanism does not lead to as much information aggregation as the theory would predict. This may lead to an emphasis on how to design sequential voting systems to correct for this irrationality and more emphasis on information provision under simultaneous voting systems. But suppose that the results stem from a fundamental difference between student and nonstudent subjects and that nonstudents' choices in a similar experiment would be more "rational." Then the results from the experiment would bias future theoretical and empirical research in certain ways until this fundamental difference is discovered. Ideally the bias is self-limiting through scientific replication. But in the meantime it can have a consequential effect as research is steered in a particular direction.

A growing experimental literature has attempted to assess the robustness of theoretical evaluations of game-theoretic models using students as subjects by comparing students to other populations. We turn to these studies next.

Game-Theoretic Models and Students

In Chapter 6 we remarked how most laboratory experiments evaluating game-theoretic predictions use repetition to allow subjects to gain experience as a more accurate way of evaluating the theory than in a one-shot game. In these games, a number of results found with student subjects have been investigated to see if they hold with nonstudents. We consider a few of these experiments in the next section. We then turn, in the following section, to a comparison of results with students in one-shot games without repetition with nonstudents. Note that we focus on those games and studies that are most relevant to the applied game-theoretic models studied in political science and thus our review is not comprehensive.[3]

Experiments with Repetition

Evidence on Mixed Strategies. As Palacios-Huerta and Volij (2008) review, considerable experimental evidence with undergraduate students suggests that the students have difficulty making choices that are predicted in mixed-strategy equilibria in games, in particular games in which the only equilibrium is for subjects to mix between strategies (see Chapter 6 for a discussion of mixed strategies). Although subject behavior in the aggregate may come close to the predicted behavior, individual choices often show choices made at variance with the predictions (nonrandom according to the predicted probabilities). How robust is this conclusion to other subject pools? Palacios-Huerta and Volij compare the behavior of professional soccer players with undergraduate students in Example 9.2.

Example 9.2 (**Soccer Player Laboratory Experiment**): *Palacios-Huerta and Volij (hereafter PHV) reported on an experiment in which they compared the choices of professional soccer players and college students in a game that is formally identical to the strategic interaction soccer players face.*

Target Population and Sample: PHV recruited 80 Spanish professional soccer players (40 kickers and 40 goalkeepers). The subjects were recruited from soccer clubs in the Primera Division and the Segunda Division A in the north

---

[3] For example, we do not explore comparisons of students and nonstudents in auction experiments.

of Spain, a region with a high density of professional teams. They recruited the subjects via telephone and interviews during their daily practice sessions. The average age of the professional subjects was 26.5 years, and the average number of years of education was 11.2. All of the subjects had played professionally for at least two years.

PHV also recruited 160 male subjects from the Universidad del Pais Vasco in Bilbao by making visits to different undergraduate classes. Students majoring in economics or mathematics were excluded. Half of the subjects had no soccer experience and half were students required to be currently participating in regular league competitions in regional amateur divisions (the Tercera Division and below). The amateur leagues used the same rules, structure, and calendar schedule as the professional leagues. The average age of the student subjects was 20.7 years and the average number of years of education was 15.1. PHV reported that both samples of students were statistically similar on these demographics.

Subject Compensation: *PHV paid subjects based on their choices in games as described in the procedures. PHV did not report if subjects received a show-up fee but did report that subjects received no endowments prior to the games, which suggests that they did not provide subjects with a show-up fee. PHV did not provide summary statistics on how much subjects earned, but it can be surmised that they earned on average roughly 75–100 euros, depending on the game played, for approximately 1 to 1.5 hours.*

Environment: *The subjects played a series of card games in which they sat opposite each other at a table. In the card games, the players held cards with identical backs and a large board across the table prevented the subjects from seeing the backs of their opponents' cards. The experimenter handed out one page with instructions in Spanish, which he then read aloud to the subjects.*

Procedures: *The subjects were divided into pairs. The professional soccer player pairs were one kicker with one goalkeeper formed randomly using the last two digits of their national ID card, making sure that subjects who were currently playing or had played in the past for the same team were not allowed to participate in the same pair. The undergraduates were formed into pairs randomly using the last two digits or their national ID card, again making sure that those amateur soccer players who were currently playing or had previously played for the same team were not allowed to participate in the same pair. The pairs then played one of two games. Of the three different subject sets – professional soccer players, students without soccer experience, and amateur soccer players – the subjects were divided equally across the two games such that 40 subjects from each set played each game (20 pairs).*

Game 1: *The pairs played a simple 2 by 2 zero-sum game. The game was modeled after the situation in soccer when there is a penalty kick. The probabilities of each outcome of the game were given from an empirical study of soccer kick interactions in professional soccer games. In the game each player had two cards, A and B. When the experimenter said "ready" each player selected a card from their hand and placed it face down on the table. When the experimenter said "turn," each player turned his card face up. Then two ten-sided dice were tossed. The faces of each die were marked from 0 to 9. One die was used to determine the first digit in a two-digit number and the other the second. If 00 was the outcome it was interpreted as 100. The winner was determined as follows.*

If there was a match AA, then the row player won if the dice yielded a number between 01 and 60; otherwise the column player won.

If there was a match BB, then the row player won if the dice yielded a number between 01 and 70; otherwise the column player won.

If there was a match AB, then the row player won if the dice yielded a number between 01 and 95; otherwise the column player won.

The subjects played the game for 15 rounds for practice and then 150 times for money. Each winner of each game received one euro. The subjects were not told how many rounds they would play.

Game 2: *The pairs played a game similar to an experiment of O'Neill (1987). Each player had four cards {Red, Brown, Purple, Green}. When the experimenter said "ready," each player selected a card from his hand and placed it face down on the table. When the experimenter said "turn," each player turned his card face up. The winner was determined as follows.*

If there was a match of Greens (two Greens played) or a mismatch of other cards (Red-Brown, for example); subject 1 won. If there was a match of cards other than Green (Purple-Purple, for example) or a mismatch of a Green (one Green, one other card), subject 2 won.

The subjects played the game for 15 rounds for practice and 200 times for money. The winner of each game received one euro.

Results: *Both game 1 and game 2 have unique mixed-strategy equilibrium predictions. Specifically, in game 1, the row and column players were predicted to choose the A card with probabilities of 0.3636 and 0.4545, respectively. In game 2, the equilibrium requires both players to choose the red, brown, purple, and green cards with probabilities of 0.2, 0.2, 0.2, and 0.4, respectively. PHV found that the professionals playing game 1 chose strategies with payoffs close to the equilibrium ones and that their sequences of choices were serially independent. In contrast, the students' choices were further from the equilibrium predictions. They found similar differences for the play in game 2. They* *also found that amateur soccer players' choices were closer to the equilibrium predictions than the students without such experience.*

Comments: *Wooders (2008) reexamined PHV's data. He found evidence suggesting that the professional soccer players were not playing the predicted strategies because they followed nonstationary mixtures, with card frequencies that are negatively correlated between the first and second halves of the games. In particular, professionals tend to switch between halves from underplaying a card relative to its equilibrium frequency to overplaying it and vice versa. Although the average play of the cards is close to the equilibrium prediction, Wooders points out that the distribution of card frequencies across professionals is far from the distribution implied by the strategy. Finally, he found that the students' choices more closely conform to these distributional predictions.*

A situation where the unique equilibrium is one in which players use mixed strategies is the game that takes place in soccer when there is a penalty kick; that is, the kicker can choose to kick either right or left and the goalkeeper can anticipate that the kicker will kick either right or left. If the kicker chooses to go right, the goalkeeper chooses to go right as well, but if the goalkeeper chooses to go right, then the kicker prefers to go left. If the kicker prefers to go left, so does the goalkeeper; and if the goalkeeper goes left, the kicker prefers to go right. Thus, there is no equilibrium in pure strategies. Interestingly, analyzing observational data from the behavior of professional soccer players, Palacios-Huerta (2003) shows that their choices were consistent with the mixed-strategy equilibrium in two ways; first, the winning probabilities were statistically identical across strategies, which means that they were indifferent between the two strategies as required by equilibrium, and second, the players' choices were serially independent and thus random as predicted.

Palacios-Huerta and Volij created a laboratory game that mirrored the soccer penalty-kick game using the probabilities of winning calculated from observed soccer games. They used as subjects professional soccer kicker–goalkeeper pairs as well as male undergraduate student pairs excluding economics and mathematics students and those with soccer backgrounds to play the game. They found that the professional soccer players performed much closer to the theoretically predicted equilibrium probabilities than the undergraduates.

However, the results do not clearly suggest that soccer players are better at choosing equilibrium strategies than undergraduates even though the soccer players appeared to mix overall at the equilibrium strategies. That is, Wooders (2008) performed additional tests on the data. He found evidence that the soccer players were not choosing according to the equilibrium predictions. In particular, he found evidence that the soccer players' choices in the first half of the experiment were correlated with their choices in the second half. That is, if players overplayed (underplayed) a card in the first half, the players underplayed (overplayed) the card in the second half. Wooders also examined the distribution of the choices of the players and found that the distribution of the choices was not as predicted if the soccer players had been using a mixed strategy, but the distribution of the choices of the students was closer to that predicted by the mixed strategy. Thus, the comparison of the subjects does not give a clear answer of whether experience with a similar game does lead individuals to be better able to choose as predicted in equilibrium.

Finally, Levitt et al. (2009) replicated the Palacios-Huerta and Volij soccer player experiments with four different subject pools: college students from the University of Arizona and three types of professionals – professional poker players from the 2006 World Series of Poker in Las Vegas, Nevada; American professional soccer players in their locker rooms; and world-class bridge players. They found little evidence that the professionals' experiences transferred to the laboratory in the games and that the choices of all four of the subject pools were generally not close to the mixed strategy predictions. They contend that their results suggest that the professionals were unable to transfer their skills at randomization from the familiar context of the field to the unfamiliar context of the laboratory.

Evidence on Backward Induction and Common Knowledge. Palacios-Huerta and Volij (2009) compare the choices of expert chess players with students in the centipede game (see Chapter 6). As we reviewed, the Nash equilibrium of the centipede game is for the first mover to choose take and for the game to be over. In game-theoretic terminology, solving for this prediction involves using what is called "backward induction." But as Palacios-Huerta and Volij point out, it is not rationality alone that implies the backward induction solution to the centipede game, but common knowledge of rationality. If rational individuals think there is a possibility that others are not rational, then it is optimal to not take on the first round. We noted in Chapter 6 that McKelvey and Palfrey propose quantal response equilibrium as an alternative equilibrium concept for the situation in which individuals are aware that others may make errors and how such knowledge coupled with errors changes the strategic nature of the game.

Palacios-Huerta and Volij used expert chess players in their experiment to manipulate subjects' beliefs about the degree of rationality in the game, as an effort to manipulate common knowledge. The presumption is that chess players are known to be able to use backward induction to figure out how best to play. They conducted two experiments, one in the field with only expert chess players and one in the lab which used mixtures of expert chess players and students. They found that both in the laboratory and the field when chess players played against chess players, the outcome was very close to the game-theoretic prediction. Furthermore, every chess player converged fully to equilibrium play by the fifth time they played the game (the games were repeated with random rematching in the lab experiments).

Even more interesting, Palacios-Huerta and Volij found that when students played against chess players, the outcome was closer to the subgame-perfect equilibrium than when students played against students. Students' choices were different when they knew that there was a probability they were playing against chess players than when the other players were not chess players. In the games in which students played chess players, by the tenth repetition college students' choices were also extremely close to equilibrium play. Palacios-Huerta and Volij suggest that their results imply that observations in other experiments in which subjects choose contrary to game-theoretic predictions may be a consequence of a failure of common knowledge of rationality rather than rationality of the subjects. Common knowledge of rationality coupled with experience leads to subjects choosing closer to the equilibrium predictions than previous experiments.

One-Shot Games. In Chapter 6 we pointed out that sometimes researchers are interested in behavior in one-shot games, either as a way of measuring subjects' other regarding preferences when confronted with a simple game such as the ultimatum game (see Section 3.3.3) or individuals' cognitive processes in a game like the guessing game (see Example 6.2). With the advent of a new experimental laboratory at Oxford University, Belot et al. (2009) conducted an interesting first experiment comparing students and nonstudents from the Oxford area on a series of one-shot games, which is presented in Example 9.3.[4] They also measure the subjects' risk preferences by having subjects participate in a series of lotteries, surveying basic demographic information, and administering an IQ test.

---

[4] Although one of the games, the public good game, is repeated for 10 periods, the composition of the groups remain the same, making it a repeated game rather than a one-shot game repeated with randomization between periods.

Example 9.3 (Student and Nonstudent Comparison Experiment): *Belot et al. (2009) reported on a set of experiments involving one-shot games in which the choices of students and nonstudents are compared holding other things constant.*

Target Population and Sample: Belot et al. recruited a subject pool that was 75% students from universities in the Oxford area. Students were registered online. Half of the students were freshmen and came from 30 different disciplines. The nonstudents were also recruited from the area. Half of the nonstudents are private employees. Significant numbers of the nonstudents are workers, self-employed, public employees, and unemployed; 57% of the subject pool (students and nonstudents combined) are female. Belot et al. reported that in total 128 subjects were used. They did not report the percentages of the total that were students and nonstudents.

Subject Compensation: Subjects were paid based on their choices. Belot et al. did not report average earnings but reported that subjects were told during recruiting that they would earn on average between 10 and 15 English pounds per hour. Apparently the pay was equivalent for both students and nonstudents. Belot et al. also reported that the typical gross pay of students working for Oxford University is 12 English pounds and that the average salary of an administrator in the United Kingdom in 2008 was 16,994 English pounds, which corresponds to an hourly rate of 8.5 English pounds.

Environment: The experiments took place in a new computer laboratory as part of the newly created Centre for Experimental Social Sciences at Oxford University. These were the first experiments conducted at the laboratory using the subject pool. Thus, no subject had participated in other experiments in the laboratory previously. All the sessions were conducted after 5:00 p.m. (at 5:30 or 6:00 p.m.) and each lasted one hour and a half. See Example 2.6 for a discussion of the computer laboratory environment.

Procedures: Six sessions were conducted – two with students, two with nonstudents, and two with a mixed population. The experiment took place in two parts. In the first part, the subjects were asked to make choices in a series of six games (described later). The games were presented in the same sequence and identified by numbers only (1, 2, 3, . . .). After the instructions for each game, subjects were asked to think of an example for each situation and were told that this would have no implication on their earnings. They did not receive any feedback except during the last game, which was a repeated game. One of the six games was drawn as payment. In the second part, subjects were given an IQ test consisting of 26 questions and were paid 0.20 English pounds for each correct answer.

The six games in the first part of the experiment were as follows (presented to the subjects in sequence below).

Trust Game: *Subjects were randomly matched. See Section 8.2.2 for a discussion of this game. In the version of the game investigated by Belot et al., first movers were given 10 English pounds and told to choose whether to transfer all to the second mover or keep all of it. If the money was sent, then it was tripled by the experimenter to 30 English pounds and the second mover decided whether to keep all of it or send back 15 English pounds.*

Guessing Game: *See Example 6.2. Subjects were asked to guess a number between 0 and 100 and told that the number closest to 2/3 times the average of the guesses would receive 20 English pounds. In case of a tie, the computer would randomly pick one of the winners to receive the 20 pounds.*

Dictator Game: *Subjects were randomly matched. The basic form of the dictator game is presented in Example 8.5. Belot et al. gave senders or proposers 10 English pounds and asked the amount they wished to transfer.*

Second-Price Sealed-Bid Auction: *Subjects were told that they would bid for an amount of money. The computer would randomly choose the amount of money that the subjects could bid for from four possibilities: 4, 6, 8, or 10 English pounds. Subjects were told that each subject had a private amount of money to bid for, drawn from the same possibilities, and that all would bid in the same auction. The person with the highest bid would win the amount of money and have to pay the amount of money corresponding to the bid of the second highest bidder. All bids were submitted simultaneously.*

Elicitation of Risk Preferences: *Subjects made choices between eight different equal-probability lotteries and a fixed sum of money. One of the eight choices was chosen for payment.*

Public Good Game: *See Section 8.2.2. Subjects were randomly divided into groups of four and given 20 tokens. They were told that they could either put a token in their private account, which would earn them 1 token each, or they could contribute it to a group project. Each member received 0.4 times the sum of the contributions to the group project. Subjects did this repeatedly for 10 periods and earnings were summed across periods. The exchange rate for tokens was 25 tokens to 1 English pound.*

Results: *Belot et al. found that students are more likely than nonstudents to make the game-theoretic predicted decisions across all games. They found the differences particularly larger for the dictator, trust, and public good games. The differences are robust in regressions in which demographic variables, cognitive differences, and risk preferences are used as controls.*

Comments: *One of the questions facing experimenters in explaining to subjects how games work is whether to provide subjects with an example of* *choices. Doing so may unduly influence subjects to make that choice. Belot et al. confront this issue by having subjects come up with their own examples as a check on how the game worked.*

Belot et al. found significant differences between students and nonstudents in these one-shot games. In particular, they found in games in which subjects typically make choices that may suggest motives of altruism, fairness, or trust, students are less likely to exhibit these alternative motives than nonstudents, even controlling for their measures of risk preferences, cognitive abilities, and demographic variables. They argue that their results suggest that, in these types of models, student choices should be seen as a lower bound for such deviations.

To some extent this evidence is not surprising given the results of other experiments on one-shot games and how dependent they can be on presentation and other factors, as found by Chou et al.'s experiment on the guessing game in Example 6.2. Whether these differences are significant if repetition with randomization is allowed is an open question.

Models of Political Elite Behavior and Students

The majority of political science experiments concern questions about voting behavior and elections. And in that case, many political scientists may see student subjects as less of a problem. However, a number are also used to test theories of political elite decision making. Suppose a theory exists about how legislators bargain over ministries. What would results from experiments testing that theory using undergraduate subjects mean? One view is that the theory, at a deep level, is a mathematical model of human behavior in a generic choice situation that happens to also be considered an applied model of legislative bargaining. In this generic sense, as argued earlier, the theory can be tested on any humans, because the underlying model is really simply a model of how humans would interact in a particular situation. Undergraduate students are as good as any other subject pool, in this perspective. The theory that is evaluated by the experiment is the generic theory; then the question about robustness of the results to other subject pools is not one of internal validity but of external validity, which we deal with more later. This is the implicit perspective of the experiments on legislative bargaining conducted by Fréchette et al. in Example 8.7.

However, if we want to think of the theory that is evaluated as an applied theory of political elite behavior, it is a question of construct validity when the subject pool is comprised of undergraduates. As noted in the previous chapter, Fréchette et al. compared the data from student subjects to observational data of actual political elites in similar bargaining situations and contend that the data are similar as an effort to establish construct validity for their results. We are aware of three recent political science experiments that have compared experimental results testing theories of political elite behavior in the laboratory with undergraduates to similar experiments with subject populations of political experts; we summarize the findings of each next.

We begin with an experiment conducted by Potters and van Winden (2000), presented in the following example. Although all three of the example experiments are interesting comparisons of students with political elites, due to space constraints we selected only one to present as a formal example. We selected the Potters and van Winden experiment because we suspect political scientists are less likely to be aware of the study and because it is the only one in which the political elites were paid for their participation in the experiment close to their market wages and thus may face stronger incentives to take the experiment seriously, as we discuss in the next chapter.

Example 9.4 (Political Elites and Students Lobbying Experiment):
Potters and van Winden (2000) reported on an experiment in which they evaluated a game-theoretic model of lobbying with lobbyists as well as students as subjects.

Target Population and Sample: *The experimenters recruited 142 student subjects from the University of Amsterdam and 30 professional lobbyists. The professionals were recruited from attendees at two different conferences on public affairs, one held in Amsterdam and the other in The Hague. They were informed by mail that participation in a one-hour experimental study of decision making, which would earn them money, was optional. Participants were public affairs and public relations officers from the private and public sectors. Subjects participated only once and had not previously participated in a similar experiment.*

Subject Compensation: *Subjects were paid according to their choices as described in the following procedures. The theoretically expected equilibrium earnings for students was 20 guilders per hour, which is above the 15 guilders per hour that was the current wage for jobs in bars or restaurants. With the advice from a public affairs consulting firm that was involved in the organization of one of the conferences, the authors multiplied the payoffs such that the expected equilibrium earnings for the professionals was 80 guilders per hour. That is, taking an estimated yearly net income of 150,000 guilders as a point of departure, the net hourly wage of professional lobbyists at the time was about 80 guilders.*

Environment: *The sessions with professionals took place at the conference center and used pen and paper (no computers). Four of the six sessions under each manipulation with students also used pen and paper at the university and the other two were conducted in a computer laboratory at the university.*

Procedures: *Subjects were first assigned as either participant A or participant B. One subject was randomly chosen to be a monitor and was paid a flat fee for his or her participation. Subjects were then randomly matched into pairs of A and B for that period. After playing the game, the subjects were randomly rematched into new pairs of A and B. The matching was designed prior to the experiment so that no match would stay the same for two (or more) consecutive periods nor would it occur more than twice during the 10 periods of a manipulation.*

The Lobbying Game: *At the beginning of each period the monitor drew a disk from an urn. In the urn were three disks, two white and one black, which was known to all subjects. The monitor then revealed the color of the disk chosen to all A's, with the color hidden from B's. Subject A then decided whether to send a message to B which could be either "white" or "black." Subject A could lie. Sending a message cost A. In the low-cost manipulation, A paid 0.5 guilders (2 guilders for professionals) and in the high-cost manipulation, A paid 1.5 guilders (6 guilders for professionals) to send a message. Subject B then chose between two options: B1 and B2. After B chose, the decision was revealed to A and the color of the disk was announced to B. The payoffs in guilders of A and B for the students (not subtracting the cost of sending a message for A) depended on the choice of B and the color of the disk as given in the following table:*

Disk	Earnings to A		Earnings to B	
Color	Choice B1	Choice B2	Choice B1	Choice B2
White	2	4	3	1
Black	2	7	0	1

As noted earlier, the payoffs for professionals was 4 times these amounts. After a period ended, then a new pair was matched. The students participated in one manipulation (either high or low cost) for 10 periods and then an additional 10 periods with the other manipulation. The professionals only participated in one manipulation for 10 periods. Only the data from the first part of the sessions with students were compared to the data from the professionals.

Results: *The professionals behaved more in line with the game-theoretic predictions, were more likely to disclose information, and earned more money.*

Nevertheless, the sizes of the differences were small and only for a minority of the subjects.

Comments: *Potters and van Winden argued that the behavior observed by the professionals can be explained by professional rules of conduct such as "avoid conflicts of interests" and "never cheat or misinform."*

Potters and van Winden present an experiment testing a game-theoretic model of lobbying with actual lobbyists, which they compare to an earlier similar experiment reported on by Potters and van Winden (1996) using undergraduates at the University of Amsterdam. They found that the lobbyists' decisions were more in keeping with the game-theoretic predictions than those of the undergraduates; however, the differences were small and the comparative static predictions were supported for both students and professionals.

Our second example is a replication of one of the classic political psychology experiments conducted with undergraduates (Quattrone and Tversky, 1988). Quattrone and Tversky presented their subjects, who were undergraduate sociology and psychology students in California, with a set of hypothetical political choices facing political elites. They found that the subjects' choices were better explained by prospect theory than expected utility theory.[5]

Fatas et al. (2007) replicated this experiment with two different subject pools, undergraduate economics and labor students at a Spanish university and a set of "experts" – Spanish PhDs in economics who were then or had been in charge of large public budgets and were or had been elected directly by voters or indirectly by political representatives in control of some public department. They found that the difference in subject pool matters for some of the tests conducted but not for all. While they found that the expert subjects were affected by the interventions as the student subjects, the experts' choices were significantly different from those of the Spanish students in some of the manipulations. Furthermore, they found that overall the fit of prospect theory to both of the Spanish subject pools' choices was not as good as that found by Quattrone and Tversky.

Our third example is a comparison of students versus professionals in another decision-making experiment over hypothetical choices facing political elites conducted by Mintz et al. (2006). In this case the

---

[5] See Quattrone and Tversky (1988) for details.

subjects were presented with a number of options to deal with a terrorist threat. Mintz et al. used a computerized decision board that allowed subjects to access information about the different choices. Two subject pools were compared – students from political science courses at the University of Wisconsin, Milwaukee, and military officers participating in a leadership course taught at the National Defense University.

The authors found significant differences in the two subject pools. Students accessed more information than the military officers and were more likely to choose the option of Do Nothing. In contrast to the study of Fatas et al., Mintz et al. found that the military officers' choices were less rational than the students, although this clearly could simply reflect the fact that the officers accessed less information. Subjects were told during the experiment that there was a time constraint on their choices and not to spend too much time gathering information, although in actuality no time constraint was enforced.

Solutions
The implication of these results for political scientists is that when a theory is applied to a situation for members in a population which are presumed to have significant experience and be experts in a decision situation, the results from experiments with a sample from a population that does not have experience or that has a lack of common knowledge of rationality may not have construct validity. The results from these experiments also suggest an asymmetry in how we should interpret experiments with undergraduates that test rational-choice-based theories of behavior of political elites or others that we may expect to have experiences with situations that are unusual for undergraduates; that is, negative results with undergraduates on these types of models of political elite behavior may not satisfy construct validity, whereas positive results may. Note that these conclusions are quite the opposite of those found by Belot et al. for one-shot games (see Example 9.3).

However, we should be cautious about drawing any conclusions from such a small number of studies. In other contexts, experimentalists have found that student subjects performed closer to the rational choice predictions than the "expert" subjects, as in Belot et al.'s study. For example, Burns (1985) found that students do better than wool traders in progressive oral auctions and Cooper et al. (1999) contend that students will perform better at certain test-taking skills than experts. Fréchette (2009) reviewed nine studies in experimental economics that compared student subjects to professionals which work with a particular theoretical construct.[6] Fréchette found that in five of the studies the professionals and students make significantly different choices but that in two of the five studies the students are closer to the theory than the professionals; in one study there are multiple possible solutions to the theory and the professionals and students coordinate on different equilibria. Thus, in only two of the nine studies is there robust evidence that students perform more poorly than professionals.

Obviously one solution to the potential problem is to recruit subjects who have the likely experience in similar games as in the experiments discussed earlier. But this is not always feasible for experiments evaluating models of political elite behavior. A second solution is to recruit undergraduates, who, like the undergraduate soccer players, are more likely to have experience in a situation like that being modeled. Models of political elite behavior may perform differently in the laboratory if the subjects recruited are active in student political life or politics in the community.

Costs Versus Benefits in Theory Evaluation Using Student Subjects

As remarked in Section 9.2.2, there is a potential cost to using a convenience sample of students for basic theory research even when the target population is humanity. But the cost should also be weighed against the benefits. As in remarks quoted from Henry earlier, we believe it would be foolish for experimentalists in political science to stop using convenience samples for this type of research given the low opportunity cost compared to that for nonstudent samples. Moreover, using student subjects provides a large methodological benefit in comparability across samples and experiments.

Although experiments are definitely increasing in political science, the predominant empirical research in political science is not laboratory research with student subjects, unlike in social psychology. Thus, we believe, it is unlikely that a given political science laboratory experiment evaluating a theory of human political behavior conducted with students would both contain results that are significantly different from those obtained with non-student subjects *and* have a consequential effect on the future of theoretical and empirical research in political science. We believe that it is more likely that the experiment with students would have results that are robust to

---

[6] His review includes the Potters and van Winden and Palacios-Huerta and Volij papers. He classifies the Potters and van Winden paper as one where the results are qualitatively the same between students and professionals and Palacios-Huerta and Volij as one where the results are qualitatively different between the two subject pools. He also reviews a tenth paper in which the authors do not test a theoretical construct.

scientific replication with nonstudents but unfortunately have only a minor effect on the future of theoretical and empirical research in political science.

9.3 External Validity and Subject Pools

9.3.1 Experiments Conducted with Multiple Subject Pools

As remarked, even if an experiment is conducted on a random sample of a target population within a given city or country, this does not mean that the experiment is externally robust if the researcher would like to generalize to other populations. Representativeness of a subject pool to a target population does not ensure external validity of the results. Habyarimana et al. faced this problem with external validity, as does any empirical researcher whether they work with experimental data or nonexperimental data. That is, Habyarimana et al. may have a higher likelihood of statistical validity for their inferences for the target population of Kampala, but whether the results generalize to the population of Paris is an open question. The results of an experiment conducted on even a random sample of U.S. citizens may not be externally valid to China.

An increasing number of experimentalists are conducting experiments in which they vary the subject pools or target population to determine the external validity of their results with respect to changes in the population. We have already addressed in the previous section a number of examples that considered the robustness of the results of theoretical evaluations from experiments with students by comparing them to other subject pools. But even if a researcher is using students as the target population in one country or region of a country, it is not obvious that the results are robust to a different country or region. To investigate the robustness of their results, Mondak et al. (Example 2.4) conducted their experiments in multiple countries. Another of the first cross-country studies was conducted by Roth et al. (1991), who compared two-person and multiperson bargaining experiments in Israel, Japan, the United States, and Yugoslavia. The authors engaged in detailed efforts to make sure that the experimental procedures were the same across countries. They found significant differences when comparing the subjects' choices across locations. However, there were some uncontrolled differences in the subject pools as well – for example, in terms of military service – so the authors can only conjecture that the differences they find are cultural.

Sometimes the comparison is not across country but simply within a particular city. Danielson and Holm (2007) reported on two trust game experiments in Tanzania, one in which the subjects were undergraduate students and the other in which the subjects were members of a local Lutheran church. We discussed the trust game earlier in Example 8.2. Danielson and Holm found that there is no significant subject pool difference in the amounts that first movers offered, but there was a significant difference in what second movers were willing to return. They found that the second movers recruited at the church were more likely to give some of their proceeds back than the undergraduate subjects.

A recent paper by Herrmann et al. (2008) reported on a set of experiments conducted in 15 different countries but with subject pools that were undergraduates and were common in terms of education, age, and relative wealth.[7] The study examined behavior in a public goods game with or without giving the subjects the ability to punish other group members.[8] They found that subjects in the public goods game without punishment behaved largely similarly across countries, particularly so with experience. However, the choices of the subjects in the game with punishment varied significantly across countries, even with experience in the game. These studies suggest that the empirical results concerning the public goods game without punishment are robust to changing the geographic locale, but not the empirical results concerning the public goods game with punishment. Subject pool changes in locale mattered in one case but not in the other.

In another noteworthy recent study, Henrich et al. (2005, 2006) compared experiments conducted in 15 diverse locales using subject pools from freshmen at Emory University in Atlanta, Georgia, to rainforest communities in Papua, New Guinea. Similar to Herrmann et al.'s experiments, they found some similarities across all subject pools and some distinctions. Again, the results appear to hinge crucially on the interaction between the subject pool and the experimental research question. There are some considerable differences in the subject pools and experimental protocols independent of culture that could explain the differences.

9.3.2 Meta-Analysis and Subject Pool Comparisons

The Ultimatum Game

One of the experimental games that has been the subject of much scientific replication in cross-country research with different subject pools (see Roth

---

[7] The countries studied were the United States, the United Kingdom, Denmark, Germany, Switzerland, Belarus, Ukraine, Russia, Greece, Turkey, Saudi Arabia, Oman, South Korea, China, and Australia.

[8] For a description of the game and experimental procedures, see Herrmann et al.'s online appendix at http://www.nottingham.ac.uk/˜lezsg1/science.htm.

et al., 1991; Henrich et al. 2004), as well as in numerous variations on the design of the experiment, is the ultimatum game. We discussed the ultimatum game in Section 3.3.3.

The cross-country research on the ultimatum game demonstrates significant variation in choices. Are these differences cultural? Does this imply that the results of the experiments on the ultimatum game, and by implication other similar models, are not generalizable across countries? Oosterbeek et al. (2004) pointed out two major problems with using cross-country studies to consider issues of generalizability of results. First, the cross-country analyses usually only compare the results from experiments in one possible location or subject pool in a country with the results from a similar single possible location or subject pool in another country. As they note (p. 172):

Nothing guarantees that the differences between (say) Pittsburgh and Jerusalem are larger than the differences that would have been observed between Pittsburgh and (say) New York, or between Jerusalem and (say) Tel Aviv. When the within country differences are of the same magnitude as the between country differences, it obviously becomes less sensible to attribute differences between subject pools to cultural differences. But since New York and Tel Aviv are not included in the experimental design, there are no data to test this. The inconsistency of the findings of Roth et al. (1991) and Buchan et al. (1999)...between the US and Japan...illustrates this problem.

Second, Oosterbeek et al. noted that in the "usual cross-country/cross-culture studies" the "cross-country differences are attributed to cultural differences without specifying the cultural traits that underlie differences in subjects' behavior."

Oosterbeek et al. took a different approach to evaluating the robustness or generalizability of the results on the ultimatum game. They conduct a meta-analysis of 37 different papers with results from ultimatum game experiments from 25 different countries. They found no significant differences between the proposals offered in the games that could be explained by geographical region.[9] Responders' behavior did significantly vary by region. To determine if cultural indicators for the different regions could explain differences in behavior, they considered the explanatory power of the cultural classifications of Hofstede (1991) and Inglehart (2000). None of Hofstede's measures and only one of Inglehart's measures were significant; specifically they found that proposers' behavior did vary with Inglehart's

---

[9] To increase the number of observations per region, they combined experiments from some countries – for example, Eastern European countries – into one region.

scale of respect for authority. A higher score implied a lower offer. There was no significant effect of the scale on responder behavior; however, this may suggest that because proposers' behavior was changed there was no effect on responder behavior.

Framing Experiments

Another experimental result that has been the subject of extensive scientific replication with different subject pools is the framing effects first discovered by Tversky and Kahneman (1981). In Tversky and Kahneman's original experiment, subjects were given a choice between two policy programs to combat a disease. In one treatment the programs were presented in terms of how many would be saved (positive frame) and in the other the treatment the programs were presented in terms of how many would die (negative frame). The programs had the same expected numbers of dead and living, but in one program the outcome was presented as nonrisky (or safe), whereas in the other the outcome was presented as risky. The subjects were more likely to choose the nonrisky option in the positive frame and the risky option in the negative frame. As with the ultimatum game, the framing effects found by Tversky and Kahneman have particular relevance in political science because they imply that public opinion can be malleable and influenced by elites. Numerous experiments have been conducted in political science studying how framing may affect public opinion (see, for instance, the experiments of Druckman and coauthors reported in Example 5.1) and it has become commonplace to accept that framing effects can alter voters' preferences; see Jacoby (2000) and Druckman (2001) for reviews of the literature.

Most of the research on framing effects involves student subject pools, but some involve nonstudent pools. Are the results robust to expanding the subject pool? Kuhberger (1998) conducted a meta-analysis of the results from 136 empirical papers on framing effects with nearly 30,000 participants. Although he found that some of the design choices in the different experiments affected the sizes of the framing effects found, he found that there was little difference between the size of the framing effect found with students compared to that found with nonstudents, suggesting that, for this particular experimental result, student subjects make choices similar to those of nonstudent subjects.

Certainly more of this type or research – scientific replication coupled with meta-analysis – is needed before we can draw many conclusions about how externally valid a particular experiment with a student subject may be.

9.4 Chapter Summary

In this chapter we have investigated the claims that student subjects can be a problem for experiments. Students are used for many laboratory experiments because they are convenient and inexpensive but also because they provide methodological advantages. That is, they constitute a relatively homogenous subject pool over time that can be refreshed with new subjects. Thus, using student subjects can increase the comparability of experiments across time and space. In many experiments, there is no particular target population for the study and therefore using students as an initial subject pool can make sense and be the most efficient way to conduct the investigation.

However, if a researcher has in mind a particular target population, using a nonrandom sample of students lessens the statistical validity (part of internal validity) of the claims made from that research. Some laboratory experimentalists have turned to recruiting nonstudent subject pools in a goal to have a subject pool more representative of their target population or to use lab-in-the-field experiments to reach a representative sample of their target population. If researchers overuse students as subjects without failing to check whether the claims generalize to other populations (external validity) and students' choices are distinctively different from those made by subjects from other populations, research directions may be affected, leading to biases in results. This may be particularly problematic in studies of behavior of political elites, but less so in studies of nonelite behavior.

A small literature has compared the impact of using different subject pools to evaluate theoretic models generally and models of political elite behavior in particular. One study of one-shot games found significant differences in the apparent prosocial behavior of students and nonstudents. However, the literature is inconclusive. For instance, one study in which political elites were given incentives comparable to those they face outside of an experiment suggests that elites make choices slightly more rationally than students. Other studies comparing professionals and students imply that experience and common knowledge of rationality may be an important determinant of the differences between student and professional choices.

Finally, a few researchers have conducted experiments using multiple subject pools or meta-analysis comparing the choices of subjects across diverse subject pools in experiments that are of relevance to political science. We believe that more such research is needed in political science. Rather than simply avoiding students as subjects or dismissing experimental research using students, we hope that political scientists will be as empirically focused as most who worry about students as subjects claim and fully investigate the true empirical implications of using students as subjects.

9.5 Money and Subjects

Laboratory experiments conducted by both political psychologists and political economists use student subjects and in this chapter we have explored the validity of their use. But the two subfields vary in how they motivate subjects in the laboratory. Political psychologists typically reward subjects with either class credit or fixed financial payments. Political economists typically reward subjects financially based on their choices in an experiment. Why do these differences exist and what do they mean for the validity of the experimental results?

Motivating subjects is also an important issue in Internet and field experiments. We investigate these issues in the next chapter.

10

Subjects' Motivations

In Chapter 1, we observed that one of the big differences between laboratory experiments conducted by political economists and those conducted by political psychologists is the use of financial incentives to motivate subjects. That is, in political economy laboratory experiments subjects' payments for participation are tied to the choices that they make, whereas in political psychology experiments subjects are typically paid a flat fee for participation or receive class credit. Why is there this difference and does it affect the validity of the experiments? In this chapter we consider these questions. We begin with the reasons why political economists use financial incentives.

10.1 Financial Incentives, Theory Testing, and Validity

10.1.1 How Financial Incentives Work in Theory Testing

Most political economy experiments involve either theory testing or stress tests of theories (see Chapter 6). The theories are largely based on formal theoretical foundations. The emphasis of the research is often on political and economic institutions (i.e., election systems, legislative committees, stock markets, first-price auctions, etc.) and the behavior of actors within those institutions. The theories make relationship (either comparative static or dynamic) and point predictions about how these institutions will affect human behavior. We discuss these types of predictions in Chapter 6.

Importantly, the theories assume that subjects have assigned particular values to each outcome in the theory, and that, given these values, the institutional differences have predictable effects on the subjects' choices. To conduct a theory-testing experiment, then, an experimentalist would like to induce subjects to have the same value orderings over outcomes as assumed in his or her theory, as we noted in Chapter 6. Moreover, the experimenter wants to populate her institution with actors who make coherent and inter-pretable decisions. Doing so increases the construct validity (Chapter 7) of the experiment because it reduces the disconnects between the motivations of subjects and those assumed by the theory.

One way to induce these values is to use financial incentives. How does this work? Suppose an experimenter wants to construct an institution in the laboratory (such as an election system) and then manipulate certain vari-ables (voting rules) and observe the effects on subjects' choices of variations on that institution (varying whether voters vote sequentially or simultane-ously) while holding other variables constant (majority rule voting). The experimenter then wants to populate the experimental institution with actors to bring the institution to life (i.e., the experimenter needs voters to make decisions under the two different institutional procedures). In this case the focus is on how institutions affect human behavior (the experi-menter wants to examine the impact of using sequential voting as opposed to simultaneous voting). This comparison is possible when the subjects' values for the outcomes of the voting are held constant.

That is, suppose the theory's prediction is that when voters have incom-plete information about the options before them and place different values on the different outcomes, the option that is most preferred by voters in pairwise comparisons (the option that would win if it faced each other option one by one or the Condorcet winner) is more likely to be chosen under sequential voting than under simultaneous voting.[1] Suppose that an experimentalist conducts an experiment testing this prediction with three options labeled Blue, Yellow, or Green. If the experimentalist uses *experimenter-induced values*, then he or she assigns a financial value for each of the possible outcomes for each of the subjects. The experimenter can assign these values so that there is disagreement among the subjects, as assumed by the theory, and also control the information voters have about these values.

Definition 10.1 (Experimenter-Induced Values): *When an experimenter assigns specific financial values to outcomes in an experiment. These values are usually assigned in the context of a theory-testing experiment and the val-ues are designed to mirror the assumed preferences of the actors in the theory.*

For example, the experimenter might have a total of 15 subjects divided into groups of 5 each. The experimenter might assign the first group to

---

[1] See Condorcet (1785).

each receive \$3 if Blue wins, \$2 if Yellow wins, and \$1 if Green wins. The experimenter might assign the second group to each receive \$1 if either Blue or Green wins, and \$3 if Yellow wins. And finally the experimenter might assign the last group to each receive \$1 if Blue wins, \$2 if Yellow wins, and \$3 if Green wins. In this setup we have both disagreement over the values of the outcomes and Yellow is the Condorcet winner if the subjects vote according to their induced values. That is, if Blue and Yellow were the only candidates, 5 of the subjects would vote for Blue and 10 would vote for Yellow; if Yellow and Green were the only candidates, again 10 of the subjects would vote for Yellow. The experimenter can then hold the information and the disagreement constant by holding the payoffs constant and compare the choices of the subjects under the two different voting systems. The financial incentives are often also called performance-based incentives. If the experimenter-induced values work (we define shortly what we mean by "work"), then the experimenter has achieved a high level of construct validity and can make the comparison between the voting systems.

What happens if the experimentalist simply pays the subjects a flat fee for participating and the outcome of the voting has no extrinsic value for the subjects – the experimenter does not explicitly attempt to induce values for the outcomes? It would be more difficult for the experimentalist to evaluate the theory. First, the experimentalist would have to figure out the subjects' preferences over the three options independent of the voting system – figure out the subjects' intrinsic motivations in the experiment to evaluate the theory's predictions. Assuming the experimentalist could do so, what happens if all the subjects are simply indifferent between the choices? Or what happens if in sequential voting all the subjects have the same values but in simultaneous voting the subjects disagree over the best option? The subjects may have as a goal finishing the experiment as soon as possible, which may outweigh intrinsic values they have over the colors, leading them to make choices that are easiest given the experimental setup. Or the subjects may be taking part in repeated elections with randomization as described earlier and may just vote for the candidate who lost the previous election because he or she feels sorry for that candidate. All of these things would create a disconnect between the theory tested and the experimental design, lessening the construct validity of the results.

10.1.2 Financial Incentives Versus Intrinsic Motivations

Some psychologists argue that reward schemes based on financial incentives may actually cause subjects to perform poorly in an experiment.

Psychologists differentiate between intrinsic and extrinsic motivations. Ryan and Deci (2000, p. 55) note: "The basic distinction is between intrinsic motivation, which refers to doing something because it is inherently interesting or enjoyable, and extrinsic motivation, which refers to doing something because it leads to separable outcomes." The authors go on to note that extrinsically motivated actions can be performed with "resentment, resistance, and disinterest". Some psychologists argue that when money is contingent on the actions of subjects within an experiment, then the intrinsic motivation is replaced by extrinsic motivation and the performance of subjects is negatively affected. Deci (1971, p. 108) comments: "If a person is engaged in some activity for reasons of intrinsic motivation, and if he begins to receive the external reward, money, for performing the activity, the degree to which he is intrinsically motivated to perform activity decreases."

A number of studies by psychologists have found evidence that financial incentives lower task performance by crowding out intrinsic motivations. Most of this research focuses on individualized decision making rather than on choices within the context of a group or game situation as in political economy experiments. A recent example is Heyman and Ariely's (2004) study of the consequences of varying payment levels on the performance of subjects engaged in individualized tasks which ranged from boring, repetitive ones to solving puzzle problems that progressed in difficulty during the experiment. They studied the effects of a small payment, a sizable one, and whether the payment was money or candy. They also ran the experiment without paying subjects for performance.

Heyman and Ariely found that when subjects were not given incentive payments (either money or candy), the number of completed tasks was higher than with small incentive payments. Furthermore, when the incentive payment was not explicitly monetary (i.e., candy), the performance was higher than in the small-monetary-payment condition. Increasing incentive payments of both types increased performance, although not always reaching the levels of task performance in the control condition with no payment. These results support the contention that financial incentives crowd out intrinsic motivations and lead to worse task performance.[2]

---

[2] Gneezy and Rustichini (2000a) found similar results when they compared no-payment treatments to insignificant small monetary payments. A reanalysis of the data by Rydval and Ortmann (2004) suggests that these differences are more reflective of cognitive differences across subjects rather than payment treatment effects.

Four possible explanations for why explicit financial incentives may worsen task performance in experiments have been proffered. One is that the cognitive effort induced by the incentives may be counter-productive, causing subjects to "overthink" a problem and miss simple solutions as subjects try more complex cognitive strategies to maximize payoffs. Financial incentives may cause subjects to think they should exert more effort than necessary when simpler decision processes such as heuristics are sufficient.[3] According to this explanation, we would expect that financial incentives are most harmful for simple, easy tasks or ones where cognitive shortcuts can be effective, even in a situation that is complicated.

A second proposed cause was suggested by Meloy et al. (2006), who found that financial incentives in experiments can elevate a subject's mood, which contributes to worsened task performance. Meloy et al. noted that the effect they and others found may be mitigated if the subjects receive feedback and experience. This suggests that financial incentives interact with feedback and experience, and failure to provide those additional features leads to inaccurate estimates of their effects. It is worth noting that the experiments conducted by economists that demonstrate advantages of financial incentives usually also include feedback and repetition, in contrast to the experiments conducted by psychologists that demonstrate disadvantages of financial incentives in which subjects typically complete tasks without such feedback and repetition. Sprinkle (2000) provided evidence in support of this hypothesis.

Endogeneity of social norm preferences has been projected as a third reason. In this view we think of the experimental subjects as workers and the experimenter as their employer. Some theorists have contended that firms who pay well regardless of performance can motivate workers by inducing them to internalize the goals and objectives of the firm, changing their preferences to care about the firm. If workers are paid on an incentive basis such that lower performance lowers wages, they are less likely to internalize these firm goals and there is less voluntary cooperation in job performance (see Bewley, 1999; James, 2005). Miller and Whitford (2002) made a similar argument about the use of incentives in general in principal agent relationships in politics.

Somewhat related is an explanation suggested by Heyman and Ariely (2004) based on their aforementioned experimental analysis. That is, they contend that, when tasks are tied to monetary incentives, individuals see

---

[3] See Arkes et al. (1999) and Camerer and Hogarth (1999).

the exchange as part of a monetary market and respond to the incentives monotonically, but if the tasks are tied to incentives that do not have clear monetary value, individuals see the exchange as part of a social market and their response is governed by the internalization of social norms outside of the experiment.[4]

Finally, a fourth explanation of crowding out is informational. Benabou and Tirole (2003) showed that when information about the nature of a job is asymmetric, incentive-based payments may signal to workers that the task is onerous and, although increasing compensation increases the probability the agent will supply effort, it also signals to the agent that the job is distasteful and affects their intrinsic motivations to complete the task.

These last two explanations (the social norm perspective and the informational theory) also suggest a nonmonotonic relationship between financial incentives and task performance. That is, when financial incentives are introduced, but are small, subjects' task performance is worsened as compared to the no-payment condition (either because they now think of the exchange with the experimenter as a market one instead of a social one or because they see the task as more onerous than before), but as financial incentives are increased, task performance increases if the financial incentives are sizable enough.

10.1.3 Is Crowding Out by Financial Incentives a Problem?

The relevant question is whether money decreases the performance of subjects in experiments using experimenter-induced financial incentives. To answer this question, we must understand what controls and financial incentives are used for – to reduce performance variability in the data. That is, they are used to reduce randomness caused by subjects making choices outside of the realm of the theory. In a noteworthy study in political science, Prior and Lupia (2005) found that giving subjects financial incentives to give correct answers in a survey experiment on political knowledge induced

---

[4] A number of studies show that individuals are more likely to volunteer and contribute to public goods when participation is not tied to financial incentives such as Titmuss's (1970) comparison of blood markets. More recently, Gneezy and Rustichini (2000a) found in a field experiment that the introduction of a fine for parents picking up children late from day-care centers increased the number of parents who came late. Brekke et al. (2003) presented a formal model in which financial incentives can have adverse effects on voluntary contributions because of moral motivations and provided survey evidence on recycling behavior and voluntary community work consistent with the model's predictions. Cappellari and Turati (2004) also found that volunteering in a variety of situations is higher when individuals are intrinsically motivated.

subjects to take more time and to give more accurate responses. Studies by economists suggest that performance-based incentives lead to reductions in framing effects, the time it takes for subjects to reach equilibrium in market experiments, and mistakes in predictions and probability calculations.[5]

Furthermore, a growing number of field and marketing experiments show that choices made by subjects in hypothetical situations are significantly different from the choices made by subjects in comparable real situations in which financial incentives are involved, suggesting that using hypothetical situations in place of financial incentives leads to biased and inefficient predictions about behavior. Bishop and Heberlein (1986) showed that willingness-to-pay values of deer-hunting permits were significantly overstated in a hypothetical condition as compared to a paid condition. List and Shogren (1998) found that the selling price for a gift is significantly higher in real situations than in hypothetical ones. List (2001) demonstrated that in a hypothetical bidding game bids were significantly higher than in one in which real payments were used. In marketing research, Ding et al. (2005) presented evidence that shows significantly better information is gathered on subjects' preferences over different attributes of meal choices when the meals are not hypothetical but real. And Voelckner (2006) found significant differences between consumers' reported willingness to pay for products in hypothetical choice situations as compared to real choices across a variety of methods used to measure willingness to pay in marketing studies. In a recent meta-analysis of experiments on preference reversals (situations in which individuals express preferences over gambles that are at odds with their rankings of the gambles individually), Berg et al. (2010) showed that when financial incentives are used, the choices of the individuals are reconcilable with a model of stable preferences with errors, whereas the choices of individuals where such incentives are not used cannot be reconciled. Thus, the evidence appears to support the conclusions of Davis and Holt (1993, p. 25): "In the absence of financial incentives, it is more common to observe nonsystematic deviations in behavior from the norm."

Fortunately, several systematic reviews of the literature have examined this question. In one survey article, Smith and Walker (1993b) examined 31 economic experimental studies on decision costs and financial incentives

---

[5] See Brase et al. (2006); Hogarth et al. (1991); Gneezy and Rustichini (2000a); Levin et al. (1988); List and Lucking-Reiling (2002); Ordóñez et al. (1995); Parco et al. (2002); Wilcox (1993); and Wright and Aboul-Ezz (1988).

and concluded that financial incentives bolstered the results. They noted (pp. 259–260):

A survey of experimental papers which report data on the comparative effects of subject monetary rewards (including no rewards) show a tendency for the error variance of the observations around the predicted optimal level to decline with increased monetary reward. ... Many of the [experimental] results are consistent with an "effort" or labor theory of decision making. According to this theory better decisions – decisions closer to the optimum, as computed from the point of view of the experimenter/theorist – require increased cognitive and response effort which is disutilitarian. ... Since increasing the reward level causes an increase in effort, the new model predicts that subject's decisions will move closer to the theorist's optimum and result in a reduction in the variance of decision error.

This conclusion has found support elsewhere. Camerer and Hogarth (1999) reviewed a wide range of studies and found that higher financial incentives lead to better task performance. Hertwig and Ortmann (2001), in a similar review, found that when payments were used, subjects' task performances were higher. Hertwig and Ortmann (2001) conducted a 10-year review of articles published in the *Journal of Behavioral Decision Making* (JBDM) and reviewed articles that systematically explored the effect of financial incentives on subject behavior. Similar to Smith and Walker's assessment, they "conclude that, although payments do not guarantee optimal decisions, in many cases they bring decisions closer to the predictions of the normality model. Moreover, and equally important, they can reduce data viability substantially" (Hertwig and Ortmann, 2001, p. 395).

Of particular interest is the systematic review of Cameron and Pierce (1994, 1996) of approximately 100 experiments in social psychology and education. These researchers found that "[financial] rewards can be used effectively to enhance or maintain intrinsic interest in activities. The only negative effect of reward occurs under a highly specific set of conditions that be easily avoided" (Cameron and Pierce, 1996, p. 49). The negative effect that Cameron and Pierce make mention of is "when subjects are offered a tangible reward (expected) that is delivered regardless of level of performance, they spend less time on a task that control subjects once the reward is removed" (Cameron and Pierce, 1994, p. 395). In other words, flat payment schemes hinder subjects' performance. Although some quibble about the methodology employed in these studies, it is clear that financial incentives based on performance have not had as negative an impact on subjects' behavior as some psychologists have argued.

To ensure that positive intrinsic behavior is not crowded out, an experimenter can attempt to make the experiment interesting and avoid repetitive tasks. As noted earlier, repetition is a hallmark for many experimental designs in political science and economics that test formal models. However, if the experiment is not interesting and the subjects are simply performing the same task repeatedly, then we can imagine cases in which intrinsic motivation will decrease and subjects will become bored and perform poorly. To avoid this type of behavior, experimental designs can incorporate greater randomness in treatments so that subjects are engaged in different tasks. Then performance-based financial incentives can ensure that the experiment is an interesting and enjoyable task for the subjects.

10.1.4 Induced Value Theory

The theory that reward media such as financial incentives can induce subjects to have preferences as theoretically assumed is called induced value theory. This theory was posited by Nobel Laureate Vernon Smith in a series of articles (Smith, 1976, 1982; Smith and Walker, 1993a). Smith (1982, p. 931) comments:

Control over preferences is the most significant element distinguishing laboratory experiments from other methods of economic inquiry. In such experiment, it is of the greatest importance that one be able to state that, as between two experiments, individual values (or derivative concepts such as demand or supply) either do or do not differ in a specified way. This control can be exercised by using a reward structure and a property right system to induce prescribed monetary value on (abstract) outcomes.

Or, as Friedman and Sunder (1994) note: "The key idea in induced-value theory is that proper use of a reward medium allows an experimenter to induce prespecified characteristics in experimental subjects, and the subject's innate characteristics become largely irrelevant." Therefore, if subjects' motivations in the experiment are guided by the reward mechanism, then other factors such as altruism, revenge, and naivety will be ruled out.

Induced Value Theory postulates that four conditions should be considered when attempting to induce experimental motivations by a reward medium (such as money) in the laboratory. First, if a reward medium is *monotonic* then subjects prefer more of the medium to less. When financial incentives are used, monotonicity requires that subjects prefer more money to less. Second, if a reward medium is *salient*, then the rewards are a by-product of a subject's labor or the choices he or she makes during the experiment. Reward mechanisms that are salient are also referred to as performance-based incentives because subjects earn rewards in the experiment based on the decisions that they make. For example, in the experiment described earlier, the subjects would receive the dollar values assigned as payment for the election in which they participated depending on which candidate won the most votes. In cases for which the researcher uses repetition, usually the subjects' rewards may be accumulated over the experiment. Alternatively, sometimes a researcher may randomly choose one of the choices of the subjects for one of the periods to reward, as we discuss later. Third, if a reward medium is *private*, then interpersonal utility considerations are minimized. That is, subjects are unaware of what other subjects are awarded. And fourth, if a reward medium is *dominant*, then the choices made in the experiment are based solely on the reward medium and not some other factors such as the rewards earned by other subjects (i.e., a subject is not concerned about the payoffs of other subjects).

Definition 10.2 (Monotonicity): *Given a costless choice between two alternatives, identical except that the first yields more of the reward medium than the second, the first will be preferred over or valued more than the second by any subject.*

Definition 10.3 (Salience): *The reward medium is consequential to the subjects; that is, they have a guaranteed right to claim the rewards based upon their actions in the experiment.*

Definition 10.4 (Dominance): *The reward structure dominates any subjective costs (or values) associated with participation in the activities of the experiment.*

Definition 10.5 (Privacy): *Each subject in an experiment is only given information about his or her own payoffs.*

Smith did not specify that these four conditions were necessary conditions to control subject behavior but rather only sufficient conditions (Smith, 1982). Guala (2005) points out that these conditions are not hardened rules but actually precepts or guidelines on how to control preferences in experiments. He states (p. 233):

[F]irst, the conditions identified by the precepts [of induced value theory] were not intended to be necessary ones; that is, according to the original formulation, a perfectly valid experiment may in principal be built that nevertheless violates some or all of the precepts. Second, the precepts should be read as hypothetical conditions ("if you want to achieve control, you should do this and that") and should emphatically not be taken as axioms to be taken for granted. ... Consider also that the precepts provide broad general guidelines concerning the control of individual preferences, which may be implemented in various ways and may require ad hoc adjustment depending on the context and particular experimental design one is using.

These guidelines were set over a quarter of a century ago when the use of financial incentives in experiments was still relatively new. How do these guidelines hold up today for political scientists who wish to use experimenter-induced values? What implications do they have for experimental design choices?

Monotonicity and Salience

In our view, the two conditions of monotonicity and salience are intricately related. Given that empirical evidence rather overwhelmingly suggests that sufficient financial incentives can work to create experimenter-induced values, the conditions of monotonicity and salience together raise the following questions for experimentalists who use financial incentives: (1) How much total should subjects expect to earn on average for them to value their participation? (2) How much should subjects' choices affect their payoffs? We consider these questions in order.

How Much Should Subjects Be Paid on Average?

Undergraduate Subject Pools. When using undergraduate students, the standard norm among experimental political economists is to structure the experimental payments so that on average subjects earn 50% to 100% above the minimum wage per hour (see Friedman and Sunder, 1994, p. 50). But this is only a rule of thumb. Does this amount have any empirical justification? Gneezy and Rustichini (2000b) conducted experiments that considered how varying the reward medium affected student performance. They conducted an experiment in which students answered questions on an IQ test. Subjects were randomly assigned to one of four treatments that varied the reward medium. In all the treatments, subjects were given a flat sum payment and treatments varied over an additional amount that the subjects could earn depending on whether they answered questions correctly. In the first treatment, subjects were not given an additional opportunity to earn more; in the second treatment, subjects were given a small amount for each question they got correct; in the third treatment, subjects were given a substantial amount for each question they answered correctly; and in the fourth treatment, subjects were given three times the amount given in the third treatment for each correct question. The authors found that the performance on the IQ tests of subjects in treatments 1 and 2 was essentially the same and significantly worse than in treatments 3 and 4.

The interesting finding is that there was no difference between the high-payoff conditions in treatments 3 and 4. Hence, what mattered in the experiment was that subjects who received substantive rewards performed better than subjects with minimum or no rewards, but there was no difference between the two types of substantive rewards. This finding suggests that financial incentives in the laboratory are not strictly monotonic in the sense that increasing the reward medium will increase the performance of subjects. Rather the subjects only have to perceive that the reward medium is sufficient. The authors foreshadow their conclusion with the title of their paper: "Pay enough or don't pay at all." This research suggests that the rule of thumb of "twice the minimum wage per hour" may be appropriate.

However, in contrast to these results, as observed earlier, Bassi et al. (2010; see Example 6.3) conducted an experiment on a voting game in which they varied the financial incentives paid to subjects. In one treatment, subjects were paid only a flat fee for participating; in another treatment, subjects were paid a normal experimental payment; and in a third treatment, the subjects were paid double the normal experimental payment. The authors also considered the effect of increasing the complexity of the voting game by reducing the information available to voters. They found a monotonic relationship between financial incentives and the tendency of voters to choose as predicted by the game-theoretic model. Furthermore, they found that this tendency was particularly strong in the complex game with incomplete information. These results suggest that, in game-theoretic experiments, particularly complex ones, increasing financial incentives does increase the attention of voters to the task. This analysis suggests that in complex games the researcher may want to pay subjects more than the standard twice the minimum wage.

Nonstudent Subject Pools. A more complex question is how much to pay nonstudent subject pools in the laboratory and how that would affect the comparison to student subjects. For example, in Palacios-Huerta and Volij's experiment with soccer players (Example 9.2), the soccer player subjects were paid the same amount as the students, yet arguably on average their income was significantly higher.[6] The payments both the students and the

---

[6] The incomes are not public information, but the authors estimate that the average income of the soccer players, excluding extra money for endorsements and the like, was between 0.5 and 2 million dollars.

soccer players received, however, were also significantly higher than that typically paid to students – a win by a subject in the two-player game earned the subject 1 euro and they played on average more than 100 games in an hour. Therefore, one may conclude the students were highly paid while the professionals were lowly paid. In their experimental study of lobbying with professionals and students (Example 9.4), Potters and van Winden paid the student subjects the conventional amount, but paid the professional lobbyists four times that amount, roughly equivalent to their hourly wages for the time spent in the experiment.

How Much Should Subjects' Choices Affect Their Pay? Both monotonicity and salience depend on subjects caring about the financial differences between choices. This may be a problem if the financial difference between two choices is only a few cents. However, in certain types of experiments the theory requires that subjects choose between extremely similar choices. For example, Morton (1993) considered an experimental game in which two candidates chose numbers representing policy positions from 0 to 1000. The candidates' payoffs were functions of the policy choices of the winning candidate and the candidates had ideal points over policy that were divergent. (Candidate payoffs were given by a standard quadratic loss function where policy positions farther from their ideal points gave them lower payoffs.) In the experiment, voters were artificial actors who voted for the candidate whose policy position was closest to their ideal points. Morton considered two treatments, one in which the candidates knew the ideal point of the median voter and one in which the ideal point of the median voter was unknown but given by a known probability distribution. Because candidates' payoffs depended on the policy position of the winning candidate, the theory predicts that they would diverge when they are uncertain about the ideal point of the median voter but converge when they knew the ideal point.[7]

In the experiment when the candidates had incomplete information they converged more than predicted by the theory. The theory predicted, for example, that candidate A would make a policy choice of 355. But subjects generally made a choice of about 375, 20 points higher. In terms of payoffs, the difference between what candidates chose and the equilibrium choice was only approximately 5 cents. Did the subjects make choices at variance with the prediction because the payoff difference was too small? Morton considered one treatment where the predicted equilibrium is the same but the payoff difference was larger – the penalty of choosing 375

---

[7] See Wittman (1983) and Calvert (1985) for the theoretical analysis.

was 15 cents. She found that the behavior of the subjects was unaffected by the change in payoff difference and there was no significant difference between the positions chosen by the candidates in the two treatments. However, the financial difference in the second treatment was still small at 15 cents, so the difference may not have been salient enough in the second treatment.

What can an experimenter do in this sort of situation? One solution is to pay the subjects more on average than the twice-minimum-wage norm to increase the payoff differences. Another option that many try is to use an artificial currency that is inflated: pay the subjects in tokens or experimental currency with an exchange rate for cash. If subjects have an intrinsic motivation to earn large numbers, then the artificial currency may tap into that motivation. Morton used this option in her experiment. Experimental currency is useful for other reasons as well. Often times the experimentalist is not sure in the design phase of the experiment what would be the best rate at which to pay subjects. Using experimental currency allows the experimenter the flexibility of designing the experiment and even conducting a trial run or two with colleagues (nonsubjects) before making a final decision as to how much to pay actual subjects. Furthermore, the researcher can also use different exchange rates for different treatments or subject groups if the experimenter believes it is necessary while not changing the overall experimental design.

In addition, to ensure the saliency condition is fulfilled, the subjects should explicitly know that they will be paid in cash the money they earned during the experiment immediately after the experiment terminates or given a cash voucher for which they can quickly receive reimbursement at the bursar's office. To further emphasize the saliency of money, one strategy that is often employed is that, before the experiment begins, the experimenter shows the subjects the cash from which they will be paid and then announces that he or she would like to get rid of as much as of the cash as possible. However, in the instructions it should be emphasized that the amount of money subjects will actually receive will depend partly on chance and partly on the decisions that they make during the experiment. This presentation will let the subjects know that the monetary incentives are real because they can see the cash.

Budget Endowments and Experimental Losses. One of the problems with using financial incentives in experiments is the difficulty in evaluating situations in which individuals can lose money. For example, in the auction experiments of Casari et al. in Example 5.2, subjects could go bankrupt.

At that point, Casari et al. dropped the subjects from the experiment. Although in personal anecdotes we have heard stories of experimentalists who actually have demanded subjects pay them at the end of the experiment when earnings have become negative, the enforcement of such procedures is likely to be difficult. Furthermore, for an experimenter to earn money from an experiment raises ethical concerns. Friedman and Sunder (1994) argued that this type of incentive scheme violates induced value theory because negative payments are not credible. They note that "when subject's earnings become negative (or threaten to become negative) you lose control over induced preferences because negative payments are not credible."

One solution is to give subjects a budget at the start of the experiment. For example, a subject could begin the experiment with $10 to play with in the experiment. Grether and Plott (1979) endowed subjects with a budget of $7 in a risk experiment. Subjects were told that they could only lose $2 on a gamble so $5 would be their minimum payment. However, such money may not be seen by the subject as his or her own money, but rather "house money," and making choices with windfall gains or house money leads to risk-seeking behavior. The experimenter loses experimental control. Thaler and Johnson (1990, p. 657) argue: "after a gain, subsequent losses that are smaller than the original gain can be integrated with the prior gain, mitigating the influence of loss-aversion and facilitating risk-seeking."

How can an experimenter deal with this problem? One solution is to allow subjects to "earn" the endowments as Eckel and Wilson did in Example 8.2 by having subjects complete a survey for payment at the beginning of the experiment. Yet, subjects may still see the endowments as not really their own money. An alternative solution is to have subjects either receive (or earn) the endowments some period prior to the experiment with the understanding that subjects will be expected to use the endowments in the subsequent experiment. Bosch-Domènech and Silvestre (2006; Example 10.1) had subjects complete a quiz on basic knowledge and earn cash paid immediately after taking the quiz based on the number of correct answers. The subjects were told that they would be called several months later for a second session where they could possibly lose money (which was promised not to be more than they had earned) and signed a promise to show up. The exact date of the second session was left unspecified.

Example 10.1 (Risk Preferences in Large Losses Experiment): *Bosch-Domènech and Silvestre (2006) reported on an experiment evaluating an assertion of prospect theory that people display risk attraction in choices* *involving high-probability losses using an experimental method that allowed subjects to view potential losses in the experiment as real.*

Target Population and Sample: *Subjects were voluntary students from the Universitat Pompeu Fabra who had not taken courses in economics or business, with a roughly equal proportion of the sexes. Twenty-four subjects participated in manipulation L and 36 subjects participated in manipulation L'.*

Subject Compensation: *Subjects were paid according to the procedures described here.*

Environment: *The experiment was conducted via paper and pencil, at a university location.*

Procedures: *Subjects were recruited to participate first in a quiz-taking session. The quiz was on basic knowledge and the subjects earned cash that was immediately paid after taking the quiz. Subjects received 90 euros if their answers were ranked in the first quartile, 60 euros if their answers were ranked in the second quartile, 45 euros if in the third quartile, and 30 euros if in the fourth quartile. The subjects were told they would be called several months later for a second session in which they could possibly lose money and they signed a promise to show up. The exact date of the second session was unspecified. Subjects were guaranteed that the eventual losses would never exceed the cash previously received at the time of the quiz.*

Four months later and after a semester break, the experimenters personally contacted each of the subjects to inform them of the date, hour, and venue for the second session. Of the subjects for manipulation L, 21 of the 24 showed up with a male-to-female ratio of 10:11. For manipulation L', 34 of the 36 showed up with a male-to-female ratio of 18:16.

Manipulation L: *Participants were told that they would be randomly assigned without replacement to one of seven classes corresponding to seven possible monetary amounts to lose in euros (3, 6, 12, 30, 45, 60, and 90), with the requirement that a participant could not be assigned to a class with an amount of money to lose exceeding the cash earned four months earlier in the quiz. Then a participant was asked to choose for each possible class and, before knowing which class he or she would be assigned, between a certain loss of 0.2 times the money amount of the class and the uncertain prospect of losing the money amount of the class with probability 0.2 and nothing with probability 0.8.*

Participants recorded their decisions in a folder containing one page for each monetary class. Participants were given no time constraint. After registering their choices, subjects were asked to answer an anonymous questionnaire about the prospective pain of losing money in the experiment. They were then called one at a time to an office where the participant's class was randomly drawn. If the participant's choice was the certain loss, he or she would pay 0.2 times the amount of money of her class. If he or she chose the uncertain prospect, then a number from 1 to 5 was randomly drawn from an urn. If the number 1 was drawn, then the participant would pay the amount of money of his or her class, otherwise he or she would pay nothing. Participants either paid the money on the spot or within a few days. All subjects ended up paying their losses.

Manipulation L': *This manipulation was exactly the same as manipulation L except that the probability of loss was 0.8 instead of 0.2. Again, all subjects paid their losses.*

Results: *Subjects are much more risk averse as the amount of possible loss grows larger. Furthermore, the majority of subjects displayed risk aversion for the high probability of a large loss and the rates of risk aversion by monetary class was not significantly different between the two manipulations, suggesting that the explanatory power of the amount of money dominates that of probability.*

Comments: *Bosch-Domènech and Silvestre found that in the questionnaire only 21% of the subjects claimed to anticipate no pain if they lost money since the money "was not actually theirs." The majority (59%) agreed that it would be very painful to lose money because "the money was theirs" and 9% said that they would feel some pain since it was "as if the money was theirs." They also compared their results to previous experiments using either hypothetical money or money given to subjects at the time of the experiment. They found significant differences between the choices made in their experiments and in the experiments using hypothetical money and similarities with those using actual money.*

As Bosch-Domènech and Silvestre reported, their survey evidence suggests that the majority of subjects, approximately 68%, viewed the money they earned in advance as their own money by the time of the experiment. They suggest that such a procedure can help reduce the "house money" effect and allow researchers to conduct experiments in which subjects can lose money.

Dominance and Privacy

Dominance and privacy are also related concepts. In its simplest interpretation, dominance is the requirement that subjects are only concerned with their own payoff and privacy is the enforcement mechanism that prevents subjects from knowing about the payoffs of other subjects. Thus, privacy seems to be an important prerequisite for payoffs to be dominant. What does it mean for subjects' payoffs to be private information? Subjects' payoffs can be private in three different ways depending on whether the payoffs are blind to other subjects and whether the identity of the subjects associated with choices and payoffs is known to the experimenter or to other subjects. We identify two types of privacy: *identity anonymous to other subjects* or *single blind privacy* and *identity anonymous to experimenter* or *double blind privacy*, whose names are largely self-explanatory.

Definition 10.6 (Identities Anonymous to Other Subjects or Single Blind Privacy): *A subject may know the choices that have been made during the experiment by others and the payoffs they received, but not the particular identity of the subjects who made each choice and received each payoff with the exception of the choice he or she made and the payoffs he or she received.*

Definition 10.7 (Identities Anonymous to Experimenter or Double Blind Privacy): *The experimenter knows the choices that have been made during the experiment and the payoffs received, but not the particular identity of the subjects who made each choice and received each payoff.*

Single Blind Privacy. Many experiments conducted by political economists can be classified as the first type, which are sometimes called single blind experiments, where subjects' identities are secret to other subjects but not always the choices made or the payoffs received. Single blind privacy goes back at least to the bargaining experiments of Siegel and Fouraker (1960). As Hoffman et al. (1994, p. 354) contend, the absence of such anonymity "brings into potential play all the social experience with people are endowed, causing the experimenter to risk losing control over preferences."

Single blind privacy also allows an experimentalist to control altruism or fairness concerns for specific individuals. In most cases, the experimentalist wishes to eliminate these concerns so that any effect of altruism or fairness observed is to a person who is anonymous to the subject. But in other cases, an experimentalist may want to manipulate the type of person that a subject is interacting with to see if type differences matter. To see how this works, consider Example 8.2, in which Eckel and Wilson investigated the choices of subjects in a trust game as a function of the attractiveness of a partner. Conducting the experiments via the Internet, they were able to both maintain subject anonymity and manipulate the attractiveness of a subject's partners.

Another reason for maintaining single blind privacy is to prevent subjects from collaborating with each other to circumvent an experiment's goal. That is, if subjects are mutually aware of each others' actual earnings, they may attempt to establish an agreement to share earnings after the experiment.

When payments are made privately, subjects have less ability to enforce such agreements and are arguably more influenced by their own private payoffs. This was one of the concerns in the Internet experiments of Egas and Riedl in Example 8.3. Specifically, if subjects could conspire to be involved in the same experiment via the Internet where a researcher cannot control subject anonymity, then they can circumvent the purpose of the experiment.

Usually single blind privacy is accomplished in the laboratory by assigning subjects experiment identities to be used during the experiment and to maintain privacy for subjects when they make their choices. Furthermore, subjects are then paid in private individually after the experiment is concluded. Single blind privacy can be implemented by not allowing a subject to discover what other subjects are doing. That is, the experimenter needs to prevent subjects from observing the choices other subjects make and needs to prevent subjects from discovering what other subjects are earning. With computer networks, it is easy to control the information that subjects have about the actions of other subjects. In a computer environment, an experimenter can protect the anonymity of subject choices, especially in laboratories specifically designed for experiments, by positioning the computer screens so that subjects cannot view other subjects' screens and by assigning subjects an anonymous subject number. In laboratories not specifically designed for experiments but rather for classroom or public use, inexpensive temporary partitions can be used to block the views of subjects' computer screens. To further ensure dominance (or anonymous payoffs) before the experiment begins, subjects should be told that after the experiment ends they will be paid in private so that only they are told their payoffs.

Single blind privacy can also be done when an experiment is conducted "by hand," that is, without a computer network, by seating subjects so that they cannot observe the choices made by others. If an experiment calls for face-to-face interaction, the reader should refer to a series of experiments conducted by McKelvey and Ordeshook (1984, 1985a,b). In these experiments, the design calls for a careful collection of responses and notification of awards so that subjects are unaware of the decisions and performances of other subjects. However, even with technological advances it is difficult to strictly implement the single blind privacy condition. Facial expressions and utterances of delight or displeasure from subjects all signal to other subjects the performance of another subject during the experiment. All the experimenter can do is attempt to monitor subject behavior as closely as possible by preventing viewing of other subjects' screens and limiting the visual and audio communication among subjects. In Internet experiments such as that of Egas and Riedl, the researcher can, as they did, use random selection in the experiment and reveal random assignment to online sessions with less than 24 hours notice to reduce the probability that subjects who know each other are in the same experiment.

Another way in which an experimenter attempts to control single blind privacy is by using hypothetical currencies such as tokens, francs, Plato dollars, or experimental currency that is converted to cash according to an exchange rate, as we have discussed in Section 10.1.4. Hypothetical currency allows the experimenter to "minimize interpersonal payoff comparisons by giving subjects different conversion ratios that are private information" (Davis and Holt, 1993, p. 25). Also hypothetical currency allows the experimenter to change the conversion rate across experiments to prevent future subjects from learning how much money they can earn.

Double Blind Privacy and Other Regarding Preferences. Experimenters endeavor to provide subjects with double blind privacy when they are especially concerned about experimental effects caused by the observation of subjects which would not occur if they were observed, such as we discussed in Section 8.4. Most of the early game-theoretic experiments that were conducted involved games in which subjects may have been in competition with each other, but there was an equalness to that competition. The early experiments demonstrated a robustness to the predictions of models of such competition, and subjects often made choices as predicted by a standard payoff-maximizing model. However, in games where the relationships between the subjects demonstrated an unequalness, subjects showed a tendency to make choices that failed to maximize their payoffs. One of the games for which this tendency is most notable is the dictator game, which we discussed in Section 8.5. The payoff-maximizing prediction is that the dictator should take all of the money, leaving none to his or her partner. Yet Forsythe et al. (1994), in an experimental test of the game, found that 20% of the subjects split the sum of money equally with their partners.

Were these subjects truly altruistic, with what are now often called other regarding preferences, or were they simply concerned about being observed to be selfish? Did the lack of privacy that the subjects had from the experimenter's observation make the payoffs no longer dominant in determining their choices? It may be one thing for a subject to behave selfishly before an experimenter in which all subjects have symmetrical opportunities to compete for the payoffs; but in the dictator game, the subjects may have been concerned that their selfish behavior was being observed by the experimenter. To evaluate whether the tendency to give to other subjects was merely induced by the fact that the dictators' choices were observed by the experimenter, Hoffman et al. (1994, 1996) conducted some of the first experiments to use double blind privacy with the dictator game. It is useful to quote from their description of the procedures they used to maintain double blind privacy (1994, p. 355):

[Fifteen] people are recruited to room A and 14 to room B. The same instructions are read by each subject, and then read orally by an experimenter in each room. . . . One of the subjects in room A is voluntarily selected to be the monitor in the experiment. The monitor is paid $10. The instructions state that 14 plain white unmarked opaque envelopes contain the following: 2 of the envelopes contain 20 blank slips of paper each, and 12 contain 10 blank slips and 10 one-dollar bills each. Each subject is given an envelope by the monitor, proceeds to the back of the room, and opens the envelope inside a large cardboard box which maintains his/her strict privacy. The subject keeps 0 to 10 of the one-dollar bills, and 10 to 0 of the blank slips of paper, so that the number of bills plus slips of paper add up to 10. For the envelopes with 20 blank slips, 10 are returned to the envelope. (In this way all returned envelopes feel equally thick. Moreover, each person in room A knows that if his/her counterpart in room B receives an envelope with 10 slips of blank paper, it could be because there was no money in the envelope originally. Thus it is really true that 'no one can know'.)

After everyone is finished in room A, the monitor goes to room B, sits outside the room, and calls each person out one at a time. The person selects an envelope, opens it, and keeps its contents, which are recorded by the monitor on a blank sheet of paper containing no names. The experimenter accompanies the monitor to answer any questions that arise, but does not participate in the process. These procedures are intended to make it transparent that room A subjects are on their own in deciding how much to leave their counterparts in room B, and that no one can possibly know how much they left their counterparts. The use of a monitor minimizes experimenter involvement and guarantees that someone from room A besides the experimenter can verify that there is actually a room B with 14 subjects, as stated in the instructions.

Hoffman et al. found that the offers made by the dictators (the individuals in room A) were significantly reduced by about half that given when the experiment was single blind. However, about one-third of the subjects did leave money for the participants in room B and room B participants earned on average approximately $1.

These results have been replicated in experiments that have increased the anonymity afforded subjects. For example, one concern is that, even though subjects were anonymous, their choices were observable by the other subjects in a fashion and they may have been motivated by that observability and possible future interaction. Koch and Normann (2008) conducted an experiment similar in design except that envelopes with money were mailed to randomly selected names from a phone book by the monitor and experimenter; envelopes without money were not mailed. Thus, Koch and Normann removed any observability of other subjects from the dictator's choices because the subjects received the monies as a free gift, without any knowledge of the source of the money and any possibility of future interaction. Surprisingly Koch and Normann also found that similar percentages of subjects gave money of approximately the same amount on average as that found in the previous experiments by Hoffman et al. Koch and Normann concluded (p. 229): "Overall, these experiments [previous research of Hoffman et al.] and our results suggest that about half of dictator giving observed in standard experiments with exogenously given pie size is internally motivated, and the other half is driven by external factors such as experimenter observability or regard by receivers."

Although the results of the experiments show that, even with a large degree of privacy, subjects still made choices that were not payoff dominant, this is a prime illustration of why it is important to test the limits of observability and payoff dominance before concluding that subjects are acting contrary to the payoff-maximizing assumption. When privacy was only single blind, subjects gave more than when it was double blind.

Privacy and Subjects' Beliefs. Establishing privacy may be extremely difficult in a game more complicated than the dictator game or in a game that is repeated. Subjects may not believe an experimenter who claims to provide double blind privacy via computers. They also may not believe that other subjects exist and are affected by their choices when they have single blind privacy. Frohlich et al. (2001) contend that one explanation for the Hoffman et al. results may be that with sufficient social and physical distance the subjects may no longer believe their partner exists. In the Internet trust experiments in Example 8.2, Eckel and Wilson found that in post-experiment interviews the subjects stated that in the treatment without the group photo they did not believe the experimenters' statements that another laboratory existed and believed that the experimenter was making the choices made by their counterparts. Anonymity via the Internet increased the experimental effect and subjects believed that the researcher was more likely to return them money (more trustworthy) than an anonymous person.

10.1.5 Risk Aversion

How Risk Averse Are Subjects in Experiments?
One concern that can arise when experimenters use financial incentives is how risk preferences may affect the subjects' choices. Loosely, we think

of individuals as risk averse if, when they are offered a gamble over two monetary options, say x and y with equal probability or a sure thing that is equal to $0.5(x + y)$, they prefer the sure thing; individuals are risk neutral if they are indifferent between the gamble and the sure thing, and risk seeking if they prefer the gamble. In most game-theoretic experiments the theoretical predictions are contingent on the assumption that the subjects are risk neutral. For example, consider the experiment of Morton (1993) described earlier. The theoretical predictions as applied to the subjects in the experiment assume that the subjects will be risk neutral.[8] If subjects are risk averse, the theory predicts that they will choose more convergent positions than that predicted when they are risk neutral. In fact, subjects did choose positions that were more convergent than predicted by the theory, although it is not possible to determine if this was due to risk aversion or simply that subjects valued winning independently of the monetary payoffs from the policy positions.

How likely is risk aversion to be a problem in the laboratory? Experimentalists who use financial incentives are naturally interested in this question and have attempted to empirically estimate risk aversion parameters. To do so, usually experimentalists assume what is called constant relative risk aversion (CRRA). With CRRA, for a given sum of money x, the utility to the subject can be represented as follows:

$$u(x) = x^{1-r}, \quad \text{for } x > 0,$$

where r is the risk parameter. If $r < 0$, the individual is risk seeking; if $r = 0$, the individual is risk neutral; and if $r > 0$, the individual is risk averse.[9]

A number of studies have estimated risk parameters of subjects in experimental games. One of the more recent influential studies is that conducted by Holt and Laury (2002, 2005). In their experiments, subjects were presented with a series of choices between lotteries. Subjects were forced to make choices and one lottery was drawn as the choice for which they were paid. From these lottery choices, Holt and Laury were able to estimate a subject's risk parameters. They found that there is a wide variation in risk preferences across subjects but that subjects were on average risk averse even for small differences in lottery choices and that the average parameter of risk

---

[8] Actually the theory as applied from Calvert (1985) and Wittman (1983) assumes that the candidates are risk averse, which is operationalized by paying subjects according to a concave function of the difference between their ideal points and the winning policy position. The experiment then assumes that subjects are risk neutral over the payments from that payoff function.

[9] We follow Holt and Laury (2002) and assume that when $r = 1$, the natural logarithm is used and division by $(1 - r)$ is necessary for increasing utility when $r > 1$.

aversion was in the 0.3–0.5 range. Furthermore, they found that, when they increased payoffs substantially, risk aversion increased significantly. They also compared real payoffs to hypothetical payoffs; they found that increasing hypothetical payoffs did not have a significant effect on risk preferences. Their research validates the results of high rates of risk aversion found by previous scholars such as Cox and Oaxaca (1996), Goeree et al. (2003), and Chen and Plott (1998).

The procedure used by Holt and Laury can be useful in experiments in which a researcher believes that risk preferences may affect the choices of their subjects. For instance, Eckel and Wilson in Example 8.2 used the Holt and Laury procedure to estimate risk preferences for their subjects, and Belot et al. in Example 9.3 used the procedure to measure risk preferences of students and nonstudents.

The Implications of Risk-Averse Subjects

Rabin (2000) and Rabin and Thaler (2001) contended that if individuals are as risk averse over small-stakes gambles as the experimental evidence suggests, then expected utility maximization means they will display a hugely implausible amount of risk aversion in large-stakes gambles. Rabin and Thaler then concluded that the evidence of risk aversion in small stakes is therefore strong evidence against expected utility theory. However, as Samuelson (2005) points out, Rabin and Thaler's argument rests on the assumption that an individual's utility is a function only of final wealth – the amount of money an individual has after the outcome of the lottery is realized, which is not an assumption of expected utility theory.[10] Samuelson remarks (2005, p. 90): "nothing in expected utility theory precludes defining utility over pairs of the form (w, y), where w is an initial wealth level and y is a gain or loss by which this wealth level is adjusted." Furthermore, Samuelson notes that to interpret expected utility theory as in Rabin and Thaler's study is contrary to how the early researchers such as Savage (1972) and Luce and Raiffa (1957) intended expected utility to be interpreted. Samuelson summarizes their view: "decision makers break the world they face into small chunks that are simple enough to be approximated with a small-worlds view. We can expect behavior in these subproblems to be described by expected utility theory, but the theory tells us nothing about relationships between behavior across problems."

---

[10] See also Cox and Sadiraj (2002) and Palacios-Huerta and Serrano (2006). For an empirical study that combines both experiments and data on income and wealth of subjects, see Schechter (2007).

What does this mean for experimentalists who work with formal models that assume that actors maximize expected utility theory? First, risk aversion over small stakes does not in itself invalidate expected utility theory. However, the small-worlds view does suggest that parameter estimates of things like risk aversion from experiments may not be generalizable. In fact, Berg et al. (2005) demonstrated that risk preferences of subjects can vary significantly according to the experimental game. They had the same subjects participate in three distinctive games involving uncertain outcomes and for which they could easily estimate the subjects' risk preferences. They found that all the subjects acted as if they were risk seeking in one of the games but risk averse in another, while in the third game, subjects split between risk seeking and risk aversion. They tested the hypotheses that for the same individuals the estimated risk coefficient across institutions was the same and found that the estimates were significantly different. As Berg et al. concluded (p. 4211): "These results suggest that researchers must be extremely careful in extrapolating a person's or group of persons', risk preferences from one institution to another. Without appropriate benchmarks on the preferences of individuals, researchers can mistake changes in behavior caused by risk preferences for change in behavior caused by other stimuli such as information or rule changes."

Can Risk Aversion Be Controlled?

Given that subjects in the laboratory are likely risk averse on average and that there is a wide variation in risk preferences, how should an experimentalist who is using financial incentives react? Friedman and Sunder (1994, pp. 45–46) point to three ways risk preferences can be dealt with in the laboratory:

1. Incorporate a procedure in the experiment that can transform subjects to be risk neutral.
2. Generate a measure of the risk attitude of subjects during the experiment.
3. Do nothing but treat the assumptions about risk aversion as technical assumptions in the model. The experimenter can then observe the data and determine for him- or herself the impact of risk attitudes for each subject.

Making Subjects Risk Neutral During the Experiment. The first method makes risk a part of the experiment by introducing it directly by specifying a binary lottery. Although there are variants to this concept, a binary lottery is a procedure in which a subject, instead of earning a specified amount of money each period, earns lottery tickets. The amount of lottery tickets accumulated increases the subject's probability of winning some prize or some payoff (Roth and Malouf, 1979; Berg et al., 1986). Samuelson (2005, p. 88) provides a nice description of why lotteries should theoretically work to transform subjects' preferences into risk-neutral ones if subjects are expected utility maximizers:

> Suppose one has in mind an experiment that would make monetary payments ranging from 0 to 100. Then replace each payoff $x \in [0, 100]$ with a lottery that offers a prize of 100 with probability $x/100$ and a prize of zero otherwise. Expected payoffs are unchanged. However, for any expected utility maximizer, regardless of risk attitudes, the expected utility of a lottery that pays 100 with probability p (and 0 otherwise) is
>
> $$pU(100) + (1 - p)U(0) = U(0) + [U(100) - U(0)]p.$$
>
> This expression is linear in p, meaning that the agent is risk neutral in the currency of probabilities.

Binary lotteries, then, theoretically eliminate subjects' individual risk preferences. Unfortunately, the evidence that these lotteries work – that they actually control for risk aversion – is, as Samuelson concludes, "not entirely encouraging."[11] Nevertheless, many experimental economists use binary lotteries, although such use is somewhat rare among political economists.

Definition 10.8 (Binary Lottery Payoff Mechanism [BLPM]): *When subjects in an experiment earn lottery tickets which are accumulated and increase the probability that the subject wins some subject-specific prize or other payoff at the end of the experiment.*

The binary lottery payoff mechanism is distinct from a payoff mechanism that has sometimes been used in experiments called a tournament reward. In this reward scheme, subjects earn points instead of money in each round and the subject who ends up with the most points wins some prize (see Ang and Schwarz, 1985). Although there are different variants, one problem with this type of reward scheme is that it can violate the dominance condition because the expectation of winning some prize is dependent on how other subjects in the experiment are performing. The subjects are in competition with each other. The tournament reward mechanism may also lead to less construct validity for the experiment because the competition creates a supergame for the subjects, which may have different equilibria

---

[11] See Berg et al. (2005), Cox and Oaxaca (1995), and Selten et al. (1999).

than the model the experiment is supposedly designed to evaluate. However, if the competition does not have these problems and dominance is not an issue, then such a payoff mechanism may be attractive.

Definition 10.9 (Tournament Reward Payoff Mechanism): *When subjects in an experiment earn points that are accumulated and the subject who earns the most points at the end of the experiment receives a reward or prize.*

Measuring Risk Preferences During the Experiment. The second approach is the attempt to measure risk preferences independent of the task performed in the experiment. One early way of using financial incentives to measure risk aversion is through eliciting buying or selling prices for simple lotteries using a procedure known as the Becker–DeGroot–Marschak (BDM) procedure (see Becker et al., 1964). In the selling version of BDM, the subject starts out owning the proceeds of a lottery with a known probability p of a payment of a fixed sum and a probability $1 - p$ of zero payment. The subject then writes down the value she places on the proceeds from the lottery. The experimenter then draws from a uniform distribution to determine whether the subject will keep the rights to the proceeds. If the number chosen is less than the subject's offer, the subject keeps the rights, but if the number is greater, the subject must sell the rights to the experimenter for an amount equal to the number drawn. After this, the lottery takes place and payments are distributed. In the buying version of the BDM procedure, the subject has an opportunity to buy, writes down a value for the purchase, and must purchase if the random number is less than that value.

Definition 10.10 (Becker–DeGroot–Marschak Procedure [BDM]): *A procedure used to measure subjects' risk preferences by having them buy and/or sell lotteries to the experimenter using a random mechanism.*

Early evidence suggests that the BDM procedure may over- or understate risk preferences depending on whether the buying or selling version is used (see Kachelmeier and Shehata, 1992). Furthermore, the evidence from Berg et al. that risk preferences can vary significantly with institution would suggest that such a procedure is not useful for all types of games. (BDM is one of the institutions that Berg et al. investigate.)

An alternative, which avoids the buying and selling frame issue, is to use Holt and Laury's procedure, or a researcher might generate an ordinal measure of risk by asking subjects risk-related questions in a survey (see Ang and Schwarz, 1985). One such measure that is commonly used in the literature is the Zuckerman SSS form V, which was used by Eckel and Wilson in Example 8.2. However, Eckel and Grossman (2002) compared the scale with subjects' decisions in an environment with financial stakes and found only a weak relationship, which is also what Eckel and Wilson found. Eckel and Wilson (2004) compared the risk preferences estimated from the survey, the Holt and Laury procedure, and a third choice between a certain amount and a risky bet with the same expected value. They found that the overall Zuckerman scale is only weakly correlated with the Holt–Laury measure. They found that neither the Zuckerman nor the Holt–Laury measures were correlated with the gamble choices.

These results suggest that estimating risk preferences from one particular institution or a survey for analysis of data in a second is problematic. However, James (2007) contends that these results may also reflect a lack of sufficient opportunity for subjects to "learn" the institution. He conducted both buying and selling versions of the BDM procedure for a longer period than previous experiments (52 periods). He found that over time the risk preferences of subjects in the buying and selling procedures converge, suggesting that the results about risk preference instability may be partly a function of subject errors.

Doing Nothing in the Design of the Experiment. Many experimental studies in political science adopt the last approach. In doing so, the experimentalist has a maintained assumption that subjects are risk neutral and risk preferences that are contrary to neutrality are one possible explanation for why subjects may choose differently from the predicted choices. The researcher can then, in the post-experiment analysis, investigate implications from the results about risk preferences if he or she thinks risk attitudes are important. An example of this approach is given by Goeree et al. (2003), who analyzed subject behavior in a series of games with unique mixed-strategy equilibria, similar to the game played by the soccer players in Example 9.2. They then estimated from the data the subjects' risk parameters after making particular assumptions about how subjects make errors and their utilities (using quantal response equilibrium [QRE] analysis as a basis; see Chapter 6). Their estimates show stability across a variety of these types of games and are comparable to those estimated by Holt and Laury.

One reason why Goeree et al. found stability in risk preferences compared to the results of Berg et al. noted earlier may be because in their estimates they control for how subjects' errors may be a function of the choices they face in the games using the QRE analysis. The results that Berg et al. found about how risk aversion is a function of game type may simply be a confounding from errors that are game dependent in measuring risk preferences.

10.1.6 Risk Aversion and Repetition

The evidence then suggests that risk preferences of subjects in experiments are susceptible to different types of games and their experience in games. It is well known that if subjects are risk averse and do not show constant absolute risk aversion – their risk preferences are affected by wealth – then if wealth changes during an experiment, the subjects' risk preferences may also change during an experiment.[12] As reviewed in Chapter 6, many experimentalists who are evaluating formal models in political science have subjects participate in a game for a number of periods with randomization between periods. We noted that one principal reason for this repetition is because, from a theoretical standpoint, the theory is meant to apply to situations that individuals have faced repeatedly in similar situations or that individuals have learned from others socially how people, through such repeated interactions, have established norms of behavior. Repetition in this case can increase construct validity.

But repetition raises an issue about how best to pay subjects. Suppose that an experimenter who uses repetition pays subjects according to an accumulated payoff mechanism (APM), for which subjects are simply paid the sum of their monetary rewards across periods. In this case subjects' wealth will increase during the experiment and their risk preferences may also change. In particular, as the experiment progresses, they may become more risk neutral.

Definition 10.11 (Accumulated Payoff Mechanism [APM]): *Where subjects participate in an experiment with repetition and are paid the accumulated sum of their payoffs across periods.*

What is the solution to this potential problem? One solution is to control for the increase in wealth that subjects experience in the data analysis. Another solution is the random round payoff mechanism (RRPM), which is also called a random lottery incentive mechanism. In RRPM, one or a few rounds are randomly chosen as the basis for subjects' payments (see Grether and Plott, 1979). In this case, monetary earnings are not accumulated during the experiment and there is theoretically no wealth effect. Again, this procedure depends on the assumption that subjects maximize expected utility as in the BLPM (see Holt, 1986). Nevertheless, there is some evidence that this procedure does work to separate the tasks for subjects and by suggestion eliminate wealth effects (see Cubitt et al., 1998; Hey and

---

[12] In Section 12.1.3, we discuss a different wealth effect: the effect of earning sizable amounts of money during an experiment on subjects.

Lee, 2005a,b; Starmer and Sugden, 1991). Lee (2008) directly compares
the two mechanisms and finds evidence that under APM there are wealth
effects on subjects' choices that are not observed under RRPM, suggesting
that RRPM is a superior payoff mechanism when the experiment involves
repetition. RRPM also has an additional advantage: using this method, the
experimenter can increase the monetary payoffs by period for each subject.
This may increase the salience to subjects of their choices.

Definition 10.12 (Random Round Payoff Mechanism [RRPM]): *Where a
subject's performance in one or a few rounds of an experiment with repetition
are randomly chosen as the basis for the subject's payments.*

10.2 Other Incentive Mechanisms

10.2.1 Home-Grown Values

Creating disconnects between the values subjects hold for the outcomes
and the theoretical assumptions may be desirable if the experimentalist is
conducting a stress test of the theory rather than a theory test. Sometimes
experimentalists work with what are called *home-grown values* where the
outcomes are not assigned financial values in order to evaluate how well the
theory predicts in such an environment. They may be assigned a value that
is a specific commodity or simply told the outcomes in terms of labels. The
key is that these values are private and intrinsic to the subject, unknown to
the experimenter. For example, Rutstrom (1998) used home-grown values
to compare different auction mechanisms by having the subjects participate in an auction for chocolate truffles. In Example 10.2, Harrison and
McDaniel (2008) use home-grown preferences in an experiment evaluating
different voting rules by having subjects vote over different music collec-
tions. Although they lost some control over the preferences of the subjects
in the experiment by using home-grown values, given a priori information about the subjects' music preferences, they structured the choices that
subjects confronted in order to manipulate the diversity of preferences.[13]

Definition 10.13 (Home-Grown Values): *When an experimenter does not
assign outcomes in the experiment with particular financial values. The experimenter may assign the outcomes values in terms of a specific commodity*

---

[13] The Harrison and McDaniel experiment is also an interesting evaluation of a proposed
voting rule that has not been the subject of previous experimental study, similar to the
experiments on storable votes in Example 8.6.

or simply rely on intrinsic values that subjects may place on the outcomes. The intrinsic values that subjects assign to the outcomes are unknown to the experimenter.

Example 10.2 (Home-Grown Values and Voting): *Harrison and McDaniel (2008) report on a voting game experiment in which subjects are given home-grown values.*

Target Population and Sample: *The researchers recruited 111 students from the University of South Carolina.*

Subject Compensation: *Subjects received compensation based on their choices as described in the procedures. They also received a $5 show-up fee.*

Environment: *The experiment was conducted by hand in the authors' experimental laboratory at the University of South Carolina.*

Procedures: *Subjects participated in six sessions that ranged from 13 to 31 subjects. First subjects were asked to rank different categories of music (as described later). They were given a list of ten CDs for each category. They were told that one category of music would be chosen for the group and that the category would be determined by a group vote. The voting procedure and the information subjects had about the procedure was manipulated as discussed later. Every individual in the group received a specific CD of his or her choice from the category determined by the group vote. Subjects made choices on a voting slip and the experimenter entered the rankings into a computer which determined, according to the voting rule, the group outcome. The subjects made choices once.*

Voting Rules: The authors compared two voting rules: random dictator (RD) and Condorcet consistent (CC). In RD, one subject was chosen at random after voting to be the dictator and his or her choice was implemented. The CC voting rule takes a ranking of voter choices and solves for the choice that maximizes the likelihood of having maximal support from the most voters given their entire preference rankings. It is solved for using integer programming.

Information: In the CC manipulations, the authors varied how much information subjects had for how the outcome was computed. In manipulation CCN, subjects were only told that the social ranking chosen would be the one which would most likely receive the support of a majority of the voters and in manipulation CCI, subjects were told how the voting rule worked explicitly and examples were worked out.

Categories of Music: The researchers also manipulated the categories of music. In the simple preferences manipulation (so called because they expected that most of the subjects would have a strong preference for Rock or Rhythm & Blues and the group would be relatively homogenous in preferences) the categories were: Jazz/Easy Listening, Classical, Rhythm & Blues, Rock, and Country & Western. In the diverse preferences manipulation (so called because they expected that with the absence of Rock and R&B the preferences of subjects would be more diverse) the categories were Jazz/Easy Listening, Classical, Heavy Metal, Rap, and Country & Western.

Results: *The authors found significant evidence of misrepresentation of preferences in the CC institution as compared in the simple preferences manipulation, assuming that the RD institution revealed sincere preferences but has no significant effect on behavior in revealing sincere preferences in the diverse preference manipulation. The effects of information are only significant in the simple preferences manipulation as well. The authors conclude that (p. 563) "[t]he provision of information on the workings of the voting rule only appears to affect behavior when subjects are in an environment in which the preference structures are simple enough [to] allow them to think that they can successfully manipulate their revealed preferences."*

Comments: *Harrison and McDaniel provided an interesting voting experiment using home-grown values in which they manipulated voter preferences by using a priori information on likely voter choices to organize the choices before voters.*

Bassi et al. (see Example 6.3) also used home-grown preferences in an experiment evaluating how voters choose in the absence of financial incentives. In their experiment, voters were assigned party identities and the experimentalists considered how these identities affect voter choices in the absence of experimenter-induced values.

As in Harrison, Harstad, and Rutstrom's (2004) study, home-grown values can also be useful in experiments in marketing, environmental damage assessment, and the general estimation of individual preferences. However, when a commodity is used for the valuation, there are particular issues involved, which Harrison et al. discuss. First of all, the existing market price for the commodity will censor the values that subjects will assign to the commodity. That is, if the experiment involves a subject purchasing a commodity, and the subject knows that the commodity has an established market price and can easily be bought, then even if the subject values the commodity more than the market price, the subject will not be willing to pay more than the market price.

Second, a subject's beliefs about the market price for the commodity may be affiliated (that is, influenced by others' evaluations of the commodity). If the experiment involves subjects sequentially revealing their values for the commodity, subjects may update their beliefs about the market price and change their evaluations during the experiment and choose differently than they would if they chose simultaneously. Finally, subjects may also have affiliated beliefs about the quality of the laboratory commodity. Again, if the experiment involves subjects sequentially revealing their values, subjects may update their beliefs about the quality of the commodity, changing their valuations during the experiment and choosing differently than they would if they chose simultaneously. These problems illustrate some of the difficulties that experimentalists who are engaging in theory testing seek to avoid with experimenter-induced values.

Harrison and McDaniel dealt with some of these issues by using CDs, which at the time of the experiment were the main way that individuals purchased music and had a generally known market price. They also conducted the experiment as one-shot games, not allowing for the possibility of subjects' beliefs being affected by others' previous choices.

10.2.2 Grades

Some experimenters have used grades and an increase in a grade to motivate subjects. We refer here to grade point incentives distinct from those sometimes used by political psychologists because they are outcome dependent. The advantages of using students in a classroom with grades as an incentive are twofold: (1) there is zero recruitment effort and (2) because their effort in the experiment is based on their grade, subjects should be highly motivated (see Williams and Walker, 1993). Kormendi and Plott (1982) compared financial incentives with grade point incentives that varied with outcomes in a majority voting game with agenda setting. They found little difference between the two incentive mechanisms. One problem with classroom experiments based on grades is that dominance cannot be controlled because subjects may believe the instructor can discover the choices they made in the experiment and think that a bad performance could potentially hurt their grade in other ways in the class. Certainly the possibilities for experimental effects, discussed in Section 8.4, are greater when subjects from classes that the experimenter teaches are used in general. Even with privacy ensured, some subjects may still believe their choices are observed and alter their choices in the experiment.

Another concern is that in many experiments that involve randomization, luck is a critical element. Some subjects may be randomly assigned to positions in the experiment where the assignment will determine their successfulness and eventual grade (Stodder, 1998). This type of grading criterion may be considered unethical because it is not based on merit. We discuss using grades as rewards for participation experiments in further detail in Chapter 12. Although we believe that using grades is unethical in experiments for research, it may be acceptable to use grades as incentives in experiments used purely for teaching purposes, not for research. In this case, the teacher may want to grade students on how well they choose as related to the theoretical predictions given others' behavior in the experiment. That is, if the point of the grades is to grade how well students understand theory and the experiment is used as a method of testing that understanding, then the grades should be relative to the roles subjects are given and how well they perform as compared to the theory they are being taught.

10.2.3 Recruiting Mechanisms

Almost all laboratory experimentalists pay subjects a fee for "showing up" independent of their earnings in an experiment. In political psychology experiments, the show-up fee may be extra credit in a class, which can raise some of the experimental effects issues discussed in Section 8.4 and ethical issues as noted in Chapters 11 and 12. As remarked previously, Kam et al. in Example 9.1 considered alternative framing for recruitment letters with nonstudent subjects, one that was neutral – simply stating the money that would be earned ($30), a second that emphasized the social utility of participation, and a third that emphasized self-interest of participation (and emphasized the $30 more than in the neutral letter). They found that the neutral letter was the most effective and that the self-interest framing was least effective. Although this chapter focuses primarily on incentives in laboratory experiments, the results of studies of incentive mechanisms to reduce missing data in surveys and field experiments are also relevant (see Section 5.5.2).

For many political economy experiments the experimental design calls for a particular number of subjects. For example, in the voting experiments conducted by Battaglini, Morton, and Palfrey in Example 2.6, the design required 14 subjects. If 13 subjects showed up, then the experiment would have to be canceled. Given that subjects' decisions to show up can be affected by unexpected effects such as illness and the weather, experimentalists often over recruit and then pay the excess subjects the show-up fee. If a show-up fee is used in an experiment with financial incentives, the presumption is that subjects understand that the fee is an amount separate from the money that they can earn in the experiment.

10.3 Motivating Subjects Without Explicit Incentives

10.3.1 Experimental Relevance and Validity

In a number of laboratory experiments, it is not possible to use explicit incentives to motivate subjects. For example, consider the experiments conducted by Druckman and Nelson in Example 5.1. The experiments took place shortly before the McCain–Feingold campaign finance reform bill was debated in the Senate. One of the arguments against the bill is that such regulation is a limitation of "free speech," while one of the arguments in favor of the bill is that the regulation would reduce the influence of "special interests." The researchers constructed two "fake" newspaper articles from the *New York Times*, each reporting on one of these two arguments.

In the framing treatments, subjects read one of these articles and a subset were assigned to discussion groups of four, some where all subjects in the group had read the same article and others where the subjects in the group had read different articles. The experimenters asked the subjects their opinions on campaign finance reform and compared the effects of the different frames and discussion combinations with each other and with a control group who did not read an article. In this experiment, as in many like it in political psychology, the subjects were paid a flat fee for participating. It does not make sense to reward subjects based on their opinions or to attempt to place some value on expressing a particular opinion. Doing so might crowd out the very thing that Druckman and Nelson are attempting to measure.

What is the motivation of subjects in such an experiment? The presumption is that the subjects, like survey respondents, are motivated to behave sincerely and to provide sincere responses to the questions asked by the experimenters. Camerer and Hogarth (1999) note that incentives interact with many other aspects of an experimental environment to motivate subjects. Druckman and Nelson (2003), by conducting their experiments at a point in time when campaign finance reform was much in the news and constructing articles that appeared "real," endeavored to give the subjects the motivation to "care" sufficiently about the issue that they would want to report their true preferences. The premise behind the experiment is that the subjects reported their opinions accurately because they were internally motivated to do so.

We present a second example of an experiment in which a researcher combines naturally occurring information in an attempt to make the choices before subjects "real" in Example 10.3, reported on by Kam (2007). In this experiment, Kam studies the effects of attitudes toward Hispanics on preferences over judicial candidates in California, using real candidates in a 2002 election. Kam explains her decision to use real candidates as follows (footnote 8):

A choice has to be made regarding whether the stimulus materials focus on fictional or real candidates. With fictional candidates, researchers can minimize prior information and maximize control over the stimulus. However, there is an obvious lack of realism. Real candidates are troublesome in that people bring real (and differing amounts of) information into the experiment, and they constrain the reasonable set of manipulations that can be imposed on subjects. I elected to use real candidates, in order to bolster the external validity of the study. The tradeoff, however, is that this is not a fully factorial design: the direction of partisanship is not manipulated; only the presence or absence of party cues is manipulated.

Kam selected judicial candidates to lessen the effects of the information that subjects may bring into the experiment. Kam notes that judicial candidate approval elections in California are typically a low-information setting where in previous research cues such as sex, ethnicity, and party can matter significantly.

Example 10.3 (Candidate Preferences and Prejudice): *Kam (2007) reported on an experiment that investigates the effects of attitudes toward Hispanics on candidate preferences using explicit and implicit priming to measure attitudes.*

Target Population and Sample: The experiment involved 234 subjects in a medium-sized California college town. Kam reports (footnote 4): "Subjects were recruited in two ways: through invitation letters sent to a representative group of 1,000 individuals living in nearby towns; and through an email invitation sent to a randomly selected group of 650 non-faculty, non-research university staff. Subjects were representative of the local area. 76% of subjects were white (10% Asian and 8% Hispanic). The modal age was between 46–55 years old (27% of the sample). 63% of subjects were female. 71% of the sample had a bachelor's degree or higher, which is only 3% higher than the Census 2000 data on the proportion of residents holding bachelor's degrees or higher. 31% of subjects identified as Republicans (strong, weak, or leaning) and 45% identified as Democrats (strong, weak, or leaning)." Subjects were told that the experiment was a study about "people and places in the news."

Subject Compensation: Subjects received $25 for participating.

Environment: The experiment was conducted via computers with between two and six subjects in each session with a mode of four subjects. Each subject was seated at his or her own computer terminal in a laboratory with six terminals. The session was scheduled for 45 minutes, but usually lasted only 30 minutes. The experiments were conducted in summer 2004. The computer software used was Inquisit 2.0 (see http://www.millisecond.com/).

Procedures: *Subjects first completed a pre-stimulus questionnaire that included questions about the upcoming presidential election, demographic and political background, economic evaluations, and policy opinions. Then they were presented with a subliminal priming task similar to that conducted by Taber in Example 4.1. The task consisted of 40 trials in which subjects were asked to categorize a target word as pleasant or unpleasant. Before seeing the target word, subjects received a forward mask of letter strings, a subliminal prime consisting of a societal group in capital letters in the center of the screen (whites, blacks, Hispanics, Asians, women, men, Democrats, or Republicans), a backward mask of letter strings, and then the target word. The societal groups were presented in a random order and each group was paired with two pleasant and two unpleasant target words taken from Bellezza et al. (1986) list of normed words (see also http://faculty.washington .edu/agg/pdf/bgb.txt). The first eight trials were neutral trials that used a nonsensical prime as a baseline measure of response to positive and negative targets.*

After the subliminal priming task, subjects completed a political information battery, a stereotype battery, and then were given the Judicial Candidates Manipulation. In this manipulation (pp. 350–351),

> *subjects were given information concerning three actual candidates who were on the ballot during the state's 2002 election for the State Supreme Court. Subjects were randomly assigned to one of two conditions: baseline or party cue. Those in the baseline condition read that the candidate's occupation was "Associate Justice of the California State Supreme Court," and this information was identical across candidates. Subjects in the party cue condition received information about which governor appointed the candidate (e.g., Kathryn M. Werdegar/Appointed by Republican Governor Pete Wilson). Beneath the names of the candidates, biographical information (culled from the Secretary of State's Official Voter Information Guide) appeared. The information was presented in tabular form, along with the following instructions: "Please consider the following slate of candidates who faced citizen confirmation for their appointments to the CALIFORNIA STATE SUPREME COURT." The slate of candidates in the party cue conditions consists of two Republican candidates (one male and one female) and one Democratic candidate (one Hispanic male).*

After reading about the candidates, the subjects continued to the next screen, which redisplayed the biographical information, followed by the question: "If you could only vote for one candidate, which candidate would you be MOST likely to vote for?"

After answering this question, subjects were debriefed and compensated.

Results: *Kam found that attitudes toward Hispanics influenced willingness to support a Hispanic candidate only in the absence of a party cue. The presence of party cues eliminates the impact of attitudes toward Hispanics on political choices in the experiment.*

Comments: *Kam used subliminal priming in the experiment mainly as a way of measuring implicit attitudes as an independent variable in explaining how individuals choose between candidates based on ethnicity or race.*

Kam claims that using real candidates increases external validity. Druckman and Nelson also remark (2003, p. 733) that the fake newspaper articles were designed to be as real as possible to increase external validity.[14] Yet, using real candidates or creating the articles to be real actually increases the ecological validity of the experiment, not necessarily the external validity, as we explored in Chapter 7. External validity, as we noted, can only be established empirically by determining if the results of an experiment hold for other target populations or other variations in the experimental design. Increasing ecological validity can increase internal validity of the results if this increases the probability that subjects are motivated to take the experiment seriously and, thus, make it easier for the researchers to establish causal inferences. The realness reduces experimental effects that can interfere with drawing causal inferences. Whether using real candidates or making the design of the newspaper articles seem real leads to more external validity is unclear because neither in itself necessarily means that the results are robust to changing the treatment parameters or the target population.

10.3.2 Task Information and Validity

Tversky and Kahneman's Study of the Availability Heuristic
We have emphasized the value of using control in experimentation to ensure that subjects' motivations are as a researcher supposes and thus increase the

---

[14] Again, this seems to be a confusion of ecological validity with external validity. Increasing the realness of the newspapers may increase the ecological validity of the experiment, making it more like the target environment, but does not imply that the results generalize to other environments.

internal validity of the results. One of the aspects of control in experimentation that affects subjects' motivations is their views of what the experiment is about. In the instructions to an experiment, the experimenter has a chance to influence these perceptions. If subjects' perceptions and, consequently, motivations are contrary to what the experimenter is assuming, then the results from the experiment may not have meaning for the experimenter's hypotheses – a failure of internal validity. Moreover, the results may not have meaning for other contexts in which the perceptions and motivations of individuals are very different from those of the subjects in the experiment – a failure of external validity.

Stapel et al. (1995) replication of one of the classic psychology experiments of Tversky and Kahneman (1973) on the "availability heuristic" in Example 10.4 illustrates this point. The heuristic approach to judgments contends that individuals use shortcuts to reach decisions because of the complexity of the world and limitations in human capacities. But it is asserted that, because the heuristics are generic, they are sometimes used inappropriately and they lead to systematic biases in judgments. The availability heuristic for retrieval maintains that things that are readily recalled or retrieved by individuals are perceived by them as relatively more frequent or numerous.

Example 10.4 (Replication of Availability Heuristic Experiment): *Stapel, Reicher, and Spears (1995) reported on a replication of Tversky and Kahneman's famous availability heuristic experiment.*

Target Population and Sample: Stapel et al. reported on three studies. Study 1 used 22 first-year undergraduates at Exeter University. Half were female and the average age was 20. Study 2 used 68 students and study 3 used 108 students who were asked to participate in a short study at the end of a lecture. The demographics on the students in studies 2 and 3 were not reported.

Subject Compensation: The authors did not report whether subjects were compensated for participation.

Environment: The authors did not report details about the environment but presumably classrooms or an experimental laboratory was used. The experiments were conducted via paper and pencil.

Procedures: The experiment comprised three studies.

Study 1 (pp. 144–145): "Four lists of names were prepared and recorded on audio tape. Each list included 39 names that were chosen from names previously rated on the concept 'fame' by 70 undergraduate students from Exeter University. All four lists contained different names. Two of these lists contained names of 'entertainers' and included 19 names of famous men and

20 names of less famous women. Two other lists contained names of 'other public figures' and included 19 names of famous women and 20 names of less famous men. Thus fame and frequency were inversely related in all four lists. The first names of all personalities always permitted an unambiguous identification of sex. Names were presented in random order.

Subjects were run individually and listened to the four tapes in turn. For half of the subjects the order of the tapes was changed so as to control for possible tape order effects. The subject was asked 'to listen to this tape attentively' and the first tape was played. The experimenter then asked 'Did this tape contain more names of men or of women?' The same procedure was then repeated for the other three tapes (with the words 'women' and 'men' being reversed in half of the frequency questions). After this the interview began. Subjects were told that we wanted to ask 'some questions about what you were thinking while you were answering the questionnaire'. The interview then covered three themes: the first had to do with participants' task expectations, the second concerned their strategies of judgment, and the third had to do with their reaction to the questions relating to gender. All interviews were recorded. Finally, subjects were debriefed and thanked for participation."

Study 2: This study was run in groups of 8 to 14 subjects who were randomly assigned to three manipulations in the introduction:

Movie Stars Manipulation: Task introduction was "Please listen attentively to this tape which contains names of movie stars and other names."

Politicians Manipulation: Task introduction mentioned politicians in place of movie stars.

Standard Frame: Task introduction was the same as in study 1.

"A tape of 39 pretested names was used consisting of 10 famous women, who were all movie stars, 10 famous men, who were all politicians, 10 less famous women and nine less famous men in neither of these categories (i.e. 20 women and 19 men). . . . All the subjects were given a blank sheet of paper and one of the three introductory texts was spoken by the experimenter and the tape with names was played. Then the experimenter asked whether there were more women or more men on the tape and told the subjects to write down their answers on the sheets of paper. Subjects were thanked and debriefed.

Study 3: Subjects were divided into groups of 20–35. After receiving general information about the task, the subjects were asked to listen 'attentively to this tape.' Then one of four tapes were played. When the tape was finished, subjects were told that they could open answer booklets and start answering questions. Upon completion, the questionnaires were collected, and the subjects thanked and debriefed" (pp. 148–149).

The study manipulated the following (each manipulation combination involved 12 subjects):

Audio Tapes (p. 152): *"Our of our stock of pre-tested names new lists of 19 (20) famous men and 20 (19) less famous women were prepared. With the help of the Exeter telephone director a list of (the same) 19 famous men (women) and 20 not-at-all famous women (men) was prepared. These four lists were recorded on audio tape."*

Recall and Frequency: *Subjects were asked to recall both names and the frequency of types of names. The experimentalists manipulated the order in which subjects were asked to complete these tasks. The frequency question had two parts: subjects were first required to judge whether the tape consisted of more names of men or of women and then had to write down actual numbers. The recall question read as follows: "Now we want you to write down all the names you can recall." Half of the subjects who were in the manipulation in which they were first asked the recall question were also given the instruction to follow, which asked subjects to rate each name for degree of "fame" on a 7-point scale with 7 implying very famous. Half of these subjects were also asked to put the names they recalled in two lists, one of men and one of women.*

Results: *In study 1 they found that the use of availability disappears when subjects learn more about the task and can adjust their use of strategy. In study 2 they found that contextual factors can influence what sort of available information is used or what becomes available. In study 3 they found that making memorability more salient enabled subjects to counteract the effects of availability by downgrading estimates of the more famous class.*

Comments: *Stapel et al.'s experiment is a good example of scientific replication of a previous experiment, demonstrating how the results of the experiment depend crucially on how it is presented to subjects.*

The availability heuristic, like a number of other heuristics studied by Kahneman and Tversky, has been used to understand political situations. For example, Andrew Gelman in his recent book, *Red State, Blue State, Rich State, Poor State,* suggests that journalists misunderstand the relationship between income and partisanship because they are using the availability heuristic. Gelman argues that most journalists are college educated and have moderately high incomes and also tend to be Democratic and that their friends and colleagues also share their characteristics. He proposes that the journalists intelligently use polls and other scientific information to understand that they are not in the majority as a first-order use of the availability heuristic would imply, but that journalists use the availability heuristic to compute second-order frequencies and as a result the journalists underestimate the extent that highly educated and wealthy voters are Republican. In a simplistic version of the argument, journalists think that voters like themselves support Democrats and voters not like themselves support Republicans.

In the original experiment of Tversky and Kahneman on the availability heuristic, student subjects were asked to listen to a list of names from a tape recording. In one treatment the list had highly famous male names and not as famous female ones and the other list was the opposite. After the subjects heard the tape they were asked to judge the frequency of occurrence of male names and of female names. In their experiment, Tversky and Kahneman expected that because subjects would be able to more readily recall or retrieve the names of the more famous, they would estimate that these were more frequent and give biased judgements. Indeed, this is what happened in the experiment; subjects who received the treatment with more famous male names estimated the percentage of males in the list as greater than what actually occurred and subjects who received the treatment with more famous female names estimated the percentage of females in the list as greater than what actually occurred.

A Replication

Stapel et al. highlight that before reading the lists of names, Tversky and Kahneman merely instructed subjects to "listen attentively" and only after the list was finished did they ask the subjects to estimate the percentage of males and females in the list. Stapel et al. suggest that, given the vagueness of the instructions and the fact that these were psychology students, the subjects believed that the task was to remember as many names as possible. In this case, remembering the more famous names may be a rational strategy. Stapel et al. argue that if the subjects had known more about the task they would be asked to engage in, they would have used a different strategy and would have provided less biased estimates. Stapel et al. conducted new experiments to evaluate their conjectures. First, they replicated the Tversky and Kahneman experiment; but instead of having different subjects in the two treatments, they had the same subjects listen to all four tapes used by Kahneman and Tversky sequentially. In this way, they anticipated that subjects would "learn" to use a different strategy to answer the questions about male and female name frequencies. Stapel et al. also questioned the subjects after this experiment about how they had perceived the task initially and as the experiment changed. Stapel et al. found that their conjecture was supported. Subjects reported that they believed initially that their job was to remember as many names as possible and that, when it became clear to them that they would not be able to do so, they concentrated on names that they could more easily remember, that is, famous names. But as the subjects repeated the task they updated their strategies and increased their accuracy in estimating the percentages of males and females. The subjects' statements were supported by the empirical analysis.

In the second experiment, Stapel et al. considered how different "frames" of the experimental task affected subjects' choices. Stapel et al. argue that the frames of the experimental task signal to the subjects what they may be asked later and what sort of judgment process would be needed for the task. In one experiment they used the same frame as Tversky and Kahneman, which they called the "fame" treatment, but in other frames they told subjects that they emphasized particular types of famous people in the instructions. That is, in one treatment, before hearing the names, subjects were told the following: "Please listen attentively to this tape which contains names of movie stars and other names" while in the other they emphasized politicians. The researchers expected that in the fame treatment the subjects would not systematically overestimate males or females (given that the percentages of famous males and females were equal), but that in the politician and movie star treatments they would overestimate males and females, respectively. The hypothesis is that the subjects will not focus on the famous politicians in movie star frame and not focus on the movie stars in the politician frame. That is, subjects would anticipate that the instructions were "signaling" to them what they needed to know about the tasks they faced after the reading.

The results supported these predictions. Stapel et al. summarized their results (p. 149):

Priming the category arguably made this whole class more salient or relevant to the task, and therefore more influential in subsequent judgements. . . . These findings provide further support for the argument that it is the way in which particular aspects of the stimuli are made relevant in terms of the task that affects judgemental performance as much as availability in any absolute sense, or as an inherent property of the stimulus. Different introductions to the same task lead to quite different judgements, suggesting that items predefined as available because of their memorability can have less influence on judgements if these are also implied to be less relevant or applicable to the task.[15]

___

[15] Stapel et al. also reported on a third experiment, which investigates the effects on subjects of being told to recall both the names and the frequencies of the names. They found that doing so counteracted the effects of availability by downgrading estimates of the percentage of more famous names. They argue that doing so allowed subjects to "become more aware of the biasing effects of availability and . . . to adjust for its effects."

The experiments of Stapel et al. highlight the fact that subjects bring with them expectations about the tasks they face in the laboratory and that these expectations interact with the instructions subjects are given about the tasks. Priming in instructions can matter. Consider the report of Stapel et al. on the interviews they conducted after the first experiment with respect to three issues – task expectation, strategy, and reactions when the actual task was revealed (pp. 145–146, italics in the original):

Task expectation The dominant view of the study was as a test of participants' abilities:

"It's the panic factor – when you turn on a tape, immediately you think 'test'."

Hence 18 of the 22 subjects expressed a desire "to do well." In this context doing well meant maximizing recall: all but one of the 22 subjects expressed a belief that their task was to remember as many of the names as they could.

Strategy choice Subjects reported that, while listening to the first tape, they became aware that there were too many names to remember. They therefore thought of strategies which would help them to remember the maximum number of names. Two strategies emerged. The first was to find ways of grouping the names:

"I tried to remember the actresses and the singers."

"I listened for certain groups: politicians, tennis players, musicians. . . ."

This strategy in which subjects tried to categorize the names into groups by "profession was reported by four of the 22 subjects (18 per cent). The alternative was to focus on well known names:

"I tried to remember the ones I knew."

"There were some familiar names. These I held on to."

This strategy was reported by the majority of subjects (14 out of 22; 64 per cent).

Reactions to actual task. The first time the subjects were asked to estimate numbers of males and females, the majority (15 out of 22: 68 per cent) reported surprise or shock:

"It wasn't at all what I'd expected."

"I hadn't thought about that at all. I'd just tried to remember the names."

"I panicked."

In response 19 of the 22 subjects (86 per cent) said that they scanned the names they had remembered in order to see how many were male and how many were female. However, the majority (13 out of 22: 59 per cent) reported that their answers had little validity:

"It's just a guess."

"No confidence whatsoever."

On the subsequent trials, subjects report that both their strategies and their level of confidence changed. By the third trial, most subjects (15 out of 22: 68 per cent) reported that they expected the gender question to re-occur and therefore devised ways of counting the relative number of men and women:

"[I] only listed to whether it was a man or woman."

"[I] balanced[d] out men and women."

As a consequence 18 of the 22 subjects (82 per cent) reported being quite certain about their responses by the last trial.

As the responses of the subjects and the results of Stapel et al.'s second experiment show, what subjects believe about an experiment can have a significant effect on how they perform the tasks that the experimenter requests. Tversky and Kahneman's first experiment on the availability heuristic shows that, given that subjects expect that their job as a subject is to remember names and adopt strategies that fit that job, if they are surprised with a new task that requires them to remember frequencies by gender, they are likely to give biased results. But if subjects view their job as remembering frequencies by gender at the outset, the results by Stapel et al. suggest that the subjects' estimates are less likely to be biased. Furthermore, if subjects believe that their job will be to remember names of a certain category such as movie stars or politicians, they will give biased estimates of frequencies as influenced by the category.

Implications for Validity

What does this mean about the relevance or external validity of the availability heuristic for applied political science research? Consider the Gelman book mentioned earlier. The empirical evidence supports his argument that journalists do not suffer from what he calls a first-order availability heuristic for estimating the strength of party support overall. Journalists likely understand that the availability heuristic would give them bad estimates of these probabilities and they do not suffer a bias in that reporting because they do not use the heuristic in making those judgments. Does the argument that journalists suffer biases because they are using an availability heuristic in categorizing the types of people who support particular parties fit the empirical evidence as well? Maybe. Certainly one may make the case that journalists see their jobs not as reporting statistics but in focusing on "human interest" stories of particular people or cases that they can investigate in depth. Perhaps journalists use an availability heuristic in their decision making about finding interesting cases.

However, the bias in reporting may also simply reflect that, to a journalist, interesting people may be those who are unlike themselves, so they look for individuals who are most unlike themselves, leading to more stories about relatively poor, less educated Republicans. Our goal here is not to determine if the availability heuristic is motivating journalists in this case, but simply to highlight the importance of subjects' perceptions about what an experiment is about before interpreting the data for extremely different situations and possible motivations.

One thing that is particularly intriguing about the Kahneman and Tversky famous names experiment is that this experiment could be replicated using financial incentives, because there is clearly a correct answer, unlike the experiment of Druckman and Nelson discussed earlier. The results of the studies discussed in the previous section on financial incentives suggest that, with large enough incentives, the subjects would perform better on the tasks. To our knowledge no such experiment has been attempted. Furthermore, "surprising" the subjects with the task of estimating male and female percentages may be difficult to implement with providing subjects sufficient information on how their payments would be determined. We suspect that if subjects could be surprised and given financial incentives, the bias would probably remain in a one-shot version of the task, but of course this is only our conjecture. We believe that the key question is what subjects perceive as their task – when subjects did not anticipate a need to know the frequencies, they used the availability heuristic, but when they did anticipate a need to know the frequencies, they used other strategies.

Certainly in such an experiment, then, variations in the way the instructions are presented, the questions asked of the subjects, and the relationship between the subjects and the experimenters can affect whether subjects express sincere opinions and whether causal inferences can be determined. For instance, suppose that the subjects were students in the researchers' political science classes and knew from class discussions that one of the researchers had a particular opinion on the campaign finance issue. Then the subjects may be motivated to please the experimenter by expressing a similar opinion. Control exercised in the experimental design to eliminate experimental effects that could cause subjects to act nonsincerely is extremely important. Random assignment also helps experimentalists in this situation control for subject-specific unobservables that may interfere with the causal relationships that the researchers wish to uncover.

10.4 Chapter Summary

In this chapter we have considered the various methods that experimentalists use to motivate subjects. Financial incentives are the standard approach in political economy experiments. Although some have concerns that financial incentives may actually have a negative effect on subjects' performance, evidence suggests that if financial incentives are sizable enough then they can motivate subjects. We have reviewed the induced value theory of Smith on how best to operationalize financial incentives and the various issues that experimentalists confront. In particular, experimentalists should consider whether the incentives maintain monotonicity, saliency, dominance, and privacy.

When using financial incentives, experimentalists may wish to control or measure the risk preferences of their subjects. Unfortunately, doing so is not easy as risk preferences appear to depend on situations that subjects confront and that are not easily measured or controlled. Wealth effects when experiments involve cumulated earnings can affect risk preferences during an experiment, which is undesirable. For this reason we recommend that random payoff mechanisms be used when possible rather than cumulated payoff mechanisms. Some experimentalists have chosen to use home-grown incentives or other incentives, such as grades, in experiments. Home-grown incentives can be useful when a researcher is interested in discovering if results found with financial incentives are valid in other situations. Grades are sometimes used to reduce the cost of conducting an experiment. Using such incentives reduces the control an experimentalist has over subjects' motivations, beliefs, and information, and, in the case of grades, is unethical.

We have also explored the issues involved in motivating subjects without incentives. In this case, many experimentalists attempt to make the experimental environment real to the subjects, increasing ecological validity. Doing so, of course, can reduce the control an experimentalist has over the manipulations because he or she is constrained by these choices. Experimentalists also attempt to motivate subjects through instructions and other material provided before and during the experiment. In many cases an experimentalist may want to keep the purpose of the experiment obscure. Nevertheless, doing so may invalidate the results if subjects' beliefs about the task before them are contrary to their beliefs about the task in a naturally occurring environment.

PART IV

ETHICS

11

History of Codes of Ethics and Human Subjects Research

11.1 Codes of Ethics and Social Science Experiments

When a researcher conducts an experiment, he or she intervenes in the data generating process, as we have discussed. Because as social scientists we are interested in studying human behavior, our interventions necessarily affect humans. Our interventions may mean that the humans affected – our subjects and, in some cases, those who are not directly considered our subjects – make choices that they would not have faced otherwise (or would have faced differently) or have experiences that they would not have been subject to otherwise. Thus, as experimentalists, we affect human lives. Of course, these are not the only ways our professional activities can affect human lives. We affect other humans in disseminating our research; in teaching students and training future scholars; in our interactions with our fellow scholars within our institutions, collaborative relationships, and professional organizations; and in our daily lives. In this way, political scientists are like members of other professions.

Most professions have codes of ethics, moral rules about how their members should conduct themselves in their interpersonal relations, which is also true for some political science professional societies. For example, the American Political Science Association (APSA) created a committee with a broad mandate to explore matters "relevant to the problems of maintaining a high sense of professional standards and responsibilities" in 1967. The committee was chaired by Marver H. Bernstein and prepared a written code of rules of professional conduct. Moreover, in 1968, a Standing Committee on Professional Ethics was created, which reviews formal grievances upon request, sometimes mediates and intercedes to other organizations, as well as issues formal advisory opinions. The code of conduct was revised in 1989 and 2008.

What does the 2008 code have to say about experimental research? The code discusses experimental research in a few short sentences in the 38-page document:

The methodology of political science includes procedures which involve human subjects: surveys and interviews, observation of public behavior, experiments, physiological testing, and examination of documents. Possible risk to human subject is something that political scientists should take into account. Under certain conditions, political scientists are also legally required to assess the risks to human subjects.

A common Federal Policy for the Protection of Human Subjects became effective on August 19, 1991, adopted by 15 major federal departments and agencies including the National Science Foundation (45 CFR Part 690) and the Department of Health and Human Services (45 CFR Part 46). The Policy has been promulgated concurrently by regulation in each department and agency. While the federal policy applies only to research subject to regulation by the federal departments and agencies involved, universities can be expected to extend the policy to all research involving human subjects.[1]

The same guide devotes twice as much space to and provides more content on matters of sexual harassment – discussing the substantive nature of the federal regulations in detail and defining sexual harassment – although arguably political scientists in the twenty-first century are more likely to engage in research involving human subjects than deal with a problem of sexual harassment. Perhaps nothing more is needed on the ethics of political science research with human subjects than these few quoted sentences. Most universities in the United States have established Institutional Review Boards (IRBs), which evaluate whether proposed research with human subjects satisfies federal policies, and many require that all research involving human subjects, whether funded by the federal government or not, must be cleared by the IRB, as the APSA guide mentions.[2] Furthermore, other developed countries are adopting similar procedures.[3] In Canada the boards are called research ethics boards and in the United Kingdom they are labeled

---

[1] *A Guide to Professional Ethics in Political Science*, 2nd Edition, Revised 2008, American Political Science Association Committee on Ethics, Rights, and Freedom, pp. 26–27.

[2] The reason for requiring even research not funded by federal sources to meet federal guidelines is because if the university receives federal funds and supports research that does not meet the guidelines, even though those funds are not explicitly used for the research that is in violation, because the university is one entity, some legal scholars believe the university is liable for losing federal funds.

[3] See Porter (2008) for a discussion of the regulation of human subjects research in Canada, and Boulton and Parker (2007) for discussions of such regulations in the United Kingdom and in other European countries.

research ethics committees. Perhaps these IRBs are working effectively and as a discipline political science can delegate ethical issues involving human subject research and experiments to university IRBs, without much further discussion.

However, political scientists often complain that the federal guidelines and the IRBs have been devised to confront concerns in medical research that are not applicable to political science. For example, in July 2008, the professional journal of APSA, *PS: Political Science and Politics*, published a symposium discussing federal policy on human subjects, in which a number of grievances were lodged.[4] Many of the criticisms relate to IRB review of research that is not experimental, such as qualitative field research and interviews, but some concern problems with review of survey research, perceived overestimation of risks to subjects, delays that impede research by graduate students and faculty that impact their careers, and denials of approval. The complaints of political scientists mirror those made by other social scientists that the IRB review process needs reform.[5]

In our view, many of these criticisms of IRBs are justified. Yet, at the same time, we believe that there are valid reasons for political science researchers, particularly experimentalists, to have concerns about ethical issues when using human subjects – concerns that are sometimes similar to those faced by experimentalists in other disciplines such as medicine, although at other times distinct. In this chapter and the next we discuss these ethical issues and how political science experimentalists can work within and sometimes outside of IRBs to deal with them. In general, three ethical principles have evolved that are seen as important for experimental research – informed consent, volunteerism, and anonymity – and IRBs have focused on these. These ethical principles have evolved primarily in response to needs in biomedical research and thus are not always applicable or translatable to social science. Many of the difficulties political scientists face in interacting with IRBs come from trying to fit social science research into a system devised for biomedical research, as we explain in this chapter. We argue that political scientists, and social scientists generally, need to be proactive in establishing ethical guidelines appropriate for social science research with human subjects and to educate both researchers and evaluators on IRBs on the merits of these guidelines. But first we begin with a brief history of IRBs

---

[4] See Hauck (2008).
[5] See, for example, the special issue in *Social Science and Medicine* in 2007 and the set of articles in the *Northwestern University Law Review* in 2007.

and ethical codes for human subject research that have evolved and that political scientists currently confront.

11.2 Early Professional Codes of Ethics

Simmerling et al. (2007) point out that the approach most used in ethical decision making concerning research on human subjects is based on the codes of ethics involved in medical decision making and a thinking of subjects or participants as patients.[6] The concept that there should be some rights afforded to human patients in medicine dates back to the eighteenth century B.C.E. to the Hammurabi code, which for the first time in recorded history placed restrictions on physicians for malpractice. Of the 282 codes, 3 addressed punishments for physicians who engaged in malpractice or unethical behavior:[7]

218 If a physician makes a large incision with the operating knife, and kill him, or open a tumor with the operating knife, and cut out the eye, his hands shall be cut off.
    219 If a physician makes a large incision in the slave of a freed man, and kill him, he shall replace the slave with another slave.
    220 If he had opened a tumor with the operating knife, and put out his eye, he shall pay half his value.

These concerns were also echoed in the fifth century B.C.E. when the physician Hippocrates proclaimed his oaths. One of the oaths reads:[8]

I will follow that system of regimen which, according to my ability and judgement, I consider for the benefit of my patients, and abstain from whatever is deleterious and mischievous.

Deleterious and mischievous referred to what we think of today as medical malpractice. Hence, in the early history of medicine there was recognition that medical treatments can be ethically harmful and that ethical norms should be established.

---

[6] The confusion between "subject" and "patient" is so much of a common problem on the subject side of biomedical experiments that it has a name: theoretical misconception. See Appelbaum et al. (1982), who found in interviews with subjects that many were unaware of the use of random assignment to control and comparison groups and believed that they were assigned a medication based on what was best for them personally. They defined theoretical misconception as occuring "when a research subject fails to appreciate the distinction between the imperatives of clinical research and of ordinary treatment, and therefore inaccurately attributes therapeutic intent to research procedures."
[7] See http://www.wsu.edu/~dee/MESO/CODE.htm.
[8] See the Oath of Hippocrates.

11.3 The Nuremberg Code

Discussion about medical ethics in academic circles began as early as the 1820s.[9] However, it was not until the events surrounding World War II that concerns about having formal norms with regard to medical research were seriously entertained. During the war, the United States federal government greatly increased the funding for experiments involving human subjects, so a lot more experiments were conducted. Also, the watershed event of the Nuremberg trial in 1948 revealed to the public the horrors that medical experimentation can inflect on human subjects. According to Faden and Beauchamp (1986, p. 153),

Although it is a common misconception that these events were the earliest examples of willfully, vicious research on unwilling human subjects, the Nazi experiments were in many respect unprecedented in the extensiveness and extremity of the harm and suffering to which they knowingly exposed their victims. Using subjects drawn from the population of concentration camps (Jews, gypsies, Poles, Russians), Nazi scientists explored the effects of ingesting poisons, intravenous injections of gasoline, immersion in ice water, and the like. Infection with epidemic jaundice and spotted fever virus were typical parts of "medical" experiments.

During the Nuremberg trial, 22 of the Nazi doctors and administrators were defendants, of which 7 were convicted and sentenced to death, 8 were sentenced to prison for 10 years to life, and 7 were found not guilty. One of the defenses used by the Nazis was that they could not have violated standards of ethical conduct in research with human subjects because no such standards existed. As part of the final verdict of the Nuremberg trial, American doctors Andrew Ivy and Leo Alexander, who served as consultants and expert witnesses on the prosecutor's team, drafted a memorandum outlining rules for permissible medical experiments, now referred to as the Nuremberg Code.[10] The code included a provision for voluntary consent and dictated that researchers should weigh the costs and benefits of any experiment, and specified that subjects in an experiment should have the ability to terminate participation at any time. The Nuremberg tribunal stated:

The voluntary consent of the human subject is absolutely essential. This means that the person involved should have legal capacity to give consent; should be situated as to be able to exercise free power of choice, without the intervention of any element

---

[9] A U.S. Army doctor in the 1820s, William Beaumont, researched stomach gunshot wounds. In his 1833 book, *Physiology of Digestion*, he mentions the idea of an informed consent (or as he referred to it, a document of indenture signed by the patient).

[10] See Ivy (1948).

of force, fraud, deceit, duress, overreaching, or other ulterior form of constraint or coercion; and should have sufficient knowledge and comprehension of the elements of the subject matter involved as to enable him to make an understanding and enlightened decision.[11]

Eventually the Nuremberg Code became the foundation for many IRB protocols, but it was initially largely ignored by the scientific community because there was no enforcement mechanism.

11.4 Regulation in the United States

11.4.1 The Impetus for Regulation

Questionable Medical Experiments Post–World War II
After World War II, a number of questionable medical experiments came to light and received prominent attention in the United States. In the 1950s, researchers at the Willowbrook school for mentally disabled children injected patients without their or their guardians' consent with a hepatitis virus in order to create a remedy. The doctors justified their actions by stating that most of the children would probably catch the hepatitis virus anyway so their actions would eventually be fruitful if they could discover a cure. In the late 1950s, without written consent and unbeknownst to them, pregnant women were given the drug thalidomide, which was supposed to control sleep and nausea during pregnancy.[12] However, the drug had a serious side effect that caused deformities in the fetus. Around 12,000 babies were born with severe deformities as a result of the drug. In the early 1960s, researchers at the Jewish Chronic Disease Hospital injected 22 senile patients with live cancer cells without their consent or knowledge. According to Faden and Beauchamp (1986, p. 161), "[t]he motivation was to discover whether in cancer patients a decline in a body's capacity to reject cancer transplants was caused by cancer or by debilitation." To examine this question, researchers needed subjects who were free of cancer.

Two long-running medical experiments were particularly horrific. From 1944 to 1974, the U.S. Atomic Energy Commission conducted around 3,000 to 5,000 radioactive iodine experiments in which subjects were injected with radiation without their consent to determine its effects on them. Some of the victims were pregnant women, newborn babies, and infants. And in the

---

[11] Warner and Al Tighe (2001, p. 401).
[12] See Warner and Al Tighe (2001).

Tuskegee syphilis experiments from 1932 to 1972, the U.S. Public Health Service conducted an experiment on approximately 400 black men in the late stages of syphilis. The subjects believed they were receiving free treatment for "bad blood," a term that was used locally to mean unrelated aliments. However, the subjects were never given treatments to heal their symptoms or a cure once one was developed; rather the researchers' intent was to generate data for the experiment from autopsies after the subjects had died.

Governmental Reactions

The proliferation of unethical experiments after the Nuremberg trial began to catch the eyes of members of the U.S. Congress and led to a call for regulation. After the failure of the drug thalidomide became public knowledge, Congress passed the Kefauver Amendments in 1962, which required drug manufacturers to provide evidence to the Food and Drug Administration (FDA) concerning the safety and effectiveness of their products before they could market them to the public. Further public attention concerning the mistreatment of human subjects was raised when Henry Beecher published an article in 1966 in the *New England Journal of Medicine* in which he documented 22 published medical studies that were risky to subjects and conducted without their knowledge or consent. Beecher recommended that editors should not publish research if no informed consent had been provided.

In 1972, newspaper reporter Jean Heller published details about the Tuskegee experiments which appeared on the first page of the *New York Times*.[13] The articles prompted the Department of Health, Education, and Welfare[14] to sponsor a Tuskegee panel to examine ethics and issues of informed consent. Congress responded to the report and in 1974 passed the National Research Act, which established the National Commission for Protection of Human Subjects of Biomedical and Behavioral Research. The act required IRBs at all institutions receiving Health, Education, and Welfare support for human subject research.

11.4.2 The Belmont Report and the Common Rule

In 1976 the commission held several discussions at the Smithsonian Institution's Belmont Conference and in 1979 released the Belmont Report, which

---

[13] Heller (1972).
[14] Now known as the Department of Health and Human Services.

was the commission's recommendations.[15] The report called for three basic ethical principles to be considered when doing biomedical research:

1. Respect for Persons. Respect for persons incorporates at least two ethical convictions: first, that individuals should be treated as autonomous agents, and second, that persons with diminished autonomy are entitled to protection. The principle of respect for persons thus divides into two separate moral requirements: the requirement to acknowledge autonomy and the requirement to protect those with diminished autonomy.

2. Beneficence. Persons are treated in an ethical manner not only by respecting their decisions and protecting them from harm, but also by making efforts to secure their well-being. Such treatment falls under the principle of beneficence. The term "beneficence" is often understood to cover acts of kindness or charity that go beyond strict obligation. In this document, beneficence is understood in a stronger sense, as an obligation. Two general rules have been formulated as complementary expressions of beneficent actions in this sense: (1) do not harm and (2) maximize possible benefits and minimize possible harms.

3. Justice. Who ought to receive the benefits of research and bear its burdens? This is a question of justice, in the sense of "fairness in distribution" or "what is deserved." An injustice occurs when some benefit to which a person is entitled is denied without good reason or when some burden is imposed unduly. Another way of conceiving the principle of justice is that equals ought to be treated equally. However, this statement requires explication. Who is equal and who is unequal? . . . It is necessary, then, to explain in what respects people should be treated equally. There are several widely accepted formulations of just ways to distribute burdens and benefits. Each formulation mentions some relevant property on the basis of which burdens and benefits should be distributed. These formulations are (1) to each person an equal share, (2) to each person according to individual need, (3) to each person according to individual effort, (4) to each person according to societal contribution, and (5) to each person according to merit.

The Belmont Report also spelled out the application of these principles in terms of informed consent. The informed consent provision specifies that subjects should have sufficient information about "the research procedure,

---

[15] See http://ohsr.od.nih.gov/guidelines/belmont.html.

their purposes, risks and anticipated benefits, alternative procedures (where therapy is involved), and a statement offering the subject the opportunity to ask questions and to withdraw at any time from the research." The Belmont Report also specifies conditions in which a fully informed consent may hamper the research efforts. It notes that when incomplete disclosure is required then it is justified only when it is clear that "(1) incomplete disclosure is truly necessary to accomplish the goals of the research, (2) there are no undisclosed risks to subjects that are more than minimal, and (3) there is an adequate plan for debriefing subjects, when appropriate, and for dissemination of research results to them." The informed consent provision also provides for a provision of comprehension; that is, subjects should have the capacity to understand what they are signing. Finally, there is a provision for voluntariness. Subjects need to give voluntarily consent to participate in an experiment and not be unduly influenced by "an offer of an excessive, unwarranted, inappropriate or improper reward or other overture in order to obtain compliance."[16]

After the Belmont Report, numerous federal agencies began to require that research funded through them meet various protocols. In 1991 these protocols were reconciled and integrated for 17 federal departments and agencies as 45 CFR 46, which has become known as the Common Rule (see Appendix A).[17] The system created by the Common Rule is decentralized. That is, the Common Rule specifies the protocols that must be followed, but it is left to the individual IRBs to make sure that research funded by the federal government meets these protocols. The system is subject to the oversight of the Office of Human Research Protections (OHRP) which is under

---

[16] See the Belmont Report for more details.

[17] The federal departments and agencies using the Common Rule are the Department of Agriculture, the Department of Energy, the National Aeronautics and Space Administration, the Department of Commerce, the Consumer Product Safety Commission, the International Development Cooperation Agency, the Agency for International Development, the Department of Housing and Urban Development, the Department of Justice, the Department of Defense, the Department of Education, the Department of Veterans Affairs, the Environmental Protection Agency, the Department of Health and Human Services, the National Science Foundation, the Department of Transportation, and the Central Intelligence Agency. The main department not included in the Common Rule is the FDA, which has concurred in the Common Rule but not adopted the policy in its entirety. The FDA rules are codified in 21 CFR 50 and 21 CFR 56. The FDA regulations apply to all research involving products regulated by the FDA, including research and marketing permits for drugs, biological products, or medical devices for human use, food and color additives, or electronic products, regardless of whether federal funds were used. Because this type of research is not typically involved in political science experiments, we do not review the FDA regulations.

the supervision of the Secretary of the Department of Health and Human Services (HHS). Before June 2000, the functions of the OHRP were carried out by the Office for Protection from Research Risks (OPRR) at the National Institutes of Health. There is also a federal advisory committee.[18] Furthermore, within the executive branch, the National Science and Technology Council's Committee on Science has a subcommittee on human subjects research which is comprised of representatives from all federal offices and agencies involved in human research and meets on a bimonthly basis to help coordinate the policies and practices of the federal government's oversight of human research. The subcommittee developed the Common Rule and continues to facilitate consistent implementation of the Common Rule across the federal government.

11.4.3 The Common Rule and Social Science Research

The Inclusion of Social Science Research

Not all the controversial research that led to codes of ethics and regulations reviewed earlier were medical experiments. Milgram (1974) conducted famous obedience experiments in which subjects, on command of the experimenter, believed that they were administering a shock to another subject. In actuality, the other subject receiving the shock was part of the experiment and, in a role-playing manner, cried out in pain whenever a shock was supposed to be administered.

Equally controversial was the "Tearoom Trade Study," conducted in the early 1970s. Researcher Laud Humphries posed as a "watch queen" outside of public restrooms and public parks to record anonymous homosexual behavior.[19] A watch queen was someone who watched out for police to warn participants if they needed to stop their encounters, and a tearoom is a place where homosexuals engaged in anonymous sex. Humphries recorded the "subjects'" license plate numbers and then went to the police department, and under a false identity persuaded police officers to reveal the addresses of the subjects using the numbers. After obtaining the addresses he went to their homes and interviewed them about their background and family life. When Humphries published his findings he wrote the report such that some of subjects' identities could be discovered. Although not an experiment, the

---

[18] Interestingly, as of this writing, 10 of the 11 members of this advisory committee have backgrounds that are predominantly biomedical.
[19] See Humphries (1970).

study demonstrated how social science research may have harmful effects on human subjects.

In 1979 the U.S. Department of Health, Education, and Welfare (now HHS) proposed guidelines that required that social science studies also be subject to IRB reviews regardless of funding sources. Social scientists protested this move as not being justified by evidence of harm from the research and some argued that the move violated First Amendment rights and could result in McCarthy era–style witch hunts.[20] The final rules in 1981 reflected these criticisms in that they allowed for exemptions and expedited review procedures for some types of research (discussed later in this chapter). In 1991 these features became part of the Common Rule. The exemption clauses of the Common Rule were interpreted to mean that much unfunded social science and almost all humanities research did not require any contact with IRBs. Gray et al. (1978) reported that two-thirds of the proposals reviewed by IRBs in the late 1970s involved medical research. He also found that more than one-half of the members of IRBs were biomedical scientists and nurses, while only one-fifth were social scientists, reflecting that domination.

Types of Exempt Research

For a list of the types of studies that are currently exempted from review, see 45 CFR 46.101(b) in Appendix A. Although most of these types of studies are not experimental in nature, some could be. Specifically, some narrow studies of educational strategies that could be experimental are considered exempt;[21] many surveys are exempt and, thus, by inference survey experiments; and research and demonstration projects designed to study, evaluate, or otherwise examine public benefit or service programs and conducted by or subject to the approval of federal department or agency heads, which could be experimental, are considered exempt. Surveys that are not exempt are those that survey either prisoners or children when funded by some agencies of the federal government (we explain these caveats further in the next chapter) or any set of subjects where information on the subjects "is recorded in such a manner that human subjects can be identified, directly or though identifiers linked to the subjects and any disclosure of the human subjects' responses outside the research could reasonably place the subjects

---

[20] See Oakes (2002) for a review of these complaints.
[21] However, if the activity or exercise is not a usual part of the curriculum or activities and is instead introduced for the purpose of research, not for the purpose of education, or if the investigator takes part in the classroom activities, then the research in the classroom does not qualify for exempt status.

at risk of criminal or civil liability or be damaging to the subjects' financial standing, employability, or reputation."

Types of Research Eligible for Expedited Review

Although research that is exempt is delineated in the Common Rule, the decision about what types of research can be expedited is made by the Secretary of HHS. Specifically, in 45 CFR 46.110(a) in Appendix A, the Common Rule refers the reader to a list of categories of studies comprised by the Secretary of HHS, published as a Notice in the *Federal Register*. Note, however, that even if research is the same as a type listed, this does not mean that the research automatically qualifies for expedited review. That is, the Common Rule requires that the research be both of a type on the list *and* of only minimal risk to the subjects. What is minimal risk? Minimal risk is defined in 45 CFR 46.102(i) as research for which "the probability and magnitude of harm or discomfort anticipated in the research are not greater in and of themselves than those ordinarily encountered in daily life or during the performance of routine physical or psychological examinations or tests." Later in this chapter and the next we explore the definition of minimal risk further and what risk means for the evaluation of particular political science experiments in general.

Definition 11.1 (Minimal Risk): *Minimal risk means that the probability and magnitude of harm or discomfort anticipated in the research are not greater in and of themselves than those ordinarily encountered in daily life or during the performance of routine physical or psychological examinations or tests.*

The list of research eligible for expedited review is also published on the Web site of the OHRP. The most current version as of this writing is presented in Appendix B of this chapter. Categories 1–4 deal with biomedical studies, categories 5–7 relate to nonmedical research, and categories 8 and 9 concern continuing review of research already approved. Category 7 is most relevant to experimental political science and refers to "research on individual or group characteristics or behavior (including, but not limited to, research on perception, cognition, motivation, identity, language, communication, cultural beliefs or practices, and social behavior) or research employing survey, interview, oral history, focus group, program evaluation, human factors evaluation, or quality assurance methodologies." In June 2008, the Social and Behavioral Research Working Group of the Human Subjects Research Subcommittee of the National Science and Technology

Council published a guidance document on expedited review of social and behavioral research activities, which presents a number of examples of research that fits within category 7 and can be experimental:

C. Experimental studies of human behavior, attitudes, opinions, and decisions, where the experimental manipulation consists of subjects reacting to hypothetical or contrived situations that are not expected to have significant lasting effects on the subjects.

For example:

A study in experimental economics in which people play an economic game that involves offering and/or accepting amounts of cash provided as part of the experiment. . . . ;

A study of adults' ability to identify accurately the perpetrators of staged thefts. . . . ;

A study attempting to validate a previously tested measure of extroversion/introversion with members of a previously untested cultural group.

. . .

D. Survey research where the respondents are approached in a natural setting, either personally or through a communications medium (e.g., by mail, telephone, or the internet), and participation is voluntary.

For example:

A research study using telephone surveys of persons who provide their names and information about their background characteristics, political beliefs, and voting behavior.

. . .

An online internet study in which undergraduate students view a video clip about economic theory and then respond to computer-simulated scenarios about individual spending decisions.

Category 9 allows IRBs considerable discretion to give expedited review to research that it has determined has minimal risks even though it does not qualify under categories 1–8. Finally, the Common Rule allows for expedited review of "minor changes in previously approved research during the period (of one year or less) for which approval is authorized."

The Expansion of IRBs into Greater Review of Social Science Research

Gradually in the late 1990s and early 2000s IRBs began to increase their focus on social science and humanities research. The change occurred for a number of apparent reasons. First, federal officials and IRBs began to recognize that "self-exemption" of research was problematic because a researcher has a conflict of interest.[22] Thus, IRBs began to require some form of certification that studies were indeed "exempt" on a case-by-case basis. Furthermore,

---

[22] See McCarty (1984) and Plattner (2003).

an institution does not have to allow for research to be exempt and can elect to review all human subjects research, even those classified as exempt according to the Common Rule. According to Guidance Report Number 95-02 dated May 5, 1995 (which is still in effect as of this writing):

Institutions should have a clear policy in place on who shall determine what research is exempt under .46.101(b). Those persons who have authority to make a determination of what research is exempt are expected to be well-acquainted with interpretation of the regulations and the exemptions. In addition, the institution should be prepared to reinforce and review, as necessary, the method of determining what is exempt. OPRR advises that investigators should not have the authority to make an independent determination that research involving human subjects is exempt and should be cautioned to check with the IRB or other designated authorities concerning the status of proposed research or changes in ongoing research.

Institutions may elect to review all research under the auspices of the institution even if the research qualifies for exemption under .46.101(b). An institution with a Multiple Project Assurance (MPA) or Cooperative Project Assurance (CPA) should indicate in its Assurance if and how exempt research is reviewed. It is incumbent on the institution to advise investigators and others involved in the conduct and administration of research involving human subjects of the institutional policies for reviewing exempt research.

Second, because of a number of incidents of violations in the biomedical field, the OPRR and later the OHRP became much more serious in its review of IRB procedures, and suspensions began to occur. Oakes (2002) cites a number of actions against universities in 1999 and 2000. Most notably, all human subject research was suspended at the University of Illinois at Chicago, the University of Alabama at Birmingham, Duke University Medical Center, the University of Oklahoma, and Johns Hopkins University. The suspension at the University of Illinois at Chicago resulted in a resignation by the chancellor of the university. Suspensions are serious and, even if the principal cause is a problem with biomedical research, when the OHRP reviews IRBs they scrutinize all research, regardless of discipline, and suspensions can seriously affect social science experimentalists as well. As Oakes remarks (2002, p. 450):

If suspended, no federally funded research may continue: Participants cannot receive treatments, enroll, or be recruited; results from time-sensitive studies cannot be reported; and data cannot be analyzed. Suspension means that there is no money to pay graduate students, travel to conferences, or purchase equipment. It means researchers may lose months, if not years, of work. Severe effects to an institution's reputation may dislodge the public's willingness to participate in research or an outstanding scientist's interest in an association. The former point is critical as there is mounting evidence that ethically improper research, by anyone, devastates a social scientist's chance to recruit from affected communities long into the future.

The third cause of increased focus on social science research has been possible legal liability to universities and IRB administrators from questionable research, whether funded by the federal government or not. Although OHRP suspensions are grim threats to universities, equally scary have been some recent suits by affected human subjects. According to Oakes, the Maryland Court of Appeals, in a case against Johns Hopkins's researchers, ruled "that an informed consent document is a binding legal contract that permits remedy through not only tort but also contract law." These suits have led a number of universities, such as New York University, to make all research subject to IRB review, whether funded by the federal government or not. Expansion of review to nonfunded research has led to more requirements for social science and humanities researchers, who are less likely to receive federal funding.

11.4.4 The Current System

Criteria for Approval

Under the current system, research involving human subjects and funded by the federal government must be reviewed, discussed, and approved by the relevant IRBs. The criteria for IRB approval are contained in the Common Rule in 45 CFR 46.111 in Appendix A. IRBs are expected to make sure that seven general requirements are met: (1) risks to subjects are minimized; (2) risks to subjects are reasonable in relation to anticipated benefits, if any, to subjects, and the importance of the short-term knowledge that may reasonably be expected to result; (3) selection of subjects is equitable given the purpose and setting of the research; (4) informed consent is sought for each prospective subject or the subject's legally authorized representative when required; (5) informed consent is appropriately documented; (6) data are monitored to ensure safety of subjects; and (7) adequate provisions are made to protect privacy of subjects and confidentiality of data. Furthermore, if some or all of the subjects are likely to be vulnerable to coercion or undue influence, additional safeguards are required to be included.

As noted earlier, some research is exempt from the full IRB review; however, the determination of whether research is exempt is made by someone other than the researcher within the institution and the IRB is responsible for making sure that these requirements are satisfied. If a research project has minimal risk and fits one of the aforementioned expedited research categories, then it can be approved on an expedited basis by only one member of the IRB, the chair or someone appointed by the chair. Under expedited review, if it is determined that the research is not qualified for expedited review, then it is not denied but referred to the entire

IRB for review. All continuing projects are subject to annual reviews; that is, approval has a 365-day limit. However, as discussed earlier, IRBs can choose to use expedited review procedures for continuing reviews of studies with minimal risks even if they do not normally qualify for expedited review.

As we explained, it is now the case in many institutions that all research involving human subjects, regardless of the source of funding, are required to be reviewed, discussed, and approved. Furthermore, although some research can be considered exempt or be given expedited review, IRBs can choose to review all research regardless. In the case of research conducted by collaborators from more than one institution, review and approval by multiple IRBs are required. So, for example, for Example 2.6, approval was secured by IRBs at the California Institute of Technology, New York University, and Princeton University, because the authors on the project were professors at these three institutions.

Training of Investigators and IRBs

Many IRBs require that all investigators who submit applications for human subjects research complete some training, usually online, and pass an exam with a minimum score before conducting human subjects research (and in some cases before an application for such research will be considered). The OHRP does not require investigators to be trained in this fashion; however, the OHRP does state that IRBs are responsible for ensuring that its investigators conducting human subjects research understand and act in accordance with the requirements of the HHS regulations for the protection of human subjects. Thus,

OHRP strongly recommends that the Institution and the designated IRB(s) . . . establish educational training and oversight mechanisms (appropriate to the nature and volume of its research) to ensure that research investigators, IRB . . . members and staff, and other appropriate personnel maintain continuing knowledge of, and comply with the following: relevant ethical principles; relevant U.S. regulations; written IRB . . . procedures; OHRP guidance; other applicable guidance; national, state and local laws; and institutional policies for the protection of human subjects. Furthermore, OHRP recommends that a) IRB . . . members and staff complete relevant educational training before reviewing human subjects research; and b) research investigators complete appropriate institutional educational training before conducting human subjects research.[23]

---

[23] See OHRP Terms of Assurance for IRBs, http://www.hhs.gov/ohrp/humansubjects/ assurance/filasurt.htm#sectionb.

As for training members of IRBs, OHRP sponsors a series of workshops on responsibilities of researchers, IRBs, and institutional officials that are open to everyone with an interest in research involving human subjects. Information on the conferences is available via the OHRP Web site and the Division of Education. The OHRP also provides tutorials and other educational materials free on their Web site.

Variety of IRBs

Catania et al. (2008) report finding 3,853 IRBs in the United States. Each IRB must have at least five members from a variety of backgrounds; at least one must be a nonscientist and one not affiliated with the institution. It is noteworthy that many IRBs continue to be dominated by biomedical professionals and that social scientists are often in the minority, according to a survey by De Vries et al. (2004). Some large institutions have more than one IRB. Catania et al. found that 85% of organizations reported having a single IRB, but those who receive large amounts of government funding were somewhat more likely to have multiple IRBs. For example, at Michigan State University there are three IRBs: a Biomedical and Health Institutional Review Board for medical professionals, a Community Research Institutional Review Board for community research, and a Social Science/Behavioral/Education Institutional Review Board for nonmedical research. In contrast, at New York University, there is only one IRB for all human subjects research. De Vries et al. found that 58% of the IRBs they surveyed reviewed both social science and medical protocols (i.e., were general rather than specific). In an early study of these boards, Gray et al. (1978) found considerable variation in procedures used by IRBs, which was similarly the case in 1995 according to Bell et al. (1998). Anecdotal evidence suggests that these variations continue.

11.5 Regulations in Other Countries

The movement toward formal regulation of human subjects research is evidenced in countries outside the United States. In 1964 at the 18th World Medical Assembly, the declaration of Helsinki set forth recommendations to guide medical doctors in biomedical research concerning human subjects.[24] As with the Nuremberg Code, the central aspect of the declaration was the principle of informed consent, but in addition the Helsinki

---

[24] These recommendations were slightly revised in 1975, 1983, 1989, and 1996.

declaration called for an independent committee to review research protocols before research with human subjects is conducted. The Canadian system, which to some extent resembles the U.S. system, is discussed at length
by Porter (2008). As noted earlier, boards and committees similar to IRBs
exist in many of these countries. One reason for the increase in regulation
in other countries is due to pressure from industry because the pharma-
ceutical industry has shown reluctance to provide funds for researchers
in countries where such institutional control does not exist.[25] However, for
many countries, either there are no such regulations or they are applied only
for medical research. University social science experimentalists in Australia,
Denmark, Germany, the Netherlands, Romania, and Spain report that they
are not required to submit their research to such boards for review although
in some cases there are reviews by internal committees comprised of faculty
members in their own discipline or reviews by deans and university administrators. In the United Kingdom, although IRB-like boards exist, the extent
to which the reviews scrutinize social science experimentalists appears to
depend on the institution.[26]

11.6 Cross-Country Research and Regulations

Officially, the OHRP requires that U.S. scholars conducting research in other
countries submit an official application to proceed with their research. In
addition, the researcher is expected to get IRB approval from the officials
in the country studied. Gilman and Garcia (2004, p. 248) described their
experience in gaining IRB approval in their 18 years of collaborative research
in Peru:

[Consider international experiments in developing countries and] collaborative
studies conducted by federally funded institutions in the United States.... For
such studies, IRBs in developing countries are required to register with the US
Office of Human Research Protections, and institutions should file a "Federalwide
Assurance," a document declaring compliance with an accepted ethical standard
for human research (e.g., the Helsinki Declaration). Studies can proceed only after
participating institution's IRB have reviewed and approved the proposed study
and consent forms. In international research, this often involves more than one,
and sometimes many, IRBs. Even the most benign study must navigate a maze of
committees, setting the research process back months and even years. For example,

---

[25] See Boulton and Parker (2007).

[26] We conducted an informal survey of experimentalists outside of the United States who are
members of the Economic Science Association listserve in 2009 and our analysis is based
on that survey. Details of the survey are available from the authors.

a simple village survey study over a five year period could require 40 separate IRB approvals (or renewals) – at a high cost of time, effort, and funding.

What does this mean for political scientists in the United States who wish to conduct field experiments in another country? Fortunately, the OHRP keeps records of the human subject research protections and a researcher should first consult this list for the relevant information. Most of the countries, however, only have regulations for biomedical research as in, for example, Denmark. What should a political scientists do then? It is our interpretation of the Common Rule that in such situations a researcher works with his or her local IRB to make sure that the university's IRB regulations are followed (which he or she should do in any case if the country does have review processes for social science experiments). If the research is federally funded, the researcher may need to get additional approval from the department or agency head to conduct the experiments. Survey experiments, because they are exempt from IRB review under certain conditions as described earlier, should similarly be exempt under the same conditions when conducted in foreign countries. We would also expect that research eligible for expedited review when conducted in the United States should be eligible for expedited review when conducted in foreign countries. Nevertheless, if an experimentalist in political science wishes to conduct research in another country, it is imperative to begin the process of IRB review as early as possible given that the review process may be longer because the local IRB may want additional assurances that IRB rules are satisfied, and approval may involve reviewing agencies in the other country.

11.7 Chapter Summary

In this chapter we have reviewed the history of codes of ethics with respect to human experimentation. The need for such codes of ethics and either government regulation or self-administered norms of conduct with respect to human experimentation is clear given some of the notorious experiments that have been conducted on human subjects in the past. As a result, a number of governments have instituted elaborate processes to regulate research with human subjects. In the United States, the process is complex and decentralized, leading to significant variations across institutions in how the regulations are administered.

Complicating the decentralized structure is that much of the regulation and the codes of ethics that have been devised have been influenced by the need to regulate biomedical experiments. Some of these regulations may be inappropriate for social science research. As IRBs both in the United States and other countries have expanded their examination of social science and humanities research, both funded and nonfunded, numerous scholars have complained that the scrutiny is unfair and unwarranted, as mentioned at the beginning of this chapter. Many of the complaints are from qualitative researchers.[27] However, social science experimentalists have also chafed under the increased regulation and scrutiny of IRBs in the past decade. Part of the difficulty has been in translating rules that were designed to ensure that biomedical research is ethical so that they work to achieve the same goal in social science research. At a general level, it would seem that the same principles discussed in the Nuremberg Code, the Helsinki Declaration, and the Belmont Report apply to all research regardless of the discipline. We agree with these general principles. But in operation there are differences that can make some of the solutions used to meet these principles in biomedical research not the best solutions for social science experiments. In the next chapter, we explore some of these differences as we discuss the benefits and costs in experiments, how the Common Rule evaluates these benefits and costs, and other requirements of the Common Rule for political science experimentalists.

11.8 Appendix A: Code of Federal Regulations: Title 45, Public Welfare, Department of Health and Human Services, Part 46, Protection of Human Subjects

Revised June 23, 2005
Effective June 23, 2005

---

[27] One complaint from qualitative researchers is that their work is not legally counted as research according to the Common Rule. Specifically, the Common Rule defines research as follows [see CFR 46.102]: "Research means a systematic investigation, including research development, testing and evaluation, designed to develop or contribute to generalizable knowledge."

Qualitative researchers have seen this definition as providing a loophole, arguing that their research is not designed to contribute to generalizable knowledge. Using this reasoning, the American Historical Association formally declared that oral history interviewing activities should not be subject to IRBs, and HHS officially accepted their position in a letter in 2003. Yet, as Seligson (2008) points out, there is clearly the possibility that these studies are as or more risky to human subjects than some quantitative social science investigations that are more easily classified as research according to the official definition. That is, historians, through reporting names and incidents, can cause possible harm to their subjects. Seligson makes the persuasive case that exemption from IRB review can lead to entrenched unethical behavior on the part of qualitative researchers.

11.8.1 Subpart A: Basic HHS Policy for Protection of Human Research Subjects

Authority: 5 U.S.C. 301; 42 U.S.C. 289(a); 42 U.S.C. 300v-1(b).

Source: 56 FR 28012, 28022, June 18, 1991, unless otherwise noted.

§46.101 To what does this policy apply?

(a) Except as provided in paragraph (b) of this section, this policy applies to all research involving human subjects conducted, supported or otherwise subject to regulation by any federal department or agency which takes appropriate administrative action to make the policy applicable to such research. This includes research conducted by federal civilian employees or military personnel, except that each department or agency head may adopt such procedural modifications as may be appropriate from an administrative standpoint. It also includes research conducted, supported, or otherwise subject to regulation by the federal government outside the United States.

(1) Research that is conducted or supported by a federal department or agency, whether or not it is regulated as defined in §46.102(e), must comply with all sections of this policy.

(2) Research that is neither conducted nor supported by a federal department or agency but is subject to regulation as defined in §46.102(e) must be reviewed and approved, in compliance with §46.101, §46.102, and §46.107 through §46.117 of this policy, by an institutional review board (IRB) that operates in accordance with the pertinent requirements of this policy.

(b) Unless otherwise required by department or agency heads, research activities in which the only involvement of human subjects will be in one or more of the following categories are exempt from this policy:

(1) Research conducted in established or commonly accepted educational settings, involving normal educational practices, such as (i) research on regular and special education instructional strategies, or (ii) research on the effectiveness of or the comparison among instructional techniques, curricula, or classroom management methods.

(2) Research involving the use of educational tests (cognitive, diagnostic, aptitude, achievement), survey procedures, interview procedures or observation of public behavior, unless:

(i) information obtained is recorded in such a manner that human subjects can be identified, directly or through identifiers linked to the subjects; and (ii) any disclosure of the human subjects' responses outside the research could reasonably place the subjects at risk of criminal or civil liability or be damaging to the subjects' financial standing, employability, or reputation.

(3) Research involving the use of educational tests (cognitive, diagnostic, aptitude, achievement), survey procedures, interview procedures, or observation of public behavior that is not exempt under paragraph (b)(2) of this section, if:

(i) the human subjects are elected or appointed public officials or candidates for public office; or (ii) federal statute(s) require(s) without exception that the confidentiality of the personally identifiable information will be maintained throughout the research and thereafter.

(4) Research involving the collection or study of existing data, documents, records, pathological specimens, or diagnostic specimens, if these sources are publicly available or if the information is recorded by the investigator in such a manner that subjects cannot be identified, directly or through identifiers linked to the subjects.

(5) Research and demonstration projects which are conducted by or subject to the approval of department or agency heads, and which are designed to study, evaluate, or otherwise examine:

(i) Public benefit or service programs; (ii) procedures for obtaining benefits or services under those programs; (iii) possible changes in or alternatives to those programs or procedures; or (iv) possible changes in methods or levels of payment for benefits or services under those programs.

(6) Taste and food quality evaluation and consumer acceptance studies, (i) if wholesome foods without additives are consumed or (ii) if a food is consumed that contains a food ingredient at or below the level and for a use found to be safe, or agricultural chemical or environmental contaminant at or below the level found to be safe, by the Food and Drug Administration or approved by the Environmental Protection Agency or the Food Safety and Inspection Service of the U.S. Department of Agriculture.

(c) Department or agency heads retain final judgment as to whether a particular activity is covered by this policy.

(d) Department or agency heads may require that specific research activities or classes of research activities conducted, supported, or otherwise subject to regulation by the department or agency but not otherwise covered by this policy, comply with some or all of the requirements of this policy.

(e) Compliance with this policy requires compliance with pertinent federal laws or regulations which provide additional protections for human subjects.

(f) This policy does not affect any state or local laws or regulations which may otherwise be applicable and which provide additional protections for human subjects.

(g) This policy does not affect any foreign laws or regulations which may otherwise be applicable and which provide additional protections to human subjects of research.

(h) When research covered by this policy takes place in foreign countries, procedures normally followed in the foreign countries to protect human subjects may differ from those set forth in this policy. [An example is a foreign institution which complies with guidelines consistent with the World Medical Assembly Declaration (Declaration of Helsinki amended 1989) issued either by sovereign states or by an organization whose function for the protection of human research subjects is internationally recognized.] In these circumstances, if a department or agency head determines that the procedures prescribed by the institution afford protections that are at least equivalent to those provided in this policy, the department or agency head may approve the substitution of the foreign procedures in lieu of the procedural requirements provided in this policy. Except when otherwise required by statute, Executive Order, or the department or agency head, notices of these actions as they occur will be published in the FEDERAL REGISTER or will be otherwise published as provided in department or agency procedures.

(i) Unless otherwise required by law, department or agency heads may waive the applicability of some or all of the provisions of this policy to specific research activities or classes or research activities otherwise covered by this policy. Except when otherwise required by statute or Executive Order, the department or agency head shall forward advance notices of these actions to the Office for Human Research Protections, Department of Health and Human Services (HHS), or any successor office, and shall also publish them in the FEDERAL REGISTER or in such other manner as provided in department or agency procedures.[28]

[56 FR 28012, 28022, June 18, 1991; 56 FR 29756, June 28, 1991, as amended at 70 FR 36328, June 23, 2005]

§46.102 Definitions.

---

[28] Institutions with HHS-approved assurances on file will abide by provisions of Title 45 CFR part 46 subparts A-D. Some of the other departments and agencies have incorporated all provisions of Title 45 CFR part 46 into their policies and procedures as well. However, the exemptions at 45 CFR 46.101(b) do not apply to research involving prisoners, subpart C. The exemption at 45 CFR 46.101(b)(2), for research involving survey or interview procedures or observation of public behavior, does not apply to research with children, subpart D, except for research involving observations of public behavior when the investigator(s) do not participate in the activities being observed.

(a) Department or agency head means the head of any federal department or agency and any other officer or employee of any department or agency to whom authority has been delegated.

(b) Institution means any public or private entity or agency (including federal, state, and other agencies).

(c) Legally authorized representative means an individual or judicial or other body authorized under applicable law to consent on behalf of a prospective subject to the subject's participation in the procedure(s) involved in the research.

(d) Research means a systematic investigation, including research development, testing and evaluation, designed to develop or contribute to generalizable knowledge. Activities which meet this definition constitute research for purposes of this policy, whether or not they are conducted or supported under a program which is considered research for other purposes. For example, some demonstration and service programs may include research activities.

(e) Research subject to regulation, and similar terms are intended to encompass those research activities for which a federal department or agency has specific responsibility for regulating as a research activity (for example, Investigational New Drug requirements administered by the Food and Drug Administration). It does not include research activities which are incidentally regulated by a federal department or agency solely as part of the department's or agency's broader responsibility to regulate certain types of activities whether research or non-research in nature (for example, Wage and Hour requirements administered by the Department of Labor).

(f) Human subject means a living individual about whom an investigator (whether professional or student) conducting research obtains

(1) Data through intervention or interaction with the individual, or

(2) Identifiable private information.

Intervention includes both physical procedures by which data are gathered (for example, venipuncture) and manipulations of the subject or the subject's environment that are performed for research purposes. Interaction includes communication or interpersonal contact between investigator and subject. Private information includes information about behavior that occurs in a context in which an individual can reasonably expect that no observation or recording is taking place, and information which has been provided for specific purposes by an individual and which the individual can reasonably expect will not be made public (for example, a medical record). Private information must be individually identifiable (i.e., the identity of the subject is or may readily be ascertained by the investigator or associated with the information) in order for obtaining the information to constitute research involving human subjects.

(g) IRB means an institutional review board established in accord with and for the purposes expressed in this policy.

(h) IRB approval means the determination of the IRB that the research has been reviewed and may be conducted at an institution within the constraints set forth by the IRB and by other institutional and federal requirements.

(i) Minimal risk means that the probability and magnitude of harm or discomfort anticipated in the research are not greater in and of themselves than those ordinarily encountered in daily life or during the performance of routine physical or psychological examinations or tests.

(j) Certification means the official notification by the institution to the supporting department or agency, in accordance with the requirements of this policy, that a research project or activity involving human subjects has been reviewed and approved by an IRB in accordance with an approved assurance.

§46.103 Assuring compliance with this policy – research conducted or supported by any Federal Department or Agency.

(a) Each institution engaged in research which is covered by this policy and which is conducted or supported by a federal department or agency shall provide written assurance satisfactory to the department or agency head that it will comply with the requirements set forth in this policy. In lieu of requiring submission of an assurance, individual department or agency heads shall accept the existence of a current assurance, appropriate for the research in question, on file with the Office for Human Research Protections, HHS, or any successor office, and approved for federalwide use by that office. When the existence of an HHS-approved assurance is accepted in lieu of requiring submission of an assurance, reports (except certification) required by this policy to be made to department and agency heads shall also be made to the Office for Human Research Protections, HHS, or any successor office.

(b) Departments and agencies will conduct or support research covered by this policy only if the institution has an assurance approved as provided in this section, and only if the institution has certified to the department or agency head that the research has been reviewed and approved by an IRB provided for in the assurance, and will be subject to continuing review by the IRB. Assurances applicable to federally supported or conducted research shall at a minimum include:

(1) A statement of principles governing the institution in the discharge of its responsibilities for protecting the rights and welfare of human subjects of

research conducted at or sponsored by the institution, regardless of whether the research is subject to Federal regulation. This may include an appropriate existing code, declaration, or statement of ethical principles, or a statement formulated by the institution itself. This requirement does not preempt provisions of this policy applicable to department- or agency-supported or regulated research and need not be applicable to any research exempted or waived under §46.101(b) or (i).

(2) Designation of one or more IRBs established in accordance with the requirements of this policy, and for which provisions are made for meeting space and sufficient staff to support the IRB's review and recordkeeping duties.

(3) A list of IRB members identified by name; earned degrees; representative capacity; indications of experience such as board certifications, licenses, etc., sufficient to describe each member's chief anticipated contributions to IRB deliberations; and any employment or other relationship between each member and the institution; for example: full-time employee, part-time employee, member of governing panel or board, stockholder, paid or unpaid consultant. Changes in IRB membership shall be reported to the department or agency head, unless in accord with §46.103(a) of this policy, the existence of an HHS-approved assurance is accepted. In this case, change in IRB membership shall be reported to the Office for Human Research Protections, HHS, or any successor office.

(4) Written procedures which the IRB will follow (i) for conducting its initial and continuing review of research and for reporting its findings and actions to the investigator and the institution; (ii) for determining which projects require review more often than annually and which projects need verification from sources other than the investigators that no material changes have occurred since previous IRB review; and (iii) for ensuring prompt reporting to the IRB of proposed changes in a research activity, and for ensuring that such changes in approved research, during the period for which IRB approval has already been given, may not be initiated without IRB review and approval except when necessary to eliminate apparent immediate hazards to the subject.

(5) Written procedures for ensuring prompt reporting to the IRB, appropriate institutional officials, and the department or agency head of (i) any unanticipated problems involving risks to subjects or others or any serious or continuing noncompliance with this policy or the requirements or determinations of the IRB; and (ii) any suspension or termination of IRB approval.

(c) The assurance shall be executed by an individual authorized to act for the institution and to assume on behalf of the institution the obligations imposed by this policy and shall be filed in such form and manner as the department or agency head prescribes.

(d) The department or agency head will evaluate all assurances submitted in accordance with this policy through such officers and employees of the department or agency and such experts or consultants engaged for this purpose as the department or agency head determines to be appropriate. The department or agency head's evaluation will take into consideration the adequacy of the proposed IRB in light of the anticipated scope of the institution's research activities and the types of subject populations likely to be involved, the appropriateness of the proposed initial and continuing review procedures in light of the probable risks, and the size and complexity of the institution.

(e) On the basis of this evaluation, the department or agency head may approve or disapprove the assurance, or enter into negotiations to develop an approvable one. The department or agency head may limit the period during which any particular approved assurance or class of approved assurances shall remain effective or otherwise condition or restrict approval.

(f) Certification is required when the research is supported by a federal department or agency and not otherwise exempted or waived under §46.101(b) or (i). An institution with an approved assurance shall certify that each application or proposal for research covered by the assurance and by §46.103 of this Policy has been reviewed and approved by the IRB. Such certification must be submitted with the application or proposal or by such later date as may be prescribed by the department or agency to which the application or proposal is submitted. Under no condition shall research covered by §46.103 of the Policy be supported prior to receipt of the certification that the research has been reviewed and approved by the IRB. Institutions without an approved assurance covering the research shall certify within 30 days after receipt of a request for such a certification from the department or agency, that the application or proposal has been approved by the IRB. If the certification is not submitted within these time limits, the application or proposal may be returned to the institution.

(Approved by the Office of Management and Budget under Control Number 0990-0260.)

[56 FR 28012, 28022, June 18, 1991; 56 FR 29756, June 28, 1991, as amended at 70 FR 36328, June 23, 2005]

§§46.104–46.106 [Reserved]

§46.107 IRB membership.

(a) Each IRB shall have at least five members, with varying backgrounds to promote complete and adequate review of research activities commonly conducted by the institution. The IRB shall be sufficiently qualified through the experience and expertise of its members, and the diversity of the members, including consideration of race, gender, and cultural backgrounds and sensitivity to such issues as community attitudes, to promote respect for its advice and counsel in safeguarding the rights and welfare of human subjects. In addition to possessing the professional competence necessary to review specific research activities, the IRB shall be able to ascertain the acceptability of proposed research in terms of institutional commitments and regulations, applicable law, and standards of professional conduct and practice. The IRB shall therefore include persons knowledgeable in these areas. If an IRB regularly reviews research that involves a vulnerable category of subjects, such as children, prisoners, pregnant women, or handicapped or mentally disabled persons, consideration shall be given to the inclusion of one or more individuals who are knowledgeable about and experienced in working with these subjects.

(b) Every nondiscriminatory effort will be made to ensure that no IRB consists entirely of men or entirely of women, including the institution's consideration of qualified persons of both sexes, so long as no selection is made to the IRB on the basis of gender. No IRB may consist entirely of members of one profession.

(c) Each IRB shall include at least one member whose primary concerns are in scientific areas and at least one member whose primary concerns are in nonscientific areas.

(d) Each IRB shall include at least one member who is not otherwise affiliated with the institution and who is not part of the immediate family of a person who is affiliated with the institution.

(e) No IRB may have a member participate in the IRB's initial or continuing review of any project in which the member has a conflicting interest, except to provide information requested by the IRB.

(f) An IRB may, in its discretion, invite individuals with competence in special areas to assist in the review of issues which require expertise beyond or in addition to that available on the IRB. These individuals may not vote with the IRB.

§46.108 IRB functions and operations.

In order to fulfill the requirements of this policy each IRB shall:

(a) Follow written procedures in the same detail as described in §46.103(b)(4) and, to the extent required by, §46.103(b)(5).

(b) Except when an expedited review procedure is used (see §46.110), review proposed research at convened meetings at which a majority of the members of the IRB are present, including at least one member whose primary concerns are in nonscientific areas. In order for the research to be approved, it shall receive the approval of a majority of those members present at the meeting

§46.109 IRB review of research.

(a) An IRB shall review and have authority to approve, require modifications in (to secure approval), or disapprove all research activities covered by this policy.

(b) An IRB shall require that information given to subjects as part of informed consent is in accordance with §46.116. The IRB may require that information, in addition to that specifically mentioned in §46.116, be given to the subjects when in the IRB's judgment the information would meaningfully add to the protection of the rights and welfare of subjects.

(c) An IRB shall require documentation of informed consent or may waive documentation in accordance with §46.117.

(d) An IRB shall notify investigators and the institution in writing of its decision to approve or disapprove the proposed research activity, or of modifications required to secure IRB approval of the research activity. If the IRB decides to disapprove a research activity, it shall include in its written notification a statement of the reasons for its decision and give the investigator an opportunity to respond in person or in writing.

(e) An IRB shall conduct continuing review of research covered by this policy at intervals appropriate to the degree of risk, but not less than once per year, and shall have authority to observe or have a third party observe the consent process and the research.

(Approved by the Office of Management and Budget under Control Number 0990-0260.)

[56 FR 28012, 28022, June 18, 1991, as amended at 70 FR 36328, June 23, 2005]

§46.110 Expedited review procedures for certain kinds of research involving no more than minimal risk, and for minor changes in approved research.

(a) The Secretary, HHS, has established, and published as a Notice in the FEDERAL REGISTER, a list of categories of research that may be reviewed by the IRB through an expedited review procedure. The list will be amended, as appropriate, after consultation with other departments and agencies, through periodic republication by the Secretary, HHS, in the FEDERAL REGISTER. A copy of the list is available from the Office for Human Research Protections, HHS, or any successor office.

(b) An IRB may use the expedited review procedure to review either or both of the following:

(1) some or all of the research appearing on the list and found by the reviewer(s) to involve no more than minimal risk,

(2) minor changes in previously approved research during the period (of one year or less) for which approval is authorized.

Under an expedited review procedure, the review may be carried out by the IRB chairperson or by one or more experienced reviewers designated by the chairperson from among members of the IRB. In reviewing the research, the reviewers may exercise all of the authorities of the IRB except that the reviewers may not disapprove the research. A research activity may be disapproved only after review in accordance with the non-expedited procedure set forth in §46.108(b).

(c) Each IRB which uses an expedited review procedure shall adopt a method for keeping all members advised of research proposals which have been approved under the procedure.

(d) The department or agency head may restrict, suspend, terminate, or choose not to authorize an institution's or IRB's use of the expedited review procedure.

[56 FR 28012, 28022, June 18, 1991, as amended at 70 FR 36328, June 23, 2005]

§46.111 Criteria for IRB approval of research.

(a) In order to approve research covered by this policy the IRB shall determine that all of the following requirements are satisfied:

(1) Risks to subjects are minimized: (i) By using procedures which are consistent with sound research design and which do not unnecessarily expose subjects to risk, and (ii) whenever appropriate, by using procedures already being performed on the subjects for diagnostic or treatment purposes.

(2) Risks to subjects are reasonable in relation to anticipated benefits, if any, to subjects, and the importance of the knowledge that may reasonably be expected to result. In evaluating risks and benefits, the IRB should consider only those risks and benefits that may result from the research (as distinguished from risks and benefits of therapies subjects would receive even if not participating in the research). The IRB should not consider possible long-range effects of applying knowledge gained in the research (for example, the possible effects of the research on public policy) as among those research risks that fall within the purview of its responsibility.

(3) Selection of subjects is equitable. In making this assessment the IRB should take into account the purposes of the research and the setting in

which the research will be conducted and should be particularly cognizant of the special problems of research involving vulnerable populations, such as children, prisoners, pregnant women, mentally disabled persons, or economically or educationally disadvantaged persons.

(4) Informed consent will be sought from each prospective subject or the subject's legally authorized representative, in accordance with, and to the extent required by §46.116.

(5) Informed consent will be appropriately documented, in accordance with, and to the extent required by §46.117.

(6) When appropriate, the research plan makes adequate provision for monitoring the data collected to ensure the safety of subjects.

(7) When appropriate, there are adequate provisions to protect the privacy of subjects and to maintain the confidentiality of data.

(b) When some or all of the subjects are likely to be vulnerable to coercion or undue influence, such as children, prisoners, pregnant women, mentally disabled persons, or economically or educationally disadvantaged persons, additional safeguards have been included in the study to protect the rights and welfare of these subjects.

§46.112 Review by institution.

Research covered by this policy that has been approved by an IRB may be subject to further appropriate review and approval or disapproval by officials of the institution. However, those officials may not approve the research if it has not been approved by an IRB.

§46.113 Suspension or termination of IRB approval of research.

An IRB shall have authority to suspend or terminate approval of research that is not being conducted in accordance with the IRB's requirements or that has been associated with unexpected serious harm to subjects. Any suspension or termination of approval shall include a statement of the reasons for the IRB's action and shall be reported promptly to the investigator, appropriate institutional officials, and the department or agency head.

(Approved by the Office of Management and Budget under Control Number 0990-0260.)

[56 FR 28012, 28022, June 18, 1991, as amended at 70 FR 36328, June 23, 2005]

§46.114 Cooperative research.

Cooperative research projects are those projects covered by this policy which involve more than one institution. In the conduct of cooperative research projects, each institution is responsible for safeguarding the rights and welfare of human subjects and for complying with this policy. With the approval of the department or agency head, an institution participating in a cooperative project may enter into a joint review arrangement, rely upon the review of another qualified IRB, or make similar arrangements for avoiding duplication of effort.

§46.115 IRB records.

(a) An institution, or when appropriate an IRB, shall prepare and maintain adequate documentation of IRB activities, including the following:

(1) Copies of all research proposals reviewed, scientific evaluations, if any, that accompany the proposals, approved sample consent documents, progress reports submitted by investigators, and reports of injuries to subjects.

(2) Minutes of IRB meetings which shall be in sufficient detail to show attendance at the meetings; actions taken by the IRB; the vote on these actions including the number of members voting for, against, and abstaining; the basis for requiring changes in or disapproving research; and a written summary of the discussion of controverted issues and their resolution.

(3) Records of continuing review activities.

(4) Copies of all correspondence between the IRB and the investigators.

(5) A list of IRB members in the same detail as described in §46.103(b)(3).

(6) Written procedures for the IRB in the same detail as described in §46.103(b)(4) and §46.103(b)(5).

(7) Statements of significant new findings provided to subjects, as required by §46.116(b)(5).

(b) The records required by this policy shall be retained for at least 3 years, and records relating to research which is conducted shall be retained for at least 3 years after completion of the research. All records shall be accessible for inspection and copying by authorized representatives of the department or agency at reasonable times and in a reasonable manner.

(Approved by the Office of Management and Budget under Control Number 0990-0260.)

[56 FR 28012, 28022, June 18, 1991, as amended at 70 FR 36328, June 23, 2005]

§46.116 General requirements for informed consent.

Except as provided elsewhere in this policy, no investigator may involve a human being as a subject in research covered by this policy unless the investigator has obtained the legally effective informed consent of the subject or the subject's legally authorized representative. An investigator shall seek such consent only under circumstances that provide the prospective subject or the representative sufficient opportunity to consider whether or not to participate and that minimize the possibility of coercion or undue influence.

The information that is given to the subject or the representative shall be in language understandable to the subject or the representative. No informed consent, whether oral or written, may include any exculpatory language through which the subject or the representative is made to waive or appear to waive any of the subject's legal rights, or releases or appears to release the investigator, the sponsor, the institution or its agents from liability for negligence.

(a) Basic elements of informed consent. Except as provided in paragraph (c) or (d) of this section, in seeking informed consent the following information shall be provided to each subject:

(1) A statement that the study involves research, an explanation of the purposes of the research and the expected duration of the subject's participation, a description of the procedures to be followed, and identification of any procedures which are experimental;

(2) A description of any reasonably foreseeable risks or discomforts to the subject;

(3) A description of any benefits to the subject or to others which may reasonably be expected from the research;

(4) A disclosure of appropriate alternative procedures or courses of treatment, if any, that might be advantageous to the subject;

(5) A statement describing the extent, if any, to which confidentiality of records identifying the subject will be maintained;

(6) For research involving more than minimal risk, an explanation as to whether any compensation and an explanation as to whether any medical treatments are available if injury occurs and, if so, what they consist of, or where further information may be obtained;

(7) An explanation of whom to contact for answers to pertinent questions about the research and research subjects' rights, and whom to contact in the event of a research-related injury to the subject; and

(8) A statement that participation is voluntary, refusal to participate will involve no penalty or loss of benefits to which the subject is otherwise entitled, and the subject may discontinue participation at any time without penalty or loss of benefits to which the subject is otherwise entitled.

(b) Additional elements of informed consent. When appropriate, one or more of the following elements of information shall also be provided to each subject:

(1) A statement that the particular treatment or procedure may involve risks to the subject (or to the embryo or fetus, if the subject is or may become pregnant) which are currently unforeseeable;

(2) Anticipated circumstances under which the subject's participation may be terminated by the investigator without regard to the subject's consent;

(3) Any additional costs to the subject that may result from participation in the research;

(4) The consequences of a subject's decision to withdraw from the research and procedures for orderly termination of participation by the subject;

(5) A statement that significant new findings developed during the course of the research which may relate to the subject's willingness to continue participation will be provided to the subject; and

(6) The approximate number of subjects involved in the study.

(c) An IRB may approve a consent procedure which does not include, or which alters, some or all of the elements of informed consent set forth above, or waive the requirement to obtain informed consent provided the IRB finds and documents that:

(1) The research or demonstration project is to be conducted by or subject to the approval of state or local government officials and is designed to study, evaluate, or otherwise examine: (i) public benefit or service programs; (ii) procedures for obtaining benefits or services under those programs; (iii) possible changes in or alternatives to those programs or procedures; or (iv) possible changes in methods or levels of payment for benefits or services under those programs; and

(2) The research could not practicably be carried out without the waiver or alteration.

(d) An IRB may approve a consent procedure which does not include, or which alters, some or all of the elements of informed consent set forth in this section, or waive the requirements to obtain informed consent provided the IRB finds and documents that:

(1) The research involves no more than minimal risk to the subjects;

(2) The waiver or alteration will not adversely affect the rights and welfare of the subjects;

(3) The research could not practicably be carried out without the waiver or alteration; and

(4) Whenever appropriate, the subjects will be provided with additional pertinent information after participation.

(e) The informed consent requirements in this policy are not intended to preempt any applicable federal, state, or local laws which require additional information to be disclosed in order for informed consent to be legally effective.

(f) Nothing in this policy is intended to limit the authority of a physician to provide emergency medical care, to the extent the physician is permitted to do so under applicable federal, state, or local law.

(Approved by the Office of Management and Budget under Control Number 0990-0260.)

[56 FR 28012, 28022, June 18, 1991, as amended at 70 FR 36328, June 23, 2005]

§46.117 Documentation of informed consent.

(a) Except as provided in paragraph (c) of this section, informed consent shall be documented by the use of a written consent form approved by the IRB and signed by the subject or the subject's legally authorized representative. A copy shall be given to the person signing the form.

(b) Except as provided in paragraph (c) of this section, the consent form may be either of the following:

(1) A written consent document that embodies the elements of informed consent required by §46.116. This form may be read to the subject or the subject's legally authorized representative, but in any event, the investigator shall give either the subject or the representative adequate opportunity to read it before it is signed; or

(2) A short form written consent document stating that the elements of informed consent required by §46.116 have been presented orally to the subject or the subject's legally authorized representative. When this method is used, there shall be a witness to the oral presentation. Also, the IRB shall approve a written summary of what is to be said to the subject or the representative. Only the short form itself is to be signed by the subject or the representative. However, the witness shall sign both the short form and a copy of the summary, and the person actually obtaining consent shall sign a copy of the summary. A copy of the summary shall be given to the subject or the representative, in addition to a copy of the short form.

(c) An IRB may waive the requirement for the investigator to obtain a signed consent form for some or all subjects if it finds either:

(1) That the only record linking the subject and the research would be the consent document and the principal risk would be potential harm resulting from a breach of confidentiality. Each subject will be asked whether the subject wants documentation linking the subject with the research, and the subject's wishes will govern; or

(2) That the research presents no more than minimal risk of harm to subjects and involves no procedures for which written consent is normally required outside of the research context.

In cases in which the documentation requirement is waived, the IRB may require the investigator to provide subjects with a written statement regarding the research.

(Approved by the Office of Management and Budget under Control Number 0990-0260.)

[56 FR 28012, 28022, June 18, 1991, as amended at 70 FR 36328, June 23, 2005]

§46.118 Applications and proposals lacking definite plans for involvement of human subjects.

Certain types of applications for grants, cooperative agreements, or contracts are submitted to departments or agencies with the knowledge that subjects may be involved within the period of support, but definite plans would not normally be set forth in the application or proposal. These include activities such as institutional type grants when selection of specific projects is the institution's responsibility; research training grants in which the activities involving subjects remain to be selected; and projects in which human subjects' involvement will depend upon completion of instruments, prior animal studies, or purification of compounds. These applications need not be reviewed by an IRB before an award may be made. However, except for research exempted or waived under §46.101(b) or (i), no human subjects may be involved in any project supported by these awards until the project has been reviewed and approved by the IRB, as provided in this policy, and certification submitted, by the institution, to the department or agency.

§46.119 Research undertaken without the intention of involving human subjects.

In the event research is undertaken without the intention of involving human subjects, but it is later proposed to involve human subjects in the research, the research shall first be reviewed and approved by an IRB, as provided in this policy, a certification submitted, by the institution, to the department or agency, and final approval given to the proposed change by the department or agency.

§46.120 Evaluation and disposition of applications and proposals for research to be conducted or supported by a Federal Department or Agency.

(a) The department or agency head will evaluate all applications and proposals involving human subjects submitted to the department or agency through such officers and employees of the department or agency and such experts and consultants as the department or agency head determines to be appropriate. This evaluation will take into consideration the risks to the subjects, the adequacy of protection against these risks, the potential benefits of the research to the subjects and others, and the importance of the knowledge gained or to be gained.

(b) On the basis of this evaluation, the department or agency head may approve or disapprove the application or proposal, or enter into negotiations to develop an approvable one.

§46.121 [Reserved]

§46.122 Use of Federal funds.

Federal funds administered by a department or agency may not be expended for research involving human subjects unless the requirements of this policy have been satisfied.

§46.123 Early termination of research support: Evaluation of applications and proposals.

(a) The department or agency head may require that department or agency support for any project be terminated or suspended in the manner prescribed in applicable program requirements, when the department or agency head finds an institution has materially failed to comply with the terms of this policy.

(b) In making decisions about supporting or approving applications or proposals covered by this policy the department or agency head may take into account, in addition to all other eligibility requirements and program criteria, factors such as whether the applicant has been subject to a termination or suspension under paragraph (a) of this section and whether the applicant or the person or persons who would direct or has/have directed the scientific and technical aspects of an activity has/have, in the judgment of the department or agency head, materially failed to discharge responsibility for the protection of the rights and welfare of human subjects (whether or not the research was subject to federal regulation).

§46.124 Conditions.

With respect to any research project or any class of research projects the department or agency head may impose additional conditions prior to or at the time of approval when in the judgment of the department or agency head additional conditions are necessary for the protection of human subjects.

11.8.2 Subpart B: Additional Protections for Pregnant Women, Human Fetuses, and Neonates Involved in Research

Source: 66 FR 56778, Nov. 13, 2001, unless otherwise noted.

§46.201 To what do these regulations apply?

(a) Except as provided in paragraph (b) of this section, this subpart applies to all research involving pregnant women, human fetuses, neonates of uncertain viability, or nonviable neonates conducted or supported by the Department of Health and Human Services (DHHS). This includes all research conducted in DHHS facilities by any person and all research conducted in any facility by DHHS employees.

(b) The exemptions at §46.101(b)(1) through (6) are applicable to this subpart.

(c) The provisions of §46.101(c) through (i) are applicable to this subpart. Reference to State or local laws in this subpart and in §46.101(f) is intended to include the laws of federally recognized American Indian and Alaska Native Tribal Governments.

(d) The requirements of this subpart are in addition to those imposed under the other subparts of this part.

§46.202 Definitions.

The definitions in §46.102 shall be applicable to this subpart as well. In addition, as used in this subpart:

(a) Dead fetus means a fetus that exhibits neither heartbeat, spontaneous respiratory activity, spontaneous movement of voluntary muscles, nor pulsation of the umbilical cord.

(b) Delivery means complete separation of the fetus from the woman by expulsion or extraction or any other means.

(c) Fetus means the product of conception from implantation until delivery.

(d) Neonate means a newborn.

(e) Nonviable neonate means a neonate after delivery that, although living, is not viable.

(f) Pregnancy encompasses the period of time from implantation until delivery. A woman shall be assumed to be pregnant if she exhibits any of the pertinent presumptive signs of pregnancy, such as missed menses, until the results of a pregnancy test are negative or until delivery.

(g) Secretary means the Secretary of Health and Human Services and any other officer or employee of the Department of Health and Human Services to whom authority has been delegated.

(h) Viable, as it pertains to the neonate, means being able, after delivery, to survive (given the benefit of available medical therapy) to the point of independently maintaining heartbeat and respiration. The Secretary may from time to time, taking into account medical advances, publish in the FEDERAL REGISTER guidelines to assist in determining whether a neonate is viable for purposes of this subpart. If a neonate is viable then it may be included in research only to the extent permitted and in accordance with the requirements of subparts A and D of this part.

§46.203 Duties of IRBs in connection with research involving pregnant women, fetuses, and neonates.

In addition to other responsibilities assigned to IRBs under this part, each IRB shall review research covered by this subpart and approve only research which satisfies the conditions of all applicable sections of this subpart and the other subparts of this part.

§46.204 Research involving pregnant women or fetuses.

Pregnant women or fetuses may be involved in research if all of the following conditions are met:

(a) Where scientifically appropriate, preclinical studies, including studies on pregnant animals, and clinical studies, including studies on nonpregnant women, have been conducted and provide data for assessing potential risks to pregnant women and fetuses;

(b) The risk to the fetus is caused solely by interventions or procedures that hold out the prospect of direct benefit for the woman or the fetus; or, if there is no such prospect of benefit, the risk to the fetus is not greater than minimal and the purpose of the research is the development of important biomedical knowledge which cannot be obtained by any other means;

(c) Any risk is the least possible for achieving the objectives of the research;

(d) If the research holds out the prospect of direct benefit to the pregnant woman, the prospect of a direct benefit both to the pregnant woman and the fetus, or no prospect of benefit for the woman nor the fetus when risk to the fetus is not greater than minimal and the purpose of the research is the development of important biomedical knowledge that cannot be obtained by any other means, her consent is obtained in accord with the informed consent provisions of subpart A of this part;

(e) If the research holds out the prospect of direct benefit solely to the fetus then the consent of the pregnant woman and the father is obtained in accord with the informed consent provisions of subpart A of this part, except that the father's consent need not be obtained if he is unable to consent because of unavailability, incompetence, or temporary incapacity or the pregnancy resulted from rape or incest.

(f) Each individual providing consent under paragraph (d) or (e) of this section is fully informed regarding the reasonably foreseeable impact of the research on the fetus or neonate;

(g) For children as defined in §46.402(a) who are pregnant, assent and permission are obtained in accord with the provisions of subpart D of this part;

(h) No inducements, monetary or otherwise, will be offered to terminate a pregnancy;

(i) Individuals engaged in the research will have no part in any decisions as to the timing, method, or procedures used to terminate a pregnancy; and

(j) Individuals engaged in the research will have no part in determining the viability of a neonate.

§46.205 Research involving neonates.

(a) Neonates of uncertain viability and nonviable neonates may be involved in research if all of the following conditions are met:

(1) Where scientifically appropriate, preclinical and clinical studies have been conducted and provide data for assessing potential risks to neonates.

(2) Each individual providing consent under paragraph (b)(2) or (c)(5) of this section is fully informed regarding the reasonably foreseeable impact of the research on the neonate.

(3) Individuals engaged in the research will have no part in determining the viability of a neonate.

(4) The requirements of paragraph (b) or (c) of this section have been met as applicable.

(b) Neonates of uncertain viability. Until it has been ascertained whether or not a neonate is viable, a neonate may not be involved in research covered by this subpart unless the following additional conditions have been met:

(1) The IRB determines that:

(i) The research holds out the prospect of enhancing the probability of survival of the neonate to the point of viability, and any risk is the least possible for achieving that objective, or

(ii) The purpose of the research is the development of important biomedical knowledge which cannot be obtained by other means and there will be no added risk to the neonate resulting from the research; and

(2) The legally effective informed consent of either parent of the neonate or, if neither parent is able to consent because of unavailability, incompetence, or temporary incapacity, the legally effective informed consent of either parent's legally authorized representative is obtained in accord with subpart A of this part, except that the consent of the father or his legally authorized representative need not be obtained if the pregnancy resulted from rape or incest.

(c) Nonviable neonates. After delivery nonviable neonate may not be involved in research covered by this subpart unless all of the following additional conditions are met:

(1) Vital functions of the neonate will not be artificially maintained;

(2) The research will not terminate the heartbeat or respiration of the neonate;

(3) There will be no added risk to the neonate resulting from the research;

(4) The purpose of the research is the development of important biomedical knowledge that cannot be obtained by other means; and

(5) The legally effective informed consent of both parents of the neonate is obtained in accord with subpart A of this part, except that the waiver and alteration provisions of §46.116(c) and (d) do not apply. However, if either parent is unable to consent because of unavailability, incompetence, or temporary incapacity, the informed consent of one parent of a nonviable neonate will suffice to meet the requirements of this paragraph (c)(5), except that the consent of the father need not be obtained if the pregnancy resulted from rape or incest. The consent of a legally authorized representative of either or both of the parents of a nonviable neonate will not suffice to meet the requirements of this paragraph (c)(5).

(d) Viable neonates. A neonate, after delivery, that has been determined to be viable may be included in research only to the extent permitted by and in accord with the requirements of subparts A and D of this part.

§46.206 Research involving, after delivery, the placenta, the dead fetus or fetal material.

(a) Research involving, after delivery, the placenta; the dead fetus; macerated fetal material; or cells, tissue, or organs excised from a dead fetus, shall be conducted only in accord with any applicable federal, state, or local laws and regulations regarding such activities.

(b) If information associated with material described in paragraph (a) of this section is recorded for research purposes in a manner that living individuals can be identified, directly or through identifiers linked to those individuals, those individuals are research subjects and all pertinent subparts of this part are applicable.

§46.207 Research not otherwise approvable which presents an opportunity to understand, prevent, or alleviate a serious problem affecting the health or welfare of pregnant women, fetuses, or neonates.

The Secretary will conduct or fund research that the IRB does not believe meets the requirements of §46.204 or §46.205 only if:

(a) The IRB finds that the research presents a reasonable opportunity to further the understanding, prevention, or alleviation of a serious problem affecting the health or welfare of pregnant women, fetuses or neonates; and

(b) The Secretary, after consultation with a panel of experts in pertinent disciplines (for example: science, medicine, ethics, law) and following opportunity for public review and comment, including a public meeting announced in the FEDERAL REGISTER, has determined either:

(1) That the research in fact satisfies the conditions of §46.204, as applicable; or

(2) The following:

(i) The research presents a reasonable opportunity to further the under-standing, prevention, or alleviation of a serious problem affecting the health or welfare of pregnant women, fetuses or neonates;

(ii) The research will be conducted in accord with sound ethical princi-ples; and

(iii) Informed consent will be obtained in accord with the informed consent provisions of subpart A and other applicable subparts of this part.

11.8.3 Subpart C: Additional Protections Pertaining to Biomedical and Behavioral Research Involving Prisoners as Subjects

Source: 43 FR 53655, Nov. 16, 1978, unless otherwise noted.

§46.301 Applicability.

(a) The regulations in this subpart are applicable to all biomedical and behavioral research conducted or supported by the Department of Health and Human Services involving prisoners as subjects.

(b) Nothing in this subpart shall be construed as indicating that compli-ance with the procedures set forth herein will authorize research involving prisoners as subjects, to the extent such research is limited or barred by applicable State or local law.

(c) The requirements of this subpart are in addition to those imposed under the other subparts of this part.

§46.302 Purpose.

Inasmuch as prisoners may be under constraints because of their incar-ceration which could affect their ability to make a truly voluntary and unco-erced decision whether or not to participate as subjects in research, it is the purpose of this subpart to provide additional safeguards for the protection of prisoners involved in activities to which this subpart is applicable.

§46.303 Definitions.

As used in this subpart:

(a) Secretary means the Secretary of Health and Human Services and any other officer or employee of the Department of Health and Human Services to whom authority has been delegated.

(b) DHHS means the Department of Health and Human Services.

(c) Prisoner means any individual involuntarily confined or detained in a penal institution. The term is intended to encompass individuals sen-tenced to such an institution under a criminal or civil statute, individuals detained in other facilities by virtue of statutes or commitment procedures which provide alternatives to criminal prosecution or incarceration in a penal institution, and individuals detained pending arraignment, trial, or sentencing.

(d) Minimal risk is the probability and magnitude of physical or psychological harm that is normally encountered in the daily lives, or in the routine medical, dental, or psychological examination of healthy persons.

§46.304 Composition of Institutional Review Boards where prisoners are involved.

In addition to satisfying the requirements in §46.107 of this part, an Institutional Review Board, carrying out responsibilities under this part with respect to research covered by this subpart, shall also meet the following specific requirements:

(a) A majority of the Board (exclusive of prisoner members) shall have no association with the prison(s) involved, apart from their membership on the Board.

(b) At least one member of the Board shall be a prisoner, or a prisoner representative with appropriate background and experience to serve in that capacity, except that where a particular research project is reviewed by more than one Board only one Board need satisfy this requirement.

[43 FR 53655, Nov. 16, 1978, as amended at 46 FR 8366, Jan. 26, 1981]

§46.305 Additional duties of the Institutional Review Boards where prisoners are involved.

(a) In addition to all other responsibilities prescribed for Institutional Review Boards under this part, the Board shall review research covered by this subpart and approve such research only if it finds that:

(1) The research under review represents one of the categories of research permissible under §46.306(a)(2);

(2) Any possible advantages accruing to the prisoner through his or her participation in the research, when compared to the general living conditions, medical care, quality of food, amenities and opportunity for earnings in the prison, are not of such a magnitude that his or her ability to weigh the risks of the research against the value of such advantages in the limited choice environment of the prison is impaired;

(3) The risks involved in the research are commensurate with risks that would be accepted by nonprisoner volunteers;

(4) Procedures for the selection of subjects within the prison are fair to all prisoners and immune from arbitrary intervention by prison authorities or prisoners. Unless the principal investigator provides to the Board justification in writing for following some other procedures, control subjects must be selected randomly from the group of available prisoners who meet the characteristics needed for that particular research project;

(5) The information is presented in language which is understandable to the subject population;

(6) Adequate assurance exists that parole boards will not take into account a prisoner's participation in the research in making decisions regarding parole, and each prisoner is clearly informed in advance that participation in the research will have no effect on his or her parole; and

(7) Where the Board finds there may be a need for follow-up examination or care of participants after the end of their participation, adequate provision has been made for such examination or care, taking into account the varying lengths of individual prisoners' sentences, and for informing participants of this fact.

(b) The Board shall carry out such other duties as may be assigned by the Secretary.

(c) The institution shall certify to the Secretary, in such form and manner as the Secretary may require, that the duties of the Board under this section have been fulfilled.

§46.306 Permitted research involving prisoners.

(a) Biomedical or behavioral research conducted or supported by DHHS may involve prisoners as subjects only if:

(1) The institution responsible for the conduct of the research has certified to the Secretary that the Institutional Review Board has approved the research under §46.305 of this subpart; and

(2) In the judgment of the Secretary the proposed research involves solely the following:

(i) Study of the possible causes, effects, and processes of incarceration, and of criminal behavior, provided that the study presents no more than minimal risk and no more than inconvenience to the subjects;

(ii) Study of prisons as institutional structures or of prisoners as incarcerated persons, provided that the study presents no more than minimal risk and no more than inconvenience to the subjects;

(iii) Research on conditions particularly affecting prisoners as a class (for example, vaccine trials and other research on hepatitis which is much more prevalent in prisons than elsewhere; and research on social and psychological problems such as alcoholism, drug addiction, and sexual assaults) provided that the study may proceed only after the Secretary has consulted with appropriate experts including experts in penology, medicine, and ethics, and published notice, in the FEDERAL REGISTER, of his intent to approve such research; or

(iv) Research on practices, both innovative and accepted, which have the intent and reasonable probability of improving the health or well-being of the subject. In cases in which those studies require the assignment of prisoners in a manner consistent with protocols approved by the IRB to control groups which may not benefit from the research, the study may proceed only after the Secretary has consulted with appropriate experts, including experts in penology, medicine, and ethics, and published notice, in the FEDERAL REGISTER, of the intent to approve such research.

(b) Except as provided in paragraph (a) of this section, biomedical or behavioral research conducted or supported by DHHS shall not involve prisoners as subjects.

11.8.4 Subpart D: Additional Protections for Children Involved as Subjects in Research

Source: 48 FR 9818, March 8, 1983, unless otherwise noted.

§46.401 To what do these regulations apply?

(a) This subpart applies to all research involving children as subjects, conducted or supported by the Department of Health and Human Services.

(1) This includes research conducted by Department employees, except that each head of an Operating Division of the Department may adopt such nonsubstantive, procedural modifications as may be appropriate from an administrative standpoint.

(2) It also includes research conducted or supported by the Department of Health and Human Services outside the United States, but in appropriate circumstances, the Secretary may, under paragraph (e) of §46.101 of subpart A, waive the applicability of some or all of the requirements of these regulations for research of this type.

(b) Exemptions at §46.101(b)(1) and (b)(3) through (b)(6) are applicable to this subpart. The exemption at §46.101(b)(2) regarding educational tests is also applicable to this subpart. However, the exemption at §46.101(b)(2) for research involving survey or interview procedures or observations of public behavior does not apply to research covered by this subpart, except for research involving observation of public behavior when the investigator(s) do not participate in the activities being observed.

(c) The exceptions, additions, and provisions for waiver as they appear in paragraphs (c) through (i) of §46.101 of subpart A are applicable to this subpart.

[48 FR 9818, Mar.8, 1983; 56 FR 28032, June 18, 1991; 56 FR 29757, June 28, 1991.]

§46.402 Definitions.

The definitions in §46.102 of subpart A shall be applicable to this subpart as well. In addition, as used in this subpart:

(a) Children are persons who have not attained the legal age for consent to treatments or procedures involved in the research, under the applicable law of the jurisdiction in which the research will be conducted.

(b) Assent means a child's affirmative agreement to participate in research. Mere failure to object should not, absent affirmative agreement, be construed as assent.

(c) Permission means the agreement of parent(s) or guardian to the participation of their child or ward in research.

(d) Parent means a child's biological or adoptive parent.

(e) Guardian means an individual who is authorized under applicable State or local law to consent on behalf of a child to general medical care.

§46.403 IRB duties.

In addition to other responsibilities assigned to IRBs under this part, each IRB shall review research covered by this subpart and approve only research which satisfies the conditions of all applicable sections of this subpart.

§46.404 Research not involving greater than minimal risk.

HHS will conduct or fund research in which the IRB finds that no greater than minimal risk to children is presented, only if the IRB finds that adequate provisions are made for soliciting the assent of the children and the permission of their parents or guardians, as set forth in §46.408.

§46.405 Research involving greater than minimal risk but presenting the prospect of direct benefit to the individual subjects.

HHS will conduct or fund research in which the IRB finds that more than minimal risk to children is presented by an intervention or procedure that holds out the prospect of direct benefit for the individual subject, or by a monitoring procedure that is likely to contribute to the subject's well-being, only if the IRB finds that:

(a) The risk is justified by the anticipated benefit to the subjects;

(b) The relation of the anticipated benefit to the risk is at least as favorable to the subjects as that presented by available alternative approaches; and

(c) Adequate provisions are made for soliciting the assent of the children and permission of their parents or guardians, as set forth in §46.408.

§46.406 Research involving greater than minimal risk and no prospect of direct benefit to individual subjects, but likely to yield generalizable knowledge about the subject's disorder or condition.

HHS will conduct or fund research in which the IRB finds that more than minimal risk to children is presented by an intervention or procedure that does not hold out the prospect of direct benefit for the individual subject, or by a monitoring procedure which is not likely to contribute to the well-being of the subject, only if the IRB finds that:

(a) The risk represents a minor increase over minimal risk;

(b) The intervention or procedure presents experiences to subjects that are reasonably commensurate with those inherent in their actual or expected medical, dental, psychological, social, or educational situations;

(c) The intervention or procedure is likely to yield generalizable knowledge about the subjects' disorder or condition which is of vital importance for the understanding or amelioration of the subjects' disorder or condition; and

(d) Adequate provisions are made for soliciting assent of the children and permission of their parents or guardians, as set forth in §46.408.

§46.407 Research not otherwise approvable which presents an opportunity to understand, prevent, or alleviate a serious problem affecting the health or welfare of children.

HHS will conduct or fund research that the IRB does not believe meets the requirements of §46.404, §46.405, or §46.406 only if:

(a) the IRB finds that the research presents a reasonable opportunity to further the understanding, prevention, or alleviation of a serious problem affecting the health or welfare of children; and

(b) the Secretary, after consultation with a panel of experts in pertinent disciplines (for example: science, medicine, education, ethics, law) and following opportunity for public review and comment, has determined either:

(1) that the research in fact satisfies the conditions of §46.404, §46.405, or §46.406, as applicable, or (2) the following:

(i) the research presents a reasonable opportunity to further the understanding, prevention, or alleviation of a serious problem affecting the health or welfare of children;

(ii) the research will be conducted in accordance with sound ethical principles;

(iii) adequate provisions are made for soliciting the assent of children and the permission of their parents or guardians, as set forth in §46.408.

§46.408 Requirements for permission by parents or guardians and for assent by children.

(a) In addition to the determinations required under other applicable sections of this subpart, the IRB shall determine that adequate provisions are made for soliciting the assent of the children, when in the judgment of the IRB the children are capable of providing assent. In determining whether children are capable of assenting, the IRB shall take into account the ages, maturity, and psychological state of the children involved. This judgment may be made for all children to be involved in research under a particular protocol, or for each child, as the IRB deems appropriate. If the IRB determines that the capability of some or all of the children is so limited that they cannot reasonably be consulted or that the intervention or procedure involved in the research holds out a prospect of direct benefit that is important to the health or well-being of the children and is available only in the context of the research, the assent of the children is not a necessary condition for proceeding with the research. Even where the IRB determines that the subjects are capable of assenting, the IRB may still waive the assent requirement under circumstances in which consent may be waived in accord with §46.116 of Subpart A.

(b) In addition to the determinations required under other applicable sections of this subpart, the IRB shall determine, in accordance with and to the extent that consent is required by §46.116 of Subpart A, that adequate provisions are made for soliciting the permission of each child's parents or guardian. Where parental permission is to be obtained, the IRB may find that the permission of one parent is sufficient for research to be conducted under §46.404 or §46.405. Where research is covered by §§46.406 and 46.407 and permission is to be obtained from parents, both parents must give their permission unless one parent is deceased, unknown, incompetent, or not reasonably available, or when only one parent has legal responsibility for the care and custody of the child.

(c) In addition to the provisions for waiver contained in §46.116 of subpart A, if the IRB determines that a research protocol is designed for conditions or for a subject population for which parental or guardian permission is not a reasonable requirement to protect the subjects (for example, neglected or abused children), it may waive the consent requirements in Subpart A of this part and paragraph (b) of this section, provided an appropriate mechanism for protecting the children who will participate as subjects in the research is substituted, and provided further that the waiver is not inconsistent with federal, state, or local law. The choice of an appropriate mechanism would depend upon the nature and purpose of the activities described in the protocol, the risk and anticipated benefit to the research subjects, and their age, maturity, status, and condition.

(d) Permission by parents or guardians shall be documented in accordance with and to the extent required by §46.117 of subpart A.

(e) When the IRB determines that assent is required, it shall also determine whether and how assent must be documented.

§46.409 Wards.

(a) Children who are wards of the state or any other agency, institution, or entity can be included in research approved under §46.406 or §46.407 only if such research is:

(1) Related to their status as wards; or

(2) Conducted in schools, camps, hospitals, institutions, or similar settings in which the majority of children involved as subjects are not wards.

(b) If the research is approved under paragraph (a) of this section, the IRB shall require appointment of an advocate for each child who is a ward, in addition to any other individual acting on behalf of the child as guardian or in loco parentis. One individual may serve as advocate for more than one child. The advocate shall be an individual who has the background and experience to act in, and agrees to act in, the best interests of the child for the duration of the child's participation in the research and who is not associated in any way (except in the role as advocate or member of the IRB) with the research, the investigator(s), or the guardian organization.

11.9 Appendix B: Categories of Research That May Be Reviewed by the Institutional Review Board (IRB) Through an Expedited Review Procedure[29]

11.9.1 Applicability

(A) Research activities that (1) present no more than minimal risk to human subjects, and (2) involve only procedures listed in one or more of the following categories, may be reviewed by the IRB through the expedited review procedure authorized by 45 CFR 46.110 and 21 CFR 56.110. The activities listed should not be deemed to be of minimal risk simply because they are included on this list. Inclusion on this list merely means that the activity is eligible for review through the expedited review procedure when the specific circumstances of the proposed research involve no more than minimal risk to human subjects.

(B) The categories in this list apply regardless of the age of subjects, except as noted.

(C) The expedited review procedure may not be used where identification of the subjects and/or their responses would reasonably place them at risk

---

[29] An expedited review procedure consists of a review of research involving human subjects by the IRB chairperson or by one or more experienced reviewers designated by the chairperson from among members of the IRB in accordance with the requirements set forth in 45 CFR 46.110 (see Appendix A).

of criminal or civil liability or be damaging to the subjects = financial standing, employability, insurability, reputation, or be stigmatizing, unless reasonable and appropriate protections will be implemented so that risks related to invasion of privacy and breach of confidentiality are no greater than minimal.

(D) The expedited review procedure may not be used for classified research involving human subjects.

(E) IRBs are reminded that the standard requirements for informed consent (or its waiver, alteration, or exception) apply regardless of the type of review – expedited or convened – utilized by the IRB.

(F) Categories one (1) through seven (7) pertain to both initial and continuing IRB review.

11.9.2 Research Categories

(1) Clinical studies of drugs and medical devices only when condition (a) or (b) is met.

(a) Research on drugs for which an investigational new drug application (21 CFR Part 312) is not required. (Note: Research on marketed drugs that significantly increases the risks or decreases the acceptability of the risks associated with the use of the product is not eligible for expedited review.)

(b) Research on medical devices for which (i) an investigational device exemption application (21 CFR Part 812) is not required; or (ii) the medical device is cleared/approved for marketing and the medical device is being used in accordance with its cleared/approved labeling.

(2) Collection of blood samples by finger stick, heel stick, ear stick, or venipuncture as follows:

(a) from healthy, nonpregnant adults who weigh at least 110 pounds. For these subjects, the amounts drawn may not exceed 550 ml in an 8 week period and collection may not occur more frequently than 2 times per week; or

(b) from other adults and children,[30] considering the age, weight, and health of the subjects, the collection procedure, the amount of blood to be collected, and the frequency with which it will be collected. For these subjects, the amount drawn may not exceed the lesser of 50 ml or 3 ml per kg

---

[30] Children are defined in the HHS regulations as "persons who have not attained the legal age for consent to treatments or procedures involved in the research, under the applicable law of the jurisdiction in which the research will be conducted." 45 CFR 46.402(a).

in an 8 week period and collection may not occur more frequently than 2 times per week.

(3) Prospective collection of biological specimens for research purposes by noninvasive means.

Examples: (a) hair and nail clippings in a nondisfiguring manner; (b) deciduous teeth at time of exfoliation or if routine patient care indicates a need for extraction; (c) permanent teeth if routine patient care indicates a need for extraction; (d) excreta and external secretions (including sweat); (e) uncannulated saliva collected either in an unstimulated fashion or stimulated by chewing gumbase or wax or by applying a dilute citric solution to the tongue; (f) placenta removed at delivery; (g) amniotic fluid obtained at the time of rupture of the membrane prior to or during labor; (h) supra- and subgingival dental plaque and calculus, provided the collection procedure is not more invasive than routine prophylactic scaling of the teeth and the process is accomplished in accordance with accepted prophylactic techniques; (i) mucosal and skin cells collected by buccal scraping or swab, skin swab, or mouth washings; (j) sputum collected after saline mist nebulization.

(4) Collection of data through noninvasive procedures (not involving general anesthesia or sedation) routinely employed in clinical practice, excluding procedures involving x-rays or microwaves. Where medical devices are employed, they must be cleared/approved for marketing. (Studies intended to evaluate the safety and effectiveness of the medical device are not generally eligible for expedited review, including studies of cleared medical devices for new indications.)

Examples: (a) physical sensors that are applied either to the surface of the body or at a distance and do not involve input of significant amounts of energy into the subject or an invasion of the subject's privacy; (b) weighing or testing sensory acuity; (c) magnetic resonance imaging; (d) electrocardiography, electroencephalography, thermography, detection of naturally occurring radioactivity, electroretinography, ultrasound, diagnostic infrared imaging, doppler blood flow, and echocardiography; (e) moderate exercise, muscular strength testing, body composition assessment, and flexibility testing where appropriate given the age, weight, and health of the individual.

(5) Research involving materials (data, documents, records, or specimens) that have been collected, or will be collected solely for nonresearch purposes (such as medical treatment or diagnosis). (NOTE: Some research in this category may be exempt from the HHS regulations for the protection

of human subjects. 45 CFR 46.101(b)(4). This listing refers only to research that is not exempt.)

(6) Collection of data from voice, video, digital, or image recordings made for research purposes.

(7) Research on individual or group characteristics or behavior (including, but not limited to, research on perception, cognition, motivation, identity, language, communication, cultural beliefs or practices, and social behavior) or research employing survey, interview, oral history, focus group, program evaluation, human factors evaluation, or quality assurance methodologies. (NOTE: Some research in this category may be exempt from the HHS regulations for the protection of human subjects. 45 CFR 46.101(b)(2) and (b)(3). This listing refers only to research that is not exempt.)

(8) Continuing review of research previously approved by the convened IRB as follows:

(a) where (i) the research is permanently closed to the enrollment of new subjects; (ii) all subjects have completed all research-related interventions; and (iii) the research remains active only for long-term follow-up of subjects; or

(b) where no subjects have been enrolled and no additional risks have been identified; or

(c) where the remaining research activities are limited to data analysis.

(9) Continuing review of research, not conducted under an investigational new drug application or investigational device exemption where categories two (2) through eight (8) do not apply but the IRB has determined and documented at a convened meeting that the research involves no greater than minimal risk and no additional risks have been identified.

Source: 63 FR 60364-60367, November 9, 1998.

Ethical Decision Making and Political Science Experiments

12.1 Expected Benefits and Costs in Experiments

12.1.1 Expectations, Probabilities, and Magnitudes

In Institutional Review Board (IRB) speak, one of the key aspects of determining whether an experiment is ethical is a consideration of the risks to subjects versus the benefits. But as the Office of Human Rights Protections (OHRP) notes in the 1993 IRB Guidebook,[1] the use of the term benefit is inaccurate. It is essentially expected benefits that are considered, not known benefits, because we cannot know for sure what will be learned through the research (otherwise there would be no point to the study). Thus, we are concerned with the product of the two – the probability that benefits can occur times the value of those benefits – or expected benefits. Calculating expected benefits means calculating both the probability of benefit and the value of benefit. Correspondingly, the term risk is confusing as well. The guidebook states at one point that risk is a measure of the probability of harm, not mentioning the magnitude. But certainly the magnitude of harm is as important as the probability (and part of the aforementioned definition of minimal risk). Expected cost (probability of harm times the magnitude of harm) is a more accurate measure to compare to expected benefits. Most IRBs and the OHRP recognize that the comparison between risk and benefit is more accurately thought of as the comparison between the expected costs of the research for the subject (probability and magnitude of harm) and the expected benefits (probability and magnitude of benefits), with risk as shorthand for expected costs and benefits as shorthand for expected benefits.

---

[1] Available online at http://www.hhs.gov/ohrp/irb/irb_guidebook.htm and in hard copy from the OHRP.

12.1.2 Expected Benefits from Experimental Research

Types of Expected Benefits

The benefits to participation in research can be divided into three types of expected benefits:[2]

1. societal benefits,
2. therapeutic benefits, and
3. collateral benefits.

The last two of these are direct benefits to subjects, whereas the first offers indirect benefits that could possibly benefit the subject as well (either through subjects' value to being altruistic or as part of society).

Societal Benefits

Anticipated societal benefits should be the ultimate reason for conducting the research in the first place. Ideally, an experimenter is engaging in human subjects research with the belief that the information he or she learns from that research will ultimately lead to more knowledge about human behavior and in political science, human behavior in political situations, and that society as a whole will benefit from this greater knowledge. We engage in experiments on voting, for example, because we hope that the research will help us understand better why individuals vote, how they vote, how different voting systems affect their choices, how different frames of voting choices affect their choices, and so on. Yet, measuring these expected benefits is extremely difficult to contemplate. We may not learn anything; our research may end up being impossible to interpret. We may learn only confirmation of facts we already know, or we may actually make our knowledge more confused by learning something that does not make sense given facts we already know.

Definition 12.1 (Societal Benefits): *Societal benefits are aspirational benefits to society from the research in the immediate and long run.*

Benefits to Subjects

Therapeutic Benefits. A therapeutic benefit from an experiment is when a subject gains some benefit in dealing with a problem in his or her daily life

---

[2] See Churchill et al. (2003), Henderson et al. (2004), King (2000), and King et al. (2005) for the development of this framework for biomedical experimental research. We present a version adapted to both social science and biomedical experiments.

due to the treatment he or she is exposed to in the experiment and the goal of the experiment is to relieve this problem. In biomedical or some psychology experiments, understanding possible therapeutic benefits from treatments is often straightforward. That is, suppose that the research involves testing a drug hypothesized to lower high blood pressure and the subjects are individuals with existing high blood pressure. Because high blood pressure is known to be a contributory cause in strokes and heart problems, if the drug works, then the subjects who receive the drug instead of a placebo may benefit. Conversely, the research may consider the effects of different measures to alleviate compulsive gambling, abstinence from gambling, or a method of controlled gambling on a group of subjects with compulsive gambling problems.[3]

Definition 12.2 (Therapeutic Benefits): *Therapeutic benefits are benefits that help alleviate a problem in a subject's daily life which is also the focus of the research.*

Of course, it is not always true that biomedical or psychological experiments involve therapeutic benefits. Sometimes these experiments use normal, healthy individuals who will not necessarily benefit directly from the treatment investigated. Or in some cases the subject pool may include patients who are terminally ill and there is none to little possibility that the therapeutic benefit would matter in their lives. However, in many cases the biomedical or psychological experiments do offer subjects the possibility of therapeutic benefits.

Do social science experiments offer therapeutic benefits? In many cases, the therapeutic benefits are minimal. Consider Example 4.2. In this experiment, Lau and Redlawsk had subjects engage in a mock election campaign and measured their ability to use information to make their vote choices closer to their own preferences in the hypothetical election. Because the design of the experiment was to be as close to a naturally occurring election as possible in the laboratory, the experiment is designed so that it is not likely to be a benefit to a subject that he or she would not gain from daily life, making the expected benefits from the treatments basically minimal (as in the definition of minimal risk discussed earlier and again later in the chapter).[4]

---

[3] See, for example, Ladouceur et al. (2009).
[4] In the experiment the authors manipulated the amount of information, number of candidates, etc., to capture different real-world scenarios.

However, it is possible for a social science experiment to provide therapeutic-like benefits. Example 12.1 reports on a field experiment conducted by Olken (2008) in Indonesia. In this experiment, Olken varied the mechanism that villages use to choose public good projects. In one treatment the mechanism was that normally used, a meeting of representatives who chose projects; in the other, the mechanism incorporated a plebiscite to determine the projects. Political science theory suggests that mechanisms that allow for greater participation through direct democracy can result in a selection of projects that better fit the preferences of the average voter and also result in greater voter satisfaction and belief in the legitimacy of the governmental choices. Some limited evidence from previous observational studies supports this argument. Thus, prior to the experiment there was not only the anticipated social benefit from the research but also the expected therapeutic benefit for the villages, which would be assigned to the direct democracy treatment, a benefit to the subject directly tied to the focus of the research. In fact, although Olken found only minor differences in the types of projects selected across treatments, he did find that in the direct democracy treatment voters were much more satisfied with the outcome and had greater feelings of legitimacy.

Example 12.1 (Direct Democracy Field Experiment): *Olken (2008) presents results from a field experiment conducted in Indonesia in which the mechanism by which villages chose two development projects were manipulated to determine if direct democracy affected the types of projects chosen and the satisfaction of villagers in the project selection process.*

Target Population and Sample: *The experiments were conducted in 10 villages in East Java Province, 18 villages in North Sumatra Province, and 18 villages in Southeast Sulawesi Province. Average village population was 2,200. For the direct democracy treatments (described later), voting cards were distributed to all adults in the village who had been eligible to vote in national parliamentary elections held approximately six months previously. Women only were allowed to vote in one part of the election. The meeting treatments (described later) were open to the public (although what that means in actual implementation – whether someone who is not an adult or not a previous voter would be allowed to attend and participate – is not addressed by Olken). On average 48 people attended each meeting. Women only participated in one part of the meeting. Those who attended the meetings were a highly selected sample: "government officials, neighborhood heads, and those selected to represent village groups compose the majority of attendees." Olken also conducted a* panel household survey, "in which five households were randomly selected in each village and surveyed each village and hamlet head."

Environment: *In the national Indonesian government program, the Keca-matan (Subdistrict) Development Project (KDP), funded through a loan from the World Bank, "participating subdistricts, which typically contain between 10 and 20 villages, receive an annual block grant for three consecutive years. Each year, each village in the subdistrict makes two proposals for small-scale infrastructure activities. The village as a whole proposes one of the projects . . . ; women's groups in the village propose the second. . . . Once the village proposals have been made, an inter-village forum . . . ranks all of the proposals . . . and projects are funded until all funds have been exhausted."*

Procedures: *Olken considered two methods by which the two proposals were generally selected by the villages; the method used by the villages normally (meeting treatment) and a method that incorporates a plebiscite or referendum to select the two proposals (direct democracy treatment). The meeting treatment proceeded as follows.*

"All Indonesian villages are comprised of between 2 and 7 dusun, or hamlets. For a period of several months, a village facilitator organizes small meetings at the hamlet level; for large hamlets multiple meetings might be held in different neighborhoods within each hamlet. These meetings aim to create a list of ideas for what projects the village should propose. These ideas are then divided into two groups – those that originated from women's only meetings and those suggested by mixed meetings or men's meetings. The village facilitator presents the women's list to a women-only village meeting and the men's and joint ideas to a village meeting open to both genders. . . . At each meeting, the representatives in attendance discuss the proposals, with substantial help from an external facilitator . . . , deciding ultimately on a single proposal from each meeting."

The direct democracy treatment used the same method for selecting the list of projects for the ballots but with a plebiscite to determine the project proposals. "Two paper ballots were prepared – one for the general project and one for the women's project. The ballots had a picture of each project along with a description of the project. . . . The voting cards also indicated the date of the election and the voting place." *Voting places were set up in each hamlet in the village (with some consolidation of nearby hamlets).* "When arriving at the voting place to vote, men received one ballot (for the general project) and women received two ballots (one for the general project, one for the women's project). The selected project (for both the general and women's project) was the proposal that received a plurality of votes in the respective vote."

Olken also conducted the two aforementioned surveys and collected data on the types of proposals selected by each treatment.

Results: *Olken found that the direct democracy treatment resulted in significantly higher satisfaction levels among villages, increased knowledge about the projects, greater perceived benefits, and higher reported willingness to contribute, compared to the meeting treatment. However, treatment had little effect on the actual projects chosen, with the exception that projects chosen by women in the direct democracy treatment tended to be located in poorer areas.*

Comments: *Olken faced some difficulties in making sure that the treatments were followed according to the experimental design. In East Java and Southeast Sulawesi, the set of projects was already fixed at the time the treatment assignment (whether the meeting or direct democracy treatment) was announced, but in North Sumatra the list of projects was selected after the treatment assignment was announced; thus, the list of projects may have been affected by the anticipated treatment. Furthermore, in Southeast Sulawesi, the treatment assigned to three villages was changed after the randomization to treatment was determined. Olken conducted robustness checks to be sure that the endogeneity of the project list did not affect the outcome and used the original treatment assignments as a measure of intent to treat (see Olken, p. 198, for a discussion).*

Olken also manipulated the methods used in the meetings to determine the winning proposed projects. He reported that these manipulations were not consequential and conducted robustness checks on the analysis, finding that they did not affect the overall results.

In our view, these benefits to subjects are best thought of as the same as therapeutic benefits in biomedical experiments in that they represent benefits subjects receive due to the treatment that alleviates a problem they face that is also the focus of the research. However, it is unclear to us whether anyone has successfully made the case to IRBs that these benefits to subjects from social science field experiments like Olken's are therapeutic benefits because IRBs, typically dominated by biomedical professionals, may narrowly define therapeutic benefits as only those that are related to health or psychological research.

Collateral Benefits. Collateral benefits are all the other benefits participants may gain from an experiment that do not relate to a personal problem he or she has that is also the focus of the experiment. These benefits can be of the following types: extrinsic financial or consumption goods, intrinsic altruistic feelings, and educational benefits.

Definition 12.3 (Collateral Benefits): *Collateral benefits are side-effect benefits to a subject from participating in research but are unrelated to the focus of the research.*

Extrinsic Goods and Intrinsic Feelings. In many experiments, subjects are compensated for participating, as explored in Chapter 10. In biomedical experiments, subjects may be offered money as well as free medical care and other inducements. In social science experiments, payments of some sort for participation are normal. Lau and Redlawsk paid some of their subjects in cash and for some others gave a contribution to a voluntary organization to which they belonged. In Example 8.5, Bahry and Wilson paid subjects in Russia sign-up fees, show-up fees, and payments based on their choices which, for the majority of the subjects, represented a week's wages. In Chapter 10 we discussed in detail why financial incentives may be used to motivate subjects in an experiment like Bahry and Wilson's using the ultimatum game.

Compensation received for participating in social science experiments may not be financial. In Example 2.1, Gerber, Kaplan, and Bergan provided subjects with free newspaper subscriptions; in Example 2.3, Clinton and Lapinski offered subjects free Internet connections for participating. In some political psychology experiments, student subjects may be offered extra credit in their classes for their participation. In experiments using functional magnetic resonance imaging (fMRI) equipment, it is normal to give subjects a "picture of their brain" as a thank you.

Beyond these selective private benefits that subjects receive for participating from the experimenter, subjects may also gain some intrinsic altruistic benefits for participating in an experiment and helping advance scientific knowledge. In some sense there is a logical difficulty in saying that someone receives a private benefit from altruism because, by definition, altruism refers to actions that solely help others; yet it is normal in social science circles to think of altruism as providing individuals with some intrinsic benefit in terms of feelings or warm glow effects. Subjects may also simply find participating in some experiments fun in the case of some of the computer interactive games (although many, of course, find them boring).

Educational Benefits and Debriefing. There is the possibility that subjects may gain knowledge from their participation in the experiment through the experience or the debriefing given by the researchers after the experiment. In particular, debriefings in some voting experiments can alert subjects to better ways to use information and make more informed voter choices. Lau and Redlawsk describe the debriefing they conducted as follows (Lau and Redlawsk, 2006, p. 295):

The experimenter explained some of the manipulations in the study, particularly those conditions the subject had not actually experienced, to illustrate the type of things we were interested in learning. Subjects were explicitly asked how realistic they thought the candidates were in the elections (the mean rating was midway between "Realistic" and "Extremely Realistic"), and whether they had remaining questions. We collected mailing addresses from subjects who desired a brief summary of the results after the experiment was completed, and paid those subjects who were working for themselves. Subjects were thanked profusely for their time (by now, approaching and often exceeding two hours) and effort, and sent on their way.

The benefits from such debriefing are hard to measure and likely to be fleeting as well. Some subjects may have been interested enough to pursue further knowledge of political science research and experimental work, but such a probability is small and whether they would have benefited themselves from such knowledge is debatable even among political scientists. Furthermore, knowledge provided to subjects through debriefing can also cause harm to subjects. For example, consider the subjects in Milgram's famous obedience experiment discussed earlier. Would the subjects benefit from or be harmed by learning the purpose of the experiment and what the experiment had shown about themselves? As the IRB Guidebook points out: "Some subjects may not benefit from being told that the research found them to be willing to inflict serious harm to others, have homosexual tendencies, or possess a borderline personality." We discuss some of the issues of debriefing when we discuss informed consent (see Section 12.2.2) and deception in social science experiments in the next chapter.

12.1.3 Expected Costs from Experimental Research

Expected Costs to Human Subjects from Experiments

As with expected benefits, expected costs from experimental research can be those borne by the human subjects directly and those that affect society in general. We first discuss expected costs to human subjects and then we discuss costs to society at large. As noted earlier, expected costs to human subjects from experiments captures the idea that what matters is the probability of harm times the magnitude of harm. The Common Rule uses "risks from an experiment" to mean this combination.[5] We can divide expected harms from experiments into three types:

1. physical harms,
2. psychological harms, and
3. social and economic harms.

Physical Harms. Many biomedical experiments can cause subjects minor to serious physical harm. Some political science experiments also have the possibility of causing physical harm. In Example 2.5, Mutz used skin conductors to measure subjects' reactions to political debates on videos. These conductors could have caused the subjects minor pain or an allergic reaction. Similarly, in Example 3.1, Spezio et al. used brain imaging equipment to measure the brain activity of subjects as subjects made judgments about candidates based on visual appearances. However, the equipment can be fatal for subjects who have cardiac pacemakers. It may also cause problems for subjects with rather ordinary metal implants such as permanent dentures or for subjects who are pregnant. Or consider Example 12.2 below, where the researchers expose some subjects to a nasal spray with a hormone to measure the hormone's effects on trusting behavior in a trust game experiment.[6] As political scientists increase their interest in the relationship between political behavior and biology, as some advocate (see Hibbing and Smith, 2007), the potential for physical harm in political science experiments can increase. Nevertheless, even with such an expansion, the possible physical harms from social science experiments are significantly less than those that can occur in biomedical experiments that may involve invasive medical procedures and drugs with unknown side effects.

Definition 12.4 (Physical Harms): *Physical harms are possible physical injuries that may be inflicted on subjects during an experiment.*

---

[5] As the IRB Guidebook relates, risks can simply refer to what someone is willing to do to achieve a goal and not harm independent of that goal. We may be willing to put up with considerable physical and mental harm in certain situations when achieving some goal demands that from us. In our analysis we mean those risks that are not goal specific. From the Guidebook: "Another confusion may arise because 'risks' can refer to two quite different things: (1) those chances that specific individuals are willing to undertake for some desired goal; or (2) the conditions that make a situation dangerous per se. The IRB is responsible for evaluating risk only in the second sense."

[6] The trust game is presented in Example 3.2.

Example 12.2 (Oxytocin and Trust Lab Experiment): *Kosfeld et al. (2005) report on an experiment on trust in which some subjects were administered a hormone that is argued to play a role in social attachment and affiliation.*

Target Population and Sample: The experimenters recruited 194 healthy male subjects from different universities in Zurich. The mean age was 22 with a standard deviation of 3.4 years. Of the total, 128 of the subjects participated in a trust experiment and 66 participated in a risk experiment. Subjects were excluded if they had significant medical or psychiatric illness, were on medication, smoked more than 15 cigarettes per day, or abused drugs or alcohol.

Subject Compensation: Subjects received a show-up fee of 80 Swiss francs and earned points during the experiment (as described later). Points were redeemed at a rate of 0.40 Swiss francs per point.

Environment: The experimental games were conducted by computer as in previously discussed political economy experiments (see Example 2.6) with the exception that, for part of the experiment, subjects interacted in a room without computers and seated around tables as described in the procedures.

Procedures: First, subjects' moods and calmness were assessed by means of a questionnaire. Then "[s]ubjects received a single intranasal does of 24 IU oxytocin (Syntocinon-Spray, Novartis; 3 puffs per nostril, each with 4 IU oxytocin) or placebo 50 minutes before the start of the trust or the risk experiment. Subjects were randomly assigned to the oxytocin or placebo group (double-blind, placebo-controlled study design). In order to avoid any subjective substance effects (for example, olfactory effects) other than those caused by oxytocin, the placebo contained all inactive ingredients except for the neuropeptide.

After substance administration, subjects completed questionnaires on a computer to measure demographic items and psychological characteristics. Owing to the crucial role of the social environment in triggering behavioural effects of oxytocin . . . , subjects were asked to wait in the rest area while the next part of the experiment was prepared. During this 5-min waiting period, subjects were seated at different tables. Subjects at the same table could talk to each other, but at the beginning of the experiment they were informed that they would not be interacting with those subjects who sat at the same table. When subjects re-entered the laboratory for both experiments, they received written instructions . . . explaining the payoff structure of the experiment and the private payment procedure at the end of the experiment. . . . After subjects had read the instructions in each experiment, we checked whether they understood the payoff structure by means of several hypothetical examples. All subjects (with one exception) answered the control questions correctly. . . . In addition, subjects received an oral summary of the instructions."

Subjects participated in either a trust game or risk game. Immediately before each game, subjects' mood and calmness were assessed again. For a review of the trust game, see Example 3.2. In this experiment the first mover received an initial endowment of 12 experimental points (called monetary units in the experiment) and could send 0, 4, 8, or 12 points to the second mover. The experimenter tripled the amount sent to the second mover and then the second mover could send any amount ranging between zero and the total amount he received back to the first mover. Each player played the same game in the same role four times, although in each game the players had different partners (randomly selected). Subjects who were first movers received no feedback about the second mover's decisions until the end of the experiment. After every decision, the first mover was asked about his belief with regard to the expected transfer he would receive back from the second mover.

In the risk game, all the subjects played a simple decision-theoretic game in which each subject received 12 experimental points and could invest 0, 4, 8, or 12 points in a risky investment that earned additional points with the same expected value as the payoffs received by the first movers in the trust game experiments.

Results: *The experimenters found that oxytocin increased the trust levels of first movers significantly. However, there was no effect of oxytocin on behavior of subjects in the risk game. Furthermore, oxytocin had no effect on the transfers from the second mover to the first. The comparison between the two games and two players suggests that oxytocin affects trusting behavior in social interactions and does not simply make individuals more willing to take risks generally or just more prosocial in their behavior.*

Comments: *Seven subjects in the trust experiment and five in the risk experiment were excluded because of incorrect substance administration. Four subjects were excluded from the trust experiment because they stated a disbelief that the opponent in the trust game was actually a human being. One subject did not answer the control questions correctly and was excluded from the data set (this subject also did not apply the substance correctly).*

Psychological Harms. More relevant to social science experiments are psychological and social and economic harms. According to the IRB Guidebook, psychological harms occur when an experiment causes "undesired changes in thought processes and emotion (e.g., episodes of depression, confusion, or hallucination from drugs, feelings of stress, guilt, and loss of self-esteem)." Many risks in political science experiments are psychological – a subject may experience regret or loss or embarrassment because of the choices he or she makes in the experiment. In Example 4.2, Lau and

Redlawsk had subjects make choices for which they had less than complete information and then gave them full information on their choices and asked them if they would change their choices given the full information. This may cause subjects some embarrassment to admit that they had made a mistake if they chose to change their choices. In Example 8.5, in which subjects made choices in ultimatum games in Russia, some subjects may have been angry with the choices provided to them by the first movers. Others may have found it psychologically stressful to have to decide whether to give money to a stranger or feel guilty or lose self-esteem if they chose not to give money to the stranger. In the Internet survey experiment conducted by Horiuchi, Imai, and Taniguchi in Japan (Example 5.3), subjects may have found answering the questions tedious or irritating or may have been uncomfortable providing their opinions. Certainly being asked to provide answers to questions in survey experiments they deem "sensitive" or "personal" may cause subjects stress and embarrassment.

Definition 12.5 (Psychological Harms): *Psychological harms are psychological costs borne by participants in an experiment.*

Subjects may face psychological harms if researchers invade their privacy (i.e., observe their behavior in a private setting without their permission), as in the Humphries study discussed in Chapter 11. Certainly, in experiments conducted in which subjects are not informed that they are participating in an experiment, as in Example 2.1, researchers are gaining information on subjects' choices that they may think of as private, such as their subscription to newspapers. The researchers may argue that the information was public information and easily found in public records, although this is not so clear because the information was provided by the newspaper and we do not know if subscribers had given the newspaper permission to share the names of its customers. Researchers who engage in experiments in which subjects are not aware that they are participating in an experiment have a special responsibility to consider the possible psychological harms such an invasion of privacy may cause the subjects.

Definition 12.6 (Invasion of Privacy): *When an experimenter learns private information about a subject without the subject's permission.*

Psychological harms can also occur when researchers violate confidentiality, which is when a researcher publicizes information that subjects have freely given the researcher under the assumption that the information would be kept private. For example, suppose that subjects are participating in a dictator game as in Example 8.5. The experimenters promise the subjects that their names, given when they sign up for the experiment, will not be revealed to the other subjects they are matched with in the experiment. If the experimenter violates that confidentiality and promise by revealing the names, the experimenter can cause the subjects psychological distress. Subjects can be upset even if there has not been an invasion of privacy but they believe there has been. For example, Michelson and Nickerson (forthcoming) reported that, when researchers told subjects that their voting turnout records would be revealed to their neighbors, some subjects were alarmed and contacted local law enforcement officials. Voting turnout records were public information in the jurisdiction and therefore not private, but from the perspective of the subjects the experiment had violated their privacy, causing them psychological harm.

Definition 12.7 (Violation of Confidentiality): *When an experimenter reveals private information freely given to him or her by a subject without the subject's permission.*

Social and Economic Harms. Invasions of privacy and violations of confidentiality can also cause social and economic harms to subjects. Humphries's revealing of the identities of the subjects he studied in his published works caused such harms to them. Similarly, in many laboratory experiments, university payment procedures require researchers to record subjects' social security numbers. Usually the experimenter promises the subjects that this information will be kept confidential. Potential economic harms can occur if the experimenter stores the subjects' data by social security number and shares the data publicly (as required by many journals for publication of results). Or consider a survey experiment in which subjects reveal political viewpoints on issues that are highly controversial. Public revelation of their views may cause the subjects social ostracism.

Definition 12.8 (Social and Economic Harms): *Social and economic harms occur when subjects face social ostracism or economic penalties as a consequence of their participation in an experiment.*

In Example 12.1, Olken varied the mechanism by which citizens in Indonesian villages decided on public projects. We already noted that this may have a therapeutic benefit for these citizens if it increases overall welfare for the community. However, the selection of the projects meant that there were winners and losers; some areas received new and improved public goods, while other areas did not. Theoretically, Olken expected that the mechanism manipulation could have a possible effect on which projects were chosen. Thus, the expectation was that, although there may be therapeutic benefits, there would be potential harms as well if some public goods were chosen that would not have been chosen in the absence of the experiment.

Some field experiments may result in subjects committing illegal acts and be subject to prosecution, causing serious social and economic harms to the subjects. In Example 12.3, Fried et al. (2010) hired confederates to commit traffic violations to determine if the police officers that stopped them would demand bribes and, if so, whether they were more likely to demand bribes from rich or poor drivers. If the officers were caught demanding bribes or accepting bribes, they potentially faced prosecution and possible loss of employment. Fried et al. note that between December 2000 and June 2006, 13% of Mexico City's police officers were arrested for committing a crime and in interviews report that officers said they took actions such as issuing warnings instead of tickets to wealthy offenders because they feared prosecution and jail because wealthy offenders could take actions against them, suggesting that the officers were worried about the possibility of prosecutions based on their choices. Fried et al.'s finding that officers were less likely to offer bribing opportunities to wealthy offenders reflected this fear of job loss and jail.

Example 12.3 (Bribery Field Experiment): *Fried et al. (2008) conducted a field experiment in Mexico City in which confederates, who either were dressed and acted "upper class" or "lower class," committed traffic violations to see whether police officers would ask for a bribe instead of giving a ticket.*

Target Population and Sample: The experiment focused on traffic officers in Mexico City. Fried et al. chose Mexico City because the income inequality is sizable and previous quantitative evidence suggests that police corruption is pervasive. The authors report that there were 42 interactions with police officers, with 27 interactions between police officers and upper class drivers and 15 interactions between police officers and lower class drivers. Presumably all of the traffic officers were male, although Fried, Lagunes, and Venkataramani did not explicitly state this information. The confederates were all male and around 30 years old.

Environment: The experiments took place at 12 intersections that the Fried et al. identified as "safe" (the criteria for safety is not explained) for making illegal left turns and as usually manned by traffic officers. The intersections were "on large, six lane roadways divided by a median" where there was a no-left-turn side or taking a left turn "involved going against traffic for a few yards." On these highways, if a driver chose to make an illegal left turn, he "had no option but to stop at the large median and wait for oncoming traffic to subside before he could continue." Fried et al. also note that "this particular infraction is highly visible – even more visible than a missing license plate or expired emissions sticker. Second, the police officer, generally on foot, has an excellent opportunity to intercept the driver while the driver is stopped at the median."

Procedures: *The upper and lower class confederates differed in physical appearance (Fried et al. report that they had phenotypic characteristics), choice of clothing, speaking patterns, and types of cars that were appropriate for their class designation. "All confederates followed the same protocol when interacting with police officers. When confronted by a traffic officer, the drivers stated that they did not know that the left turn they had made was illegal. This allowed police officers to set the terms of each encounter and freely choose to write a ticket, give a warning, or ask for a bribe." Although there was a script for drivers' responses, drivers were also given leeway to sound natural.*

Drivers visited the intersections in the morning and in the afternoon, since shift changes took place early in the afternoon. "The confederates drove to each intersection according to a predetermined, random assigned ordering. If in the afternoon run a driver observed that a police officer with whom an encounter had already occurred was still present, then that intersection was skipped. The details of the encounter were recorded immediately."

Results: *First, the traffic officers "never explicitly asked for money, but instead said something along the lines of 'We can solve this the easy way,' or 'Together we can fix this.' Second, not a single ticket was written for the violations. Police officers either did not stop the driver, requested a bribe, or issued a warning. Third, the authors find that the police officers did not distinguish between rich and poor drivers when choosing whether to stop the car, but were more likely to demand a bribe from lower class drivers.*

Comments: *Fried et al. did not relate whether any of the police officers interacted with both an upper and a lower class driver, although they are clear that each driver interacted with a particular police officer only once. Fried et al. also did not report how many confederates of each type were hired and if confederates of the same type interacted with the same police officer. Thus, it is unclear how many interactions are independent observations from the report. Furthermore, it is unclear whether the confederates used their own clothes,* *cars, and speaking patterns or were "acting," and how much confederates were monitored by the researchers during the experiment.*

Fried et al. investigated two other traffic violations – driving without a license plate and driving while talking on mobile phones – but found little evidence that traffic officers enforced these violations in comparison to illegal left turns. Finally, Fried et al. interviewed 10 police officers, 7 of whom were traffic police and 3 of whom had different duties, in an effort to determine why officers may be more likely to demand bribes from lower class drivers. Fried et al. suggested that the discrimination arises because the officers fear that they are more likely to be caught if they ask for a bribe from wealthy drivers and that wealthy drivers are more likely to use their influence to avoid traffic fines.

Finally, subjects incur economic opportunity costs from participating in an experiment. That is, in almost any experiment, subjects spend time completing experimental tasks. This time could be spent working in a job, doing course work for students, or in personal leisure. Some subjects may also have the additional financial cost of coming to an experimental laboratory.

Wealth Effects from Collateral Benefits and Harms to Subjects. In Example 8.5, the payments Bahry and Wilson offered subjects could cause a "wealth effect" from the experiment, which could be seen as a harm to subjects. The wealth effect is when an individual receives a large sum of money and as a result increases his or her spending or otherwise modifies his or her behavior. Researchers have not systematically studied this effect, because funding agencies in the United States rarely fund research that rewards subjects a "substantially large" sum of money. Depending on which country is selected to be studied, it is often possible to pay subjects in U.S. currency where the value of the dollar is overvalued. For example, $20 in U.S. currency is worth $200 in a foreign country's currency. For researchers, this scenario is attractive because it allows them to overcome the criticism that the behavior of subjects does not adhere to the dictates of various behavioral models because the payments they receive are not high enough. But running an experiment in a country that overvalues the "American" dollar allows a researcher to skirt this criticism. To illustrate how overvalued currency can translate into high subject payments, Kachelmeier and Shehata (1992) conducted field experiments about risk aversion in China in which a 25-round experiment was conducted where the top prize of 10 yuan could be earned in each round. The authors note that the average salary of the subjects was

60 yuan a month (or $15). Kachelmeier and Shehata, in explaining their currency exchange rate, commented (1992, p. 1123):

Government-subsidized living accommodations cost only 3–5 yuan per month, but monthly food expenditures could easily run over 50 yuan. This left subjects with essentially no savings and no monthly net income after food costs. In the course of a two-hour experiment, group-I subjects accumulated about 180 yuan, on average, or about three times their total monthly revenue. Subject reactions convinced us that they viewed 10-yuan prizes as very large, much as a student subject in the United States might view a series of lotteries for real $100 prizes.

Robert Slonim and Alvin E. Roth (1998) reported on another experiment that was conducted in the Slovak Republic in 1994, which examined an ultimatum bargaining game with very high stakes. They note (p. 570):

The stakes were varied by a factor of 25, from 60 Slovak Crowns (Sk) to 1500, with an intermediate stakes condition of 300 Sk. The smallest stakes condition (60 Sk) was chosen because it is similar to the experimental rewards per hour subjects get in experiments run in the U.S., where the stakes are often between 2 and 3 hours of wages. Subjects in the 60, 300, and 1500 sessions were bargaining over approximately 2.5, 12.5, and 62.5 hours of wages, respectively. The average monthly wage rate in the Slovak Republic at the time of the experiment was 5500 Sk.

The worry is that, when tangible stakes are at the table, the behavior of subjects after the experiment ends may be altered. Subjects may go into a spending frenzy and make unwise choices if they are unused to having large sums of money, or if they missed out on the "jackpot" they may experience depression.

Expected Costs to Nonsubjects

Some of the risks in an experiment are borne by others who are not subjects. We identify two types of risks to nonsubjects:

1. harms to confederates and researchers and
2. harms to third parties or societal risks.

Harms to Confederates. Some laboratory experiments use confederates, who are individuals who participate in the experiment but who are part of the treatments administered to subjects. Such individuals do not generally make choices, but they behave according to a script given to them by the researcher. In some cases the role of confederate is innocuous. In Example 2.6, Battaglini, Morton, and Palfrey selected one individual originally recruited as a subject to serve as a monitor and who helped with the randomization procedure used to determine the true state of the world in a voting game. All the subjects in the experiment knew that the individual was playing this role and would be paid a fixed amount for doing so. In other cases, subjects do not know that one of the participants is a confederate. In Milgram's famous obedience experiment, discussed in Chapter 11, research assistants were used as confederates to pretend to be getting electric shocks administered by the subjects. In Example 12.3, Fried, Lagunes, and Venkataramani used confederates who engaged in traffic crimes to see if police officers would ticket them or demand a bribe.

Definition 12.9 (Confederates): *Individuals who participate in an experiment not as subjects but as part of the experimental treatment administered to subjects. Confederates generally have no choices to make in the experiment but behave according to a script provided to them by the researcher.*

Confederates face risks as well. A confederate who is told to pretend to do something they would not normally do may face psychological harms. In Fried, Lagunes, and Venkataramani's experiment, confederates faced the potential of physical harm because they were asked to commit traffic violations (illegal left turns) that presumably were illegal because they could cause an accident. In our view, although the stated subjects of the experiments were the police officers, the researchers have an ethical responsibility to all humans who participated in the research, and the risks to confederates should also be considered.

Harms to Third Parties. All experiments potentially cause risks for individuals who are neither subjects nor confederates, but are nevertheless affected by the experiment, which we call third parties. Certainly there can be long-term societal costs from the knowledge gained in research in terms of future public policy that is difficult to foresee or other unexpected negative effects, which affect society and many third parties as we explained earlier with respect to societal benefits. But such costs can also be more specific and identifiable. For example, a laboratory experiment that negatively affects a subject's health or psychological well-being also affects his or her family and colleagues. Example 12.3 caused risks for third parties as well in that the families of the police officers would have suffered if the officers who were bribed had been caught, and the traffic offenses committed by the confederates could have potentially led to accidents, injuring other drivers and pedestrians.

Definition 12.10 (Third Parties): *Individuals who are affected by an experiment but are not subjects, researchers, or confederates of researchers.*

Field experiments in political science can be particularly consequential for third parties because they often involve the intervention into events such as elections that affect potentially many individuals. For example, researchers who conduct field experiments that study voter turnout in elections often vary turnout mechanisms, such as giving more information to some voters than to others or calling one group of voters to remind them to vote and not another group.[7] In Example 2.1, Gerber, Karlan, and Bergan provided voters with free newspapers that they expected would affect how subjects in the experiments would vote in an upcoming election.

The treatments may inadvertently alter election outcomes. It may be argued that only a small number of voters would have their behavior altered and that any increase or decrease in turnout as a result of the experiment would not change the election outcome. However, elections can be "very" close as we have witnessed recently (the U.S. 2000 presidential election and the 2008 Minnesota senatorial election are just two examples) and a field experiment intervention would have the potential to dictate the outcome. How could this happen? We expect theoretically that information can affect voters' preferences over candidates and parties as well as their willingness to turn out. Moreover, the effect can be differential, depending on voters' cognitive abilities, prior information, education, and wealth. If, for example, the manipulation has a greater effect on voters who have particular characteristics and induces them to vote differently or more often than they would normally, then the experiment may affect the distribution of voters in the election and consequently the outcome of the election.

12.1.4 IRB Assessment of Benefits and Risks

Rules About Types of Research to Be Reviewed
After assessing expected benefits and harms, the determination of whether an experiment is ethical depends on whether the expected benefits from the research outweigh the expected harms. If the expected benefits outweigh the expected harms, then, according to this approach, the research is ethical. Essentially this evaluation is what IRBs are supposed to do. According to

---

[7] For examples see Gosnell (1927); Gerber and Green (2000); and Gerber et al. (2003).

the IRB Guidebook, "Evaluation of the risk/benefit ratio is the major ethical judgment that IRBs must make in reviewing research proposals."

How is the evaluation accomplished? It would be nice if there were some hard and fast rules that would make such evaluations easy. A few such rules exist. For example, the Common Rule designates that some research is exempt from the evaluation, as noted in Chapter 11. It is our interpretation that survey experiments in which subjects' identities are kept confidential are largely exempt because such surveys are generally exempt. Although surveys certainly have the potential to cause psychological harm, as discussed earlier, we believe that in general these risks are not significant enough to outweigh the benefits that can be gained from the research.

Two other guidelines have been established by the Common Rule or OHRP that govern which types of benefits and risks can be counted. Specifically, IRBs are told not to consider collateral benefits or long-term societal risks. We address the rationale for each of these rules, beginning with a discussion of the merits of counting third-party harms in general, of which long-term societal risks are one type.

Rules that Exclude Benefits or Risks

On Third-Party and Confederate Harms. The uncertainty inherent in estimating and valuing future societal risks is acknowledged in the Common Rule in that IRBs are told not to attempt to anticipate much in terms of long-term risks. Specifically, the Common Rule in 45 CFR 46.111 states that IRBs "should not consider possible long-range effects of applying knowledge gained in the research (for example, the possible effects of the research on public policy) as among those research risks that fall within the purview of its responsibility." We agree with the view that IRBs should not consider these long-term societal risks. We take the position that ultimately greater knowledge is our goal and, although it is possible that this greater knowledge may make society worse off in some cases or instances, we maintain the belief that the ultimate good of greater knowledge outweighs these negative possibilities.

Although societal risks are not to be counted, it is unclear whether the Common Rule or IRBs are expected to consider other third-party harms, particular if they involve affecting real-world events such as elections. It is our view that other third-party harms should be evaluated. We believe these third-party harms are indirect harms from the experiment and that to be ethical a researcher should take a broad view of the potential harms that can occur as a consequence of his or her research. The Belmont Report's definition of unethical injustice is that "[a]n injustice occurs when some benefit to which a person is entitled is denied without good reason or when some burden is imposed unduly." We think that an intervention of a random controlled experiment that biases an election qualifies as denial of a benefit to a political candidate who would have won the election if it had not been for the intervention and a significant harm to a third party.

That said, most other potential harms to third parties are likely to be minor if the risks to the subjects are minor. That is, if a laboratory experiment has a small risk of affecting a subject's health, then it also has a minimal risk of affecting that subject's family and colleagues as a consequence. Even so, such third-party harms, in our opinion, should be considered in IRB evaluations.

Finally, the Common Rule and OHRP are silent when it comes to the possible harms to confederates. We suspect the silence stems from the fact that the use of confederates in experiments is not normal in biomedical experiments and if they are used in social science laboratory experiments, they face few potential harms. However, as field experiments increase in social science, we expect that more and more researchers will use confederates, as in Example 12.3, and the potential harms they are confronted with will increase. We believe that when confederates are recruited specifically to participate in an experiment, even though they are not the subjects of the experiment, the possible harms that may be inflicted on them as a consequence of their participation should be considered in the risk assessment of the research.

On Collateral Benefits. According to the Common Rule, collateral benefits, in contrast to therapeutic benefits, do not count toward the benefit–cost analysis of the research and societal risks. The IRB Guidebook states:

Direct payments or other forms of remuneration offered to potential subjects as an incentive or reward for participation should not be considered a "benefit" to be gained from research.... Although participation in research may be a personally rewarding activity or a humanitarian contribution, these subjective benefits should not enter into the IRB's analysis of benefits and risks.

What is the justification for the position that these benefits do not count? It appears that the reason for not counting such compensation, whether extrinsic or intrinsic, is to avoid approving research that uses compensation as an undue influence to circumvent voluntary participation in an especially risky experiment. Suppose that compensation is sizable and expected costs are sizable as well. If compensation is used in benefit–cost comparisons, then the research may be undertaken even when the other expected benefits (therapeutic and societal) are much smaller than the expected costs to the subjects. Essentially, the view is that such research, which does not provide enough expected therapeutic or societal benefit to offset the expected costs to the subjects, should not be undertaken, even if subjects are compensated sufficiently to offset these expected costs.

If we think of participation as purely voluntarily, then if subjects are willing to accept payments to participate or altruistically desire to participate, and these payments or altruistic feelings are sufficient to offset the difference between the expected costs to the subjects and the therapeutic and societal benefits, why should that experiment be unethical? This is an issue that has been oft debated in the ethics of biomedical research, particularly research involving terminally ill patients.[8] When the experiment has no expected social value or benefit, it seems fairly simple that conducting the research is not ethical because the researcher is basically paying subjects to participate in a costly activity without any demonstrable social value. This would not be research in our view.

But what about experiments that do have some social value albeit not sufficient to offset the expected costs to subjects of the research? Given the inherent difficulty in measuring societal benefits mentioned in Section 12.1.2, it may be the case that the estimated social value is insufficient for justifying the research for experiments in which the costs are greater than minimal. In this case, what is the problem with counting the compensation to subjects as a benefit given that therapeutic benefits to subjects in biomedical experiments are counted? First, the comparison is not accurate. Expected social benefits are typically positively related to the expected therapeutic benefits to subjects and, as a consequence, because the social benefits by definition involve effects on a larger group of individuals, greater than those received directly by subjects. Thus, it is unlikely that human subjects could expect to receive therapeutic benefits that would be greater than the social benefits and the issue does not arise for therapeutic benefits. In contrast, it is possible for the compensation of subjects to be larger than the expected social benefits of the research, making compensatory benefits distinctive.

Second, if compensatory benefits are counted as offsetting expected costs, the fear is that subjects offered compensation to participate may not be "real"

---

[8] See for example Nycum and Reid's (2008) discussion of the ethics of "gene transfer research for glioblastoma multiforme, a malignant and rapidly progressing brain tumor with a median survival from time of diagnosis with best treament – surgery, radiotherapy and chemotherapy – of 8–12 months."

volunteers. That is, the presumption is that, if the expected social benefits alone do not mitigate the expected costs to the subjects when there are no therapeutic benefits, then the compensation must be sizable and can cause subjects to be unduly influenced to either act irrationally and ignore their own peril, or act super-rationally and circumvent the experiment to receive the compensation. Consider the statement in the IRB Guidebook on compensation:

Undue inducements may be troublesome because: (1) offers that are too attractive may blind prospective subjects to the risks or impair their ability to exercise proper judgment; and (2) they may prompt subjects to lie or conceal information that, if known, would disqualify them from enrolling or continuing as participants in the research project.

Such a statement suggests that IRBs should not allow any sizable compensation for subjects to participate in research. IRBs may also worry about the harms of wealth effects, discussed in Section 12.1.3. However, as the Guidebook notes later in the same section, deciding what is a too sizable an inducement is difficult. Moreover, the Guidebook remarks that many IRB members argue "that normal healthy volunteers are able to exercise free choice, and that, since judging the acceptability of risk and weighing the benefits is a personal matter, IRBs should refrain from imposing their own views on potential subjects. On this view, IRB responsibility should be confined to ensuring that consent is properly informed." Because there is disagreement over the issue, the Guidebook recommends that decisions on whether compensations provided to subjects, either monetary or nonmonetary, are problematic are left to individual IRBs to decide on a case-by-case basis.[9] It seems to us that the two positions on how to view compensation to subjects are inconsistent. If decisions on the size of compensation should be made on a case-by-case basis, then deciding how to evaluate compensation to subjects as expected benefits should also be decided on a case-by-case basis.

Rules on Assessing Benefits and Risks that Count
Calculating Societal Benefits and Design Questions. With the exceptions of long-term societal risks and collateral benefits, the presumption is that IRBs will consider all other harms and benefits in making their assessment of the research. Given that collateral benefits are not counted and that in most social science experiments therapeutic benefits are rare, the

---

[9] We address the issue of sizable compensation again in our discussion of special subjects and informed consent later in this chapter.

principal benefits to be evaluated are societal benefits from the research. The IRB Guidebook states that IRBs "should assure that the . . . knowledge researchers expect to gain" is clearly identified. Making sure that these knowledge benefits are clear involves evaluating the research design and the expected validity (both internal and external; see Chapter 7) of the research. If the design is fundamentally flawed, then the research cannot add to our scientific knowledge. But how much should IRBs evaluate research design and what does that mean for what we can learn? The federal regulations are not clear because, as the Guidebook notes, they "do not clearly call for IRB review of the scientific validity of the research design. Nevertheless, the regulations do require that IRBs determine whether '[r]isks to subjects are reasonable in relation to . . . the importance of the knowledge that may reasonably be expected to result.'"

What then are IRBs supposed to do? The Guidebook states that most IRBs use the following strategy: If the research is funded by an agency that engages in peer review, then the IRB assumes that the agency has undertaken a rigorous review of the science and that the science does have the societal benefits claimed by the researcher. However, if the proposed human subjects research has not undergone such an external peer review, the IRB itself reviews "the research design with much more care, perhaps with the assistance of consultants, if the IRB itself does not possess sufficient expertise to perform such a review." It is interesting that the Guidebook presents this as what IRBs do, rather than a recommendation about what they should do, leaving it up to individual IRBs to deal with the conundrum. We only have anecdotal evidence of how IRBs review societal benefits from research because no comprehensive study of the substantive nature of IRB decision making has been conducted to our knowledge.[10]

The fact that IRBs see it as their responsibility to evaluate research design and the societal benefits of research in a number of cases has led to some of the criticisms of IRBs by humanities and social science scholars. In particular, researchers have complained that IRBs use a model for proper research design that is inappropriate for qualitative research, as in Yanow and Schwartz-Shea's (2008) article in the symposium on IRBs in *PS: Political Science and Politics.* Yanow and Schwartz-Shea suggest that survey research and experimental work in political science find IRB procedures less

---

[10] There have been surveys of IRB membership and workload. The most comprehensive recent such survey of which we are aware is by Catania et al. (2008), which was published in the new *Journal of Empirical Research on Human Research Ethics.* This new journal, which began publication in 2006, promises to be a good source for researchers interested in empirical evidence on ethical issues in experimental research.

problematic because they see less of a disconnect between the research designs used by political scientists in these areas and biomedical experimental procedures than there is between the approaches used by qualitative researchers and biomedical research. We agree that they are correct in that there are more commonalities between experimentalists in social science and those in the biomedical field. That said, there are many cases where social science experiments are distinct from those typical in biomedical research. As a result, social science experimentalists sometimes face difficulties in justifying their research designs with IRBs dominated by biomedical researchers as well. Many of these hurdles result because the norms of informed consent, anonymity, and voluntaryism fit well within standard research designs for most biomedical experiments but in many cases do not fit well within the standard research designs for social science experiments, as we discuss later in this chapter.[11]

Defining Minimal Risk

Probability and Magnitude of Harm. One of the issues for IRB assessment of risks is to determine when the risks are minimal. As noted in Chapter 11, one of the requirements for expedited review by IRBs is that only minimal risks exist in the research. The implication is that if risks can be shown to be minimal, then the research has merit even if the benefits from the research are minimal as well. Given the fact that few social science experiments have therapeutic benefits and that there are difficulties in assessing societal benefits, assessing whether the risks of the experiments are minimal becomes more important for social scientists, probably more so than for biomedical experiments with possible therapeutic benefits.

Recall that "minimal risk means that the probability and magnitude of harm or discomfort anticipated in the research are not greater in and of themselves than those ordinarily encountered in daily life or during the performance of routine physical or psychological examinations or tests." This one sentence has a lot of content. Two aspects of the definition in particular merit explanation: (1) the relationship between probability and magnitude of harm and (2) the standards for comparison.

A researcher needs to distinguish between the probability of harm or discomfort and the magnitude of harm or discomfort. Both of these aspects of the research require evaluation. For example, an experiment may have

---

[11] The lack of fit between biomedical research concepts of informed consent, anonymity, and voluntaryism and research designs standardly used in qualitative research is also a source of the problems for such research designs as well.

an extremely low probability of harm but the magnitude of that harm could be sizable or the experiment may have a high probability of harm but the possible magnitude is extremely low. Consider, for example, the fMRI experiments in Example 3.1. The probability that a subject will be harmed by having a heart pacemaker on during the experiment is extremely small when the researchers screen subjects in advance for the device, but, if it does happen, the subject could die from the experience. Thus, the probability of this particular harm with screening is small but the potential harm itself is large. But even in an experiment as in Example 2.6, where Battaglini, Morton, and Palfrey had subjects participate in a series of voting games, there is a low probability that a subject may experience a sudden cardiac arrest because of an underlying heart condition unknown to the experimenter. Rare harmful events can certainly take place during any experiment.

Alternatively, in Example 2.3, Clinton and Lapinski show ads to subjects via the Internet in an Internet survey experiment. One of the potential harms is the opportunity cost to the subjects of spending the time watching the ads and responding to the questions. The probability of this harm is high, although it varies with subjects (some subjects may prefer to spend their time this way, but let's assume that most would rather do something else, either on or off the Internet), but the harm itself is likely small. Clearly then, all experiments have almost 100% probability of harm in terms of these opportunity costs.

Standards for Comparison. Given that expected risk is always positive – that there is always at least a small probability of a sizable harm occurring to subjects during an experiment and a near 100% probability of minor harms to the subjects – what does it mean for risk to be minimized? How low is minimal? What matters then is the standard for comparison. The Common Rule offers three alternative standards for comparison:

1. daily life,
2. the performance of routine physical examinations or tests, and
3. the performance of routine psychological examinations or tests.

We consider these standards in reverse order. The third standard is likely relevant for most laboratory experiments that do not involve biomedical equipment or procedures and do resemble routine psychological examinations or tests. Using this standard, many laboratory experiments conducted by political scientists are designated by the OHRP as eligible for expedited review according to category 7 in Appendix C in Chapter 11.

The second standard is typically used as a measure of minimal risks for biomedical experiments. But this criterion can also be relevant to political science experiments that measure biological responses, as in the fMRI experiments in Example 3.1. In Example 2.5, Mutz not only had subjects watch videos but also used skin conductors to measure their reactions to the videos. Thus, the appropriate standard for establishing minimal risk with respect to Mutz's use of the skin conductors is whether the experience of a subject having the skin conductors attached was similar to a routine physical examination or test in terms of probability and magnitude of harm or discomfort. If we consult the list of types of research that the OHRP allows for expedited review, presented in Appendix C in Chapter 11, we see that such experiments are eligible under categories 1–4.

Finally, the first standard, daily life, is most applicable to political science field experiments. A field experiment, then, would provide a subject with minimal risk if the experiment had an equivalent probability and magnitude of harm to the subject as events in his or her daily life. Consider Example 2.1, where Gerber, Kaplan, and Bergan randomly provided households in the Washington, D.C., area with free temporary newspaper subscriptions. Obviously, this experience would be no different from what the recipients could experience in their daily lives, as often newspapers and magazines offer temporary free subscriptions to induce future subscriptions. Or consider Example 2.2, where Wantchekon induced political candidates to vary their messages in Benin elections. The messages that the voters (subjects) heard, although manipulated by the experimenter, were no different from messages that were ordinarily heard in other political campaigns in Benin and were delivered willingly by actual candidates. Thus, by the standard of daily life, it would appear that the probability of harm or discomfort experienced by the subjects would be no different from their normal daily experiences.[12]

What about the risks to subjects in Example 12.3 in which the experimental design by Fried, Lagunes, and Venkataramani gave subjects the opportunity to commit illegal acts (accept bribes from the researcher's confederates)? As noted earlier, the risk to subjects of accepting bribes is a

---

[12] Of course both of these experiments (see Section 12.1.3) have potential harms to third parties in that they may affect the elections in which they are embedded. For these experiments to be deemed to have minimal risks, we argue that these potential harms to third parties should also be compared to their potential in daily life. That is, for these field experiments to have minimal risks, we believe that the probabilities that they would affect the outcomes of the elections in which they occurred and possibly harm third parties should be equivalent to other possible events that may occur during an election that could affect the outcome of the election. Making such an assessment can be difficult.

serious risk with significant potential social and economic harm. One viewpoint might be that in Mexico City corruption is widespread and the fact that many police officers have been arrested in the past for crimes suggests that the acts they engaged in were part of their normal daily life. Moreover, the design of the experiment in which confederates were supposed to read a script in which they never offered a bribe, but instead the officer had to ask for one for a bribe to occur, was not a case where the confederate was purposely inducing the officer to commit a criminal act (i.e., not entrapment) and thus less problematic.[13]

An alternative perspective is that the experiment put officers more at risk than they are in daily life in that the confederates committed the crimes in situations in which it is unlikely that many such crimes may have occurred in daily life. That is, the confederates acted in full view of police officers, and committed a crime in which they could easily be caught by the officers, which one could argue is not a normal occurrence. Also, in daily life it may be less likely that lower class and poor individuals would commit such crimes because the relative cost of doing so is higher for them than for wealthy individuals. Since Fried, Lagunes, and Venkataramani found that officers were more likely to ask for bribes from these confederates, experimentally having confederates who appeared low class and poor commit the crimes may have led officers to demand more bribes than would have occurred in their normal daily life. A similar point can be made about the consequences of all random assignment mechanisms in field experiments as having a disconnect with daily life when subjects are exposed to treatments that would occur in daily life, but rarely. For example, although the campaign messages subjects heard in Wantchekon's experiment were like those heard in nonexperimental political campaigns, the distribution of the messages was purposely manipulated and thus subjects likely heard a different distribution of messages than they would normally have heard.

What is the appropriate standard for daily life, then, in a field experiment? Is it whether an event occurs in daily life or whether it occurs frequently and under the same conditions as in the experiment? Obviously the second comparison will always lead to the conclusion that experimental research has greater than minimal risks because if the event occurred in daily life under the same conditions as in the experiment, there would be no point to

---

[13] However, one could argue that entrapment is also something that police officers could face in daily life, because it used as a mechanism of law enforcement and oftentimes to catch corrupt government officials.

conducting the experiment. Such a standard would mean that virtually all field experiments would exceed minimal risks and not be eligible for expedited review, although it would not mean that the experiments themselves are unethical, as we discuss later in this chapter.

In the comparisons just made, we used what is called a "relative standard" – comparing the subjects to the same specific proportion of individuals outside of the research. Sometimes, the comparison is made using a "uniform standard," that is, comparing the subjects to a population of "normal" healthy individuals. Why is this important? It may be that the use of a relative standard takes unfair advantage of a population of subjects who are already vulnerable in some fashion. For example, imagine an experiment that is the reverse of the Fried, Lagunes, and Venkataramani bribery experiment, and confederates are used to pose as police officers in Mexico City who then demand bribes from randomly selected traffic violators who are visibly poor or lower class. It may be the case that it is normal for these subjects to be asked for bribes in this fashion in Mexico City; however, as the Fried, Lagunes, and Venkataramani results suggest, it is not so normal for higher class subjects to experience such demands nor is it normal in other countries. Whether the risks are evaluated in comparison to a relative standard (poor, low class individuals) or uniform standard (all individuals) affects how we think of the potential harms from this hypothetical experiment.

Minimizing More than Minimal Risks. Suppose an experiment has more than minimal risks. As part of the assessment of risks, IRBs are expected to make sure that risks are minimized. How can researchers minimize risks? Certainly doing so is more art than science. There are some obvious ways to minimize physical harms. In experiments that involve the use of biomedical equipment as in the fMRI experiments in Example 3.1, researchers can minimize physical risks by screening subjects for medical devices that could interfere with the fMRI equipment. Similarly, in Example 12.2, where experimenters exposed subjects to oxytocin to consider its effects on trust, the researchers screened subjects for prior health conditions that could be affected by the hormone administration. Note that the presumption in making these types of experiments eligible for expedited review is that they will be conducted in this fashion, minimizing the risks faced by subjects.

Minimizing psychological harms is not as easy for social scientists, particularly if the point of the research is to explore psychological responses that may be unpleasant for subjects. In Example 2.5, Mutz exposes subjects to in-your-face television videos to measure the psychological responses that subjects have to such situations, which we posit may lead them to form negative opinions. Similarly, the purpose of Oxley et al.'s (2008) experiment was to confront subjects with sudden noises and threatening visual images to measure the relationship between subjects' physiological responses to these manipulations and their political attitudes on a number of issues. The experimental design calls for making the subjects uncomfortable and unhappy. Minimizing the response would defeat the purpose of the experiment.

What about minimizing social and economic harms? The principal mechanism by which most social and economic harms are minimized in experimental research is through maintaining confidentiality of the identity of the subjects and storing the data by experiment-specific subject identification numbers that are not associated with names or other sensitive identification measures such as social security numbers.

But as with psychological harms, some social and economic harms often cannot be minimized without making the research less valid. In the bribery experiment in Example 12.3, the point of the research on bribery is to study corruption and the effects it has on citizens. The social and economic harms occur because in order to examine corruption the researchers need a situation where an individual has the potential to commit a corrupt act. Certainly the researchers could have used a more serious crime as their manipulation as a stronger test of corruption with greater potential social and economic harms to the subjects (i.e., the confederates could have engaged in the sale of illegal drugs), so in one sense the researchers have chosen what some may argue is an extremely low-level offense. Are there ways that the social and economic harms to the subjects in the experiment could have been further minimized while maintaining the research design? It is difficult to conceive of an alternative crime that the confederates could have committed that had lower potential for social and economic harm for the subjects.[14]

What about harms to third parties in field experiments? Of particular relevance are social science field experiments that may alter the outcome of events such as elections that can affect many beyond the subjects in the experiment and in some cases (candidates, parties) have substantial effects. Recall that Wantchekon's field experiments in Benin, in Example 2.2, are

---

[14] The authors did consider two alternative traffic crimes – driving without a license plate and talking on a cell phone while driving – but chose not to use these treatments because the confederates were never stopped by traffic officers. Driving without a license plate would have minimized the physical harm to confederates and third parties.

a case where the outcome of an election could have been affected by the research. Wantchekon (2003, p. 405) discussed how he minimized the third-party effects of his experiment:

[T]he distribution of votes in previous elections was such that the risks of a field experiment seriously affecting the outcome of the 2001 election was nonexistent. This is because (1) the nationwide election outcomes have always revealed a significant gap between the top two candidates (Kerekou and Soglo) and the remaining candidates and (2) electoral support for those top two candidates has always been between 27 and 37 percent. As a result, a second round election opposing Kerekou and Soglo in the 2001 presidential elections was a near certainty. This together with the fact that the experiment took place mostly in the candidates' stronghold means the experiment is not risk for the parties.

Hence, while his experiment could have resulted in an effect on the election outcome, Wantchekon's careful accounting of the political environment and the calculation for bias helped to minimize the risk that such an event would happen. Wantchekon's discussion of the possible effects from his intervention is unfortunately an exception as many of the researchers who are conducting field experiments do not address these potential harms for third parties or how they could minimize them. We believe that there should be a greater recognition of these harms and greater efforts made to minimize them when possible, although we understand that, at some point, reducing these harms further would lead to research that would no longer be worthwhile and at that point, the decision must be made whether the benefits from the research merit the harms that are imposed on not only the participants but also third parties.

12.2 Other Criteria in the Common Rule

12.2.1 Subject Selection

Vulnerable Subjects and IRB Review
Determining whether benefits merit risks and that risks are minimized are criteria that must be satisfied for IRBs to approve human subjects research according to the Common Rule. But the Common Rule also lists additional criteria in 45 CFR 46.111 (see Appendix A, Chapter 11) that must also be satisfied. The Common Rule requires that IRBs make sure that the selection of subjects is equitable, informed consent is sought and documented except under certain exceptions, and the data are monitored and kept confidential. Most of these requirements stem from perceived unethical biomedical experiments in the past. How relevant are they to social science experiments?

We explore first the selection of subjects. Many of the infamous experiments that have led to regulation by governments were conducted using populations of subjects who are seen as especially vulnerable and, as a consequence, the Common Rule states in 45 CFR 46.111(b) that IRBs must ensure that "[w]hen some or all of the subjects are likely to be vulnerable to coercion or undue influence, such as children, prisoners, pregnant women, mentally disabled persons, or economically or educationally disadvantaged persons, additional safeguards have been included in the study to protect the rights and welfare of these subjects." Moreover, the Common Rule has three separate parts with particular rules for pregnant women and fetuses, prisoners, and children (see Subparts B, C, and D). Of particular interest to political scientists, the National Science Foundation (NSF) has not adopted Subparts B, C, and D and thus presumably these additional regulations on human subjects research with pregnant women, prisoners, and children do not apply to research funded by the NSF, although 45 CFR 46.111(b) does apply to NSF-funded research. Although the NSF has not adopted these subparts, IRBs may use procedures in these subparts for all research that qualifies regardless of funding, so political scientists, even if receiving just NSF funding or no outside funding, could be affected.

What does this mean for social science experiments using these types of subjects? There are three primary implications. First, if research involves a subject population that is considered "not normal" – because the subjects are cognitively impaired, have serious illnesses, are elderly or aged, or are disadvantaged in some way – IRBs are expected to give the research special scrutiny to be sure that the subjects are protected. What this means in practice is that research is permitted with such groups when (1) there is a research reason for choosing the population (i.e., the population is not chosen simply for convenience, but because using the population is essential to investigate the research question) and (2) the research has minimal risks. If the research has more than minimal risks, it should have some therapeutic benefit for the population. Research with more than minimal risks and no therapeutic benefit for the subjects may be permitted, but only if the research is of vital importance for understanding or eventually alleviating the subjects' disorder or condition.

Second, surveys, and by extension survey experiments, are not exempt from IRB review if they involve children, prisoners, or pregnant women under Subparts B, C, and D. The restriction on surveys with pregnant women is probably a surprise to some readers; many political science survey experiments likely have respondents who are pregnant, but the researcher has no way of knowing if that is the case. Presumably, the restriction is for survey experiments where the focus is on pregnant women and only pregnant women are surveyed and, because this does not apply to NSF-funded grants, it is not a large concern for many political scientists. Although surveys are not exempt for these populations when Subparts B, C, and D apply, if they have minimal risks, they are likely to be approved.

Third, IRBs can approve research for federal funding with children, prisoners, or pregnant women only if they involve minimal risks. If the research involves more than minimal risks, then the Secretary of HHS (or his or her representative on these matters) must approve the research for it to receive federal funding. Of course, research that is not federally funded and involves more than minimal risk would not go to the Secretary of HHS, presumably, but then whether local IRBs are willing to approve such research appears to depend on the institutions' rules.

More on Research with Prisoners

How relevant are these issues with subject selection for political scientists? It is true that using these groups of subjects in political science experiments is rare because most of the focus of such experiments is on the political behavior of the nonprisoner adult population, which might include pregnant women but not purposely, nor do the experiments single out pregnant women. Yet, we expect as experimentation increases that political scientists will find it desirable to conduct experiments using these populations. For example, much research has investigated the effects of felon disenfranchisement laws in the United States under the assumption that, if these laws were changed, the disenfranchised population's votes may affect electoral outcomes. Yet little is known about the political sophistication of these potential voters. One could imagine that an experiment using prisoners where voting in prison is permitted (as in Vermont) and where it is not (many other states) would yield new and interesting information on how this population of citizens views voting and elections.

If political scientists wish to use prison populations for experiments to study these questions, in Subpart C the Common Rule requires that IRBs include at least one prisoner representative to evaluate the research proposal, that the incentives used in the research not be so sizable that subjects ignore possible risks (which in a contained environment is likely to mean that even small incentives may be viewed as sizable), and that the selection of who participates from the prison population is equitable.

More on Research with Children

Similarly, political scientists have been interested in the development of partisan identities for over half a century. Observational research has been conducted on partisanship development over time. One could imagine that experiments using children could give new insight into how partisan identities develop. To see how such an experiment may be conducted, consider Example 12.4. Bettinger and Slonim (2007) were interested in the effects of winning a lottery for a voucher toward private school tuition on altruism of both parents and children. They exploited a natural experiment conducted in Toledo in which vouchers were given to families by lottery and recruited families who were both winners and losers of the lottery and conducted a set of dictator game experiments (for information on the dictator game, see Example 8.5). They also conducted other experiments that evaluated children's levels of patience by giving them choices between receiving a prize at the time of the experiment as compared to larger prizes in the future (see Bettinger and Slonim, 2007).

In these experiments with children, the researchers faced a number of challenges. In particular, in these types of experiments, as discussed in Chapter 10, researchers standardly use financial incentives to motivate subjects. But financial incentives present a problem for children because (1) the children may not have a strong concept of what money means to them in terms of their daily life – money may not be salient in the same way that it is for adults – and (2) children may feel that decisions on how the money is spent will be made by their parents or adult guardians and thus not care much about the size of their prizes. Bettinger and Slonim attempted to mitigate this problem by giving the children Toys-R-Us gift certificates. Harbaugh and Krause (2000), who pioneered game-theoretic and decision-theoretic experiments with children, gave their child subjects tokens as rewards, which the children could redeem for toys and other prizes after the experiment.

As with prisoners, if an experimenter uses children in a school setting, the experimenter should be careful that participation is open on an equitable basis to the children and that the children who participate are not unduly influenced by the incentives from participation. For example, is it fair for children who participate in an experiment to be able to go to a special party with cake and ice cream during school time but the children who do not cannot enjoy the treats and must have a study hall instead? We think that such an inducement, highly visible to all students and social in nature, may put undue pressure on children to falsify permission slips or otherwise attempt to force parents to let them participate. A better system would be for the experiments to take place outside of school hours and for the incentives for participation to be child-specific rather than social events during periods where nonparticipants would feel especially excluded.

A further challenge for experimenters using children is that state laws vary regarding the age of maturity. Moreover, identifying the legal guardians of children may not be as clear-cut as it seems if a researcher is unaware of court rulings that affect the children studied. Finally, if the children are institutionalized, then it is important that the researcher is not simply using these children – who may be more vulnerable to coercion – to participate because the sample is convenient, but because the subjects are particularly suited for the research question.

Example 12.4 (Combined Natural and Laboratory Experiment on Altruism of Children): *Bettinger and Slonim (2006) conducted an experiment examining how a voucher program affects students' and parents' altruism.*

Target Population and Sample: The researchers used subjects who had applied for a scholarship for private school tuition from the Children's Scholarship Fund (CSF) of Toledo, Ohio. The CSF offers four-year renewable, private school scholarships to K-8 students in Northwest Ohio for students who qualify for federal/free lunch programs via a lottery program. The researchers used as their initial population for their sample 2,424 families who applied for scholarships in the fall of 1997 and spring of 1998. CSF divided the applicants into two groups: those who had self-reported that at least one child was attending private school at the time of the lottery (1,265) and those who had none in private schools (1,159). Each group of applicants participated in a separate lottery. If a family won a lottery, all children were eligible to use the voucher for one-half of a private school tuition.

During 2001 and 2002, the researchers attempted to contact via mail, phone, and home visits a random sample of 438 families including nearly 900 children. The researchers then surveyed 260 of these families, gathering information on both parents and children. From this group, they recruited both parents and children to attend "evaluation events." A total of 212 students and 111 parents attended the events. Each child was accompanied by at least one parent. The students who attended were insignificantly younger than those who did not attend and African Americans were more likely to attend. Of those who attended, African-American lottery winners were less likely to attend than African-American lottery losers, and the percentage of attendees who were lottery winners was greater than those who were lottery losers (although approximately 45% of attendees were lottery losers).

Subject Compensation: *Each parent was given $15 in cash for attending and each child $5 in Toys-R-Us gift certificates for early sessions. The show-up fee for parents was increased to $50 for later sessions to increase attendance. Parents and children were also compensated with either cash or Toys-R-Us gift certificates for their decisions in the experiments. The experimenters used gift certificates for toys to increase the salience of the money to the children and to mitigate fears they may have had that their parents would confiscate their earnings or at least partially influence how the money would be spent. The researchers report that all of the children were familiar with the Toys-R-Us store.*

Environment: *The experiments were conducted at the Central Catholic High School in Toledo. The experimenters separated the parents and children into rooms for the experiments and used a common room for before and after the experiments. Most of the events were conducted in groups of families (101 families), but some involved just an individual family (26 families). The experiments were conducted using pencil and paper.*

Procedures: *The events lasted up to 2.5 hours. Each event used the following schedule.*

1. Parents and children registered and were randomly given identification tags, and consent forms were provided, read, and signed.

2. In a central room everyone gathered and received refreshments (fruit, drinks, cookies) and heard an informal description of where each family member would be located.

3. Subjects were separated into different rooms and participated in the experiments after an ice-breaker penny jar guessing game. After the experiments, students took the California Achievement Test and parents completed a survey with an informal discussion. The survey measured attitudes and contained a manipulation check where the parents were asked to assess on a scale from 1 (strongly disagree) to 5 (strongly agree) whether they felt the procedures had preserved anonymity, had confidence that the experimenters would pay as promised, and whether the instructions were clear and easy to follow.

4. Everyone returned to the central room and had pizza, fruit, cookies, and beverages. Parents and children were called one at a time for private payments.

The subjects (both parents and students) participated in a set of three dictator games. For information on the dictator game, see Example 8.5. In the first set, each subject was sequentially matched to three nonprofit organizations as recipients and each subject played the role of dictator in the following order: the American Red Cross, the Make-A-Wish Foundation, and the Children's Scholarship Fund. Each subject was given a brief written description of each organization (a simplified version for children) and there were envelopes addressed to the organizations prepared. Subjects were also given an option to receive a "thank you" letter from each organization. In each decision, children were endowed with $10 (which they could use as Toys-R-Us gift certificates) and parents were endowed with $50. Each subject was given a simple sheet of paper that listed possible choices as follows:

My Choice	KEEP for Myself	SEND to organization
	$10	$0
	$9	$1
	$8	$2
	$7	$3
	$6	$4
	$5	$5
	$4	$6
	$3	$7
	$2	$8
	$1	$9
	$0	$10

Subjects were asked to mark in the first column their choice.

In sessions with five or more children, the researchers conducted a second set of dictator games. In these games, the subjects had the same endowments. In each decision, subjects chose how much of the endowment to keep and how much to give to another person (another child if the decision maker was a child, and another parent if the decision maker was a parent). The amount given to the other person was multiplied by the researchers by an exchange rate which varied from 50% to 150% and the subjects were given a modified version of the preceding table reflecting the exchange rate. The recipients of the amounts given away were randomly and anonymously selected at the end of the session, so subjects did not know who they were paired with at the time of the decision and were not told at the end of session.

Results: The researchers found that students who had been lottery recipients were more generous toward charitable organizations but not toward their peers. They found no statistically significant effect of the vouchers on parents' altruism or student test scores.

Comments: Greater than 90% of all responses to the manipulation check were 4 or 5. Several families left before the test administration and in the early sessions students above the 7th grade were not tested. The authors considered whether reciprocity is driving the results of greater charitable giving by voucher winners and contended that the evidence suggests a form of negative reciprocity with voucher losers decreasing the amount they give. Bettinger and Slonim

(2007) reported on a decision-making experiment the researchers conducted with the children on patience in which children were given a choice about whether to receive payments today versus larger payments in the future.

Students and Employees

The Common Rule statement about vulnerable subjects who may be subject to undue influence has been interpreted by some IRBs to also include students and employees. As noted in Chapter 10, giving students grades based on their performance in experiments may be unethical because presumably their grades should be based on what they learn in the classroom and not their performance in experimental research. That said, is it ethical to give students extra credit in course work for participating in experiments where the credit is not tied to performance? Is it ethical to require that students participate in experiments as part of their course work, again where the credit is not tied to performance? Many psychology departments make such requirements or offer extra credit for such participation and political psychologists also often use students in this fashion.

Is the use of course credit for participation in experiments undue coercion and unethical? Whether the credit is considered a normal part of course work or "extra," students who choose to participate will make higher grades than those who choose not to. In our view, grades granted in this fashion give students very little choice if they do not wish to participate in experiments. That is, there are no other ways to make up for the disadvantage of not earning the course credit from participation. In contrast, although students may be similarly motivated by financial incentives, students have other opportunities to earn money in part-time employment, so a student who chooses not to participate is not necessarily without options. We believe that students should be given the option of earning the same course credit by other activities that consume equivalent amounts of time if they choose not to participate, such as attending seminars or writing short research reports, which are evaluated under the expectation that students who complete these assignments spend as much time on them as the time spent participating in experiments. The IRB Guidebook describes such possible alternatives that have been used at universities.

An additional ethical problem with using students in experiments is that it may be more difficult to maintain the confidentiality of student choices. In the close quarters of a university it is more likely that data on subjects' identities linked to their choices in experiments, if they are not adequately kept confidential, will fall into the hands of those who know the subjects and can lead to embarrassment for the subjects in some cases. Thus, in political science experiments using students as subjects, unless there is a particularly good research reason for keeping subjects' information by name or university or social security identification number, we suggest that experimenters use experiment-specific identification numbers to store data. If a researcher does plan on perhaps using students grades or other information as covariates in understanding the experimental results (with permission from the students, of course) or if the researcher plans to use subjects repeatedly over time and needs to make sure that they are aware of the identity of the participants over time, then the researcher should take extra care to maintain data confidentiality.

In Chapter 9, we remarked that Kam et al. investigated the use of university employees as an alternative convenience sample of subjects (see Example 9.1). Yet, it is also possible that special ethical concerns exist when researchers use university employees; that is, employees who work with or are associated with a researcher may feel compelled to participate in an experiment even if she or he does not wish to. Ideally, a researcher should only use employees who work in departments or institutes that are outside of his or her own. Furthermore, as with students, in a university setting it may be more difficult for researchers to maintain data confidentiality and thus we recommend, when possible, that researchers use only experiment-specific random identification numbers to store data, as recommended earlier.

12.2.2 Informed Consent

Problems with Informed Consent and Social Science Research
The Belmont Report called for all human subjects to provide informed consent before agreeing to participate in an experiment. As a result, the Common Rule is specific in requiring that researchers provide their subjects with the opportunity to make an informed decision to consent to participation and that the consent is documented. The basic elements of informed consent are specified in 45 CFR 46.116(a), in Appendix A of Chapter 11. Informed consent, as a requirement for research, makes ethical sense and is hard to argue against. Yet it is the requirement of informed consent that leads to some of the most vigorous complaints from social scientists about the Common Rule and IRB research regulation.

Why? There are three main reasons. First, many social scientists conduct research in cultures where securing a Westernized notion of informed consent is problematic. Consider the issues faced by a black South African doing fieldwork in South Africa during the apartheid rule (Goduka, 1990, p. 333):

Can the black people of South Africa, particularly those who live in homelands, resettlements, and white-owned farm areas, give truly informed consent? What if the research content is so embedded in authoritarian relations that individuals cannot meaningfully exercise choice? How does a researcher secure informed consent when more than half of the subjects in her study are illiterate and not familiar with research enterprise. Such people may think refusing to participate would create problems for them and their children. On the other hand, agreeing to participate may reflect their submission to the school, or to the researcher, who represents authority in the eyes of black families.

Even when these problems of authoritarianism do not exist, there may be cultural reasons why potential subjects are confused by informed consent requirements, as Fontes (1998) recalls when attempting to secure informed consent for field experiments on family violence in an underdeveloped country (p. 55):

I sat with ten shantytown residents and leaders, reading them the consent-to-participate form that I had carefully prepared, translated, and moved through the approval process of the human subjects review committee at my university in the United States. One of the potential participants raised a concern that I had not anticipated. Why would I fail to give them credit by disguising their names and identifying information?

Thus, many social scientists working with subjects in other countries find the requirement to secure informed consent difficult to fulfill.

Second, qualitative researchers argue that informed consent is not possible in soak-and-poke activities because it is not possible to predict in advance when the research will end or the extent of the involvement of possible subjects. These and other criticisms of informed consent for qualitative research can be found in the literature (Yanow and Schwartz-Shea, 2008). The inability to forecast the path of research and the involvement of participants can also be relevant in political science field experiments. In the bribery experiment presented in Example 12.3, which police officers would be involved in the experiment was not predictable until the experiment was already in progress. Moreover, in some cases traffic violations were committed in front of traffic officers who did not stop the violators but were also technically subjects in the experiment; however, the researchers have no information on these subjects other than where the violations took place. Thus, in some field experiments, identifying subjects before research begins and securing informed consent is not possible.

Third, providing full information to subjects in a social science experiment about the purpose of the research may invalidate the results in experiments. In a medical experiment, informed consent has been interpreted to require that a researcher provide subjects with detailed information about the purpose of the study as well as the possible benefits and harms that subjects may experience as a consequence of participating in the study. But consider Example 2.6, in which the researchers used experiments to evaluate the Swing Voter's Curse model, which predicts that uninformed voters abstain or vote contrary to their a priori information. If the researchers were to tell the subjects in advance the purpose of the experiment, then the subjects may behave differently because they will be "told" how they are expected to choose as predicted by the theory. The research question – do subjects behave as predicted – would not be answerable by the study if subjects are influenced by the presentation of the theoretical results. Similarly, in Experiment 2.5, Mutz has subjects view videos of mock debates to measure the effects of television discourse on the subjects' views of issues and those on different sides of issues. If she had revealed to the subjects in advance of the experiment that the videos they are watching were created for the experiment and the purpose of the different treatments, then this is likely to have influenced how the subjects responded to the videos and to her post-experiment survey. If an experiment uses more active deception, such as the confederates who commit traffic violations in Example 12.3, informing the subjects such as the traffic officers in this example that they are participating in an experiment and that the violators are confederates of a researcher would make the experiment invalid.

Waiving or Reducing Informed Consent Requirements

Given these difficulties, is it ethical to conduct experiments without securing informed consent from subjects? Informed consent has become a mainstay of research with human subjects because it serves two purposes: (1) it ensures that the subjects are voluntarily participating and that their autonomy is protected and (2) it provides researchers with legal protections in case of unexpected events. When research is conducted and subjects do not give their informed consent, then both subjects and researchers, including those that fund and support the research, face risks. The risks to subjects when they act in an experiment without informed consent should be included when evaluating the possible harms that can be a consequence of the research. If we use a risk–benefit comparison to determine if research is ethical, then if the benefits outweigh all the risks, including those to the subject from acting without informed consent, then the research is ethical.

Does the Common Rule allow for experimenters to forgo informed consent? Certainly exempt research such as survey experiments do not require that researchers secure informed consent. For nonexempt research, the Common Rule allows for IRBs to waive informed consent under certain conditions. First, IRBs can waive informed consent under 45 CFR 46.116(c) (see Appendix A in Chapter 11), which allows for waiver or alteration of informed consent requirements when "(1) The research or demonstration project is to be conducted by or subject to the approval of state or local government officials and is designed to study, evaluate, or otherwise examine: (i) public benefit or service programs; (ii) procedures for obtaining benefits or services under those programs; (iii) possible changes in or alternatives to those programs or procedures; or (iv) possible changes in methods or levels of payment for benefits or services under those programs; and (2) The research could not practicably be carried out without the waiver or alteration." Second, IRBs can waive informed consent under 45 CFR 46.116(d) (see Appendix A in Chapter 11), which allows for waiver or alteration of informed consent requirements when an "IRB finds and documents that: (1) The research involves no more than minimal risk to the subjects; (2) The waiver or alteration will not adversely affect the rights and welfare of the subjects; (3) The research could not practicably be carried out without the waiver or alteration; and (4) Whenever appropriate, the subjects will be provided with additional pertinent information after participation."

It is our interpretation of the Common Rule that these exceptions provide social scientists with the opportunity to make the case for waiver or alteration of informed consent when it is necessary for the research to be valid. Most political economists and many political psychologists who conduct laboratory experiments in which providing full information on the experiments would invalidate the results secure informed consent that is vague about the purpose of the research. In some cases when researchers use deception, they debrief the subjects after the experiment, although as mentioned in Section 12.1.2, such debriefing could be harmful to subjects and such harms need to be considered before debriefing. Informed consent in these laboratory experiments is usually straightforward; subjects are given a document similar to Appendix D, used by one of the authors at Michigan State University.

In contrast, in many field experiments, researchers do not secure even a limited version of informed consent from subjects because doing so would completely invalidate the research and make the research impossible. It is impossible to imagine how many of the field experiments we have reported on in this book, such as the newspaper and voting experiment of Gerber,

Karlan, and Bergan in Example 2.1 and the voters in Wantchekon's experiment in Benin in Example 2.2 or in the direct democracy experiment in Indonesia in Example 12.1, in which subjects were not granted the opportunity to choose whether to consent to participation in an experiment that had the potential of affecting the government goods and services they received.[15] In these cases, researchers face an ethical responsibility to be sure that the risks facing subjects are less than the benefits from the experiment, including the risks inherent in subjects making choices without the autonomy that informed consent provides them.

12.3 Chapter Summary

In this chapter we have reviewed the costs and benefits from political science experiments. In general, the quantifiable benefits that can be used to justify political science experiments are few or nonexistent. Social benefits are not easy to calculate or estimate, therapeutic benefits are extremely rare, and it is generally believed to be unethical to count collateral benefits. However, although there can be risks in political science experiments, in many cases these risks are minimal and, thus, the experiments are justifiable. That said, in some cases the risks can be greater than minimal and involve possible physical, psychological, social, or economic harms to subjects or third parties. In this case it is imperative that experimentalists attempt to design experiments to minimize such harms. We have discussed some of the ways in which experimentalists have attempted to do so.

Experimentation is intervention in the data generating process and, as we noted in the beginning of this chapter, that means that experimentalists directly affect human lives, particularly when their research is successful. As a result, experimentalists have an ethical responsibility to weigh the costs and benefits of their research before undertaking that research. In the United States and a number of other countries, such as Canada and the United Kingdom, elaborate regulatory processes exist with the goal of preventing unethical research. But oftentimes these regulatory processes seem more of a problem to social scientists than the benefit gained, primarily because many of the procedures were originally designed to evaluate biomedical research, and the decentralized nature of the process can mean that researchers are subject to decisions that can vary depending on the institution. For example,

---

[15] Interestingly, in the Indonesian direct democracy experiments, subjects presumably had full information that they were participating in an experiment, so were informed unlike other field experiments, but had no choice whether to participate.

in some institutions it is acceptable for subjects to provide informed consent for laboratory experiments when they sign up for a subject pool, whereas in other institutions subjects must sign new consent forms designed for each particular experiment. Institutions vary in whether they allow for those types of experiments eligible for expedited review under the Common Rule to actually undergo expedited review. There are numerous anecdotes of researchers who failed to get approval sufficiently in advance for time-sensitive studies and as a result the research was not completed. The time involved in securing consent has affected the ability of graduate students and assistant professors to meet deadlines.[16]

We believe, as do many, that there are good reasons to advocate some reform of the U.S. IRB process as well as the process of review in other countries. In the meantime, though, experimentalists must work within the system as it exists. For this reason, we advocate that political science experimentalists become informed about the process and involved in it. To be active participants it is important that we have a good understanding of the costs and benefits from experimentation, and we hope this chapter provides a useful starting point for that knowledge. As experimentation in political science increases, we believe that we should also make sure that graduate students learn not only the method of experimentation but also the ethical considerations involved as well as how to navigate the IRB bureaucracy. Similarly, we should provide advice and help to colleagues with not only methodological questions on experimentation but these ethical issues as well. The code of ethics of the American Political Science Association and other national and international political science associations should not simply delegate ethical issues to institutional IRBs but consider specifically the ethical needs and concerns involved in political science experimentation.

12.4 Appendix: Sample Consent Letter for Laboratory Experiments

You will participate in a series of simulated elections. The experiment examines how different types of information affects election outcomes. The experiment will take place on computer terminals. Before the experiment you will be given an identification number. Throughout the experiment you will only be identified through this number. As such any decisions that you make will be anonymous. Also in any future reporting of the results your identity will remain confidential. For your participation you will be paid anywhere from 5 to 9 dollars a hour and the experiment will last approximately $2\frac{1}{2}$ hours. You will be paid in cash, an hour

---

[16] See, for example, the special issue in *Social Science and Medicine* in 2007 and the set of articles in the *Northwestern University Law Review* in 2007.

confidentially, after the experiment has ended. The monetary payoff cited above is just an average payment. Each subject may be paid a different amount depending on actual decisions that are made. You will be allowed to terminate the experiment at any time without any penalty to you. After the series of experiments are completed you may contact Professor Kenneth Williams for the results of the experiment. He may be contacted by calling xxx-xxxx. Also, if you have any further questions about this study please contact Professor Williams at xxx-xxxx, or the Institutional Review Board officer who approved this project at xxx-xxxx.

I voluntarily consent to participate in the experiment described above:

Written proper name_____   Date _____

Signed Signature_____   Date _____

Best time to contact me if by phone _____

Phone contact information _____

E-mail contact information _____

Student ID number _____

13

Deception in Experiments

13.1 Deception in Political Science Experiments

In the previous chapter we highlighted a number of ethical issues in experimentation, one of which is the use of deception. Many consider deception
not unethical per se and believe it is permissible to engage in deception when
it is required to do so for the research and the risks are minimal or sufficiently minimized as discussed in the previous chapter. Deception occurs
in many political psychology experiments, such as Druckman and Nelson's
use of fake *New York Times* articles (see Example 5.1). In this sense, political
psychology uses deception in the same way that it is used in social psychology experiments generally. Deception is widespread in social psychology;
Hertwig and Ortmann (2001) reported that deception in experimental articles in the top-ranked journal in social psychology, the *Journal of Personality
and Social Psychology*, averaged between 31% and 47% from 1986 to 1997.
Deception is even more common in field experiments in political science,
where it is standard practice for subjects not to even know they are participating in an experiment, as in the newspaper experiment of Gerber et al.
(see Example 2.1). In some cases, deception in field experiments can also
involve confederates posing in roles such as in the bribery experiment in
Mexico City (see Example 12.3).

Deception is also used in political economy experiments. Almost all
political economy experiments, as in the Swing Voter's Curse experiment
in Example 2.6, do not tell subjects the truth about the purpose of the
experiment; instead subjects are provided with vague information about
the point of the research. But deception in political economy experiments has occasionally been similar to that used in experiments in political psychology or in the field. For example, Scharlemann et al. (2001)

500

reported on a trust experiment similar to Example 8.2 in which subjects were given pictures of individuals and told that they were participating in a trust game with the individual in the picture, but actually they were not; the pictures were from a stock of photos chosen for particular characteristics. One of us has previously conducted an experiment with deception. In Collier et al. (1989) voting experiment, the authors had graduate students pose as subjects and the graduate students were chosen as candidates for the voting game and left the room. The subjects were told that the choice of who was a candidate had been a random draw. The subjects were then assigned to be voters and were told that the candidates were choosing positions in the other room, while in actuality the candidate positions in the experiment had been chosen by the experimentalists in advance of the experiment.

Although deception is used, the experimental community is divided over whether this practice should be employed. Some experimentalists feel that deception is necessary for their research questions, whereas others believe it is a "public bad" that can contaminate a subject pool and alter the behavior of subjects in future experiments. This chapter attempts to clarify what is considered to be deception, then examines the pros and cons of using deception in experiments, and finally offers suggestions for dealing with deception.

13.2 What Is Deception?

Deception in an experiment essentially involves lying to subjects prior to or during an experiment. Hertwig and Ortmann (2001, p. 4) analyzed 14 social psychological studies that used deception and concluded that "[e]xamination of their criteria for defining deception reveals that intentional and explicit misrepresentation of, that is, lying about, for instance, the purpose of the investigation and the identity of the researcher and confederate, is unanimously considered to be deception."

Definition 13.1 (Deception): *Deception occurs in an experiment when the experimenter uses intentional and explicit misrepresentations before, during, or after an experiment.*

The use of deception in experiments is something that, according to codes of ethics, is not taken lightly. According to the American Psychological

Association 2002 ethics guidelines, deception is a procedure of last resort. The guidelines note (2002, p. 11, 12):

(a) Psychologists do not conduct a study involving deception unless they have determined that the use of deceptive techniques is justified by the study's significant prospective scientific, educational, or applied value and that effective nondeceptive alternative procedures are not feasible.

(b) psychologists do not deceive prospective participants about research that is reasonably expected to cause physical pain or severe emotional distress;

(c) psychologists explain any deception that is an integral feature of the design and conduct of an experiment to participants as early as is feasible, preferably at the conclusion of their participation, but no later than at the conclusion of the data collection, and permit participants to withdraw their data.

13.3 Types of Deception

13.3.1 Deceptive Purpose

Most would distinguish between different types of deception. For example, an experimenter may simply deceive subjects about the purpose of the experiment by giving only vague information about the purpose. As noted earlier, many of the experiments discussed in this book used deception in this manner. In the Swing Voter's Curse experiments of Example 2.6, the researchers told subjects only that they would be participating in an experiment on voting, not about the details of the theory. In other cases, researchers may actually mislead subjects as to the purpose of an experiment. For instance, in Example 10.3, Kam told subjects that she was conducting a survey of public opinion and did not reveal that she was studying the effects of attitudes toward Hispanics on their preferences between candidates.

Definition 13.2 (Deceptive Purpose): *When the subjects are not told the purpose of the experiment or they are told a falsehood about the purpose of the experiment.*

13.3.2 Deceptive Materials and Information

Kam not only deceived subjects about the purpose of the experiment, but she also used deceptive materials and information. She had subjects complete a survey on public opinion to fit the cover story of the purpose of the experiment. An elaborate use of deceptive materials is given in Example 2.5, where Mutz created professional videos and actors that she told subjects were actual candidates engaged in a debate. Druckman and Nelson in Example 5.1 went to great lengths as well to create materials for their experiment that would mislead subjects to think that they were reading articles from the *New York Times*. An example of an experiment with deceptive information is that of Weimann (1994), in which subjects participated in a public goods game (see Example 8.3 for a discussion of a public goods game) and were given false reports about others' contributions in previous periods before being asked their contribution for a current period. Weimann considered two different variations – a low-contributions condition, where each subject was told that the others had contributed 15.75% of their endowments on average, and a high-contributions condition, where each subject was told that the others had contributed 89.75% on average.

In some cases, experimentalists provide subjects with incomplete information rather than false information. We have already discussed an example of such incomplete information – when subjects are not told the purpose of an experiment. But the incomplete information may extend to other aspects of the experimental design. For example, an experimentalist may not tell subjects precisely when the end of the experiment will occur or that there is a second part to an experiment because he or she wishes to avoid last-period effects or possible contamination of knowledge of a second period on choices in a first period. Such procedures are often routine in laboratory experiments in both political psychology and political economics.

Definition 13.3 (Deceptive Materials and Information): *When the materials used in the experiment are deceptive or subjects are given deceptive or incomplete information.*

13.3.3 Deceptive Identities

Consider the field experiment of Gerber, Karlan, and Bergan in Example 2.1. In this experiment, the subjects were randomly provided with free newspapers to gauge the effect of media-provided information on their voting choices. The subjects were not told the purpose of the free newspapers and that other subjects would not be receiving newspapers. The experimenters engaged in deceptive identities. In the bribery experiment (Example 12.3) conducted in Mexico City, the researchers hired confederates who were given identities (to be either rich or poor) and the police officers were not told they were confederates. But deceptive identities are not just used in the field. Deceptive identities may be used in the laboratory if a researcher has a confederate pretend to be a subject and make pre-programmed choices as in the Collier et al. experiment by Collier, Ordeshook, and Williams discussed in the introduction to this chapter; or subjects may be shown a photo of a subject that they are told is the other player but the other player is a computer, as in the Scharlemann et al. experiment also referred to in the introduction.

Definition 13.4 (Deceptive Identities): *When the subjects are not told the identity of the experimenters or confederates of the experimenters.*

13.4 Arguments for Deception

13.4.1 Control over Perceived Artificiality and Subjects' Motivations

Most experimentalists who use deception argue that it is needed to achieve control over a subject's behavior; that is, revealing the information is argued to lead to the problematic experimental effects discussed in Section 8.4 and to a loss of control over subjects' motivations. Obviously, if the subjects in the bribery experiment had known that they were participating in an experiment, then their choices would have been different than what was observed. The experimentalists would have lost control by creating an artificial experimental effect and changing the subjects' motivations.

But controlling perceptions of artificiality and subjects' motivations are also reasons for using deception in experiments in the laboratory. Consider an experiment on strategic voting (as in Example 6.3) in which a researcher is interested in the conditions under which a subject would vote strategically, but the subjects are only told that the purpose of the research is to examine voting behavior. In this case subjects are deceived about the hypothesis that is being tested because revealing information about the hypothesis to subjects may alter their behavior during the experiment; that is, they may vote strategically more or less often if they knew this was the purpose of the experiment. Consequently, it is argued that deception is needed to achieve "natural" responses from subjects.

Kam, mentioned earlier, and Taber (see Example 4.1) both used deception in their laboratory experiments when they did not tell the subjects that they were being exposed to subliminal priming; if they had done so, the subjects would have no doubt tried to control or change their responses. Collier et al. used deception so that they could control the choices made by candidates that voters faced, but they wanted to maintain the fiction that the choices were real to motivate the subjects to take the experiment seriously. Similarly,

Weinmann used deception because he wanted to determine how subjects would react to a situation in which contributions were either high or low. Druckman and Nelson wanted subjects' experiences not to be artificial and wanted to control their perceptions of the articles independent of their manipulations. Mutz similarly desired to use control over the videos so that subjects would believe that the videos and debates were real. If subjects were fully informed about all aspects of the experimental design, then they might behave in an "unnatural" manner during the experiment, the experimentalist would lose control, and the subjects may not have the motivations that are desired.

Bortolotti and Mameli (2006, pp. 260–261) note that:

In most cases, the purpose of deceptive methods in psychology is to make sure that the research participants are not aware of what aspect of their psychology is being studied and in what ways. Deception regarding the main purpose of the experiment is often used to avoid the so-called Hawthorne effects, the tendency of research participants to behave in accordance to what they think the experimenter's expectations are.

Elaborating on the need to control subject behavior, Bassett et al. (1992, p. 203) state: "Using deception may protect the experimenter from certain 'subject problems.' This argument is based on the assumption that a subject's motive can profoundly affect how he or she responds to the experimental situation. It has been argued that some motives place subjects in roles that threaten the validity of research results." Bassett et al. cite three commonly addressed problems with subject behavior. The first is the "negativistic subject," whose incentive is to disconfirm whatever hypotheses they think the researcher is trying to prove (Cook et al. 1970). The second is the "good subject," who wants to help the researcher confirm his or her hypotheses (Orne, 1962). The last is the "apprehensive subject," who wants "to look good" in the eyes of the researcher (Rosenberg, 1965). By using deception, a researcher can attempt to control the behavior of subjects and prevent them from making "unnatural"choices.

13.4.2 Experiments on Rare Situations

Another reason cited for using deception is that some situations of interest do not arise naturally, even in some experimental situations. The Collier et al. experiment used deception partly for this reason because they wanted to be sure that voters had the opportunity to react to certain candidate policy positions that they did not anticipate subjects as candidates actually choosing.

Similarly, there are many studies that attempt to examine the behavior of subjects in "realistic" emergency situations and the only way to induce this environment in an experiment is by using deception. For example, Berkum et al. (1962) conducted a study in which military personnel were deceived to think they were in imminent danger from a misdirected artillery shell. To protect themselves, their task was to repair a faulty radio transmitter so that they could contact someone to help them. In this case, if the military personnel did not believe they were in imminent danger, then the researcher would not be able to gauge natural responses to this scenario. In another experiment, Latané and Darely (1970), to examine how bystanders may react, placed subjects in a waiting room and then filtered smoke through the air vent to determine the reaction of subjects (e.g., which type of subject would seek help first). In both cases it is argued that deception was needed to measure the true reactions of subjects to an emergency.

13.4.3 Deception as a Method of Lowering Costs of Experiments

Deception can also have the benefit of lowering subject costs for experiments that pay subjects to participate or that pay subjects based on performance in the experiment (Bonetti, 1998). Say that a researcher wants to conduct an experiment in which subjects believe they are participating in a large-scale election. The researcher could tell the subjects that there are 500 other subjects at various universities, when in fact there are only 20 subjects based in her laboratory. A computer program then generates responses for the 480 other subjects. Instead of having to pay the cost of 500 subjects, the researcher only has to pay the cost of 20 subjects. Hence, as Bonetti (1998, p. 388) notes, "very large groups are possible using this technique when they would be prohibitively expensive if deception was prohibited." However, recent experimental evidence suggests that this ruse may not be that successful, as discussed in relation to the Eckel and Wilson experiments via the Internet (Example 8.2).

13.4.4 Deception as an Educational Benefit

Deception has been cited as an educational benefit to subjects. Smith and Richardson (1983) argue that subjects who are deceived and then debriefed afterward have a better educational experience and enjoy the experimental experience more than subjects who are not deceived. One reason is that researchers who deceive must take more time and thoroughly explain the deception during the debriefing session. They note (p. 1081):

To some extent, the greater educational benefit reported by the deception group may be a function of the investigators care in explaining the rationale for deception and the purpose of the study. Perhaps those investigators who had not exposed their participants to any deception felt less need to spend a great deal of time and/or effort on the debriefing. . . . Deceived participants had relatively positive evaluations of the entire research participation may arise from their greater enjoyment and perception of greater educational benefit as well.

13.4.5 The Societal Costs of Prohibiting Deception

Some contend that not using deception in some experiments when it is needed to attain knowledge has a societal cost. Christensen (1988, p. 670) states:

[O]ne issue that is seldom considered by the critics of deception is the moral cost of not doing research on important issues. . . . To smugly fail to investigate these issues or to use an approach that invites bias can also be viewed as immoral. This is not meant to imply that a concern for the advancement of knowledge should override the concern and welfare of the research participant. Rather, there are also moral costs to not doing research and this fact must also be considered when evaluating the ethical acceptability of deception.

Of course, as we noted in Section 12.1.2, societal benefits from research are exceedingly difficult to calculate. Relying simply on such unstated benefits to justify deception is a weak argument, in our opinion, unless a researcher can be confident that the deception used has minimal risks as discussed in the previous chapters.

13.4.6 Deception Is Part of Everyday Life

Others argue that deception is part of our everyday society, and we should embrace it if it allows us to attain knowledge. As reported in Vedantum (2004), Nass a professor of communication, commented: "We spend enormous amounts of time teaching children to deceive – it's called being polite or social. The history of all advertising is about deceiving. In education, it's often important to deceive people – sometimes you say, 'Boy you are really doing good,' not because you meant it but because you thought it would be helpful." Thus, the argument is that deception is in the category of a minimal risk (see Definition 11.1) and, thus, acceptable. We address this claim later in Section 13.6.1.

13.5 Objections to Deception

13.5.1 Ethical Concerns

There are two kinds of arguments against the use of deception in experiments – ethical and methodological. The ethical concerns are twofold: first, some argue that deception causes harm to subjects, and second, others contend that deception is morally wrong independent of possible harms. In the previous chapter, we outlined the harms that can occur in experiments and in Section 13.6.1 we explore whether the potential harms from deception are more than minimal.

The moral argument is well expressed by Miller et al. (2005, p. 585):

[D]eception in research raises ethical concern because it can be corrupting for the professionals who practice it, and for those who witness it. According to ancient perspective in moral philosophy, moral character depends on habits of conduct. The use of deception in research may interfere with the disposition not to lie or deceive persons. . . . Those who witness deception, especially if performed or sanctioned by professionals in positions of authority, may develop skewed perceptions of the ethics of deception, which may have negative consequences for the development of moral character. In sum, deception in research is prima facie wrongful, and it may be harmful not only to those who are deceived but also to those who practice or witness it.

13.5.2 Methodological Concerns

Political economists and psychologists have voiced objections to the use of deception as a methodological tool in laboratory experiments, particularly the use of deceptive materials and identities, because many see no problem with a deceptive purpose experiment. The primary objection is that these types of deceptions as methodological tools have the potential to negatively affect subjects who participate in future experiments. The notion of contaminating the subject pool was summed up by Kelman (1967, p. 7): "As we continue to carry out research of this kind, our subjects become increasingly distrustful of us, and our future relations with them are likely to be undermined. Thus we are confronted with the anomalous circumstance that the more research we do, the more difficult and questionable it becomes."

Political economists are more adamant about the use of deceptive materials and identities and some have decreed a ban on the practice of these types of deception and deem them negative externalities. Davis and Holt (1993, pp. 23, 24) express this point of view:

The researcher should also be careful to avoid deceiving participants. Most economists are very concerned about developing and maintaining a reputation among the student population for honesty in order to ensure that subject actions are motivated by the induced monetary rewards rather than by psychological reactions to suspected manipulation. Subjects may suspect deception if it is present. Moreover, even if subjects fail to detect deception within a session, it may jeopardize future experiments if the subjects ever find out that they were deceived and report this information to friends.

This sentiment is further explained by John Ledyard (1995, p. 134):

It is believed by many undergraduates that psychologists are intentionally deceptive in most experiments. If undergraduates believe the same about economists, we have lost control. It is for this reason that modern experimental economists have been carefully nurturing a reputation for absolute honesty in all their experiments . . . if the data are to be valid. Honesty in procedures is absolutely crucial. Any deception can be discovered and contaminate a subject pool not only for the experimenter but for others. Honesty is a methodological public good and deception is not contributing.

Finally, Friedman and Sunder (1994, p. 17) warn:

Do not deceive subjects or lie to them. It is true that social psychologists have run interesting experiments based on deception. . . . However, experimental economists require credibility because salience and dominance are lost if subjects doubt the announced relation between actions and rewards, or if subjects hedge against possible tricks. Deception harms your own credibility and that of other experimentalists, thereby, undermining the ability to achieve experimental control.

As these quotes demonstrate, many political economists believe that the social costs from deception are greater than the private benefits to an individual experimentalist. In this sense, the subject's expectation that they will not be deceived in an experiment is viewed as a common good. The fear is that subjects who have been deceived in experiments may suspect deception in future experiments and alter their behavior accordingly even when deception is not being used. For example, suppose an experimenter is evaluating a model of choice under uncertainty and some outcomes are affected by random factors. If subjects do not believe the experimenter about how the outcomes are randomly determined, then their choices may be influenced. When the subjects in Eckel and Wilson's experiment (Example 8.2) did not believe that there were other subjects at a different university but that the experimenter was lying to them, they contributed more in the trust game than they did when they did believe that there were other subjects at a different university. Beliefs that subjects have about the truth of what an experimenter tells them can possibly have consequential effects on their behavior.

There is also a potential problem with the use of deceptive materials, such as fake newspaper articles as in Druckman and Nelson's study or fake candidates and news shows as in Mutz's study. That is, if subjects are aware that the materials are fake, then their choices may be affected. Research shows that, in many situations where hypothetical choices are compared to actual choices involving monetary amounts, the hypothetical choices are significantly different (see, for example, Alpizar et al., 2008; Bishop and Heberlein, 1986; Ding et al., 2005; List, 2001; List and Shogren, 1998; Voelckner, 2006). We reviewed these studies in Section 10.1.3. It is unclear whether subjects' choices with known hypothetical political options are different from those that are not hypothetical and we know of no study that has investigated this question.

Are these methodological problems real? We examine this question more expansively in the next section.

13.6 Effects of Deception

13.6.1 Are Harms from Deception Minimal?

Does deception, as some argue, have minimal risk because it is prevalent in naturally occurring environments? Some argue that the answer depends on the type of deception and that some types of deception should not even be classified in this fashion. For example, in an experiment in which the subjects are simply not told full information, either by not being told the true purpose of an experiment or by not being given information about how many periods the experiment will last, subjects are not explicitly lied to and thus the deception is not viewed as more than minimal by researchers. Consider Hey's remark (1998, p. 397), "there is a world of difference between not telling subjects things and telling them the wrong things. The latter is deception, the former is not." Thus, many, like Hey, believe that not telling subjects the entire truth about an experiment is not really deception. Certainly, the harm from not telling subjects precisely when an experiment will end or that a second part will occur is likely to cause the subjects only minimal discomfort.

What about Kam's and Taber's experiments using subliminal priming? In this case, the experimenters did not tell subjects about the priming but misled them about the purpose of the experiment. Is giving subjects subliminal priming without their knowledge risky to subjects? Evidence that subliminal priming does have persistent and nontrivial effects has been reported by Sohlberg and Birgegard (2003). They discovered that the exposure to subliminal messages significantly affected subjects' responses as compared to subjects not exposed 7–14 days after the experiment.[1] Lowery et al. (2007) found that subliminal priming has effects that last one to four days and Carnelley and Rowe (2007) found that such priming, when given across three days, was in evidence two days after the last treatment. Thus, subliminal priming may affect subjects' choices in the period after an experiment in a fashion that may not be desirable to them. Whether these effects are more than minimal is unclear.

What about deceptive identities? Certainly being deceived may cause subjects psychological harms, as discussed in the previous chapter. But the potential harms again depend on the situation. In laboratory experiments the subjects may be angry or increase their distrust of the experimenters, but given that it is probably not their first encounter with deception and they may already expect deception (which we discuss later), the psychological harms are likely minimal. But in some cases the harms may be more significant; that is, the potential harms for subjects and third parties from the deceptive identities in the Mexico City are arguably more of an issue than those that can occur in Collier et al. or Scharlemann et al.'s studies.

13.6.2 Does Deception Affect Subjects' Behavior in Future Experiments?

As noted earlier, one of the principal arguments of political economists is that deceived subjects will contaminate the subject pool, thus changing a subject's performance in future experiments. MacCoun and Kerr (1987) provide classic anecdotal evidence that subjects' behavior has been affected by being deceived in past experiments. During an experiment they were conducting, a subject had an epileptic seizure. Other participants initially thought this seizure was part of the experiment and ignored the subject. The student who did help the other subject was not a psychology major. How systematic are such effects?

Ortmann and Hertwig (2002) and Hertwig and Ortman (2008) provide an excellent review of the research on the effects of deception in the psychology literature. Most research on the effects of deception considers whether being deceived makes subjects suspicious and then whether that suspicion affects their behavior in experiments. In general, Ortmann and Hertwig found mixed results from this literature. On the one hand, some studies found that deceived subjects did not become more resentful (Christensen, 1988; Kimmel, 1998); on the other hand, other studies have found that

---

[1] However, Fudin (2006) challenges their conclusion and says that the findings are not compelling evidence for the claims.

resentfulness in subjects affected their behavior (Allen, 1983; Cook et al., 1970; Straits et al. 1972).

Fewer studies have examined the effects of deception in one experiment on performance in a subsequent experiment. Ortmann and Hertwig reviewed nine papers that examine the effects of past deception on the behavior of subjects in future experiments in psychology. Most of these studies examine the effects on subjects of a deceptive purpose or materials rather than deceptive identities. They found that, although in some cases deception in an experiment leads to changes in behavior in a second experiment, again the results are mixed. Some of the work suggests that the effects depend on whether the two experiments are similar in design (see Brock and Becker, 1966; Cook et al., 1970). Jamison et al. (2008) point out that many of these studies suffer from methodological problems in that baseline manipulations without deception were not used or the second experiment was conducted immediately after the first, which does not capture the reality of experimental recruitment.

We are aware of only one experiment by political economists on deception. Jamison et al. (2008) examined the effects of deceptive identities on future performance in other experiments, shown in Example 13.1. In the experiment, some subjects were deceived that they were playing against a human partner in a trust game (see Example 8.2) when they were actually playing against a computer. In the baseline manipulation, subjects played against other subjects. The researchers were careful to make the computer choices close to those chosen by the human subjects so that the only difference between the subjects deceived and those not deceived was deception. They then revealed to the deceived subjects that they had been deceived. Two to three weeks later, both the deceived and undeceived subjects were recruited for a second experiment involving other well-known games and choice situations. They found some minor effects of deception on the likelihood that subjects chose to return for the second session and on their behavior in the second session.

Example 13.1 (Effects of Deception): *Jamison et al. (2008) report on a public goods game experiment in which they purposely deceived participants to examine the effects of deception on their subsequent behavior.*

Target Population and Sample: Jamison et al. recruited 261 from the subject pool of largely undergraduates and a few graduate students of Xlab, which is the experimental social science laboratory at the University of California at Berkeley. The lab maintains two subject pool lists – one in which a no-deception rule is maintained and the other (a smaller list) in which deception is allowed.

The authors recruited the subjects from the no-deception rule list and after the experiment these subjects were "moved" to the other list. Note that the psychology department at Berkeley maintains a separate pool of subjects and the researchers do not know if there is overlap of subjects on the two lists.

Subject Compensation: *Subjects were compensated based on their choices as explained in the procedures. Subjects received an additional $5 for participating in the first set of sessions and an additional $10 for participating in the second set of sessions.*

Environment: *The experiment took place in a computer lab using procedures similar to those of Example 2.6.*

Procedures: *The researchers conducted a sequential experiment, similar to those discussed in Examples 5.1 and 5.2.*

First Set of Sessions: *In the first set of sessions, the subjects played a trust game (see Example 8.2) with a $20 endowment to the first mover. The game was programmed in z-Tree (see Section 1.3.1). The first mover could send any amount to the second mover and this amount was tripled by the experimenter. In these sessions subjects played the trust game for six periods, with the first two periods as practice and the remaining four as counting for payment. They used a partners matching procedure (see Definition 6.14). That is, initially subjects were randomly assigned to anonymous partners and subjects stayed in the same pairs throughout the experiment. One of the four rounds was randomly chosen for payment, using a random round payoff mechanism (Definition 10.12). After the session was completed, payoffs were calculated and subjects waited approximately 15 minutes for individual checks to be filled out and distributed. The researchers conducted 10 sessions of the trust game, 5 with deception (described next) using 129 subjects and 5 without using 132 subjects.*

The first set of sessions was conducted in two stages. In the first stage, the researchers conducted three nondeception sessions. Using the data from the nondeception sessions, the researchers programmed computer play for the deception sessions so that it would match human play as much as possible. They categorized first movers into five types and second movers into three types. The authors also included a "trigger strategy" for all types of first movers: if the second mover ever sent back less than what was invested, the first mover never again invested anything. In the deception sessions, subjects were randomly matched with computer players programmed in this fashion but were told that their partners were other subjects. During the check processing time, these subjects were told about the deception. They were told that the deception was necessary for the research without further details and were asked to sign a second consent form allowing their data to be used. All subjects gave their consent.

Second Set of Sessions (pp. 479–480): "_Two to three weeks later, all subjects from the first round were sent a recruitment email for new experimental sessions using the name of a researcher different from that in the first round. This email was identical to the standard Xlab recruitment email, except that it promised $10 above and beyond the normal earnings in order to facilitate sufficient return rates. Subjects did not know that only they had received this particular email, although it is possible that some of them checked with friends and noticed that it had not gone out to the entire pool. However, that in itself is not an uncommon occurrence given various screening criteria used by other researchers at the lab._

In all, 142 people returned for one of the eight sessions that took place 3–4 weeks after the first sessions in round one. These lasted slightly under an hour, and each consisted of a mixture of both deceived and non-deceived subjects. A different researcher than in the first round was physically present in the room for these sessions. Subjects signed a standard consent form, were given instructions, and completed the experiment as three separate interactions on the VeconLab website." See Section 1.3.1 for information on the VeconLab Web site.

The three separate manipulations were the following.

(1) Subjects played a dictator game (see Example 8.5) with an endowment of $20 in which all subjects made choices as a dictator and were assigned randomly a receiver, but only half of the dictators' choices were implemented (so half of the subjects ended up being dictators and had receivers).

(2) Subjects played a series of 10 gambles as in Holt and Laury's study (2002) and Example 8.2. The first choice was between a lottery that paid $11 with 10% probability and $8.80 with a 90% chance and a lottery that paid $21.20 with a 10% chance and $0.55 with a 90% chance. As the choices progressed, the probability of the higher payoff in each lottery increased by 10% until the final choice was between $11 for sure and $21.20 for sure.

(3) Subjects played a prisoner's dilemma game as in Example 6.1. The payoffs in the game were that both subjects received $10 if both chose to cooperate, both received $6 if both chose defection, and if one chose to cooperate and the other chose defection, the person who cooperated received $1 and the person who defected received $15.

One of the three games was randomly chosen to determine the payoffs and if the risk game was chosen, one decision was randomly chosen.

Results: Deception had no significant effect on return rates; 51% of those deceived returned for the subsequent session and 58% returned who were not deceived. Women who had been deceived were significantly less likely to return than women who had not been deceived, while men displayed the opposite relationship. The authors found that deception most influenced an individual's decision to return to the laboratory when he or she was not lucky *in the game. The effect for women survived a correction for making multiple comparisons (see Section 8.3.4), but none of the other effects survived the correction. The authors also found that there is no significant differences in the prisoner's dilemma game, but that subjects who had been previously deceived were more likely to answer risk-aversion questions inconsistently and made more inconsistent choices in the lotteries. In the dictator game, subjects who were first movers, especially those who were either female or inexperienced (participated in fewer previous experiments), kept more of their money.*

Comments: *The authors' study is unusual because they willingly "burned" subjects in the subject pool and risked the possible contamination that many experimental political economists fear from conducting an experiment with deception.*

Although interesting, Jamison et al.'s study does not clear up the controversy over whether deception matters or not because the effects they found, although real, were weak. They note (p. 486):

We have discussed these results with both psychologists and economists and are struck by their reactions: both see the data as supporting their priors! . . . We fully understand that although we do find clear differences in behavior, they are subject to interpretation as to their economic (or psychological) importance, as well as to further refinement regarding their magnitude and generalizability. The irony is that further study of how deception influences behavior, both in the laboratory and in the real world, requires relaxing the no-deception rule.

13.6.3 Debriefing and Removing Effects of Deception

Promoters of the use of deception argue that negative effects of deception can be removed by *debriefing*. In some cases, debriefing involves two stages: *dehoaxing*, which is revealing the deceptive practice to the subjects, and *desensitizing*, which attempts to remove any undesirable consequences of the experiment (Holmes, 1976a,b). Debriefing by explaining the nature of the deception and the purpose of the experiment may undo the harm that a subject may have endured.

Definition 13.5 (Debriefing): *Revealing deceptive practices to subjects after an experiment is completed (dehoaxing) and attempting to remove any undesirable consequences of the experiment (desensitizing).*

Does debriefing work? Holmes (1976a,b) show in experiments that debriefing can effectively remove any lingering psychological damage done to a subject during a deceptive experiment. One interesting example of effective debriefing is given by Holmes and Bennett (1974). They conducted an experiment in which stress was induced in one treatment by warning one group of subjects that an electric shock could be administered to them, and in another treatment a group of subjects knew that an electric shock would not be administered to them. In both cases an electric shock was not administered (p. 366):

[I]t was found that debriefing after stress-producing deception returned the subjects' levels of performance to the levels of nondeceived subjects which offers strong and consistent support for the contention that debriefing is effective in eliminating deceptions and the stress associated with them.... [T]he effectiveness of debriefing can be generalized across experiments involving different types of deceptions.

However, other researchers counter that debriefing is not always effective in removing psychological damage done to subjects. Bok (1978, p. 191) argues:

Unfortunately, debriefing does not always succeed. The disappointment may remain; the anxiety or loss of privacy may not be overcome. The experiment might reveal something to subjects about themselves that no debriefing will erase. Subjects may become more suspicious after the explanation, and thus less useful for further studies. And they may suffer from the discovery that someone in a position of a model and authority figure resorted to such devious tactics.

Sieber (1992, p. 72) and Berscheid et al. (1967) found evidence that debriefing is not that effective in removing the psychological harm that may be caused by deception. Baumrind (1985, p. 169) also points out that although self-reported surveys during debriefing sessions may indicate that subjects are not harmed by the deception, in reality these instruments cannot measure a subject's true feelings.

Recent studies on debriefing are rare. One particularly interesting study is Birgegard and Sohlberg's (2008) investigation of whether debriefing eliminates the lingering effects of subliminal priming (discussed earlier in Section 13.6.1). They find that simple debriefing about the stimulus was effective in preventing effects, whereas more elaborate debriefing, also describing the effects and mechanisms, for them was less effective.

Thus, the evidence on the positive effects of debriefing to eliminate harms from deception is mixed. Should experimentalists debrief subjects at all? Or perhaps only use simple debriefing procedures as in Birgegard and Sohlberg's study? Some researchers argue that debriefing is desirable ethically, independent of whether it works to remove harmful effects of deception (see Miller et al., 2008). That is, debriefing is seen as a chance to rectify the unethical or immoral act of deception by the researcher.

13.7 The Conditional Information Lottery Procedure and Avoiding Deception

Most political scientists who use deception do so because they see it as the only way to address the research question of interest. Scharlemann et al. contend (pp. 628–629):

> In our experiment, control requires that subjects be presented with paired sets of faces. A single face is presented in two versions: one smiling, and one unsmiling. Without this control we cannot be certain whether our result is due to a smile, or due to some other difference between any two different faces. This led us to control the facial expressions by setting them ahead of time.

Is this the only way Scharlemann et al. could have conducted the experiment? Two of the coauthors of the study conducted a later experiment (Eckel and Wilson, 2006) that looked at beauty and the effect on behavior without using deception, which we discuss in Example 8.2. In the later experiment, the subjects participated in ten separate trust games in which they were shown the face of the other player in each game. However, only one of the faces shown was actually a subject in the experiment; the other faces were from photos that the experimentalists had taken previously from a different experiment. Subjects knew that only one photo was real but did not know which one. Hence, Eckel and Wilson were able to show the same photos to subjects both smiling and unsmiling, as in Scharlemann et al.'s study, but not engage in deception. That is, they were able to control what subjects saw in the same way that Scharlemann et al. did, but without using deception.

The method used by Eckel and Wilson to avoid deception is a version of that first proposed by Bardsley (2000), which he labeled the conditional information lottery (CIL) design. The CIL design is a variation of the random round payoff mechanism (RRPM; see Definition 10.12). Recall that in an experiment with repetition, RRPM randomly selects one or several periods for payment of the subjects. In CIL the subject participates in a full set of tasks, but some are hypothetical. Subjects are not told which tasks are "real." Subjects are then paid only for the real tasks. The lottery is involved in determining in which period or round subjects experience the real task and subjects are told the likelihood of a task being real (the percentage of real tasks they face). At the end of the experiment, the real tasks are revealed to the subjects.

Definition 13.6 (Conditional Information Lottery): *When subjects participate in a set of tasks, some of which are hypothetical. Subjects are told that some tasks are real and others unreal, but not which tasks are of which type. Subjects are paid only for the real tasks.*

Bardsley used such a procedure in a replication of the Weimann experiment discussed in Section 13.3.2. Interestingly, Bardsley found that the results were similar to those Weimann discovered with deception. The advantage of the Bardsley procedure, of course, is that he was able to conduct almost the same experiment but without deceiving the subjects and risking possible negative effects on the subject pool for the future.

Bardsley points out that CIL can be argued to give accurate representations of subjects' choices if it can be argued that subjects treat each task independently. CIL is similar to the strategy method used in many game-theoretic experiments (see Definition 3.10). However, the main difference is that in CIL a subject may play against a computer for the entire period or round, whereas in the strategy method a subject will simply specify in advance of the period and the strategy is then implemented. To see the difference, consider a simple trust game as in the Eckel and Wilson experiments. In the strategy method, the second mover would be asked to specify how he or she would respond to all the possible offers he or she might receive. In the CIL procedure, the second mover chooses in a set of situations, some hypothetical and some real, without knowing which ones are real. We can imagine a more complicated game with multiple players choosing sequentially and the CIL method being used, in which sometimes a subject is playing against one or more computers and other times the subject is playing against other subjects. The strategy method would be difficult to implement in such a complex game.

Could a CIL-like procedure be used in political psychology experiments? In some cases, if the deception is in materials or information, using something like CIL may work. Consider the Druckman and Nelson newspaper experiment. Subjects may be randomly assigned to both real and unreal manipulations and told that some are real but others are not. The experimentalist loses control by using some real manipulations but avoids deceiving the subjects about the hypothetical manipulations. Such a design would be costly, however, given the loss of control that can occur and thus data would be "wasted." On the other hand, such an experiment could be an interesting check on the artificiality of the hypothetical manipulations if the experimentalists ask the subjects to predict which manipulation is real and pay them accordingly. Examples exist in which political psychologists use nonhypothetical choices. Kam's experiment, while she deceived subjects about the purpose of the experiment and the subliminal priming, used real candidates rather than hypothetical ones. Spezio et al., in Example 3.1, similarly used real candidates. Political psychologists have also avoided using deceptive materials by telling subjects that their choices are hypothetical or by not being specific as to where the choices come from, as in Tomz and Van Houweling's experiment in Example 8.1. A CIL-like procedure would mix both Kam and Spezia et al.'s approach with Tomz and Van Houweling's.

Nevertheless, CIL-like procedures are not useful in avoiding deception in the subliminal priming experiments of Kam and Taber or in most field experiments, such as the newspaper example. That said, CIL is certainly an attractive alternative for many laboratory experimentalists who would like to avoid deception but would like to have greater control than is normally possible without deception.

13.8 How Much Deception Should Be Allowed in Political Science Experiments?

Roth (2001) makes an interesting point about the methodological costs of deception in economics-style experiments, such as those conducted by political economists, versus psychology-style experiments, such as those conducted by political psychologists. That is, given that deception is used widely in psychology experiments and it is well known that psychologists have used such deception (taught in classes, etc.), then it would take many years for a rule of no deception to actually have a positive effect, if any. Thus, the benefits from adopting such a norm for psychology are not as large. As a consequence, it probably is the case that the benefits of deception in such experiments outweigh the costs because subjects are likely to believe deception exists already.

However, in experiments conducted by political economists, where only minimal deception principally involving omission of information is the norm, introducing deception could have a greater negative effect to the extent that subjects perceive and recognize that political economy experiments are distinctive from political psychology ones. And the benefits of relaxing the norm of little to no deception could have large consequences for what researchers can do in future experiments.

Given that political science is a discipline where both types of experiments are conducted and the trend, which we hope continues, is of more collaboration between experimentalists of both heritages, what is the solution? In pure political economic experiments conducted in the laboratory, we believe that minimizing deception and subjects' perception that deception occurs in experiments is best. The CIL procedure advocated and used by Bardsley can be effectively used for almost all of the incidents in which political economists may desire deception. Although using such a procedure may increase the cost of the experiment, the advantage of the procedure in maintaining honesty with subjects is in our view worth the cost. Political economists can also maintain separate subject pools and laboratories or collaborate with economists on subject pools and laboratories such that the perception of no deception in the experiments is maintained by preventing overlaps with experimentalists who use deception.

We also believe that political psychologists should make more of an effort to reduce deception in experiments that involve hypothetical situations or materials. We recognize that the benefits from doing so may be small given that subjects may already expect some deception and that the additional cost of creating treatments in which deception is not used and the loss of control may be greater. Yet, we believe that procedures like CIL can possibly allow for as much control as occurs in experiments in which such deceptive situations and materials are used. Certainly such procedures are one way for political psychologists and economists to collaborate on experiments that combine both approaches.

Of course, some deception in political psychology experiments cannot be avoided, as in the subliminal priming experiments of Kam and Taber. Yet, although the effects of such priming are a bit unclear, the use of deception in omission of information about the nature of an experiment's purpose is not very different from the types of deception that are used in political economy experiments and are not viewed as problematic.

As for experiments conducted in the field, the methodological effects of such deception are less problematic because subjects are not typically debriefed and there is not much overlap in the subjects used across experiments. Nevertheless, we believe that when deception can possibly cause more than minimal harms as discussed in the previous chapter, it should be minimized in the field as well. We believe that reducing deception in the field should not be a goal in itself, but that deception should be considered a possible cause of harms to subjects, confederates, and third parties, and that these harms should be minimized to the extent possible.

13.9 Chapter Summary

In this chapter we have reviewed the types of deception used in political science experiments, the arguments for and against deception, and the evidence on the effects of deception. Deception varies in degree – some types of deception that involve omission of information are generally viewed as less problematic than other types of deception that involve deceptive identities. Deception is desirable because it allows researchers a greater degree of control without artificiality and problematic effects on subjects' motivations. However, deception can harm subjects, make subjects more suspicious in future experiments, and affect their behavior in future experiments.

Debriefing can somewhat reduce these effects, but the evidence on the benefits from debriefing is mixed. The CIL procedure is a method that can be used in political economic experiments to mimic the control gained with deception without deceiving the subjects. CIL-like procedures may also be possible in political psychology experiments to reduce the need for deception. We argue for a norm of minimal deception and use of CIL procedures in all types of laboratory experiments in political science, but we recognize that deception may be necessary in field experiments.

PART V

CONCLUSION

14

The Future of Experimental Political Science

14.1 The Promise of Collaboration

In May 2009, a group of experimental political scientists from all three heritages – political psychology, political economics, and statistics – met at Northwestern University. The meeting will soon lead to a new *Handbook of Experimental Political Science* with essays by the various attendees. We see this handbook as an important companion to our book. This meeting, like two previous ones at New York University (NYU) in February 2008 and February 2009 (the first two meetings of the now Annual NYU Center of Experimental Social Sciences Experimental Political Science Conference), are the first conferences of which we are aware (our collective memories reach back over 20 years) in which such a broad range of experimentalists in political science have interacted. Typically experimentalists in political science have interacted mainly with those in their respective subfields within the experimental community or with non–political scientists who take similar focuses.

We believe the movement of more interaction between experimentalists in political science across heritages has the potential of adding significantly to our knowledge of political behavior and institutions. The possible collaborations are many. Consider the experimental literature on voting, one of the most studied aspects of political behavior. Although the purpose of this book is not a substantive review of experimental literature on particular topics, we have presented a number of examples of experiments on voting to illustrate various methodological issues. Nevertheless, the diverse nature of the experimental literature on voting is striking in the nonrepresentative sample of experiments we have discussed, both in the field in the lab, and by all three stripes of experimentalists. Some differences in this literature are obvious. The laboratory work tends to be more theoretically driven, while the field research is largely less connected to particular theories.

First, one promising avenue would be to take a more theoretical approach in the field – to focus on how experimental designs could evaluate some of the theoretical results that have already been considered in the laboratory. Doing so will not be easy. Field experimentalists will need to become more familiar with both the theory and the laboratory work. The literature reviews in the forthcoming handbook can be helpful in this regard.[1] Moreover, because working in the field means a loss of control, researchers will need to be more creative in design than is required of the laboratory experimentalists. For instance, evaluating the nuances of the predictions of the Swing Voter's Curse theory proved illusive for Lassen's nonexperimental study that came close to what can be done in a standard field experiment (Example 2.8). But given the interest of political scientists in field experimentation on voting, we hope that this will lead to imaginative designs that can more directly confront theory.

Second, laboratory work on voting has the potential of focusing on some of the mechanisms underlying the phenomena that have been found in the field experiments on voting. A large field-experimental literature now exists on different types of mobilization methods (for a review see Michelson and Nickerson, forthcoming). The laboratory can be a way of examining the mechanisms through which successful and unsuccessful mobilization strategies in the field work on cognitive processes. Again, to do so, laboratory experimentalists will need to be more familiar with the field literature and to create designs that can actually capture the phenomena observed in the field in the laboratory (not likely to be an easy task). But ultimately we want to understand these mechanisms that underlie the behavior we observe in field experiments and the laboratory, and lab-in-the-field research is often the only way to study such mechanisms because of the control and measurement capabilities of the laboratory.

Third, collaboration between the two types of laboratory experimentalists – political economists and political psychologists – on experiments in voting has the potential of enriching our understanding of the voting process. How robust are the results in political psychology when financial incentives are used? When the decision context is more interactive rather

---

[1] Unfortunately, the review essays in the handbook, due to constraints on length, are mostly heritage specific. There are separate chapters on types of experiments by political economists, political psychologists, and field experimentalists with only a little overlap. So the essays can serve as good introductions to areas a researcher does not know, but not as the syntheses we believe are needed.

than individual decision-making? When methods are used that avoid deception? How robust are the results in political economics when more contextually relevant materials are used? When nonstudents are used as subjects? When incorporating theories from political psychology into the designs? Doing so requires familiarity with both literatures and inventive experimental designs. But the promise of possibilities is real. Already we see such collaboration. For instance, NYU experimental political scientist Eric Dickson, whose training is in the political economics tradition, received the 2007 Roberta Sigel Award from the International Society of Political Psychology for the best paper at their annual meetings by anyone within eight years of receiving their Ph.D.

The promise of cooperation between political psychologists and political economists is of course not just in the literature on voting. Diermeier (forthcoming), in his review of the experimental literature on coalition experiments, makes a similar point about the potential for more partnerships between different stripes of experimentalists to address research questions in that area. Dickson's paper was not a voting experiment but examined bargaining and conflict. The potential of collaboration between laboratory and field experimentalists also extends beyond the substantive area of voting. In general, both laboratory and field experimentalists would benefit from thinking about the other venue and how their skills can translate. Laboratory experimentalists have considerable knowledge on how control and incentives can be used in the laboratory; the potential exists from laboratory experimentalists, considering how they can translate these methods to the field in productive ways, expanding what we can learn from field research and reducing the excessive reliance on random assignment, which is not always successful. Field experimentalists' knowledge of statistics can help laboratory experimentalists deal with areas where control and random assignment are less successful. Field experimentalists interested in evaluating methods used on their data can use the laboratory as a behavioral testbed (see Section 8.6).

Finally, there is the promise of more collaboration between nonexperimentalists and experimental political scientists. Often observational studies are disconnected from experimental work on the same research question. Just as there are potentials for laboratory and field experimentalists to combine forces, the commonalities in how causality is addressed in observational research and in experiments (which is one of the points of Part II of this book, on causality) mean there are also considerable opportunities for more communication and collaboration. As we have shown, the control in experiments is the same sort of control that researchers working with observational data seek when they use control functions in regressions, panel data, or matching. Instrumental variables are an attempt to mimic random assignment in experimentation. The principal tools of observational research and experimental work are at a base level the same and, thus, collaboration on how these tools can be used with both types of data to answer common questions can lead to a greater understanding of political processes.

14.2 The Difficulties Ahead

We see the outlook for experimental political science exciting, particularly the collaborations that we hope to see in the future. Yet, there are a number of difficulties ahead for experimental political science in achieving its promise. First, collaboration of the type we have discussed needs a fuller understanding and appreciation of the methodologies used across experimental political science. We hope this book helps. We need to continue active participation of the broad range of experimentalists in meetings where discussions and collaborations can be encouraged. Rather than debate over methodological differences, we need more discussion of how different methods can be combined to investigate common questions. Although we argue for a reduction in the use of deception in political psychology experiments in the previous chapter, we recognize the benefits from deception and advocate the development of new methods that can both achieve these benefits and lead to fewer ethical and methodological problems.

Second, although experimental political science is more visible and respected in the discipline than in previous years, experimentalists still face challenges in relating the experimental results (particularly those in the laboratory) to questions of interest of political scientists who work primarily with observational data. Outside the experimental community (and to some extent within), many political scientists are dismissive of the use of students in laboratory experiments, experiments that appear less "real" to them, or experiments that appear to address what to them are trivial questions. But as we have explored in this book, sometimes there are important advantages to using students as subjects, using artificial-appearing experimental environments, or answering old questions in new ways. Educating our colleagues on the value of experimental methods will be a continual test for experimentalists.

Third, experimental political scientists need to become more visible and active on Institutional Review Boards. In Chapters 11 and 12, we reviewed how most of these boards were created with a focus on biomedical experiments and how such a focus can limit the understanding of the costs and benefits of experimental research. Experimentalists in political science can educate these boards so that the members understand better the methods we use. However, to do so, experimental political scientists need to think more deeply about the ethical considerations in experiments, particularly the newer experiments being conducted in the field.

Fourth, one of the questions that experimental political scientists will confront in the coming years is the extent that we incorporate the study of biological and neural processes in our understanding of politics. What can we learn from fMRI experiments and other similar approaches about politics? Is it worth the investment in time and resources? Or are these processes best left to other biomedical disciplines? In economics, there is currently an active debate over the value of such work to address questions of interest (see the recent edited volume of Caplin and Schotter, 2008). Experimentalists in political science are in the vanguard of the movement toward incorporating more of this type of research into their studies, but doing so may distance experimentalists further from others in the field who work with more traditional data sources.

While we see these difficulties, we remain optimistic about experimental political science. We hope that this book is the first of many books on experimental political science methods and that the promise of future collaboration between both types of laboratory experimentalists, laboratory and field experimentalists, and experimentalists and nonexperimentalists will be realized.

Appendix: The Experimentalist's To Do List

Throughout this book we have attempted both to describe the methodology of experimental political science and to give advice to new experimentalists. In this appendix we provide an experimentalist's to do list that summarizes what an experimentalist needs to consider in designing and conducting an experiment as well as in analyzing experimental data. We reference parts of the book that are relevant for each item. Note that, although the items are numbered, they should not be viewed as chronological; that is, a researcher may address how he or she plans to evaluate a causal relationship before figuring out the specific target population for the experiment.

15.1 The Target Population and Subject Pools

An experimentalist should identify the target population for the study and how that target population relates to the subjects recruited for the experiment (see Definition 2.2).

15.1.1 Nonspecific Target Populations

If the target population is "humanity," as discussed in Chapter 9, then the experimentalist can reasonably use any subject pool for a first investigation of a particular experimental design. In such a case, the target population for the experiment becomes the subject pool from which the subjects are drawn and the results are valid for that pool (assuming that the subjects are randomly drawn from that pool). The subject pool is defined as the set of recruited subjects who are willing to participate. Using a subject pool similar to those used by other experimentalists who have investigated related questions means that the results of the research are more comparable to these other studies and can have methodological advantages. Undergraduate students are useful as a subject pool when the target population is humanity because they are homogeneous over time, can be compared relatively easily across universities, and are automatically refreshed with new potential subjects over time. Other options, which may be less homogeneous within a pool but are still homogeneous over time, are university staff and individuals in the local community (although refreshment is not automatic and researchers should be wary of professional subject pools developing). Researchers should be aware of the special ethical issues involved in using students and university staff and make sure that the students used are not students in their classes and that university staff used are not those who have a working relationship with the researcher (see Chapter 12). If the experiment is an exact replication of some previous study using the same subject pool, then the researcher may want to consider using a different subject pool to consider the external validity of the study to a different target population (although statistical replication can still be of use). Researchers should be aware of the pitfalls of rejecting (or accepting) theories based on excessive use of the same target population as well. Evidence on comparisons of subject pools shows that for one-shot games students may be more likely to choose "rationally," although games where learning is allowed or comparisons using populations likely to be familiar with the situation in the game suggest the opposite relationship.

15.1.2 Specific Target Populations

If the target population is more specific, such as particular types of political elites or registered voters in a particular election such as the New York Senate contest in 2010, then the researcher should consider how the subject pool used for the experiment relates to this target population. If it is not a random sample from that population, the researcher should consider the extent that the results can be generalized to that population by examining the differences between the subject pool and the target population in terms of demographics and known differences from previous experiments. Conducting such an experiment is not problematic in itself because sometimes it is impossible to recruit sufficient numbers of subjects from a desired target population. For example, recruiting members of the U.S. Congress in sizable numbers to evaluate a theory of congressional bargaining is likely to be exceedingly difficult. Some specific target populations, such as children and prisoners, may require special ethical considerations (see Chapter 12).

15.2 Location of the Experiment

An experimentalist needs to decide if the experiment will be conducted in a traditional experimental laboratory, in a lab in the field, in a virtual laboratory over the Internet, through a survey, or in the field. See Chapter 8 for a discussion of the advantages and disadvantages of different location choices.

15.2.1 Traditional Laboratory Experiments

Experiments conducted in traditional laboratories provide researchers with significant control over the experimental environment and are particularly useful for interactive experiments or experiments using biomedical equipment. In interactive experiments, subjects who see other participants recruited like themselves are more likely to believe that they are engaging in interactions with other humans than may be true in experiments conducted via the Internet. Biomedical equipment may not be available outside of the laboratory. Laboratory experiments can also use within-subjects designs, which often are not possible outside of the laboratory (see Section 3.3.3). However, traditional laboratory experiments can reach smaller numbers of subjects than are available outside of the laboratory. As compared to some field experiments but not necessarily Internet experiments, the subjects willing to participate in a traditional laboratory experiment may be significantly different from those who are recruited in the field.

15.2.2 Lab-in-the-Field Experiments

Experiments conducted in labs in the field can also provide the same control and usefulness as traditional laboratory experiments, depending on the arrangements that a researcher can make with outside entities who manage the locations. They have the potential to draw from a wider target population, although they may be less comparable over time and across studies because of differences in target populations. They provide excellent opportunities for evaluating the external validity of an experiment previously conducted in a traditional laboratory.

15.2.3 Internet Experiments

Experiments conducted in virtual laboratories can similarly be useful for interactive situations and draw from an even wider potential target population (although not necessarily a random sample given that Internet use varies by demographics). They can be used for much larger sample sizes than in traditional laboratory experiments, which is a decided plus. They also provide excellent opportunities for evaluating the external validity of an experiment previously conducted in a traditional laboratory. However, subjects may not believe that their choices in interactive experiments affect other human beings. In this way and in others, the experimentalist loses the strong control he or she has in a laboratory (either traditional or in the field). And the data may be less comparable over time and across studies because of differences in target populations.

15.2.4 Survey Experiments

Experiments conducted through surveys (either through the Internet or using traditional methods) also have the potential to draw from a wider population in greater numbers than in laboratories and are excellent opportunities to explore the external validity of results previously found in decision-making experiments conducted in laboratories. However, the researcher loses the strong control he or she has in a laboratory and only very simple interactive experiments can be conducted via surveys (such as a dictator game or ultimatum game using the strategy method for the second mover; see Example 8.5). And as with Internet experiments, they may be less comparable over time and across studies because of differences in target populations.

15.2.5 Field Experiments

Experiments conducted in the field have the same advantages as experiments conducted in surveys. Field experiments can also be embedded in a naturally occurring event (e.g., an election) and, thus, the ecological validity of the experiment is high. But these experiments have the same disadvantages that survey experiments have in terms of loss of control, difficulty in conducting interactive experiments, and problems with comparability across studies because of differences in target populations.

15.3 Motivation and Recruitment of Subjects

An experimentalist should consider how he or she plans to recruit the subjects and motivate them during the experiment (see Chapter 10 for a review).

15.3.1 Financial Incentives Related to Subjects' Choices

If financial incentives are to be used to motivate subjects, an experimentalist should make sure that the incentives are sizable enough compared to the earnings that a subject could make outside of the experiment. For students, a norm of roughly twice the minimum wage has been shown to be successful for most experiments; however, in complex experiments, some research suggests that higher payoffs can make a difference. If the subjects are participating in a number of tasks over time, to prevent wealth effects researchers should use the random round payoff mechanism (RRPM; see Definition 10.12). Researchers may find it useful to use experimental currency with a known exchange rate, both for ease of design and to increase the saliency of the payments. Researchers should be careful to provide subjects with privacy during the experiment and when payments are made for ethical reasons, to prevent subjects from collaborating against the experimentalist, and to keep subjects from being motivated by concerns about the payments to other subjects whose identity they know. If the degree of risk aversion of the subjects is a serious concern as a possible confounding factor in an experiment, a researcher may want to conduct the manipulations described in Chapter 10 to measure risk aversion or to attempt to induce risk-neutral preferences; however, the evidence is mixed on the effectiveness of such procedures.

15.3.2 Other Types of Incentives Related to Subjects' Choices

If home-grown values are used as incentives (see Definition 10.13), the researcher should be aware of the loss of control that can occur, particularly in experiments in which subjects make choices sequentially and the commodities used for incentives are perceived to have a fixed monetary value and level of quality, but these may be unknown to all subjects. Grades should not be used to motivate subjects in experiments for research purposes, although in classroom situations where the experiment is a teaching tool, then grades may be acceptable as a motivation. Researchers should avoid using tournament reward payoffs – that is, lottery points as a payoff mechanism in a lottery in which all subjects compete (see Definition 10.9) – because doing so introduces confounding supergame effects that may affect the subjects' choices in the experiment.

15.3.3 Motivating Subjects in Other Ways and the Role of Frames and Scripts

When it is not obvious how to relate incentives to subjects' choices, as in many political psychology experiments, experimentalists usually attempt to motivate subjects through the framing of the experiment – the script and instructions. Scripts and frames are also important because the type of information provided to subjects may affect how they choose in the experiment even when experiments use incentives based on choices. Researchers should carefully consider whether the script or frame makes it easier or more difficult for particular types of subjects to understand the experimental tasks. Researchers may want to evaluate the effectiveness of different alternative frames in trial runs or as evaluations of the external validity of previous experiments. For some subject pools, it may be desirable to express the experiment in a frame that is contextual, to increase their interest in the task, while in other cases researchers may want to use a more neutral frame if subjects come to the experiment from a wide variety of backgrounds.

15.3.4 Subject Recruitment

Typically most experimentalists who use students, university staff, or community members recruit subjects via the Internet, through flyers, and so on, to be part of a general subject pool that is then drawn from by a group of experimentalists at their institution. Software for recruitment is available; one free option is ORSEE (Online Recruitment System for Economic Experiments) devised by Ben Greiner at the University of New South Wales (see ttp://www.orsee.org/). Because of differences in the extent that deception is used, sometimes experimentalists maintain separate subject pools for experiments with deception and for those without. Many experimentalists use show-up fees ranging from $5 to $10 to further induce subjects to participate. In some group experiments in which the researcher needs a specific number, it is normal to over-recruit, paying subjects the show-up fee if they are not used for the experiment and they arrive before the experiment starts.

15.4 Relationship to Theory, Manipulations, and Baselines

The experimentalist needs to consider the relationship between the theory underpinning the possible causal relationships studied and the experimental design and post-experimental data analysis.

15.4.1 When Working from a Formal Theory

In some cases researchers have an explicit theory about the effects of causes that they wish to evaluate in the experiment. If that is the case and the theory is formally derived, a researcher may want to approach the design of the experiment and the post-data analysis using the Formal Theory Approach, as explained in Chapter 6. When researchers take this approach, they standardly attempt for the design and any post-experimental data analysis to be logically consistent with the equations underlying the theory and to engage in manipulations (and appropriate baselines) that evaluate the predictions from the theory (as well as sometimes the assumptions of the theory). The parameters of the experiment are carefully chosen so that the researcher can evaluate the predictions. In some cases a researcher may wish to conduct a stress test of the theory (see Section 6.4.2), in which a researcher relaxes some of the connections or varies aspects of the experiment that are not expected to matter.

15.4.2 When Working from a Nonformal Theory or a Prediction That Is Inspired by a Formal Theory

Sometimes a researcher works with a less-specified theoretical hypothesis about the effects of causes, either because it comes from a less-specified theory or because the researcher is not interested in evaluating the formal theory underlying the theoretical prediction explicitly. In either case, a researcher uses a Rubin Causal Model (RCM) approach, as discussed in Chapters 3, 4, and 5. The researcher makes the theoretical consistency assumption, as noted in Chapter 6. The manipulations and baselines chosen should come from the hypotheses investigated. When using an RCM approach, the researcher makes the stable unit treatment value assumption (SUTVA; see Definition 3.15) and must be aware of the implications of SUTVA for drawing conclusions about causal relationships from the experimental research.

15.5 Operationalizing Random Assignment

The experimentalist needs to consider how to operationalize random assignment. Random assignment to manipulations, along with control, is a principal tool used by experimentalists to evaluate causal relationships. A full discussion of why random assignment is valuable and how random assignment can be operationalized can be found in Chapter 5.

15.5.1 Random Assignment in Laboratories, Both Traditional and in the Field

For simple decision-making experiments, subjects can be randomly assigned to manipulations when they arrive at the laboratory, which should control for subjects arriving at different times as well as for idiosyncratic subject-specific differences. For more complex group interactive experiments, manipulations can be randomly assigned in a within-subjects design or across sessions, although possible confounding differences in session times should be considered. Typically, researchers do not have to worry about nonresponse or noncompliance in laboratory experiments; however, in sequential experiments (see Definition 5.6) conducted in the laboratory, researchers may need to consider how to control for subjects failing to show up for subsequent sessions.

15.5.2 Random Assignment Outside the Laboratory

Researchers should be prepared for problems of noncompliance and non-response as well as timing issues when conducting experiments outside of the laboratory. There are many methods (both in the design and in the post-analysis of the data) to deal with these problems, which are explained in depth in Chapter 5.

15.6 Considering Ethical Issues Involved in the Experiment and Securing IRB Approval

Because experiments with human subjects have direct effects on others' lives, experimentalists should be aware of the ethical issues involved in their experimental design and in a growing number of countries must get approval from Institutional Review Boards (IRBs) before conducting experiments. These issues are explored in Chapters 11, 12, and 13.

15.6.1 Benefit and Cost Evaluation

Researchers should consider explicitly the benefits and costs of their experimental design on their subjects, confederates, and third parties. Chapter 12 defines and gives examples of these benefits and costs. Societal benefits (and costs), because they are so difficult to measure and anticipate in most social science research, should not weigh heavily on whether an experiment is conducted. Similarly, collateral benefits such as payment for participation should not be given weight either. However, risks and harms to individuals involved should matter considerably and researchers should attempt to minimize risk and, when possible, engage in experiments with only minimal risks (see Definition 11.1).

15.6.2 IRB Approval

Before even beginning the design of an experiment, researchers should discover the IRB requirements for experimentation at their institution. Typically, regardless of where the experiment will be conducted (in the laboratory or the field, even outside of their home country), researchers in the United States and a growing number of other countries must get approval from the IRB at their institution before conducting experiments. IRBs requirements can vary significantly across institutions and in some cases the wait time for approval can be substantial, which researchers need to consider in their research plans. Chapters 11 and 12 explain how the process works in the United States and in several other countries that use IRB procedures.

15.6.3 Deception

Experimentalists need to consider how much deception is needed for an experiment. We believe that researchers should minimize deception for both ethical and methodological reasons. In Chapter 13 we advocate that researchers consider using a method similar to a conditional information lottery design (see Definition 13.6) as a substitute for deception when possible.

15.7 Post-Experimental Analysis

In contrast to observational research, experimentalists have the opportunity to use the design stage to use control and random assignment to deal with confounding observable and unobservable variables. Yet, sometimes, because control is lacking or random assignment is not perfect, experimentalists need to approach their data in the same ways that researchers approach observational data, using control in regressions, matching, or panel data as discussed in Chapter 4; using methods to correct to deal with problems in random assignment as reviewed in Chapter 5; or using FTA-based methods typically used on observational data (empirical estimating equations directly derived from a formal model), as explored in Chapter 6. Ideally, an experimentalist relies as much as possible on the design stage rather than the analysis stage, but in some situations it is not possible to devise a completely "clean" design. To the extent that the design fails in control and random assignment, the researcher can turn to the methods used for observational data to deal with these deficiencies in the design.

References

Abbring, Jaap H. and James J. Heckman. 2007. "Econometric Evaluation of Social Programs, Part III: Distributional Treatment Effects, Dynamic Treatment Effects, Dynamic Discrete Choice, and General Equilibrium Policy Evaluation," in *Handbook of Econometrics* (James J. Heckman and Edward E. Leamer, eds.). New York: Elsevier, pp. 4779–4874.

Allen, D. F. 1983. "Follow-up Analysis of Use of Forewarning and Deception in Psychological Experiments," *Psychological Reports* 52:899–906.

Alpizar, Francisco, Frederick Carlsson, and Olof Johnsson-Stenman. 2008. "Does Context Matter More for Hypothetical than for Actual Contributions? Evidence from a Natural Field Experiment," *Experimental Economics* 11:299–314.

Altman, Micah and Michael P. McDonald. 2003. "Replication with Attention to Numerical Accuracy," *Political Analysis* 11:302–307.

American Psychological Association. 2002. "Ethical Principals of Psychologists and Code of Conduct," *American Psychologist* 57:1–16.

Andreoni, James. 1988. "Why Free Ride? Strategies and Learning in Public Goods Experiments," *Journal of Public Economics* 37:291–304.

Andreoni, James and John Miller. 2002. "Giving According to GARP: An Experimental Test of the Consistency of Preferences for Altruism," *Econometrica* 70(2):737–753.

Ang, J. S. and T. Schwarz 1985. "Risk Aversion and Information Structure: An Experimental Study of Price Variability in the Securities Markets," *Journal of Finance* 40:825–844.

Angrist, J. 1998. "Estimating the Labor Market Impact of Voluntary Military Service Using Social Security Data on Military Applicants," *Econometrica* 66(2):249–288.

Angrist, Joshua D. and Alan B. Kreuger. 2001. "Instrumental Variables and the Search for Identification: From Supply and Demand to Natural Experiments," *Journal of Economic Perspectives* 15(4):69–85.

Angrist, Joshua D., Guido W. Imbens, and Donald B. Rubin. 1996. "Identification of Casual Effects Using Instrumental Variables," *Journal of the American Statistical Association* 91(June):444–455.

Ansolabehere, Stephen and Shanto Iyengar. 1997. *Going Negative: How Political Advertisements Shrink & Polarize the Electorate.* New York: Free Press.

Ansolabehere, Stephen, A. Strauss, James Snyder, and Michael Ting. 2005. "Voting Weights and Formateur Advantages in the Formation of Coalition Governments," *American Journal of Political Science* July 49(3):550–563.

539

Ansolabehere, Stephen, Jonathan Rodden, and James Snyder. 2008. "The Strength of Issues: Using Multiple Measures to Gauge Preference Stability, Ideological Constraint, and Issue Voting," *American Political Science Review* 102(2, May):215–232.

Appelbaum, P. S., L. H. Roth, and C. W. Lidz. 1982. "The Therapeutic Misconception: Informed Consent in Psychiatric Research," *International Journal of Law and Psychiatry* 5:319–329.

Aragones, Enriequeta and Thomas R. Palfrey. 2004. "The Effect of Candidate Quality on Electoral Equilibrium: An Experimental Study," *American Political Science Review* 89(1, February):77–90.

Arceneaux, K. 2005. "Using Cluster Randomized Field Experiments to Study Voting Behavior," *Annals of the American Academy of Political and Social Science* 601:169–179.

Arkes, Hal R., Robyn M. Dawes, and Caryn Christensen. 1999. "Factors Influencing the Use of a Decision Rule in a Probabilistic Task," *Organizational Behavior and Human Decision Processes* 37:93–110.

Athey, Susan and Philip Haile. 2002. "Identification in Standard Auction Models," *Econometrica* 70(6):2107–2140.

Aviv, A. L., J. M. Zelenski, L. Rallo, and R. J. Larsen. 2002. "Who Comes When: Personality Differences in Early and Later Participation in a University Subject Pool," *Personality and Individual Differences* 33(3):487–496.

Bahry, Donna L. and Rick K. Wilson. 2004. "Trust in Transitional Societies: Experimental Results from Russia," in American Political Science Association Meetings. Chicago: American Political Science Association.

Bahry, Donna and Rick Wilson. 2006. "Confusion or Fairness in the Field? Rejections in the Ultimatum Game under the Strategy Method," *Journal of Economic Behavior and Organization* 60:37–54.

Bahry, Donna P., Mikhail Kosolapov, Polina Kozyreva, and Rick Wilson. 2005. "Ethnicity and Trust: Evidence from Russia," *American Political Science Review* 99(4):521–532.

Bajari, Patrick and Ali Hortacsu. 2005. "Are Structural Estimates of Auction Models Reasonable? Evidence from Experimental Data," *Journal of Political Economy* 113(4):703–741.

Bangert-Downs, Robert L. 1986. "Review of Developments in Meta-Analytic Method," *Psychological Bulletin* 99(3):388–399.

Barabas, Jason. 2004. "How Deliberation Affects Public Opinions," *American Political Science Review* 98(4):687–701.

Bardsley, Nicholas. 2000. "Control Without Deception: Individual Behaviour in Free-Riding Experiments Revisited," *Experimental Economics* 3:215–240.

Bardsley, Nicholas. 2008. "Dictator Game Giving: Altruism or Artefact?" *Experimental Economics* 11(2):122–133.

Barnard, J., C., Frangakis, J. L., Hill, and D. B. Rubin. 2002. "School Choice in NY City: A Bayesian Analysis of an Imperfect Randomized Experiment" in *Case Studies in Bayesian Statistics*, vol. V, C., Gatsonis, R. E. Kass, B. Carlin, A., Cariiguiry, A. Gelman, I. Verdinelli, and M. West, eds. New York: Springer-Verlag, pp. 3–97.

Baron, David and John Ferejohn. 1989. "Bargaining in Legislatures," *American Political Science Review* 83:1181–1206.

Baron, R. M. and D. A. Kenny. 1986. "The Moderator-Mediator Variable Distinction in Social Psychological Research: Conceptual, Strategic and Statistical Considerations," *Journal of Personality and Social Psychology* 51:1173–1182.

Bartels, Larry M. 1996. "Uninformed Votes: Information Effects in Presidential Elections," *American Journal of Political Science* 40(1, February):194–230.

Basinger, S. J. and H. Lavine. 2005. "Ambivalence, Information, and Electoral Choice," *American Political Science Review* 99(2):169–184.

Bassett, R. L., D. Basinger, and P. Livermore. 1992. "Lying in the Laboratory: Deception in Human Research from Psychological, Philosophical, and Theological Perspectives," *Journal of the American Scientific Affiliation* 34:201–212.

Bassi, Anna. 2006. "Experiments on Approval Voting," Working paper, New York University.

Bassi, A., R. Morton, and K. Williams. 2010. "The Effect of Identities, Incentives, and Information on Voting." Working Paper.

Battaglini, M., R. Morton, and T. Palfrey. 2007. "Efficiency, Equity, and Timing of Voting Mechanisms," *American Political Science Review* 101:409–424.

Battaglini, M., R. B. Morton, and T. R. Palfrey. 2008. "Information Aggregation and Strategic Abstention in Large Laboratory Elections," *American Economic Review* 98(2):194–200.

Battaglini, M., R. B. Morton, and T. R. Palfrey. 2010. "The Swing Voter's Curse in the Laboratory," *Review of Economic Studies* 77(1):61–89.

Baumrind, D. 1985. "Research Using Intentional Deception: Ethical Issues Revisited," *American Psychologist*, 40:165–174.

Beaumont, Williams. 1833. *Physiology of Digestion.* Plattsburgh: F. P. Allen.

Beck, Nathaniel. 2000. "Political Methodology: A Welcoming Discipline," *Journal of the American Statistical Association* 95(450):651–654.

Becker, G., M. H. DeGroot, and J. Marschak. 1964. "Measuring Utility by a Single-Response Sequential Method," *Behavioral Science* 8:41–55.

Beecher, Henry. 1966. "Special Article: Ethics and Clinical Research," *New England Journal of Medicine* 274:1354–1360.

Bell, J., J. Whiton, and S. Connelly. 1998. "Evaluation of NIH Implementation of Section 491 of the Public Health Service Act, Mandating a Program of Protection for Research Subjects." Report prepared under National Institutes of Health contract N01-OD-2-2109. Washington, D.C.: U.S. Department of Health and Human Services.

Bellemare, Charles, Sabine Kroger, and Arthur Van Soest. 2008. "Measuring Inequity Aversion in a Heterogeneous Population Using Experimental Decisions and Subjective Probabilities," *Econometrica* 76(4, July):815–839.

Bellezza, F. S., A. G. Greenwald, and M. R. Banaji. 1986. "Words High and Low in Pleasantness as Rated by Male and Female College Students," *Behavior Research Methods, Instruments, and Computers* 18:299–303.

Belot, Michele, Raymond Duch, and Luis Miller. 2009. *Who Should Be Called to the Lab?* Oxford, UK: CESS, Nuffield College.

Benabou, Roland and Jean Tirole. 2003. "Intrinsic and Extrinsic Motivation," *Review of Economic Studies* 70(3):489–520.

Benjamini, Y. and Y. Hochberg. 2000. "On the Adaptive Control of the False Discovery Fate in Multiple Testing with Independent Statistics," *Journal of Educational and Behavioral Statistics* 25(1):60–83.

Berelson, Bernard, Paul F. Lazarsfeld, and William N. McPhee. 1954. *Voting.* Chicago: The University of Chicago Press.

Berg, J., J. Dickhaut, and K. Mccabe. 1995. "Trust, Reciprocity, and Social-History," *Games and Economic Behavior* 10(1):122–142.

Berg, J., R. Forsythe, F. Nelson, and T. Rietz. 2008. "Results from a Dozen Years of Election Futures Markets Research," in *Handbook of Experimental Economics Results* (C. R. Plott and V. L. Smith, eds.). Oxford, UK: Elsevier, vol. 1, pp. 742–751.

Berg, Joyce E., John W. Dickhaut, and Thomnas A. Rietz. 2010. "Preference Reversals: The Impact of Truth-Revealing Monetary Incentives," *Games and Economic Behavior* 68(2):443–468.

Berg, Joyce, L. Daley, J. Dickhaut, and J. O'Brien. 1986. "Controlling Preferences for Lotteries on Units of Experimental Exchange," *Quarterly Journal of Economics* 101:281–306.

Berg, Joyce, John Dickhaut, and Kevin McCabe. 2005. "Risk Preference Instability Across Institutions: A Dilemma," *Proceedings of the National Academy of Sciences* 102(11, March):4209–4214.

Berkum, M. M., H. M. Bialek, R. P. Kern, and K. E. Yagi. 1962. "Experimental Studies of Psychological Stress in Man," *Psychological Monograph* 76(15):534.

Berry, Steven, James Levinsohn, and Ariel Pakes. 1995. "Automobile Prices in Market Equilibrium," *Econometrica* 63(4):841–890.

Berscheid, E., D. Abrahams, and E. Aronson. 1967. "Effectiveness Debriefing Following Deception Experiments," *Journal of Personality and Social Psychology* 6:371–380.

Bertrand, Marianne, Esther Duflo, and Sendhil Mullainathan. 2004. "How Much Should We Trust Differences-in-Differences Estimates," *Quarterly Journal of Economics* (February) 119(1):249–275.

Bettinger, Eric and Robert Slonim. 2007. "Patience among Children," *Journal of Public Economics* 91(1–2):343–363.

Bewley, Truman F. 1999. *Why Wages Don't Fall During a Recession*. Cambridge: Harvard University Press.

Binmore, Ken. 2005. "Economic Man – or Straw Man? A Commentary on Henrich et al.," Working paper, University College London.

Binmore, Kenneth, Peter Morgan, Avner Shaked, and John Sutton. 1991. "Do People Exploit Their Bargaining Power? An Experimental Study," *Games and Economic Behavior* 3:295–322.

Birgegard, A. and S. Sohlberg. 2008. "Persistent Effects of Subliminal Stimulation: Sex Differences and the Effectiveness of Debriefing," *Scandinavian Journal of Psychology* 49(1):19–29.

Bishop, R. and T. A. Heberlein. 1986. "Does Contingent Valuation Work?" in *Valuing Environmental Goods: A State of the Arts Assessment of Contingent Valuation Method* (R. Cummings, D. Brookshire, and W. Schulze, eds.). Totowa, NJ: Rowman and Allenheld. 123–147.

Blanton, Hart and James Jaccard. 2008. "Representing Versus Generalizing: Two Approaches to External Validity and Their Implications for the Study of Prejudice," *Psychological Inquiry* 19(2):99–105.

Blydenburgh, J. C. 1971. "A Controlled Experiment to Measure the Effects of Personal Contact Campaigning," *Midwest Journal of Political Science* 15:365–381.

Bok, S. 1978. *Lying Moral Choices in Public and Private Life*. New York: Pantheon Books.

Bolck, Annabel, Marcel Croon, and Jacques Hagenaars. 2004. "Estimating Latent Structure Models with Categorical Variables: One-Step Versus Three-Step Estimators," *Political Analysis* 12:3–27.

Bolton, Gary E. and Axel Ockenfels. 1998. "Strategy and Equity: An ERC Analysis of the Guth-van Damme Game," Levine's Working Paper Archive 2060, David K. Levine.

Bonetti, S. 1998. "Experimental Economics and Deception," *Journal of Economic Psychology* 19:377–395.

Bortolotti, L. and M. Mameli. 2006. "Deception in Psychology: Moral Costs and Benefits of Unsought Self-Knowledge," *Accountability in Research* 13:259–275.

Bosch-Domènech, Antoni and Joaquim Silvestre. 2006. "Reflections on Gains and Losses: A $2 \times 2 \times 7$ Experiment," *Journal of Risk and Uncertainty* 33(3):217–235.

Bositis, David A. and Douglas Steinel. 1987. "A Synoptic History and Typology of Experimental Research in Political Science" *Political Behavior* 9:263–84.

Boulton, M. and M. Parker. 2007. "Informed Consent in a Changing Environment," *Social Science and Medicine* 65:2187–2198.

Bound, John, David A. Jaeger, and Regina M. Baker. 1995. "Problems with Instrumental Variables Estimation When the Correlation between the Instruments and the Endogenous Explanatory Variables is Weak," *Journal of the American Statistical Association* 90(430):443–450.

Brady, Henry. 2000. "Contributions of Survey Research to Political Science," *PS: Political Science and Politics* 33(1, March):47–57.

Brambor, Thomas, William Clark, and Matt Golder. 2006. "Understanding Interactive Models: Improving Empirical Analyses," *Political Analysis* 14:63–82.

Brams, Steven and Peter Fishburn. 1983. *Approval Voting*. Cambridge, MA: Birkhauser.

Brase, Gary L., Laurence Fiddick, and Clare Harries. 2006. "Participant Recruitment Methods and Statistical Reasoning Performance," *Quarterly Journal of Experimental Psychology* 59(5):965–976.

Brekke, Kjell Arne, Snorre Kverndokk, and Karine Nyborg. 2003. "An Economic Model of Moral Motivation," *Journal of Public Economics* 87:1967–1983.

Brock, T. C. and L. A. Becker. 1966. "Debriefing and Susceptibility to Subsequent Experimental Manipulations," *Journal of Experimental Social Psychology* 2:314–323.

Brody, Richard and Charles Brownstein. 1975. "Experimentation and Simulation," in *Handbook of Political Science* (Fred Greenstein and Nelson Polsby, eds.). Reading, MA: Addison-Wesley, vol. 7, pp. 211–264.

Burns, P. 1985. "Experience and Decisionmaking: A Comparison of Students and Businessmen in a Simulated Progressive Auction," in *Research in Experimental Economics* (V. Smith, ed.). Greenwich: JAI Press, 2:139–157.

Calvert, Randall. 1985. "Robustness of the Multidimensional Voting Model: Candidate Motivations, Uncertainty, and Convergence," *American Journal of Political Science* 29(February):69–95.

Camerer, Colin F. 2003. *Behavioral Game Theory: Experiments in Strategic Interaction.* New York: Russell Sage Foundation.

Camerer, Colin and Robin Hogarth. 1999. "The Effects of Financial Incentives in Experiments: A Review and Capital-Labor-Production Framework," *Journal of Risk and Uncertainty* 19:1–3, 7–41.

Camerer, Colin, George Loewenstein, and Matthew Rabin, eds. 2004. *Advances in Behavioral Economics.* Princeton: Russell Sage Foundation and Princeton University Press.

Cameron, Charles and Rebecca Morton. 2002. "Formal Theory Meets Data," in *The State of the Discipline of Political Science* (Ira Katznelson and Helen Milner, eds.). Washington, DC: American Political Science Association.

Cameron, J. and W. D. Pierce. 1994. "Reinforcement, Reward and Intrinsic Motivation: A Meta-analysis," *Review of Educational Research* 64:363–423.

Cameron, J. and W. D. Pierce. 1996. "The Debate about Rewards and Intrinsic Motivation: Protests and Accusations Do Not Alter the Results," *Review of Educational Research* 66:39–51.

Campbell, Donald T. 1957. "Factors Relevant to the Validity of Experiments in Social Settings," *Psychological Bulletin* 54:297–312.

Canache, Damarys, Jeffrey J. Mondak, and Ernesto Cabrera. 2000. "Voters and the Personal Vote: A Counterfactual Simulation," *Political Research Quarterly* 53(3):663–676.

Caplin, Andrew and Andrew Schotter, eds. 2008. *The Foundations of Positive and Normative Economics: A Handbook.* Oxford: Oxford University Press.

Cappellari, Lorenzo and Gilberto Tuarti. 2004. "Volunteer Labour Supply: The Role of Workers' Motivations," *Annals of Public and Cooperative Economics* 75(4):619–643.

Carnelley, K. B. and A. C. Rowe. 2007. "Repeated Priming of Attachment Security Influences Later Views of Self and Relationships," *Personal Relationships* 14(2):307–320.

Caroll, J. S. and E. J. Johnson. 1990. *Decision Research – A Field Guide.* London: Sage Publications.

Casella, A., T. Palfrey, and R. Riezman. 2008. "Minorities and Storable Votes," *Quarterly Journal of Political Science* 3(2):165–200.

Casella, Alessandra. 2005. "Storable Votes," *Games and Economic Behavior* 51:391–419.

Catania, Joseph A., Bernard Lo, Leslie E. Wolf, M. Margaret Dolcini, Lance M. Pollack, Judith C. Barker, Stacey Wertlieb, and Jeff Henne. 2008. "Survey of U.S. Human Research Protection Organizations: Workload and Membership," *Journal of Empirical Research on Human Research Ethics* 3(4):57–69.

Cesari, Marco, John C. Ham, and John H. Kagel. 2007. "Selection Bias, Demographic Effects, and Ability Effects in Common Value Auction Experiments," *American Economic Review* 97(4, September):1278–1304.

Charness, Gary and Matthew Rabin. 2002. "Understanding Social Preferences with Simple Tests," *Quarterly Journal of Economics* 117(3):817–869.

Chaudhuri, Ananish, Andrew Schotter, and Barry Sopher. 2009. "Talking Ourselves to Efficiency: Coordination in Inter-Generational Minimum Effort Games with Private, Almost Common and Common Knowledge of Advice," *Economic Journal* 119(534):91–122.

Chen, Kay-Yut and Charles R. Plott. 1998. "Nonlinear Behavior in Sealed Bid First-Price Auctions," *Games and Economic Behavior* 25(1, October):34–78.

Chong, Dennis and James N. Druckman. 2007. "Framing Theory," *Annual Review of Political Science* 10:103–126.

Chong, Dennis and James Druckman. 2009. "Durability of Framing Effects on Public Opinion." Paper presented at the annual meeting of the ISPP 32nd Annual Scientific Meeting, Trinity College, Dublin, Ireland.

Chou, Eileen, Margaret McConnell, Rosemarie Nagel, and Charles Plott. 2009. "The Control of Game Form Recognition in Experiments: Understanding Dominant Strategy Failures in a Simple Two Person 'Guessing' Game," *Experimental Economics* 12(2):159–179.

Christensen, L. 1988. "Deception in Psychological Research: When Is Its Use Justified?" *Personality and Social Psychology Bulletin* 14:664–675.

Church, Alan H. 1993. "Estimating the Effect of Incentives on Mail Survey Response Rates: A Meta-analysis," *Public Opinion Quarterly* 57:62–79.

Churchill, Larry R., Daniel K. Nelson, Gail E. Henderson, Nancy M. P. King, Arlene M. Davis, Erin Leahey, and Benjamin S. Wilfond. 2003. "Assessing Benefits in Clinical Research: Why Diversity in Benefit Assessment Can Be Risky," *IRB* 25(3):1–8.

Clinton, Joshua and John Lapinski. 2004. "'Targeted' Advertising and Voter Turnout: An Experimental Study of the 2000 Presidential Election," *Journal of Politics* 66(February):69–96.

Coate, Stephen and Michael Conlin. 2004. "A Group Rule-Utilitarian Approach to Voter Turnout: Theory and Evidence," *American Economic Review* 94(5, December):1476–1504.

Collier, K. E., R. D. McKelvey, P. C. Ordeshook, and K. Williams. 1987. "Retrospective Voting – An Experimental-Study," *Public Choice* 53(2):101–130.

Collier, K., P. C. Ordeshook, and K. Williams. 1989. "The Rationally Uninformed Electorate – Some Experimental Evidence," *Public Choice* 60(1):3–29.

Condorcet, Marquis de. 1785. Éssai sur L'application L'analyse à la probabilité des dés Décisions Rendues à la Pluralité des Voix [Essay on the Application of Mathematics to the Theory of Decision-Making]. Paris.

Connelly, Gordon M. and Harry H. Field. 1944. "The Non-Voter – Who He Is, What He Thinks," *Public Opinion Quarterly* 8:175–187.

Cook, T. D., J. R. Bean, B. J. Calder, R. Frey, M. L. Krovetz, and S. R. Reisman. 1970. "Demand Characteristics and Three Conceptions of the Frequently Deceived Subject," *Journal of Personality and Social Psychology* 14:185–194.

Cook, T. D. and D. T. Campbell. 1979. *Quasi-Experimentation: Design and Analysis for Field Settings*. Chicago: Rand McNally.

Cooper, D. J., J. H. Kagel, W. Lo, and Q. L. Gu. 1999. "Gaming Against Managers in Incentive Systems: Experimental Results with Chinese Students and Chinese Managers," *American Economic Review* 89:781–804.

Cooper, D. J. and J. B. Van Huyck. 2003. "Evidence on the equivalence of the strategic and extensive form representation of games," *Journal of Economic Theory* 110(2):290–308.

Costa-Gomes, Miguel A. and Vincent P. Crawford. 2006. "Cognition and Behavior in Two-Person Guessing Games: An Experimental Study," *American Economic Review* 96(5):1737–1768.

Cox, D. R. and N. Reid. 2000. *The Theory of the Design of Experiments*. Monographs on Statistics & Applied Probability. Boston, MA: Chapman & Hall.

Cox, James C. and Ronald L. Oaxaca. 1995. "Inducing Risk-Neutral Preferences: Further Analysis of the Data," *Journal of Risk and Uncertainty* 11(1):65–79.

Cox, James C. and Rondal L. Oaxaca. 1996. "Is Bidding Behavior Consistent with Bidding Theory for Private Value Auctions," in *Research in Experimental Economics* (R. M. Isaac, ed.). Greenwich, CT: JAI Press, vol. 6, pp. 131–148.

Cox, James C. and Vjollca Sadiraj. 2002. "Risk Aversion and Expected-Utility Theory: Coherence for Small- and Large-Stakes Gambles," Working paper, University of Arizona.

Cronbach, L. J. 1982. *Designing Evaluations of Educational and Social Programs.* San Francisco: Jossey-Bass.

Cubitt, Robin P., Chris Starmer, and Robert Sugden. 1998. "On the Validity of the Random Lottery Incentive System," *Experimental Economics* 1:115–132.

Dal Bó, Pedro. 2005. "Cooperation under the Shadow of the Future: Experimental Evidence from Infinitely Repeated Games," *American Economic Review* 95(5):1591–1604.

Danielson, Anders J. and Hakan J. Holm. 2007. "Do You Trust Your Brethen? Eliciting Trust Attitudes and Trust Behavior in a Tanzanian Congregation," *Journal of Economic Behavior and Organization* 62:255–271.

Dasgupta, Sugato and Kenneth Williams. 2002. "A Principal-Agent Model of Elections with Novice Incumbents: Some Experimental Results," *Journal of Theoretical Politics* 14(October):409–438.

Davern, Michael, Todd H. Rockwood, Randy Sherrod, and Stephen Campbell. 2003. "Prepaid Monetary Incentives and Data Quality in Face-to-Face Interviews: Data from the 1996 Survey of Income and Program Participation Incentive Experiment," *Public Opinion Quarterly* 67:139–147.

Davis, D. D. and C. A. Holt. 1993. *Experimental Economics.* Princeton, NJ: Princeton University Press.

Dawid, A. 2000. "Causal Inference Without Counterfactuals," *Journal of the American Statistical Association* 95(450):407–424.

De La O, Ana L. 2008. "Do Poverty Relief Funds Affect Electoral Behavior? Evidence from a Randomized Experiment in Mexico," Typescript, Yale University.

De Vries, R., D. A. DeBruin, and A. Goodgame. 2004. "Ethics Review of Social, Behavioral, and Economic Research: Where Should We Go from Here?" *Ethics & Behavior* 14(4):351–368.

Deci, E. L. 1971. "Effects of Externally Mediated Rewards on Intrinsic Motivation," *Journal of Personality and Social Psychology* 18:105–115.

Dehejia, Rajeev H. and Sadek Wahba. 1999. "Causal Effects in Nonexperimental Studies: Reevaluating the Evaluation of Training Programs," *Journal of the American Statistical Association* 94(448):1053–1062.

Delgado-Rodriguez, Miguel. 2006. "Systematic Reviews of Meta-Analyses: Applications and Limitations," *Journal of Epidemiology and Community Health* 60:90–92.

Dickson, Eric, Catherine Hafer, and Dimitri Landa. 2008. "Cognition and Strategy: A Deliberation Experiment," *Journal of Politics* 70(4).

Diermeier, Daniel. Forthcoming. "Coalition Experiments," in *Cambridge Handbook of Experimental Political Science* (James N. Druckman, Donald P. Green, James H. Kuklinski, and Arthur Lupia, eds.). Cambridge, UK: Cambridge University Press.

Diermeier, Daniel and Rebecca Morton. 2005. "Experiments in Majoritarian Bargaining," in *Social Choice and Strategic Decisions: Essays in Honor of Jeffrey S. Banks* (David Austen-Smith and John Duggan, eds.). Berlin and New York: Springer, pp. 201–236.

Ding, Min, Rajdeep Grewal, and John Liechty. 2005. "Incentive-Aligned Conjoint Analysis," *Journal of Marketing Research* XLII(February):67–82.

Doucouliagos, Hristos and Mehmet Ali Ulubasoglu. 2008. "Democracy and Economic Growth: A Meta-Analysis," *American Journal of Political Science* 52(1, January):61–83.

Druckman, James. 2001a. "Evaluating Framing Effects," *Journal of Economic Psychology* 22(February):91–101.

Druckman, James. 2001b. "On the Limits of Framing Effects," *Journal of Politics* 63(November):1041–1066.

Druckman, James, Donald Green, James Kuklinski, and Arthur Lupia. 2006. "The Growth and Development of Experimental Research in Political Science," *American Political Science Review* 100:627–635.

Druckman, James N. and Cindy D. Kam. Forthcoming. "Students as Experimental Participants: A Defense of the 'Narrow Data Base'." In *Cambridge Handbook of Experimental Political Science* (James N. Druckman, Donald P. Green, James H. Kuklinski, and Arthur Lupia, eds.). Cambridge, UK: Cambridge University Press.

Druckman, James and Kjersten R. Nelson. 2003. "Framing and Deliberation: How Citizens' Conversations Limit Elite Influence," *American Journal of Political Science* 47:729–745.

Eckel, C. C. and P. J. Grossman. 2002. "Sex Differences and Statistical Stereotyping in Attitudes Toward Financial Risk," *Evolution and Human Behavior* 23(4):281–295.

Eckel, Catherine C. and Rick Wilson. 2004. "Is Trust a Risky Decision?" *Journal of Economic Behavior and Organization* 55(4):447–465.

Eckel, Catherine C. and Rick Wilson. 2006a. "Internet Cautions," *Experimental Economics* 9(1):53–66.

Eckel, Catherine C. and Rick Wilson. 2006b. "Judging a Book by Its Cover: Beauty and Expectations in the Trust Game," *Political Research Quarterly* 59(2):189–202.

Egas, Martijn and Arno Riedl. 2008. "The Economics of Altruistic Punishment and the Maintenance of Cooperation," *Proceedings of the Royal Society* 275:871–878.

Egger, M. and G. D. Smith. 1997. "Meta-Analysis: Potentials and Problems," *British Medical Journal* 315:1371–1374.

Eldersveld, S. 1956. "Experimental Propaganda Techniques and Voting Behavior," *American Political Science Review* 50:154–166.

Enders, Walter. 2003. *Applied Econometric Time Series, 2nd Edition*. New York, NY: John Wiley & Sons.

Erikson, Robert, Michael MacKuen, and James Stimson. 1998. "What Moves Macropartisanship? A Response to Green, Palmquist, and Schickler," *American Political Science Review* 93(4, December):901–912.

Erikson, R. and C. Wlezien. 2008. "Are Political Markets Really Superior to Public Opinion Polls," *Public Opinion Quarterly* 72(2):190–215.

Evans, W. N. and R. M. Schwab. 1995. "Finishing High School and Starting College: Do Catholic Schools Make a Difference," *The Quarterly Journal of Economics* 110(3):941–974.

Faden, Ruth R. and Tom L. Beauchamp with Nancy M. P. King. 1986. *A History and Theory of Informed Consent*. Oxford, UK: Oxford University Press.

Fatas, Enrique, Tibor Neugebauer, and Pilar Tamborero. 2007. "How Politicians Make Decisions: A Political Choice Experiment," *Journal of Economics* 92(2):167–196.

Feddersen, T., S. Gailmard, and A. Sandroni. 2009. "Moral Bias in Large Elections: Theory and Experimental Evidence," *American Political Science Review* 103(2):175–192.

Feddersen, Timothy and Wolfgang Pesendorfer. 1996. "The Swing Voter's Curse," *American Economic Review* 86(3):404–424.

Feddersen, T. and A. Sandroni. 2006. "A Theory of Participation in Elections," *American Economic Review* 96(4):1271–1282.

Fehr, E. and S. Gächter. 2002. "Altruistic Punishment in Humans," *Nature* 415:137–140.

Fehr, E., G. Kirchsteiger, and A. Riedl. 1993. "Does Fairness Prevent Market Clearing? An Experimental Investigation," *Quarterly Journal of Economics* 108:437–460.

Fehr, E. and M. Klaus Schmidt. 1999. "A Theory of Fairness, Competition, and Cooperation," *The Quarterly Journal of Economics* 114(3):817–868.

Feldman, Stanley and Huddy Leonie. 2005. "Racial Resentment and White Opposition to Race-Conscious Programs: Principles or Prejudice?" *American Journal of Political Science* 49 (1):168–183.

Fishkin, James S. 1991. *Democracy and Deliberation: New Directions for Democratic Reform.* New Haven, CT: Yale University Press.

Fishkin, James S. 1992. *The Dialogue of Justice.* New Haven, CT: Yale University Press.

Fishkin, James S. 1997. *The Voice of the People.* New Haven, CT: Yale University Press.

Fleiss, J. L. 1994. "Measures of Effect Size for Categorical Data," in *Handbook of Research Synthesis* (H. Cooper and and L.V. Hedges, eds.). New York: Russell Sage Foundation, pp. 245–260.

Fontes, Lisa A. 1998. "Ethics in Family Violence Research: Cross-Cultural Issues," *Family Relations* 47(1):53–61.

Forsythe, Robert, Joel L. Horowitz, N. E. Savin, and Martin Sefton. 1994. "Fairness in Simple Bargaining Experiments," *Games and Economic Behavior* 6:347–369.

Forsythe, Robert, John Kennan, and Barry Sopher. 1991. "An Experimental Analysis of Strikes in Bargaining Games with One-Sided Private Information," *American Economic Review* 81(1):253–278.

Forsythe, R., F. Nelson, G. R. Neumann, John Wright. 1992. "Anatomy of an Experimental Political Stock-Market," *American Economic Review* 82(5):1142–1161.

Fox, R. J., M. R. Crask, and J. Kim. 1988. "Mail Survey Response Rate: A Meta-Analysis of Selected Techniques for Inducing Response," *Public Opinion Quarterly* 52:467–491.

Frangakis, C. E. and D. B. Rubin. 1999. "Addressing Complications of Intention-to-Treat Analysis in the Presence of All-or-None Treatment-Noncompliance and Subsequent Missing Outcomes," *Biometrika* 86:365–379.

Fréchette, Guillaume. 2009. "Laboratory Experiments: Professionals versus Students," Working paper, New York University Department of Economics.

Fréchette, Guillaume, John Kagel, and Massimo Morelli. 2005. "Behavioral Identification in Coalitional Bargaining: An Experimental Analysis of Demand Bargaining and Alternating Offers," *Econometrica* 73(6):1893–1937.

Freedman, David A. 2008a. "On Regression Adjustments to Experimental Data," *Advances in Applied Mathematics* 40:180–193.

Freedman, David A. 2008b. "On Regression Adjustment in Experiments with Several Treatments," *Annals of Applied Statistics* 2:176–196.

Fried, Brian J., Paul Lagunes, and Atheendar Venkataramani. 2010. "Corruption and Inequality at the Crossroad: A Multi-Method Study of Bribery and Discrimination in Latin America," *Latin American Research Review* 45(1):76–97.

Friedman, D. and S. Sunder. 1994. *Experiment Methods: A Primer for Economists.* Cambridge: Cambridge University Press.

Frohlich, Norman, Joe Oppenheimer, and J. Bernard Moore. 2001. "Some Doubts About Measuring Self-Interest Using Dictator Experiments: The Costs of Anonymity," *Journal of Economic Behavior and Organization* 46:271–90.

Fudenberg, Drew. 2006. "Advancing Beyond *Advances in Behavioral Economics*," *Journal of Economic Literature* 44(September):694–711.

Fudin, R. 2006. "Critique of Sohlberg and Birgegard's Report of Persistent Complex Effects of Subliminal Psychodynamic Activation Messages," *Perceptual and Motor Skills* 103(2):551–564.

Gachter, S., and A. Falk. 2002. "Reputation and Reciprocity: Consequences for the Labour Relation," *Scandinavian Journal of Economics* 104:1–26.

Gaines, Brian J. and James H. Kuklinski. 2008. "A Case for Including Self-Selection alongside Randomization in the Assignment of Experimental Treatments." Manuscript.

Gaines, B. J., J. H. Kuklinski, and P. J. Quirk. 2007a. "The Logic of the Survey Experiment Reexamined," *Political Analysis* 15(1):1–20.

Gaines, Brian, James H. Kuklinski, and Paul J. Quirk, 2007b. "Same Facts, Different Interpretations: Partisan Motivation and Opinion on Iraq," *Journal of Politics* 15:1–21.

Gelman, Andrew. 2008. *Red State, Blue State, Rich State, Poor State*. Princeton University Press.

Gentzkow, Matthew. 2006. "Television and Turnout," *Quarterly Journal of Economics* (August):931–972.

Gerber, Alan and Donald Green. 2000. "The Effects of Canvassing, Direct Mail, and Telephone Calls on Voter Turnout: A Field Experiment," *American Political Science Review* 94(3):653–663.

Gerber, Alan and Donald Green. 2002. "Reclaiming the Experimental Tradition in Political Science," in *Political Science: State of the Discipline* (Ira Katznelson and Helen V. Milner, eds.). New York: W.W. Norton, pp. 805–832.

Gerber, Alan, and Donald Green. 2005. "Correction to Gerber and Green (2000), Replication of Disputed Findings, and Reply by Imai (2005)," *American Political Science Review* 99(2):301–313.

Gerber, Alan S., Donald P. Green, and Roni Shachar. 2003. "Voting May Be Habit Forming: Evidence from a Randomized Field Experiment," *American Journal of Political Science* 47(3):540–50.

Gerber, Alan, Dean Karlan, and Daniel Bergan. 2007. "Does the Media Matter? A Field Experiment Measuring the Effect of Newspapers on Voting Behavior and Political Opinions," Working paper, Yale University.

Gerber, Elisabeth R. and Rebecca B. Morton. 1998. "Primary Election Systems and Representation," *Journal of Law, Economics, and Organization* 14(2):304–324.

Gerber, Elisabeth, Rebeca Morton, and Thomas Rietz. 1998. "Minority Representation in Multimember Districts," *American Political Science Review* 92(March):127–144.

Gerring, John. 2004. "What Is a Case Study and What Is It Good For?" *American Political Science Review* 98(2, May):341–354.

Gerring, John and Rose McDermott. 2007. "An Experimental Template for Case Study Research," *American Journal of Political Science* 51(3, July):688–701.

Ghirardato, Paolo and Jonathan Katz. 2002. "Indecision Theory: Explaining Selective Abstention in Multiple Elections," Working paper, California Institute of Technology.

Gilman, Robert H. and Hector H. Garcia. 2004. "Ethics Review Procedures for Research in Developing Countries: A Basic Presumption of Guilt," *Canadian Medical Association* 171(3):248–249.

Glass, G. V. 1976. "Primary, Secondary, and Meta-Analysis Research," *Educational Researcher* 8:12–14.

Gneezy, Uri and Aldo Rustichini. 2000a. "A Fine Is a Price," *Journal of Legal Studies* 29:1–17.

Gneezy, Uri and Aldo Rustichini. 2000b. "Pay Enough or Don't Pay at All," *The Quarterly Journal of Economics* 115(3):791–810.

Goduka, Ivy N. 1990. "Ethics and Politics of Field Research in South Africa," *Social Problems* 37(3):329–340.

Goeree, J. K., C. A. Holt, and T. R. Palfrey. 2003. "Risk Averse Behavior in Generalized Matching Pennies Games," *Games and Economic Behavior* 45(1):97–113.

Goeree, Jacob K. and Charles A. Holt. 1999. "Classroom Games: Rent-Seeking and the Inefficiency of Non-market Allocations," *Journal of Economic Perspectives* 13(3):217–226.

Goeree, Jacob K., Charles A. Holt, and Thomas R. Palfrey. 2005. "Regular Quantal Response Equilibrium," *Experimental Economics* 8(4):347–367.

Goldstein, Daniel G. and Gerd Gigerenzer. 2002. "Models of Ecological Rationality: The Recognition Heuristic," *Psychological Review* 109(1):75–90.

Gosnell, Harold. 1927. *Getting Out the Vote: An Experiment in the Stimulation of Voting.* Chicago: University of Chicago Press.

Gray, Bradford H., Robert A. Cooke, and Arnold S. Tannebaum. 1978. "Research Involving Human Subjects," *Science* 201:1094–1101.

Green, Donald P. 2009. "Regression Adjustments to Experimental Data: Do David Freedman's Concerns Apply to Political Science?" Available at SSRN: http://ssrn.com/abstract=1466886 (August 9).

Green, Donald P., Alan S. Gerber, and David W. Nickerson. 2003. "Getting Out the Vote in Local Elections: Results from Six Door-to-Door Canvassing Experiments," *Journal of Politics* 65(4):1083–1096.

Green, Donald P. and Lynn Vavreck. 2008. "The Analysis of Cluster-Randomized Field Experiments," *Political Analysis* 16:138–152.

Green, Donald, Brad Palmquist, and Eric Schickler. 1998. "Macropartisanship: A Replication and Critique," *American Political Science Review* 92(4, December):883–899.

Greene, William. 2000. *Econometric Analysis.* New York: Prentice Hall.

Greenland, Sander and Babette Brumback. 2002. "An Overview of Relations Among Causal Modelling Methods," *International Journal of Epidemiology* 31:1030–1037.

Grether, David M. and Charles R. Plott. 1979. "Economic Theory of Choice and the Preference Reversal Phenomenon," *American Economic Review* 69:623–638.

Groseclose, T. and J. Milyo. 2005. "A Measure of Media Bias," *Quarterly Journal of Economics* 120(4):1191–1237.

Grosskopf, Brit and Rosemarie Nagel. 2008. "The Two-Person Beauty Contest," *Games and Economic Behavior* 62(1):93–99.

Guala, Francesco. 2005. *The Methodology of Experimental Economics.* Cambridge: Cambridge University Press.

Guerre, Emmanuel, Isabelle Perrigne, and Quang Vuong, 2000. "Optimal Nonparametric Estimation of First-Price Auctions," *Econometrica* 68(3):525–574.

Guetzkow, Harold and Lloyd Jensen. 1966. "Research Activities on Simulated International Processes," *Background* 9(4):261–274.

Guetzkow, Harold and J. J. Valadez. 1981. "International Relations Theory Contributions of Simulated International Processes," in *Simulated International Processes: Theories and Research in Global Modeling* (H. Guetzkow and J. J. Valadez, eds.). Beverly Hills: Sage, pp. 253–330.

Guth, W., R. Schmittberger, and B. Schwarz. 1982. "An Experimental Analysis of Ultimatum Bargaining," *Journal of Economics, Behavior, and Organization* 3:367–388.

Habyarimana, James, Macartan Humphreys, Daniel Posner, and Jeremy Weinstein. 2007. "Why Does Ethnic Diversity Undermine Public Goods Provision?" *American Political Science Review* 101(4, November):709–725.

Haddock, C. K., D. Rindskopf, and W. R. Shadisn. 1998. "Using Odds Ratios as Effect Sizes for Meta-Analysis of Dichotomous Data: A Primer on Methods and Issues," *Psychological Methods* 3:339–353.

Haile, Philip A., Ali Horacsu, and Grigory Kosenok. 2008. "On the Empirical Content of Quantal Response Equilibrium," *American Economic Review* 98(1): 180–200.

Hamermesh, Daniel S. 2007. "Viewpoint: Replication in Economics," *Canadian Journal of Economics* 40(3, August):715–733.

Hamilton, James. 1994. *Time Series Analysis.* Princeton: Princeton University Press.

Harbaugh, William T. and Kate Krause. 2000. "Children's Altruism in Public Good and Dictator Experiments," *Economic Inquiry* 38(1):95–109.

Hardle, Wolfgang and Oliver Linton. 1986. "Applied Nonparametric Methods," in *Handbook of Econometrics*, 1st edition (R. F. Engle and D. McFadden, eds.). Elsevier, vol. 4, pp. 2295–2339.

Härdle, Wolfgang and Oliver Linton. 1994. "Applied Nonparametric Methods," Cowles Foundation Discussion Papers 1069, Cowles Foundation, Yale University.

Harrison, Glenn W., Ronald M. Harstad, and E. Elisabet Rutstrom. 2004. "Experimental Methods and Elicitation of Values," *Experimental Economics* 7:123–140.

Harrison, Glenn, Eric Johnson, Melayne M. McInnes, and E. Elisabet Rutstrom. 2005b. "Risk Aversion and Incentive Effects: A Comment," *American Economic Review* 95(3, June):897–901.

Harrison, Glenn, M. I. Lau, E. E. Rutstrom, and M. B. Sullivan. 2005a. "Eliciting Risk and Time Preferences Using Field Experiments: Some Methodological Issues," in *Field Experimetns in Economices, Research in Experimental Economics* (J. Carpenter, G. W. Harrison, and J.A. List, eds.). Greenwich CT: JAI Press, vol. 10, pp. 125–218.

Harrison, Glenn W., M. I. Lau, and M. B. Williams. 2002. "Estimating Individual Discount Rates for Denmark: A Field Experiment," *American Economic Review* 92(5):1606–1617.

Harrison, Glenn and John List. 2004. "Field Experiments," *Journal of Economic Literature* 42:1009–1055.

Harrison, Glenn W. and Tanga McDaniel. 2008. "Voting Games and Computational Complexity," *Oxford Economic Papers* 60(3):546–565.

Hartmann, G. 1936. A field experiment on the comparative effectiveness of "emotional" and "rational" political leaflets in determining election results. *Journal of Abnormal and Social Psychology* 31:99–114.

Hauck, R. J. P. 2008. "Protecting Human Research Participants, IRBs, and Political Science Redux: Editor's Introduction," *PS-Political Science and Politics* 41(3):475–476.

Heckman, J. J. 2005a. "The Scientific Model of Causality," in *Sociological Methodology*, vol. 35, pp. 1–97.

Heckman, J. J. 2005b. "Rejoinder: Response to Sobel," in *Sociological Methodology*, vol. 35, pp. 135–162.

Heckman, J. J. and E. J. Vytlacil. 2001. "Local Instrumental Variables," in *Nonlinear Statistical Modeling: Proceedings of the Thirteenth International Symposium in Economic Theory and Econometrics: Essays in Honor of Takeshi Amemiya* (C. Hsiao, K. Morimue, and J. L. Powell, eds.). New York: Cambridge University Press, pp. 1–46.

Heckman, J. J., H. Ichimura, and P. E. Todd. 1997. "Matching as an Econometric Evaluation Estimator: Evidence from Evaluating a Job Training Programme," *Review of Economic Studies* 64(4):605–654.

Heckman, James J. 1997. "Instrumental Variables: A Study of Implicit Behavioral Assumptions Used in Making Program Evaluations," *Journal of Human Resources* 32:441–62.

Heckman, James J. and Edward J. Vytlacil. 2007a. "Econometric Evaluation of Social Programs, Part I: Causal Models, Structural Models, and Econometric Policy Evaluation," in *Handbook of Econometrics* (James J. Heckman and Edward E. Leamer, eds.). New York: Elsevier, pp. 4779–4874.

Heckman, James J. and Edward J. Vytlacil. 2007b. "Econometric Evaluation of Social Programs, Part II: Using the Marginal Treatment Effect to Organize Alternative Econometric Estimators to Evaluate Social Programs, and to Forecast their Effects in New Environments," in *Handbook of Econometrics* (James J. Heckman and Edward E. Leamer, eds.). New York: Elsevier, pp. 4875–5144.

Heckman, James J. and R. Robb. 1985. "Alternative Methods for Evaluating the Impact of Interventions," in *Longitudinal Analysis of Labor Market Data* (J. Heckman and B. Singer, eds.). New York: Cambridge University Press, vol. 10, pp. 156–245.

Heckman, James J. and R. Robb. 1986. "Alternative Methods for Solving the Problem of Selection Bias in Evaluating the Impact of Treatments on Outcomes," in *Drawing Inferences from Self-Selected Samples* (H. Wainer, ed.). New York: Springer-Verlag, pp. 63–107.

Hedges, Larry V. and Ingram Olkin. 1985. *Statistical Analysis for Meta-Analysis*. New York, NY: Academic Press.

Heller, Jean. 1972. "Syphilis Victims in U.S. Study Went Untreated for 40 years," *New York Times*, July 26, sec. 1, p. 8.

Henderson, Gail E., Arlene M. Davis, Nancy M. P. King, Michele M. Easter, Catherine R. Zimmer, Barbra Bluestone Rothschild, Benjamin S. Wilfond, Daniel K. Nelson, and Larry R. Churchill. 2004. "Uncertain Benefit: Investigators' Views and Communications in Early Phase Gene Transfer Trials," *Molecular therapy: The Journal of the American Society of Gene Therapy* 10(2):225–231.

Henrich, Joeseph, Robert Boyd, Samuel Bowles, Colin Camerer, Ernst Fehr, Herbert Gintis, and Richard McElreath. 2001. "In Search of Homo Economicus: Behavioral Experiments in 15 Small-Scale Societies," *American Economic Review* 91:73–78.

Henrich, Joseph, Richard McElreath, Abigail Barr, Jean Ensminger, Clark Barrett, Alexander Bolyanatz, Juan Camil Cardenas, Michael Gurven, Edwins Gwako, Natalie Henrich, Carolyn Lesorogol, Frank Marlowe, David Tracer, and John Ziker. 2006. "Costly Punishment Across Human Societies," *Science* 312(June):1767–1770.

Henrich, Joseph, Robert Boyd, Samuel Bowles, Colin Camerer, Ernst Fehr, and Herbert Gintis. 2004. *Foundations of Human Sociality: Economic Experiments and Ethnographic Evidence from Fifteen Small-Scale Societies.* New York: Oxford University Press.

Henrich, Joseph, Robert Boyd, Samuel Bowles, Colin Camerer, Ernst Fehr, Herbert Ginitis, Richard McElreath, Michael Alvard, Abigail Barr, Jean Ensminger, Natalie Smith Henrich, Kim Hill, Franciso Gil-White, Michael Gurven, Frank W. Marlowe, John Q. Patton, and David Tracer. 2005. "'Economic May' in Cross-Cultural Perspective: Behavioral Experiments in 15 Small-Scale Societies," *Behavioral and Brain Sciences* 28:795–855.

Henry, P. J. 2008a. "College Sophomores in the Laboratory Redux: Influences of a Narrow Data Base on Social Psychology's View of the Nature of Prejudice," *Psychological Inquiry* 19(2):49–71.

Henry, P. J. 2008b. "Student Sampling as a Theoretical Problem." *Psychological Inquiry* 19(2):114–126.

Herrmann, Benedikt, Christian Thoni, and Simon Gachter. 2008. "Antisocial Punishment Across Societies," *Science* 319:1362–1367.

Hertwig, R. and A. Ortmann. 2001. *Deception in Experiments: The Costs of an Alleged Method of Last Resort.* Working Paper. Berlin: Max Planck Institute for Human, Development, pp. 1–45.

Hertwig, R. and A. Ortmann. 2008. "Deception in Experiments: Revisiting the Arguments in its Defense," *Ethics & Behavior* 18(1):59–92.

Hey, J. D. 1998. "Experimental Economics and Deception," *Journal of Economic Psychology* 19:397–401.

Hey, John D. and Jinkwon Lee. 2005a. "Do Subjects Separate (or Are They Sophisticated)?" *Experimental Economics* 8:233–265.

Hey, John D. and Jinkwon Lee. 2005b. "Do Subjects Remember the Past?" *Applied Economics* 37:9–18.

Heyman, James and Dan Ariely. 2004. "Effort for Payment: A Tale of Two Markets," *Psychological Science* 15(11):787–793.

Hibbing, J. R. and K. B. Smith. 2007. "The Biology of Political Behavior: An Introduction," *Annals of the American Academy of Political and Social Science* 614:6–14.

Hirano, K., G. Imbens, D. Rubin, and X. Zhou. 2000. "Causal Inference in Encouragement Designs with Covariates," *Biostatistics* 1:69–88.

Ho, Daniel E., Kosuke Imai, Gary King, and Elizabeth Stuart. Forthcoming. "Match It: Nonparametric Preprocessing for Parametric Causal Inference," *Journal of Statistical Software.*

Hoffman, Elizabeth, Kevin McCabe, Keith Shachat, and Vernon Smith. 1994. "Preferences, Property Rights, and Anonymity in Bargaining Games," *Games and Economic Behavior* 7:346–380.

Hoffman, Elizabeth, Kevin McCabe, and Vernon L. Smith. 1996. "Social Distance and Other-Regarding Behavior in Dictator Games," *American Economic Review* 76(September):728–41.

Hofstede, G. 1991. *Cultures and Organizations: Software of the Mind.* New York: McGraw-Hill.

Hogarth, Robin M., Brian H. Gibbs, Craig R. McKenzie, and Margaret A. Marquis. 1991. "Learning from Feedback: Exactingness and Incentives," *Journal of Experimental Psychology: Learning, Memory, and Cognition* 17(July):734–752.

Holbrook, T. and S. D. McClurg. 2005. "Presidential Campaigns and the Mobilization of Core Supporters," *American Journal of Political Science* 49(4):659–703.

Holland, Paul W. 1986. "Statistics and Causal Inference," *Journal of the American Statistical Association* 81:941–970 (with discussion).

Holland, P. W. 1988. "Causal Inference, Path Analysis, and Recursive Structural Equation Models" in *Sociological Methodology* (C. C. Clogg, ed.). Washington, DC: American Sociological Association, pp. 449–493 (with discussion).

Holm, H. and P. Nystedt. 2008. "Trust in Surveys and Games – A Methodological Contribution on the Influence of Money and Location," *Journal of Economic Psychology* 29(4):522–542.

Holmes, D. S. 1976a. "Debriefing After Psychological Experiments: I Effectiveness of Postexperimental Debriefing," *American Psychologist* 31:858–867.

Holmes, D. S. 1976b. "Debriefing After Psychological Experiments: II Effectiveness of Postexperimental Desensitizing," *American Psychologist* 31:868–875.

Holmes, D. S. and D. H. Bennett. 1974. "Experiments to Answer Questions Raised by the Use of Deception in Psychology Research," *Journal of Personality and Social Psychology* 29(3):358–367.

Holt, C. A. and S. K. Laury. 2005. "Risk Aversion and Incentive Effects: New Data without Order Effects," *American Economic Review* 95(3):902–904.

Holt, Charles A., 1986. "Preference Reversals and the Independence Axiom," *American Economic Review* 76(3):508–515.

Holt, Charles and Susan K. Laury. 2002. "Risk Aversion and Incentive Effects," *American Economic Review* 92(5):1644–1655.

Horiuchi, Yusaku, Kosuke Imai, and Naoko Taniguchi. 2007. "Designing and Analyzing Randomized Experiments: Application to a Japanese Election Survey Experiment," *American Journal of Political Science* 51(3):669–687.

Hovland, C., A. A. Lumsdaine, and F. Sheffield. 1949. *Experiments in Mass Communications.* Princeton: Princeton University Press.

Humphreys, Macartan. 2009. "Bounds on Least Squares Estimates of Causal Effects in the Presence of Heterogeneous Assignment Probabilities," Working paper, Columbia University Department of Politics.

Humphries, Laud. 1970. *Tearoom Trade: Impersonal Sex in Public Places.* London: Duckworth.

Hunter, John. 2001. "The Desperate Need for Replications," *Journal of Consumer Research* 28:149–158.

Hunter, J. E. and F. L. Schmidt. 1990. *Methods in Meta-Analysis – Correcting Errors and Bias in Research Findings.* London: Sage.

Imai, Kosuke, Gary King, and Clayton Nall. 2009. "Rejoinder: Matched Pairs and the Future of Cluster-Randomized Experiments," *Statistical Science* 24(1):65–72.

Imai, Kosuke, Luke Keele, and Dustin Tingley. 2009. "A General Approach to Causal Mediation Analysis," Working paper, Princeton University Department of Politics.

Imai, Kosuke, Luke Keele, and Teppei Yamamoto. 2008 "Identification, Inference, and Sensitivity Analysis for Causal Mediation Effects," Working paper, Princeton University Department of Politics.

Imai, Kosuke. 2005. "Go Get-Out-The-Vote Calls Reduce Turnout? The Importance of Statistical Methods for Field Experiments," *American Political Science Review* 99(2):283–300.

Imbens, G. and D. B. Rubin. 1997a. "Bayesian Inference for Causal Effects in Randomized Experiments with Noncompliance," *Annals of Statistics* 25:305–327.

Imbens, Guido and Donald Rubin. 1997b. "Estimating Outcome Distributions for Compliers in Instrumental Variable Models," *Review of Economic Studies* 64(4):555–574.

Imbens, Guido W. and Joshua D. Angrist. 1994. "Identification and Estimation of Local Average Treatment Effects," *Econometrica* 62(2):467–475.

Inglehart, Ronald. 1990. *Culture Shift in Advanced Industrial Society.* Princeton, NJ: Princeton University Press.

Inglehart, Ronald. 2000. "Culture and Democracy," in *Culture Matters: How Values Shape Human Progress* (L. E. Harrison and S. P. Huntington, eds.). New York: Basic Books, pp. 80–97.

Ivy, A. C. 1948. "The History and Ethics of Use of Humans Subjects in Medical Experiments," *Science* 108(2, July):1–5.

Iyengar, Raghuram and Andrew Schotter. 2008. "Learning Under Supervision: An Experimental Study," *Experimental Economics* 11(2):154–173.

Iyengar, Shanto and Donald Kinder. 1987. *News That Matters.* Chicago: University of Chicago Press.

Iyengar, Shanto. 1987. "Television News and Citizens' Explanations of National Affairs," *American Political Science Review* 81(3, September):815–831.

Iyengar, Shanto. Forthcoming. "Laboratory Experiments in Political Science," in *Cambridge Handbook of Experimental Political Science* (James N. Druckman, Donald P. Green, James H. Kuklinski, and Arthur Lupia, eds.). Cambridge, UK: Cambridge University Press.

Jacoby, W. 2000. "Issue Framing and Public Opinion on Government Spending," *American Journal of Political Science* 44:750–767.

James, Duncan. 2007. "Stability of Risk Preference Parameter Estimates Within the Becker-DeGroot-Marschak Procedure," *Experimental Economics* 10:123–141.

James, Harvey S. 2005. "Why Did You Do That? An Economic Explanation of the Effect of Extrinsic Compensation on Intrinsic Motivation and Performance," *Journal of Economic Psychology* 26:549–566.

James, Tracey. 1997. "Results for the Wave 1 Incentive Experiment in the 1996 Survey of Income and Program Participation," in *Proceedings of the Survey Research Section of the American Statistical Association.* Baltimore: American Statistical Association, pp. 834–839.

Jamison, J., D. Karlan, and L. Schechter. 2008. "To Deceive or Not to Deceive: The Effect of Deception on Behavior in Future Laboratory Experiments," *Journal of Economic Behavior & Organization* 68(3–4):477–488.

Kachelmeier, Steven J. and Mohamed Shehata. 1992. "Examining Risk Preferences Under High Monetary Incentives: Experimental Evidence from the People's Republic of China," *American Economic Review* 82:1120–1141.

Kagel, John and Dan Levin. 2009. "Auctions: A Survey of Experimental Research, 1995–2008," Working paper, Department of Economics, Ohio State University.

Kagel, John H. and H. Dan Levin 1993. "Independent Private Value Auctions: Bidder Behaviour in First-, Second- and Third-Price Auctions with Varying Numbers of Bidders Independent Private Value Auctions: Bidder Behaviour in First-, Second- and Third-Price Auctions with Varying Numbers of Bidders," *Economic Journal* 103(419):868–879.

Kahneman, D., P. Slovic, and A. Tversky, 1982. *Judgment under uncertainty: Heuristics and biases.* Cambridge University Press.

Kahneman, D., J. Knetsch, and R. Thaler. 1986. "Fairness and the Assumptions of Economics," in *Rational Choice* (R. M. Hogarth and M. W. Reder, eds.). Chicago: University of Chicago Press, pp. 101–116.

Kam, C. D. 2007. "Implicit Attitudes, Explicit Choices: When Subliminal Priming Predicts Candidate Preference," *Political Behavior* 29(3):343–367.

Kam, Cindy D., Jennifer R. Wilking, and Elizabeth Zechmeister. 2007. "Beyond the 'Narrow Data Base': Another Convenience Sample for Experimental Research," *Political Behavior* 29:415–440.

Karpowitz, Christopher and Tali Mendelberg. Forthcoming. "An Experimental Approach to Citizen Deliberation," in *Cambridge Handbook of Experimental Political Science* (James N. Druckman, Donald P. Green, James H. Kuklinski, and Arthur Lupia, eds.). Cambridge, UK: Cambridge University Press.

Keane, Michael P. and Kenneth I. Wolpin. 2007. "Exploring the Usefulness of a Nonrandom Holdout Sample for Model Validation: Welfare Effects on Female Behavior," *International Economic Review* 48(4, November):1351–1378.

Kelejian, Harry H. 1971. "Two Stage Least Squares and Econometric Models Linear in the Parameters but NonLinear in the Endogenous Variables," *Journal of the American Statistical Association* 66:373–374.

Kelman, H. C. 1967. "Human Use of Human Subjects: The Problem of Deception in Social Psychology," *Psychological Bulletin* 67:1–11.

Keynes, John Maynard. 1936. *The General Theory of Employment, Interest and Money.* London, MacMillian: Harcourt, Brace.

Kimmel, A. J. 1998. "In Defense of Deception," *American Psychologist* 53:803–805.

Kinder, Donald and Thomas R. Palfrey. 1993a. "On Behalf of an Experimental Political Science," in *Experimental Foundations of Political Science* (Donald Kinder and Thomas Palfrey, eds.). Ann Arbor, MI: University of Michigan Press, pp. 1–42.

Kinder, Donald and Lynn Sanders. 1990a. "Mimicking Political Debate with Survey Questions," *Social Cognition* 81(1):73–103.

Kinder, Donald R. and Thomas Palfrey, eds. 1993b. *Experimental Foundations of Political Sciences (Michigan Studies in Political Analysis).* Ann Arbor, MI: University of Michigan Press.

King, G., E. Gakidou, N. Ravishankar, R. T. Moore, J. Lakin, M. Vargas, M. M. Téllez-Rojo, J. E. H. Ávila, M. H. Ávila, and H. H. Llamas. 2007. "A 'Politically Robust' Experimental Design for Public Policy Evaluation, with Application to the Mexican Universal Health Insurance Program," *Journal Policy Analysis Management* 26:479–506.

King, Gary, Robert O. Keohane, and Sidney Verba. 1994. *Designing Social Inquiry.* Princeton: Princeton University Press.

King, N. M. 2000. "Defining and Describing Benefit Appropriately in Clinical Trials," *Journal of Law, Medicine & Ethics* 28(4):332–343.

King, Nancy M. P., Gail E. Henderson, Larry R. Churchill, Arlene M. Davis, Sara Chandros Hull, Daniel K. Nelson, P. Christy Parham-Vetter, Barbara Bluestone Rothschild, Michele M. Easter, and Benjamin S. Wilfond. 2005. "Consent Forms and the Therapeutic Misconception: The Example of Gene Transfer Research," *IRB* 27(1):1–8.

Koch, Alexander K. and Hans-Theo Normann. 2008. "Giving in Dictator Games: Regard for Others or Regard by Others?" *Southern Economic Journal* 75(1):223–231.

Kollman, K., J. H. Miller, and S. E. Page. 1992. "Adaptive Parties in Spatial Elections," *American Political Science Review* 86(4):929–937.

Kormendi, Roger C. and Charles R. Plott. 1982. "Committee Decisions under Alternative Procedural Rules: An Experimental Study Applying a New Non-monetary Method of Preference Inducement," *Journal of Economic Behavior & Organization* 3(2–3):175–195.

Kosfeld, Michael, Markus Heinrichs, Paul J. Zak, Urs Fischbacher, and Ernst Fehr. 2005. "Oxytocin Increases Trust in Humans," *Nature* 435(2):673–676.

Krosnick, Jon A. and Donald R. Kinder. 1990. "Altering the Foundations of Support for the President Through Priming," *American Political Science Review* 84(2, June):497–512.

Krugman, S. 1986. "The Willowbrook Hepatitis Studies Revisited: Ethical Aspects," *Reviews of Infectious Diseases* 8(1):157–162.

Kuhberger, Anton. 1998. "The Influence of Framing on Risky Decisions," *Organizational Behavior and Human Decision Processes* 75(July):23–55.

Kuklinski, James H., Paul M. Sniderman, Kathleen Knight, Thomas Piazza, Philip E. Tetlock, Gordon R. Lawrence, and Barbara Mellers. 1997. "Racial Prejudice and Attitudes Toward Affirmative Action," *American Journal of Political Science* 41(2, April):402–419.

Kulisheck, Michael R. and Jeffrey J. Mondak. 1996. "Candidate Quality and the Congressional Vote: A Causal Connection," *Electoral Studies* 15(2):237–253.

Kulka, Richard A. 1992. "A Brief Reivew of the Use of Monetary Incentives in Federal Statistical Surveys," paper presented at the Symposium on Providing Incentives to Survey Respondents, convened by the Council of Professional Associations on Federal Statistics for the Office of Management and Budget, Harvard University, John F. Kennedy School of Government, Cambridge, MA.

Ladouceur, Robert, Stella Lachance, and Patricia-Maude Fournier. 2009. "Is Control a Viable Goal in the Treatment of Pathological Gambling?" *Behaviour Research and Therapy* 47(3):189–197.

Laffont, Jean-Jacques and Quang Vuong. 1995. "Structural Analysis of Auction Data," *American Economic Review Papers and Proceedings* 86(May):414–420.

LaLonde, R. 1986. "Evaluating the Econometric Evaluations of Training Programs," *American Economic Review* 76:604–620.

Larcinese, Valentino. 2007. "Does Political Knowledge Increase Turnout? Evidence from the 1997 British General Election," *Public Choice* 131(3):387–411.

Lassen, David Dreyer. 2005. "The Effect of Information on Voter Turnout: Evidence from a Natural Experiment," *American Journal of Political Science* 49(1):103–118.

Latané, B. and J. Darely. 1970. *The Unresponsive Bystander: Why Doesn't He Help?* New York: Appleton-Century-Crofts.

Lau, Richard R. 1982. "Negativity in Political Perception," *Political Behavior* 4(December):353–378.

Lau, Richard R. 1985. "Two Explanations for Negativity Effects in Political Behavior," *American Journal of Political Science* 29(February):119–138.

Lau, Richard R. and David P. Redlawsk. 1997. "Voting Correctly," *American Political Science Review* 91(3, September):585–598.

Lau, Richard R. and David P. Redlawsk. 2001. "Advantages and Disadvantages of Cognitive Heuristics in Political Decision Making," *American Journal of Political Science* 45(4):951–971.

Lau, Richard R. and David P. Redlawsk. 2006. *How Voters Decide: Information Processing During Election Campaigns.* Cambridge University Press.

Lau, Richard R., Lee Sigelman, Caroline Heldman, and Paul Babbitt. 1999. "The Effects of Negative Political Advertisements: A Meta-Analytic Assessment," *American Political Science Review* 93(4, December):851–875.

Lau, Richard R., Lee Sigelman, and Ivy Brown Rovner. 2007. "The Effects of Negative Political Campaigns: A Meta-Analytic Reassessment," *Journal of Politics* 69(4, November):1176–1209.

Ledyard, J. O. 1995. "Public Goods: A Survey of Experimental Research," in *Handbook of Experimental Economics* (J. Kagel and A. E. Roth, eds.). Princeton, NJ: Princeton University Press, pp. 111–194.

Lee, Jinkwon. 2008. "The Effect of the Background Risk in a Simple Chance Improving Decision Model," *Journal of Risk and Uncertainty* 36:19–41.

Levin, Irwin P., Daniel P. Chapman, and Richard D. Johnson. 1988. "Confidence in Judgements Based on Incomplete Information: An Investigation Using Both Hypothetical and Real Gambles," *Journal of Behavioral Decision Making* 1(March):29–41.

Levine, David and Thomas Palfrey. 2005. "A Laboratory Test of the Rational Choice Theory of Voter Turnout," *American Political Science Review* 101(1, February):143–158.

Levitt, Steven and John A. List. 2007a. "What Do Laboratory Experiments Measuring Social Preferences Reveal About the Real World?" *Journal of Economic Perspectives* 21(2, Spring):153–174.

Levitt, Steven and John A. List. 2007b. "Viewpoint: On the Generalizability of Lab Behaviour to the Field," *Canadian Journal of Economics* 40(2, May):347–370.

Levitt, Steven D., John A. List, and David Reiley. 2009. "What Happens in the Field Stays in the Field: Professionals Do Not Play Minimax in Laboratory Experiments," *Econometrica* 76:71–115.

Lewis, David K. 1963. *Counterfactuals.* Cambridge, MA: Harvard University Press.

Lijphart, A. 1971. "The Comparable-Cases Strategy in Comparative Research," *Comparative Political Studies* 8:158–177.

List, John A. 2001. "Do Explicit Warnings Eliminate the Hypothetical Bias in Elicitation Procedures? Evidence from Field Auctions for Sportscards," *American Economic Review* 91(5):1498–1507.

List, John A. and David Lucking-Reiling. 2002. "Bidding Behavior and Decision Costs in Field Experiments," *Economic Inquiry* 40(4, October):611–619.

List, John A. and Jason F. Shogren. 1998. "The Deadweight Loss of Christmas: Comment," *American Economic Review* 88:1350–1355.

Little, R. J. A. and D. B. Rubin. 1987. *Statistical Analysis with Missing Data.* New York: John Wiley.

Lodge, M. and C. S. Taber. 2005. "The Automaticity of Affect for Political Leaders, Groups, and Issues: An Experimental Test of the Hot Cognition Hypothesis," *Political Psychology* 26(3):455–482.

Lodge, M., K. M. Mcgraw, and P. Stroh. 1989. "An Impression-Driven Model of Candidate Evaluation," *American Political Science Review* 83(2):399–419.

Lodge, M., M. R. Steenbergen, and S. Brau. 1995. "The Responsive Voter – Campaign Information and the Dynamics of Candidate Evaluation," *American Political Science Review* 89(2):309–326.

Lowery, B. S., N. I. Eisenberger, C. D. Hardin, and S. Sinclair. 2007. "The Persistense of Priming Effects on Academic Performance," *Basic and Applied Social Psychology* 29(2):151–157.

Luce, Duncan and Howard Raiffa. 1957. *Games and Decisions.* New York: Wiley.

Lund, F. 1925. "The Psychology of Belief," *Journal of Abnormal and Social Psychology* 20:174–196.

Luskin, R. C., J. S. Fishkin, and R. Jowell. 2002. "Considered Opinions: Deliberative Polling in Britain," *British Journal of Political Science* 32:455–487.

MacCoun, R. J. and N. L. Kerr. 1987. "Suspicion in the Psychological Laboratory: Kelman's Prophecy Revisited," *American Psychologist* 42:199.

MacKuen, Michael B., Robert S. Erikson, and James A. Stimson. 1989. "Macropartisanship," *American Political Science Review* 83(December):1125–1142.

MacKuen, Michael B., Robert S. Erikson, and James A. Stimson. 1992. "Question-Wording and Macropartisanship," *American Political Science Review* 86(June):475–481.

Mahoney, R. and D. Druckman. 1975. "Simulation, Experimentation, and Context – Dimensions of Design and Inference," *Simulation & Gaming* 6(3):235–270.

Majumder, S. R., D. Diermeier, T. A. Rietz, and L. A. Amaral. 2009. "Price Dynamics in Political Prediction Markets," *Proceedings of the National Academy of Sciences* 106(3):679–684.

Manski, Charles. 1995. *Identification Problems in the Social Sciences.* Cambridge: Harvard University Press.

Manski, Charles. 2003. "Identification Problems in the Social Sciences and Everyday Life," *Southern Economic Journal* 70(1):11–21.

Matsusaka, John, 1995. "Explaining Voter Turnout Patterns: An Information Theory," *Public Choice* 84:91–117.

Maxwell, Scott E. and Harold D. Delaney. 2004. *Designing Experiments and Analyzing Data 2.* Mahwah, NJ: Lawrence Erlbaum.

McCabe, K., D. Houser, L. Ryan, V. Smith, and T. Trouard. 2001. "A Functional Imaging Study of Cooperation in Two Person Reciprocal Exchange," *Proceedings of the National Academy of Sciences* 98:11832–11835.

McCarty, Charles R. 1984. "Introduction: The IRB and Social and Behavioral Research," in *NIH Readings on the Protection of Human Subjects in Behavioral and Social Science Research* (J. E. Sieber, ed.). Frederick, MD: University Publications, pp. 8–9.

McCarty, Nolan and Adam Meirowitz. 2006. *Political Game Theory: An Introduction.* Cambridge University Press.

McCray, J. A., M. D. Bailly, and A. R. King. 2005. "The External Validity of MMPI-2 Research Conducted on College Samples Disproportionately Represented by Psychology Majors," *Personality and Individual Differences* 38:1097–1105.

McDermott, Rose. 2002. "Experimental Methods in Political Science," *Annual Review of Political Science* 5(June):31–61.

McFadden, D. 1977. *Urban Travel Demand Forecasting Project Final Report,* vol. 5, Berkeley, CA: Institute of Transportation Studies, University of California.

McGraw, Kathleen and Valerie Hoekstra. 1994. "Experimentation in Political Science: Historical Trends and Future Directions," in *Research in Micropolitics* (M. Delli Carpini, Leoni Huddy, and Robert Y. Shapiro, eds.). Greenwood, CT: JAI Press, vol. iv, pp. 3–30.

McKelvey, Richard and Peter C. Ordeshook. 1985a. "Elections with Limited Information: A Fulfilled Expectations Model using Contemporaneous Poll and Endorsement Data as Information Sources," *Journal of Economic Theory* 36:55–85.

McKelvey, Richard D. and Peter Ordeshook. 1985b. "Sequential Elections with Limited Information," *American Journal of Political Science* 29:480–512.

McKelvey, R. D. and P. C. Ordeshook. 1986a. "Sequential Elections with Limited Information – A Formal Analysis," *Social Choice and Welfare* 3(3):199–211.

McKelvey, Richard D. and Peter Ordeshook. 1986b. "Information, Electoral Equilibria, and the Democratic Ideal," *Journal of Politics* 48:909–937.

McKelvey, Richard D. and Thomas R. Palfrey. 1992. "An Experimental Study of the Centipede Game," *Econometrica* 60:803–836.

McKelvey, Richard D. and Thomas R. Palfrey. 1995. "Quantal Response Equilibrium for Normal Form Games," *Games and Economic Behavior* 10:6–38.

McKelvey, Richard D. and Thomas R. Palfrey. 1998. "Quantal Response Equilibrium for Extensive Form Games," *Experimental Economics* 1(1):9–41.

McKelvey, Richard and P. C. Ordeshook. 1984. "Rational Expectations in Elections: Some Experimental Results Based on a Multidimensional Model," *Public Choice* 44:61–102.

Mealli, F., GW, Imbens, and S. Ferro, et al. 2004. "Analyzing a Randomized Trial on Breast Self-Examination with Noncompliance and Missing Outcomes," *Biostatics* 5(2):207–222.

Meloy, Margaret G., J. Edward Russo, and Elizabeth Gelfand Miller. 2006. "Monetary Incentives and Mood," *Journal of Marketing Research* 43(May):267–275.

Mendelberg, Tali. 2005. "Bringing the Group Back Into Political Psychology: Erik H. Erikson Early Career Award Address," *Political Psychology* 26(4):638–650.

Michelitch, Kristin. 2010. "Do Elections Manipulate Citizens' Everyday Economic Decisions? Field Experiments in Ghana." Working Paper, New York University.

Michelson, Melissa R. and David W. Nickerson. Forthcoming. "Voter Mobilization," in *Cambridge Handbook of Experimental Political Science* (James N. Druckman, Donald P. Green, James H. Kuklinski, and Arthur Lupia, eds.). Cambridge, UK: Cambridge University Press.

Milgram, S. 1974. *Obedience and Authority*. New York: Harper and Row.

Miller, R. E. 1981. "Experimental studies," in *Handbook of Political Communication*. Dan D. Nimmo and Keith R. Sanders, (eds.). Beverly Hills: Sage, pp. 561–589.

Miller, F. G., J. P. Gluck, and D. Wendler. 2008. "Debriefing and Accountability in Deceptive Research," *Kennedy Institute of Ethics Journal* 18(3):235–251.

Miller, F. G., D. Wendler, and L. C. Swartzman. 2005. "Deception in Research on the Placebo Effect," *PLoS Med* 2(9):e262, doi:10.1371/journal.pmed.0020262.

Miller, Gary M. and A. Whitford. 2002. "Trust and Incentives in Principal-Agent Negotiations: The 'Insurance/Incentive Tradeoff'," *Journal of Theoretical Politics* 14(2):231–267.

Mintz, Alex, Steven B. Redd, and Arnold Vedlitz. 2006. "Can We Generalize from Student Experiments to the Real World in Political Science, Military Affairs, and International Relations," *Journal of Conflict Resolution* 50(5, October):757–776.

Moffitt, Robert A. 1996. "Identification of Causal Effects Using Instrumental Variables: Comment," *Journal of the American Statistical Association* 91(434):462–465.

Mondak, Jeffrey J. and Robert Huckfeldt. 2006. "The Accessibility and Utility of Candidate Character in Electoral Decision Making," *Electoral Studies* 25:20–34.

Montori, Victor, Marc F. Swiontkowski, and Deborah J. Cook. 2003. "Methodologic Issues in Systematic Reviews and Meta-Analyses," *Clinical Orthopaedics and Related Research* 413:43–54.

Morelli, Massimo. 1999. "Demand Competition and Policy Compromise in Legislative Bargaining," *American Political Science Review* 93:809–820.

Morton, Rebecca B. 1987. "A Group Majority Voting Model of Public Good Provision," *Social Choice and Welfare* 4:117–131.

Morton, Rebecca B. 1991. "Groups in Rational Turnout Models," *American Journal of Political Science* 3:758–776.

Morton, Rebecca B. 1993. "Incomplete Information and Ideological Explanations of Platform Divergence," *American Political Science Review* 87:382–392.

Morton, Rebecca. 1999. *Methods and Models: A Guide to the Empirical Analysis of Formal Models in Political Science.* Cambridge: Cambridge University Press.

Morton, Rebecca. 2006. *Analyzing Elections.* New York: W.W. Norton.

Murnighan, J. K. and A. E. Roth. 1978. "Large Group Bargaining in a Characteristic Function Game," *Journal of Conflict Resolution* 22:299–317.

Mutz, Diana C. 2007. "Effects of 'In-Your-Face' Television Discourse on Perceptions of a Legitimate Opposition," *American Political Science Review* 101(4, November):621–635.

Nagel, Rosemarie. 1995. "Unraveling in Guessing Games: An Experimental Study," *American Economic Review* 85(5):1313–1326.

Nelson, Thomas E. and Donald Kinder. 1996. "Issue Frames and Group-Centrism in American Public Opinion," *Journal of Politics* 58(4):1055–1078.

Neyman, Jerzy S. 1923 (1990). "On the Application of Probability Theory to Agricultural Experiments. Essay on Principles. Section 9," *Statistical Science* 4:465–480 (with discussion).

Nickerson, David W. 2008. "Is Voting Contagious? Evidence from Two Field Experiments," *American Political Science Review* 102(February):49–57.

Nyarko, Yaw, Andrew Schotter, and Barry Sopher. 2006. "On the Informational Content of Advice: A Theoretical and Experimental Study," *Economic Theory* 29(2):433–452.

Nycum, Gillian and Lynette Reid. 2008. "The Harm-Benefit Tradeoff in 'Bad Deal' Trials," *Kennedy Institute of Ethics journal* 17(4):321–350.

Oakes, J. M. 2002. "Risks and Wrongs in Social Science Research – An evaluator's guide to the IRB," in *Evaluation Review* 26(5):443–479.

Oath of Hippocrates. 1910. In *Harvard Clasics*, vol. 38, Boston: P. F. Collier and Son.

Ochs, Jack and Alvin E. Roth. 1989. "An Experimental Study of Sequential Bargaining," *American Economic Review* 79:355–384.

Olken, Benjamin A. 2008. "Direct Democracy and Local Public Goods: Evidence from a Field Experiment in Indonesia," NBER Working Paper 14123, National Bureau of Economic Research.

O'Neill, Barry. 1987. "Nonmetric Test of the Minimax Theory of Two-Person Zero-Sum Games," *Proceedings of the National Academy of Sciences* 84:2106–2109.

Ones, D. S., Viswesvaran, C., Schmidt, F. L., 1993. "Comprehensive Metaanalysis of Integrity Test Validities – Findings and Implications for Personnel-Selection and Theories of Job-Performance," *Journal of Applied Psychology* 78(4):679–703.

Oosterbeek, Hessel, Randolph Sloof, and Gijs Van de Kulien. 2004. "Cultural Differences in Ultimatum Game Experiments: Evidence from a Meta-Analysis," *Experimental Economics* 7:171–188.

Ordóñez, Lisa D., Barbara A. Mellers, Shi-Jie Chang, and Jordan Roberts. 1995. "Are Preference Reversals Reduced When Made Explicit?" *Journal of Behavioral Decision Making* 8(December):265–277.

Orne, M. T. 1962. "On the Social Psychology of the Psychological Experiment: With Particular Reference to Demand Characteristics and Their Implications," *American Psychologist* 17:776–783.

Ortmann, A. and R. Hertwig. 2002. "The Costs of Deception: Evidence from Psychology," *Experimental Economics* 5:111–131.

Ostrom, Elinor. 1998. "A Behavioral Approach to the Rational Choice Theory of Collective Action: Presidential Address, American Political Science Association, 1997," *American Political Science Review* 92(March, 1):1–22.

Ostrom, Elinor. 2007. "Why Do We Need Laboratory Experiments in Political Science," paper presented at the 2007 American Political Science Association annual meeting, Chicago.

Oxley, Douglas R., Kevin B. Smith, John R. Alford, Matthew V. Hibbing, Jennifer L. Miller, Mario Scalora, Peter K. Hatemi, and John R. Hibbing. 2008. "Political Attitudes Vary with Physiological Traits," *Science* 321:1667–1670.

Paarsch, Harry J. 1992. "Deciding Between the Common and Private Value Paradigms in Empirical Models of Auctions," *Journal of Econometrics* 51(January-February):191–215.

Paarsch, Harry J. 1994. "A Comparison of Estimators for Empirical Models of Auctions," *Annales d'Economie et de Statistique* 34(6):143–157.

Pagan, J. L., Eaton, N., Turkheimer, E., and Oltmanns, T. F. 2006. Peer-reported personality problems of research nonparticipants: Are our samples biased? *Personality and Individual Differences* 41:1131–1142.

Page, Benjamin I. and Robert Y. Shapiro. 1992. *The Rational Public: Fifty Years of Trends in Americans' Policy Preferences.* Chicago: University of Chicago Press.

Palacios-Huerta, I. and O. Volij. 2009. "Field Centipedes," *American Economic Review* 99(4):1619–1635.

Palacios-Huerta, Ignacio and Oscar Volij. 2008. "Experientia Docet: Professionals Play Minimax in Laboratory Experiments," *Econometrica* 76(1):71–115.

Palacios-Huerta, Ignacio and Roberto Serrano. 2006. "Rejecting Small Gambles under Expected Utility," *Economics Letters* 91(2):250–259.

Palacios-Huerta, Ignacio. 2003. "Professionals Play Minimax," *Review of Economic Studies* 70:395–415.

Palfrey, Thomas. 1991. *Laboratory Research in Political Economy.* Ann Arbor, MI: University of Michigan Press.

Panagopoulos, Costas and Donald Green. 2008. "Field Experiments Testing the Impact of Radio Advertisements on Electoral Competition," *American Journal of Political Science* 52(1):156–168.

Parco, James E., Amnon Rapoport, and William E. Stein. 2002. "Effects of Financial Incentives on the Breakdown of Mutual Trust," *Psychological Science* 13(May):292–297.

Parker, M. 2007. "Ethnography/Ethics," *Social Science and Medicine* 65(11):2248–2259.

Pearl, Judea. 2000. *Causality.* Cambridge, UK: Cambridge University Press.

Plattner, S. 2003. "Human Subjects Protection and Cultural Anthropology," *Anthropological Quarterly* 76(2):287–297.

Plott, C. R. 2000. "Markets and Information Gathering Tools," *Southern Economic Journal* 67(1):1–15.

Poole, Keith and Howard Rosenthal. 1997. *Congress: A Political-Economic History of Roll Call Voting.* New York: Oxford University Press.

Porter, S. R. and M. E. Whitcomb. 2005a. "Email Subject Lines and Their Effect on Web Survey Viewing and Response," *Social Science Computer Review* 23(3):380–387.

Porter, S. R. and M. E. Whitcomb. 2005b. "Nonresponse in Student Surveys: the Role of Demographics, Engagement and Personality," *Research in Higher Education* 46(2):127–152.

Porter, Tony. 2008. "Research Ethics Governance and Political Science in Canada," *PS: Political Science and Politics* 41(July):495–99.

Potters, Jan and Frans van Winden. 1996. "Comparative Statics of a Signaling Game. An Experimental Study," *International Journal of Game Theory* 25:329–354.

Potters, Jan and Frans van Winden. 2000. "Professionals and Students in a Lobbying Experiment Professional Rules of Conduct and Subject Surrogacy," *Journal of Economic Behavior and Organization* 43:499–522.

Powell, J. L. 1994. "Estimation of Semiparametric Models," in *Handbook of Econometrics* (R. F. Engle and D. McFadden, eds.). Amsterdam: North Holland, vol. 4, pp. 2443–2521.

Prior, Markus and Arthur Lupia. 2005. "What Citizens Know Depends on How You Ask Them: Experiments on Time, Money, and Political Knowledge," Working paper, Princeton University.

Przeworski, A. 2004. "Institutions Matter?" *Government and Opposition* 39(4):527–540.

Quandt, R. E. 1958. "The Estimation of the Parameters of a Linear Regression System Obeying Two Separate Regimes," *Journal of the American Statistical Association* 53(284):873–880.

Quandt, R. E. 1972. "A New Approach to Estimating Switching Regressions," *Journal of American Statistical Association* 67:306–310.

Quattrone, G. A. and A. Tversky. 1988. "Contrasting Rational and Psychological Analyses of Political Choice," *American Political Science Review* 82:719–736.

Rabin, Matthew. 2000. "Risk Aversion and Expected Utility Theory: A Calibration Theorem," *Econometrica* 68(5, January):1281–1292.

Rabin, Matthew and R. H. Thaler. 2001. "Anomalies. Risk Aversion," *Journal of Economic Perspective* 15:219–232.

Reiss, Peter C. and Frank A. Wolak. 2007. "Structural Econometric Modeling: Rationales and Examples From Industrial Organization," in *Handbook of Econometrics* (James J. Heckman and Edward E. Leamer, eds.). New York: Elsevier, vol. 6A, pp. 4277–4416.

Rice, S. 1929. "Contagious Bias in the Interview: A Methodological Note," *American Journal of Sociology* 35:420–423.

Riker, William H. 1967. "Experimental Verification of Two Theories about *n*-Person Games," in *Mathematical Applications in Political Science III* (Joseph L. Bernd, ed.). Charlottesville, VA: University Press of Virginia, pp. 52–66.

Rivers, Douglas and Quang H. Vuong. 1988. "Limited Information Estimators and Exogeneity Tests for Simultaneous Probit Models," *Journal of Econometrics* 39(3):347–366.

Rodriguez, Aroldo and Robert Levine, eds. 1999. *Reflections on 100 Years of Experimental Social Psychology*. New York: Basic Books/Perseus.

Rosenbaum, Paul R. 1987. "The Role of a Second Control Group in an Observational Study (with Discussion)," *Statistical Science* 2:292–316.

Rosenbaum, Paul R. 2002. *Observational Studies*, 2nd edition. New York: Springer.

Rosenbaum, Paul R. and Donald B. Rubin. 1983. "The Central Role of the Propensity Score in Observational Studies for Causal Effects," *Biometrika* 70:41–55.

Rosenberg, M. J. 1965. "When Dissonance Fails: On Eliminating Evaluations Apprehension from Attitude Measurements," *Journal of Personality and Social Psychology* I:28–42.

Rosenstone, Steven J. and John Mark Hansen. 1993. *Mobilization, Participation, and Democracy in America*. New York: Macmillan.

Rosenthal, R. and D. B. Rubin. 1978. "Interpersonal Expectancy Effects: The First 345 Studies," *Behavioral and Brain Sciences* 1:377–386.

Rosenthal, R. and D. B. Rubin. 2003. "r Equivalent: A Simple Effect Size Indicator," *Psychological Methods* 8:492–496.

Roth, Alvin. 1993. "On the Early History of Experimental Economics," *Journal of History of Economic Thought* 15(Fall):184–209.

Roth A. E. 1995. "Introduction," in *The Handbook of Experimental Economics* (J. H. Kagel and A. E. Roth, eds.). Princeton, NJ: Princeton University Press.

Roth, A. E. 2001. "Form and Function in Experimental Design," *Behavioral and Brain Sciences* 24(3):427.

Roth, A. E. and J. K. Murnighan. 1978. "Equilibrium Behavior and Repeated Play of Prisoners-Dilemma," *Journal of Mathematical Psychology* 17(2):189–198.

Roth, A. E. and M. Malouf. 1979. "Game-Theoretic Models and the Role of Information in Bargaining," *Psychological Review* 86:574–594.

Roth, Alvin E., Vesna Prasnikar, Masahiro Okuno-Fujiwara, and Shmuel Zamir. 1991. "Bargaining and Market Behavior in Jerusalem, Ljubljana, Pittsburgh and Tokyo: An Experimental Study," *American Economic Review* 81:1068–1095.

Roy, A. 1951. "Some Thoughts on the Distribution of Earnings," *Oxford Economic Papers* 3(2):135–146.

Rubin, Donald B. 1976. "Inference and Missing Data," *Biometrika* 63:581–592.

Rubin, Donald B. 1980. "Comment on 'Randomization Analysis of Experimental Data: The Fisher Randomization Test,' by D. Basu," *Journal of the American Statistical Association* 75:591–593.

Rubin, Donald B. 1990. "On the Application of Probability Theory to Agricultural Experiments: Essay on Principles," *Statistical Science* 5(4):472–480.

Rudman, Laurie A. 2008. "On Babies and Bathwater: A Call for Diversification and Diagnosis," *Psychological Inquiry* 19(2):84–89.

Rutstrom, Elisabet E. 1998. "Home-Grown Values and the Design of Incentive Compatible Auctions," *International Journal of Game Theory* 27(3):427–441.

Ryan, R. M. and E. L. Deci. 2000. "Intrinsic and Extrinsic Motivations: Classic Definitions and New Directions," *Contemporary Educational Psychology* 25(1):54–67.

Rydval, Ondrej and Andreas Ortmann. 2004. "How Financial Incentives and Cognitive Abilities Affect Task Performance in Laboratory Settings: An Illustration," *Economics Letters* 85:315–320.

Sager, Fritz. 2006. "Policy Coordination in the European Metropolis: A Meta-Analysis," *West European Politics* 29(3):433–460.

Samuelson, Larry. 2005. "Economic Theory and Experimental Economics," *Journal of Economic Literature* 43(March):65–107.

Savage, Leonard J. 1972. *The Foundations of Statistics*. New York: Dover.

Schafer, J. L. 1997. *Analysis of Incomplete Multivariate Data*. London: Chapman & Hall.

Scharlemann, J. P. W., C. C. Eckel, A. Kacelnik, and R. Wilson. 2001. "The Value of a Smile: Game Theory with a Human Face," *Journal of Economic Psychology* 22(5):617–640.

Schechter, Laura. 2007. "Risk Aversion and Expected-Utility Theory: A Calibration Exercise," *Journal of Risk and Uncertainty* 35:67–76.

Schotter, Andrew and Barry Sopher. 2007. "Advice and Behavior in Intergenerational Ultimatum Games: An Experimental Approach," *Games and Economic Behavior* 58(2):365–393.

Schotter, Andrew and Barry Sopher. 2003. "Social Learning and Coordination Conventions in Intergenerational Games: An Experimental Study," *Journal of Political Economy* 111(3):498–529.

Schotter, Andrew and Barry Sopher. 2006. "Trust and Trustworthiness in Games: An Experimental Study of Intergenerational Advice," *Experimental Economics* 9(2):123–145.

Schram, Arthur. 1989. "Voter Behavior in Economic Perspective," PhD dissertation, University of Amsterdam.

Schram, Arthur and Joep Sonnemans. 1996a. "Why People Vote: Experimental evidence," *Journal of Economic Psychology* 17(4):417–442.

Schram, Arthur and Joep Sonnemans. 1996b. "Voter Turnout as a Participation Game: An Experimental Investigation," *International Journal of Game Theory* 25(3):385–406.

Schuessler, Alexander A. 2000. *A Logic of Expressive Choice*. Princeton: Princeton University Press.

Sears, David O. 1986. "College Sophomores in the Laboratory," *Journal of Personality and Social Psychology* 51(3):515–30.

Sears, David O. 2008. "College Student-itis Redux," *Psychological Inquiry* 19(2):72–77.

Sekhon, Jasjeet. 2005. "The Varying Role of Voter Information Across Democratic Societies," Working paper, University of California, Berkeley Department of Political Science.

Seligson, Mitchell A. 2008. "Human Subjects Projection and Large-N Research: When Exempt is Non-Exempt, and Research is Non-Research," *PS: Political Science and Politics* July:477–482.

Selten, R., 1967. "Die Strategiemethode zur Erforschung des eingeschr ankt rationalen Verhaltens im Rahmen eines Oligopolexperiments," in *Beitrage zur experimentellen Wirtschaftsforschung* (H. Sauermann, ed.). Tubingen: J. C. B. Mohr, pp. 136–168.

Selten, Reinhard, Abodolkarim Sadrieh, and Klaus Abbink. 1999. "Money Does Not Induce Risk Neutral Behavior, but Binary Lotteries Do Even Worse," *Theory and Decision* 46:211–249.

Shadish, W. R. and C. K. Haddock. 1994. "Combining Estimates of Effect Size," in *The Handbook of Research Synthesis* (H. Cooper and L.V. Hedges, eds.). New York: Russell Sage Foundation, 261–281.

Shadish, William R., Thomas D. Cook, and Donald T. Campbell. 2002. *Experimental and Quasi-Experimental Designs for Generalized Causal Inference.* Boston: Houghton Mifflin.

Shaw, M. J., T. J. Beebe, H. L. Jensen, and S. A. Adlis. 2001. "The Use of Monetary Incentives in a Community Survey: Impact on Response Rates, Data Quality, and Cost," *Health Services Research* 35:1339–1346.

Shettle, Carolyn and Geraldine Mooney. 1999. "Monetary Incentives in U.S. Government Surveys," *Journal of Official Statistics* 15(2):217–230.

Sieber, J. 1992. "Planning Ethically Responsible Research: A Guide for Students and Internal Review Boards," *Applied Social Research Methods Series*. Newbury Park, CA: Sage Publications, vol. 31.

Siegel, Sidney and Lawrence E. Fouraker. 1960. *Bargaining and Group Decision Making: Experiments in Bilateral Monopoly*. New York: McGraw-Hill.

Sigelman, Lee, Caol K. Sigelman, and Barbara J. Walkosz. 1992. "The Public and the Paradox of Leadership: An Experimental Analysis," *American Journal of Political Science* 36(2, May):366–385.

Signorino, Curtis. 1999. "Strategic Interaction and Statistical Analysis of International Conflict," *American Political Science Review* 93(June):279–298.

Simmerling, M., B. Schwegler, J. Sieber, and J. Lindgren. 2007. "Introducing a New Paradigm for Ethical Research in the Social, Behavioral, and Biomedical Sciences: Part I," *Northwestern University Law Review* 101(2).

Sinclair, Betsy. 2009. *Design and Analysis of Experiments in Multilevel Populations*, Druckman and Kim Cite (Jamie Druckman, ed.).

Singer, Eleanor, John Van Hoewyk, N. Gerbler, T. Raghunathan, and K. McGonagle. 1999. "The Effects of Incentives on Response Rates in Interviewer-Mediated Surveys," *Journal of Official Statistics* 15(2):217–230.

Singer, Eleanor, John Van Hoewyk, and Mary Maher. 2000. "Experiments with Incentives in Telephone Surveys," *Public Opinion Quarterly* 64(2):171–188.

Skrondal, Anders and Sophia Rabe-Hesketh. 2007. "Latent Variable Modelling: A Survey," *Scandinavian Journal of Statistics* 34:712–745.

Slonim, Robert and Alvin E. Roth. 1998. "Learning in High Stakes Ultimatum Games: An Experiment in the Slovak Republic," *Econometrica* 66(3, May):569–596.

Smith, M. L. and G. V. Glass. 1977. "Meta-Analysis of Psychotherapy Outcome Studies," *American Psychologist* 32:752–760.

Smith, Rogers M. 2002. "Should We Make Political Science More of a Science or More About Politics?" *PS: Political Science and Politics* 35(2, June):199–201.

Smith, S. S. and D. Richardson. 1983. "Amelioration of Deception and Harm in Psychological Research: The Important Role of Debriefing," *Journal of Personality and Social Psychology* 44:1075–1082.

Smith, Vernon. 1976. "Experimental Economics: Induced Value Theory," *American Economic Review* 66:274–279.

Smith, Vernon. 1982. "Microeconomic Systems as an Experimental Science," *American Economic Review* 72(5):923–955.

Smith, Vernon. 2003. "Constructivist and Ecological Rationality in Economics," *American Economic Review* 93(3, June):465–508.

Smith, Vernon L. and James M. Walker. 1993a. "Money Rewards and Decision Cost in Experimental Economics," *Economic Inquiry* 15:245–261.

Sniderman, P. M. and D. B. Grob. 1996. "Innovations in Experimental Design in Attitude Surveys," *Annual Review of Sociology* 22:377–399.

Sniderman, Paul M. and Edward G. Carmines. 1997. *Reaching Beyond Race.* Cambridge, MA: Harvard University Press.

Sniderman, Paul M., Richard A. Brody, and Philip E. Tetlock. 1991. *Reasoning and Choice: Explorations in Political Psychology.* New York: Cambridge University Press.

Sobel, Michael. 2005. "Discussion: 'The Scientific Model of Causality'," *Sociological Methodology* 35:99–133.

Sohlberg, S. and A. Birgegard. 2003. "Persistent Complex. Subliminal Activation Effects: First Experimental Observations," *Journal of Personality and Social Psychology* 85(2):302–316.

Sondheimer, Rachel. Forthcoming. "Analyzing the Downstream Effects of Randomized Experiments," in *Cambridge Handbook of Experimental Political Science* (James N. Druckman, Donald P. Green, James H. Kuklinski, and Arthur Lupia, eds.). Cambridge, UK: Cambridge University Press.

Spezio, Michael L., Antonio Rangel, Ramon Michael Alvarez, John P. O'Doherty, Kyle Mattes, Alexander Todorov, Hackjin Kim, and Ralph Adolphs. 2008. "A Neural Basis for the Effect of Candidate Appearance on Election Outcomes," *Social Cognition and Affective Neuroscience* 3(4):344–352.

Sprinkle, Geoffrey B. 2000. "The Effect of Incentive Contracts on Learning and Performance," *The Accounting Review* 75(July):299–326.

Stahl, Dale O. and Ernan Haruvy. 2008. "Subgame Perfection in Ultimatum Bargaining Trees," *Games and Economic Behavior* 63:292–307.

Stanca, Luca. 2009. "Measuring Indirect Reciprocity: Whose Back Do We Scratch?" *Journal of Economic Psychology* 30:190–202.

Stanley, T. D. and Stephen B. Jarrell. 1989. "Meta-Regression Analysis: A Quantitative Method of Literature Surveys," *Journal of Economic Surveys* 3(2):161–70.

Stapel, Diederik A., Stephen D. Reicher, and Russell Spears. 1995. "Contextual Determinants of Strategic Choice: Some Moderators of the Availability Bias," *European Journal of Social Psychology* 25:141–158.

Starmer, C. and R. Sugden. 1991. "Does the Random-Lottery Incentive System Elicit True Preferences? An Experimental Investigation," *American Economic Review* 81:971–978.

Stigler, George. 1965. *Essays in the History of Economics.* Chicago: University of Chicago Press.

Stodder, James. 1998. "Experimental Moralities: Ethics in Classroom Experiments," *Journal of Economic Education* 29(2):127–138.

Straits, B. C., P. L. Wuebben, and T. J. Majka. 1972. "Influences on Subjects' Perceptions of Experimental Research Situations," *Sociometry* 35(4):499–518.

Strandberg, Kim. 2008. "Online Electoral Competition in Different Settings," *Party Politics* 14(2):223–244.

Stromberg, David. 2008. "How the Electoral College Influences Campaigns and Policy: The Probability of Being Florida," *American Economic Review* 98(3):769–807.

Sullivan, John L., James E. Piereson, and George E. Marcus. 1978. "Ideological Constraint in the Mass Public: A Methodological Critique and Some New Findings," *American Journal of Political Science* 22:233–249.

Taber, Charles. 2009. "Principles of Color: Implicit Race, Ideology, and Opposition to Race-Conscious Policies," Working paper, Department of Political Science, SUNY Stony Brook.

Tetlock, Philip E. and Aaron Belkin, eds. 1996. *Counterfactual Thought Experiments in World Politics: Logical, Methodological, and Psychological Perspectives.* Princeton: Princeton University Press.

Tetlock, Philip E., Richard Lebow, and Geoffrey Parker, eds. 2006. *Unmaking the West "What-If?" Scenarios That Rewrite World History.* Ann Arbor, MI: University of Michigan Press.

Thaler, R. and E. Johnson. 1990. "Gambling with the House Money and Trying to Break Even: The Effects of Prior Outcomes in Risky Choice," *Management Science* 36(6):643–660.

Thurstone, L. 1930. *The Fundamentals of Statistics.* New York: Macmillan.

Titmuss, Richard M. 1970. *The Gift Relationship: From Human Blood to Social Policy.* London: George Allen and Unwin.

Todorov, A. and J. S. Uleman. 2003. "The Efficiency of Binding Spontaneous Trait Inferences to Actors' Faces," *Journal of Experimental Social Psychology* 39:549–562.

Todorov, A., A. N. Mandisodza, A. Goren, and C. C. Hall. 2005. "Inferences of Competence from Faces Predict Election Outcomes," *Science* 308:1623–1626.

Tomz, Michael, with Robert Van Houweling. 2008. "Candidate Positioning and Voter Choice," *American Political Science Review* 102(3):303–318.

Tversky, A. and D. Kahneman. 1981. "The Framing of Decisions and the Psychology of Choice," *Science* 211(4481):453–458.

Tversky, Amos and Daniel Kahneman. 1973. "Availability: A Heuristic for Judging Frequency and Probability," *Cognitive Psychology* 5:207–232.

Uhlaner, Carole. 1989. "Rational Turnout – The Neglected Role of Groups," *American Journal of Political Science* 33(2):390–422.

Vedantum, S. 2004. *Human Responses to Technology Scrutinized: Emotional Interactions Draw Interest of Psychologists and Marketers.* Washington Post; Sect A: 14.

Voelckner, Fanziska. 2006. "An Empirical Comparison of Methods for Measuring Consumers' Willingness to Pay," *Marketing Letters* 17:137–149.

Wang, A. Y. and F. G. Jentsch. 1998. "Point-of-Time Effects across the Semester: Is There a Sampling Bias?" *The Journal of Psychology* 132:211–219.

Wantchekon, Leonard. 2003. "Clientelism and Voting Behavior: Evidence from a Field Experiment in Benin," *World Politics* 55(3):399–422.

Warner, John Harley and Janet A. Tighe. 2001. *Majors Problems in the History of American Medicine and Public Health.* New York: Houghton Mifflin.

Warnere, John H. and Janet Al Tighe, eds. 2001. *Major Problems in the History of American and Public Health.* New York: Houghton Mifflin.

Warriner, Keith, John Goyder, Heidi Gjertsen, Paula Hohner, and Kathleen McSpurren. 1996. "Charities, No; Lotteries, No; Cash, Yes: Main Effects and Interactions in a Canadian Incentives Experiment," *Public Opinion Quarterly* 60(4):542–562.

Warwick, Paul and James Druckman. 2001. "Portfolio Salience and the Proportionality of Payoffs in Coalition Government," *British Journal of Political Science* 31:627–649.

Weimann, J. 1994. "Individual Behaviour in a Free-Riding Experiment," *Journal of Public Economics* 54:185–200.

Whitt, S. and R. Wilson. 2007. "Public Goods in the Field: Katrina Evacuees in Houston," *Southern Economic Journal* 74(2):377–387.

Wilcox, N. 1993. "Lottery Choice: Incentives, Complexity, and Decision Time," *Economic Journal* 103:1397–1417.

Wilde, Louis. 1981. "On the Use of Laboratory Experiments in Economics," in *The Philosophy of Economics* (Joseph Pitt, ed.). Dordrecht: Reidel, 137–148.

Williams, Arlington W. and James M. Walker. 1993. "Computerized Laboratory Exercises for Microeconomics Education: Three Applications Motivated by Experimental Economics," *Journal of Economic Education* 24(Fall):291–315.

Winship, Christopher and Stephen Morgan. 1999. "The Estimation of Causal Effects from Observational Data," *Annual Review of Sociology* 25:659–707.

Wittman, Donald. 1983. "Candidate Motivations: A Synthesis of Alternative Theories," *American Political Science Review* 77(March):142–157.

Wolak, F. A. 1994. "An Econometric Analysis of the Asymmetric Information, Regulator-Utility Interaction," *Annales d'Economie et de Statistique* 34:12–69.

Wolf, Leslie E., Joseph A. Catania, M. Margaret Dolcini, Lance M. Pollack, and Bernard Lo. 2008. "IRB Chairs' Perspectives on Genomics Research Involving Stored Biological Materials: Ethical Concerns and Proposed Solutions Abstract," *Journal of Empirical Research on Human Research Ethics* 3(4):99–111.

Wolpin, Kenneth I. 2007. "Ex Ante Policy Evaluation, Structural Estimation, and Model Selection," *American Economic Association Papers and Proceedings* (May) 97(2):48–52.

Wooders, J. 2008. "Does Experience Teach? Professionals and Mini-Max Play in the Lab," University of Arizona, Working paper 08-04.

Wooldridge, Jeffrey M. 1999. "Distribution-Free Estimation of Some Nonlinear Panel Data Models," *Journal of Econometrics* 90:77–97.

Wooldridge, Jeffrey M. 2002. *Econometric Analysis of Cross Section and Panel Data.* Cambridge, MA: MIT Press.

Woolfolk, A. E. 1998. *Readings in Educational Psychology*, 2nd edition. Boston, MA: Allyn & Bacon.

Wright, William F. and Mohamed E. Aboul-Ezz. 1988. "Effects of Extrinsic Incentives on the Quality of Frequency Assessments," *Organizational Behavior and Human Decision Processes* 41(April):143–152.

Yammarino, Francis, Steven Skinner, and Terry Childers. 1991. "Understanding Mail Survey Response Behavior: A Meta Analysis," *Public Opinion Quarterly* 55:613–639.

Yanow, Dvora and Schwartz-Shea. 2008. "Reforming Institutional Review Board Policy: Issues in Implementation and Field Research," *PS: Political Science and Politics* 41(3):483–494.

Zelenski, J. M., C. L. Rusting, and R. J. Larsen. 2003. "Consistency in the Time of Experiment Participation and Personality Correlates: A Methodological Note," *Personality and Individual Differences* 34(4):547–558.

Zeng, Langche. 2003. "Improving Prediction and Causal Inference with Graphical Methods and Models," Paper presented at the annual meeting of the American Political Science Association, Philadelphia Marriott Hotel, Philadelphia, PA, August 27. http://www.allacademic.com/meta/p64597_index.html (accessed May 26, 2009).

Author Index

Subject Index